■ THERE'S NO TIME LIKE FREE TIME—
LET THIS BESTSELLING BOOK
SHOW YOU HOW TO FIND IT ——————

Ray Josephs tells you how to make your time your own. From
streamlining your morning routine to making decisions faster
and getting more done at work, he offers hundreds of suggestions
and commonsense strategies designed to help you get more out
of every minute and make the most of faxes, computers, and
other time-saving technologies. With this remarkable guide you
will be able to gain control of your time—and fill your days with
rewarding activities.

RAY JOSEPHS is a pioneer in the field of public relations who
has written nine books on international relations and management. Originally published in 1955, *How to Gain an Extra Hour
Every Day* is still regarded as the bible of efficiency in Japan. Now
completely revised and updated for the 1990s, this resource will
give Americans what has become a rare commodity: *time*.

- RAY JOSEPHS ··········

HOW TO GAIN AN EXTRA HOUR EVERY DAY

MORE THAN 500 TIME-SAVING TIPS

COMPLETELY REVISED AND UPDATED

A PLUME BOOK

PLUME

Published by the Penguin Group
Penguin Books USA Inc., 375 Hudson Street, New York, New York 10014, U.S.A.
Penguin Books Ltd, 27 Wrights Lane, London W8 5TZ, England
Penguin Books Australia Ltd, Ringwood, Victoria, Australia
Penguin Books Canada Ltd, 10 Alcorn Avenue, Toronto, Ontario, Canada
M4V 3B2
Penguin Books (N.Z.) Ltd, 182–190 Wairau Road, Auckland 10, New Zealand

Penguin Books Ltd, Registered Offices:
Harmondsworth, Middlesex, England

First published by Plume, an imprint of Dutton Signet,
a division of Penguin Books USA Inc.

First Printing, April, 1992
12 11 10 9 8 7 6 5 4 3

 REGISTERED TRADEMARK—MARCA REGISTRADA

LIBRARY OF CONGRESS CATALOGING-IN-PUBLICATION DATA:

Josephs, Ray.
    How to gain an extra hour every day : more than 500 time-saving tips /
Ray Josephs.
        p.   cm.
    Originally published: New York : Dutton, 1955.
    ISBN 0-452-26783-8
    1. Time management.   I. Title.
BF637.T5J67   1992
640'.43—dc20   91-36467
                                                                        CIP

Printed in the United States of America
Set in Bodoni Book

Designed by Steven N. Stathakis

To Hanny

Who made all those extra hours worth gaining

■

▪ Contents ▪ ▪ ▪ ▪ ▪ ▪ ▪ ▪ ▪ ▪ ▪

▪ Introduction ▪ ▪ ▪ ▪ ▪ ▪ ▪ ▪ ▪ ▪

"I don't know where my days go. There are so many things I never seem to have time to . . .

"accomplish all my business tasks . . .

"have time with my spouse and children . . .

"listen to music or go to movies . . .

"read the books I hear about . . .

"help others in my community, and take part in civic, church, and religious activities . . .

"undertake the projects I'm always hoping to undertake . . .

"If I only had the time!"

Have you ever expressed these frustrations? Do you often feel rushed and harassed? Under strain and pressure, with countless things to do?

Are you missing out on new and interesting experiences?

As we move toward the year 2000, more and more Americans feel that they are in this position. *Time* magazine—an even more appropriate name now than when it began—recently reported that Americans were simply running out of time. According to a Harris survey, the amount of leisure time enjoyed by the average American had dropped 37 percent from 1973 to 1990. Over the same period, the average work week, including commuting, jumped from under forty-one to nearly forty-seven hours. In some professions—particularly law, finance, and medicine—demands often stretch to eighty-plus hours weekly. Vacations have been shortened to a degree that, in comparison with years past, they seem not much more than long weekends. The Sabbath is for—what else—shopping!

If all of this continues, time could end up being in the nineties what money was to the eighties—the ultimate goal—with time to enjoy life becoming the hardest thing to obtain.

▪ THE SECRETS OF MANAGING TIME ——

Some of the world's busiest people are not only able to develop highly successful careers, but constantly find time for all of the nonbusiness activities they enjoy.

What's their secret?

I began to ask this question back in the fifties, when the first edition of this book appeared in America (followed by other editions in the United Kingdom, France, Germany, Italy, Spain, Japan, Taiwan, and elsewhere). I found that the answer was in learning how to do what you had to do and wanted to do in less time—and usually with less effort, so that you truly worked smarter, not harder.

I discovered that something called time management might well be the answer. But that term, as Todd L. Pearson of Time Masters notes, is really a misnomer: We can't *manage* time; we can only manage ourselves in relation to the clock. This requires both organization and structure.

Over the past three decades, I have been relentlessly pursuing the time-saving secrets of successful—and often famous—

people around the world. I have sought out countless experts, teachers, writers, doers, and others who, while perhaps less known, have managed to develop and employ a tremendous variety of time savers. In this book I hope to share some of these techniques with you, and to offer a wide range of practical tips, to help you find those that can put you one step ahead in your job, career, and home and community lives.

▪ YOU HAVE 1,440 MINUTES A DAY ————

All of us start with the same twenty-four hours a day. Your day is, in effect, a time bank from which to draw your assets in minutes and hours. The supply is limited. Your use of them is not. As an old friend, Fred Decker, one-time publisher of the late, lamented *Printer's Ink* magazine explained it: Suppose you had a bank that credited your account each morning with $86,400, and every evening canceled whatever amount you failed to use that day. Call that bank *time* and the dollars, *seconds*. Every morning it credits you with 86,400 seconds—and every night makes irrecoverable whatever part you fail to invest to good purpose. The bank has 365 days a year, allows no overdrafts, and carries no ongoing balance. Each day it opens a new account for you; each night it burns the day's records. There's no drawing against tomorrow.

There is no mistaking the message, as Decker says. Time has no value before it is used or after it has been wasted. The instant in which your eyes are reading this sentence has value right now. It had only potential value an instant ago, and will have lost all value an instant from now—unless its use has created value for you.

What happens to your twenty-four hours a day? Well, you probably spend eight hours, or 480 of the 1,440 minutes, in sleep. The same number, in all likelihood, goes to your workday. The rest, for most, offers the greatest freedom of choice.

In practice, however, we find these hours hardly enough for half of the things we want to accomplish. There never seems to be enough time available to avoid that constant sense of pressure. Our pace appears set for us, leaving scant opportunity to do the wonderful, full-flavor activities of which we dream.

The secret of achieving your objectives and diminishing both strain and its tension, is to gain that extra hour you need every day. You can do so by accruing minutes, for those sixty or more extra minutes daily can provide time to share your life with others and to improve yourself, opportunities for accomplishment in your job or career, moments for rewarding leisure, a chance to live life more fully, and time to use and expand all of your creativity. Sixty minutes a day is enough in ten years to have earned a college degree.

■ WHY DO YOU WANT TIME? ————————

Before we go into the question of how to gain that extra time, let's stop for a moment to decide why we really want it.

Having a goal, something you want to do with the time you gain, is almost indispensable in achieving that time. Obviously, we haven't sought extra time because we are lazy.

If you are reading this book and want to put it to work for you, your motivation is self-evident. You want to do more in less time. You want accomplishments achieved in the simplest, most practical way. You want to give more time to yourself, your interests, your family and friends, and a host of other things.

As I noted, borrowing a thought from writer Ted Malone, in the very first edition of this book: "Never in history has it been possible to live as colorful and interesting a life as you can in our world today. *There's almost nothing you can't do if you have the time.* There's travel. Entertainment. Books. Gardens. Study. Music. Trips at home and throughout the country. Overseas.

Photography. The most beautiful rose garden in town. All these and others . . . are really possible."

We need, all of us, time to grow, to develop new interests, gain new friends, and carry out plans or projects and activities that we can really be excited about. We need, and can use time, to go to new places and learn about stimulating and fun things. This is one of the most important parts of living. It enlivens and invigorates social time and relationships; it enhances your workaday hours and your entire life.

Yet, when it comes to most of the things we really want to do, the things we dream about, we find ourselves so cluttered, so seemingly filled with what we *ought* to do, that we put off what we really *want* to do until we have more time.

Next week, next year, we tell ourselves. Still, that time never comes. It never will—unless we plan ways and means of getting that extra hour or more out of every twenty-four.

▪ TIME COMES IN MINUTES ────────────

Time rushes past us constantly. We must look for and collect, and even hoard minutes. Forget big, hour-saving ideas. Concentrate instead on twenty five-minute time savers. Or, ten ten-minute minders.

Those who appear to accomplish more say that time-saving can be boiled down to three essentials:

1. Eliminate the unnecessary, slave-of-habit things that fritter away so much time.
2. Stop doing what you must the hard way; simpler is usually easier and faster.
3. Teach yourself to do two or three things together.

Learning to spend a minimum of time on those things that are extravagant because they are not worth that much time, requires looking at your daily activities with a fresh eye, as we will explore in subsequent chapters. Business has efficiency engineers who seek to cut down wasted motion. They work constantly to make even the simplest-seeming task easier through shortcuts. Finding and using your best systems will do the same for you.

Many experts I consulted estimate that we are all—unless absolutely focused—likely to waste as much as 50 to 70 percent of our time and energy doing irrelevant, nonworthwhile things in the least effective way. Many an inventor or creator of a service business has grown rich devising ways to make machines or processes 5 or 10 percent more efficient. Now more and more specialists are trying to do that with individual time-consuming tasks.

We can accomplish more in less time and do it better if we put our minds to it—not only reading about such techniques as described herein, but adopting and following them, and, in the process, discovering still other, better approaches that work for us.

Dr. Frederick W. Taylor, founder of what is known as scientific management of factories, has explained: "Most of us can do three or four times as much as we ordinarily do—without lengthening working hours, or driving ourselves so that we are exhausted when day's work ends." Even if we have apparently reached the highest level of effectiveness, it is usually possible to improve what we actually do. Such is the aim of this new edition of *How to Gain an Extra Hour Every Day*.

▪ YOU WILL AGREE AND DISAGREE ———

You will find yourself in immediate agreement with many of the points in these pages. You will find others with which you will hardly agree. Bravo! In fact, you will discover any number of contradictory suggestions. This is natural; the system *you* find effective may be absolutely ridiculous for someone else.

Nevertheless, if I give you enough ideas to start you thinking about how to get out of some of the ruts and habits into which we all naturally fall, if I help you clarify and freshen your own thinking, if I force you to stand off and take a hard, critical look at yourself and your lifestyle, this book will have been successful for the one person who matters most—you!

Start with a Time and Motion Study

If you could hire the country's best time-and-motion study person to work for you and you alone, to analyze your work habits and produce a personal report of recommendations to follow, you wouldn't need this book. There are such experts, but hiring them is expensive.

You might also take an extensive course on time management and go through its steps with a top teacher. Perhaps you will; I have listed some of the best in the appendix. However, if those alternatives aren't now available to you, and if you want to see what my findings can do for you before you probe more deeply, take heed of the following:

■ For every example cited here, there was somebody who looked at a problem exactly like yours and, by trial and error, worked out a solution to it or rediscovered an existing one.

■ As will be noted, you can't save time and effort wholesale: If you need to accomplish more with less effort, to do the things you really want to do, you have to use every possible practical technique to handle many of your necessary tasks more easily and quickly—and eliminate or delegate those tasks that you don't have to do.

■ You have to cut the interruptions and shorten many of the actions that now consume so much of your time. You have to mind the 480 minutes in your eight-hour or more working day to liberate time rather than become a mechanical robot.

■ You must have an open mind on time saving. Challenge everything you do to see if there is a simpler, faster, better way to do it. Then you are bound to come up with notions that will make you ask, Why didn't I think of this before?

■ BUDGETING YOUR TIME ──────────

As you get into these pages, you will find yourself budgeting your time as you budget your income—trimming and cutting wasted minutes as you would cut squandered dollars to keep yourself financially sound. You will discover that just as your budgeting and regular savings enable you to buy that new CD player or take that trip to Cancun, so the budgeting and better use of your time will give you that extra hour daily to expand your life, find adventure, develop, grow, and enjoy living.

The methods presented here—with the self-discipline only you can supply—can help you gain command over the march of daily events. They will take some of the burden of detail off your back, and give you the freedom and leisure that results from throwing off the slave chains of must-do.

■ PUT IDEAS INTO PRACTICE ──────────

Recall how you learned to drive a car. Theory was necessary, but you really started to become a good, effortless driver when you sat behind the wheel, stepped on the gas, and began moving down the road. Mistakes? You made them. Practice, however, did make perfect, or almost so. It was the same when you learned to type, bake a cake, or sail a boat. Doing is the essential of learning. The doer is the learner.

This book may cause you to shed some of your pet notions. Too often we retain and lug around wasteful, old-fashioned ways and approaches, unwilling to discard them even though we know there are better methods. Finding the easiest way is not lazy; it is being smart. Using your brain instead of your muscle proves you have the intelligence to find better ways of doing things. As you discover easier, more relaxed methods for chores, you will derive more satisfaction from accomplishment. The duller and more routine the task, the more worthwhile it is to trim the time it takes to do it.

Instead of rebelling, pour your dislike of a chore into constructive channels. Keep a happy, adventurous attitude. Constantly seek out the center of interest in what you are doing—a better, quicker, and more efficient way of doing it. Ask, as well, why you should be doing it, or whether it should be done at all. In these and the points that follow, you will have a key to finding time for everything.

I think it adds up to this: The ineffective individual struggles endlessly with a job; the successful one has leisure to enjoy both work and play. With concentration and control, the use of just a portion of your untapped reserve, and with an arrangement of your own time to produce ideas that work and plans that achieve results, you will no longer have to dream of the accomplishment you seek. You have the ability to achieve it. Working together, let's see if we can't get you the time.

In Chapter 2, we will start with your morning routine, and then go through all of the steps of your working day, followed by time-saving chapters on chores, health, home, education, and much more. Don't read through the book quickly and inattentively—take a chapter at a time. Consider. Apply. Go back another time. You will have jump-started your way to more than an extra hour every day.

■ Chapter Two ■ ■ ■ ■ ■ ■ ■ ■ ■

The Morning Routine

No matter what you do, no matter where and how you live, there is one way in which you will have to start your day: You have to wake up. As you have certainly long since discovered, *how you wake up* has a genuine bearing on what you get out of the day that follows. How you start, in fact, often makes all the difference in what you accomplish in your household, workplace, and other activities. It determines how you interact with the people you encounter and the spirit in which you live your day.

Missed alarms, misplaced personal effects, an empty cereal box and sour milk, scattered papers and an empty glass on a TV table—all are small minute stealers that set the tone for the day. So, to start your minute-gaining steps, let's begin with a group of morning routines that can help you get going better and faster even before you get to the workplace, and that set your day's pace.

▪ GETTING UP —————————————————————

The comedian and television personality Arthur Godfrey, whose relaxed manner gained him an audience of millions, once told me, "Long ago I learned one method that saves anywhere from twenty to fifty minutes a day. I simply get up when I wake up. Lingering in bed, hoping somehow it isn't as late as you know it always is, only delays the inevitable. Besides, you aren't getting any real rest anyway. Developing the habit of popping out of the covers when your eyes open in the morning may give you an extra hour right then and there."

Many people I have encountered say that setting yourself a wake-up hour realistic to the needs of your day—and following it even against the stay-abed temptations—is one of the best ways to save morning minutes.

Making Yourself Want to Get Up —————————

Everyone, of course, has their idea on how to make themselves want to get up. One of the best-motivated persons I know told me, "I try thinking of the pleasantest, most enjoyable thing I have to do that day. This concentration, rather than dwelling on the discouragers that might want to make me stay under cover, gives me the spirit and energy to motivate my rise right then and there."

Elsa Maxwell, the famed socialite party-giver, columnist, and writer who exemplified the joy of living, said, "I never have trouble getting up. No matter how late the night before, I look forward to each day with a zest of a child anticipating Christmas morning. A picnic in the woods, or a birthday party—these things always worked magic for you as a child. They can be just as effective, no matter what your age. Getting up this way eliminates the time-wasting, spirit-deflating morning start which makes everything you do subsequently rushed and harassed."

■ GET AN EARLY START ——————————————

S. I. Newhouse, Jr., head of Advance Publications, which in-cludes the Newhouse newspapers, Condé Nast magazines, Ran-dom House publishers, and a wide variety of other media, has long followed the early rising system. He is often at his office in midtown Manhattan by 6:00 A.M.—a habit developed because, as younger men, he and his brother Donald had key positions in family newspapers requiring such schedules for their daytime editions. In his modern, sparkling white office, he goes through his most important tasks long before many of his editors and publishers have come in. He examines an array of figures on advertising revenues, circulation, and a host of other variables. He then totals results, percentages, and projections without wait-ing for associates to calculate these for him. Result: A finger on the crucial elements that involve many of the highly successful family properties.

Like his father, S. I. Newhouse, Sr., who became one of America's leading publishers, he keeps written communications to a minimum, personally dealing with his key people, many during brief, early morning, very-much-to-the-point meetings. His business luncheons at his favorite restaurant, Manhattan's Four Seasons, are often on a regular weekly schedule. These meetings are minimally social and concentrated on the business at hand in a direct (critics sometimes say often abrupt) manner—but highly efficient, successful, and time-saving.

Early Risers Do Get It ————————————————

Two of America's wealthiest men are early risers. Sam Walton, who turned a five-and-dime store into the huge Wal-mart chain he runs today, is the type of manager who shows up at 4:00 A.M. at one of his warehouses to swap information with the stockmen.

His people-oriented style, combined with a deep understanding of retailing and a sixteen-hour workday, has built him what is believed to be the largest personal fortune in America.

America's newest claimant to membership in the "big rich" is David Geffen, owner of Geffen Records, who sold his company to entertainment giant MCA Inc., which in turn agreed to be purchased by the Japanese consumer electronics conglomerate Matsushita Electric Industrial Company for a total of $8 billion. Geffen, who had made his deal just eight months before, netted a cool $710 million for his shares. But, at 7:00 A.M., the day the deal was announced, he was back to uninterrupted wheeling-and-dealing, producing the big-name records that sell into the millions.

Newsweek, reporting on Geffen's amazing success and dynamic personality, revealed another time-saving tip. Singer Bruce Springsteen's manager Jon Landau agonized at length over a business option; he finally approached Geffen for advice. Thirty seconds into his labored explanation of the problem, *Newsweek* reports, Geffen told Landau what to do. Landau tried to carry on with his explanation, but Geffen interrupted: "No! Now do! Stop thinking and do it!" No morning minutes wasted there!

▪ PLAN A PRE-WORK, PRE-BREAKFAST ACTIVITY

One time saver many busy people—particularly when working on important projects—establish is a pre-breakfast work segment. Breakfast serves as a reward for completion of that extra thirty- to sixty-minute activity. If there is a place in your home particularly suitable for concentrated work, so much the better; use it. You may find that despite hunger pangs, working before roommate or spouse and the rest of the family arise will give you the treasure of uninterrupted concentration, whose efficiency can be many times that of later daytime periods.

■ PRE-DAWN ACTIVITY —————————————

Executive Tom Mahoney once told me that over a big fireplace in the Saturn Club, in Buffalo, New York, hangs a motto: The best of all ways to lengthen our days is to steal a few hours from the night. This idea can be followed many ways. One writer I know, William J. Lederer, put the idea into working practice. Starting his writing career, he rose at 4:00 A.M. and worked until 8:00, explaining, "I disliked it—especially in winter—but it made writing possible. I'd have to drink about a pint of hot tea or soup, then take a wake-up shower. Sometimes I'd just sit around moping and thinking before wanting to tackle the typewriter. Finally did, however. The house was quiet. I felt alert, fresh, and full of anticipation. With that practice, I became more productive. Today I can do the same amount of work I did previously by rising at 5:30 and going on to 8:00. The habit has become so ingrained that it's now almost automatic." Lederer's output makes it clear that no one is too busy to write—or to do something else on which one's heart is set.

■ ALL RIGHT, STAY THERE THEN —————

That blanketed wake-up time period can be turned into extra, worthwhile minutes. I know one fashion industry executive who established her own unique program to get almost two day's work done in one. She sets the automatic coffee maker beside her bed to ring at 6:00 A.M. Instead of bustling about, she stays abed. At hand are stacks of papers, reports, pads, stamped envelopes, and a bowl of sharp pencils.

She says, "Without disturbing the family and without interruptions, I get done in two hours what would take five in the office." She writes important reports and studies American retailing, handles personal and business correspondence, works out new ideas, and reads clippings held for this thinking time. She has learned to remain relaxed while accelerated. She also rarely feels fatigue later in the day, explaining, "If I'm going out in the evening and can't retire early, I take a nap. I'm just as refreshed during long days as others who work what might be called more normal schedules, yet I manage to do all the things I want to do."

Other Stay-Abed Ideas

Winston Churchill long used a similar system. Sir Winston didn't wake at 6:00 A.M.—although he did so for many of his younger years. When he reached the prime ministership, he made it a rule to get up between 7:00 and 8:00. Pillow-propped, he waded through a mountain of London and provincial newspapers. By 9:00, he was ready to start dictating, frequently remaining in bed until luncheon.

An aide with whom I corresponded about this idea told me, "The Prime Minister has always felt it's foolish to stand when he can sit, or sit when he can lie." This way he satisfied his desire for more rest—especially during the wartime crisis days of late hours (and even received such official visitors as the U.S. ambassador while in bed). He felt the method gave him two extra hours a day, yet conserved his strength and mental agility. In fact, he edited his entire series of World War II books through this very routine.

▪ HAVE YOU MADE YOUR BATHROOM TIME EFFICIENT?

Assuming you are awake and up, one of the many problems most of us face in essential morning routines is the fact that many houses and apartments still have too few bathrooms—especially for families at rush hour. Whether you have your own or share, it is most important to look things over with the deliberate eye of a time-and-motion expert to discover delay makers. For example, are items you use daily up forward in the medicine chest and bathroom closet for handy access, and less used items on upper shelves or at the back of shelves? Not long ago someone checked 100 bathroom closets: 78 percent, or three out of every four, were helter-skelter minute wasters.

Other Bathroom Ideas

Are there enough shelves to keep everything needed forward? Have you grouped items used together in one place, for example, shaving and related accessories in one group; toothbrushes, dental floss, and the like in another; and makeup, toiletries, and eye care in a third? Here are some other hints:

■ To stretch space, try installing a few extra shelves, cabinets, and towel racks. An infinite variety is available in department stores and specialty shops, helping you increase space for minute-minding convenience without wall expansion.

■ Another good time saver: Giving each family member his or her own racks saves countless minutes unscrambling someone else's things.

■ If you don't already have one, consider a small, portable bathroom radio. It not only gives you the news while completing your morning toilet but its time signals can speed you up.

■ A small TV in the bathroom offers news visually after bath or shower. First introduced in luxury hotels, they are increasingly becoming popular home time savers.

■ If you share a bathroom, consider installing double wash basins. They are relatively inexpensive and take surprisingly little extra floor room.

■ If space permits, the addition of bathroom partitions or dividers enables two to have greater privacy while saving minutes waiting.

▪ VERTICAL IS FASTER THAN HORIZONTAL ──────────────────

If you are accustomed to a morning bath, but time is important, showering is a really welcome change, cutting time by a third.

▪ TIME SAVERS FOR MEN ────────────────

Every man who has to shave daily should consider the following points:

▪ If you are going to shower, shave first so that you can eliminate rinsing at the sink.

▪ Use a push-button lathering device, instead of brushes or your hands.

▪ Try one of the new electric razors. Many safety or straight razor fans attempt these briefly, but find them unsatisfactory and refuse to stick out the week or ten days necessary to make an electric razor really effective. Electric razors not only save time by eliminating the lathering process, cleanup, and cuts, but give a close-as-a-blade shave, to quote Remington's Victor Kiam. If you are an electric shaver, use preshave preparations that help you set up the stubble for a quick whisk and that can be rubbed in when shaving's done. Some men have taught themselves to electric shave without even looking in the mirror—and can thus read the paper or carry on other tasks while clearing off their whiskers. I know a number of busy men who use batteried portables while driving to work.

■ TELEPHONE IN THE BATHROOM ──────

A bathroom wall telephone is today virtually standard equipment at first-class hotels here and abroad. This saves the telephone dash at embarrassing moments. If you are adroit, there is no need for your caller to know where you are. You will also find that with bathroom calls you will likely be far more to the point than in more conventionally located early morning minute-stealing telephone exchanges.

■ SAVE MORNING TIME AT NIGHT ──────

Many people prefer bathing at night—making it a long, relaxed, tension-relieving session instead of taking the normal morning shower. A stretch-out soak is also often good reading time. One executive told me, "When I go to bed after a bedtime bath, I fall asleep more easily—saving me at least thirty minutes a day."

■ SPEEDING UP YOUR DRESSING ──────

Dressing is one of the big time-consumers of almost everybody's morning routine. The material that follows can help you cut down the amount of time you spend dressing. *Woman's Day* magazine offers the following suggestions:

For Women ─────────────────────

Your Clothes

■ Limit your wardrobe, period. Having fewer choices saves time.

- Wear one handbag with all of your daytime clothes.
- Choose clothes in a coordinated color scheme so that it is easy to pull together separates.
- Wear the same pants and skirt several times a week, with different sweaters, blouses, and jackets. A straight, black skirt (just above the knee) is a godsend at the office.
- Buy easy-on, easy maintenance clothes such as sweaters in knits that are virtually wrinkle-free.
- To avoid makeup stains on clothes—and frantic spot removal—put a shower cap over your face when you pull on a tight top.
- As you dress, keep looking in the mirror to catch a mistake—a run, perhaps—right away, so that you don't have to make a last-minute change.
- Organize your closet by category (pants, skirts, and so on) and color so that you can find things quickly.
- Don't store your jewelry dumped together. Sort it by what you use most often. If you wear a lot of earrings, for instance, divide them into gold, silver, and novelty earrings, and store each group in its own compartment in your drawer or jewelry box.
- Hang scarves on hangers to prevent wrinkles and last-minute ironing.
- Use a shoe polish sponge to spiff up shoes fast.

Makeup In Minutes

- For a fast base, just use concealer—in a shade one tone lighter than your natural skin color—under eyes and over any blemishes. Then powder and go.
- For every day, stick to an earth-tone shadow, advises makeup artist Ken-ichi. It looks good with most colors. The following are shortcut products:

  – Aziza's Mink Coat mascara makes lashes look three times as thick in just one fast coat.

– Any pink or brownish blush can double as eye shadow.

– A foundation with sunscreen, such as Maybelline's Active Wear, means putting on one product instead of two.

Manic Manicures

■ Pick sheer, pale colors. They show chips less than deeper tones and have to be done less often.

■ If you want to go bright for a weekend party, put the color over your pale base—don't redo the entire manicure.

■ Try one-coat polish, long-wearing polish, and two-in-one basecoat/topcoat.

■ Apply polish in thin coats and in a minimum of layers. Your manicure will dry faster, especially if you dip your finished nails into a basin of water filled with ice cubes.

For Men

Your Clothes

■ You will save pressing time and make suits, jackets, trousers, and so on look better and last longer if you always put them away on good wooden hangers. Don't button buttons. To keep creases sharp, use trouser hangers instead of bars or coat hangers; let wrinkles hang out.

■ Let suits hang a day or two between wearings so that they regain their preworn shape. Both ideas provide better appearance and give longer wear and save pressing time.

■ You can take out many spots by rubbing a material lightly with plain water.

■ Hang ties by colors and dark to light to make for speedy selection.

■ Much time-consuming dry cleaning of expensive sportswear
has been eliminated by new fabrics. Many blends are time-saver
home washables. The same idea applies to no-iron dress shirts: no
time wasted on laundry that's always late.

■ When dressing, select your suit or casual jacket first; then the
shirt, tie, and socks follow. Have a coordinating-color belt or
suspenders attached to each pair of trousers. This saves time
taking them on and off. If you are resting the suits between
wearings, this will also extend the life of your accessories.

Take-Alongs: Be sure to keep supplies of essential items that help
sidestep delays: plenty of change for tolls and a newspaper, if
bought en route. Cash lets you avoid a rush to the bank. Also
have handy pens and pencils, a memo pad, and your daily orga-
nizer/scheduler (of which more in another chapter).

■ IMPROVING CLOSETS AND STORAGE

You will find investment in a local closet specialist or in department specialty stores can be a tremendous time saver if you are
unable to organize your storage space yourself. Really adequate
organization also helps keep things in top condition.

Some favor keeping all like items in one place. Others try
grouping as closely as possible those items used together. For
example, socks near shoes and ties near shirts. (For further ideas,
see Chapters 25 and 26.)

■ THOSE EASILY LOST OR MISPLACED ITEMS

Keep an empty plastic ice-cube or muffin tray in a top dresser
drawer. Into this, when you come home, dump change, car keys,

cufflinks, tie clasps, earrings, and so on. In the morning, you can see everything—saving minutes daily rummaging.

Another Variation: Hang one of the new compartmentalized shelves available at many stores inside your clothes closet. These have places to toss your change, watch, wallet, and pocket paraphernalia. The less complicated the compartments, the better.

■ REORGANIZING POCKETS AND BAGS

Cluttered pockets, jumbled handbags, messy attaché cases, and carry-alls are often minute-wasting annoyances. There is no need to go around like a walking roll-top desk if you take a few minutes out every now and then to organize pockets and handbags. The following are some suggestions:

■ Look at your wallet now. It is probably stuffed with useless cards, assorted photos five to ten years old, folded clippings and other assorted impedimenta. Just pretend, even if you don't want to switch, that you are now going to carry a money clip. Sort out cards you really use. If you carry photos, pick two or three; don't make pockets or pocketbooks walking albums.

■ Keep an essential key set in every suit and handbag—and let some change accumulate in them. When dressing in a hurry, you may forget coins, identification, or keys. Duplicates can be time and frustration savers.

■ A single credit card can generally be found to meet virtually all of your requirements. As will be noted in another chapter, one card used in every possible place means far fewer individual bills to be paid.

▪ PLAN YOUR BREAKFAST-MAKING STEPS

Study and systematize a preparation routine to make only one kitchen circuit. For example, do you start at the sink for coffee water, then move to the stove, then to the refrigerator, and finally to the table? Circulating in what you find to be a most efficient order will help you avoid wasted motions and minutes. (For more on this, see Chapters 25 and 26.)

▪ *Breakfast Trays:* Set individual trays for each family member as evening dishes are put away. In this way, the entire breakfast can go to, and return from, the table in one trip per person. Where possible, prepare the morning meal the night before; you are likely to be slower in the morning.

▪ *Avoid Dishpan Hands:* Have a set of inexpensive breakfast dishes to be washed with others later. Many people conscientiously wash and dry after breakfast and every other meal, even though it is more sanitary, and faster, to scald dishes and let them air dry.

Other Breakfast Ideas

▪ To avoid newspaper reading, have a small radio for news everyone can share—or a kitchen TV. Or better still, use breakfast time for a full family discussion and agreement on the day's plans, to be jotted on a pad and posted.

▪ Instant coffees have now achieved much of the flavor of brewed varieties. Eliminate waiting for the percolator or coffee machine.

▪ Take advantage of the wide variety of items that can be quickly toasted or microwaved.

▪ Vitamins, pills, and so on should be kept easily at hand on the table.

■ A container filled with individual cereals on the table eliminates table-to-cupboard dash.

■ IF THERE ARE CHILDREN ─────────────

Trying to save time while administering to children's needs obviously depends on their ages, but also on your ability to help them
develop morning routines that meet family requirements. But
this is a book in itself; my only point here is that routines can be
worked out to meet the time needs of all members and reduce the
morning-routine crisis.

Now that we've started the day, let's get to the workplace
and begin on priorities and programs.

Organizers
and Schedulers

"He who every morning plans the day's transactions, and follows out that plan, carries the thread that will guide him through the maze of the busiest life. But, where no plan is laid, where the disposal of time is surrendered merely to chance, chaos soon reigns."

That quote comes not from any management consultant or time-and-motion study expert, but from one of the most prestigious of all writers, France's Victor Hugo.

Nothing is more helpful in gaining an extra hour every day—and accomplishing the goals you have chosen for your personal life, your work, and every phase of your activities— than planning.

Despite the fact that this point is usually conceded by everyone at all conscious of the value of time, far more lip service than actual practice is given to this vital need.

In this chapter we will concentrate on what most authorities describe as scheduling, or getting right down to the immediate problem: How to best handle your workload, and implement action toward your determined goals in the next hour, day, week, and as far ahead as practical.

British author C. Northcote Parkinson, of Parkinson's Law fame (work expands to the time available to do it), has said, "Too many people find their workloads heavy because they're unable to schedule, evaluate, and coordinate their daily tasks. They keep themselves loaded with, or diverted by, that which in actuality is trivial. They may not think everything they're doing so unimportant—but are first to notice the minor matters with which other executives fill their day."

▪ WHY MAKE A TO-DO SCHEDULING LIST

Would you think of building a house without a blueprint, or try driving to a destination hundreds of miles away without a road map? Of course not, says the Day-Timers company, which produce a wide range of effective scheduling materials—some of which I have used for a quarter-century. Their guidelines ask why you would entrust your career or life to chance or the whims of others. "You need a way to plan and measure each day's progress as you strive to reach your goals."

This means first establishing goals and priorities, as noted; then making the translation into an actual to-do list: individual actions set into your daily organizer/scheduler in a form that they can be executed by you on a planned schedule. Most important, at the end of the day they will help put you back on track when, as is inevitable, you will be diverted by interruptions and other factors outside your control.

You might think that a constantly updated and reprioritized to-do list would hinder creativity and kill spontaneity. Quite the contrary: Maintaining an awareness of what you must do to make each day count actually increases time you have available for thinking, creating, and planning how to use your leisure for maximum enjoyment.

Day-Timers adds: "Instead of dragging around a lot of guilt because you left important tasks undone, you'll be knocking off each task in your order of priority. Instead of waking up with a start as you suddenly remember the vital meeting you forgot to prepare for, you'll get the rest you need before a big presentation. And you can go in prepared."

■ MEASURING YOUR TO-DO LIST AGAINST YOUR OWN GOALS

The first step in effective time saving is to set goals to help you steer a steady course. You must make intelligent choices, deciding what is first, what is postponable, and what can be dropped. Once this has been done, you are ready to organize and schedule the time ahead.

As Day-Timers literature explains, "Some people say they can remember everything—appointments, assignments, deadlines, steps and projects . . . everything. They don't need lists to tell them what to do."

This might be true for you, but the act of remembering is costly—in moments and effort. It wastes valuable energy by requiring a mental clinging to the details of what must be done.

The lists many people make serve no real purpose; they lack a plan, an order of priority or sequence, and a commitment to evaluate or track progress on each item. It is these people who say, "I don't know where the day's gone." This is true. They are not in control.

Day-Timers notes that controlling your time requires control of self. Begin by getting into the habit of writing a to-do list daily—things to be done this day, and the time when they are to be done, if possible. If you can't slot something immediately, use such headings as Things to Be Done This Week and Things for Following Weeks (or months).

If you have never used such lists before, begin slowly. Failure is just as frequently the result of trying to do too much as too little. The most effective lists are those kept in some permanent form.

Concludes Joseph D. Cooper in his book *How to Get More Done in Less Time:*

> *To get through a day successfully and satisfyingly, you cannot approach it as though it were a period of time of and by itself. The day is an action period in the stream of your total time budget. How effectively you get your day's work done depends partly on the institutional resources supporting your efforts; your own self-organization and your own working habits. All these in combination are the basis for coursing successfully through each day.*

▪ PRIORITIZE YOUR TO-DO LIST —————

Your organizer, with its sections for each day and summaries for the months ahead, is best used with two types of systems: numerical and alphabetical. The simpler numbering system is probably best if you have fewer than ten items daily. Enter each into your To Be Done Today list. When they are all down, determine their order of importance and write those numbers next to each item. This reminds you to do your most important task first and encourages consolidating steps that can be taken together, a valuable time saver.

The alpha system usually requires a combination of letters and numbers. Once you decide which items are vital (i.e., important and urgent), designate these as *A*'s. Use *B* for important, but not urgent. Use *C* for items of some value.

You will find that once you have written something into your organizer you will probably do it. This is why many organizational experts urge people to use only one organizer and to review it not just once a day, but constantly. It is always before you as a reminder of what has to be done; a place into which you can write new steps as they occur. A pocket-size organizer is something you can have with you as a constant indispensable—as important as a wallet or reading glasses.

■ OTHER POINTS ON
ORGANIZER/SCHEDULER USE ―――――――

To gain the greatest time-saving benefit from your organizer, assign all items to a specific date—an immediate one or for whatever opening you see available. This technique encourages timely completion of each item and saves you the bother of rewriting and rescheduling. Use ink for set items and pencil for those that might change. Check off completions rather than obliterating them so as to be unreadable; the lists can be invaluable when you go back to review or evaluate.

■ SCHEDULING AND ORGANIZING WHERE
OTHERS ARE INVOLVED ―――――――

One good tip: Schedule early in the day those things you must do that require others' actions. That is, contact people who must ship you goods, complete a service, work in your behalf, and so on. Reaching them early, you are more likely to get them to work in your behalf that day. In addition, you won't discover too late that what you want is no longer available.

This concept also applies to secretaries, assistants, and so on. Don't be like the boss who comes in at 4:45 P.M. demanding something to go out in the evening mail if, in actuality, you could have delegated this item for action early, when it could be fit into a subordinate's workload.

▪ DIVIDE AND CONQUER WITH COLOR

Another way to improve your organizer/scheduler is to use color. Write in various colors or highlight items with a marker to represent priorities and levels of importance. A less elaborate system is to use red to indicate urgent items and black to indicate items of marginal importance. Choices depend on your needs and to some extent where you are in your time-management skills.

Write down items as they come up, and prioritize them after you have analyzed their relative importance. Color is often more effective as an eye-catching signal than priority numbers. I prefer to use highlighters to assign priority color codes because highlighting can be read through. Highlighters also offer the advantages of not showing obtrusively on copies and enabling you to see at a glance how many top priorities and secondaries you have to accomplish. Colors can also be used to designate the same types of work to be scheduled in sequence rather than hit and miss—saving many minutes in make-ready time.

▪ TICKLER REMINDERS

Use your to-do list to break down large projects into manageable bites; write tickler reminders to schedule time blocks for work on each part. If you must write a report, for example, and have estimated that it will take four hours, schedule a half-hour block in your appointment column to do an outline. On subsequent pages, write in additional blocks for writing, preferably by sections.

Tickler reminders made well in advance of deadlines can help roadmark steady progress, ensuring on-time performance. *This concept of making an appointment with yourself, so to speak, is the surest way to reserve time for important projects.*

Scheduling the time in your appointment column and treating it with the same respect as other important dates can help you concentrate on doing the most essential things first. It is also a good procrastination avoider.

▪ SCHEDULE A DAILY PLANNING SESSION

Virtually all time-management sources agree that the most productive minutes of your day are those devoted to planning the remaining hours or the days ahead. Some executives say that every hour invested in planning produces a dividend of two to three. Thus, twenty minutes a day planning can help save an hour; doing it daily could save five hours weekly. A year means 250 hours: over two extra weeks of time to achieve your goals.

Day-Timers urges setting aside a specific time daily for your organizer sessions. Some like to do this quietly at home before leaving for the office. Others plan first thing on arrival; still others before leaving for the night, while events are still fresh in their minds. I personally prefer the last approach.

Planning and writing those plans down, and scheduling and organizing should be done whenever and wherever it suits your lifestyle. Its effectiveness as a minute minder requires that it become a fixed part of your daily routine. Picking a time and place to focus on how you are going to use each day to move closer to goals can show results now.

▪ ALLOCATING AND ANALYZING YOUR TIME

As Parkinson's Law puts it, if you have one task to complete in an eight-hour day, it may take that long. If you have only two hours, you will probably do it in two, even though it might not be done quite as well as if it were done in eight.

One difficulty we all face is determining how much time we want to devote to each project, and doing it realistically. Almost everyone feels that he or she can do more in fewer minutes than is actually required. To help keep you within your self-determined time allocation, note in your organizer/scheduler the time you have available to allocate to any given task, and then press to stay within your own deadline.

If you have developed a good eye for estimating time, says Day-Timers, you can cram a lot of work into the day's nooks and crannies, the time, between appointments and other tasks, that many let go to waste. *Tip:* Try estimating required time as you write your to-do list. Then compare your performance with the estimate. Your estimating skills will grow ever sharper. The procedure is also useful when delegating tasks to subordinates or making requests: "Give an hour to this and see what you can come up with. It's not worth more than sixty minutes."

▪ JUDGING YOUR SCHEDULE

Quality of accomplishment, rather than *quantity of activities*, is really the basic purpose of all scheduling explains Werner C. Brown of Hercules Powder, noting, "It isn't what an executive *does*, but *what gets done.*" A good method to make certain your top priorities stay highest on your to-do list is to concentrate on the ten most important irons currently in the fire. The late Fred Lazarus, Jr., long-time president of Federated Department Stores, once said to me, "The big secret is frequent reevaluation to determine matters of highest priority. I list the toughest first. Then I stick to that schedule. Postponing the nasty chore only prolongs it."

▪ ADDITIONAL ORGANIZER/SCHEDULER USES

For travel, I always write set schedules in my organizer to be sure that I have data always at hand. For plane trips, specifically, it is best to write in pencil, and then ink when a flight is confirmed, because actual times often change.

Another use of an organizer is to log the names, addresses, phone numbers, and so on of people you might want to see or contact later. When I do not remember a name or where I have put a business card, I will recall, for instance, the meeting at which I met the person, look up the pages for those dates, and find the name and other information right there.

▪ SIMPLER ORGANIZERS

Lucy Hedrick, a time management consultant and author of *Five Days to an Organized Life*, recommends simpler organizers available at stationers: a pocket notebook and a calendar. In the notebook, she says, you write down everything you have to do under four categories: phone calls, errands, something to write, and something to do. You simply cross them off as they are done.

In the calendar section she notes personal appointments with doctors, her son's teachers, appointments with herself, and so on, explaining, "When you put it on the calendar, chances are much better that you'll accomplish it. You shouldn't try to carry your life around in your head. The reason you write things down is so you can free your brain for more creative pursuits."

■ WALL CHARTS AS ORGANIZER/SCHEDULERS ─────────

In addition to the foregoing organizers, consider wall charts and similar items. Among other companies, **Remarkable Products** [245 Pegasus Avenue, Northvale, NJ 07647-9941; tel: 201-784-0900] produces "remarkable" (meaning you can wipe off and write on again general wall calendars, vacation calendars, project/personnel and other charts, and a wide variety of other products that help you share prescheduled items with others in the workplace.

Divided on a day-by-day, week-by-week, or month-by-month basis (or even a year at a glance), these products are claimed to "turn any empty wall into a communications center"—putting before everyone what has to be done: deadlines, appointments, meetings, production schedules, and itineraries. They are also useful in keeping track of payment dates, sales analyses, trafficking, and inventory control.

■ CHOOSING THE BEST SYSTEM ─────────

As noted, I have been a long-time user of **Day-Timers** [Allentown, PA 18195-1551], but there are a variety of other systems, each with its advantages and disadvantages.

Filofax, originated in the United Kingdom, is very popular internationally with those familiar with its functions. It contains not only an organizer/scheduler, but a host of optional factual information at your fingertips: maps of major cities, local holidays and customs, airport data, and so on.

Road-Runner is another system that offers a wide variety of alternatives. There are all kinds of specialized bound-book organizer/schedulers, heavily advertised toward year's end and displayed in stationery and department stores. My personal advice:

Concentrate on the smallest of these that meets your basic needs. Use one such as the Day-Timer, which you can slip into your shirt pocket or purse (they come as a twelve-book yearly set, together with a storage box). Also available are an identically sized six-year planner, a permanent address book, and use tips. Day-Timers claims that more than three million busy and successful executives, managers, and professionals renew orders annually and that users' suggestions are constantly incorporated.

▪ ACCELERATING TASK COMPLETION TIME

Once you have learned to schedule your tasks, and have found a comfortable working pace, try gaining time by squeezing in just one more to-do item a day. Becoming accustomed to this addition (provided it doesn't produce a counterproductive attitude) can help accomplish more, freeing time to be used the next day.

A good way to speed up a schedule is to set time slots and learn to compress many activities that ordinarily take longer into such periods.

Dr. Daniel Pawling, a clergyman, author of twenty-three books, and one-time president of World Christian Endeavor, once told me: "Years ago I started dividing my day into fifteen-minute segments and scheduling programs for each period. I learned to squeeze into a quarter-hour what might have previously taken twenty to twenty-five minutes. Thus, I gained an extra hour or more daily. Now I no longer need to be reminded of the segments. The habit is practically automatic."

▪ AN EXTRA-HOUR-DAILY CLOCK

Morton Rachofsky of Dallas, Texas [800-637-8583], has developed the **Xtraour clock,** which is divided into 25 hours, each hour with 60 "minutes," but each minute consisting of 57.6 seconds. The 2.4 seconds borrowed from each minute are used to create an extra "hour" each day. The clock is in sync with a normal clock at noon daily. Use it to guide your own schedule and you will speed up your activities, with daily efficiency improving over 4 percent.

▪ ORGANIZING AND MANAGING ACTIVITIES ON COMPUTER —————

Organizing and scheduling your activities on a personal computer is offered by a variety of software programs. One of the best I have encountered is the Lotus Agenda 2.0, from the developers of the 1–2–3 spread sheet, said to be one of the most widely used in the United States and abroad. (See also Chapter 16.)

Paul Hatchett, director of **Agenda Marketing** [800-343-5414] explains:

> *Every morning you face a wall of information: calls, memos, meetings, letters, plans, schedules, reminders, notes, conversation. Just when you think you have it all under control, something changes and you know you're going to need more than a paperclip and staples to hold it together. With Lotus Agenda, your computer becomes a powerful personal information manager, and you become calmer. What it does is to track your appointments, projects, people, and ideas so that they relate to each other.*
>
> *You simply enter the information into your PC (any IBM personal or 100-percent certified compatible), whether it's a memo, day and time of an important meeting, or an idea or a project. You don't even have to structure it in advance. Agenda automatically arranges, updates, and cross-references everything for you—any way you want.*

> *By consolidating all your information in one place, Agenda gives you the flexibility to view it in numerous ways: by people, by projects, by dates. It can handle everything from appointments and reminders to telephone numbers and ideas for the future. It organizes so that you get what you need when you need it—feel more in control and able to make informed decisions.*

If, for example, as part of your job, you need to work with Jones in Mergers and Acquisitions to see how you can support his department in an upcoming deal, you type yourself a note: Call Jones at 2:00 P.M. about preparation for meeting on merger such and such a date. Agenda says it can read information as unstructured as this and know exactly where to put it. Once it is input, you can look at this information under the name of Jones, under mergers, or under today. Agenda will do more than just remind you to check on preparation with Jones, it will even give you his phone number so that you don't have to spend minutes hunting.

If you decide to include someone else in the preparation, you can type the change wherever you are working at the time, and the information is added anywhere else it relates. All of this enables you to see how these various steps affect your personal priorities and those of your company, work in progress, and even other steps. The system offers an activities planner, a people manager, an account manager, and a template to show you how Agenda can help you organize information sent to you by electronic mail or on compact discs.

The makers claim that additions are so easy to incorporate into your daily routine that you can start using it productively in half an hour, thus making it useful for those who don't have much time to learn utilization. Agenda's unstructured format allows information to be entered on the fly—at the desk, on a laptop computer while traveling, or wherever you have access to a keyboard. *Note:* For an upgrade, look into Magellan 2.0, Lotus File Manager Software, which offers a host of additional features.

Computerized Organizer/Schedulers ——————

The Sharp Electronics Wizard Electronic Organizer is marketed with the idea that if you need to have important personal and business information, schedules, and so on wherever you go, the Wizard is compact and light enough to make this possible. The organizer features a typewriter-style keyboard with raised keys, and is packed with useful features: a 200-year calendar and schedule mode for easy entry and recall of appointments; three telephone directories for storing names, numbers, and addresses; and more. The system also offers an electronic memo pad, an anniversary function, a calculator, a world clock, and to-do and expense functions.

Sharp organizers also allow you to mark any information as secret, protected by a password only you know. With optional links, you can exchange information with IBM or Macintosh compatible computers or with other Sharp organizers that range from shirt pocket to palm size.

Wizard electronic organizers can include the following packages: Time Expense Manager, Thesaurus Dictionary, Eight-Language Translator, Money Planner, North American City Guide, Work Sheet Manager, and Scientific Computer. You can also download from your computer to your Wizard to travel light with heavyweight information in your pocket.

Atari claims to be the producer of the world's first pocket-size MS–DOS command–compatible computer, which has five built-in applications. These include an address book that can store and retrieve hundreds of addresses and telephone numbers, a diary to help you plan business and social schedules, and a sophisticated calculator with five memories. The computer also carries a Lotus file–compatible worksheet for planning and calculating a budget or keeping track of expenses, and a text editor for typing memos and letters.

The Schedule function of the Atari lists appointments and

can include a programmable alarm to remind you of your key dates. Entries can be repeated daily, monthly, or yearly.

The popular Sidekick 2.0 program, from Borland International, is an executive organizing tool emphasizing a graphics command system with drop-down menus and windows. Using either keyboard or mouse commands, it allows you to choose from pop-up applications new and old (with a million users, it is claimed). Substantially improved features include time management tools, an electronic address book with auto-dialer, an alarm clock, a notepad, a calculator, and communications software. Most programs stay out of the way until needed; vanish to sidelines after utilization. [Information: 212-599-3110]

The Manager's Organizer software program is claimed to "give you all the tools you need to organize tasks, time, and people in one place . . . [and] manage the sometimes overwhelming number of obligations you currently handle manually or just never seem to handle at all." Reportedly developed with input from 10,000 managers in a wide variety of disciplines, it includes the following software: time organizer, business card file, telephone log, personnel manager, expense reports, automobile log, trip reports, business calculator, and agreements. Manager's Organizer "centralizes the huge mass of information you're expected to keep organized, accurate, and current, with everything you might be called on to produce at a moment's notice accessible with a keypress or two." Other features include pull-down menus for simple navigation, a memory resident option, instant pop-ups, a new-user tutorial to get you started quickly, and an on-screen Help function with just a keystroke. [Information: MECA, 203-222-9150]

The Chronos Portable Organizer software management system, available from **Chronos** [555 DeHaro Street, Suite 240, San Francisco, CA 94107], offers an appointment calendar with an alarm, conflict checking, a priority to-do list, an office scheduler, group names, project schedules, milestone and deadlines files, time charts, card file categories, client and contact histories, delegation and follow-up files, "intelligent" dates, an auto-dialer, a memo pad, "hot" keys, and more. The system also fits the Day-Timer, Day-Runner, and Franklin Organizer systems, permitting transfer from one to the other.

A word of caution: Although all of these organizer/schedulers claim to be simple to operate, it takes some understanding to know how to input and take out information. The incredible miniaturization that provides for so many functions in so small a space has made it likely that these devices will be increasingly used as time savers. To help gain an extra hour every day, decide now to get on board and to learn how to use an electronic organizer effectively.

▪ ORGANIZER/SCHEDULERS ───────

Among the companies offering the best overall systems—whose catalogues you can request without charge—are the following:

Day-Timers
One Day Timer Plaza
Allentown, PA 18195-1551
(215-395-5884)

Day-Focus Inc.
31921 Camino Capistrano
San Juan Capistrano, CA 92675
(800-662-5300)

Dartnell
4660 Ravenswood Avenue
Chicago, IL 60640-9981
(800-621-5463; fax: 312-561-3801)

Franklin International Institute Inc.
2640 Decker Lake Boulevard
Salt Lake City, UT 84119-0127
(801-975-1776, 800-767-1776)

Time Management Center
1590 Woodlake Drive
Chesterfield, MO 63017
(800-458-6468)

Routine Repetitive Tasks

When you fully use your organizer/scheduler, you will certainly find that you are spending many minutes on routine, repetitive activities. Finding short-cuts for these is vital. In both business and personal activities, we repeat innumerable tasks day after day. Many of these can be effectively systemized so as to be completed in less time and to keep the time others spent on them to a minimum.

Two central strategies are required:

1. *Simplify:* If paperwork is involved, develop a variety of procedures and forms that are most efficient for you.
2. *Delegate:* Assign tasks to secretaries, aides, or subordinates.

Such simplification and delegation is derived from industrial engineering, whose basic principles were well formulated years ago, and which have been constantly refined and improved. J. M. Sinclair, in *Public Relations Journal,* explains:

Industrial engineers work on the premise that if a procedure is repeated frequently, even slight method improvements can result in substantial productivity gains. Consequently, they analyze integrated systems of people, machines, and materials to design and install the best. They may eliminate even a slight hand movement in the process. Or design an entire plant, all in the cause of increased efficiency.

Because of repeated procedure emphasis, industrial engineering principles have been utilized primarily in mass production. But, some can be applied to people in offices, even for those who think their work different every day. Ask yourself how often you open mail, answer correspondence, make telephone calls, attend staff meetings, read trade papers or journals, go to suppliers, write varied items, and more.

In all of these, Sinclair continues, it becomes apparent that while the job content changes constantly, processes remain the same. After tracking your activities, you will also find a remarkable day-to-day similarity in the sequences by which you perform many of your functions.

Sinclair says he looked at his own job not with a stop-watch or slide-rule, as might an industrial engineer, but with two assumptions in mind that show the spirit of the industrial engineer:

1. *A better way of doing every job can be found.* Industrial engineers are optimists; even when they develop an improvement, they seldom refer to it as the best, but are more likely to call it the best available or the best yet devised, assuming further progress inevitable.

2. *Adopting a constant questioning attitude toward every repeated action* allows one to discover improvements. Before industrial engineers suggest changes, says Sinclair, they study

them. By keeping the same type of daily log as noted elsewhere, along with time requirements for tasks, they begin to see which routines can be divided into smaller steps and units, which can be combined or short-cut, and which can be systemized and simplified.

Through such analysis, says Sinclair, you have done exactly what an industrial engineer would; you have taken the process apart and rebuilt it to establish the best available method. While the time saved may at first seem insignificant, engineers would remind you that, when you repeat any activity, small method improvements can result in substantial total time and energy savings.

After an industrial engineer has determined the best available method, he or she figures out how long it will take. Realistically calculating time enables you to determine in advance how much you can likely do in given time periods, enabling you to set more realistic goals. Such calculations are valuable because they are based on direct observations of how long activities take (as opposed to the time you would like them to take).

Recognizing your time needs early instead of at day's end allows you to make better decisions about what to do first, about what may have to be cut from later periods, and about what can simply be delegated. Sinclair notes that this strategy led him to—

■ Cut morning reading time of the *Wall Street Journal* and other trade publications.

■ Ask for deliveries of certain things he normally might have picked up by hand.

■ Get scheduled meetings postponed or streamlined to gain time.

■ Allocate to the next day those things that could wait.

Sinclair concludes, "When an industrial engineer projects how much an operator can complete in a day, he doesn't assume

100 percent efficiency. He figures in lost time due to personal needs and fatigue; percentages varied by job and performance conditions. Adopting these principles to your own repetitive tasks can enable you to get more done in less time."

What worked for Sinclair works just as well for others, and can for you if you look at your routine repetitive activities and try to save minutes on each. The increasing aim of many firms such as Sea-Land, a major international transport company, is to enable workers to get rid of wasteful, repetitive tasks—a particularly important goal in light of the downsizing of business, with fewer employees to do the job. An unexpected result for Sea-Land has been that many job descriptions have shrunk from five pages to a single sheet. This is so, for example, because salespeople no longer have to write overly detailed routine reports that often go unread. A blunt but effective test Sea-Land now uses to determine task necessity, according to *Fortune,* is this: If somebody else's department needs it more than you, let that group do it. Often, the other department doesn't need the task done either.

Digital Equipment Corporation, undergoing restructuring, has invited employees to look for routine, repetitive work inefficiencies. Among other things, Digital compared shop-floor control systems at U.S. and Japanese automakers with their own, seeking simpler, time-saving ways to move materials through factories. The result: *Fortune* quotes John F. Smith, senior vice president for operations, as saying that employees themselves choose routine tasks to be eliminated.

Pizza Hut, another labor-intensive operation, has taken the time pressure off many employees by having them suggest ways to redesign the routine, repetitive aspects of their work themselves. *Fortune* says: "Sales and morale increased when store managers helped decide what paperwork the parent company could scuttle. One opted out of its payroll system and started his own, with more generous bonuses responsible for the 40-percent sales growth."

Maids International, a franchise house-cleaning service with

$16 million in annual sales, taught employees how to speed up their routine, repetitive procedures, enabling them to complete more work in less time and earn more in the process.

▪ HANDLING TASKS ASSIGNED TO YOU ──────────────

The opposite of routine, repetitive tasks you must undertake are the new assignments you may be given. Virtually every job you have involves a series of assignments, either self-imposed or given to you by higher-ups to whom you report. Some assignments take minutes, some months or years, but, says Lauchland A. Henry in *The Professional's Guide to Working Smarter,* no matter what the assignment, certain basic steps can help you accomplish them in less time and with greater satisfaction with the assurance that you don't have to go back and redo them. Henry offers the following tips:

▪ *Define the assignment clearly.* Many important new assignments are frequently misinterpreted, even in settings in which the employee basically knows what is to be done. Repeat the assignment in your own words if given directly. You might be leaping ahead, thinking about how you will carry out the task being explained to you, perhaps missing an important element. If required facts are not put before you, clarify through your own questions what you have to produce, the expected finishing time, any special circumstances, and possible sources of help and other resources. Seek an opportunity to review progress periodically if the task is complex.

▪ *Keep dated notes.* Assignments often change during execution. Notes will give you a running record of what you are seeking to do and how well you are moving toward its accomplishment. If something important becomes unclear, return to the assigner of the task and get clarification. Don't rely on the oft expressed "Do thus and so. *You know what I mean.*"

■ *Avoid unreasonable deadlines.* Sometimes assigners will say something such as "Don't make a federal case out of it," meaning not to take forever. The amount of time spent on a project obviously should be based on the importance of the assignment itself and its priority to the assigner.

■ *Read every word if an assignment is written.* Don't skim written directions. Identify targeted results, information sources, reports required, and due dates. Note what you don't understand, being sure that you haven't overlooked anything that would clarify these questions. Contact the assigner and discuss such matters until they are clear. If changes result from the discussion, put these in writing and date the notes so that you are sure at any moment to be working with the latest version of the assignment and not wasting time.

■ *Execute your assignment plan flexibly.* In executing your plan, don't discard it at the first point at which it seems to fail—but don't adhere too blindly to it either. Plans are always subject to change as you move along. Also, don't fail to bring important difficulties to the attention of your assigner.

I would add this tip: If the assignment has been a long process, consider leading your report with an executive summary, highlighting points in terms of most benefit to the assigner. Keep documentation, backup, and so on with the report, or include a note to the assigner simply saying what else you have available. As former U.S. Senator William Benton, whose Encyclopedia Britannica was my long-time client, once explained, "Don't make the obvious irrefutable." By providing everything significant directly and in the fewest possible words, you will not only save the time of those for whom the assignment has been done, but ensure that it will be read and heeded.

Using Your Most Effective Hours

When should you undertake the many tasks noted in your organizer/scheduler? Given a choice (for we often have no control over when many things must be done), when is your best time to undertake your most important tasks?

No one would think of operating complex machines without a wide variety of gauges and measuring devices to provide the essential data on what was going on inside. Yet, we are apt to overlook the fact that we ourselves are complex machines with our own personal gauges—indicators that make clear our physical condition throughout the day and its effect on our ability to accomplish more in less of our best time.

Doing your *most important tasks* at your *most productive hours* and saving the hours of least personal efficiency for less essential jobs is another overlooked time-saving principle I can't stress too much.

It seems as though this formula shouldn't require elaboration. Yet, so many people become so set in their routines that they use their most productive hours for handling the relatively unimportant, and tackle big, priority problems during some of their poorer hours.

Dr. Nathaniel Kleitman, a University of Chicago physiologist, is a noted expert on both sleep and wakefulness. Using what he calls the clinical thermometer, Kleitman discovered that how fast you get started in the morning is largely a matter of body temperature. A normal temperature for the body is 98.6°F. Actually, Dr. Kleitman notes, this varies as much as three degrees during the day, even if a person is perfectly well. Variations in body temperature—lower when asleep than when awake—reflect your basal metabolism, a complicated process in which your body burns up oxygen and, so to speak, stokes your furnace.

Temperature variation patterns coincide with the rise and fall of your working efficiency, mental alertness, and feeling of well-being.

Though not everyone is alike, you're likely to fall in one of three categories:

■ *Morning*—You wake up with your furnace hot and ready to go full blast; you're packed with drive. You reach your peak around noon, then cool off gradually. By evening, you're often pretty well burned out for the day.

■ *Evening*—You hate getting up, and go through morning listless, lethargic, even sulky; by afternoon, you begin to glow. In the late afternoon, you're just as much a fireball as the Morning type was at ten o'clock. By the time you start to wind down, the sun has long set.

■ *Ever-Ready*—This happy individual has the virtues of both others' personal thermostats—starts early, cools at midday lunch period, fires up again in the afternoon.

▪ YOUR EFFICIENCY PATTERN ─────────

During the course of each day, your mental and physical efficiency varies greatly. In every twenty-four hours there is a time when your built-in efficiency is highest and another when it is lowest. These ups and downs occur about the same time daily, constituting what could be called your efficiency pattern. Most of us hit our peak about an hour after breakfast. From then on, we decline, slowly at first, then more rapidly, beginning shortly after lunch.

If you are like the average person, your daily low may be about 4:00 P.M. However, you pop back a bit after dinner, then down again about 10:00. Even then, you are apt to be more efficient than during your afternoon doldrums.

All of this is provided that you are in the norm. Most of us, however, aren't just average. Because of different habits and lifestyles, each individual varies somewhat from this mean. You can, however, talk yourself into thinking that you are a morning or night person and act accordingly.

The fact that morning hours are best for most has been demonstrated by many studies. A few rare types can turn it on at 9:00, and turn it off at 5:00, but a majority say they are tops before the day's hustle and bustle begins.

▪ DETERMINING YOUR OWN CYCLE ─────────

There are many ways to determine your own cycle's peak periods. Here are some tips:

▪ Keep your own chart for two to three weeks to spot best and poorest times.

▪ If you want to raise your body heat, and thus your morning efficiency, take a longer, warmer shower or bath. Or, do up to a half hour of jogging or aerobics. Once elevated, your temperature will stay high, lifting your entire day's cycle.

■ If you don't function well at day's start, consider whether you are getting enough sleep. Additionally, adequate nutrition at breakfast, rather than a hurried cup of coffee and toast, can be a big boost. You need to raise blood sugar levels, bringing your body up to full functioning capacity.

■ ADAPT TO WORKPLACE REALITIES

If your boss is groggy in the morning and wide awake in the afternoon, and you exhibit just the opposite cycle, you might have to learn to live with this pattern until you become the boss yourself.

If your workplace habit is to use morning time for colleague greetings, inventorying the news, and rehashing last night's game—cut the palaver. While it is nice to exchange greetings, these pleasantries can be brief. The head start achieved by singleness of purpose can make all the difference in your day.

Most important, don't waste high-efficiency morning time on the newspapers, nonessential correspondence, and cleaning up the little matters. Tackle the big things.

■ MAKING THE BEST USE OF PEAK PERIODS

Once you have identified your high-energy periods, concentrate on—

■ Major problems on your to-do schedule.
■ Creative thinking.
■ Discussions and working out matters of first importance.

Tackle unpleasant or difficult jobs in the optimum period. Leaving them to later or slower times only makes them more difficult and unpleasant. (Schedule the largest or hardest jobs for Mondays or Tuesdays. Chances are that you will have more high-energy time free then. Doing the tough jobs early gives you a psychological boost in feeling that the week's "hump" is over.)

For medium efficiency times concentrate on—

- Interchanges with others at your office or other workplace.
- Dictation of routine letters and memos.
- Further planning and scheduling.

For low efficiency times concentrate on—

- Preliminary sorting and study of mail.
- Talking with visitors on routine subjects.
- Telephone calls.

A personal note: I found that my best period was in the morning. For many years, I arose before breakfast to put in an hour writing. During some of those years as a long-time Long Island Railroad commuter, I also discovered how to make use of the ride time. I was at an energy high at that time of day and simply blocked out interruptions. I did original creative work, managing to write two books and innumerable articles in this daily 30-minute period. Tempting headlines in the news were limited to a glance; detailed news reading was saved for later, less effective moments. I also taught myself to tackle the most important creative assignments in the best time-saving period, using techniques detailed elsewhere in this book.

Procrastination

Procrastination is often the result of self-delusion—perfectly good reasons we give ourselves to put off a report that can be done tomorrow (when we are at our peak) instead of today (when we are "not inspired"). However, putting off the things you ought to do, things you know are your high priorities, can double or triple the time it takes to do what has to be done. The very thought of having more to get done than you appear to have time to do often paralyzes the will. Doing nothing, or doing something less important, piles up to-be-dones like snow before a plow until there is a mountain.

Caught in this self-created predicament, we are apt to go slightly haywire. Our subconscious mind protests. We get nervous, feel constantly under pressure, lose our tempers, get frustrated and bark at anyone around, and, most of all, hate ourselves. All of this is counterproductive and unnecessary.

■ ARE YOU A PROCRASTINATOR? ———————

If the answer is yes, congratulations on your honesty. To some degree, we all are. Procrastination is so universal that there is now reportedly a national procrastination club. Members have been planning to meet for some time—they just haven't gotten around to it.

Procrastination is often difficult to detect because it is a nonentity. The tasks you perform are what you get done. The rest are left undone, or are postponed. Dale Carnegie once wrote: "Procrastination becomes a problem because neglect and delay in doing the things important to you and your advancement become a continuing road block."

Do You Recognize These? ————————————

Procrastination, say Dr. Merrill E. Douglass and Dr. Larry B. Baker of the Time Management Center, is—

■ Doing low-priority tasks rather than higher-priority ones.
■ Straightening your desk when you should be working on a vital report.
■ Calling on the friendly customer who buys very little instead of preparing a presentation for the tough prospect who could purchase much more.
■ Postponing the time you know you should spend with your children until they are half grown and it is too late.

Douglass and Baker add: "It's avoiding co-workers rather than telling them bad news. Staying away from the office so you don't have to discipline a subordinate." By keeping us from tackling the truly important or most vital tasks, "procrastination is an insidious habit that can ruin careers, destroy happiness and even shorter lives—preventing success in all areas."

Procrastination costs you untold minutes, hours, and days. Controlling the urge to put things off takes discipline, but the good news is, once tackled, the procrastinated task usually isn't half as difficult to overcome as it had seemed.

■ CAUSES OF PROCRASTINATION ⸻

Habit is one of the main causes of procrastination. We all have a tendency to develop certain patterns and to continue them rather than accepting the challenge of change.

We most often procrastinate on certain tasks because they are unpleasant, difficult, or make us feel indecisive. We tend not to put off things that are easy or enjoyable. Procrastinating about the unpleasant rarely makes it disappear; it only increases your anxiety level, for the things that must be done are still there, nagging, and frequently causing irritability.

■ PROCRASTINATION-BREAKING APPROACHES ⸻

Here are some of the best minute-making procrastination-breaking approaches:

■ *Do the unpleasant thing first.* Try scheduling your most unpleasant task—the one you tend to put off most often—at the beginning of the day. This gets the matter behind you, rather than being left to dread and continually put off. (Douglass and Baker)

■ *Reserve a small amount of time* for the prospective procrastination item. Resolve to work on manageable components of a problem for ten to thirty minutes each day. Quit when the time is up. Such large problems as preparing a budget or taking inventory can be handled this way. *(Japan Times)*

Unfortunately, some unpleasant tasks don't lend themselves to this approach. Firing an employee or being the bearer of bad news can't really be handled piecemeal. The best suggestion for this is simply do it and let it be done. Not tackling unpleasant-nesses today only ensures that you will feel equally burdened with such problems, and other procrastination-inducers, tomorrow. *(Japan Times)*

■ *Make a deadline commitment to yourself.* Wager with some-one to force yourself to action. For example, tell your boss you will have the budget prepared a week early or buy her the dinner of her choice. If you are a sales rep, tell one or more of your colleagues that you will up your last month's sales by 20 percent or buy a round at a future happy hour. If you bet with someone, there is something in it for you if you win. You want both an incentive for reaching your goal and a penalty for falling short. *(Japan Times)*

■ *Reward yourself for accomplishment.* For example, make a special lunch date with your spouse for finishing the project you have been putting off. Self-rewards can be anything appealing to you, large or small. If you don't earn the reward, don't give it to yourself; if you do, be sure to take it. Occasional rewards make life more interesting and help you conquer your tendency to procrastinate on dreaded tasks.

■ *Work backward to break jobs down into subunits.* Start with the desired results—the finished task—and then keep asking yourself what would have to precede this. Thus, the most com-plex task can be broken into units as small as necessary to reduce the overwhelming nature of a project. (Douglass and Baker)

■ *After you have divided large tasks into smaller ones,* add milestones so that you are conscious of your progress. Research shows that outstanding managers of time build their own sense of urgency and overcome procrastination by planning target time. (Dr. James Steffin)

The fear of not achieving immediate perfection is another common cause of putting things off. *A tip:* Do your best the first

time around, with the implicit self-understanding that you will
return later for improvements. Knowing that there will be a
second or third review, you will move ahead with far greater
speed and confidence.

■ *Go ahead with what you have.* If you delay starting a report
because you don't have every last piece of information, remember that 80 percent will be a more than passing grade. If you
jump right in and get the job done the best possible way *now,*
you will avoid the drawbacks and downers of procrastination.
(Dr. James Steffin)

■ *Consider delegating* a dull or unpleasant task. Assign the
project, or part of it, to a subordinate; hire an outside service; or
swap tasks with a colleague who doesn't have the same mental
block.

■ *Give in to procrastination.* Do nothing for fifteen minutes.
"You should become very uneasy and, in effect, jump-start yourself. Finally, if you clear everything off your desk or workplace
except the task at hand and work on nothing else for at least an
hour, you'll probably find yourself overcoming many of the procrastination causers." (Alan Lakein)

■ BREAKING A PROCRASTINATION HABIT

Lester R. Bittel, in *Right on Time,* says that the best ways to beat
procrastination are the following:

■ *Make a definite, even radical, change in your routine.* That
is, eliminate behavior associated with the habit you want to
change. For example, if you procrastinate by drinking coffee and
chatting with co-workers, stop doing this completely for a while
and reward yourself for periods during which you stick to your
new habit.

■ *Allow no exceptions to your new habit* early in your campaign. If you decide to put your work in priority order and always complete the highest priority items before tackling the next, do so consistently.

■ *Begin immediately.* We don't usually follow through with resolutions for a change effective next week. Bittel notes: "If you have time-wasting habits that need elimination, start right now. The rudiments of a successful habit-breaking campaign can be worked out in minutes."

■ *Finally, set up barriers to procrastination.* These include setting a starting time for each planned task; generating momentum in an easy, routine manner; and, as suggested earlier, breaking major tasks into subtasks.

■ CREATING SELF-PRESSURE

Some procrastinate because they believe they work better under pressure, says Thomas J. Quirk. There is a grain of truth to this. A certain amount of pressure *can* help you get moving, but if your habit is routinely to wait until the last minute to start, you are more likely to turn out shoddy work, or at least a lower quality than you are capable of producing.

Not putting things off but beginning major projects well in advance of due dates offers two advantages, says Quirk: You are prepared for crises that might demand your attention, and you don't need to come up with a plausible excuse when the boss asks, "What do you mean you won't have the report ready on time?"

Quirk also offers the following tips:

■ *Substantially reduce one time-waster weekly.* You might never eliminate it altogether, but you can cut down on wasted time.

■ *Keep track of time wasters* you feel you have licked over the course of a week. If, at the end of a year, you have fifty-two of these, you will be well on your way toward being a skillful time user, rather than one who can't keep track of those time-wasting minutes.

▪ THE PLEASANT VERSUS THE IMPORTANT

Time management consultant James Steffin concludes:

> *Many people regularly encourage procrastination by asking "What do I feel like doing now?" instead of asking themselves what is most important to do now. By keeping importance uppermost, you concentrate on what is significant related to your goals—not the pleasantness of the moment. . . . You could well discover, as many do, that when you push yourself to be totally involved in the procrastinable activity that is really your Most Important Now, what started out to be unpleasant can become the reverse due to the progress you're making toward where you want to go.*

Making Your Desk a Time-Saving Work Station

Your key thinking, planning, organizing, and scheduling can be done in a variety of locations, but your daily work is likely to be concentrated at a desk in an office or other workplace. Laying out your desk as an effective personal work station, one best suited to your needs, can be a most important time saver. Considering the time you spend there, it is worth examining in detail.

The danger is that too often a desk becomes a prop, a place in which to conveniently bury papers and all types of infrequently used reference materials, rather than to advance the tasks you must or wish to do. Hence, an increasing number of alert business people are keen about clean desktops—to reflect streamlined, minute-minding control.

If you have a choice, look for a desk with spaces specially fitted for your specific job: choices include drawer trays, which help eliminate surface clutter; personal files with special guides; and a removable wastebasket, which saves floor space and is especially useful in banks or front offices where you are in public view.

If you are assigned a desk, your need is to use what you have in the most effective way.

▪ MAKING YOUR OFFICE AS WELL ORGANIZED AS YOUR HOME ─────────

Whether you realize it or not, says Day-Timers, your home is a model of efficient design: the bed is in the bedroom; the stove is in the kitchen; the TV is wherever you like to stretch out and relax. The same usually can't be said for your office. Many people attempt to work in offices that actually impede productivity. Files are lost or out of place; papers are piled high; desktops are cluttered.

If this description applies to your office, don't worry, you are in good company, says Day-Timers. The answer to this problem is to consider how you can best arrange your equipment and supplies for maximum time-saving productivity. Efficient files will keep paperwork from piling up while providing the papers you really need *now*. Once you are effectively organized, it is relatively easy to maintain the place in which you earn a living. Offices ought to be thought of as a country divided into three space provinces, says Day-Timers. They are:

1. *Work* (where you perform your daily responsibilities)
2. *Storage* (where you keep resources needed for performance)
3. *Visitors*

These divisions are primarily functional rather than physical. There is bound to be some overlap—as, for example, with work and storage space—but the best organized offices are those with the most clearly defined areas.

▪ WHERE TO PLACE YOUR DESK ─────

Many managers prefer positioning desks so that they face the outer office, with a view of it. This allows greeting visitors comfortably while enjoying a pleasing sense of command over your space, but there is a drawback: You might find yourself being distracted by every passing co-worker. Given the option, either angle your desk so that outside traffic doesn't directly pass in front of your sightline, or, as many do, face it inward to a wall. This also leaves the most space for other furniture and fittings. Remember, you are not there for the view.

More and more, executives who can, add another desk or work surface. It is often simply a tabletop with enough room to spread out large jobs and other items that would otherwise clutter primary space. A credenza provides added storage space and allows you to switch back-and-forth from one project to another without having to clear away or reestablish components each work period—a definite time waster. Day-Timers notes: "Even if you don't require project space, you might use a separate stand-up unit to vary routine and relieve the fatigue often plaguing the desk-bound."

Another worthwhile option is a right-angle table for telephone, notepads, file holder, and other accessories wanted within arm's reach. These can also accommodate a typewriter or PC.

Knowing exactly where an item can be located and being able to get to it easily save more minutes over the course of a year than you might imagine.

▪ DESKS AND PERSONNEL PLACEMENT ─────

More work can usually be turned out if desks are not facing windows, open doorways, or busy corridors—sources of a large number of distractions. If this is a problem, and furniture move-ment is out of the question, it might be financially beneficial in the long run for you to invest in some partitions.

Additionally, if you have a say in desk and personnel loca-tion, examine the human element. One expert says: "Whether we like it or not, it's a fact that some people cannot work in a group environment without habitually creating useless conversation. This leads to wasted time and can deteriorate into a series of gossip sessions. Even though this particular problem is not al-ways easy to correct, it is usually solvable. Begin with a careful review of the physical placement of each employee. After this is completed, try separating personnel who have a tendency to take time talking too much. One approach: Strategically locate in-dividuals who will not be at specific workplaces long enough to engage in lengthy peer discussions. For example, filing clerks are excellent people to place in this fashion since their respon-sibilities generally entail continuous movement from desks to recording areas."

▪ HOW DISORDERLY DESKS IMPAIR EFFECTIVENESS AND WASTE TIME ──

Day-Timers notes these consequences of constantly disorderly desks:

▪ Loss of control over your work.
▪ Diminished productivity.
▪ Distraction, fatigue, and stress.
▪ A poor image with colleagues and others who see you at your helter-skelter workplace.

There is also the strong likelihood of constantly misplacing important documents, correspondence, and projects—something many executives say is one of the most frustrating time wasters.

I agree with "clean desk" advocates, who insist that only your current project belongs on your desktop. Get rid of everything that doesn't have to be there: unfiled papers, books, personal momentos, writing tools, and everything else that could either be disposed of or put somewhere out of the way.

▪ PILE-A-MANIA

As Jeffrey Mayer described it in *Cosmopolitan,*

> *You've probably seen offices that look as if they've gone through the spin cycle of a washing machine, or as if a dump truck had backed up and dropped its load. There are piles of paper everywhere—on the desk, credenza, floor, and couch. Newspapers, magazines, books, pink phone slips, yellow, blue, and green Post-It notes. Pads and pads of paper. New files. Used files. Colored files and papers—big, little, new, and old. How can any work be accomplished with such Pile-a-Mania? The person behind that desk may look busy, but is the job really getting done? The main reason for cluttered desktops and files is fear of putting anything away because you'll never find it again. Or will forget about it. By leaving everything out, we can see all our unfinished work—right there in front of us spread out—but unfortunately everybody else can see it, too.*

▪ THE DOUGLASS LAW OF CLUTTER

Authorities Merrill E. and Donna N. Douglass, writers on time management, have developed what they call their desk-applicable Law of Clutter, explaining: "Clutter tends to expand to fill space available for retention. If you're a disorganized person with a small desk, your desk will be cluttered. Get a desk five times larger, it will still become totally cluttered." Why do desks become cluttered so easily? The answer is that many people lack criteria for determining what goes into or on top of a desk. They use the desk for the wrong purpose, they have sloppy work habits, or they fail to think through the problem. Solutions require a certain amount of discipline and new habits.

▪ CLEARING AWAY DESK CLUTTER IN FIVE EASY STEPS

Clear your desk of clutter by following these five easy steps suggested by Day-Timers:

1. *Set aside a definite block of time* to tackle the problem head-on. Be prepared to spend a few slow periods or after-work hours for this task. The worst part about desk debris is getting rid of the accumulated clutter; afterward, it can be simply routine preventive maintenance.

2. *Use the "salami" technique,* if clutter is truly overwhelming. Cut the cleanup operation into more manageable "slices." For instance, you might clear just desktop or a single desk drawer, saving the rest for another time.

3. *Eliminate those items that are dispensable.* Photos, gadgets, and other odds and ends have no place. Books, magazines, and old reports not essential to work at hand should be cleared away. Too many desks are filled with "someday" items that, in fact, are rarely used.

4. *Have a few inexpensive bookshelves put in one office corner.* Ready-made, easily assembled units are best placed behind the desk so that you can get to them without rising. These can be placed in another corner if there isn't a daily reference requirement.

5. *Gather all loose papers into a single pile or into a box.* Position your wastebasket or a plastic garbage bag within easy

range and start going through the pile, passing judgment on each item. Has it been used in the past month? Year? How soon do you expect use? What is the worst that can happen if you decide to chuck an item? Bear in mind the old adage "When in doubt, throw it out" (except legal and tax documents, of course).

Discard as much as you can. If you are unsure about certain items, move them into inactive storage areas, and make an organizer/scheduler notation to deal with them at a set time. Act on items that must be acted upon and get rid of the rest—by category and, if needed for the future, in clearly marked folders.

▪ THE ART OF WASTEBASKETRY ─────

The wastebasket is a functional link in paper flow, say the Douglasses, offering the following advice on making it a valuable tool:

> *Get a wastebasket big enough to hold all you can feed it without its being an eyesore. It should be convenient for your use, not placed to suit janitor or interior decorator whims. Set up your own goes-in and stays-out rules. Objective: to throw out as much as possible. For some, throwing things out is a decisive act; for others, it creates an unusually high level of apprehension. Try getting over your emotional attachment to paper—and don't avoid your trauma by routing your junk to somebody else. As you learn to master these desk organizing principles, you'll recognize a significant increase in both quality and quantity of accomplishment—and be able to do more in less time.*

Once existing clutter is cleared, you will be ready to start your own preventive maintenance program: a system for sorting and handling the papers that cross your desk (see Chapter 8). Meanwhile, doesn't it feel good to see the top of your desk again?

▪ OTHER DESK AND OFFICE ORGANIZING TECHNIQUES —————————————————————

There are any number of desk-organizing techniques that have been developed by highly regarded experts; ideas that you can adopt.

R. Alec Mackenzie, developer of the Time Management Methods course, believes that 95 percent of executives are affected by what he calls stacked desk syndrome. Many executives say that they desk-pile items because they don't want to forget about them—but every time they see the pile, their train of thought is broken. As the stack mounts, they are unable to remember what is at the bottom and begin looking. So much time is wasted retrieving lost items and rediscovering all of the things not to be forgotten that the minutes lost would be hard to calculate. The following are Mackenzie's three working rules to help cure the stacked desk syndrome:

1. Clear your desk of everything that is not related to the project at hand.
2. Don't allow any other items to be deposited on your desk or other workspace until you are ready for them.
3. Integrate papers for action gradually into your daily processing routine. Pay personal attention to what you must, and delegate what you can. Divide publications into must and might read, tossing out as many of the latter as possible.

Set up your office for ease of performance through the following guidelines:

▪ Position yourself according to whether you are right- or left-handed, with your typical movements in mind.
▪ Create work space in front of you for the job that you are currently doing. If necessary, move the telephone and other

equipment, as well as the most often consulted references, to side extensions or to a rear credenza within reach.

■ Place the most frequently used items in immediately accessible areas.

■ Place priority starting materials on your desk the night before, and let them be the only items on your desk.

Mackenzie notes that Ralph Cordiner, one-time chairman of General Electric company, disclosed another reason for having no papers atop a desk: "When I have a visitor to whom I've committed time, I want that person to have my full attention. No distractions. That's another reason I demand a clean desk."

■ A FINGERTIP DESK MANAGEMENT PLAN

Think of your office area as a target, urges Charles R. Hobbs, author of *Time Power*, adding: "The desk where you sit is the bull's-eye. Your most valuable space is what you fill personally. Next most valuable: that directly within reach. What might be called *Area A* includes a scheduler/organizer at your fingertips—on desk or in pocket when outside. *Area B* is for things less frequently used; *Area C*, those not often used."

Hobbs offers the following tips:

■ *Take time to clean out your desk, back-up furniture, and everything else around you.* Evaluate each according to frequency of use. Then, put such things as paperclips, staplers, and scissors in their proper places.

■ *Use an A-B-C system to organize all papers in your work area.* Papers designated *A* are for immediate action, *B* papers should be easily accessed, and *C* papers are to be put away for review at a later time.

■ *Don't take out all the interesting materials and leave only an austere cell.* A tropical plant, an oil painting—the accoutrements that make you *you*—are desirable. Make your office a comfort zone so that when others are there they feel accepted, at ease, and personally productive—but within reason. A special sofa arrangement or place to sit and talk in comfort often improves discussions and conversation if such decor is available in your position. However, there is a point at which too much comfort distracts one from productivity.

▪ ORGANIZER ESSENTIALS ——————————

Robert C. Lowery, in *The Organized Workplace,* suggests a desk work station set-up containing, among other things, the following items:

▪ *An in-basket,* an urgent basket, and an out-basket should handle, respectively, receiving, reviewing, and returning documents.

▪ *A desk drawer file* to hold materials and documents awaiting processing, and a pull-out desk tray to which are taped a list of most frequently called numbers.

▪ *A personal "databank" of essential,* frequently needed facts, such as addresses, dimensions, sizes, capacities, social security numbers, credit card numbers, and so on.

▪ *An answer/speaker phone,* along with a calendar and clock—preferably one with an alarm. A typewriter or word processor or PC with keyboard, display screen, printer, modem and interconnect input/output devices. A computer can also serve as an out-basket if connected with other work stations, as noted in another chapter.

Of course, you also need a truly comfortable chair (preferably the swivel variety) and a *very large* wastebasket.

▪ THE U-SHAPED WORK STATION ——————

Lester R. Bittel, in *Right on Time,* says that the most desk time saving for paper flow should be U-shaped, explaining: "That is, incoming mail or requests received by telephone or in person should be placed in the in-basket in the upper right-hand corner. Incoming documents should be sorted as soon as possible and routed toward you for immediate action in your urgent now-basket or filed in the holding file of your desk drawer. Urgent items move as soon as possible to your work surface for action—to be completed or acted upon and moved out as soon as possible."

In this system, incoming items judged to be not for immediate attention go into a location divided by those needing action, review, or response within a week; those requiring longer-range action; and those to be put away for review at one's convenience, with the use of a wastebasket and permanent file.

It is vital to review *A* items constantly for their placement in their order of urgency. Keep your pending file slim, says Bittel: no more than five day's work.

▪ A FOUR-PHASE SYSTEM ——————

Full-scale reorganization to make your desk and workplace a time saver probably requires at least two or three Saturdays for the job, and a lot of trashbags, says Stephanie Winston in *The Organized Executive.* This is her procedure:

In your mind's eye, block your desk into four rough quadrants. Select a starting pile—either one containing critical materials or the one nearest at hand. If papers are scattered rather than stacked, block out a square foot of space and begin there. Treat each item according to the *TRAF* system. *T,* Throw it away; *R,* Refer it to someone else; *A,* Act on it; and *F,* File for future use or to read.

Next, divide drawers into thirds and work on one section at a time, sorting, consolidating, and discarding dog-eared index cards and antique sugar packets. Now, TRAF all accumulated papers on windowsills, shelves, credenza, bulletin board, and so on. The time-wasters will soon be minimized.

■ THE DESKLESS OFFICE ─────────

A growing number of executives have actually eliminated their desks completely—on the theory that if you don't have anywhere to hide your paperwork, you do it much more quickly. One-time American Management Association president Lawrence A. Appley introduced me to the deskless office concept, explaining: "I keep no files or papers myself; my aides bring in items needing attention. I act as quickly as possible on new matters or, if they can't be settled, jot down thoughts, either on a memo sheet or a Post-It note routed to those who can add ideas and material. Some can be tickled for a second look when other materials are assembled. I simply refuse to be buried in paper."

I have found that numerous top executives follow the same idea—keeping a few required papers on a low coffee table in an office without a desk, to promote informal conversation and to speed up meetings. Louis Hausman, of Columbia Broadcasting, explained:

> *Establishing a new office, I asked myself why I needed a desk. Answer: I don't. Specifically, an executive job involves signing mail, making notes on reports or correspondence, running meetings, dictating, telephoning by the hour, going to or having people in for discussions. None required a desk. Take paperwork: Three or four times a day my secretary brings in a correspondence folder, memos, and reports. Since the only place I can put it down is the coffee table, I do the*

*job right then and there. The informal setting makes
it easier to move around, dictate, and think.*

David C. Hurley, Jr., believes many executives use conventional
desks primarily as symbols of office prestige, adding: "They feel
more important; the individual in front, less. Neither is relaxed.
Eliminating the desk brings about informality and rapidity of
approach."

I unchained myself from a desk when I founded and chaired
International Public Relations Company, Ltd., associated with
the Tokyo company of the same name. Because the majority of
my work involved meeting with clients, prospects, and staff, and
reading reports and studies and then dictating responses, I set up
a deskless office with a Japanese-American decor. Decorator Bar-
bara Cohen chose restful colors, couches, easy chairs, and a
clipboard on which to write. My outgoing basket was in a side-
board. All minor necessities were in small, built-in bookshelves,
along with a Dictaphone Time Master. A single personal file held
all necessary current reference material.

I found the simpler way of office life rich with other rewards.
I could be very busy, yet the noncommercial atmosphere of my
deskless, attractively curtained, flower-and-leaf decorated workplace removed feelings of office stress and strain. As a public
relations executive, I gained other benefits. Clients enjoyed coming without feeling in a secondary position. I didn't always have
to go to them. We often served lunch, and *The New Yorker* and
Newsweek magazines and others ran stories and pictures about
the concept, bringing new prospects with them.

Many large companies, of course, predetermine the general
decor of offices. You might not be able to call all of the shots, but
selecting furniture and even artwork from the company's collection might be possible.

▪ UNCLUTTERING COURSES ─────────

For professional guidance on ridding yourself of time-killing desk, office, and home clutter, consider the many schools—particularly adult learning centers—providing courses with such unabashed titles as Getting Rid of Clutter. One such school is the **Learning Center** in New York [tel: 212-580-2828], whose course cost (in 1991) $21 for members and $29 for nonmembers. It is taught by Daralee Schulman, a private-practice career and stress counselor.

The course literature asks:

> *Are you overwhelmed by the continued buildup of clutter—tense and anxious about your inability to handle the problem? If you have difficulty getting rid of newspaper articles, old books, and other material things, the Managing Clutter workshop may be the answer. Through discussion, pencil-and-paper exercises, and visualization, participants explore reasons for clutter and accumulation and learn effective ways of reducing it and the accompanying anxiety. Class topics include: Reasons for Accumulating Clutter, Separating from the Past, Organizing Your Papers and Files, and Procrastination.*

▪ ORGANIZING CONSULTANTS ─────────

Finally, if you can't or won't do your own desk and clutter reorganization, consider getting outside help. The National Association of Professional Organizers has 300 members who provide professional services. In 1990, such services charged anywhere from $30 an hour to $1,500 a day—sometimes doing the job in three or four hours, sometimes longer.

Services provided by Sue McMillin of Time to Spare, as

reported in *Changing Times,* are typical. Her cardinal rule: Break large projects into small chunks—clearing out desks to show immediate results. Gathering up every stray paper scrap that barges in, she divides desk papers into four piles: (1) needed at fingertips, (2) close by for quick reference, (3) archival paper delegated to background files, and (4) eminently trashable reading material to be tossed in the wastebasket.

Changing Times notes that organization experts swear that the vast majority of time-management problems can be solved by setting up systems that match your method of working—or your lifestyle. That is, organize by activity.

Another consultant is Stephanie Schur, head of Spaceorganizers. One of her clients has been Edwina McLaughlin, Personnel Director at Kaye, Scholer, Feirman, Hayes & Handler, a New York law firm. *Working Woman* reported that Ms. McLaughlin had never really taken ownership of her office, though there for two years—but felt she could make her space a tool for success by using it and her time more effectively. The desktop was the first problem—with papers, problems, and priorities competing for attention. Toning down the "visual noise" increased her productivity. She imposed order with coordinated accessories and a personalized filing system: red Hot Files on the desktop for day-to-day priorities, project files on a nearby shelf, and less active files stored in a drawer.

McLaughlin no longer needs stacks of folders to remind her to do something; a To-Do list in the Hot Files keeps her on track. A clip for message slips encourages returning calls at set intervals.

To free up desk space, *Working Woman* adds, Schur had a wall phone put in and had two shelves installed to hold Post-It notes, tape, and other necessities. Ms. McLaughlin concludes: "I wasn't hopelessly disorganized before the makeover, but I no longer feel the pressure of the clock as intensely. I don't have to work long hours to play catch-up—as formerly. Moments once spent of getting it together now are pockets of peace and quiet." And time-saving productivity.

Handling Your Paperwork

One story you are likely to hear at any convention is that of the executive who, after an especially hard day, comes home to be asked, "Mom, what do you *really* do at work?" Executives and other office people who on some days aren't sure themselves just what they have or haven't accomplished, are often frustrated trying to explain. Most would agree that a good portion of their time is spent fighting a paper battle—one that never seems to offer sight of victory.

"People in business today are battling their paperwork with a velocity akin to Don Quixote's tilting at windmills," *Business Week* reported not long ago. "Unfortunately, the result is often chaos and frustration." Each day there are more pieces of correspondence, memos, reports, office forms, journals, and increasingly, E-mail, faxes, and other information on paper.

However, paperwork is a price you pay for steady employment—there is simply no way to avoid it. Once you accept this fact, you will find it easier to deal with the steady paper influx to your desk—a new batch arriving just when you have taken care of the old. The following are time-saving suggestions concerning paperwork from a wide variety of sources.

▪ TIME-STEALING PAPERWORK ─────

The problem of too much paperwork is growing, and fast, says Dianna Dooher, a nationally recognized business writing consultant whose *Cutting Paperwork in The Corporate Culture* cites these statistics:

▪ American business spends 50 to 70 percent of all working hours on paperwork—preparing, writing, reading, interpreting, filing, and searching. And it is getting worse.
▪ Americans create thirty billion original documents yearly (a 1987 statistic that has undoubtedly risen since).
▪ We never again look at 75 to 85 percent of the documents we file.

Many of us strew desks with paper—which usually means delays, work slowdowns, and limited productivity. To cure the disease, says Ms. Booher in her excellent, very specific approach, the goal must be not to eliminate *all* paperwork but *unnecessary* paperwork. Examples include the customary cover letter that says only that something is being sent and that the recipient now has it, memos written as self-protectors, forms that collect duplicate information, computer printouts of data that needs interpretation before it can be used, reports that go unread, routine-activity and trip summaries, fifty-page documents sent to those who want only a page of conclusions and recommendations, most boilerplate proposals, and lengthy sales letters.

▪ HOW AND WHEN TO HANDLE YOUR PAPERWORK ─────────────────

The most efficient executives I know follow a few key procedures in cleaning up their paperwork:

▪ First and foremost, try setting aside your best—meaning highest-energy, clearest-thinking—time for handling the *important* incoming flow.

If you have an administrative aide or secretary, capable or trained by you to do this, the day might begin with a look at *only the most vital incoming papers*—without a glance at all others, which should be handled at a later time. Using the most efficient part of your day for routine correspondence is a no-no. There is always the temptation to look for good news, bad news, unexpected news, and so on, but the minutes wasted on what is often trivial can get you off to a poor start.

▪ If you are too busy or too paper-inundated to handle each nonpriority item as it enters your orbit, you or your secretary should put these items aside—preferably out of sight—for a daily lull in which you deal with what is not absolutely urgent.

▪ Rerouting things that can or should be handled by others can reduce your minute-stealing incoming pile.

▪ SORTING FOR SUCCESS ─────────────────

Once key papers are before you, Day-Timers suggests you then ask yourself, Does this piece of paper fit into my plan? If not, toss it (what's the worst that can happen?). If it does, ask, *How* does this piece of paper fit into my plan? This is the tricky part. You don't want to waste time agonizing over each item; therefore, categorize items as follows:

A. *To Do:* Something you should act on or delegate to someone who will act on it (*examples:* assignments, invoices, and business inquiries).

B. *To Read:* Information you want to digest as soon as practical (*examples:* professional journals, catalogues, and in-house reports).

C. *To File:* Something for future reference (*examples:* personnel policy handouts, tax records, and legal documents).

Note: Keep the To-Do pile front and center on your desk. Take the B and C piles and place them where they won't catch your eye and attention, under labels marked To Read and To File. You will find that virtually every item you have decided to save falls into one of these three groups.

When you go through your A pile (or file), pull out any items you think should be delegated and attach a directive Post-It note unless the item requires talking to the individual. *Tip:* If you have several subordinates, have folders for each; put items there at once.

Most important: Make an immediate decision to bounce back any unneeded or unwanted materials that have made their way to your desk. Getting rid of any paper you don't need until you are ready to work on it and keeping only one major item on your desk at a time will keep your eyes away from things that can precipitate mental side trips. Unnecessary clutter makes concentrating on what you are doing difficult.

▪ THE DOT METHOD ——————————

If you want to check your own efficiency in handling paper, consider the dot method. The idea is simple. Each time you pick up a letter, memo, or other material from your desk, place a small dot in the upper left-hand corner of the page, explains Bernie

Rooney, an executive with the Institute of Business Technology, in Washington, D.C. After a day or two, you might be surprised by the results of your experiment. Some papers will look as though they have measles. You will make it clear to yourself that you have fallen into the habit of time-consuming paper shuffling. Adds Rooney: "You save eight full days over a year if you gain just the fifteen minutes a day wasted in such meaningless actions as picking up the same piece of paper ten times (the average) before you act on it."

■ COLOR-CODING SYSTEMS

An administrative aide who handles hundreds of letters weekly for a very busy executive uses a system in which all incoming letters are quickly read and then marked in red with one of three marks corresponding to the following: (1) refer to an assistant of the initials noted, (2) to be answered by the recipient during dictation, or (3) to be acted upon after referral to the subject file.

One traveling executive uses three marked letter folders. Red indicates "must" matters requiring immediate attention; orange indicates a second priority; and green indicates matters to be handled whenever it is convenient. The three tab folders thus give an immediate picture of the daily paperwork ahead.

Whatever minute-minding system you adopt, the important thing is to establish a methodology with which you are comfortable and that puts the most important topside and moves the less important below (or into the wastebasket).

■ MOVING PAPERWORK IN ONE STEP

Many people find that at least 80 percent of their mail can be answered when first read. Handle each piece only once, they insist. Never setting it down, but responding then and there can efficiently process a substantial part of your daily deluge. Consider the following points:

■ A quick, handwritten note on an original letter, accompanied by a stamp such as Handwritten Response for Quick Reply, can save both personal and secretarial time—and speed answers to senders awaiting response. If you keep originals, write your note and make a copy of the original and send it back.

■ Devising your own form letters, with handwritten notes attached, can be a great time saver where recurring questions and answers are involved. If you feel form letters inappropriate, prepare form paragraphs, answering with a note to your secretary such as: Respond with paragraphs 2, 4, and 7. Only your own staffers should know that your response is boilerplate. Compose these routine responses so that they don't sound that way.

■ ANSWERING WITH A DICTATING MACHINE

Dictating responses at once can be helpful. The following is my own system:

■ Dictate preliminary drafts immediately on every important item, worded as closely as possible to a final version. For example, for information requests, I dictate the response and outline accompanying material. If it involves something as complicated as a program, I note major points, leaving spaces for subsequent fill-ins. Doing this speeds up my thought process. Once something is on paper, I can revise and improve it far more effectively than if I were to simply put the item aside and later go through the how-shall-I-answer process.

■ Instead of merely rerouting an item or "bucking it along," I put down my own ideas and then give associates, superiors, or subordinates thought stimulators.

■ I have always trained secretaries to notice the slightest reference to related material I might want to include or comment on, and to collect this from files—frequently with other materials I had overlooked—and return it with the draft. I can then speedily complete the final version.

■ REQUEST SPOKEN RATHER THAN WRITTEN REPORTS

To cut the incoming flow of written reports, some executives have subordinates report on tape, which can be listened to at any time and place, saving many minutes. Such reports often give both detail and flavor; for example, what a prospect said and how it was stated.

There is a tendency for oral reports to be longer than written, but they take less time to prepare, and the added detail might be vital. You also get a much clearer picture from tone of voice and emphasis applied. Tapes can be transcribed later if the material is important.

■ OTHER PAPERWORK-CONDENSING TIPS

■ *Double-space drafts:* When preparing important paperwork, double- or triple-space drafts, which facilitates editing. Although new word processors make editing easier than ever, starting with at least a double-spaced draft, finishing it to perfection, and then having it typed or printed out single-spaced can save much time *and pain* for yourself and whoever is transcribing.

■ *Use charts and graphs:* Computers and their ability to turn factual information into the widest range of charts, graphs, diagrams, and so on has encouraged many to adopt a visually oriented system for noncomputer-generated documents. This can be a vital time saver for readers—and for you in organizing information in fewer words. The Japanese have employed charts to perfection because of the complexity of their language; charts either need no translation or are easily translated into other languages.

▪ CUTTING OFF JUNK MAIL ——————

If you feel you are drowning in time-stealing junk mail coming across your desk or doorstep, send your name and address to the **Direct Marketing Association Mail Reference Service** [11 West 42nd Street, P.O. Box 3861, New York, NY 10163-3861]. Ask to have your name deleted from member lists. *Time* magazine (November 26, 1990) reported that the 3,500-member association has had over a million deletion requests.

To get off credit card membership mailing lists, write to **Bank Card Center** [P.O. Box 15443, Wilmington, DE 19885-9416]. Include your account numbers, name, address with zip code, and signature. It takes eight to ten weeks for the request to be in effect.

The Buyer's Market is a new service that sends you a questionnaire on mail you want and don't want, and advises list users of your preferences so that you can stop time-consuming junk mail. [For information contact them at 801 Pennsylvania Avenue, Washington, DC 20004; tel: 1-800-289-7658.]

Talking Your Way to a Shorter Day

In Chapter 8 I noted that dictating is an important time saver. Hence, I would like to elaborate with additional tips and techniques for making "talking your way to a shorter day" more than a slogan of the Dictaphone Time-Master people. Executives say the phrase makes sense, for it's a rare manager who doesn't spend a great deal of time communicating ideas to others, preparing studies, reports, and other written materials; and analyzing information to be passed along. All of these tasks involve time-consuming word processing.

Skillful dictating can save many minutes weekly in your writing—getting ideas from brain to paper, where they can start operating for you and your interests. Yet, as good a time saver as dictating is, it is amazing how many executives don't use it. Look around many offices; you will probably find unused dictating machines.

Dictating instruments have become marvels of efficiency: They are small, compact, accessible by telephone inside or outside the office, and portable (some minirecorders are not much larger than cigarette packs).

The recorder's ability to aid your minute minding comes from the fact that you can literally talk your work away—gaining that extra hour if you organize effectively and use dictation to the fullest. A machine into which you can pour written work renders a clearer desk and a clearer mind. Ideas don't stay very well in cold storage.

■ TIME-SAVING DICTATION METHODS ──

Here, adapted from my book *Streamlining Your Executive Workload* are some thoughts on dictation:

■ *Dictating devices obviate shorthand.* Writing or communicating through dictation-taking devices is completely different from shorthand. Your machine can be constantly before you—on a desk, in a briefcase, or even in your pocket. New machines allow you to simply talk into a telephone extension while a centrally placed machine records. Other systems can put a microphone on your desk, and a recorder on your secretary's in another office. No waiting—for you or your secretary. You dictate when you are ready, and work doesn't pile up.

■ *There is no need to slow down.* With recording, you never have to slow down to shorthand speed. You will never hear "Sorry, I missed the last few words." Everything is captured without interruption of your train of thought.

■ *Changes are easy.* You can pause as often as you like, and make changes without embarrassment or apology. Corrections can be made so as to replace whatever was originally recorded.

■ *Shorthand fright is eliminated.* Without someone at your elbow, hanging onto your every word, there is no "shorthand fright." You concentrate better and words and phrases come more readily.

■ *No fixed hour for dictation is necessary.* Before offices open, or late at night when things are quiet, during business days, after hours at home—in a car, plane, or train, hotel or other locale—your recorder is more dependable than a scratch pad. What were once fleeting ideas can be put to use.

■ CORRESPONDENCE

Most dictating machine users think of them as being primarily for letters and correspondence. The following are some time-saving steps for this primary use:

1. Have a secretary open and sort mail and incoming reports by major groups.
2. Pull out papers requiring the fastest action. Quickly move those needing only initialing or brief comments to outgoing. With each desk pile lower, you are free to tackle the most important items.
3. Proceed with dictating drafts then and there. Do you lack required information? Don't waste time—leave blank spaces for subsequent insertion. With your first draft done, action has started. Save less important items for dictation at lower energy periods.
4. Have drafts typed on green or other colored paper to instantly spot jobs in progress. Even rough drafts crystalize thoughts. Moreover, if others have to work on the material, you can pass along the original, with your draft, instead of having another time-consuming interruption or conference.
5. As each note is dictated, put the original and accompanying papers in a special folder with the dictated cassette tape. Everything then leaves your desk. When drafts are returned, your secretary or assistant should add pertinent data files you have cited. There is no time out to spell requests. It's all on paper. While you are busy with your work, associates can be completing theirs.

6. Dictating immediate first drafts rather than starting a memo series often eliminates several intermediate steps. For example, instead of first writing several people to ask for opinions about an incoming proposal, dictate draft answers and let others work in specifics.

7. Always jump as far as possible toward the ultimate objective, whether it involves a letter, report, or study. While the final version might be changed, it will usually be clearer, more direct, better thought out, and done in far fewer minutes if you use this tactic.

▪ DICTATING INSTRUCTIONS TO OTHERS

Whenever you have to instruct others in a complicated matter, instead of lifting the telephone, pressing a buzzer, or writing a note, reach for your dictating microphone. The following are some points to keep in mind:

▪ Talk to your associates, branch managers, salesmen, plant foremen, club members, or anyone else as though they were present. What you say can be transcribed and delivered. Save even more time by mailing a cassette to them.

▪ Secretarial reminders need never be typed at all. Instructions can simply be dictated, then executed.

▪ You can't pass the buck and make others guess your meaning if you dictate. Statements are for the most part transcribed as you have dictated them. This necessitates clarity.

▪ Because realization of almost every task in office, factory, or community requires a series of separate steps, another good idea is to detail instructions in separate paragraphs. This helps you to think out just what needs doing. Once a draft is before you, you will frequently redictate another, clearer version without the painful editing or correcting process.

▪ Chapter Ten ▪ ▪ ▪ ▪ ▪ ▪ ▪ ▪ ▪ ▪

Secretaries and Administrative Aides

In scheduling, prioritizing, dictating your work away, and in scores of other tasks, no one individual can be more helpful to an executive in handling the daily workload—more effectively in less time—than a good secretary. A good secretary is one who not only shares the chores but who, because of intimate, specialized knowledge and abilities, can relieve you of much detail through imaginative planning and work execution.

Working with your secretary or administrative assistant (a term increasingly used where the individual responsibilities have been upgraded) to produce a smoothly functioning minute-minding operation requires mutual liking and response, real team work, considerable mental telepathy, large doses of mutual patience, and, above all, a desire to see the job through in the best and most efficient manner. Of course, you expect your secretary to handle your mail, make and receive calls, type or word process, file, receive callers, and perform other routine tasks detailed in these pages. Otherwise, he or she wouldn't be there. However, if that is all you expect, or allow, you are cheating yourself of what for many individuals in many types of businesses is their number one support.

My own long-term top secretaries, the late Peggy Rollason, for ten years, and her successor, Shirley McGowan, with me more than twenty, both became expert in the widest variety of activities, including editing. So did Cathy Gallagher, with me for years and now running her own typing and word-processing service. Peggy, before her lamented passing, wrote a book—inspired, she said, by me—called *The High Priced Secretary*. It is still the outstanding guide in this field, and I have—to turn the tables—borrowed some ideas from it.

▪ CHECK YOUR OWN ATTITUDE ——————

If you are desirous of handing over more and more of your incoming headaches or pleasures to your secretary, saving you time for those career-advancing things only you can do, hold off a minute and take stock. First ask yourself the following questions:

1. Are you prepared to not only give a secretary more responsibility but allow the individual to develop in his or her own way, make many decisions, and carry the job through? You would be surprised how difficult this is for many executives, and no more so than for the less experienced or knowledgeable.
2. Have you helped work out an efficient, regular routine that permits work on extracurricular activities without feeling pressured? If you are a one-letter-at-time dictator, a buzzer fiend who allows constant break-ins and considers your telephone calls more important than your aide, you are making it impossible for your secretary to develop or stick to any efficient minute-minding schedule.
3. Do you allow your secretary to organize a priority list for chores, just as you do for yours? It isn't always possible for every

job to be completed at the moment or on the day it comes up. Flexibility is one of the greatest strain savers. Your realization that the business or enterprise won't collapse if every report or letter doesn't go out tonight, or if every request doesn't get top-priority, on-the-double response, will make you a pleasure to assist.

4. Are you willing to share credit? The individual who takes all the glory for an outstanding achievement and treats the secretary as a robot, will either lose that person completely or so stifle initiative as to wind up with just that—a machine.

If you pass this self-test and decide to upgrade your secretary, you will be in outstanding company. Let's look at how some busy people save time by working effectively with their assistants.

■ DEVELOPING RELATIONSHIPS ————

How do you best develop this vital, cooperative secretarial relationship? Like every other human encounter, it is an art, but here are some specific tips from a variety of polled secretaries:

■ *Hold a brief daily morning conference.* Inquire how your secretary can help you accomplish more. If your previous relationship has been strictly "do as I tell you—and fast," your secretary may think you are implying a need to speed up, or worse yet, that you are feeling ill. Be reassuring and suggest a joint compilation of every job in the works.

■ *Encourage your secretary to assume jobs.* Hand over those in which some preliminary research can be done or even taken over entirely. If your aide is new, young, or inexperienced, it might require some time for the person to realize you expect initiative, to take each project as far as possible.

■ *Foster responsibility.* Do this always with the understanding that you will be kept informed. Many executive secretaries not only keep their bosses' pending schedules, but include their own agendas for boss approval.

■ *Use strengths.* Learn to analyze your secretary's strongest and weakest points; don't expect all-around miracle aides. Do rely on outstanding capabilities, and try to help strengthen the weakest.

■ *Take suggestions from colleagues.* Many times another viewpoint can shed an entirely new light on a problem. There is also a converse benefit: Secretaries whose opinions are respected are much more amenable to a boss's suggestions about *their* work.

■ *Back up your secretary.* When a mistake in judgment is made, stand by your assistant. Loyalty will be appreciated. From that demonstration of your faith, you will get better results than from reproofs. Moreover, it is not likely that errors will be repeated.

■ *Reprimand in private.* This is a direct corollary to the previous suggestion; it is especially important when your secretary is representing you to others in the firm. Mistakes can be noted privately without undermining status and authority.

■ *Channel work.* Nothing is more disconcerting to a secretary than to learn the boss has given assignments to another assistant on the "Q.T."

■ *Let your secretary know what you expect.* Going to lunch, taking a coffee break, or leaving should all be based on a definite understanding. Late conferences in or out of the office can wreak havoc with loyalty unless your secretary knows exactly what is expected. Consideration begets consideration.

■ *Give credence to intuition.* This is developed largely from a secretary's "receiving set" for information from various sources not always open to you—and the ability to piece them together into a pattern often complementing your radar. This doesn't mean being stationed on the office grapevine, but that isn't to be ignored entirely either.

■ *Depend on your secretary's sense of orderliness.* This can smooth your daily routine. If your assistant is not naturally tidy and you take the lead eliminating your own desk and workplace clutter, you will find the example you set as boss far more likely to be followed than admonitions. If you turn out to be the type of odd couple depicted in film and television, I don't know the answer. If anything has to give, it's obviously going to be the can't-see-the-desk-for-the-papers approach.

■ *Teach your secretary to act as a second pair of eyes.* Encourage reading of business and trade publications with an eye to your interests, business and personal. A miscellaneous intelligence file can be a vital source of information in reports, letters, speeches, and so on.

■ *Develop that sense of humor.* It stands to reason that even the most efficient executive—and secretary—will pull occasional bloopers. Learn to take time, either jointly or singly, to laugh at the funny or preposterous. Many secretaries and administrative aides rate this the greatest pressure reliever.

■ ACCESS AND APPOINTMENTS ─────

Many chief executive officers leave it to their secretaries or administrative aides to handle appointments for all but the very highest peers. They are not necessarily arbiters of access, but are, rather, the individual making the appointments subject to confirmation. Some top executives, like advertising agency Omnicon's Allen Rosenshine, even have two secretaries: one to do the more or less routine typing, filing, and traditional secretarial chores; the other to help him better manage time, both by keeping appointments straight and by serving as a go-between when he can't immediately get in touch with someone he needs information from or must otherwise deal with.

Says Rosenshine, quoted by Fred Worthy in *Fortune*, "Rather than play tag, I can brief her or him on what I'm trying to find out from someone and let her or him follow through, even at the risk I won't get everything wanted."

Some top company executives say that their secretaries "almost totally" control access to people, both outside and inside, and know who should be able to walk in, who can wait, and whose request can be cared for by others. Such extensive delegation can backfire, of course, so it needs careful working out.

■ TAKING TIME TO TRAIN ───────────

Before your secretary or administrative aide can provide all of the time savers you would like, you must do some coaching and teaching. This can, at first, be another time drain says Andrew S. Gove in *Working Woman*, adding:

> *Investing time in training will pay off. The training should specifically focus on the concept of your job so that your secretary understands what you do and why—and then be able to aid consistently. . . . Don't stop with just the basic familiarization—have your regular morning meetings, your weekly reviews of what's happened and what's coming for the week ahead, to fine-tune your secretary's knowledge of the job and enhance assistance. Investing time in your secretary may be the best time- and effort-saving investment you ever make—it will be repaid with dividends in time saved.*

■ A MUTUAL TEACHING PROCESS ────────

In the mutual teaching process, says the Time Management Center, these tips are also important:

■ Hire the best. Expect the best. Pay the best.
■ Encourage others to deal directly with your secretary for things they can handle.
■ Ask what he or she could do that you are now doing—how you could manage time better.

■ Take the necessary time to provide good instructions—using good feedback techniques in allowing for initiatives.

■ OTHER TIME-SAVING IDEAS FOR YOUR SECRETARY

■ *Schedule your morning and afternoon conferences at a fixed time.* This leaves both of you with uninterrupted hours for other work. Consider these get-togethers as sacrosanct as any other on your schedule—not to be put off repeatedly because "something more important has come up."

■ *Go easy on the buzzer.* Keep your own notes and reminders in your organizer and give directions at one time; most can wait. Suggest the same in reverse if you don't require immediate notification.

■ *Keep your secretary up to date.* Inform him or her of all department changes, ongoing projects, assignments given others, files you have loaned out, telephone developments (especially important call alerts), and so on.

■ *Keep a current-file drawer.* Have this near you with most active project material, instead of constantly buzzing. As each is completed, turn the folder over to be placed in permanent files.

■ *Keep a continuing file on those weekly, semimonthly, or monthly tasks.* This will allow you to avoid last-minute scrambling to assemble necessary data.

■ *Let your secretary answer as many of your letters as possible.* Many become so skillful, that they can draft replies for signature as mail comes in or take an oral yes, no, or maybe and turn it into the form of response you like to give—keeping it short.

■ *Give your secretary or aide complete responsibility for many routine jobs.* Many inquiries can be referred directly, especially if subordinates know of the authority in this area. Otherwise, time is wasted assuring callers that their problems will be well handled. The manner of speaking, the authority conveyed, and the avoidance of talking down or an obvious air of irritation can assure many callers that they will get attention faster and better.

■ *Investigate new methods, materials, and office equipment.* This makes the job easier for both of you. There is no need to stick to the same old routine out of habit.

■ *Help build a library of reference and textbooks.* These are useful time savers.

■ *Consider having your secretary join a professional association to keep up progress.* There are many, local and national.

■ *Treat your secretary to a seminar or lecture course in your field.* If advancement in the professional secretary area is sought, consider what is available at local adult education courses.

■ *Get your secretary out of the office once in a while.* If your secretary can be spared for a day, an out-of-town trip for a special research project can be truly rewarding—and that same day can be yours away from the desk to work on important projects.

■ *Suggest that your secretary read this book.* Don't be surprised if he or she comes up with even better time-saving suggestions.

A final reminder: Never forget the stimulus and morale-building inherent in those two little words: thank you. When you have had a particularly hectic day, with every minute used to the maximum, or when some miracle has been accomplished for you despite constant interruptions, let your secretary know how much help and time you have gained from that action.

■ IF YOU ARE THE SECRETARY OR AIDE

Phillip Diminna, who has held top positions in New York, offers these tips:

Supplies: Always keep critical supplies close at hand. A big time saver in processing important jobs on a rush basis is to never, never run out of important items in the middle of a job. If that happens, important time can be lost in a sometimes futile search.

Spares such as typewriter ribbons, tape, staples, and so on should be at your desk. This way, if supplies are low or (as in some cases) completely out, you still have backup supplies. Don't forget computer disks, blank cassettes for recording, an extra headset for the dictaphone (in case of malfunction), and so on.

A good assistant also keeps spare supplies that the boss might need (such as erased cassettes) at his or her own station for emergency. Another time saver: Always check your desk at night before going home; this is the best time to make sure you are stocked up on whatever is needed, because it saves doing it during the morning hours—when jobs are rushed and time is at a premium.

Mail Flow: If you don't have it, get the free booklet *Five Creative Ways to Save Time and Money on Your Business Mail* [Marketing Department, U.S. Postal Service, P.O. Box 7897, Mt. Prospect, IL 60056-9821].

▪ Chapter Eleven ▪ ▪ ▪ ▪ ▪ ▪ ▪ ▪

Making the Fax Work for You

Increasingly, written communications are being conveyed by facsimile, or "fax." During the past decade, this channel has evolved from a slow, relatively expensive communications option to an off-the-shelf, easy-to-use tool, affordable even for individuals and the smallest businesses. Knowing how to use the fax effectively can be another important daily time saver.

The relative ease of fax use has a lot to do with its current popularity and fast growth. New features will propel acceptance even further. Kevin Shea, vice president of facsimile field operations for Xerox Corporation, notes: "Some machines can now be preset so that you can simply point to a touch screen overlay—a list of names, series of photographs, a map—and have a document faxed to your designated list.

John Lemke, vice president for marketing operations at Fujitsu Imaging Systems, says: "Short-term, many companies are thinking about new ways to network fax machines, maximizing utilization and minimizing transmission costs, plus developing some really powerful applications using combinations of older and emerging machines. As fax utilization expands, you'll be able to apply more of a systems approach. Suppliers of almost any related product or service will take an increasing role in the process."

▪ USING YOUR FAX AS A TIME-SAVER

Today, faxes are not limited to big offices; more and more smaller companies, individuals, and homes have them. They can provide a wide range of time-saving benefits, such as the following:

▪ *Immediate delivery:* When you hang up—it's there.

▪ *Brevity:* Most faxes are short and to the point—quicker to compose and more likely to be read at once and draw speedy responses, especially if you take the trouble to phrase your points to make replies easier. The writing and communications tips in previous chapters are thus applicable to your faxes—in spades!

▪ *Multiple designees:* You can simultaneously send the identical fax to a wide list—depending on your machine's capabilities.

▪ *Delayed transmission:* This enables you to preset transmission to take advantage of the lowest telephone rate hours.

▪ *Automatic document feeders:* Some machines stack up to thirty letter-size documents for transmission, and automatically cut and collate pages in the order in which they are received. A document stamp appears on each item faxed so that you can be sure it has been sent.

▪ *Memory reception:* Up to twenty pages of information storage guarantees that you will not lose incoming information, even if the unit runs out of paper.

▪ *Outgoing message and fax tele-auto switchover:* By combining a programmable twelve-second outgoing message with the auto switchover feature, you are able to let callers know that the unit is in a fax mode. Their voice switches the unit to a telephone mode so that you can also talk, as well as send and receive automatically.

▪ MULTIPLE FUNCTIONS IN ONE MACHINE ─────────────

You can now get a machine that combines the fax with a telephone, an answering machine, a printer, a scanner, and a personal computer with top-rated software—all at your fingertips, and affordably priced.

You can fax while updating your data base, talk with a client while creating an illustration, and much more—without moving from your desk or work station.

▪ ONE-WAY FAXING ─────────────────────

It used to take two to fax, but that is no longer true, thanks to DHL Worldwide Express FAX LYNK Service, an ingenious combination of facsimile and overnight delivery to those lacking units but seeking to save time. You can transmit to the remotest locations by faxing DHL in Cincinnati. From there, documents are transmitted overseas via satellite, then laser printed on bond paper, sealed in an envelope, and delivered by courier the old-fashioned way—by hand. The U.S. Postal Service has a similar international service.

If you don't have your own fax, you will find many services and even stores that make one available.

▪ NEWSPAPERS BY FAX ───────────────────

The *Chicago Tribune,* in 1990, sought to be the first to put news bulletins in its Tribfax service—sending one-page summaries of business headlines to customers. They had hoped to have between one and two thousand subscribers at $400 annually to their nationally available service. Despite extensive promotion however, Tribfax had poor earnings; it has now been dropped.

The *Minneapolis Star Tribune* and the Times Mirror Company's *Hartford Courant* (Connecticut) remain in the fax business—sending news by fax—valuable if you need the latest in writing and are willing to pay for such a time-saving service. Dow-Jones and Company, publisher of the *Wall Street Journal;* Knight-Ridder Company; and *The New York Times* are producing, testing, or studying various facsimile products.

■ PORTABLE FAX

The smallest fax of which I have heard—saving time by offering service wherever you go—is Ricoh's PF-1, which measures just 11 × 7 inches, fits on a sheet of typing paper, and weighs just 5.5 pounds. The unit holds thirty letter-size pages, prints out faxes at high or low resolution, and has error-correction circuitry that keeps phone-line static to a minimum. It even serves as a portable copier and can transmit or receive via cellular phone. Indoors, it plugs into a regular electrical outlet and telephone line.

■ FIX IT BY FAX

It is now possible to have your fax, business telephone, medical equipment, or a wide range of other items fixed via fax, without wasting time waiting for the repairman. Remote diagnosis and repair systems, accessed via a fax message—or telephone call—can allow some equipment suppliers to decrease the number of calls requiring response by making repairs without someone actually going to the site. As reported in *The New York Times*, Arthur Ryan, of AT&T, explains: "Remote diagnosis and repair systems permit some equipment suppliers to sharply reduce their service calls and cut time spent on problems that must still be dealt with at the locale, because remote diagnosis frequently allows dispatching the repairer with proper tools and parts. For the user, it means vital equipment back on line in minutes, instead of hours or days."

■ JUNK FAXES

These time wasters—fax messages from suppliers, solicitors, or others seeking your business—have been proliferating. Once your machine is operating, you can't stop incoming messages any more than you can block unwanted telephone calls. They use your paper and machine time, impeding other messages. This, and minutes you or your secretary or assistant may take to read the message, are definite minute wasters. The best solution to this problem is to advise senders that you will do no future business with them if they continue unsolicited transmissions.

Flash: One machine will do the blocking for you. The new Fujitsu Dex 80 lets you program up to fifty numbers for "selective rejection." If you are getting unwanted faxes from advertisers and the like, you can plug their numbers into your machine; Dex will automatically block transmission.

Electronic Messaging

Faxing is generally individual—one originator to one or many recipients. However, with many larger message senders or receivers—corporations, agencies, and so on—the sheer volume of message interchange takes so much time that new systems have been developed, with new features constantly added.

Consider your present telephone communications, for example. It often takes four or five telephone calls for two people to complete a single round of "telephone tag." In *The Electronic Mailbox*, Ira Meyer explains: "Party A initiates the call only to be told by a secretary that B is in a meeting. The call is returned and B is told A is unavailable right now. When the call is returned again, B is out of the office. Another try or two and the odds begin favoring one reaching the other." This is as true for offices in the same building as those across the continent or over the ocean, says Meyer. The not uncommon situation is exacerbated as you cross time zones.

Meyer notes that the new electronic mail—dubbed E-mail—has become an important time saver in overcoming these problems. You call, reach a machine, and leave a full spoken message the first time, whatever the hour or locale. Your intended recipient doesn't have to be there to get it or otherwise deal with your message until it is convenient. When a response is ready, there is no waiting for the original sender to be available; the answering message can be sent to that person's electronic mailbox, where it will wait patiently. Depending on system sophistication or user desires, some form of notification is registered whenever a message is waiting at either end. Based on usage volume, the unit cost is low and the convenience great—and the market is growing, says Meyer, whose book answers the questions of where and how the various types of electronic mail can save you and your firm both money and time.

With the continued explosion in the number of PC users connected to local and wide area networks, E-mail is also being used by individuals other than those in large organizations.

The use of electronic messaging isn't something you may be able to do on your own if you are employed by a large company where, obviously, installation is a corporate decision, but if you are in an individual or small business where your situation permits you to review and recommend when and how your operations can adapt these new approaches, it would be worthwhile considering.

▪ SAVING TIME USING E-MAIL ────────────

If you are the caller, follow these guidelines:

- Make your message short and to the point.
- Give whatever facts are needed to evoke a specific reply—and request return ASAP.
- In requesting a return telephone call, tell when you will be available.
- In requesting E-mail reply, tell when you check your box.

If you are the recipient, follow these guidelines:

■ Claim your messages at the time you have scheduled for their reading.
■ Respond as quickly as you feel the importance and urgency indicates.

■ MULTIPLE MESSAGING ─────────────

With these systems, you can also send identical messages to a wide number of individuals on your network—leaving the same spoken or written item for any group. Obviously, this eliminates time spent on multiple copies and their delivery or mailing. Responses are also gathered this way, for reading or replay later. The cost of these systems is high, requiring company-wide operations, but they are becoming increasingly popular because of their time and effort savings.

■ MAKE YOUR VOICE MAIL
EASY TO USE ───────────────────

Nancy Friedman, the St. Louis "Telephone Doctor," notes that the wide-spread adaptation of automated voice messaging, or voice mail, has turned what many had long considered basically an energy saver into a source of heated disagreement as to its use and effectiveness.

Despite the debate, says Ms. Friedman, automated message-taking systems can be time and productivity enhancers if you learn their proper use. She notes: "Voice mail industry statistics say that half of all business calls convey information only one way, making person-to-person links unnecessary. Seventy-five percent of all business calls accomplish nothing on the first attempt, resulting in the familiar back-and-forth 'tennis calling' syndrome. Despite the public outcry against voice mail, there are solid reasons why so many companies are purchasing these systems." The following are Friedman's tips to make your own voice mail system friendlier and your telephone encounters with others more productive:

■ *Record your message in your own voice, identifying yourself and your department.* For example, "You've reached Carolyn Schmidt in Sales."

■ *Use personal, informational messages.* Avoid the "I'm not able to come to the phone right now" type of message. A better statement would be: "I'm in a sales meeting until three. You can reach my secretary at extension four-four-five if you need immediate information, or press zero to speak to a live operator." This type of message, however, requires constant updating.

■ *Let caller know that you check your machine for messages.* "Please be sure to leave a message. I check this machine often." Most people will leave a message if they feel recorders get periodic checks.

■ *Practice recording until you sound conversational.* Don't let callers know you are reading. *Smile* while recording. Nobody wants to talk to a gruff machine.

■ *Make sure to change your message before going on vacation.* Salespeople often lose important clients because calls weren't returned for weeks.

■ *Return all messages or have them returned in your behalf.* Otherwise, there is little value to the system.

■ *When your voice messaging system is installed, inform key people with whom you do business of the fact.* A short, personalized letter explaining the change and brief instructions on how to use the system will be a welcome gesture.

▪ USING OTHER PEOPLE'S VOICE MAIL SYSTEMS ─────────────

Ms. Friedman offers these tips:

■ *The vast majority of systems allow bypassing the initial recorded message.* Pressing the zero button can connect a human operator immediately. Habitually jot down frequently used extension numbers so that you can get right through the next time.

■ *If you are on the calling end and reach a machine, leave a detailed, complete message for your party.* Get value out of every call. Ask for the information you need; that way the other person can get the ball rolling before they call back.

■ *Stay calm.* As frustrating as initial experiences using voice mail with certain systems can be, remember that eventually everyone works out their bugs.

■ *Learn from other people's mistakes.* Make notes about what irritates you about other company's systems. Note effective messages. Make sure your company's automated voice messaging system is as user-friendly as possible and you will gain untold minutes every day.

▪ OTHER VOICE MESSAGING BENEFITS ─────────────

Voice Tel Enterprises of Hudson, Ohio 44262, a system developer, explains that voice messaging is an effective time saver for these additional reasons:

■ It enables you to leave a message more quickly and more accurately than a fast scribble on paper—resulting in fewer callback questions.

■ Unauthorized personnel can't look at your messages.

■ Calls are shorter. With voice messaging, people don't gab, they talk business.

■ You get freedom from time zone differences and the constraints of 9 to 5 business hours. The benefits increase as the distance expands.

■ Message slips are reduced. Secretaries and administrative assistants are left alone for more productive tasks.

■ There is less paging of called parties. If you page, you have to wait for the person to find a telephone and either answer or call back. With voice mail connected to a paging system, the former can be programmed to activate a beeper each time a new message enters the electronic mailbox. The called party can dial the system when it is convenient to play back messages.

■ E-MAIL FOR INDIVIDUALS

CompuServe Mail claims to be the world's largest group of potential recipients of electronic mail. This system saves time by allowing you to send and receive written messages twenty-four hours a day, regardless of distance or time zone, directly from your personal computer. As a member, you get a software "address book," which stores up to fifty names and electronic addresses.

In addition to CompuServe members, you can communicate electronically with users of CompuServe's private corporation E-mail system. A link between CompuServe and MCI Mail allows you to exchange electronic mail with MCI telephone company mail users and users of Internet, the widely used research-oriented electronic mail system. A CompuServe-to-Telex link allows exchange of messages with Telex users worldwide, and users can send messages to fax machines globally. [Information: 800-848-8199]

Chapter Thirteen

Delegation

There is the story of a young, would-be executive who, when applying to the personnel manager, was asked what position he previously held.

"I was a doer, sir," he replied.

"A doer! What's that?"

"Well, sir, you see, when my employer wanted anything done, he would tell the cashier. The cashier would tell the bookkeeper. The bookkeeper would tell the clerk. And the clerk would tell me."

"And what would happen then?"

"Well, since I hadn't anyone to tell it to, I'd do it."

That popular misconception of the extent to which delegation supposedly goes has many variations. Yet, popular mythology aside, delegation is another major key to saving minutes, hours, days, and months.

While the concept of delegation might seem simple, it is often complex because it involves relationships with the world's most complicated and sensitive machines: people. And, as we all know, with people, one plus one doesn't always equal two.

Undertaking broad delegation is about the most difficult thing executives on the way up ever have to do. This is particularly true in family-owned businesses. To build the team, you have to encourage others to run the risk of making mistakes with your own money; otherwise, they can never grow. I once asked C. R. Smith, then president of American Airlines, the key step that really started him on the way up. He said:

> *When I got my first assistant, I was dissatisfied with almost everything he did. It took me so long to explain what I wanted and so long for him to do it half as well as I, that I figured more time was being wasted than gained. Then one day I realized that, so long as I'd be limited to doing only what I could myself accomplish, I'd always be time short, with no real advancement opportunity. So I concentrated on getting, and training, aides. I looked for people both industrious and competent, even if not operating exactly my way. Each pair of hands and brains I trained helped give me more time to develop myself further and move ahead.*

As you advance up the ladder, dropping things that got you to your post is not easy. Yet, if you insist, even subconsciously, on involvement with those duties you previously handled, you won't be able to do the broad planning and coordinating required by your new job or your desire for advancement.

■ THE DETOUR THE DETAILS SYSTEM

Not all of us can use the "detour the details" system of Admiral Robert P. Carney, longtime chief of U.S. Naval Operations. However, one of his approaches may be for you. He explained:

For years I had an officer expert in internal administrative organization. His unique function: screening away everything not properly my business.

Any matter which could be handled by a competent subordinate was not permitted to reach my desk. Loopholes in policy and major issues were brought to my attention. By actual analysis, this system reduced the number of items I handled to about 50 percent of those covered by my predecessor.

I don't believe Navy administration suffered. On the contrary, I had more time to think about things that were solely my responsibility. Plus I could have leisurely, contemplative discussions with my deputies, subordinate commanders, superiors, and civilians— all contributing something to the Navy's business and thinking on policy matters.

■ A MASTER DELEGATING PLAN ————————

Delegating just to make your job simpler can be hazardous explain Drs. Donald and Eleanor Laird, adding:

On the other hand, when your motivation is to strengthen the organization, you're more likely to look for unused talents among your workers (and at home with the family) and delegate accordingly. Either way requires considerable self-discipline.

If you insist upon keeping your hand on all details, you discourage subordinates by competing with them. Capable people are likely to quit. Others sit back and let you do the work. Remember: The person to whom you delegate doesn't want to become simply a pack horse. On the other hand, they may be more anxious and able than you realize, to take on tasks they perceive are important.

The Laird Master Delegation Plan, published in *Management Methods*, includes these highlights:

1. *Pinpoint delegated functions.* Draw up a list of department activities and name individuals to whom each job is, or should be, specifically delegated. This might reveal gaps that are being filled by default and others that are unnecessarily being delegated to several people.

2. *Clearly define delegation goals and scope.* Subordinates should be told in unmistakable terms how much authority they have been granted and the expected results—*not how to do the job.*

3. *Define the problem or assignment.* There are no solutions to unknown problems. If you can't clearly and concisely state the issue, you have some more brainwork to do before delegating. Asking somebody to go to Department X to "make themselves useful" is a prime example of bad delegation.

4. *Go slowly.* Start with minor missions. It is the act of delegation that matters, rather than project size. Besides, executives who dislike sharing responsibility find it easier to relinquish by degrees as they develop confidence in subordinates' judgment.

5. *Consider the work group effect.* Delegation should be planned to fit the characteristics of those with whom you work, as well as the individual's task-handling ability. When discussing a problem at a staff meeting, make it plain who is carrying the ball. If you are the executive in charge, you are, in effect, the quarterback—but the team needs to know the play.

6. *Start with short-run delegation.* This helps you test more people at a greater variety of tasks with less risk. Also, you have a chance to make accurate individual capability appraisals.

7. *Rotate delegations.* Organization-motivated executives won't delegate only to a proven few; they will try to develop their group by giving everyone a chance.

8. *Redelegate.* This method should be used not to pass the buck but to develop second and third teams. General Electric, a man-

agement methods leader, believes executives should use redelega-
tion to set up a team ten years younger than themselves. Every
business needs trained personnel reserves if it is to grow.

9. *Include delegatees in planning.* This prepares them for the
job and makes them feel they are sharing a common goal. Moreover, being close to the firing line, such individuals can offer
sound advice.

It is wise to set target dates and make clear how often, and
exactly when, you want progress reports. Both you and your
delegatee should note them in your organizer/schedulers. Otherwise, it is like asking a friend to dinner "some evening," or
suggesting lunch "one of these days." It rarely comes off.

10. *Tailor delegations to minimize consequences and mistakes.*
Because errors are inevitable, it is wise to arrange first missions
so that blunders don't become catastrophies. Often, the so-called
mistake is merely action you yourself would not have taken.
Effective delegation, as a time saver, requires trying various
methods so that others can learn from experience. Delegatees
shouldn't be frightened if they find themselves in disagreement
with you over methods—nor should you if you disagree with your
superiors. Each individual brings a fresh, personal, unique approach, assuring a wide array of talent.

▪ DELEGATION IS CONTROLLING THROUGH OTHERS

Charles R. Hobbs, developer of the unique Time Power system,
notes that as an organization expands and your position increases
in responsibility, you can no longer directly control the growing
number of events under your personal span of activity. Someone
has to be brought in, trained, and prepared to carry part of the
load. Successful executives with an eye on the best use of their
time and effort follow two basic delegation rules, says Hobbs:

1. Decisions should be made at the lowest level that has the necessary information and judgment.
2. Those answering to you should bring answers, not problems.

Hobbs quotes Peter Drucker's *How to Manage Your Time* in raising two initial questions to be asked if you are to best use delegation as a minute-minder: They are:

1. What am I doing now that doesn't have to be done by me; what is being done by others at a level higher than is necessary?
2. What am I doing now that those answering to me can do or be trained to do?

Once you have determined from these questions the need and desirability of delegating, Hobbs says, follow these nine steps in the delegation process.

1. Select people with the ability to do the job.
2. See that those selected understand what you expect.
3. Let associates know that you sincerely believe in their ability to carry out their tasks.
4. Negotiate deadlines.
5. Secure follow-through commitments from associates.
6. Let associates know at the beginning that you are going to follow up; then do it.
7. Provide latitude for other imaginations and initiatives.
8. Don't do the job for others.
9. Reward commensurately with results produced.

Hobbs adds:

Behavior persists when rewarded. Best are rewards that build an associate's self-esteem: a pat on the back or special recognition; sometimes a bonus, if grantable; a promotion; or an extra day off. Ironically, one of

*the best rewards is receiving more stimulating projects.
Bear in mind that if the delegation fails, you may
not have selected the best person for the job, perhaps
did not clearly communicate what was expected, or
failed to set proper deadlines or secure realizable
commitments.*

▪ WHOM TO CHOOSE WHEN DELEGATING —————————————

If you are in an executive position, finding the best person to
delegate to takes thinking and planning on your part. In *The
Techniques of Delegating*, the Lairds say:

▪ *Find persons with unused abilities.* Executives often tend to
judge people by routine job efforts—even though such work
contains little real challenge. Experience shows that average
workers are usually capable of much more, given a chance. There
might be someone in your own office, organization, shop, or plant
with undiscovered talents that could make them effective delegatees and time savers for you, if properly guided.

▪ *Delegate to a wide range.* Every company has all types of
small problems requiring solutions. Many can be delegated, and
are are good tests of associates' handling of responsibility. Successes also help build confidence.

▪ *Find the not-so-obviously qualified.* Your natural inclination
might be to delegate to the handiest person or to one who handled
a task before. This isn't always the wisest course because it—

> Overloads a willing horse.
> May generate jealously and opposition to favorites.
> Often creates one or more overconfident princes or
> princesses.

Fails to develop your work team or group in depth. While delegating to the not-so-obvious requires more explanation, and possibly produces slower results, your benefit comes as each person masters a new job and in turn trains the next.

■ *Delegate to individuals with a weakness.* You can often help such people with heart-to-heart talks, lectures—even threats. You will do infinitely more, however, by delegating jobs that develop new skills and that will give you minute-minding future support.

In some cases, the Lairds say, the most important ingredient of delegation is the trust your subordinates have that you won't—

Desert them in battle.

Withdraw their authority.

Condemn them for blunders.

Make decisions in their absence.

Hold back secrets.

Delegate someone else to spy on them.

Withhold advice and the benefits of experience.

■ *Delegate to suppliers.* Suppliers can often do important jobs for you, given the opportunity. They can gather information, set up work plans, and show you ways to use materials more effectively. Often they will do these things even if there is no immediate prospective order.

■ *Share your ability.* You are the boss probably because you have superior ability. Share it with delegatees. Tell them what you have learned about the delegated problem. Keep yourself accessible for legitimate progress reports and questions to which only you have answers. It pays to take occasional progress readings.

■ CHECK YOUR DELEGATION TECHNIQUE

One reason delegation often fails and wastes time is the poor way it is handled. Some think that giving the fullest instructions— military style—and exercising tight-reined follow-through control is good delegation. Authorities disagree. The following steps will help you check your own delegation techniques:

1. *Indicate your real goal.* This means defining, as concisely as possible, the results you expect. Suppose you assign someone to handle a study of one phase of shipments. Results will be far better if you explain the overall plan to cut costs and make salary increases possible. Letting delegatees know department, division, company, and even industry-wide goals gives them better perspective. In addition, you help clarify *why* the job should be done, as well as who is to do it.

2. *Allow delegatees decision-making participation.* As far as possible, let people not only use their own initiative and share in decisions affecting their work but, when two ideas come up, favor the one offered by the individual who will eventually have to carry it out. No one produces as effectively as someone trying to prove his or her idea's worth.

3. *Build in challenges.* If it is a tough assignment, stress that you have chosen the person because you believe they can succeed. Explain that you feel it will not only prove ability but increase their own experience, technique, and understanding, thus helping their advancement.

4. *Cite information sources.* Let the delegatee know where to go for help, especially on touchy questions. If you promise other people's assistance or the use of facilities, make their availability certain. Let your delegatee determine what aids are needed; then, realistically check to be sure there are neither too many or too few of these.

5. *Give the delegatee a chance.* Let them evaluate their own progress by measuring their accomplishment at any specific time against the jointly outlined goal.

6. *Prepare for errors.* Mistakes are inevitable. If you aim at over-all accomplishment, minor mistakes en route shouldn't affect you unduly. Obviously, when delegatees make an error, they have responsibility as far as you are concerned, even though ultimate responsibility properly falls on you.

7. *Criticism should be constructive.* Rather than irate and thus destructive reactions, show where the mistake occurred and how the problem might be handled next time. Scolding alone causes delegatees to avoid decisions involving risk. They will either follow previous patterns exactly or keep referring decisions to you or someone else—meaning that you are right back to the time-consuming, effort-diverting patterns that delegation was supposed to address.

8. *Avoid overruling or reversing delegatees' decisions.* When delegatees have responsibility for certain results and the authority to take the necessary steps to achieve them, they are far more likely to make the right decision.

▪ THE HEART ATTACK APPROACH ——

Suppose, for example, that because of a heart attack, you were able to be on your job only four hours a day instead of the eight or more that you now spend. Which functions would you elect to keep? Which would you eliminate or delegate?

Can you say that you simply couldn't carry on your job if it had to be done in half the time? Or would you, as in the most famous case I know of—former President Dwight D. Eisenhower after his heart attack—classify your workload into essentials and nonessentials? And, like Ike, evaluate and eliminate some tasks altogether and reduce others to the minimum?

In drawing up his own list of essentials, President Eisenhower found he needed to—

- Act as Commander-in-Chief of the armed forces.
- Preside over the National Security Council.
- Watch and direct major foreign policies.
- Supervise key economic matters.

All of that was a big order in itself, but Eisenhower did cut down on what he considered nonessential activities, including:

- Entertainment (less)
- Appointments (fewer)
- Travel (curtailed)
- Correspondence (drafted by others)
- Routine jobs (delegated)

Following this procedure eliminated much of Eisenhower's time-consuming workload until he was able to resume full-time. Even then, he never got back into quite as much of a heavy schedule as before, having turned a crisis into an asset.

A heart attack approach is admittedly drastic, but thinking about it helps dramatize the undoubted number of things you are presently doing that you could do less of, do more quickly and efficiently, or delegate.

To return to the main time-saver: Determine what is essential and what is not, what should get priority and what goes to the bottom of your list, and how to delegate better every day, in a business climate in which priorities are constantly changing. Doing this can gain you that extra hour every day.

▪ ENCOURAGING ACCEPTANCE OF DELEGATED RESPONSIBILITY ———————

If you are in a position in which you direct the activities of others, it is important to encourage subordinates to do more of their own thinking about delegated tasks. Many young people, particularly when transferred from line to staff jobs, flounder when delegated assignments. During orientation, they may seek as much help and guidance as possible. Up to a point, this is not only understandable but desirable. However, continued too long, it becomes a crutch, destroying their ability to get things done on their own.

Oliver L. Niehouse, of the Canadian industrial concern TFC, once told me:

One such individual I recall had boundless enthusiasm for his work, but after several months, he was still dropping into my office five or six times a day to discuss relatively minor problems. Not only was he not doing his job properly, he constantly interrupted me. When I presented him with a tally of the time he'd been in during the preceding week, he agreed it was excessive and promised to list what he wanted to talk about twice weekly. As I suspected, many items didn't have the importance he thought they had when they first came up. Others could be self-solved with more thought. He became more proficient, carried out more responsibility, and took a lot less of my time and his own.

Another young man clearly demonstrated the ability to analyze problems, but stopped there. All too often, I had to suggest solutions. So, I turned to sitting in silence for several minutes when he presented a problem. Then I asked what he recommended. After less than a half dozen times, he realized that whenever

*presenting a problem, he also had to offer a recom-
mended solution or two. More often than not, his
recommendations were adopted.*

■ YOU ARE STILL RESPONSIBLE ———

In the long run, say Merrill E. and Donna Douglass in *Manage
Your Time, Work, Yourself,* delegation never relieves you of any
responsibility, explaining: "In fact, delegation creates more *total
responsibility.* For after delegating, you're still responsible or
accountable to your superiors, even if your subordinate is also
responsible to you. If you're not delegating adequately now,
learning to do so could be more time-consuming than doing it
yourself. But, failure to delegate is disastrous. You cheat your
subordinates and wind up buried under a mountain of detail."

The Douglasses emphasize differences between delegation
and job assignment: "The former should always include results
to be achieved, as well as required activities and their intended
results. Work assignment is simply instructing a subordinate to
complete a particular task in a specific manner. Assigning work,
don't expect the same results as when you delegate. Subordinates
may not become more motivated or improve their skills. The
assignment may not save you time."

▪ Chapter Fourteen ▪ ▪ ▪ ▪ ▪

Avoiding Interruptions

Delegating to expand your performance should leave you more time for *effective* action if you can lick another major minute stealer: interruptions. Greatest of these is the boast: My door is always open.

Many executives, even up to and including top levels, frequently like making this claim. However, such a policy actually wastes an amazing amount of expensive time and produces minimum results. As you go down the line, the "open door" impact becomes even greater. Obviously, no one in business wants to remain so well hidden as to be virtually inaccessible, but your door should be closed a good portion of the day to permit you to work on really important matters without minute-wasting interruptions. The individual who welcomes everyone who wants to drop in will get plenty of one thing: conversation. In most cases, this doesn't add up to accomplishment.

Some interruptions shouldn't worry you; they go with every job. If your visitor's chair is getting dusty, it is perhaps a sign that you aren't getting to see people who might be important for your activities. A far-reaching contact network can be an invaluable resource. If, on the other hand, the chair is getting worn from overuse, remember that its occupants—delegatees or others—are not always sensitive to the time demands they are making on you.

The most important minute-minding technique is to pay attention to the *type* of interruptions you are getting. This calls for some checking into these major categories:

■ Are others constantly interrupting to pass the buck to you?
■ Are others bypassing channels when they come to you?
■ Are company policies, objectives, procedures unclear, so that too many hazy-area decisions are coming to you on a daily basis?
■ Do unannounced visitors keep coming around—from inside and outside?
■ Are emergencies always popping up?

■ THE OPEN DOOR MYTH

The always-available executive finds it impossible to get his or her own work done, to think through objectives and priorities, and to concentrate on getting priority tasks accomplished. Closed-door, controlled time is when you are doing what you want and need to do. Response time is when you accept time-stealing interruptions.

The idea of making oneself unavailable, says Jonathan Cotes in *Industrial and Commercial Training* magazine, discomforts many, adding:

> But, to meet your work priorities, you need to think about the best time of day to be unavailable and how to communicate this fact, especially between team members who have both controlled and response time obligations. It also requires that you develop nonoffensive ways to protect yourself from casual callers.

*Top managers are virtually unanimous in condemna-
tion of open door; they agree on the imperative need
for planned unavailability whether achieved by a
"quiet hour" and a skillful secretary taking call-
backs, a hideaway, or simply staying at home for a
few hours of concentration without interruption.*

Kevin Daley, president of Communispond, uses a variation of the
open door policy. His door is ajar—not fully open; not fully
closed. Its hidden meaning is: Kevin really doesn't want you to
come in, but you can if it is *really* important. Obviously, you
would think twice before pushing open that half-opened door.

▪ TO MINIMIZE YOUR INTERRUPTIONS —

▪ *Go after the buck-passers and bypassers.* They can, and
should be, stopped—the quicker the better.

▪ *Reduce as many subordinate transactions to the shortest
time possible.* Do this through discussion of responsibilities and
things that they can do on their own *without* asking you. Obviously, this doesn't mean producing a manual that tries to anticipate every possible situation. Planning, however, can cover
most routine situations—and in virtually all businesses, routines
dominate.

▪ *Draw a line and stick to it.* No matter what you do about
visitors, someone may well take offense. You will see certain
visitors; others will have to see somebody else. Moreover, try to
see those you must see, in periods away from your most important, high-effectiveness periods.

A study by the Young President's Organization—whose
members are corporate heads under age forty—in the *Harvard
Business Review*, reveals that members spend about 80 percent
of each business day talking to people. The average had seven

prearranged appointments a day and innumerable people who "just dropped by" or "stuck their heads in the door."

Obviously, no business person is ever completely free from the unexpected emergency. Saving time from visitor interruptions means cutting them to the minimum—to diminish as far as possible those that limit your effectiveness—and adopting techniques of handling visitors that make the best use of your time.

■ MAKING YOUR OWN INTERRUPTIONS —

You might be excessively developing some of the following self-interruptions:

■ Wandering around the office or plant to "get the feel of things."
■ Chatting with employees at all levels—particularly subordinates—just to get to know them better.
■ Slipping away for nonvital visits to branch offices or plants.
■ Playing "visiting fireman" yourself.

A time log in your organizer/scheduler kept for a week or two, with interruptions noted and minutes required, can help you to realize the following points:

■ Avoid interrupting yourself subconsciously because you are really bored with what you are doing. Sticking to the important, and following self-set priorities or those given you with deadlines, requires concentration.
■ Instead of being diverted by a bright idea or sudden thought, have a scratch pad ready. Use your dictating device or write it into your own scheduler as a to-do task for a specific time. Record only enough to express your notion; then get back to it later without having lost a good idea that might not return.

▪ INTERRUPTIONS BY SUPERIORS ———

The most difficult interruptions to control are those by superiors. First, however, consider if *you* are doing the same thing with those under you.

How frequently have you encountered company heads who insist that their people come on the double when called? Often, they give little consideration to the fact that *you* might be busy handling vital, undroppable tasks. All too often, these same individuals think nothing of keeping aides at doorside or sitting at the desk while they go on and on with the previous caller. The following are some tips to help deal with this problem:

▪ One executive I know never goes to see the company vice president or president without a job in progress on which to work while waiting: editing a report, revising drafts, or reading required material. This individual simultaneously gets work done and impresses higher-ups.

▪ The brisk, interrupting command to a subordinate submitted through a secretary is less and less in favor. So is the buzzer. Today's top executives prefer telephoning subordinates themselves and giving an idea of the best time to meet and an alternative. They also explain the reason for the meeting, in at least general terms, so that the person requested can be prepared.

▪ When office geography permits, ranking officers on occasion trot down to a subordinate's quarters to take the curse off of the summons. One executive explained: "It relaxes me to get away from my desk, and I think, bucks up a junior when I make the visiting gesture. Often, you'll get your business done quicker, frequently completing it without even a sit-down."

Who could get angry at one's boss when interruptions are so democratic, civilized, and downright friendly? However, there are other types of bosses, says Merrill E. Douglass, of Time-

Management Center, in his brochure "What to Do if Your Boss Is Wasting Your Time." Douglass writes: "Sometimes the boss is a time-waster, but other times he or she may simply be the focus of a subordinate's generalized frustrations. If your boss is well organized, clarifies objectives, specifies priorities, maintains consistent priority signals, and avoids frequently interrupting your work, you can judge whether or not your chief is wasting your time."

If you have identified an interruption problem, the next step is to bring it to the boss's attention, which is often easier said than done. Says Douglass, "Some bosses are aware they create subordinates' time problems. Others aren't. Still others refuse to even admit the possibility."

Reaching a workable solution requires joint action. The first decision is whether or not to tackle the problem. Many of us, Douglass says, shy away from dealing with such issues, feeling it is easier and less painful if we don't rock the boat. As you begin addressing your problem, remember that until both of you recognize that the boss's interruptions are wasting your time and ability to perform, *you* will have to talk to your boss about it—as a colleague, not as an adversary. As long as you do little but privately complain, no solution is possible.

■ INTERRUPTIONS BY SUBORDINATES ——

Consider the following questions about subordinates' interruptions:

■ Do you train your aides to consolidate interruptions and make daily or weekly presentations and plans at one time?

■ Do you make reporting by groups a routine wherever possible?

■ Do you reserve a specific daily time during which subordinates can come to you with questions—and make sure that if something changes your schedule, you advise them when you can meet?

People—even kids—quickly learn the difference between such periods and uninterruptible times and act accordingly. People like clearly defined boundaries and tend to respect those most clearly marked. To this end, ask yourself the following questions:

■ Have you encouraged the use of brief written notes in preference to personal interruptions?

■ Do you promptly *answer* subordinates' communications, so that they don't feel they must interrupt you for prompt answers?

■ INTERRUPTIONS BY PEERS —————

Whereas you probably have to take it when the boss interrupts and you can set the subordinate interruption pattern, handling interruptions from those of the same or relatively equal rank requires even more diplomacy and tact. The following are some points to remember:

■ *Begin by mutual agreement.* Make necessary contacts at periodic, predesignated times. This can be worked out only face-to-face—based on a real look at respective schedules. Some 20 percent of peers are likely to bring you 80 percent of the emergencies you face. They try to have you drop whatever you are doing when *they* need help. At the same time, they might be disinclined to sidetrack *their* activities when *you* require assistance. Says Jay Levinson in *The 90-Minute Hour:* "Be compassionate, sympathetic, helpful, and sensitive to their needs—but also make it clear that they're getting in the way of your efficiency."

■ *Don't be a "dropper-inner" yourself.* Taking the time to call your peers—making appointments rather than interrupting them—is an unexpected courtesy that begets like treatment.

■ *Consider why your interruptions have gotten out of hand.* You don't like offending people. You love to be involved in everything. It makes you feel important to be consulted often. You aren't very good at terminating visits. You've gotten people accustomed to checking with you. You just like talking. Allow any of these to continue and you end up the loser.

■ HANDLING OUTSIDE VISITORS ————

Although it is impossible to completely halt outside visitor interruptions, there are many steps you can take to better control such drop-ins.

The best alternative, says Charles R. Hobbs in *Time Power*, is to take charge by observing two rules:

1. The other person's self-esteem is a prized possession; therefore, do the necessary graciously.
2. Don't violate your unifying principles. There are no reasons to lie, but there are techniques for reducing overlong stays by visitors, including the following:

■ Maintain a businesslike stance and a formal tone with drop-ins. Be quick and alert. Sit at the edge of your seat. Give the visitor your complete attention.

■ Set a specific time limit, if possible—obviously, depending on the visitor and your own time pressures.

■ When the moment comes for visit's end, stand up. Don't interrupt, but when it is your turn to speak, express thanks as you walk toward your visitor; he or she will probably then be standing as well. Walk toward the door or escort visitors to the elevator or their cars. A bit of personal attention, Hobbs finds, works well for him.

■ Always keep a timepiece you, and preferably also your visitor, can see.

- Use body language such as closing your date book, shuffling papers, or moving to the edge of your seat.
- When you feel that the interruption has to end, you can well make such statements as, "I guess that sums it up" or "I certainly appreciate your dropping in."
- Summarize the action to be taken. That is, what you will do to follow up or look into the matter.

I have sometimes dictated a note in the visitor's presence when a point was reached at which I knew clearly what was wanted. In this way, visitors knew I had registered their requests. Usually, visitors overstay and repeat themselves because they think you don't understand or will forget.

Bring Out the Visitor's Objective

Dr. Harry Stack Sullivan, long a leading figure in American psychology, wrote:

> The person who comes to see you usually has something specific in mind—even if unclearly expressed. Everything you can do to bring it out most quickly and effectively will save both of you time; make things easier all around.
>
> Don't be afraid to ask questions. Often callers expect you to both listen and suggest action. Direct questions can get them to say at the beginning what they might ordinarily say at the end.

I know one leading executive who, after the preliminaries, does this and cuts through all of the time-wasting palaver by specifically asking, "Exactly what can I do for you?" Having established the main point, he seeks additional information on significant details. If he can give the caller the desired information or help, he does so promptly. If it will take follow-up, he requests a memo;

many time-wasting interrupters never follow up. Both participants are more quickly satisfied.

A construction company president I know signals visitor
conclusion by putting on his hat to walk his visitors out. A retired
army general, now in private business, claps his hands together
smartly when he feels everything has been covered, asking,
"Well, now, does that answer all of your questions?" It usually so
disconcerts callers that they make a quick answer and wind up.

Don't Coffee-or-Tea Unexpected Visitors ————————

In many instances, you prolong visits with questions such as
"Can I get you a cup of coffee?" or "Would you like a drink?"
When the visitor accepts the offer, you have automatically tied up
a portion of your valuable time with someone who might not be
a positive influence on work.

If you have fallen into this time-wasting habit, consider not
offering every caller refreshments. You can work your way into
this concept gradually by mentally evaluating each visitor according to his or her potential effect on your output. Naturally, drinks
and coffee should be eliminated first for those who have little or
nothing to do with your ability to fulfill your duties. Within a
short time, you should be able to omit most of the unnecessary
servings and in the process make your work more enjoyable and
productive.

Have your secretary interrupt, if necessary—through inter-
com or personally. The latter shows greater urgency, but doesn't
make the mechanics of interruption too obvious.

Special Rooms for Visitor Calls ————————————

In most Japanese companies, and some in the United States,
visitors don't come to the offices of those on whom they are

calling—often because the person called on has no office. Even top executives frequently lack private quarters and work in large bull pens. Firms have one or more visitors' rooms, furnished simply or elegantly, according to rank and corporate size. Invariably, the Japanese have "tea ladies" who serve tea, coffee, or a soft drink; visitors sit on one side of a low table and host or company representatives on the other. After a few pleasantries, they get right down to business. While the Japanese generally run on an exact-minute appointment basis, drop-in "courtesy call" visitors are not unknown. Because good manners are a habitual part of the lifestyle, such visitors are generally received—but briefly.

Other Techniques in Handling Unexpected Callers

Realize that interruptions are a part of your job. They can't be completely eliminated, and you wouldn't want them to be, even if it were possible. However, you can manage them better with these tips:

■ *Set another specific date.* After taking a moment to say hello to the unexpected visitor, apologize for a crowded schedule and try setting up a specific, later date. Serious visitors won't mind; others probably shouldn't have stolen your minutes in the first place.
■ *Find the right person to handle the visitor.* Frequently, someone else is better qualified to handle a particular question, if the visitor actually has one. Making this clear, and setting up an introduction then and there, often avoids upsets. Thus, even if you don't spend much time with the caller, your recognition, greeting, and assurance that the visitor is in the best hands makes your interest clear.

The Telephone

There is a story of a New England farmer, his telephone continuously ringing, talking to a passerby outside his door. The latter can barely hold himself back from going in to answer. The farmer only shifts his pipe. "Pay it no mind," he replies calmly. "I put that phone in for *my* convenience."

A lot of us often feel that telephones *are* for our own convenience, not just to be answered—and wish we knew how to make them function that way. There is hardly any device that can do more to save minutes in our daily activities—or waste us so many more.

Although telephones undoubtedly make many of our activities possible, we are sometimes thoroughly tempted to try business without them. Whereas many incoming calls might be the bane of your existence, outgoing calls—those you want to make—are frequently the lifeblood of what you want to do. The trick is to master the telephone to enable you to save minutes and more each day—so that it is there, like the telephone of the New England farmer, for *your* convenience.

In this chapter, we will deal with the following key aspects of telephone use:

■ Ways to save time and to use your telephone more effectively in the calls *you* make—or that are made for you.
■ Handling incoming calls—both those you want and those you would sooner put off or avoid altogether.
■ Some of the new equipment now available that can make telephones more useful to you.

We will also explore telephone techniques, particularly as they apply to saving time.

■ FACE-TO-FACE IS BETTER ─────────

Phone conversations are inferior to talking to someone face-to-face, explains Richard Saul Worman in his excellent work *Information Anxiety*, because "We're deprived of the nonverbal signals that add to the richness of communication—the eye contact, facial expressions, hand gestures, and body language. But, the speed, convenience, and low cost has made telephones the dominant form of communications in business and increasingly in our personal lives. There are many people who have strong relationships, social and we assume business, with individuals whom they actually haven't seen in years, but know only from the telephone."

■ HANDLING OUTGOING CALLS ─────────

The first time-saving step before any call is to consider the call's necessity. Keep its purpose clear in your own mind. If you need to cover more than one subject, jot down the points you need to make. Then, get right to it. Half of the conviviality many people adopt so that they won't sound too brusque is really just a waste of other people's time. Save the game descriptions, bridge tallies, and social tidings for appropriate hours. Busy and effective people appreciate directness. Keep the following in mind:

- Consider actually clocking your own calls to see that you finish soon—using anything from an egg timer to a stopwatch. This will teach you to handle your calls more efficiently.
- Keep a record of times when people you call regularly are in and least busy. You can organize your tries to avoid that "occupied" or "out" response.
- Make appointments to call important contacts and enter them into your organizer/scheduler. Not only are the individuals called likely to be there, you will both be prepared to get right down to business.
- Place action-requesting calls in the morning. The party you called can gather the necessary papers, consider decisions, or otherwise start early on whatever is wanted.

▪ WHEN SOMEBODY ELSE MAKES YOUR CALLS

Undoubtedly you have had secretaries say "Wait a minute, please, Mr. Smith would like to talk to you." Finally, the long-lost Smith is on the line. You know how annoying it can be. Presumably Smith is busy and thinks he can save his minutes by telling his secretary to get you on the line and then advise him. Smith somehow forgets that he is the one asking the favor of time and requires you to waste your minutes waiting for him.

Some executives say that when they are kept waiting in this fashion by secretaries, they promptly hang up—except, of course, for important customers or the spouse. Others add that waiting requesters invariably are those who get most indignant when you use the same gambit on them.

The telephone company stresses that always being ready to greet people you have called when they answer is only courteous, reflecting on you and your company. Said one busy executive: "My time is precious. So is that of the people with whom I usually talk. They don't like me to keep them waiting. I share the sentiment when the situation's reversed."

▪ SPEAKERPHONE ADVANTAGES AND DRAWBACKS

Increasingly prevelant, speakerphones have real advantages. Whether or not there is an automatic dialer, your hands (and mind) are free for something else until the other party picks up or you get a message center. Speakerphones can also eliminate ear fatigue—important for frequent callers.

In many offices, speakerphones help by letting users easily refer to papers, blueprints, and so on while telephoning. In other situations, users can even operate a PC, typewriter, or other device and still talk without the other party being aware of this. At home, a wide variety of tasks can be carried on while telephoning—a valuable minute-minder.

Sometimes, of course, speakerphones sound as if you are calling from the bottom of a well. When told of this, I immediately pick up and talk in the normal way—but I have still saved holding on while getting the other party.

Another speakerphone advantage: When the operator or receptionist at the other end says Mr. X is on long-distance or otherwise occupied, doing something else productive while waiting saves many minutes. Moreover, the fact that you are waiting, and tying up the other person's line, usually persuades your party's deputy to put your call through promptly.

Speakerphones are also vital when you have calls to make to airlines and others with heavy phone traffic, for which a recorded voice says "All of our agents are busy serving other customers.

Your call will be answered by the first available operator." With
the speakerphone, waiting-time annoyance is minimized because
you can accomplish something else in the interim.

Picking up your speaker as soon as the other party is on the
line is a good decision. Accountemps recently surveyed the largest U.S. companies and found that more than 45 percent said they
disliked being put on a speaker; two percent said that they actually refuse such calls. Objections cited were a perceived lack of
privacy (50 percent), poor voice quality (34 percent), a feeling of
being patronized (12 percent), and concern that the other party
is being distracted (4 percent).

▪ USING A HEADSET

If you make a great many calls, consider an operator-type headset. Once heavy and bulky, today they are extremely light and
compact. Unlike speakerphones, on these you sound completely
natural. They leave your hands free and eliminate neck pains
resulting from bracing receivers between shoulder and ear. Don't
worry if you are downgraded in colleague estimation if you use
these instead of a regular phone—the time and energy advantages
are tremendous.

▪ USING OUTGOING CALLS TO INFORM AND SELL

The following, from New York Telephone, are a number of
time-saving tips for telephone users. Although some are intended
for sales telephoning, many apply to any outgoing call.

▪ *Plan calls to speed information.* For example, you could
reach twenty customers—no matter where they might be
located—by telephone in less than a day, to answer questions,
solve problems, make sales, and speed up information exchange.

■ *Make a calling blitz.* If you have a new product or service, make a priority list and quickly inform customers or sales representatives of features, prices, selling methods, special rates, and so on—getting directly to the best prospects more quickly than by almost any other means. Put your cues on paper before calling.

■ *Confirm correspondence.* Clarify what has been put in writing. Letters are slow and easily misinterpreted. Quick calls allow you to make sure that what your letter says is what the recipient really understands.

■ *Make appointments.* Calling for appointments is nothing new, but if you schedule and then call to fit dates to your optimum routing, you can cut backtracking. A confirming call shows consideration for the other person's time, as well as your own.

■ *Plan your calling day.* Even if it is just a matter of checking in with an important customer, telephone sessions can prove invaluable. Use your organizer/scheduler to plan a week's business calls in advance. This, and your follow-up card file, can do wonders for organizing telephoning schedules.

■ *Make friends of secretaries.* It never hurts to be cordial and friendly. Get names, first and last, and include them in your file so that you will remember them for the next call.

■ THREE-WAY CALLING AND OTHER SERVICES

A number of new services allow you to reach two or more persons at different places in the same call. New York Telephone, for example, has a unit that allows you to dial a second number to add another person to your call. Three-way calling helps avoid back and forth when planning social or business activities. Call forwarding lets you forward calls to another number. Speed calling lets you dial important numbers locally or long-distance—almost instantaneously—using just two or three digits.

■ CALLING WITHOUT PRESSING BUTTONS OR DIALING ———————————

Late in 1990, A&S, the New York department store, introduced a new "voice print" telephone, which automatically dials calls from the sound of your voice. The telephone stores up to fifty names, in just about any language, for voice command dialing, and 100 numbers for easy speed dialing.

■ INCOMING TELEPHONE CALLS ————————

Incoming calls—especially the unwanted or the inappropriately timed—are the bane of many people in their business and personal lives. Although some top executives can claim that they always answer their own telephones, with no screening whatsoever, following this practice can subject you to an infinite number of time-stealing moments every day. According to Michael Fortotino, president of Priority Management, *Business Week* reports, middle managers are telephoned every five minutes.

Consider this: You wouldn't let anyone barge into your office at any busy moment. Hence, is there any real reason you should let the telephone do the same? I think not, especially if you want to save those precious minutes. The following are useful tactics concerning telephone calls:

■ *Have all calls screened.* In many cases someone else can supply the information or handle the job as well, or even better, than you. Don't give in to the temptation of feeling that only you can respond sufficiently to take care of a majority of callers' needs.

■ *Be "out," not in conference.* Have your secretary or assistant explain that you are out of the office, rather than in a meeting. In-conference or in-meeting putoffs seem to annoy many callers,

who can't quite figure what all of those time-consuming sessions
are about, or why they are more important than their calls.

■ *Explain absences.* Have your secretary refrain from saying
that you are not in just now; rather, have him or her say when you
will be available. Give a specific call-back time or promise to
respond. This also takes the sting out of your inability to answer
and preserves a caller's self-esteem. However, all of this doesn't
mean that your secretary has to explain your private business.

■ *Call back punctually.* If you promise to call back at a certain
time, do it.

■ *Use tact and courtesy.* Much of your call-screening success
depends on the tact and courtesy of your telephone answerer.
That person must, at all costs, avoid the impression that they are
there just to prevent anyone from getting through to you. Callers should feel that, although you are unavailable at the moment, their needs will be cared for as specifically and directly
as possible.

■ *Make the best calling times known.* Letting essential callers
who call you regularly know when you are most likely to be
available and best able to take their calls eliminates many un-
desired interruptions.

■ TAKING CALLS WHEN YOU HAVE PEOPLE IN YOUR OFFICE ─────────

One of the most frustrating time-wasters are calls taken by others
when you are with them. It is both embarrassing and an imposi-
tion to have to sit, squirm, gawk, and pretend not to listen while
someone takes a long call, or several calls.

  If, on the other hand, *you* take calls while a visitor is in your
office, remember that you are imposing on their time. The best
approach is to anticipate as many calls as possible. Explain in
advance that you are likely to be interrupted and the importance
of the call. If possible, step outside to take the interrupting

call. Handled with tact, this procedure is generally easier for all concerned.

Some executives make this distinction: Customer calls always get the right-of-way; practically everybody else is called back. I find taking calls while I'm occupied with someone else particularly annoying, especially in the dentist's chair, where, not infrequently, work inside my mouth stops for a colleague's or family member's largely social call. Some individuals make it a point to accept their children's calls no matter who is in the office—on the theory that the kids should always feel that they can gain access. My judgment: Unless it is a real crisis, children past a certain age should be placed under some of the same constraints as anyone else—and know when parents can be called at business and when not.

▪ TOO MUCH TALK ——————————————

R. Alec MacKenzie, author of *New Time Management Methods*, quotes Shirley Belz of the National Home Study Council as a strong advocate of staying *off* the telephone when possible— adding that those who hang on for half an hour or longer are often using you as a substitute therapist. To short-circuit such people, introduce some of your own problems into the conversation.

Recognize the danger of involvement in every detail of every caller, MacKenzie says, and preserve the ability to divorce yourself from routine matters and unessential details. The inability to terminate long-winded telephone callers is another time-waster. Learn and practice such techniques as setting a time limit— signaling your ending with such prases as "Before we hang up."

Extensive telephone socializing, particularly during business hours, might make for pleasant relationships, but it can steal your time and drain your productive concentration. Socializing can be reduced without your becoming antisocial.

MacKenzie notes that another reason many people take

every call that comes along is *ego*—a feeling of self-importance or a desire to be involved and informed.

▪ USING ANSWERING MACHINES ─────────

If you don't have one, I urge you to consider getting an answering machine as a most important telephone-interruption preventer. More and more companies supply them; if your company can't or won't, you can purchase your own inexpensive model. Their use is also growing for homes. Answering machines offer many time-saving advantages. The following tips should help you maximize this potential:

▪ It is perfectly reasonable to make your message short and to the point: "This is [your name and number]. Please leave a message and I'll get back to you as soon as possible." Lengthy responses or asking that a message be left when the tone sounds are no longer necessary; answering machines are so common-place these days that virtually everyone who calls knows this procedure.

▪ New machines allow you to see the caller's number so that you can decide whether to have a message recorded or pick up. This system is being challenged in some states on the theory that it is an invasion of the caller's privacy—the logic of that completely escapes me.

It is forecast that digital answering machines will replace cassette tape models. Microchips for messages give immediate access instead of the seconds or minutes it takes for a tape to rewind. You can even take your personal answering machine on the road. The Cobra Traveler, for instance, hooks up to any hotel phone and works like your office or home unit. It also serves as a dictation machine and alarm clock.

To sum up: Use your answering machine to control your

telephone time. Because the majority of incoming calls will not be that urgent, resist the temptation to find out who is calling when you are doing something else—or even when you have just returned to the office. Your highest priority should always be the most important thing you have to do, based on your schedule. That is rarely attending the telephone.

▪ KEEPING A TELEPHONE LOG ─────────

Keeping organizer/scheduler entries for all of your business calls can be a valuable time saver says W. R. Rossnagel in *Supervisory Management*. He explains: "Noting significant events—subjects discussed, follow-up information, verbal agreements, and arrangements for return calls—then and there can help ensure you have a memory jogger for accurate recall." Unresolved matters should be listed on your next day's sheet so that you can attend to them immediately.

▪ TELECONFERENCING ─────────────

Another increasingly popular time-saving trend is the teleconference. AT&T explains that, in minutes, without operator assistance, you can set up call meetings with as many as fifty-eight locations, nationally and internationally.

AT&T can also arrange for you to make it possible to allow other people to dial directly to your prearranged call meetings. Specialized firms arrange to have each participant on line for discussion—the service is billed as if you had individually made person-to-person calls. Also available are systems that tie into video cameras, microphones, large screens, and satellite technology. These can be considered individual time-savers for all participants—something to keep in mind if you have to organize.

■ INFORMATION-SEEKING CALLS ──────

If you don't already know it, you will be surprised how often you can get information on the telephone that would take hours to obtain in person. You can save many minutes by making information-seeking calls to other businesses, government offices, civic agencies, stores, schools, and so on. The following are some useful tips:

■ *Use a direct approach.* State that you want to talk to the person who can give you the most complete information on a specific problem. For example: "I want to talk to the person in charge of the butterfly collection—and may I have the name and title before you switch me." Request the extension number in case you are cut off, as so frequently happens with internal systems requiring a touch-tone transfer. The more concise and specific you are, the more quickly you will get the person best qualified to handle your problem.

■ Always get the name of the person supplying information. Before you get into the conversation, write down the name in your organizer/scheduler for future reference. In the conversation, use language such as "Tell me, Ms. Gallagher. . . ." This establishes a rapport, more quickly producing needed information without being overly familiar. Give your own name and business when calling; frequently, information calls get cut off and you have to start all over again.

■ *Make advance notes on what you want to learn.* Tick off items as you get the information.

■ *Stick to the point.* Don't go through a lot of roundabout explanations in seeking information; just say what you want to know as simply and as directly as possible.

■ *Have available all relevant numbers.* This eliminates having to hold while looking. We have all been taught to do this when telephone shopping with credit cards. In many cases you will get a series of questions in a certain order. For example, inquiries about publication subscriptions usually begin with a request for your zip code—even before your name—because records are filed by this number.

▪ CHECK TELEPHONE LOCATIONS ──────

To save time, make sure that your telephones at home or office are located where they are answerable with the fewest steps taken. You actually walk many unnecessary miles, and waste countless minutes, if your telephone hasn't been conveniently placed. Yet, often people go on using telephones located for the previous occupants of their house or office because they don't want to take the time or make the effort to change telephone locations.

▪ TRANSLATIONS BY TELEPHONE ──────

Do you need a foreign-language interpreter at your beck and call any time of day from almost any telephone in the world? AT&T's **Language Line** gives you just that by providing immediate telephone access to highly trained interpreters of virtually any language or dialect (more than 140 at last count). When might the service be useful? If you were traveling abroad, and became ill and couldn't explain the symptoms to a doctor, you could call Language Line and have an interpreter on the line. If you needed to deal with a non–English speaking prospect at home or overseas, you could call Language Line and have an interpreter help you with the call. The cost is $3.50 per minute of actual on-line time, which can be billed to a major credit card. [To reach an interpreter in the U.S. call toll-free 800-628-8486; outside the U.S. call either AT&T's USADirect service or 408-648-5971.]

In addition to telephone-based interpretation, AT&T Language Line offers a variety of other time-saving convenience services, including written document translation and foreign-language voice recordings. [800-752-0096]

■ CELLULAR PORTABLES: ON-THE-GO TIME SAVERS

In recent years there has been an avalanche of new cellular, mobile telephones, which at one time could be used only in an automobile, subsequently on a train, and later on airplanes—but which are now completely portable and becoming ever smaller in size. If you are constantly on the go, you can choose from the following types of telephones:

■ *Car Phones:* These are permanently installed, with the antenna hard-wired to the electrical system. They contain full-power, 3-watt transmitter-receivers. Their use is restricted to your vehicle.

■ *Transportables:* These are cellulars, with their own powerful battery packs, that can be carried in an attaché case.

■ *Pocket Phones:* Small, portable, fitting into a jacket pocket or purse, these lack the power of transportable or car versions and the batteries need frequent recharging. You are also more likely to find some areas unreachable.

■ *Cordless:* These are noncellular telephones with a detachable handset and a radio-based "station" from which the call comes. This type of telephone is wireless from handset to the base and can be carried around the house or office. The base, however, is connected to regular telephone wires.

Some Leading New Models

Motorola offers a compact, lightweight 4.2-pound unit enabling you to dial from a keypad or memory. It offers super-speed dialing, mute, and other control features.

New York Telephone and many other Bell companies claim

that their telephone has maximum calling channels in the area so that even during congested hours you can be busy talking business instead of waiting on line. Coverage is reportedly better because of more strategically located cell sites. The service for this telephone offers emergency 911 dialing, auto-answer after two rings, and a fifty-number memory with automatic storage into vacant memory locations. Multicity registration allows frequent travelers to subscribe to several cellular services, thus reducing the roamer charges when outside your primary subscription area.

Mitsubishi offers the Model 800 transportable cellular, claimed to be equally at home in a car, boat, or briefcase, with asserted "top performance in a sleek package." Weighing less than five pounds, it comes with a retractable antenna and rechargeable battery.

The Cincinnati Microwave Portable is offered "30 days risk free." Its price seems considerably higher than others on the market. It weighs 18.6 ounces, or only 16.5 ounces with the optional slim battery. A one-touch button instantly connects you toll-free to an operator who can answer all questions about the telephone and service.

Fujitsu calls its Pocket Commander "the cellular phone with a whole new dimension"—it has all of the most popular features in a pocket size. Chrysler has announced Visor Phone, a sophisticated cellular telephone built into a car's sun visor. Described as a "convenient location that lets you keep your hands on the wheel and eyes on the road," you can talk without holding the instrument. The unit features one-touch dialing, 100-number memory, radio mute when calls come in, and an automatic redial.

Cellular Telephone Benefits

The major advantages of cellular telephones, users tell me, are the following:

■ You can make calls on the go. If plans or requirements change and there isn't time to get to a regular telephone, a cellular can be a lifesaver.

■ You save time by making use of traveling minutes to call those you have to reach—whether you are in a car or public conveyance or even, in fact, walking on the street.

■ You save time by getting necessary calls done at available moments between desk-bound activities—not simply when en route, but during waiting minutes.

■ You can save time by calling the office en route—with orders, instructions, and so on—without having to use the telephones of those you are visiting.

■ Calls are easily made while commuting back-and-forth between suburban locations and in-town offices, to and from airports, and so on. While waiting for a flight or other transportation, you can bypass airport facilities—so frequently tied up when most wanted.

Robert Dilenschneider of one of the leading public relations firms, Hill & Knowlton, tells of typical use: He was in Stamford, Connecticut, and about to be driven back to New York; he asked how long it might take. Told forty minutes, he called his secretary on his portable, was connected with the switchboard, and handled twenty calls in the interim.

Pagers

Pagers are also an increasingly used time saver. A variety of wristwatch or pocket-size models feature numeric display combined with a digital watch to create a personal communications tool. Originally used only by emergency personnel, battery-powered pagers are now used by nine million Americans in all walks of life. The pager simply alerts you to make a return call at the most convenient time. They display callback numbers or other messages and beep, flash, or vibrate to alert you.

Motorola is the world's largest maker—for a variety of life-styles. Its most popular pager is a wristwatch model with numeric display and a digital timepiece weighing 2.1 ounces. Seiko also makes a wristwatch-size digital timepiece, which displays long-distance messages received over FM radio waves. Conventional beepers can signal you to call the office or your home, or to dial a specific displayed number. Messages are relayed in about one minute through a telephone network, FM transmitters, and a miniature receiver inside the watchband. Most beepers cost far less than cellular phones.

Sky-Tel offers a 2.5-ounce paging system called SkyPage. When someone needs to reach you, they dial a central toll-free number and your personal identification number (PIN). Messages are relayed from a central computer to a satellite, which connects with downlinks in every metropolitan area across America. You receive a numeric message—either the telephone number of the person trying to reach you or a code. Sky-Tel says: You hear about opportunities sooner; get information faster and gain the competitive edge. Moreover, since all network cities are paged simultaneously, you don't have to alert your callers or SkyPage to travel plans. You respond at your convenience, calling in toll-free. If on do-not-disturb, the system saves messages for up to ninety-nine hours. You control who gets your PIN. Special features: Priority Paging for urgent messages, Group Page to alert many people at once, and Time-of-the-Day Paging to program and send messages up to fourteen days in advance.

Computers Can Be Time Savers

In this and subsequent chapters, we will deal with the increasingly ubiquitous computer for office, home, and every locale in between. More than ten million personal computers (PCs) are now in use in the United States.

Obviously, if you are working in a big, or even a medium-size, business that has installed its own computer system, you need only learn how best to use what you are given to save corporate and personal time. On the other hand, if you have the chance to study computers—particularly those directly impacting your efforts—understanding the ever-growing range of options can enable you to suggest additions of software programs, upgrading of equipment, and other steps that can benefit both you and fellow users.

▪ PERSONAL ORGANIZER COMPUTER PROGRAMS

How can computers be best used by an individual concerned with time saving? One place to start is in personal organization: using the computer for many of the functions outlined in Chapter 3, on organizing and scheduling. The following are some of the best such software programs.

Lotus Agenda 2.0

This new software program from the widely used Lotus 1–2–3 is described as the "personal information manager for your PC or laptop portable helping you get better control of appointments, personnel, figures, projects, stray thoughts, and more in just thirty minutes." Lotus says: "Just type it all in; Agenda sorts it out, grouping relevant information in an organized, easy-to-read format. You get a choice of ready-to-use starter applications, including Activities Planner, People Manager, Account Manager, or Information Sifter, plus customized specific applications."

Lotus claims that the system, designed for individuals, eliminates all of the notes, pads, and slips of paper that once littered desks. It allows you to easily enter information into individual files. Agenda software concentrates on the two most important management requirements: follow-up and follow-through.

Chronos Time Management Software

This is a system designed for people, projects, and time management that claims the following advantages: The system enables you to better manage people, including yourself, as well as projects, goals, tasks, to-dos, and deadlines. A single integrated system, Who-What-When, understands the need for power and simplicity, and gives you a three-way view of people, projects, and time from the big picture down to specific task details so that you will always know who is working on what and when it is due.

R & R Associates' Shoebox

This program provides a place to fill in a calendar, which is expandable to fit in all appointments. Reminder flags are placeable as much as three months in advance, and the system automatically sets up a tickler file, eliminating the need to page through your calendar and make duplicate entries. If you are booked months ahead, a search routine can rapidly find open time blocks.

Shoebox 2 can be used by more than one person at a time—and links their calendars—thus enabling several people to fill in dates, appointments, and so on and to check for scheduling conflicts before setting up a group meeting. The expense tracker turns out group reports while monitoring individual accounts.

Tandy

The Tandy 1000RL computer and software is claimed to save time by organizing vital everyday information and placing it at your fingertips. Advertising for the Tandy states:

It's so easy—just point, click, and you're on your way. Create investment plans and keep track of credit and bank accounts. Keep detailed personal possessions inventory for insurance purposes. Create vacation or business trip itineraries, along with packing lists. Keep an idea journal. Even make time-saving computerized grocery lists. Possibilities are endless, but what-

ever the task, the RL Desk Mat Home Organizer soft-
ware handles details for you. Uses popular business,
home education, and entertainment programs.

Compaq

Compaq offers a 7.5-pound high-performance new generation
portable. It is claimed to be faster and more powerful than most
PCs because it provides either a 30- or 60-megabyte hard disk for
storage. That is comparable to 15,000 and 30,000 typewritten
pages, respectively.

Expense It!

Made by On-The-Go Software this program saves hours by auto-
mating documentation of business receipts. Run on an IBM-
compatible laptop, it enables you to punch in expenses en route.
Pop-up windows make it easy to bill clients and enter such expenses as hotels, meals, entertainment, and auto mileage. The
program sorts entries by dates, and even has a currency con-
verter. It comes with eight IRS-acceptable expense forms, saving
minutes for anyone who has to bill or collect on out-of-pocket
travel expenses.

▪ COMPUTERS USED TO PRODUCE DOCUMENTS

If yours is the responsibility to develop effective presentations for
your business or personal interest or to issue any type of newsletter, flyer, mail piece, bulletin board notice, and so on, you will
want to look into the wide range of software applications enabling you to speedily improve your output. There is a wide range

of desktop publishing options that offer software that prepares single- or many-page documents with effective headlines and body type, illustrations, attractive layouts, and so on—all without physically going to outside printers and the expensive processes they employ.

Presentations of every type—whether to be used in a subsequent printout or in videocassette form—can also be easily prepared. Typical is the IBM Personal System/2 (PS2) computers with Micro Channel software. The maker says:

> They're opening people's eyes and ears to more involving presentations—more stimulating classes and training programs—more interesting demonstrations. With this hardware and software, you can combine full-motion video, slides, photographs, illustrations, text, graphics, animation, as well as your existing database—a full plate, indeed. You can also capture and manipulate sounds and images from video cameras, disks and tapes, from CD and audio players and from an IBM CD–ROM player.
>
> You can show them right on your PS/2. Share them across a network. Or, project on a big screen. Then, instead of passively reading a report or hearing a lecture, your audience can experience what you communicate: An auto mechanic can hear the sounds made by a failing brake and see how to replace the part in animated sequence. A travel agency client can surf Hawaii's waves. Or, a real estate prospect can stroll through houses for sale.

Less sophisticated is IBM's new PS/1, described as a new type of personal computer that "brings it all home" with ease of use, power, and value to satisfy family needs. PS/1 provides a high-resolution IBM Photo Graphic display, an IBM Selectric Touch keyboard, an operations mouse, and a built-in modem—as well as the DOS/Microsoft Works, called the best-selling integrated software package. All of this lets you do word processing, spreadsheets, or financial calculations. In one offer, PS/1 provides the Prodigy Databank Service (described in Chapter 17) for three months at no charge—providing access to all types of information, convenient home shopping, banking, travel arrangements, and more. One extra feature is Support System, which brings you answers 365 days a year, eighteen hours a day, right to your own screen. The system can be expanded if you and your family's personal computer needs change.

▪ NOTEPAD PERSONAL COMPUTERS ─────

New notepad personal computers, introduced in 1991, are based not on the typewriter, as are most conventional machines, but on the standard 8½ × 11 notepad sheet—about the size of a clipboard. They have a large, liquid-crystal screen and a small electronic pen stylus. You carry it with you on any job. *Time* magazine explains:

> *Want to draft a note? Just write directly on the etched-glass screen as you would on a piece of paper; the writing is transformed into letters that appear as if by magic. Want to change a word? Just circle it. Want to cross out a sentence? Scratch it out. Want to add a phrase? Just draw a little caret under the insertion point and start writing. Capitalizing on 30 years of research and handwriting recognition, the Go Corp system can identify carefully printed letters, numbers and punctuation marks and turn them into clean, crisp, computer readable typescript—a tool as simple as a pencil or a postcard, but with the power of a computer behind it.*

Microsoft Pen Windows is a new system that works with application programs written for its Windows graphics software. Grid Systems Corporation is among the first to market this pen system, and intends to offer Microsoft's Pen Windows as well as Go's Pen Point option—at least until the market determines which is more popular. *Fortune,* noting that the new devices are the "friendliest, most totable computers yet," states that experts think these machines will relieve keyboard phobia, change how people work, and dramatically increase demand.

Chapter Seventeen

Obtaining, Absorbing, and Applying Information

Whatever your concerns—in business or career—there is always the need to keep up with continuing developments in your field and the wide range of fast-moving information that affects your professional and personal interests your daily life. How to best access information you need in the shortest time and most efficient manner, using computers and a wide variety of other channels, is this chapter's subject.

We live in an age of information, which is likely to exert an even greater influence on our lives in the decades ahead. As Richard Saul Werman explains in *Information Anxiety*, one *New York Times* issue contains more written information than the average person in seventeenth-century England would likely come across in a lifetime. Today, he adds, both our professional and personal lives are judged by the information we pursue— information that shapes our personalities, contributes to the ideas we formulate, and colors our world view. Says Werman, "The information explosion didn't occur solely because of an increase in information. . . . Advances in the technology of transmitting and storing it are as much a factor—affecting us as much by its flow as by its production."

With the quantity of information reportedly doubling every four years, it becomes increasingly important to select the best time-saving techniques to—

■ Pinpoint the information you really need.
■ Constantly update your ability to obtain it quickly and usefully.
■ Avoid the time-consuming distractions of an information excess.

Werman quotes Linda C. Lederman's *Communications in the Workplace:* "In one year, the average American will read or complete 3,000 notices and forms; scan 100 newspapers and 36 magazines; watch 2,463 hours of television; listen to 730 hours of radio; buy 20 records; talk on the telephone almost 61 hours; read three books and spend countless hours exchanging information in conversation. Thus, we spend most of our waking hours with information."

■ SAVING MINUTES IN INFORMATION ABSORPTION

The following are some tips on how to process information sources efficiently:

■ Read selectively. Concentrate on one general newspaper.
■ Examine news indexes—both general and business—before reading.
■ Learn to speed up your reading.
■ If you want to keep material, put a topical code word in the corner of the article and later cut out and file it for reference. Discard the rest of the publication at once, rather than letting it

pile up for subsequent browsing. Most times, you won't find much you missed on the first go-around, and you will avoid distracting clutter.

■ Cancel publications you don't want or don't get a chance to read.

■ Get others interested in the same field to read publications you can't—exchanging clippings to save both parties' time.

■ TELEVISION NEWS ─────────────────

■ Concentrate on one international broadcast, reading during commercials.

■ Limit local television news absorption to a single broadcast.

■ When minutes are tight and you have to get news faster, select single, all-news radio programs, which are usually broadcast on the hour. Major stories can be absorbed in as little as five minutes.

■ PLAN YOUR SEARCH ─────────────────

Planning is as important to speeding fact-finding and information-gathering and absorption as it is to any other activity you undertake. Written outlines are great time savers, even if not yet backed by facts. This is not as paradoxical as it sounds. Setting forth your ultimate objectives and noting the details you have at that point solves the very first step of reducing the search from your research. My project writing approach has always been as follows:

1. Sketch out areas to be covered.
2. Dictate the facts you know and the questions these and initial thinking produce.
3. Research only for what you then believe you will really need, rather than fact-gathering and trying to give discoveries meaning.

Time-driven, scientific problem-solving is based on such a method of research, which involves the following steps:

a. Assemble observable facts.
b. Form a hypothesis about the collected facts.
c. Test the hypothesis.
d. Deduce the course of action indicated by the accepted or rejected hypothesis—keeping both the hypothesis and course of action open for alterations as new facts are acquired.

Your essential directive must be not only to find facts, but to see beyond to the principles they illustrate. This is a mark of professional understanding—not only in business, but in law, medicine, the sciences, and many other fields.

You see a slogan in some offices that reads: Don't confuse me with the facts—my mind is made up. Many business executives are so strong-willed that subordinates fear to offend them by coming out with facts, or indicated solutions, that might upset conventional wisdom. Hence, this warning: If you lose your integrity and capacity to make judgments because you fear offending a superior, you will lose both your ability to reach sound decisions and to ferret out the facts on which decisions must be based. The solution to this problem is to use tact and ingenuity in presenting information that leads to your conclusions.

▪ WHERE TO LOOK IT UP

Books, trade journals, and specialized reports can provide the answers to many questions you might need to probe. Microfilm, audiocassette, and videotape also carry vast information stores. Being aware of this, it is surprising how many business people fail to use valuable available data fully. Quincy Munford, Librarian of Congress, once told me, "Probably 95 out of 100 people never take advantage of short-cuts learned by other's experience because they don't know the information they need, and could put to use, is available—or where to get it quickly and effectively."

Many business people who say that they don't have time to read and conduct research usually want to leave you with the impression that they are so busy on practical matters that they can't waste precious minutes on such fact-finding. These "school of experience" individuals fail to realize that even their favorite school operates a lot better with good researching from the best sources, done in the most effective way.

▪ SAVE TIME BY NOT REINVENTING THE WHEEL

Whatever your need or problem, you can probably find somebody else who has done it many times before. Starting with research into what is available on past performance or trends and directions in your area of interest can save tremendous time.

Writing this work is one example. My first step in planning this edition was to look up all available books and articles on the subject. Many are referred to and quoted and credited in this book—supplementing and expanding my own ideas on the subject. To find related magazine articles, I went to the monthly and annual *Reader's Guide to Periodical Literature*, which indexes a vast number of publications with references to titles, authors, dates, and pages. For most subjects, you will find its indexing outstanding. *Note:* Not all libraries carry all of the magazines indexed—but once you have established your target, getting to what you need is relatively easy. Trade magazines are separately listed.

I then made use of all of the computer databases described later in this chapter, consulted with key authorities and corresponded with scores of contacts, assembled data in file folders by chapter, and then started the process of dictation, transcription, and editing.

▪ USE YOUR LIBRARY MORE FULLY ———

The best quick-information source is your own public library. Usually, central or main branches are best, although in many cities, downtown satellites might have the largest business-related information availability. Outline your requirements and then contact the professionals who can lead you to the best available materials. My experience is that librarians are most congenial and generally helpful, but they can be most helpful if you do your homework first and go to them with specific questions.

Many libraries also offer help by telephone—at least giving you the addresses and numbers of certain sources. If they can't give you an answer right away, they will call back. A good library self-starter is *Instant Information* by Joel Mackower and Alan Green. It notes resources for almost any imaginable subject— many with phone numbers and descriptions. Another good source is *The Yearbook of Experts, Authorities and Spokespersons: An Encyclopedia of Sources From Broadcast Interviews.*

Using Specialized Libraries ———————

If your own local library doesn't have what you seek, many specialized libraries are worth checking. *The Special Libraries Association Directory* lists those in business, technical, and professional areas—most permitting interlibrary borrowing. You can find this directory through your own librarian.

There are also such libraries as the Academy of Medicine, Institute of Life Insurance, Dun & Bradstreet, and so on. Often overlooked are clippings, leaflets, and similar matter on a wide variety of subjects. Morton Yarmon, a public relations executive and writer, also suggests:

▪ *The Guide to Reference Books*
▪ *Sources of Business Information*

Government Information

The U.S. Department of Commerce, Washington, with many local offices, issues a wide variety of trade directories and other business publications with factual, authentic data, although usually two to three years behind. Go to an office in your community to examine the material. Specialized directories are constantly increasing and indexes vastly improved. The Government Printing Office lists thousands of publications, ranging from heavy law books to four-page leaflets. [For free descriptive matter, write: Superintendent of Documents, U.S. Government Printing Office, Washington, DC 20402.]

Using Local and State Libraries

Your state university or almost any college can also give you information to help solve business problems. The Graduate School of Business Administration at Harvard University publishes many books, pamphlets, and other materials, as well as the *Harvard Business Review*. So do the Wharton School, the University of Pennsylvania, Stanford University, and the University of Chicago. Many constantly issue new books and publications, some of which are probably in your field. Typical is Long Island University, C. W. Post Campus. According to Director Mary N. Grant, "The business library contains over 1,100 business magazines, many specialized trade journals, annual reports of listed New York and American Stock Exchange companies, numerous financial services, indexes, subject files, reference books and directories for in-depth industry information, and library staff and specialists." They contract for special-project research, with a fast turn-around—usually twenty-four hours. Their charges are based on hours spent.

The American Management Association ————

This nonprofit national organization [135 West 50th Street, New York, NY 10021; tel: 212-586-8100] publishes a vast range of books aimed at both small businesses, marketing, finance, human resources, career development, general business, and general management. If you can't drop in for a free look at what is available, request a catalogue. Your community bookstore with the greatest assortment of business books and catalogues is the best place to start.

Saving Time Through Telephone Information ——

You can get a lot of information by astute use of the telephone.
Call directly to the highest level of a targeted source. Lee Levitt, a New York management consultant, says that there has been a real change in the business telephone culture, adding that executives once shielded by secretaries are now proud to answer themselves. There are, of course, exceptions, Levitt says, but the basic change is unmistakable, especially in large companies. Follow these tips when calling:

■ Prepare an outline of what you want to learn.
■ Do a little advance checking to determine if the target source is knowledgeable on this subject.
■ Ask questions directly. Chances are that you will be surprised who you can reach and how much they can tell you.

800 Numbers ————————————————

One increasingly valuable source is the availability of toll-free 800 numbers offering from-the-source information. Most companies list numbers in their ads—aware that by providing this service, customers and prospects are more likely to call. Always get the names, titles, and extensions of those you reach so that you can contact them again.

AT&T's *Toll-Free 800 Directory: Business Edition* and *Consumer Edition* are two valuable sources that are updated annually. The business edition contains about 120,000 numbers, the consumer about half that.

Paid Information Services via Telephone ——————

The 900 lines provided by the major telephone companies enable you to call various information services.

For details contact: **The National Association for Information Services** [Helen M. Phlig, Managing Director, 1150 Connecticut Avenue N.W., Suite 1050, Washington, DC 20036; tel: 202-833-2545] *Note:* Beware high-cost, inconsequential, or erotic information available on 900 numbers.

Information From Specialized Resources ——————

Increasingly available in most cities across the country are information services and bureaus who can undertake your information gathering, special research projects, market studies and surveys, computer-base searches—virtually any information needed. **Find/SVP** [500 Fifth Avenue, New York, NY 10110; tel: 212-645-4500] is one of the nation's leading information-on-demand services, with its own worldwide network.

Find/SVP claims they will "cost-effectively find, screen, and sort the information you need via a unique combination of information consulting, analytical skills, and primary and secondary research capabilities—anything from a quick search of published literature to an in-depth customer study." They can be time-saving in the following areas:

■ *The Competition:* Competitors' marketing strategies; consumer and trade press coverage (including copies of articles); advertisements; speeches given by top management; merger and acquisition activities; major SEC filings, including annual reports, quarterly reports, 8Ks, and 10ks; R&D expenditures; identification of leading companies, along with names, addresses, and telephone numbers; and biographies of top executives.

■ *Industries:* The latest trends in health care, food and beverages, chemicals, energy, finance, and dozens of other industries; economic forecasts; major technological breakthroughs; business-segment breakdowns; wage and employment trends; suppliers, wholesalers, and retailers; consultants and experts; bibliographies; relevant books, research reports, and photographs; government regulations, policies, and documents; available equipment meeting certain specifications; and typical profit margins, costs, and budgets.

■ *Markets:* Historical, current, and projected market size; demographics (age, sex, income, education data, and so on); dominant companies in specific market segments; major market research reports, studies, and surveys; and profiles of shopping patterns.

■ *Products:* Use and demand, product samples, product literature, wholesale and retail prices, trademarks and patents, and number and success rate of new products.

■ *International:* International crises; annual reports of foreign companies; potential overseas market opportunities; identification of foreign manufacturers, importers, and distributors; currency exchange rates; translations; overseas telephone numbers and addresses; import and export statistics, projections, and regulations; current and anticipated policies of foreign governments; and economic, political, and social climates in foreign countries.

Personal Newsletter

Information and articles from many sources selected to match an interest profile you select from a memo of names or concepts distributed by fax or E-mail to reach you by 8:00 each morning is now offered by **Individual Inc.** [Cambridge, MA], headed by Yosi Amram. This supplier notes: "You don't have to log on to a computer or learn an on-line search protocol. You simply arrive at your desk in the morning and your news is there. We use filtering software called Smart, under an exclusive license from Cornell University, to sift articles from nine sources, including two press release news wires. Costs depend on complexity of your search profile and number of copies distributed. A typical personal newsletter contains five to ten articles."

Everything You Always Wanted to Know—By PC

Whatever the question, fact, or figure—about almost any subject, competitor, or interest—if you own a personal computer, a modem, and the required communications software, you are a few keystrokes away from quantities of information in minimum time and cost. Once the domain of reference librarians, these electronic in-depth storehouses can now be reached by anyone. They are very useful for a wide range of information; but be warned, without guidance, you could end up spending hundreds of dollars running down dead-end roads to the 5,000 or so U.S. sources. Databanks are now a $272 million annual U.S. business expected to double by 1994, according to Link Resources, a New York electronics consulting firm.

Ads for some services appear in both general and business publications.

Recommended for further reading:

- *How to Look It Up Online.* Alfred Glossbrenner (St. Martin's Press).
- *The Directory of All Online Databases* (Cuadra/Elsevier).
- Knowledge Industry Publications
  (These guides tell you how to connect to each base.)
- Gale Research, Detroit, publishes *Computer Readable Databases*, which lists some 5,500 sources.

The Database World

Databases come in three basic types. One simply locates articles you are seeking. A second type offers summaries of material. A third produces complete texts to read on your screen or download to print. Most services offer all three. The trend is toward full-text databases, because summaries, while fast, often don't give you what you are really looking for.

Providers of database services usually charge a per-month rate and an on-line per-minute fee for each search. Others charge a start-up fee with a five-minute minimum per search. To get what you want in the least time and at the lowest cost, Paula Ingraham of Arthur Andersen & Company, in *Personal Computing*, recommends the following:

- Define—on paper—the specific information needed before the search begins.
- Use catalogues to determine the best database to tap.
- If possible, use cross-referencing functions that search over several databases.
- List synonyms and variations of search terms to pinpoint desired information.

Each database has its own structure, documentation, and procedure. After you write or call for information catalogues, be sure to look at price lists and determine what you wish to spend on information. Charges can run up in very short time if not kept under control. Information on some of the best database services follows.

CompuServe Information Services [P.O. Box 20212, 5000 Arlington Center Blvd., Columbus, OH 43220; tel: 800-848-8199] says: "No matter what you need to know, we can inform you faster and more economically than any other data retrieval method. Simply pose your question, select the database and capture the relative data. Never before has getting information you need been so easy—to find, read, print out, or download right from your personal computer keyboard."

Founded in 1979, and now with 700,000 subscribers globally, CompuServe stresses that its services "can make your own desk a research center to study business opportunities, market patterns, foreign trade data, and housing starts. Or, keep up with new products. Read press releases. Stay atop your industry's hot topics. Monitor competition. Even check weather forecasting for traveling."

Other databases let you "browse and buy business products and services. Pre-shop latest computer and software system competitive analysis. With instant access to current news and technical reports, you can support your business proposals and decisions with cited information. Back up your reports, memos, etc."

The service also helps you "investigate market potential of any state geographic area; access feasibility of proposed ventures by examining economic forecasts, sales potential, and reports of similar ventures successes. There are also census and demographic data to plan direct mail, media activity; analyze competition."

The following are areas of CompuServe services:

■ *Investment:* Get instant information on companies of interest—their histories, financial statements, stock performance, products or services, major shareholders, and latest reports.

■ *Personal Research:* Hobbies and personal interests take on new dimensions when you expand your knowledge with current and historical information. Use the most recent, accurate statistics to support your personal views; give weight to political arguments and make smarter personal decisions or enhance your general knowledge.

■ *Home Buying:* Take a close look at a neighborhood before buying a house. Investigate income, age, family status, and other characteristics. Check out an area's professional makeup or sports affiliations. Learn about your own neighborhood and compare it with others across the country.

■ *National News:* From services not carried locally.

■ *Sports:* Follow favorite teams.

■ *Weather Information:* For local community information and details on points of destination.

■ *Professional:* Perhaps few have greater time demands and more of a need to stay atop current developments than doctors, lawyers, and other professionals. CompuServe databases enable you to follow current technology, economic trends, and political activities and news topics affecting your work. An electronic clipping service searches for, and retrieves, news stories important to you. A medical database keeps doctors abreast of current research, treatments, and issues, and speeds investigation of unusual or unheard-of symptoms. Writers and journalists find the service invaluable in researching and tracking contemporary issues.

Dow-Jones Retrieval

This service from the *Wall Street Journal*, offers "corporate membership for fee, account or location; a 33⅓ percent discount on standard prime and non–prime time per minute charges; ten free hours; no annual service fee; user's guide. Standard membership about $30 with three free hours and first year annual fee waived. Blue Chip membership about $100 with discounts and no annual service fee."

Dow-Jones News Retrieval says:

> [*This is the*] *only on-line resource specifically designed for business and financial professionals, and serious personal investors . . . who need up-to-the-minute data about companies, markets, industries and investments.*
>
> *Users have stock quotes and detailed financial data on thousands of companies on call, along with historical information as solid action foundation. Easy-to-use format.* Wall Street Journal *full text on-line. Plus selected articles from* Barron's, Business Week, Forbes, Fortune, Money, Inc. *and* Washington Post. *Regional newspapers and business publications unavailable on other services.*
>
> *In just seconds get information that could take days to compile via other sources. Enter industry or category code, company name, stock symbol, or key words/phrase and information is displayed.*

In addition to financial data, Dow Jones Retrieval offers access to reference library text search services; all airline fares, schedules, reservations, and ticketing; electronic mail and communications; a shopping service for more than 250,000 discounted brand name products, including appliances, office products, sporting goods, gourmet foods, and much more; an encyclopedia with more than 32,000 articles, covering industry and finance, as well as academic services; college selection services; movie and book reviews; and customer information and updates.

Dialogue Information Services ───────────────

This company [Palo Alto, CA; tel: 415-858-2700 or 800-3-DIA-LOG] calls itself "the world's largest on-line knowledgeable bank." Established in 1972 by leading newspaper publisher Knight-Ridder, Dialogue offers, among other services: Dialogue ("the world's most comprehensive on-line databank"), Knowledge Index (after-hours on-line access for the home computer user), Dialogue Business Connection (applications-oriented service for business professionals), Dialogue Medical Connection (information for practicing physicians and biomedical researchers), and Corporate Connection (access to over 220 Dialogue databases for companies offering Dialogue passwords to twenty-five or more employees).

Many of these services are contracted by companies and organizations. Individual users have literally hundreds of different files to draw on—from agriculture and nutrition to the social sciences and the humanities.

Dialogue was first used primarily by information specialists and librarians. As resources have become more accessible, users have expanded across the spectrum. Dialogue puts on your computer screen what is available in thousands of publications—stimulating your creativity so that you can extend your ideas into areas you may not have even considered exploring if you had to physically search out every published source. The major claims—similar to those made by others—of the service is that Dialogue lets you choose the best options for retrieving vital information—selecting from on-line services or disk-based products.

Lexis/Nexis ─────────────────────────────

This service [Mead Data Central, Inc., 9393 Springboro Pike, P.O. Box 933, Dayton, OH 45401; information: 800-227-4908] claims to be the world's leading full-text, on-line legal, news, and business information source—with customers in nearly fifty countries. Mead Data Central notes that between them Lexis and Nexis access 2,400 databases; more than 230 billion characters— with about 650,000 topics added weekly to the more than 85 million documents on line.

Lexis legal research service contains major archives of federal and state laws, codes, and regulations, as well as twenty-nine specialized libraries covering such fields as tax, securities, banking, the environment, and insurance. It also offers libraries of English and French law.

Nexis, introduced in 1979, is a "full-text news and business information service with more than 750 on-line sources, including *The New York Times* (exclusively), the *Washington Post,* the *Los Angeles Times, Business Week, Fortune,* and *The Economist,* and the news services AP, UPI, Reuters, Tass of the USSR, and Xinhua of China." It also provides *Wall Street Journal* abstracts, and specializes in international news, by country, region, and topic. Services include the following:

Apolic (information on elections, political issues, polls, and candidates), NAARS (accounting information), Medis (over forty current medical journals and textbooks and access to the National Library of Medicine and various specialized libraries), Lexpat (full text of patent and trademark information for more than a million U.S. patents issued since 1975), Eclipse (an electronic clipping service—you can request daily, business days, weekly, or monthly), and Lexod (which orders copies of public records documents retrieved from any jurisdiction, state or local, in the U.S., Canada, and the Virgin Islands). Additionally, a private database service can "provide or build litigation support files, private libraries, and other proprietary databases for law firms and corporations. Paback allows access to your use information on a weekly basis in a private and secure file, on-line or through magnetic tapes."

■ DATABASES BY TELEPHONE ——————

If you lack a computer, try **Nexis Express**, a service of Mead Data Central [in Ohio: 800-843-6476; elsewhere: 800-227-8379, ext. 5501]. Call to have research specialists help define your request. In twenty-four hours, or faster if essential, everything requested is mailed or messenger delivered. The cost, Nexis comments, is "probably a lot less than you think. You'll be quoted expected charges before go-ahead."

Prodigy ——————————————————————————————

Used primarily at home, **Prodigy** calls itself an interactive personal service. Developed by IBM and Sears Roebuck, it now claims 400,000 household subscribers. Advertising for the service reads:

> *Once you get the software and service start-up kit, you connect your home computer via your telephone line and sit back and enjoy its benefits, which are aimed at families. Designed like a magazine with advertising, often catering specifically to user age, gender, and zip code. In addition to providing information, lets you pay bills without writing checks; find great buys and then immediately purchase; get stock quotes before the morning paper, and sports scores before the evening news.* [Information: 212-947-2121 or 800-778-3449]

The 750 features of the service available day and night, include Travel (book your own airline flights, hotels, car rentals, and more), Communicate (exchange messages, advice, and information with members), Play (games, fun contests, and exciting quizzes for kids of all ages), Shop (thousands of values), Finance (buy and sell stocks, get quotes, do your banking), Learn (encyclopedia, educational games, and more), News (check the latest), Weather (current local and foreign), and Sports (latest standings and more).

Book Information on Database

You can access a variety of bases dealing with books. Available twenty-four hours a day, they save you time by providing a precis before you head for the library or bookstore. They are updated more frequently than printed guides and, once you get the hang of it, are easier to use than thumbing through reference volumes.

The following, with codes, are among the most widely used:

■ Computer Database Plus (GO COMPDB) offers computer-related book reviews.
■ Literary Forum (GO LITFORUM) offers book reviews.
■ McGraw-Hill (GO MH) offers a full line of books.
■ Time-Life Books (GO TL) offers computer books and a general interest book series.

▪ Chapter Eighteen ▪ ▪ ▪ ▪ ▪ ▪

Reading and Remembering in Less Time

Most of the information we gather comes from reading. With so much reading required these days, we next address how to speed up reading while retaining the information.

Centuries ago in Tibet, Lamaist priests devised a time-and-effort-saver for this requirement that would be mighty useful to many in our busy world. Like most of us, these religious men faced a reading time problem. Their solution was to write prayers on long strips of paper and wind these around a revolving cylinder. When devotions had to be expressed, there was no need to read them—they just spun the prayer wheel. Presumably, a god to whom messages were addressed could keep up with any speed.

E. Wayne Marjarum, in *How to Use a Book* (Rutgers University Press), adds that today's flood of papers, magazines, books, circulars, pamphlets, and every other type of reading matter makes one wish for the powers of the Tibetan god. Lacking such supernatural endowments, we are forced to do the next best thing: read more rapidly and selectively. At the same time, we need a concurrent level of comprehension so that we retain what we read. Because reading is one of our most important skills—directly influencing income, pleasure, and often business success—saving time in reading, comprehending, and remembering is a vital minute-minder.

▪ FINDING MORE READING MINUTES ——

A key step in improving your reading is to create more time to read—time otherwise wasted or perhaps devoted to reading of little real interest or importance to you. The following are some tips to help put you on this track:

▪ *Keep good reading handy.* Put articles, reports, and other material you *want* to read in the most conspicuous place, such as the after-dinner easy chair rather than out on the hall table where you are tempted to let it sit. Always carry reading with you. Have tearsheets in your pocket, your briefcase, beside your bed, and even in the bathroom.

▪ *Use travel time for reading.* Free time often opens up while traveling; capture such essential minutes.

▪ *Do your most important reading when freshest.* If you devote all of your morning reading time to the newspaper, you will miss the opportunity to go through a lot of other far more important must-reads when at your best and energy highest. After you have read the important news highlights, or have absorbed them from radio or TV while bathing or breakfasting, save more detailed news reading for a daytime break or day's end, when creative energy is less, but absorption still strong. Use your best time for the most involved business and technical report or material requiring the fullest response.

▪ *Read while waiting.* Time spent waiting for meals, transportation, the doctor or dentist, the barber, the telephone, or even for your spouse to finish dressing can be spent on reading. It is amazing how these minutes add up. Reading also helps you overcome waiting annoyance.

■ *Read early editions the night before.* Many major city executives get ahead on the next day's news features this way. However, avoid becoming a news junky of the sort who has to get news at night and a repeat in the morning.

■ *Use lunchtimes.* Take an occasional lunch for yourself and simply read while eating.

■ *Read before going to sleep.* Read for fifteen to thirty minutes before bedtime. Don't necessarily read business books alone, but books for inspiration and entertainment. Developing the habit can lead you to a wide variety of topics.

■ BOOK CONDENSATIONS AND DIGESTS —

The amount of professional reading we want to do—trend forecasts, shrewd management techniques, powerful marketing strategies, valuable techniques, and so on—requires an impossible amount of time. Depending on one's definition, there are reportedly 1,200 to 1,500 U.S. business and management books published annually—far more than any human being can possibly skim, let alone read.

The average executive reads only six books yearly—missing many that might be valuable, reports *Profile.* Yet, not reading important books could be a serious and expensive mistake. Why? Because their ideas and insights are often available nowhere else. To be really informed, you should be keeping up with this important source of business intelligence and doing it in less time. One solution is to take advantage of **Executive Book Summaries** from Soundview [5 Main Street, Bristol, VT 05443; tel: 800-521-1227]. Each month, Cynthia Langley Folino, publisher, and her staff seek out what they believe are the best business books. They read all of them and choose only the best to summarize. Their criteria include subscriber usefulness, timeliness and relevance, and nature of content, looking for ideas that will help save time, increase profits, avoid problems, increase productivity, and advance careers. When books meet these standards, they're assigned to professional business writers, who extract every useful idea and produce an eight-page summary for publication. These are not reviews (somebody's opinion) or digests (book excerpts strung together), but a "skillful distillation preserving the entire book's content and spirit."

Other Book Summary Sources

■ *Fortune Digest:* Condenses five business-related must-read best-sellers—sold direct [tel: 800-765-6400] and in book stores.
■ **Business Week Book Club:** Selects a monthly main selection and offers bonus books on special terms [Blue Ridge, Summit, PA 17294-0795].
■ **Productivity, Inc.:** [Box 3007, Cambridge, MA 02140; tel: 800-274-9911]. Publishes English translations of Japanese quality experts, as well as its own titles and books related to quality, productivity, customer service, continued improvement, and employee involvement.
■ *Publishers Weekly:* A trade magazine for publishers and libraries, it reviews about 100 books each issue, often months prior to the popular press. Two or three business books are reviewed weekly. [Information: 800-842-1669]
■ **The Executive Program:** Offers groups of books—ideas, strategies, time savers—at bonus prices, with audiotaped books as free gifts. [3000 Cindel Drive, Delran, NJ 08075-9889].

■ READING SELF-IMPROVEMENT

To improve your own reading speed and retention, try the following strategies:

■ *Read with a purpose, not aimlessly.* Whatever the subject, read for everything in it. This aids your absorption and fixes ideas in memory. Don't permit lagging attention. Your mind should be working like a nest of termites—riddling, reducing, digesting, and consuming the ideas underlying the printed word.

■ *Concentrate on first sentences.* In much reading matter, they express the basic ideas. Learn to spot content signposts: chapter headings, subtitles, lines in boldface or italic type, and everything else set off from the text. Today, many magazines abstract and color highlight key phrases—not simply to add visual interest, but to call attention to must-note passages.

■ *Make sure you are not moving your lips as you read.* Vocalizing or mouthing slows reading speed.

■ *Avoid word-by-word reading.* Because ideas are seldom found in single words, but are conveyed by groups of words, the essential of speed-up reading is to train your eyes to absorb such groups—the whole, rather than the part. The eyes of a good, fast reader pause only to seize word groups embodying ideas. With experience, you can group-read as easily as you read individual words. You grasp such phrases when you listen to someone talk. The same idea extends to your reading.

Act As Your Own Reading Accelerator ————

In effect, constantly force yourself to read faster than formerly. For example, try pretending the words disappear as your eyes pass over them. You will probably be surprised to find that you didn't miss anything important. Estimate the number of words in an article or chapter and determine a time limit for how long completion should take. Set a timer for this period and gradually you will raise your target to secure more effective results.

■ *Pause and summarize.* After reading a section at top speed, pause and summarize in your mind the author's main points. Check this by reviewing the material at greater length. Once formed, the habit becomes automatic.

■ *Mark freely.* Don't be afraid to mark articles and books as you read—especially this one. The best way is to use any of the light-colored markers to highlight pertinent information. Other writing instruments are slower for this purpose.

■ *Have the confidence to dismiss the trivial.* Skip unimportant words or ideas, clichés, and trite phrases. Find the beef!

■ *Check unfamiliar words later.* Make either a mental or written note for dictionary perusal. The greater your vocabulary, the higher your reading speed. Efficiency requires a knowledge of 20,000 to 30,000 words, say experts. Not understanding single vital words can make you miss sentence or paragraph meaning—a frequent cause of rereading.

Reading Skill Requires Practice ─────────

Another reading speed-up variation comes from Dr. Phyllis A. Miller, in her book *Managing Your Reading.* Dr. Miller says that most of us read only half or possibly a third as fast as we could, given instruction and practice. Reading is a skill and, like other skills, simply reading how to do it isn't enough. Acquiring the skill requires practice. Breaking bad reading habits is another necessary ingredient, and the exercises contained in Dr. Miller's excellent book can help. A wealth of other publications are also available to help you read better and faster.

Dr. Miller's most useful technique is called pace setting. Using either your hand or a blank index card, run down the page and keep your attention on the reading spot to improve concentration and build your reading rate. Try pacing to get accustomed to a higher reading speed—considerably faster than your present pace. Keep this up regardless of your retention level until you have added speed and concurrent comprehension to your reading ability. Then work on reading, and retaining what you read, at the new rate.

Skimming and Scanning

When reading, don't limit yourself to plodding along from start to finish, word by word, page by page, says Robert Moskowitz in *How to Organize Your Work and Your Life*, adding:

> Skimming *is the act of running your eyes quickly over a printed page, picking out headings, charts and other eye-catching items . . . trying to grasp the main point by reading only the prominent details. First and last sentences of paragraphs, too, usually offer good clues.*
>
> *Scanning, on the other hand, is a careful examination of the outline or construction of a piece of writing with a view toward understanding it without full reading. Look at table of contents, illustrations, charts and/or tables, index and appendices to determine what it's about. Then zero in on the juiciest meat.*

Moskowitz says that the breakaway from word-by-word reading doesn't occur overnight—it takes a while to crack old reading habits or get comfortable reading so few words per page. Nevertheless, skimming and scanning are valuable means to cover more reading ground in less time.

Speed Reading to Win

Some fifty time-saving ways to read faster and smarter, guaranteed, is the promise of an audiocassette program by management consultants Kathleen Hawkins and Peter Turla for Day-Timers. A three-volume set of six audiocassettes—with complete transcripts, workbooks, and storage albums—this accelerated course has been specially designed to help you "identify [your] personal reading style, better master complicated technical material, go through your in-basket in a fraction of previous time, and absorb new data quickly and easily."

Professional Reading Courses ────────────────

Reading clinics, many at schools and universities (especially those with extension or adult education courses), usually last a few weeks and are moderately priced. Instructors generally employ mechanical training aids. New York's Reading Laboratory, for example, uses these methods:

■ *Eye Check:* You may simply require new glasses. Improving vision enables you to teach your eyes to move faster and see more.

■ *Improving Total Eye Span:* Students are taught reading by "thought units"—ideas conveyed by word groups.

■ *Word on Screen:* After checking eye span weaknesses, eye pauses, and duration, experts flash words on a screen. You can learn to scan and retain seven-digit numbers and entire sentences from a glance.

■ *Reading Accelerator:* This machine uses a pacing instrument with an opaque shutter, which lowers over the page like a curtain as you read. Set at specific rates, it not only tells you how fast you are reading, but sharpens concentration, prods you into more rapid reading, and prevents backtracking, a common time-consuming habit.

These courses are well worth investigating if home study is impractical.

Books on Faster Reading

There are many good books on increasing reading speed. One of the best is *Speed Reading* (third edition) by Tony Buzan. Buzan has applied his expert knowledge of human brain function to create a ground-breaking, speed-reading method—including many new self-help tests, each designed to stimulate interest in a difficult knowledge area. Buzan discusses various approaches to reading, combining traditional information on speed with the latest discoveries about brain functioning.

Another Buzan book, *Use Your Perfect Memory*, offers an ingenious system for memory improvement. It is geared toward handling specific memory problems—from facts and figures to faces and dreams. Memory-expansion exercises combine imaginative power with techniques for remembering names, telephone numbers, dates, vocabulary, and appointments. Buzan even provides special cardplayer programs, particularly for poker and bridge, and, for students, the how-to of studying the most effectively and preparing for exams for optimum results.

▪ A COOPERATIVE READING APPROACH

In many companies and organizations with a heavy flow of printed matter that contains vital material, one time-saving approach to covering a lot of material is a shared-reading team. Individuals in a department decide among themselves to each read more closely a selected number of publications and other sources. They note items of group or individual interest and then circulate so that each member gets a turn to talk to the reader. This is often effective where subjects are of considerable importance to all members.

Another time-saver: Instead of reading and then having to

sit down and abstract the most important points, have each group member take a different color of highlighter and mark points felt to be significant and then circulate his or her own material. You then see what each reader has emphasized. Most highlighters won't damage originals or affect copies.

▪ STREAMLINING YOUR INCOMING OFFICE READING

If you are in a position to influence reports coming to you from subordinates, get them into the habit of providing a brief—no more than ten lines—Executive Summary; adopt the habit yourself. An increasing number of companies and organizations use this time-saving reading format. If you do it, you will find others with whom you exchange must-read material will pick up the same system—saving the time and improving the comprehension of both reader and writer.

▪ TIME-SAVING MEMORY

Through training, you can improve your memory and save the countless minutes trying to recall names, places, dates, and other facts. Forgetting what you have read wastes a lot of time. Books, laptop computers, and other devices make much information easily available, and minimize what you have to keep in your head. However, individuals who know the most important things about their field of interest—and can talk about these without constant reference to notes—are often successful and always widely envied.

Dr. Bruno Furst, a top authority on memory and an author of many books on this subject, believes that one of the best memory aids is to associate a name or a fact with a familiar object you are sure to come across. Dr. Furst cites this example:

> *When my wife asks me to contact our insurance man*
> *to change our fire policy, I immediately picture my*
> *desk at the office on fire. The moment I open my office*
> *door, the vivid mental image of my burning desk re-*
> *minds me to write the note—and no time's required*
> *trying to recall what I'm supposed to. To ensure mail-*
> *ing it, I picture the insurance man standing at the*
> *mailbox. The sight of the box reminds me of him and*
> *the letter simultaneously. The same method works*
> *with names, facts, and numbers.*

Memory, Dr. Furst notes, is like a muscle. It weakens through idleness; strengthens through constant use. However, he says, don't burden your memory by crowding it; many simple reminders are better written down. However, the more experiences you store and the more easily you receive impressions, the better you are able to retain them, and to recall them the moment needed. Keep in mind, though, that personal computers and software that record and permit quick retrieval of all types of information should be used to supplement rather than substitute for developing our own memory.

▪ WHEN TO MEMORIZE ────────────

Professor Donald Laird, an authority on human relations and personal efficiency, has said, "If your memory is naturally poor, it's likely you'll never be able to make it as good as someone born with a better gift of recall. But, before you decide yours is hopeless, try using it properly. Many people with serviceable memories were born with poor ones. Results depend a great deal on the way in which you memorize." The following are some of Laird's tips:

- ▪ Give closest attention to the things you want to remember.
- ▪ Talk and think over to yourself what you have read, heard,

or seen. By making this a firmly fixed habit, you will reinforce your memory.

■ Associate everything new with what you have already stored in your memory. If a problem is remembering to buy someone a gift, remember a gift that particularly pleases *you*. When you run across a new word, think of others like it and where you might use it. In short, use association to remember.

■ The best time for most people to memorize is before noon, particularly from 8:00 to 10:00 in the morning. The reason is that at that time your nervous system has fewer new impressions. In the evening, efficiency and memory are 6 to 10 percent less. Your retentive powers lose strength gradually from waking to retiring. Sunday, by the way, seems to be the worst day for remembering. Probably because we want to take it easiest then.

■ SEVEN SIMPLE TRICKS YOU WON'T FORGET ——————————————————

Here are a few excellent memory-improving tricks from Leanne Kleinmann, editor-in-chief of *Memphis* magazine, writing in *Self*:

1. *Concentrate on being mindful.* Work with information, don't just notice it. If, for example, your boss asks you to remember several important names that have no meaning for you, ask yourself questions about the names. Do they sound unusual? Are they similar to those of other people you know? Giving yourself clues helps you to remember more easily.

2. *Break out of your routine.* Novelty helps make things easier to remember. As you get older, you have to put effort into making the familiar novel. Do you repeatedly have trouble remembering whether or not you have locked the front door? Try using your other hand to lock it. Making a mindless process novel or markedly different makes it more memorable.

3. *Picture what you want to remember.* Giving yourself visual hints as to a person's name or job helps you remember it. When you meet Mrs. Fox, for example, think about the animal and the features they share—a long nose, red hair, whatever. (A potential pitfall might be confusing the image and calling her Ms. Wolf, instead.)

4. *Make up mnemonic devices.* You might remember this trick from school, where you learned that ROY G BIV was the first letters of the colors of the rainbow: red, orange, yellow, green, blue, indigo, and violet. Making acronyms, rhymes, and other mnemonics helps you to recall complex or lenghty items. "Spring forward, fall back" is a mnemonic for the switch from standard to daylight time.

5. *Write it down.* Putting things on paper often ensures that you will later remember them.

6. *Be more organized.* The more organized, the better your chances of recalling where you put things. Examples of strategies include hanging hooks by the door for your car keys, always putting your sunglasses in a set locale, and saving items in individually colored folders.

7. *Be aware of other factors influencing your memory.* Medications affecting the central nervous system—such as antihistamines, sleeping pills, and pain relievers—can affect memory. Alcohol and cigarettes, which deprive the brain of oxygen, can also hinder memory.

▪ Chapter Nineteen ▪ ▪ ▪ ▪ ▪

Self-Education

It used to be that when you finished college, you considered lifetime education complete—save perhaps for an occasional special course in some subject related to your career or personal interest. Today, however, adult education has proliferated to a truly amazing degree. Hardly a university or college, educational system, or specialized school or organization doesn't offer a wide range of courses in virtually every field—from hands-on personal computing to speaking Japanese or virtually any other language. In some fields—medicine, for instance—states mandate continuing education or loss of license.

Many of these courses can be a most valuable place to learn the time-saving skills and information most directly applicable to your job. To broaden your horizons, gain the personal and career satisfaction of a degree for advancement, or enjoy the pure fun of learning and broadening your mind, take advantage of them.

▪ LIFETIME LEARNING TIPS ─────────

▪ *Set aside a study place.* Have all necessary supplies ready—everything from markers for highlighting noteworthy passages to disks for your computer. Don't waste valuable time searching for needed supplies at crucial moments.

▪ *Use commuting time.* Read assignments on the way in to work in the morning; try recalling them on the way home.

▪ *Study with a friend.* Select someone with a complimentary learning style. This works well studying foreign languages. You may understand grammar; your friend accent. Each catches the other's mistakes.

▪ *Consider hiring help.* A housecleaner, babysitter, or handyman can relieve you of some of the energy-draining, time-consuming chores. While they are working—and you force yourself to stay away from them—you can leave the house and study.

▪ *Get a tutor.* The cost is often moderate. No one expects you to remember everything you learned at age nineteen. If you suspect that you are not keeping up, a tutor can pay off.

▪ UNIVERSITY COURSES IN MINIMAL TIME ─────────────────────

The Wharton Experience in Five Days ───────

The Wharton School of the University of Pennsylvania offers "the learning experience of a lifetime"—condensing lengthy graduate programs into intense, stimulating, five-day executive seminars that are taught by a world-class faculty at the school's Steinberg Conference Center, a state-of-the-art residential learning facility in which you relax and exchange ideas with today's business leaders. Recent seminars included Finance and Accounting for the Non-

Financial Manager, Advanced Competitive Marketing Strategy, Salesforce Management, and Strategic Alliances.

Columbia Business School, New York ───────

The school offers the opportunity to earn an MBA without interrupting your career, giving up your salary, or attending night school. Your company must sponsor your attendance full-time for three consecutive summers—an investment in continuing education without career interruption.

▪ COURSES LONG ON LEARNING ───────

Another important development has been the establishment of "short courses long on learning." Typical are those provided by the New York University School of Continuing Education, which offers more than 150—each held for a minimum of six weeks. Typical courses: How to Run Your Life, Learning How to Learn, Designing Your Career, Managing Business, and Computer Programming. You can register by telephone, using MasterCard, VISA, or American Express. Similar courses might be available in your community.

▪ A NEW CONCEPT IN ADULT EDUCATION ───────

A new concept in spare-time, speedily taught adult education is the Learning Annex, now operating in some fifteen cities across the United States. Developed by Bill Zanker, who describes himself as a perennial student, Learning Annex courses range from the practical How to Open Your Own Bookstore to the off-beat How to Begin and Continue a Conversation. Courses are short and inexpensive, and are geared toward people who have little time and many interests, and who want fast-paced learning that is fun and, in Zanker's words, has "sex appeal."

Zanker began by offering courses in film for New Yorkers interested in making, directing, producing, and marketing. Offerings now fill a magazine-size brochure—distributed every other month—which lists old favorites and the constantly added new classes. For teachers, Zanker recruited moonlighting professors and professionals, encouraging them to teach, if possible, at their own offices and studios to keep overhead low. The curriculum combines the best elements of practical self-improvement and trendy fun in short, inexpensive courses. If traditional adult education is like a textbook, Zanker's program is more like a magazine—timely and easily digested. Learning Annex courses last from four to ten hours, vary in tuition (in 1990) from $21 to $140, and are constantly innovative.

For one of the 3,000,000 catalogues printed annually, call 212-580-2920.

▪ HOME STUDY BY CASSETTES ──────

Another time saver in your adult education is to probe the growing number of home study courses on audio- and videocassette. There are so many audiotape listening courses available that a list of them would fill a book. If you have an audiocassette player and want to gain an extra hour every day by saving minutes learning in free time or while engaged in another activity, you can regularly listen to your recorder as a major weapon in goal achievement.

The variety of information and materials on cassette tapes grows daily. Selecting those best meeting your particular needs—whether on the job or on your personal activities—pays off for the following reasons:

■ You can listen and learn—or simply enjoy—while doing something else.

■ Combining two activities does not necessarily minimize the benefits gained. In fact, as Jay Conrad Levinson points out in the *90-Minute Hour,* you can play tapes driving to or from work; during any exercise such as jogging, walking, or cycling; while flying on business or pleasure; or while waiting for almost anything. Listen while doing the dishes or other home chores or while engaged in hobbies, taking a bath, or working in the garden (or any other place in the house). Best of all, listen in place of watching TV.

Harvey MacKay, author of *Beware the Naked Man Who Offers You His Shirt,* says he has more than 300 tapes to listen to while traveling, adding: "Most people drive 12,000 miles a year. If you live to be 72, that's three-and-a-half years in a car. Why not turn your car into a university." Others listen while moving about by using lightweight headphones and a portable tape player.

To gain the most from listening to cassette tapes, start by clarifying what you want to get out of each program, such as information needed or simply wanted for its interest, improvement of specific skills, or keeping in touch with business, professional, or other trends.

■ Keep your tape player in a strategic location. Because they are small, compact, and designed to be listened to whenever and wherever you like, units such as a battery-operated Sony V-O-R can be kept in numerous places and are easily carried.

■ Listen to specific programs in selected locations. For example, listen to a diet program in your kitchen, a stress control program in your car (great for easing tensions in traffic), or a management skills tape in your office.

Steve Rowley, Day-Timers president, notes: "As you hear theories and ideas presented and adopt suggested techniques and skills, you'll discover new, strong resources to handle varied situations more successfully. Scientists studying how people retain information find that while for some seeing is best, for others, hearing is better. Even when you're not paying close attention, or distracted or going to sleep, your subconscious mind picks up an amazing amount with no extra time expenditure."

The Best Way to Use Educational Tapes ———

There is no right way to listen to educational audiocassettes— except the one that works best for you. Day-Timers offers these techniques:

■ *Listening Versus Hearing.* Often you hear much but pay attention to and mull over very little. You might have to replay a tape or segment several times before its ideas really sink in and you truly listen. Decide what time of day you are most relaxed and open to new ideas. Create a learning environment by eliminating as much external noise as possible. Chances are you will absorb far more.

■ *Deep Listening.* Start with side A of each cassette and employ the "deep listening" technique, picturing what is going on. Closing your eyes and picturing yourself performing effectively in the situation being described can also provide a reflex reaction to a given real-life situation.

■ *Stopping Tapes for Good Ideas.* Listening and then stopping to take notes of what you hear, or to respond mentally (especially if physically acted out), enhances benefits.

■ *Follow-Up.* When you read over your notes, keep a first-thoughts record for follow-up action. In some cases, audio teaching tapes come with self-testing and exercise workbooks, stressing your own situation to enhance learning. Many exercises are designed to train you to choose new approaches to given situations.

■ *Repeat Listening.* An old adage says, Three times and it's yours. There's no question, the more you immerse yourself in listening and learning, the more your imagination and mind will be stimulated—the subconscious as well as the conscious. Repeated listening helps. Having heard something only once, you might recall a third a day later and almost none in sixty days. However, with cassette programs—as opposed to seminars, workshops, and college courses—you can "sit in on"—that is, replay—programs as frequently as desired until they are thoroughly understood.

■ *The Key Tip:* Adopt new concepts and techniques *as soon as possible.* Unimplemented ideas—which simply go around in your mind with no practical use—mean wasted listening time.

■ AUDIOTAPE SUGGESTIONS

There are so many audiotape learning materials that it is impossible to mention more than a few. One good course on tape is *Listening Power* by Dr. Robert L. Montgomery. It shows you how to concentrate, to remember what you have heard, to recognize speakers' motives, to strengthen friendships, and to build business success by using active listening techniques. Montgomery notes: "As you become skilled in expert listening, you develop new insights and find yourself picking up body language signals . . . get along better with boss, associates and staff—everyone. Listening skills can . . . pay off as you negotiate, plan, and sell more effectively—even . . . win a much deserved promotion."

The following are other especially interesting tapes:

■ The Teaching Company puts out a series of eight 45-minute lectures on audio- or videocassettes called the Superstar Teachers College Lecture Courses. With the cooperation of the Smithsonian Institution resident associate program, top-rated professors at leading universities are individually brought to Washington to have their famed lecture courses preserved. Each tape is a condensed version of the professor's one-semester course. [Information: The Teaching Company, P.O. Box 17524, Arlington, VA 22216; tel: 800-832-2421]

■ A One-Day MBA is an even more unique university-level course on audiotape. The course was developed by Dr. Paul Lerman and Dr. John H. Turner, who between them share more than forty years of experience teaching MBA courses designed for "busy get-ahead achievers who simply can't spare time and energy demanded for a conventional MBA." The six-cassette audio course strips away "the fluff and time-wasters of graduate school; hones in on immediately usable key concepts." The description of the course adds: "You quickly learn how the six major divisions of the business world function; pick up valuable practical tips in management, marketing, accounting, finance, decision-making and human resources."

A sides of cassettes are for listening only; the B sides are for workbook follow-along. If you don't use the workbook, you can listen to the tapes while doing something else. Read transcripts as you listen; review at another time when you don't have access to a player. The contents of each volume are independent so that you can complete as much—or as little—of the entire program as you desire at any one time. [From Day-Timers]

Language Learning on Tape

Language learning from tapes is more popular than ever. Developers promise easy language mastery in a month or less. Courses in Spanish, French, German, Italian, Russian, Hebrew, and Greek—among others—are available.

Many have learned foreign languages through audiotapes. Burt S. Cross, president of 3M—whose far-flung operations include factories in many Spanish-speaking countries—long fretted over his inability to communicate in Spanish. He decided to use the drive between his home and office to listen to Spanish lessons on a tape recorder—and achieved an excellent working knowledge of the language, if not the ability to translate Cervantes.

The American Medical Association provides taped medical readings to thousands of physicians across the nation. This helps them to keep up with new developments in their specialties when they are unable to go through medical journals and reports.

▪ BOOKS ON TAPE

An increasingly wide range of books are available on two- to six-cassette sets. The **Nightingale-Conant Corporation**, which calls itself the "human resources company," claims to be the world's largest audiocassette program producer [7300 North Lehigh Avenue, Chicago, IL 60648; tel: 800-323-5552]. The following tapes are among those it offers:

The One-Minute Manager, by Dr. Kenneth Blanchard and Dr. Spencer Johnson, stresses "simple, action-oriented techniques that get immediate employee results." This program is claimed to be a revolutionary, effective system used in hundreds of corporations. *How to Exceed Yourself*, by Joe Batten, is an innovative teacher of high-performance skills, "giving a fresh, encouraging, workable approach to becoming more than you've ever been . . . achieving more than you've ever achieved and enjoying yourself more than ever before." *Peak Performance*, by Dr. Charles Garfield, offers an action plan that "helps you channel all resources into goal-related projects" and "teaches surpassing earlier accomplishment and reaching higher success pinnacles."

▪ GOING TO HARVARD BY VIDEO ──────

It is not a Harvard degree in minutes, but the Harvard Business School has introduced a series of video programs for education at home. Says Harvard: "You won't need to leave the office or reschedule priorities to view these programs—they're modular, for screening in segments as your schedule permits." They are also price competitive, making them affordable management seminars for both the individual and groups. You can view them as many times as you like at one fixed price. Presenters are Harvard Business School professors and leading CEOs, who "examine proven strategies for competitive success; share insights of the country's most innovative and productive industry leaders."

Each program focuses on a unique and relevant aspect of competitive advantage, such as practical, implementable options for building competitive power and recognizing market opportunities and meeting the goals targeted by strategies. Examples include *Competing Through Quality* (accelerating market demand and increasing profitability through innovative customer-driven approaches to quality), *Synergies, Alliances and New Ventures* (how to leverage core strengths while conserving costs), and *Competing Through Information Technology* (rewriting the roles of competition in your favor, developing competitive strategy, and building market share through sound competitive conditioning). [Information: 800-227-7703]

Other Film and Video Programs ──────────

Dartnell offers a vast library of film and video programs intended to help improve training in customer service, human resource development, sales, and health care and safety. Typical of programs are the Power Close to Successful Selling, Sales Training Motivation, Personal Training, and Human Resource Development. [Information: 4660 Ravenwood Avenue, Chicago, IL 60640; tel: 800-621-5463] Dartnell catalogues a wide range of training handbooks, manuals, periodicals, and audiocassettes.

▪ SUBLIMINAL MESSAGE LEARNING ——

Subliminal tapes—that is, audiocassettes that register a self-selected message on your subconscious mind—are an increasingly used time-saving self-education tool. **Randolph Success International** [P.O. Box 90608, San Diego, CA 92109-3602; tel: 800-248-2737] offers over 150 such tapes aimed at "success, health, and mega-learning." Betty Lee Randolph, Ph.D., has said:

> *Advances in computerized audio recording technology have allowed subliminal motivation experts like Dr. Paul Tuthill to create programs permitting you to literally reprogram your own subconscious mind with specific directions you select. For the past decade, Dr. Tuthill has created programs to effectively reduce stress and promote rapid healing. Perhaps the most effective and most easily measured were weight-loss programs—giving messages you play over and over against the sound of music similar to that of FM easy listening stations.*
>
> *You simply put the tape in your player, press the play button, and let enjoyable music become a pleasant background as you go about your normal activities. No special effort is required to listen or concentrate. Consciously, you hear only the music. Subliminal messages you have selected become an irresistible whisper, closely heard by your subconscious mind. Use them as you work, play, or relax. Results claimed are not miraculous; they simply let you unify*

*your conscious goals and desires with a positive new,
subconscious program. Mental harmony achieved not
only gives you an incredible feeling of confidence and
well-being, it can allow you to finally make changes
you want in your life.*

Available subliminal message tapes include those on stress and
time management, computer phobia, decision-making, goal-
setting, improving health and losing weight, and many of the
business and personal concerns covered in this book. Messages
are brief and to the point, heard audibly for three to five minutes
and then subliminally for the remainder of the tape. Audible
stereo sounds over the subliminal message typically feature the
ocean or music. Messages are directed to both the right and left
brain for whole-brain learning, and intermittent rest spaces ensure assimilation. Dr. Randolph says that clients include, among
others, many leading Fortune 500 companies, insurance agencies,
public administration and law firms, and naval bases.

Chapter Twenty

Saving Wasted Time

There are many moments during your day in which no matter how much you plan and how carefully you schedule you are forced to wait. At first glance, these might appear to be minutes never fully recoverable—increasing the ire and disaffection that often accompanies forced waits when you have a lot to do and too little time to do it.

However, there are many things you can do to turn waiting time to your own advantage. This is gained time that can add significantly to that extra hour a day. The following are some ideas on how to make use of otherwise idle moments.

■ DON'T JUST KILL TIME

When waiting is inevitable, don't consider it time you have to kill. Make these minutes work for you. We have noted that such moments can be used for reading, with five minutes here and ten there adding up to an hour a day. Regardless of your schedule or how carefully appointments are made, *be certain to always bring your own reading and study matter*. A briefcase or folder into which you can put items such as office reports, periodicals, and clippings can house a treasure-trove. Always take a highlighter to note important things you come across, which helps you to concentrate on what you are reading, even in such distracting places as bank or other service lines and flight check-in queues. A pad of Post-It notes to tag items you want to revisit is also a useful item to have along in utilizing what frequently are wasted minutes.

When you have to wait at the doctor's or dentist's office, your own reading matter will undoubtedly be superior to the standard fare. It has always surprised me how many companies don't keep—for a visitor's self-briefing—a corporate brochure or annual report in reception rooms. Keep company materials in your reception area so that visitors can use their time getting to know your firm.

▪ RELAX WHILE WAITING

If you don't want to read, waiting can give you an excellent relaxation opportunity. Try, if occasion permits, to shut your eyes, isometrically stretching as completely as possible. Depending on the location, you might even be able to take brief catnaps. For places where there is nowhere to sit, many learn to relax standing up—by leaning, or by standing still in balance. Some have told me that they can acquire the equivalent of an hour or two of sleep each day through these methods—gaining time later in increased productivity.

■ PICK THE BEST LIMITED WAITING TIME

Other waiting-time cutters include the following examples:

■ *When Going to Films:* Arrive no more than fifteen minutes ahead of the film's starting time. If you go to the theater on weekends, go to the first show, when lines are likely to be shorter. Many cinemas now accept prepurchased firm seat orders on credit cards. Take advantage of this time saver.

■ *For Museum Shows:* Check out the starting dates and daily hours of the more popular shows you want to see. The last days of, and later hours of days within, show schedules often involve long lines. Schedule yourself accordingly.

■ MAKING THEM WAIT

One business leader, who understandably wants to remain anonymous, told me: "I get an extra hour out of every day by *deliberately* arriving fifteen minutes late for meetings—whether business appointments or even PTA get-togethers. Sometimes I suspect people realize my inevitable lateness isn't entirely coincidental. But, since most sessions get off to a slow start, I find I can use the fifteen minutes to accomplish other things."

Every reader will react differently to this idea—especially if you are the one calling the meeting and expect others to get there promptly. Keeping people waiting is a "one-up" practice with both negative and positive sides.

Chapter Twenty-one

Travel

My wife and I have been frequent travelers from the moment we met in Buenos Aires, half a century ago. A young man, I had traveled there from my home city of Philadelphia; she from Europe. Having been on the go all these years—for both business and personal activities in my global enterprise, International Public Relations Company, Limited (New York), with ninety associates at sixty locations around the world—we couldn't help but develop some travel time savers to share with you.

■ PREPLANNING: THE KEY TO TRAVEL TIME-SAVING

In that trips are often sudden rushes, you need the know-how and stamina for facing increasing numbers of people on the move, the inconvenience of crowds, the unexpected (but virtually certain) delays, and all of the other frustrations of mere movement in a go-go age. Accept lines, delays, bad weather, and traffic jams as part of the territory. Anticipating them, you will not waste time, energy, or good humor—realizing that the occasional non-calamitous trip is a blessing.

Before you make a trip, ask yourself the following questions: Is the trip necessary? Can others make it? Would an associate be able to handle most of the business? Can it be done by mail or telephone? Can I get them to come here instead of my going there? Thinking it through might provide a way of avoiding the trip altogether.

Once you have decided to make the trip, create a list that includes the names of those you are going to meet, along with telephone and fax numbers, addresses, and other relevant information. Prepare an itinerary with all information in one place: departure times, flight or train numbers, and so on. This is better than having objectives here, individuals and telephone numbers there. Copies should go to family, secretary, and anyone else with a need to know where you can be reached.

Write out the purpose and objectives, each in a separate paragraph, of your trip to facilitate prioritizing. While traveling, you can get right to the execution of desired objectives. Always target your most vital goals first—leaving remaining items as optionals.

Set appointments with fixed, instead of vague, times. Then, reconfirm these times on arrival. Robert A. Whitney, one-time president of the National Sales Executives, says: "I'm constantly amazed at how many traveling businesspeople waste time on undefined dates when a little advance call would likely ensure promptness."

Send your business agenda ahead of you. Letting those you are meeting know what you want to review and what you are bringing to put before them is useful to both parties.

If you have a number of appointments to keep and tasks to accomplish while traveling, try, where possible, to cut the distance between appointments. Leave enough scheduling lee-way between meetings so that you won't have to rush from uncompleted business only to have a nervous breakdown getting to your next appointment on time. Avoid crossing town three or four times by scheduling appointments geographically whenever possible.

■ Leave enough time between appointments—especially between arrival time and your first appointment—to get some clean-up time or a rest if going directly from the airport to a meeting location. Cabs are not necessarily easily obtained. If you have several appointments, consider a car and driver or a friendly taxi for the day—and make sure the rates are agreed on beforehand.

■ Don't plan too many things for a single trip. Travel is costly, and achieving multiple objectives saves minutes and money, but it is more important to do a few things well than many things poorly.

■ Keep a separate file folder for each locale. Memos, proposals, vital background papers, and correspondence should all be in one place.

■ If you are going to cities frequently visited, or to others for the first time, take folders for each that contain clips on local activities, restaurants, and historical or cultural attractions. Mrs. Josephs and I have long done this for every city and country visited over the course of many years. Whether Paris or Peoria, chances are we have a list of "some day" things to see there after business. Showing that you know a bit about the place also makes a good impression on contacts or hosts.

■ PERSONAL TRAVEL ─────────────

A few words about holiday travel planning before proceeding: If planning a holiday to some location you've never before visited, don't limit inquiries to one travel agent. Shop around and weigh counterproposals. Big companies such as American Express,

Thomas Cook, and so on, offer videocassettes of leading resorts by category and location. They have found letting you see their properties and services on VCR in your own home far more effective than a load of brightly colored brochures. In a ten-minute video (usually loaned against a deposit), you get an overall sight, sound, and color impression never achieved from print or slides.

Obviously, these presentations put on only the best face (they won't tell you about dissatisfied customers or any disadvantages), but videos can be an important and effective starting-point time saver. Also, the further ahead you can plan, the greater the likelihood of pleasurable travel. Excellent sources for this purpose are *Stern's Guide to the Greatest Resorts of the World*, edited by Steven B. Stern [29 South LaSalle Street, Suite 617, Chicago, IL 60603; tel: 312-368-4481] and *Leading Hotels of the World*, an association with 190 offices worldwide [747 Third Avenue, New York, NY 10017-2847; tel: (U.S. and Canada) 800-223-6800].

▪ SCHEDULING AND TICKETING BUSINESS TRIPS ─────────────

If you have, within your company or outside, a good, reliable, and caring travel agent, contacting them might be the best way to book your journey. Travel is today America's third largest retail business; therefore, competition is keen. If you use an agency infrequently, you might not get the all-out service regular customers get in finding the best flights and prices; hence, consider consolidating your business with one supplier to increase clout.

More and more people seeking the best travel services are turning to their personal computers to call up a wide variety of information services available. The following are a few of such services:

■ *CompuServe's Travelshopper, Official Airline Guide Electronic Edition (OAG), and EAASY Sabre* computer databases provide continually updated information on schedules and fares for virtually every world airline. They let you shop for the lowest fare matching scheduling requirements, then actually book on-line. Hotel and car rental information are also available. [800-323-4000]

■ *The ABC Worldwide Hotel Index* offers complete reservation and lodging descriptions of more than 35,000 hotels worldwide—enabling you to research price ranges, locations, and other factors.

■ CompuServe provides up-to-date advice on overseas visas, immigration laws, political environments, and more. Its Go Travel service lets you act as your own travel agent—ensuring that flights, hotels, and rental cars are obtained for the right times and at the best prices. You can set everything up on-line so that tickets and confirmations are mailed to you right away.

Airline Reservations by Telephone

If you lack computer access or a travel agent, and have to make airline reservations directly, consider the following points:

■ Virtually all airlines now have 800 numbers and experienced agents. Waiting for an agent takes time during peak hours; therefore, call early or late in the day.

■ Try for bulkhead or aisle seats, which are roomier. Free aircraft seating guides can help you choose this seating.

■ When calling specific airlines for schedules and reservations, ask for alternates that are earlier or later than your intended departure. If you don't ask, they are unlikely to suggest the possibilities; if you do, the majority are more than willing to do so. If reservations are made by telephone, request the locater number and the best times for picking up tickets and boarding passes at in-town locations, rather than at invariably busy airports where delays can cause missed flights.

■ If there is time, have tickets sent to you by Federal Express—the service charge, if any, is worth your time saved.

■ Try always to book the most direct, nonstop flight. Fewer changes mean less chance of delays, lost luggage, and other mishaps. Problem: The hub-and-spoke system of many airlines often means that you "can't get there from here" without changing in Atlanta for Chicago, St. Louis for Denver, or whatever. Avoid hubs where possible.

■ KNOW YOUR OPTIONS ─────────────

Sophisticated travelers ask airline reservation agents for on-time ratings of desired flights, an underused service. While past performance is no future guarantee, ratings can tell you how often (in percentage terms) a regular flight has arrived on schedule over the past two months. Although airlines have begun increasing their estimated flight times to appear more punctual, on-time ratings still provide a good guideline. *Note:* American Airlines has added a new automated time-saver information system—offering flight arrival, departure, gate, fare, and schedule information directly from its SABRE Computer Reservation System. You can get options for flight arrivals, fares, and schedule information. Use the system's BARGE-IN feature to interrupt recorded instructions and get faster service. Once your selection is announced, you can enter a response immediately. Arrivals and departures on all lines are updated every ten minutes (available from CompuServe) so that you can check, for instance, to see when an incoming flight is actually coming in.

Another easily employed time-saving approach with these systems is to get a list of several flights leaving before and after those you have booked. If you reserve on these, and need to make a quick change to an earlier flight or miss your airplane or get bumped or canceled, you will already have an alternative. Be sure not to make reservations for which you'll be charged if you cancel.

Peter J. Tanous, Director of Bank Audi USA, uses his portable equipment when he has to change an airline ticket. Dialing the American Express Travel Service 800 number on his cellular phone, he gets the needed information and, if possible, a reservation while others are still waiting in what is all too frequently a long ticketing agent line. Caution: Be certain you are not charged for unused flights. As the airlines often state: "Certain restrictions may apply."

▪ AN ORGANIZER'S TIPS ─────────────

Neil Balter, president and founder of the California Closet Company, has logged more than 938,000 frequent-flyer miles traversing the country visiting his franchisees. He offers these tips for getting in and out of the airport with a minimum of stress and delay:

▪ Fly only with carry-on luggage if at all possible.

▪ Check in at the gate, not the counter.

▪ Stay away from Friday travel, if possible—always a nightmare.

▪ Avoid early morning flights. Airports are busiest between 6:30 and 10:00 A.M. and slowest mid-afternoons.

▪ Always call ahead to make sure your flight is leaving on time. What they tell you isn't always guaranteed, but it helps.

▪ Taking the "red-eye" doesn't pay. The time saved never adds up, and you never feel quite right the next day.

▪ SAVING TIME CHECKING IN ─────

Checking in used to mean long lines and waits, an hour and a half being standard on international routes. However, even with heightened security checks, it is getting better. Curbside check-in has returned. Most airlines now provide special counters for first- and business-class check-in. Internationally, Swissair passengers can, in many places, check in by telephone. Arriving at the airport, they find that boarding passes and bag tags have been prepared, reducing the wait for a flight to the recommended thirty minutes before boarding.

Airline baggage check-in at hotels has proved extremely popular in Europe, the Far East, and some U.S. locations. Also growing in popularity is the downtown check-in. Overseas, American Airlines provides check-in service at London's Victoria Station, next to the Gatwick Express platform. You get seat assignments, and then catch the special airport train. Cathay Pacific has a check-in point in Kowloon, Hong Kong, and Korean Air has one at its Seoul air terminal. Downtown check-in is also possible in Tokyo and many other Far Eastern cities.

When you are in Switzerland, you can use Fly Rail, enabling you to check in your bags with Swissair in the United States or at Zurich and Geneva air and rail stations and pick them up at your destination.

▪ USING TRAVEL MINUTES FOR WORK ─────────

Recognizing that business travelers often need to work on board, many airlines have made office equipment available gratis. Some have installed air telephones or even portable cellulars. Others, usually overseas, have calculators on board. Singapore Airlines and JAL promise fax service. However, by and large, business travelers or professionals with work to do aloft are taking along their own equipment.

Many executives point out that they have to take defensive measures to be sure that if they are planning to work they won't be interrupted by seatmates. Showing that you are busy usually works, but the best tactic is to ask to be seated next to a free space if available.

If traveling alone, learn to tune out travel noises so as to concentrate, and take advantage of precious quiet time. One executive, Jimmy Williams, CEO of SunTrust, puts on airline earphones with the volume off to do his reading and other work, and to discourage interruptions. Others, such as Robert Crandall, CEO of American Airlines, get flight attendants to bring a trash-bag in which to throw away unwanted paperwork. Lawrence A. Appley, one-time president of the American Management Association, says he invariably selects the seat immediately under the movie screen, where viewing is so inconvenient that he isn't tempted. He also begins work immediately so that his seatmate doesn't strike up idle conversation.

Portable tape recorders and dictating machines are, I have found, the best en-route time savers. Because they are small, you can record without physically disturbing those around you, stopping and starting as word flow requires. Dictate correspondence, memoranda, reports, observations, and ideas and suggestions. Then, when you step off the plane, your cassette tape is ready for transcription—and action.

Listening to audiocassettes is another significant time saver—most often more interesting and rewarding than the airline headset music or the movie, which almost invariably turns out to be something you have either seen or don't want to see.

As noted elsewhere, laptop computers continue shrinking in weight and size, while expanding in speed and capabilities. Such market leaders as Toshiba, Zenith, Epson, and Tandy/Radio Shack are now at weights that impose no air travel hardship or inconvenience. These can contain an array of work-aiding software or simply serve as word processors.

■ THE RED-EYE SPECIAL ——————————

If rushed for time, consider flying by night instead of by day. The following are some tips on making red-eye flights opportunities for sleep:

■ Teach yourself to sleep in the air, even in airplanes that lack stretch-out space. The Red Eye coast-to-coast is hardly recommendable for comfort, but it might be necessary when you finish business late at one coast and have to speed to the other.

■ Always wear an easy-fitting suit or dress, preferably crease-resistant. You will be more comfortable snoozing and won't look like the proverbial unmade bed on arrival.

■ Be sure to take off your shoes. Some long-distance flights provide pull-on slippers. Ask for an extra pillow or two and a blanket.

■ Encourage sleep with an eye-mask (no longer given as generously, so it is wise to take your own) and use an inflatable U-shaped travel pillow. These pillows give you the comfort even if the seat doesn't recline much.

■ GET TRAVELERS CHECKS BEFORE GOING ABROAD ——————————

If you are going to several countries abroad, and time is important, consider purchasing travelers checks in German marks, Swiss francs or French francs, Italian lira, and so on, so that you won't have the time-wasting hassle of changing over there. Money exchange is available from many sources at *no commis-*

sion charge. Many leading banks also offer checks without the 1-percent fee I consider a rip-off. Checks provide refunds in case of loss or theft and unused ones can be saved for a later trip.

▪ TIME-SAVING CUSTOMS TIPS

If you are going abroad—even if knowledgeable—be sure to get the new brochure (Publication No. 512, Department of the Treasury, U.S. Customs Service) "Know Before You Go." It contains information on restrictions on what you bring home, exemptions, penalties, customs pointers, duty-free sales slips, and more. You can save many minutes trying to find out what you can or can't do when returning—and eliminate possible problems. Customs offices, listed under U.S. Government in major city phonebooks, are happy to provide answers. For passport information, contact the nearest office of the U.S. Department of State.

▪ OVERSEAS SECURITY CHECK

Save time determining whether or not destination is safe by calling the U.S. State Department's Civilian Emergency Center, which lists current travel advisories. [Information: 202-647-5222 or 647-0900]

▪ SAVE TIME GETTING THE NEWS WHILE TRAVELING

Traveling domestically, there is a wide range of quick-access news sources—with newspapers, television, and radio freely available. Overseas, it is a different matter. However, you will find these time-saving media available abroad:

■ *The International Herald Tribune* is on sale in a growing numbers of locations. A joint publication of *The New York Times*, *Washington Post*, and *Los Angeles Times*, it is printed in several overseas locations and is usually available in the morning the day of issue. It gives you all of the advantages of the U.S.-oriented news, including many of the by-liners from the American originating papers. Usually shorter, and often with features from all three original papers, it offers compact reporting.

■ The *Wall Street Journal* is also available in European and Far Eastern editions, and is generally the most up-to-date.

■ Many leading overseas hotels now provide an English-language and a local daily *on request*, without charge.

■ *CNN*, running twenty-four hours a day, is available in many leading hotels globally. It gained an even wider following for its outstanding Persian Gulf War reportage.

■ You might consider one of the new shortwave radios. Thanks to electronic advances, they are now smaller, cheaper, and sound better. For as little as $75, you can keep up with "Voice of America" or the BBC, with many points of view, in many languages, from Hindi to Farsi to Estonian. Battery-operated, sets can be tucked into a backpack, briefcase, or pocket. Like other electronic equipment, they might be inspected closely at airport security stations at crisis times. International travelers are often asked to remove radios from hand luggage and demonstrate that they are not really an explosive device.

▪ HOTEL TIME SAVERS ─────────────

Your hotel can be your home away from home, as well as a major time and effort saver, say Kristin Sandberg and Donna Simmons of Hyatt International, Chicago. Hyatt operates over 160 hotels in the United States and overseas. The following are their tips:

■ *Always confirm reservations.* Get written confirmation or make a note of your confirmation number.

■ *Locate the best hotel.* Major chains often have several locations in key cities. One reason many travelers today stay at airport hotels: With meeting attendees coming from a variety of locations, there is really no time-consuming need to go downtown.

■ *If your travel budget permits:* If you have membership or upgrade coupons or can otherwise afford it, try to get booked on the executive floors (example: Hyatt's Regency Club). These floors offer helpful service people, morning papers, and often a wide range of additional amenities, including a light breakfast in a private lounge only a few steps from your room, which eliminates the inconvenience of eating in a main, often crowded, dining room or coffee shop.

■ *If you are booking directly:* Use toll-free 800 numbers. Virtually all leading hotels and chains, domestic and international, offer these, making it easy to shop for the best deal. Reserve as far ahead as possible; confirm with a credit card number. If you cancel by 6:00 P.M., you have lost nothing. If you go, there is far better choice.

■ *Take advantage of time-saving departure innovations.* Hyatt Hotels and Resorts now allows you to actually check in by telephone. Dial 800-CHECKIN and your accommodation is ready and waiting on arrival. The same system works in reverse on departure. At increasing numbers of hotels you can call up your bill on your television screen, check it for accuracy and, if there are no errors, simply sign your bill and leave it with your key as you depart. There is no need to go to the desk and wait, especially annoying during rushed departures.

▪ Chapter Twenty-two ▪▪▪▪▪

Personal but Not Private

Here are some tips to help ensure that you give the fullest possible attention to your personal health and needs, yet with the same type of goal-setting, planning, and activity time control dealt with in other sections. In short, good health in less time.

▪ SEDUCE YOURSELF INTO SHAPE ——————

Throughout the United States and worldwide people are realizing that adequate exercise is the key to good health. In a recent survey, 93 percent of respondents agreed. However, busy, ambitious people often neglect this vital need. Dr. James M. Rippe, M.D., in a special *Newsweek* health supplement, noted recently that inactive people face almost twice the risk of heart disease as active people. To help you see how easy it is to get started on and stay with regular exercise in a minimum of time, Dr. Rippe offered the following ten tips to "seduce yourself into shape"—

based on a study he did for the President's Council on Physical Fitness and Sport:

1. *Develop a specific plan.* Don't leave exercise to chance. It can end up at the bottom of your daily schedule and simply not get done. If you know that you are going to be busy, plan from day's beginning to gain a miniworkout by taking the stairs to appointments or a brisk walk at lunchtime, using such minutes for a healthy self-benefit.

2. *Set realistic goals.* In planning an exercise program to be done in limited available time, you might forget that it might have taken a number of years to fall into sedentary ways. Don't make the mistake of trying to go out and run or walk briskly for two or three miles the first time out. The result will be soreness, discouragement, and injury. Base your realistic goals on your current conditioning level.

3. *Use motivational equipment.* Don't falter on preliminaries preparing for exercise programs. Significant advances in equipment over the past five years make regular exercise easier, safer, and more motivational in less time. If you intend to walk, purchase fitness shoes. Running shoes are, of course, vital to joggers, and nylon or water-resistant exercise suits allow you to exercise outdoors during inclement weather. Many stationary cycles and other home fitness equipment allow you to see elapsed workout time, calories burned, and miles pedaled—all motivators.

4. *Establish a definite time and place.* Treat your exercise session as an organizer/scheduler priority appointment. If you set up a definite exercise time and place, you are more likely to do it than leaving opportunities to chance.

5. *Involve family and friends.* Studies show that individuals who involve others in their exercise decision are more likely to stick with programs than go-it-aloners. Spousal support is particularly critical. Kids can join in, too—a great way to make it part of family life.

6. *Vary activities*. The best way to fight exercise boredom is to prevent it from happening. Diversify daily and seasonally. Walk one day and swim another.

7. *Avoid injury*. Use proper techniques, wear and use correct equipment, and warm up and cool down. Well-designed and maintained equipment also reduces the risk of injury.

8. *Build up gradually*. Fitness change occurs slowly. The goal: To establish a consistent, life-long increased activity pattern. Most research studies show fitness improvements in increased aerobic capacity or strength increases about 1 to 2 percent weekly. Therefore, build gradually.

9. *Keep records*. Most experienced athletes keep exercise records—a good non-pro idea. It is very motivational to be able to look back over the weeks and months, and eventually years, to see how your own efforts have led to an increase in personal health and happiness. Don't be elaborate; a wall calendar or your scheduler marked with an X is enough.

10. *Reward yourself*. If you decide to exercise twice weekly, when you have made it through the month, go to your bookstore and buy as a reward the book you have been wanting. Or take your spouse to dinner to congratulate yourselves on the healthier life. Simple rewards remind you that you are the one in charge and that your own efforts can determine your life quality. Concludes Dr. Rippe: "Seducing yourself into shape just involves these simple, everyday opportunities each of us has to make increased activity a natural and fun part of our lives."

If you exercise at home, use television viewing time to get your much-needed exercise by putting equipment in the same room.

One exerciser I have found of particular interest—especially for those perhaps not into body-building—is Nordic Track, a home exerciser based on the cross-country skiing motion. Replacing exercise bicycles and rowing machines, Nordic is said to be used by five-year owners an average of three times weekly for twenty-two minutes a session—rather than the typical pattern of buying equipment and leaving it alone, as with so many unsustained exercise enthusiasms.

■ MEDICAL AND DENTAL VISITS

With the increasing patient loads of medical, dental, and other health specialists, going often becomes such a time-consuming matter that people often put off the necessary, knowing that a ten-minute date with a practitioner can mean an hour's waiting time or use up half a day. To speed this process, consider the following:

■ Try to set your appointments for mornings, before going to your job, by explaining the time pressures you are under and asking for the day's first appointment. Getting up earlier to be the initial patient can save considerable elapsed time.

■ With medical people under such pressure, you often find the explanations they give you on *your* problem or need not fully comprehensible. *Medical Tests and Diagnostic Procedures* by Dr. Phillip Shatsel claims to take the mystery out of medical testing. Reading up on your problem (or what you think you have) and bringing this to the attention of your doctor or dentist can save time. They might not agree, but having authoritative information on which to base your own questions speeds responses.

■ Use a home computer database for health information written for lay audiences. The Medline Database System from CompuServe is an electronic library of more than 40,000 indexed and abstracted publications containing a total of over 3.6 million references. You can also tap the IAC Health Database and Healthnet for general health and medical information. These contain the latest information on such concerns as arthritis, cancer, cholesterol, drug side effects, the risks and benefits of aero-

Typical is Beth Israel Medical Center in New York, which has over 650 such professionals on its list—noted by location, specialty, and language requirements. There is no fee. This institution, like many others throughout the country, also has a department of health education and information, which publishes a health news bulletin. Free of charge, the bulletin offers authoritative and useful data on new medical developments. It also lists a wide range of services—medical and dental, child and family, seniors, and much more. If your hospital experience is limited, you will probably be surprised at how much time-saving information institutions now make available without charge.

■ HEALTH MEASUREMENTS AT HOME

It used to be that getting your blood pressure, cholesterol, or a wide variety of other readings required time out to schedule a doctor's or clinic visit, with all of the attendant time-stealing requirements. Now, an increasingly wide variety of devices allow you to do this at home. If your reading is out of line with what your doctor says is your norm, call to get the necessary advice. MediSense has developed a gadget to let you measure your own cholesterol level, much as diabetics check blood glucose levels. Until now, reports the *Wall Street Journal,* cholesterol testing required technicians using lab machines. The new device (which in December 1990 still required regulatory approval) will be pen-size.

■ MEDICAL INFORMATION BY TELEPHONE

Increasing numbers of hospitals in many parts of the country offer free health information by telephone twenty-four hours a day. For example, Lenox Hill Hospital, New York, offers Tel-Med Health Line, which is described as "An anonymous way to get doctor's answers to 300 different health questions and disease indicators 24 hours a day." A directory and services listing is available from Lenox Hill Health Education Center [1080 Lexington Avenue, New York, NY 10021; tel: 212-439-2980]. Choose a topic you want to learn more about, find its corresponding number, call Tel-Med, and listen for recorded instructions and dial the topic program number given to you.

▪ PSYCHOTHERAPY BY TELEPHONE ———

If you use psychotherapy, as do so many high-profile achievers these days, be aware of the latest manifestation of our mobile and anxious society: telephone therapy. Says Emily Joffe in *Newsweek* (November 19, 1990): "It's an answer for people working through psychological transference when they move to another city and, because of tight schedules and time-zone differences, find themselves keeping in touch with therapists from pay phones, hotel rooms or offices."

Newsweek quotes Dr. Ellen McGrath, a New York psychologist, as saying: "I think telephone therapy is one of the major therapies of the future." Dr. McGrath's own move from Los Angeles prompted her to begin counseling from another area code. Her counseling group brought a speaker phone so that she could continue conducting sessions from the East Coast. Because Dr. McGrath has limited time to see everyone in person, patients telephone from wherever they are for discussions they believe help them with a variety of health problems. *Drawbacks:* The therapist misses your body language and facial expression and vice versa. Telephone therapy lends itself more to quick fixes than the free association believed to be a key to successful treatment. Still, it is a time saver for some; noted here for potential value.

▪ SAVING TIME ON YOUR HEALTH BILLINGS

The mere thought of time and effort required to fill out health insurance forms is enough to make most people sick, said *Fortune*. Now American Express has voluntarily entered this hassle-filled jungle of paper and pain—with a new card called Quattro. Designed for people covered by corporate health plans, at offices of participating doctors you pay with a card. AMEX pays the doctor's fees in two weeks; it then files an electronic claim with your insurer, which pays the portion covered by your policy, and then bills you for the remainder.

Medicare

New regulations require doctors or other health care providers to fill out and file forms. Many complain about the burden, but it is a time saver for you, the patient, and certain to improve proper payments. Seek a doctor or provider who accepts this assignment. It eliminates your paperwork and adjusting between payments and reimbursables.

Chapter Twenty-three

Personal Chores

You need your health for yourself, your family, your job, and all of the other activities of your daily life, not the least so that you can speedily attend to all of the personal chores that crowd your schedule. Fortunately, as our activities pace increases, new minute-minding techniques, services, machines, systems, and organizations are available to help cut down the time required.

What follows are a series of ideas you might be able to successfully adopt in handling your own range of personal chores. They deal with individuals, men and women and families. Select those that appear practical for you—knowing that once you get the time-saving habit, you will think of many others on your own. Other tips dealing specifically with home and family are detailed in a following chapter.

▪ BANKING ───────────────────────────────

Many aspects of our personal banking needs are now being short-cut through new approaches that can save personal time. The following are some tips from *Working Woman* magazine and others:

▪ Direct-deposit your salary and your Social Security and other government checks in your bank account, eliminating mail delays and waiting in line. Thousands of companies offer such services.

▪ If your bank provides such service, have them automatically pay such regular bills as mortgage and utility fees. You won't waste time writing and mailing checks. Some handle this by telephone—simply punching in the amount and the code for the company it goes to. However, it is important to check payment statements to catch errors if you use either of these services.

▪ If you need money regularly, ask your bank or credit union to transfer a specific amount from higher-interest savings to checking each month.

▪ Buy prestamped envelopes and keep them with your checkbook for paying bills.

▪ Use a rubber stamp or gummed labels (500 for as little as a dollar or two) with your name and address so that you don't have to constantly write them out.

▪ Put bills in a folder as soon as they arrive—or attach them to a clipboard along with your checkbook and a pen. You can pay bills during commercial breaks while watching TV, or at other spare moments.

▪ Consolidate your banking so that all information about checking and savings accounts, CDs, and so on come in one statement. Some banks offer consolidation.

▪ If you need a loan, consider such time savers as the Bank of New York's 60 Minute Loan—enabling you to get a telephone answer on any installment request in under an hour. Many banks offer this service.

■   Choose a bank with automatic teller machines (ATMs) closest to your home and office, and with national and international connections.

■ INSURANCE CONSOLIDATION TO SAVE TIME

Many of us have policies with several insurance companies— bought at various times and for long-forgotten reasons. Consider a single, independent agent who can handle all of your insurance needs—saving you considerable time in dealing with multiple insurers. Many national financial concerns offer an array of one-stop sources.

■   Cut the number of your payments. For example, pay annually, if possible, to save writing monthly checks and avoid the service charges companies often tack on to cover multiple-payment processing costs.

■   Be sure to list various insurance policy numbers, due dates, and family numbers in your personal organizer/scheduler so that they are handy when needed.

■   As investment time savers, choose one or more of the best-performing mutual funds—which buy a diversified portfolio of stocks and bonds. Evaluate the pros and cons, low and high risks, tax-free and overseas investments, front load management fees, and so on. Then you have an immediate, often daily, reading on *your* values, rather than the time-consuming task of selecting and constantly monitoring an individualized portfolio.

■ TAX RETURNS BY COMPUTER

The popularity of computer software systems in saving time in personal tax preparation is demonstrated by *TurboTax,* used by a reported three million tax filers in 1990, and during the last half of the eighties by more persons for tax preparation than any other. Says the maker: "Just start up on your PC or Macintosh and it guides you through all aspects of tax preparation. The system explains tax terminology, suggests ways of keeping more of your hard-earned money, reviews return for errors, and even warns you if anything might flag the IRS. Lift a finger and in a keystroke it does all of the necessary calculations. You can then print out and file your return right off your computer. More than sixty federal forms, schedules, and worksheets are included. State filing packages are also available.

Other Leading Computerized Tax Preparation Software

A good package is *Taxcut*—from **NECA Software** [203-222-9150]. *Quicken* and *Checkwriter Plus* software handle budgeting and checkwriting, organizing bill paying, and record-keeping to make these tasks faster and more accurate than you could do them without the use of a computer. *Note:* Federal tax returns can now be filed by fax, which saves mailings and copies and speeds up refunds.

▪ PERSONAL COMPUTER FINANCIAL SYSTEMS

Today's tax-related software can do a lot more than fill out IRS forms. Many are time-saving, tax-savvy, and valuable in shaping your investment and savings strategy. Some offer advice on state taxes and insurance. In that many share data with one or more tax preparation programs, they should save many hours at tax time, says *Business Week* (November 12, 1990).

Getting up to speed with these programs, however, can be a

real pain for those still practicing unstructured accounting. Software forces you to think meticulously about your financial affairs. Categorizing expenses and income sources is just the beginning. It will take some hours to start on even a simple program; a weekend to scratch the surface of something as rich in features as *Managing Your Money* or *Wealth Builder* software programs, says *Business Week*.

Developed by expert Andrew Tobias, *Checkwriter* writes and prints any size checks, has an electronic bill payment option, handles multiple bank accounts, prints invoices, handles credit cards, and much more. [Information: 800-962-5583]

CompuServe Information Service has a personal finance program to help you balance checkbooks, calculate net worth, and even determine mortgage amortization schedules.

If you have a personal or family investment portfolio, there is a wide range of computer software for your home PC. If time is at a premium, but you feel it is essential to stay atop your stocks and news affecting them, CompuServe offers *Go Money*. By giving the proper instructions, your holding valuations and other information are offered on a real-time basis via modem connection to the service provider.

▪ PROFESSIONAL "CHOREGANIZERS" ──

Changing Times reports that any chore you have to do can probably be done faster by a professional, given the experience gained in serving many people. Professional organizers' charges are not cheap, but the results might be worth it. The National Association of Professional Organizers has 200 members. For a directory, write: 23824 Ocean View Blvd., Montrose, CA 91020.

▪ STAMPS BY TELEPHONE OR MAIL ———

No longer is it necessary to stand in an endless line for stamps. The U.S. Postal Service is now selling stamps by telephone, twenty-four hours a day, seven days a week—delivered in three to five business days. These may be charged to Visa, MasterCard, or Discover credit cards only. There is a $3 service fee [800-782-6724]. Stamps are also available in many supermarket chains. To order by mail with no service fee, get a stack of postage-free order forms at all post offices.

▪ TIME SAVINGS FOR SENIORS ———

Seniors and retirees have many of the same time-saving objectives as individuals in mid career. They are past the years of standard 9-to-5 jobs, may lack the support services of their younger years, and are often partially restricted by health or other problems.

One leading organization dedicated to their needs—and highly conscious of the best use of time—is the American Association of Retired Persons (AARP). Described as the world's largest, nonprofit, nonpartisan membership organization, it has four goals: (1) enhancing the quality of life of older persons, (2) promoting independence, dignity, and purpose for older individuals, (3) leading the way in determining the role and place of older persons in society, and (4) improving the image of aging.

AARP has developed a vast variety of programs, services, activities, and information sources expressly designed to meet these four goals with less time and effort. At the same time, many of the activities it offers give members an opportunity to become more involved as community volunteers—close to home.

By using the facilities and resources of AARP, whose one-year membership is only $5, you can tap many services otherwise difficult to obtain and time-consuming to both investigate and put to use. [Information: P.O. Box 199, Long Beach, CA 90801]

▪ GETTING OUTSIDE HELP

If you are a busy individual or family and simply can't get all of the household chores done within your available time, consider the proliferation of household service agencies in virtually every city. They come in to do the cleaning and straightening out— even windows. Many firms send in teams—ensuring the provision of experts in various home tasks who complete your jobs in fewer hours at less cost. However, charges are not inexpensive. Services can be useful perhaps for heavy cleaning jobs once a month so that you or your spouse or family can do the less arduous items in between.

You will also find a wide variety of other services available— at a cost. They run from stand-ins who will line up for tickets and renew your driver's licenses and passports to part-time helpers who will wait for deliveries and perform the range of household chores.

See the Yellow Pages under such headings as Personal Concierges and Domestic Help.

▪ TIME-CONSUMING CHRISTMAS CHORES

We all love to give gifts at Christmastime. However, the process (on which retailers often depend for half their total annual earnings) takes a great deal of time—often at that period of the year when you are least able to afford it. The following are some tips from Kate Marvin, reported in "A Fifth Avenue Christmas," a supplement distributed with *The New York Times*:

▪ Write out enclosure cards for gift recipients ahead of time to take along as you shop so that they can go right into your store-sent packages.

■ Many stores have prewrapped gifts; buy several, including extras for people you will think of long after you have left the store.

■ Use messenger services to deliver last-minute gifts.

■ Consider gift buying at major museums. They, and even libraries, concert halls, and so on now often have gift shops offering the unusual and unexpected. You can get better-than-market prices with member discounts.

■ Use telephone shopping. Many stores have holiday season twenty-four-hour gift shopping services that accept their own or major credit cards.

■ Make a master list. Note what you bought for whom to keep in your organizer/scheduler for Christmastime the following year. Include addresses, with zip codes, and keep receipts in a separate folder.

Chapter Twenty-four

Sleeping and Resting Better

Getting enough of the right kind of sleep can ensure that you are always at your best and gain the benefits of your minute-saving day. One of the greatest time gainers is reducing sleeping time. The other is improving your ability to fully gain the benefits of essential rest when you are under the sheets.

Individuals who, in periods of stress and high activity, are able to employ condensed sleep patterns without adverse impact, can actually run at a supercharged pace for the time required to complete major assignments. Famed film producer Richard deRochemont, who created *The March of Time*, used a system of brief sleeping periods during intense work sessions. He would sleep three or four hours, wake with a fresh drive and work for four, and then return to sleep—repeating the pattern. He explained: "It breaks my working tension; gives me refreshment. And I reduce the normal eight-hour sleeping period to five, gaining three hours in every twenty-four."

For most of us, however, getting more good rest from our time abed will do the trick. Here are a few suggestions:

■ *Get the sleep you really require.* If you arise fresh, without the need for an alarm clock, you have had sufficient rest. If you find that you have to force yourself to get up in the morning, you are cheating yourself—and will pay in subsequent time-consuming strain and lack of energy.

■ *We sleep deepest, most restfully, during the first hour or two of sleep.* Muscles are most relaxed, blood pressure lowest, and skin sensitivity at its minimum during this period. Sleeping late mornings isn't as restful as the initial sleep after retiring.

■ *To sleep most easily, try taking a soporific bath.* Heat water to which one tablespoon of mustard powder or pine essence has been added to exactly 100°F. Soak twenty minutes. This normalizes and tranquilizes your circulation. Pat your skin dry instead of rubbing. Be sure your bed is already prepared and hop right in.

■ *Carefully relax every body muscle.* Once abed, deliberately let your arms, legs, trunk, and neck muscles go. Get out of any cramped position. S-T-R-E-T-C-H.

■ *Create monotony. Excitement prevents sleep;* try making your bedroom as dark and quiet as possible, or use an eye mask.

■ *Eliminate noise.* Try one of the previously mentioned tapes, which give you the sound of the ocean and a subliminal message you select on any one of a wide range of subjects. This helps lull you to sleep while making use of your brain process (without harming your rest).

■ IMPROVING YOUR SLEEP QUALITY ─────────────────────────

Improving your sleep quality is another way to save time by gaining its benefits in fewer minutes each day. Michael J. Thorpy, director of the Sleep-Wake Center at Montefiore Hospital, New York, is quoted by George Sullivan in *Work Smart, Not Hard,* as saying: "How long you spend in bed isn't all-important when you consider the sleep you need; what's important is the *quality* of the sleep you get." To do this, says Sullivan, try daily exercise. This will produce more rest from fewer hours in bed. However, don't exercise later than two hours before bedtime. Avoid stimulants such as caffeine during the day. There are so many decaffeinated coffees and teas now on the market that you can get much of the flavor and pleasure sought without the adverse effects. A glass of wine or a bottle of beer before bed actually interferes with sleep; too much can trigger insomnia. A bath and a glass of warm milk are much more effective, Sullivan says.

Try cutting back your time abed. By fifteen-minute increments weekly—returning to the higher level if you really feel fatigued during the day or your efficiency level drops—reduce your sleeping time. People's need for sleep covers quite a range: Thomas Edison claimed to have slept only about four hours a night; Albert Einstein reportedly slept half the day.

▪ BETTER BEDS IMPROVE REST ——————

You will rest best in a bed that doesn't exert pressure against your body while sleeping. Use open-weave sheets, foam pillows and mattresses, and in winter, either an electric blanket (eliminating the heavy, circulation-stopping blanket pile), quilts, or thermoweave blankets that provide warmth yet let air circulate.

Your mattress should be at least 39 inches wide so that you can turn during the night without being halfwakened with the fear of falling. It should never be so soft that your body is buried, making it necessary to wake to turn over. Look out for springs that aren't up to the job.

All these steps can help you fall asleep more quickly; and you get more good rest. Often, they'll enable you to arise an hour earlier than normal and still have benefits of an additional hour abed.

■ TAKE FEWER HOURS FOR SLEEP ──────

Godfrey M. Lebhar, in *The Use of Time*, says that many people sleep more hours than they generally need. There is no formula for sleep required—even for those engaged in the same type of work. How much sleep you need depends on your constitution, work, and personal inclinations. As noted, some of history's greatest figures have found it possible to get along with as few as four or five hours a day. Others require seven to nine. Lebhar adds:

> *By experimentation, you can determine just how much you need, ascertaining a safe minimum. Time spent sleeping beyond what's required for bodily and mental refreshment is wanton waste, shortening your life by the number of minutes of what might be called the "over-sleeping" you actually do.*
>
> *You may be getting more sleep than you need and still not want to change your habits. You may enjoy sleeping so much that it's your major pleasure. Yet the common belief that everyone needs a minimum of eight hours in 24 is baseless. In large measure the amount depends on sleep habits. And they can be altered.*

University of Chicago professor Nathaniel Kleitman—who specializes in sleep and energy studies—says that experiments prove that sleep requirements are unique to the individual. Most animals get the total rest they need through a series of naps. If you would like to save time in sleep, try these experiments:

■ If you are now sleeping nine hours daily, try getting along with eight. See if it doesn't satisfy—perhaps not the first time, but after at least ten days.

- Whatever your sleep pattern, try cutting your total sleep time by half an hour without necessarily going to bed later.
- Set your alarm at least fifteen minutes earlier each day for a certain period. Use the time gained for something you really want to do. You can always accomplish more in less time in the morning with the rest and relaxation from a really good night's sleep.

Associate Professor Thomas J. Quirk of Webster University in St. Louis notes: "Actually most adults only need six or seven hours of sleep nightly. If you're getting more, it's likely a habit, not a need. Most of our parents drummed this daily sleep requirement into us as children. Why? Probably because they needed at least an eight-hour break from us. If you slept less, could you get more done and still function properly? It's worth considering."

▪ THE INSOMNIAC —————————————————

Sleeplessness makes it hard to be a model executive who comes on quick and sharp-creased—able to do more in less time. According to the best estimates, says Walter Kiechell, III, in *Fortune* (October 8, 1990), in any given year upwards of 50 million Americans have trouble sleeping. Managerial types are as prone to insomnia as the rest of the population, perhaps a little more so. So-called A-type active personalities suffer sleeplessness in disproportionate numbers. Experts attribute the problem variously to stress, required evening socializing, heavy travel across time zones, and general workaholism.

Says Kiechell: "If you count yourself among the occasionally afflicted, have hope. Slightly. You may not be able to exactly manage the sleep process, which means falling asleep immediately and getting five hours of uninterrupted, deeply satisfying shuteye. But, you can take steps to improve your chances of ending up in the arms of Morpheus."

Kiechell suggests beginning by understanding normal sleep.

While the experts still don't know why we sleep and why we dream, much has been learned about the basic physiology. At night there are two types of sleep: rapid-eye movement, or REM, and the non-REM, called orthodox, quiet, or slow-wave sleep. At night, the two types alternate. This explains why you are more likely to wake up at four in the morning from a nightmare about your boss's latest lunatic move than you are at midnight. *Fortune* says that researchers suspect that creativity is most affected by lack of adequate sleep. The following are Kiechell's suggestions:

■ Try establishing a regular time for daily rising. This can help avoid so-called Sunday night insomnia.

■ Realize that you can't work feverishly right up to bedtime, and expect immediate drift-off. Leave at least an hour or two before bedtime for winding down.

■ In bed, don't work, watch television, or argue with your significant other. Your mind won't learn to associate going to bed with going to sleep.

■ Beginning six hours before hitting the hay, avoid caffeine or foods that may stimulate—chocolate, for instance. Cut off alcohol intake at least two hours before bedtime.

■ Regular exercise can promote better rest.

If you can't sleep, Kiechell suggests the following:

■ Go elsewhere, turn on a light, and read something boring—or do some other unstimulating diversion—until you feel sleepy.

■ Resist the sleeping pill temptation. All sleep disorder specialists say that taking sedatives more than once weekly is too often.

Kiechell concludes: "Some experts say the biggest hurdle in treating sleepless executives is their unwillingness to take time to improve sleep habits. What folly. How much better to view ability to sleep as a sort of test of how in tune we are with the natural order."

▪ SLEEPING LESS TO THRIVE ─────────

For so many who mourn the fact that we sleep away a third of our lives, magazine publisher Dale Hanson Bourke has come up with a radical solution: sleep less. You might feel better and accomplish more. Her *Sleep Management Plan* offers a six-step program claimed to "add hours to your week, increase energy, and bring balance to a more active, more fulfilling life."

Bourke explores many of what she describes as myths concerning sleep. Sleep reduction actually has known benefits, especially for insomniacs and people suffering chronic depression, she says. For the millions of on-the-go men and women who can't find enough time in their day to satisfy personal, professional, and parental responsibilities and needs, her plan claims a unique approach to what she describes as "a more balanced life."

Bourke supplements her plan with self-assessment quizzes, time charts, activity planners, sleep logs, and data about sleep. She gives sage advice about nutrition, covering alcohol, fats, and sugars; which drugs contain caffeine; and which foods are high in sleep-inducing tryptophan. She adds an informative appendix answering what are described as the eighteen most commonly asked questions about sleep. Over 130 sleep disorder clinics are listed by state.

Although not a doctor, scientist, nutritionist, or trainer—but simply an individual who has become absorbed in the question of sleep management as a corollary to time management—Bourke's own experimentation challenges many of our most basic assumptions about sleep and exposes many of these beliefs as "unscientific myths." Bourke offers the following:

▪ Eight hours of sleep are not a necessity. Specialists put the norm between six and nine. Many of the world's greatest achievers slept fewer than six without compromising their health and well-being.

■ You are not necessarily an insomniac if you have trouble falling and staying asleep. You might simply be by nature a short sleeper.

■ If you feel tired, you are not necessarily lacking sleep. Being tired is just as often a symptom of stress, depression, or poor nutrition—none of which will be solved by sleeping more.

Bourke believes that not everyone is a candidate for sleep reduction as a time saver, which could add minutes or hours to your day, and hundreds of hours per year. Pregnant women, nursing mothers, children and adolescents, and those with medical problems should stay in bed, she advises. So should anyone "who can't think of anything better to do with their time." She explains: "If you find there aren't enough hours in the day for you to pursue your own interests—whether exercise, reading, a hobby or just plain relaxation—then you're ready to dip into the wonderful grab-bag of time you've been wasting on sleep."

This well-written and challenging book notes that the best trade-off of sleep time for waking time is exercise. In her own approach, she rises half an hour earlier than she really needs to, using the time for riding her bike. Improved blood circulation, stress reduction, and an increase in body temperature from exercising give her the energy and alertness needed for her business schedule, she says, as well as the impetus to cut more deeply into her sleep time. She notes: "The sleep management plan is not really about sleeping. It's about living."

■ GIVE YOURSELF A BREAK

Working so that you best use every moment to gain time doesn't mean putting relentless pressure on yourself. A relaxing break in your routine can often do much to improve the energy and enthusiasm levels of what follows that break—so that your post-relaxation intervals let you work faster and better. The following are techniques cited by Lester R. Bittel in *Right on Time*:

- A ten-minute break can be an excellent recharger.
- If time pressures are prolonged, take a relief day or a long weekend.
- If change has been turbulent in your organization, try stabilizing work schedules to reestablish a degree of normality.
- Try alternate deep and shallow breathing. This is a performance-enhancement technique commonly used to psyche up or calm down athletes.
- An exercise break clears the mind and relaxes the body, lessening pressure. In many parts of the world, particularly China, Japan, and Korea, production plant group exercises are done morning and afternoon by everyone, including top managers. Take fresh-start rest breaks.

■ NAPS AS FRESH STARTERS ─────────────

Some people with the facilities, often the highest ranking officials, find a cat nap after lunch worth up to three hours of nightly rest. President Franklin D. Roosevelt, who had great energy despite being wheelchair-bound, learned that a thirty-minute cat nap after lunch gave him a powerful lift. His successor, Harry S Truman, had the same idea—as well as the ability to sleep almost anywhere, any time. While in the White House, President Truman liked odd-time brief naps, especially before important speeches. From fifteen to thirty minutes of rest he gained the pep for two hours of intensive talks or conferences.

A nap when you arrive home at day's end can make you much more energetic for the balance of the evening—especially useful if you are going out. Ten to fifteen minutes stretched out and a change before dinner is an effective pepper-upper. Some prefer ten minutes of relaxation in a tepid tub, others shower. Regardless of the method, this rest break can give you a fresh, perked-up feeling for both dinner and evening schedules.

In Latin America, where I lived for many years, we unfailingly took after-lunch siestas. It became one of the day's most precious times. In many places, the midday siesta is usually impractical, and air-conditioning has minimized its imperative in hot climates. A before-dinner rest, however, provides the same benefits as a nap at any other time.

▪ Chapter Twenty-five ▪ ▪ ▪ ▪ ▪

Household Tasks

Keeping a home and raising 2.4 children (the U.S. average) is a full-time job, says *Time* magazine—as anyone who has ever done it already knows. The increasing rarity of the homemaker has done more to eat into everyone's leisure time than any other factor. In 57 percent of U.S. families, both mother and father work to make ends meet. Still, someone has to find time to make lunch, set up pediatrician appointments, shop, cook, fix the washer, do the laundry, take the children to choir practice and much, much more. In single-parent households the squeeze is tighter.

Families are coping, adds *Time*, by sharing chores, teaching children to put the roast in the oven after school; enrolling kids in day-care; hiring nannies; swapping play-date babysitting with other parents; sending out laundry and ordering in pizza. In short, they are spending a lot of time buying minutes by contracting out for family and household care.

Some of the increasing number of services available to help

are well worth their costs in minutes freed up—assuming you can afford them, judged by setting a monetary value on your time. Outside help is dealt with in the next chapter; here, however, I would first like to cover how you—and family—can save time at home on what you have to do to gain more time for what you want to do.

Start with the following:

■ Analyze the things that you and your family have to do with the same precision of office, shop, or working world.
■ Set goals and priorities so that you can more effectively allocate time available to those of greatest importance to loved ones and yourself.
■ At the same time, you have to cull those tasks that can be eliminated from your personal chore list; in a sense, delegated to or shared by spouse, children, and others within your household or close family group.

■ HOMEMAKERS HAVE NO EASY JOB ──────

You put in many hard labor hours daily—and get little praise or reward. However, at the risk of raising your hackles, it is a pretty good bet that if you are the homemaker, you could do your job in a third less time, with better results, by giving some concentrated thought and action to simplifying and improving your operations. Fully as much planning might be needed, even in a two-person household, as in many a small office. One must also deal with the constant changes—not all foreseen. How to improve?

▪ ORGANIZING EASES THE HOME LOAD ——————————————

Organizing time is as important at home as at work, but often more difficult, explains Kathryn Walker, a home economist writing in *US News and World Report* (January 25, 1982). She explains: "Each family must set its own standards for what's considered important and what's wasted time. This applies from hours with the children to minutes for cleaning. Regarding the latter, a decision on how clean is clean is a key to determining what housekeeping time is needed."

Ms. Walker notes that a home schedule can, at best, only be a guideline. Alternative routes are always essential. With your workaday life, the goals you set and values you establish are guidelines to planning and organizing your own time for accomplishing more with less effort. Similar goals and values should guide your home time management.

Many homemakers are doing just that—especially as more and more women, once the traditional keepers of the house, work full- or part-time, often necessitating an equal spousal sharing of housekeeping responsibilities.

Household tasks, of course, vary widely with the nature of living quarters, economic status, and lifestyle. The ideas that follow obviously can't apply to everyone; however, as with other time savers, if you find two or three you can use with some regularity, our joint efforts might be well worthwhile.

▪ ADAPT WORKPLACE ORGANIZATION TO YOUR HOME ——————————————

They are not exactly the same, of course. Time-saving problems of organizing home activities are, in many ways, far *greater* than those of an office. This is primarily because, at the workplace, one objective rules: accomplish tasks and be profitable at the same time. At home, the objective is to make your "castle" as pleasant and rewarding as possible for all who share its roof. However, the means to this objective are more fluid and multifarious than simply completing tasks.

In most homes, there are continuing needs to be met: purchasing and putting food on the table, the chores of operation, adjusting the expected differences of viewpoint between family members. Children come with their own complex sets of needs and desires. However, once you determine how long it takes to prepare a meal, vacuum the house, and so on, you can begin to allocate minutes according to an essential planned and written schedule.

▪ DAILY AND WEEKLY LISTS OF HOME CHORES SAVE TIME ———————————

Attorney Christine Beshar, who practices law in a major Manhattan firm and who has raised a family of four, says a logical sense of order helps her budget time for the equally demanding jobs of wife, mother, and lawyer, reported the *Christian Science Monitor*. In less than ten minutes each day she lists matters to be accomplished. Her children do almost all of the food shopping and marketing; two nights a week, they cook dinner. Other nights Mrs. Beshar is home in time to cook for her husband, also a lawyer, and the youngsters. Through good organization, Mrs. Beshar has been able to not only handle her professional work and family, but has been involved in church, college, her childrens' school, and New York City Bar Association activities— and done them all well.

Regarding household management to save time, Dr. Doris Williams, a Bowling Green State University home economist, suggests the following:

■ Write schedules for each of the various home processes; that is, meal management and so on.

■ Use time in relation to energy levels.

■ Employ "dovetailing": one task helps advance another.

■ Understand your own motivations and value systems relative to time use.

■ Achieve a balance of work and leisure in relation to personal goals.

Finally, realize that time is a valuable resource that at times warrants extravagant use of other resources such as money. Sometimes it is worth paying for an outside service if it relieves you of your need to do the job.

■ GENERAL HOUSEHOLD SCHEDULE ———

For all of your household activities, planning and developing improved methods can help save the minutes that add up to hours. Just as setting priorities, delegating responsibilities, and adapting good schedules based on experience works in business, so it can be effective at home. To do this, you, your roommate, spouse, and/or family members (including children when they are old enough) should first list those things done daily, weekly, and only occasionally. Divide these chores into the following time periods:

Before the Workday: Establish staggered wake-up times for individuals and morning-routine schedules to avoid the strain on bathrooms. Note other morning-routine steps.

Daytime Activities: In coordinating schedules, note the day's needs of the children (who needs to be taken to school or wherever, and who can make their own way), scheduled deliveries or repairs, and so on in relation to who will be at home and who out.

At Day's End: List evening activities by groups, with each major weekday item assigned only half an evening. Then two can be done on nights when you feel energetic.

Once all this is on paper, you can talk it out. Divide the responsibilities and post them on a wall chart.

Don't go forward without taking into account those who can be your greatest supporters. Children or others under your roof would like to, and must be, consulted about family plans and included in the rewards of joint labor. As noted previously, many husbands feel it is the wife's job to manage the home, even if she also works. However, evidence is piling up that of necessity households share everything.

The Best Ways to Get Cooperation

Decide jointly, by talking things out, who will do what. Obviously, everybody can't have the ideal home chore, but apportion, as in business, according to abilities, needs, and desires. There is no longer any obligatory, cast-in-stone activity for man or woman.

The following are some tips toward getting family members to cooperate:

■ Drawing up a list of unavoidable household chores will appall you perhaps, but also give you a chance to apportion work according to the capabilities and interests of all, oldest to youngest. Don't be quick to scorn youngsters' time-saving suggestions; they are often not bound by habit and can have interesting, original ideas.

■ Assign chores by the week. Rotate tasks so that no one gets permanently stuck with the less desirable. Nobody can be enthusiastic about everything. Cooperation is likely to be better—and time saved greater—if household tasks alternate.

■ Praise, all too rarely given at home, is an easy cooperation builder. When daughter knows you appreciate her care, or dad realizes you are aware he's made a contribution no one else could, old reluctances diminish. By praising them, you will not only get more help, but kudos for your own job well done in fewer minutes—with more time for enjoying individual and family pleasures.

■ WORK SIMPLIFICATION SAVES TIME

Time-saving ideas for everyday tasks come from many sources. Those in industry or office are frequently difficult to put into effect because others might be involved. However, when the laborer is *you* and the place *your* abode, the time saved is gained by you, your spouse, and your children, not others—and thus is infinitely more valuable.

Some concepts herewith come from an examination originally developed for the New York Heart Association by Dr. Lillian Gilbreth. Her aim was to show people suffering from heart disease how to accomplish more with less energy and in fewer minutes. Her ideas work just as well for any homemaker. Another pioneer, Dr. Eugene S. Murphy of the Veterans Administration, New York, made similar studies for disabled veterans. He has said: "Most homemakers make unnecessary work for themselves. They're victims of habit and tradition. It's time they stop to consider how much of their work could be eliminated."

Naturally, time you spend on any phase of your homemaking must be related to the degree of satisfaction gained. If you are a gourmet cook, for example, planning and preparing a meal is worth considerable time expenditure. However, if the objective is to serve one or two persons in the least time—with flavorsome variety well prepared and well served, but without three-star Michelin guide treatment—you will want to use all available techniques and as much new equipment as you can afford to do the best possible in the least time.

Get Extras ─────────────────────────────────

■ Make a small investment in duplicates of items needed frequently in every home. *Toiletries:* Buy several instead of individually—often at better prices. This saves constantly shopping for essentials. *Umbrellas:* An extra at the office might save you untold waiting time, keep your clothes in condition, and save annoyance.

■ *Household Working Tools:* Keep them together, and return them after each use. Pencils, pads, extra scissors, tissue packets, and so on in drawers in many places can avoid a search when such items are required.

■ *Extra hangers* in a guest closet avoids chasing around every time there are visitors.

Put Things Where You Can Find Them ─────────

Finding things is often the first and most time-consuming household chore. Having everything in its place, easily located, is an ideal few attain. You might insist the reason the goal is unachievable is that you don't want to be a slave to a "mania for orderliness." Yet, the fact is, with a system, it is actually easier to put things in the right place than to leave them around helter-skelter.

Establishing a place for everything and returning items there as your first priority so that it becomes an engrained habit can save many minutes each day. For example, even if you can't see past the end of your nose, with an eyeglasses holder sitting on a desk or nightstand, or mounted on a wall or dashboard, you can find them if you make it a habit to put your glasses in the same place at each locale. Do the same with anything you want to keep track of.

Lessening Household Clutter ———————————

Time-wasting aspects of household clutter can make us feel weak, incompetent, and guilty for letting it control us, says Stephanie Culp, author of *How to Conquer Clutter*, quoted by Beverly Hall Lawrence in *Newsday*:

> *You've lived with disorganization for years—but you managed. But, then one day it dawns on you that you've got an organization problem of biblical proportions. You may be unproductively disorganized if your day starts with a crisis: keys can't be located; you can't find anything to wear; you're now late for work and it gets worse. If saving time isn't a motivator, saving money might be.*
>
> *You rent or pay the mortgage on a fixed amount of space—if clutter occupies 10 percent of an apartment renting for $650, the renter really pays $65 monthly, or $780 annually to warehouse clutter.*

An industry of clutter-busters has been spawned because people sense its time-stealing impact and want to take control of their lives. Manufacturers are offering a variety of products to help you get organized. There is even a store devoted solely to the subject: Hold Everything, a national mail-order/retailer selling hundreds of items for hanging, hooking up, and hiding your "junk." "Clutter therapists" Pauline Hatch and Alice Fulton of Kennewick, Washington, estimate that they remove forty-five to fifty 30-gallon garbage bags of clutter from the average 2,000-square-foot house they are hired to reorganize.

Closet Organizing Tips

Neil Balter, president, California Closet Company, suggests the following:

■ Hang pieces of an outfit or suit separately. This allows you to envision other combination possibilities more easily. Categorize garments; that is, put all the blouses together, slacks together, skirts and jackets together, and so on.

■ Don't put into drawers what can be folded and placed on open shelves. You forget what you have if it's not in front of you.

■ Store handbags flat, loosely stuffed with tissue, on a shelf or in a drawer.

■ Keep a closet door list of what is at the cleaners and what needs repairing or tailoring and of outfits you have put together and loved but whose pairings you might forget.

■ Wispy scarves can be folded in a small set of drawers. If the drawers are transparent, scarves are easily visible without having to pull out each drawer. Scarves can also be draped on a kitchen mug rack nailed to a door or wall, hung on short towel bars, or clothespin clipped to a conventional hanger.

■ Keep hosiery snag-free. Line drawers or store hose in clear plastic bags. Separate stockings by color and store them separately. Label each bag with its intended use, including those with runs for pants only. Stuff hose and socks into small shopping bags looped over hangers, in stacked plastic carry-all bins, or in clear plastic boxes.

■ Don't put sweaters, knits, or bias-cut clothing on hangers. Fold them to maintain their shape, thus avoiding time-consuming ironing.

■ Plastic mesh wall grids are useful for keeping jewelry visible and accessible. Jewelry can also be kept neatly in a drawer with the use of a kitchen utensil divider. Earrings store neatly in ice cube trays.

■ Keep "shedding" fabrics, such as angora, away from those that pick up lint, such as velvet.

■ Don't immediately closet hang what you have just taken off. Hang them in the bathroom to release odors (such as smoke) and to smooth out wrinkles.

■ Clear out anything with a stain that's never going to come out, anything you like but never wear, your surplus of ratty weekend clothes (there will always be more), shoes with turned-up toes that haven't been worn in over a year, and anything that doesn't match the quality of what you are wearing now.

■ Old purses almost always look shabby and outdate what you are wearing. *Outdated basics:* the dirndl that came with your first suit; the white blouse with the large, pointed collars; exhausted lingerie; the coat that won't fit over your jackets and that is too short for your dresses; the skirt or pants that have been just a little too small for the past three years.

■ Every time you buy something new, get rid of something old. This doesn't mean you have to throw away your old letterman's jacket or your prom dress. It does mean you should carefully pack them up in tissue and store them in the garage or attic. These unusable, but sentimental, items should not be taking up valuable space in your closet.

Household Key Center

Keys should be kept together where they are accessible and out of the reach of small children. Consider the **Easy Key Finder**—a key ring that responds. Clap your hands four times and it will chirp electronically. How much time do you waste searching for your keys? [Mogalog Marketing, P.O. Box 3006, Lakewood, NJ 08701; tel: 800-365-8493]

Like Items Together

Examples: golf or other sporting things, overnight trip requirements, special party items. One woman immediately returns all
of her tennis paraphernalia to a single bag—knowing that whenever she goes out to play, everything is together, and no gathering
is necessary. Similar planning and prelocating applies to many of
your interests.

The Linen Closet

Keep sheets with matching pillowcases and bath towels with hand
towels and washcloths, rather than, for instance, all sheets in one
area, and all pillowcases in another.

▪ THE BATHROOM

The most used room in the house, after the kitchen, should be
both functional and pleasing. Look at the wasted space—on
walls, above toilet or tub, and under the sink or toilet tank.
Shelves can be used throughout. Add hooks and towel racks to
the backs of doors. Use empty space above the tub for shelves and
narrow cabinets. Consider drawer dividers or flatware trays for
makeup and jewelry storage. Hang shower caddies from shower
heads. If you are low on counter space but have space in the
room, use a small table or chest to store toiletries and personal
grooming supplies.

▪ CHILD'S ROOM

Scale storage space to a child's size with shelves that adjust to growth and changing needs. Store toys by categories. Children are natural collectors; provide them with pegboards that let them display collections. Put wheels on toy boxes so that kids can pull them around for quick pickup. Consider a small hammock for holding dolls and stuffed animals. Use cubbyholes for school and art supplies. Bulletin boards and colorful stacking baskets keep things orderly. For safety's sake, don't store toys on shelves your child can see but not reach. This invites climbing to get a favorite toy, and thus, possible falls.

▪ THE HOME OFFICE

If there is space, consider converting a large closet into a minioffice. Create a desktop out of a corner of a room by suspending a large piece of wood or door atop stacked modular boxes or filing cabinets. Flank a wide, wood desktop with two bookcases. Install an entire wall of shelves; they will unclutter left-abouts. Organize your home filing system for personal and family papers. Index exactly as you would at the office or workplace—depending on the utility of the system. Consider these time savers:

▪ General categories: household warranties and guarantees, home repair, suppliers, insurance, out-of-town trips, birthday lists, house, car, taxes, receipts, clothing, investments, medical, prospects, gifts, and miscellaneous.

▪ Correspondence to be retained—business and personal—should be filed according to your own needs. Writer Dorothy M. Johnson notes that in her Gifts folder she records birthday and Christmas gifts given and received, avoiding the usual year-later family argument. List persons with whom you exchanged collector's items. Beside each name, note everything exchanged to avoid sending duplicates and minutes trying to think what you did last go-around.

■ Individual files for children, family pictures, information on fraternal or community organizations, and so on should be kept apart from other files. Make your system simple or fancy—but make it. Avoid, however, one so complex that it takes more time to figure out than the minutes saved in using it.

■ RECORDS OF FAMILY DOCUMENTS SAVE TIME AND MONEY ————————————————————

Keeping family records is not only a time saver but can result in collecting money and benefits otherwise lost or overlooked. American banks, for example, have millions of unclaimed depositors' dollars in misplaced or forgotten accounts.

Under abandoned-property laws, unclaimed policies, accounts, and other valuables are returned to states after a minimum period. Your family might be one that could have recovered rightful property if you had kept papers in order. A separate essential facts and figures record makes claim establishment quick and easy.

■ If you keep records in a bank safe-deposit box, make xerox copies with identification dated on issuers and numbers. This makes tracing quick and easy. If you need to collect Social Security or other health, pension, or compensation benefits, having numbers saves untold hours—often without going to the original.

■ Licenses, draft papers, mortgage agreements, and contracts are valuable. If they are ever lost or misplaced, you will bless the day you made a record of the numbers and other data and kept this separately in an unassailable, fire-resistant home container.

Get Your Family's Help

Setting up family files, get everybody's help. Note car key numbers, bank account numbers, marriage certificate dates, Social Security numbers, military record serial numbers, organization memberships, and so on.

Use as a checklist. When you find documents missing, write for notarized copies and get replacement certificates or lost-instrument bonds for missing securities. Throw nothing away until checking with your insurance agent, bank, lawyer, accountant, or other authority. Then get rid of the unnecessary, pronto.

▪ SAVING TIME WHILE MOVING

Moving is a time-consuming home trauma for many families. Allied Van Lines, purportedly the world's largest household goods mover, annually transporting possessions of thousands of families, suggests the following pointers to make moving easier and faster:

▪ *Make floor plans of your new home before moving.* Give these to your moving people, saving time and energy placing major items at journey's end. Tape a letter, about where you want each item to go, to each box.

▪ *Let moving men do your packing.* They know how to protect stemware, bone china, and other fragile valuable goods to come through unscathed. Time and worry savings alone are usually worth the professional knowledge cost.

▪ *Take advantage of special wardrobe containers movers send in advance.* Clothes can be hung by you directly from closets into wardrobes and then back into new closets. There is no fuss, mess, or time wasted.

■ *If you and your family undertake packing chores yourselves,
be sure to list carton contents.* An easy system is to assign a
number to each box and then list the corresponding contents on
a sheet of paper. Avoid rummaging in pots, pans, and barrels
when you want something quickly.

• Chapter Twenty-six • • • • •

More Household Tasks

Herewith a round-up of tips on this vital time-saving activity.

• THE KITCHEN ───────────────────

The kitchen is the heart of most homes and the place for the majority of continuing tasks that take so much time and contribute so much to family welfare. Experts say one-third of most housekeeping time is spent in meal preparation and cleanup. Hence, if you can save as much as six or seven hours weekly by new and improved methods, rearranging utensils and equipment and fully employing the many new ideas now circulating, you have gained a prize.

The availability of pre-prepared foods—needing only microwave heating—has cut kitchen time even more. Improving your existing setup with better organization; added storage units; portable, easily installed shelves; additional work counters; and so on can help until that day—if ever—when your "dream kitchen" becomes more than just a dream.

Start by clearing the deck. Put away all appliances unless you really make waffles every day. Hang pots and pans; they make great decorations. Stop stuffing those use-some-day grocery bags between refrigerator and stove; they only attract bugs and more bags. Unless you are going to file and use recipes, don't clip them.

Organizing the Kitchen

Whatever your kitchen size, make certain major equipment is fairly close together, particularly the sink and the stove. It is between these two that most trips are made. Allow enough space to work efficiently without crowding, but not so much you are marathon running.

■ *Work Heights:* All work surface heights should be comfortable for tasks at area where done. You should be able to stand or sit in a relaxed position, working without stooping or raising your hands above elbow height. Kitchen sinks, for example, are frequently too low for comfort. Because it is difficult to change them, try adjusting your work chair height so that elbow relation to work surface remains constant, standing or sitting.

■ *Sitting Versus Standing:* You can sit when you are cleaning up, preparing things, and so on if everything needed is at hand. Standing takes 14 percent more energy. Although you might *feel* you are getting things done faster by standing, sitting gives you greater efficiency for longer periods. Sit well back with your feet flat on the floor and the upper part of your body forming a straight line. Bend forward from the hips, not the waist.

■ *Arranging Work Surfaces:* Your work counter shouldn't be so wide that you must stretch to reach the back of it. Set up work surfaces so that you can reach sixteen inches from each elbow in all directions. In many cases, a pull-out counter, lapboard, or portable table brings work closer to you, an important time and energy saver. Remove everything from kitchen counters not used often. It is easier to clean with fewer items on top, invariably getting dirty.

■ *"Where Do I Use This Article Most Often?":* Store as closely to where they are used as possible. Throw or give away rarely used accumulated single-purpose gadgets. Chances are that with a bit of drawer, and soul, searching, you can gather a boxful.

■ *Portable Tables and Carriers:* These provide extra work space and are useful for assembling and transporting dishes, food, groceries, cleaning supplies, and other items.

Storage and Preparation ——————————

Saving time in food storage and preparation requires both equipment and a system. The following are some ideas in this regard:

■ *Incoming Supplies:* Make sure that new supplies can be stored efficiently with a minimum of handling. Six-inch deep shelves are adequate for almost all supermarket items. Line up supplies in single file, eliminating the need to remove front items when looking for something.

Some people like the color and convenience of open-shelved canned and packaged food. Others call them distracting dust collectors. Ask yourself which you prefer: time spent opening and closing doors or time spent dusting. Prefer closed? Consider convenient metal or glass sliding doors, or accordion folds.

■ *Refrigerator Near Door:* If possible, locate the refrigerator near an outside-access door. Have an unloading surface nearby, where you can set things down while you take out and store purchases.

■ *Shelves Set at Various Clearances:* Bowls take space; cups need little. Few homes have adequate shelves, but kitchen reorganizers often start installing adjustables. Attach hooks under shelves to hang cups. Use vertical dish racks and glide-aways. Seek practicality rather than uniformity.

■ *Storing Table Needs: Condiments, napkins, breakfast cereals, extra silver, and so on* should be within arm's length on shelves above the dining table to eliminate mealtime kitchen trips.

■ *Lazy Susans:* Circular shelves revolving around an upright pole provide space otherwise wasted. They enable you to reach such large utensils as mixing bowls by turning shelves instead of rummaging in cupboard depths. Also practical is a series of upright partitions built into a cupboard for storing platters and trays vertically, for free pulling rather than lifting out over other objects.

■ *Less Accessible Shelves:* Store everydays on adjustable, open shelves between kitchen and dining areas.

■ *Sliding Trays:* These placed in deep drawers make minor items reachable.

■ *Unnecessary Motions:* Keep knives on racks on walls; pans suspended over the stove. With such strategies as these you avoid stooping and other unnecessary motions. This also encourages keeping such items spotless.

A Mixing Center

This is essential to any time-saving kitchen. Keep frequently used tools within arm's reach. Files above the mixing center can hold pie plates and cake tins vertically. Adjustable upright stands make pan selection easy without groping through stacks. Store baking equipment and needed utensils close together. Gravity feed bins to hold sugar and flour mean that the oldest ingredients, at bottom, are drawn first, keeping everything its freshest. Keep measuring spoons in every canister.

The Sink and Food Preparation —————————

■ Pans and tools used in preparing food with water should be stored within sink reach.

■ The cabinet under the sink can hold dish towels for easy access.

■ Store seldom-used pans as far out of the way as possible.

■ In suburban homes, a disposal is a real help. If you lack one, put a special bin under the sink to hold a quickly dispensible plastic bag.

■ Vegetable and fruit preparations should center around the sink. Vegetables that don't need refrigeration should always be stored close to the sink.

Cooking and Serving ——————————————

Have shelves with needed items at the cooking location—with an adjoining cabinet with utensils and dishes. Keep roasters, casseroles, and other bakeware close to the stove. Use easily cleaned adjustable file dividers to hold items upright. A pot-lid rack eliminates rummaging. Storing crackers and ready-to-eat cereals in stove side bins helps keep them fresh because bins are often warm.

Microwaves ——————————————————————

Your microwave can be, in Toshiba's words, "Your passport to a versatile and innovative cooking experience." It is also a great time saver. The range of foods simply and easily made with microwaves is growing. Many are now offered specifically for this device, packed in single or double servings to save even more preparation, serving, and cleanup time and effort.

Dishwashing ———————————————

No matter what your kitchen size, a dishwasher can save many, many minutes and ensure sparkling cleanliness. Also bear in mind the wide array of environmentally acceptable, recyclable paper products that save washing dishes.

Table Setting ———————————————

Busy homemakers with few minutes to spare know how every minute saved *before* serving is worth twice its number afterward. The following are some tips to help you employ this strategy:

■ *Always use a tray or cart when setting or clearing a table.* Make sure it is not employed for anything else; time savings will be lost. Store china used most frequently on lower pantry or kitchen shelves. Easily wiped plastic placemats eliminate table-cloth laundering.

■ *When setting a table, stand close to it.* This allows you to place most things on it without having to walk around it an undue amount. One trip around to arrange glasses and napkins carried on tray or cart should be sufficient. Use cart with hotplate attachments. An entire meal can be brought to the table at once with dishes placed on the lower portion of the cart.

■ SAVING TIME IN CLEANING ———————

No household activity offers more time-saving tricks than cleaning. It is estimated that the average family spends up to seventeen hours weekly in vacuuming, keeping mirrors and windows spotless, dusting furniture, polishing floors, and other household cleanups. Yet, many people who have the latest wonder appli-

ances squander minutes and footwork by using them ineffi-
ciently. In the home, as in industry, the essence of efficiency is to
preposition appliances within easy reach; make every move do
double duty. The Rutgers University Extension Serve/New Jersey checked some 300 homemakers to simplify regular chores.
They were, on average, able to effect a 41-percent time and 56-
percent "mileage" saving in household cleaning.

Learning to clean your home the easy way doesn't mean you
are lazy; it means you are employing the same techniques and
approaches covered in this book for the business world. The
following are some examples of this principle:

■ *Basic Procedure:* Reread instruction booklets for every appliance you own, or telephone makers for demonstration locales.
Leading firms report that relatively few take advantage of this
service, which can be highly useful.
■ *Supplies:* Follow the system hotels have found most effective.
Always group cleaning things in a storage basket or cart, and
keep basic cleaning supplies in *each* bathroom and kitchen.
■ *A Large Apron With Several Big Pockets:* Carpenter and
gardener varieties are good. As you go about your cleaning, pick
up small misplaced objects and "file them" in the apron. Whenever you reach a designated place, check the appropriate pocket
and drop off the item. This eliminates many steps and beats
making piles for distribution. *Tip:* Getting the family to restore
things where they belong, as suggested earlier, is an even better
minute-minder.

■ WINDOWS

The University of California, Los Angeles, extensively tested
washing methods for a 72-inch window; then reported: Using a
double pail or two joint pails, one with warm water and soap, the
other with rinse and cloths for washing, drying, and polishing

required 3.52 minutes. Using clear water and newspapers for drying took 2.3 minutes. Using *Glass Wax* and a cloth took 3.45 minutes. A patented spray preparation and polishing cloths took 3.5 minutes. Ammonia and a sponge squeegee favored as the least time and energy consuming. *Another idea:* Wearing old cotton gloves lets you clean and dry corners easily with the fingertips, but first apply hand lotion to the fingers.

■ YOUR VACUUM CLEANER ───────

Almost every home today has one, but many don't take advantage of all of the time-saving tasks this appliance can perform. They fail to use the vacuum properly or make use of all of its attachments.

■ *Use a dusting brush* for woodwork, walls, furniture, lamp shades, pictures, and even reflectors. This eliminates bending, prevents dust from recirculating, and gets into hidden crevices.
■ *Don't cart ashtrays.* Use one light vacuum touch.
■ *Eliminate dust in high places.* With cleaner extensions, regularly dust high windows, doors, and picture frames, with no more scrub brushes or stretching.
■ *Don't lift out heavy drawers for cleaning.* First, empty their contents. Then, one vacuum pass clears the dust. Stooping and bending take a lot of time and effort. Crevice tools work just as well in drawing out dust and crumbs from ovens and other difficult-to-get-at locations.

■ SILVER ─────────────────

Polish metal jewelry when doing silverware. For more frequent cleaning, use a chemically processed cloth. Rub silver to a shine with soft flannels, one in each hand for speed. An old toothbrush cleans hard-to-get-out spots.

■ *Consider stainless steel flatware instead of silver.* Stainless steel requires no polishing or special cleaning. Chrome-plated hollowware serves the same purpose.

■ You can also boil silver dinnerware in a vinegar solution (2 tbsp./gallon) to remove tarnish. Don't boil knives, though; there is often glue in the handles.

■ BEDMAKING

There are many good suggestions on improving bedmaking. Mitered-corner contour sheets can save half your bedmaking time, and cost no more than others of comparable quality.

■ Sew colored labels on sheet corners so that you can tell at a glance if they are singles or doubles. Keep same-set sheets and pillowcases together, rather than in different piles, to save handling.

■ In bedmaking, completely make the upper left-hand corner, from bottom sheet to pillow and spread. Then throw the loose portion across bed. At the lower left, anchor bottom sheet and other bedding in the proper order. Proceed to the lower right and anchor, making certain everything is smooth. Finally, finish the job at the upper right.

■ If you don't have mitered contour sheets, make hospital corners, tucking sheets in smoothly and evenly under the mattress. Consider a bed on rollers, which is easy to pull out and push back without lifting.

■ Abolish bedspreads altogether. With a wide range of colorful sheets now available, beds look well-dressed without spreads.

▪ Conclusion: ▪ ▪ ▪ ▪ ▪ ▪ ▪ ▪ ▪ ▪

Using the Time You Gain

Picture the scene: A group of harried business types pulls up to a drive-through window sign that reads, Time "Is" Us. They place their urgent orders. "Can I get a spare minute?" says one. "Give me a couple of hours" asks the second. "Could I have 'till tomorrow morning?" pleads the third.

The time they seek might not be as available as the play things kiddies and parents can shop for at Toys "R" Us, but the desirability is fully as great—if not greater.

My hope in these pages has been to give you ways to gain some of the precious minutes that can add up to an hour—or more—each day, and to offer you my own storeful of goodies you can adapt; not like a child with a new toy, but with a technique or two you can use for a lifetime.

It has not been my objective in this work to try to outline all of the things you can do with the time you save. Suffice it to say that the very fact that you bought or borrowed this book, and have read this far, provides ample evidence that you want to gain that extra hour every day because there are so many things you want to do "if you only had the time."

■ SOME SUGGESTIONS TO SPUR YOU ON

Try listing all of the things you like to do and have been wanting to do for so long: where you would *travel,* and how; what you would *read; recreation* you would seek; and *useful activities* you might be able to undertake. Then note the time you would like to devote to these activities—and begin to build your own "time bank" of an hour, day, week, month, or more.

Explains Godfrey M. Lebhar in *The Use of Time:* If you make up a pretty complete list of things you'd like to do, you'll find *you can enjoy many of them now* with the time saved this week, next week, and in the months ahead. The more complete and detailed the list and the more hours you gain, the more things you will find you can do right now because you have the time.

Obviously, you'll not be able to achieve as much in the salvaged hours as you could if all your time were your own. But that's not the point. It's what can be done now and tomorrow with the gainable hours within your reach.

Some will feel too young to begin—sensing a lifetime ahead; others too old to change. But, time-thrift is never too late for adoption. It will never be too late to spend your time more wisely as long as you have any time to spend at all . . . indeed, the less time you figure you have left, the more you may profit, relatively speaking, by utilizing it carefully. On the reverse, if you feel you are too young, you'll find it even more important to manage your time, for then you'll get the most out of it during your maximum years.

My good wishes to you all the way!

▪ WHERE TO LEARN MORE ─────────────

Obviously, as numerous as my tips and techniques have been, they are only the beginning. There is far more available: an entire, burgeoning time-management industry with no shortage of firms offering public seminars and private consultations. The following is a selection of recommended consultants, offering many courses on personal time management for you, your family, and your staff.

COURSE	AUTHOR	SOURCE
New Time Management Methods	R. Alec MacKenzie	*Dartnell* 4660 Ravenswood Ave. Chicago, IL 60640-4595 (800-621-5463)
Time Power Seminars	Charles R. Hobbs	*Hobbs Corporation* 4505 S. Wasatch Blvd. Salt Lake City, UT 84124-4757 (800-332-9929)
The New Time Management	Dr. Merrill Douglass Dr. Larry Baker	*Nightingale-Conant Corp.* 7300 N. LeHigh Ave. Chicago, IL 60648 (800-323-5552)
Time Management Center	Dr. Larry Baker	1590 Woodlake Dr. Chesterfield, MO 63017 (314-576-9995)
Time Mastery Seminars	Steffen-Steffen & Associates	52 Glenbrook Rd. Stamford, CT 06906 (800-831-0946)
Dale Carnegie Training	Dale Carnegie Training	100 E. 42nd St. New York, NY 10017 (212-986-0054)
Time Masters Institute for Personal Excellence	Todd L. Pearson	776 South 980 East Pleasant Grove, UT 84062 (801-785-1105)
Franklin International Institute	Hyrum W. Smith, Board Chairman	2640 Decker Lake Blvd. Salt Lake City, UT 84119 (800-767-1776)

▪ Index ▪ ▪ ▪ ▪ ▪ ▪ ▪ ▪ ▪ ▪ ▪ ▪ ▪

DOUGHBOY WAR

The American Expeditionary Force
in World War I

Edited by
James H. Hallas

STACKPOLE
BOOKS

Published in paperback in 2009 by
STACKPOLE BOOKS
5067 Ritter Road
Mechanicsburg, PA 17055
www.stackpolebooks.com

Cover design by Tracy Patterson

Printed in the United States of America

10 9 8 7 6 5 4 3 2 1

ISBN 0-8117-3467-6 (Stackpole paperback)
ISBN 978-0-8117-3467-7 (Stackpole paperback)

The Library of Congress has cataloged the hardcover edition as follows:

Hallas, James H.
    Doughboy War : the American Expeditionary Force in World War I / James H. Hallas
    Includes bibliographical references and index.
    ISBN 1-55587-855-5 (alk. paper)
    1. World War, 1914–1918—United States. 2. World War, 1914–1918—Personal narratives, American. I. Title.
D570.H25   1999
940.3'73—dc221   99-28754

DOUGHBOY WAR

The Stackpole Military History Series

Contents

Where the Americans Fought in France

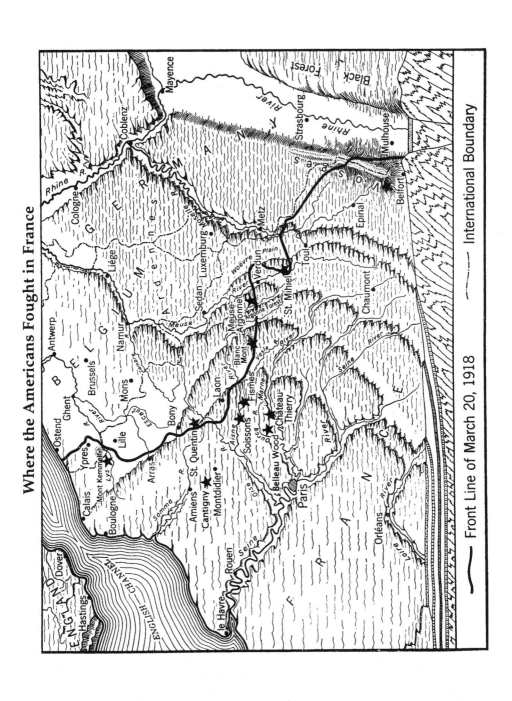

—— Front Line of March 20, 1918   ----- International Boundary

Introduction

Why write about them now?

They are gone and largely forgotten, those once jaunty young men with the quaint dishpan helmets, the spiral puttees, and high-collared wool tunics. The songs they sang, the weapons they used—their very concept of the world—are mere curiosities to most of us today.

But they were so American! A latter-day historian referred to them as "the fierce lambs." Fierce they certainly were; their combat record brooks no dispute. And yes, they were lambs, their lack of sophistication and worldliness sometimes humorous, often touching and sometimes sad and a bit pathetic. They were farmers and mill workers, students and clerks, men whose roots went back to the original 13 colonies and men who were barely off the boat from Europe and had yet to master the English language. Few in the ranks were well educated, a surprising number (by today's standards, at least) were illiterate.

Nearly 5 million Americans served in the armed forces during World War I—the largest fighting force the country had ever seen. Some 2 million of them served in Europe where U.S. presidents had traditionally promised never to interfere. Nearly 80,000 of them died there.

They went because they had to go, most of them; because they were expected to go; and many because they wanted to go. They went to save France, to repay LaFayette, to skin the Kaiser or just, as one Marine veteran recalled, "to see what all the noise was about."

Of course they were innocents. So was their country.

When the United States entered the war in the spring of 1917, the standing army numbered less than 130,000 men—this at a time when millions were engaged on the Western Front. The largest organization in the U.S. Army at the time was the regiment—a unit numbering some 2,000 men. The military owned 55 aircraft, of which General John J. Pershing, the soon-to-be commander of the American Expeditionary Force (A.E.F.), recalled, "51 were obsolete and the other 4 obsolescent." There were not enough machine guns, not enough artillery pieces, not enough uniforms, not enough ships to transport an army to Europe.

No wonder the Germans scoffed.

And yet the U.S. contribution did ultimately save the Allied cause. It had been a near thing. The French had come close to collapse in 1917 and the British were hard pressed. But the flood of American manpower arriving in France in 1918 erased any hope Germany had for outright victory.

Two out of every three American soldiers who reached France took part in battle. A total of 2,084,000 U.S. soldiers reached France. Of these, 1,390,000 saw active service in the front lines. Forty-two American divisions reached France before war's end. Of these, 29 took part in active combat service. The rest were used for replacements or arrived as the hostilities ended.

The places they fought, many of them, would be spoken of with reverence for years afterward in American Legion Halls, at Memorial Day Parades, by Gold Star Mothers, and in the mills and on the farms, on city streets, and in every corner of America they called home: the Marne, Soissons, Belleau Wood, the Vesle, the Hindenburg Line, St. Mihiel, the Argonne . . . always "the Argonne."

The following pages do not touch on the "romance" of the air war—if incineration thousands of feet above mother earth can be considered romantic. Rather, it is the story of the ground soldier— the combat infantryman, the artilleryman, the engineer, who slept in the rain, ate corned beef from a can, and fervently hoped the next German artillery shell would fall far from his personal funk hole.

A few of the participants became legends: Sergeant Alvin York, the conscientious objector turned warrior who earned a Medal of Honor; Marine Sergeant Dan Daley, who rose up out of the wheat at Belleau Wood, turned to his mates, too many of whom had only a brief time left on this earth, and cried, "Come on you sons of bitches! Do you want to live forever?"; and Ulysses Alexander, whose regiment of the 3rd Division stood on the shore of the Marne River like a rock and shattered one of the last great German attacks of the war.

The bulk of them just did what they were told and tried to stay alive. Most of them found that war was nothing like what they expected.

The English called them Sammies, at first, a play on Uncle Sam, but the American soldiers never took to the name. Some called them Yanks. But they have gone down in time as "the doughboys."

Perhaps, even now, at this late date, they have something to teach us about what it means to be an American.

This was their war.

CHAPTER 1

War

*I*t was 8:20 P.M. Monday, April 2, 1917. A light rain was falling in Washington as President Woodrow Wilson ducked into a waiting car and set out toward Capitol Hill, a cavalry escort clattering protectively alongside. As of that early spring evening, Europe had been at war for over two and a half years. Millions had been killed or maimed. Now, in a few moments, Wilson intended to ask Congress to commit the United States to the European abattoir.

The decision had not come easily. From the start of the great conflagration in Europe in the summer of 1914—the inevitable result of years of rivalries and entangling alliances—Wilson had urged the United States to remain neutral in both heart and deed. Isolationist sentiment had prevailed at first, reinforced by what one historian termed "134 years of studious disengagement from the affairs of Europe."[1] But as the months passed and the war in Europe settled into a stalemate of mud and blood on the Western Front, neutrality became more and more problematic. Lucrative U.S. trade with the Allies, clever British propaganda, the seeming brutality of German submarine warfare, the natural ties of blood and national origin, all contrived to impel American sympathies toward the Allies.

As 1917 arrived, relations with Germany deteriorated further with the German announcement that unrestricted submarine warfare—halted less than a year earlier due to U.S. protests—would be resumed. Wilson broke diplomatic relations with Germany in early February. Then came the revelation that the German foreign minister had proposed a treaty with Mexico to come into the war on the German side should the United States join the Allies. In March, three U.S. ships were torpedoed as German submarines once again began to take their toll. Anti-German fever swept the country. And now Wilson, a one-time college professor who only five months before had narrowly won re-election on promises of peace, was about to ask for war.

He arrived to find many of the Congressmen wearing or carrying small

American flags. "The world must be made safe for democracy," he told them. He asked the nation to "accept the status of belligerent which has . . . been thrust upon it . . . [and] to exert all its power and employ all its resources to bring the Government of the German Empire to terms and end the war." And finally, "To such a task we can dedicate our lives and our fortunes, everything that we are and everything we have, with the pride of those who know that the day has come when America is privileged to spend her blood and her might for the principles that gave her birth and happiness and the peace which she has treasured. God helping her, she can do no other."

Congress gave him a standing ovation.

"Think of what it was they were applauding," Wilson remarked to his secretary as they rode back to the White House. "My message today was a message of death for our young men. How strange it seems to applaud that."[2]

Four days later, Congress formally approved a declaration of war.

●

The evening of April 2nd I had accepted an invitation to dine and go to the opera in New York City. Our party occupied a box on the right-hand side of the stage, about halfway to the front. The opera was "Canterbury Pilgrims," by DeKoven, with a German cast. During the entr'acte many of the men in the audience rushed out to Seventh Avenue to buy newspapers. There was an "Extra," reporting that the President had asked Congress for a declaration of war. This newspaper, the New York *Evening Telegram*, was then printed in pink. It was the most unusual sight, looking down from our box, to see every fourth or fifth person sitting in the orchestra, "dressed to kill," (for in those days no one would have thought of going to the opera without the man wearing a dress suit and the woman in a low-necked gown), reading a pink newspaper! At the end of the next act, the leading soprano, Margarete Ober, a German, fainted dead away.

After the opera was over the curtain went up again. The audience all stood, the entire cast appeared, and led by them the audience joined in singing the "Star-Spangled Banner." It was impressive and moving.

Congress did not delay in declaring war. From then on it was only a question of time as to how and where and when those of my age would serve. We knew nothing of the mutinies in the French army, the result of the bloody failure of the French Commander-in-Chief Neville's offensive. We were full of hope and enthusiasm.[3]

—*Robert W. Kean*
New York

I happened to be in Boston that day [war was declared] and while walking up Washington Street saw a terrific mob of people in front of the *Boston Globe* office, reading the bulletins.

In the crowd in front of the *Globe* office, many people were expressing their thoughts, and from the consensus I heard, they were one hundred percent behind our president. It was said that the sinking of the *Lusitania*[4] was the last straw that led us into war; also that the French had their backs right up against the wall and needed our help. Remembering our history and how General Lafayette came to our assistance during those dark days of our first fight for independence, perhaps we had an obligation to our sister republic, the Republic of France.

Papers were selling like hotcakes. On my way home I bought an *Evening Globe* and as I sat in the surface car I started reading the paper and I observed that everybody else was doing the same.[5]

—*Connell Albertine*
Massachusetts

When the U.S. entered the World War I knew I would be called from reserve. But without waiting I reenlisted—in fact, I joined up that same day, April 6, 1917.

All of the men at the ranch wanted to go along with me. Half of them barely knew where the war was and didn't give a damn.

We caught the train to Waco, and soon as we got there all of us, 32-strong, trotted right up to the recruiting office and took the oath. That was sure one happy crowd.[6]

—*Dan Edwards*
Texas

I quit my job at the steel mill and went to see Mr. George Hainey, chief electrician, and Mr. Elliott Lewis, assistant chief electrician, and told them I was enlisting in the Navy. They wished me good luck and assured me my job would be waiting for me when I got back and I thanked them. Shook hands with the boys. I was the first from the line gang to enlist. Next morning I went to Cleveland and stayed for three days to get away from home until Mother stopped her crying.

I went and registered to be drafted. Some of my friends were there and I asked them to come with me and join the Navy, but none wanted to, so I went alone. The first man I met was a U.S. Marine. He sure looked fine, too. He showed me the Marines' posters, first to fight on land or sea, and I was so impressed that I signed. He was a fast worker all right. I got back home and told Mother and Dad that

I had enlisted and nobody was going to stop me. It was like a funeral around home.[7]

—*Joseph E. Rendinell*
Pennsylvania

On the 14th of April I made my decision to enter the Marine Corps, at which time I'd learned that I couldn't be an aviator because of faulty eyesight. There wasn't any main recruiting station in Minneapolis, so knowing that I probably couldn't even pass the eye examination for the Marine Corps, I went up to the sub-station and memorized the eye chart which was in plain view in those days with a big capital "A" and a "T" and "F" getting smaller as it went down the column. I then went over to St. Paul, and the recruiting office was on the fourth floor of an office building and one had to get his name in the book in order to get an appointment for a physical examination. That line, to get your name in the book, extended up the office down the hall and down four flights of steps, down on the sidewalk and around the corner—just to give you an idea of the enthusiasm. Now, this was on the 14th of April, eight days after the [declaration of] war. This will just give you an idea of the enthusiasm which the youth of that city at least, and I know from all other cities, responded to the call of arms. It was something that I'm afraid is a thing of the past now (in 1973).[8]

—*Merwin H. Silverthorn*
Minnesota

I was 17, unmarried, of course, and had no responsibilities to hold me back. I felt that I looked old enough to pass a recruiting sergeant and that the call for men was urgent enough to justify me in camouflaging my age by one year. Anyhow, I thought, I can go to France and grow up with the war.

In the midst of the intense recruiting campaign for the National Guard, I was at the theater one night when a call was made for volunteers. During the speech of the recruiting agent, I made up my mind. He wound up by asking all the men willing to serve the country, to see her through her present emergency with rifles in hand, to step upon the stage. As I sat very near to the stage, I was the first to present myself. When I filled out my application, I chose the old New York 69th—because it and I were Irish.

Next morning we recruits of the night before went to the armory. There we were taken in charge; passed through our physical examinations, and five of us were sent to Company K, Captain J.P. Hurley's company. All five of us were young; all about my age, and, when the captain had been called out to look us over by the first sergeant, his eyes traveled up and down our line, and he exclaimed, "What are we getting now, sergeant, a Boy Scout outfit?"[9]

—Corporal Martin J. Hogan
69th New York Regiment

To young enthusiasts, such as we, war consisted of following the flag over a shell torn field, with fixed bayonet. Hadn't we stood for hours gazing at the recruiting posters? We could picture ourselves in the near future as pushing the Hun back from trench to trench, stopping only now and then to cut notches in the stocks of our rifles.[10]

—Justin M. Klingenberger
West Virginia

What strikes me most, I think, is the eagerness of the men to get to France and above all to reach the front. One would think that, after almost four years of war, after the most detailed and realistic accounts of the murderous fighting on the Somme and around Verdun, to say nothing of the day-to-day agony of trench warfare, it would have been all but impossible to get anyone to serve without duress. But it was not so. We and many thousands of others volunteered. Perhaps we were offended by the arrogance of the German U-boat campaign and convinced that Kaiserism must be smashed, once and for all. Possibly we already felt that, in the American interest, Western democracy must not be allowed to go under. But I doubt it. I can hardly remember a single instance of serious discussion of American policy or of larger war issues. We men, most of us young, were simply fascinated by the prospect of adventure and heroism. Most of us, I think, had the feeling that life, if we survived, would run in the familiar, routine channels. Here was our one great chance for excitement and risk. We could not afford to pass it up.[11]

—William L. Langer
Massachusetts

*A*bout 4,000,000 men served in the U.S. Army during World War I— another 800,000 served in the Navy, Marine Corps, and other services. Five out of every 100 American citizens took up arms. New York, Pennsylvania, Illinois, Ohio, and Texas furnished the most troops— 367,864, 297,891, 251,074, 200,293, and 161,065 respectively. The Regular Army numbered only 127,500 officers and men at the start of the war. The largest organization was the 2,000-man regiment—this at a time when whole corps and armies were fighting on the Western Front. More men were needed. The most obvious and immediate pool of manpower were the so-called citizen soldiers—the National Guard, numbering 174,008 men

from every state except Nevada. Some 77,000 of the Guardsmen were
already in federal service, mobilized for duty during the Mexican border
troubles in 1916.

•

The second line of defense, the National Guard, under mobilization
orders since the declaration of war, was called into active service at
twelve noon, July 25, 1917, and mobilized in their respective
armories all over the Union.

On that unforgettable day, at exactly noon, fire bells, whistles,
and sirens were shrieking out their message in multiples of five, for
the alarm call to arms was 5-5-5. Startled people ran into the streets
in wonder, leaving their noonday meals untouched. Such excitement
prevailed, with everybody talking about war, that one would have
got the impression that the enemy was only miles away.

Bidding a hasty farewell to my employer and fellow workers,
my fingers tingling from their earnest handshakes and my ears ringing with "Good luck," "Don't forget to write," and "Bring me back a
German helmet," and the like, I started for the Somerville Armory,
where Companies M and K of the 8th Massachusetts Regiment were
stationed.

The streetcar which I boarded hardly seemed to move. All along
the route we picked up other Guardsmen, who like myself were
answering their country's call. Fares were forgotten, as the conductor, imbued with the spirit of patriotism, thought only of getting us
to the armory as soon as possible.

The bells and sirens were still sounding as we arrived at the
armory. We had to fight our way in as there were hundreds of people milling around on the sidewalk around the wide-open doors,
many of them looking through the windows. Inside the armory
there were many Guardsmen already in uniform and discussing the
situation. I immediately got into my uniform and proceeded to the
drill hall, shaking hands with others of my buddies . . .

How true it was, as someone on the streetcar we were riding on
remarked, "Well, a lot of us will never see the armory or home
again." Of course, each one's chance of coming home was as good as
the next fellow's, so no one gave it much thought.[12]

—Private Connell Albertine
Massachusetts National Guard

I remember looking around the room after my physical examination
and enrollment. Here were the men I was going out with to war.
Larry Williams was playing ragtime on the piano and singing.

Someone told me his name. Everyone was talking and laughing. I felt a little thrill of emotion, and the phrase "comrades-in-arms" came into my head. A year later, on July 19th, Larry was killed by German shellfire on the edge of a thicket at Belleau Woods, and his parents received their telegram from the War Department.

My parents bravely kept their deepest thoughts to themselves, but I can guess now what they were. They had me photographed in my uniform; I didn't see why! I attended a few evening drills at the armory, with my parents watching from the gallery. I learned a few men's names, and then the word came that the Massachusetts Militia was to be called out July 25. I had been living in a mental fog, not thinking of anything, but feeling relieved that there was nothing more to be decided.

The packing up was all Greek to me. I had never seen a gun close to, and I would have called it a cannon offhand. Someone told me to get on a truck piled high with packing boxes, and the truck jounced out of the paddock onto the macadam of Commonwealth Avenue. At the corner of the street stood a man on the sidewalk with a straw hat in his hand. He looked up. It was my father. He smiled, and I saw him still waving his hand as the truck turned the next corner. A great lump came into my throat and I winked back tears.[13]

—Corporal Horatio Rogers
Massachusetts National Guard

The National Guard was to provide 16 divisions, numbered from 26 to 42. To this were added seven Regular Army divisions to be raised by voluntary enlistments. It was not enough. There was only one solution— the draft. Drafted men would be formed into the National Army, which, with the Regulars and the Guard, would comprise the U.S. Army. By war's end, more than three quarters of all troops would have come in through the Selective Service or National Army enlistments. Of every 100 men, 10 were National Guardsmen, 13 were Regulars and 77 belonged to the National Army.

The original plans called for 16 National Army divisions, numbered 76 to 92, to be mobilized and trained at sixteen cantonments, and to be composed of men chosen by the operation of the Selective Service Act from 16 Draft Areas throughout the United States. The first registration, June 5, 1917, covered men ages 21 to 31. The second, on June 5 and August 24, 1918, included those who had turned 21 since the first registration. The third registration, on September 12, 1918, extended the age limits from 18 to 45. When war broke out, the total male population of the United States was about 54,000,000. During the war, about 26,000,000 men were either registered under the Selective Service Act or serving in the armed forces without being registered.

•

A diminutive Italian, Tony Monaco by name, water boy by occupation, presented himself at the Selective Service office early one morning.

A clerk at the desk, his eyes still clouded—their hours of rest were not long in those days—not recognizing the young man as a possible registrant, said: "What can I do for you?"

"Ma name Tony Monaco. In dees countra seex months. Gimme da gun."

Had Tony descended from a passenger on the good ship Mayflower he could scarcely have been more intensely American.

Not all at first blush, however, were able to see their duty. An example of that class was presented by a grocery boy who had driven to the City Hall in his employer's wagon. He had answered all the questions until the clerk asked him if he desired to claim exemption from the draft.

"What's that?" he queried.

"Is there any reason why you shouldn't go to war in case you are called by Uncle Sam?" said the clerk.

"Who the hell would drive the horse?" was the somewhat apprehensive answer.

A photographer wrote to the City Clerk advising him that he would be busy with a June wedding on June 5th and that some other day would have to be set for the registration as he positively could not appear on June 5th.[14]

—*Daniel J. Sweeney*
World War History Committee, Buffalo, New York

Summoned by the "Order of Induction" to appear at our respective local boards, we donned our least desirable suits of clothes and reported at the appointed hour. The assembled group of recruits was put under the supervision of one of their number, selected by the local board chairman, and this important personage was given the title of "district leader." Moving to the point of entertainment, we boarded troop trains while relatives and friends bade us good luck and God-speed. Arriving at Medford, the last stop before Camp Upton, an army officer boarded the train and called on the district leaders to surrender the records of the men of their groups. Upon detrainment at camp we were formed in double rank and answered roll call. There we stood, soldiers, yet still civilians, home and friends behind us and before us we knew not what. Our feelings ranged from drunken hilarity to sober, quiet pondering.[15]

—*Sergeant Francis L. Field*
306th Field Artillery, 77th Division

*C*onstruction of camps to house the hundreds of thousands of new soldiers was turned over to the Cantonment Division. Wooden barracks for the 16 National Army divisions and an equal number of National Guard camps with tents were required. All would soon become household names—Devens in Massachusetts, Dix in New Jersey, Custer in Michigan, Gordon in Georgia, Grant in Illinois, Upton in New York, Meade in Maryland, Lewis in Washington state, and so on.

The magnitude of the effort was staggering—one statistician estimated enough lumber had been used to build a boardwalk an inch thick and 12 inches wide to the moon and halfway back. Inevitably there were problems, but by September the cantonments were two-thirds done with space for over 400,000 draftees. It was one of the great achievements of the war mobilization effort.

•

The troop train on which I rode to Camp Funston, Kansas, April 29, 1918, was crowded. There were several hundred of us aboard and no time was lost in formal introductions. While passing through towns along the way, heads and shoulders were thrust out of car windows and loud yells greeted those townspeople who went to the trouble to go down to see the "boys pass through."

Inside the coaches "crap" games were in full blast and drinks were freely passed around. Most of us were asleep when we arrived at Camp Funston near Fort Riley, Kansas, at 1 o'clock at night. A sergeant came aboard and ordered us to "hit the cinders" pronto. Outside we formed a column four abreast and, directed by the sergeant, marched to our barracks where we were assigned cots and then told to hit the hay "right now." In 15 minutes the lights were turned out and we were ordered to go to sleep.[16]

—*Corporal Asa B. Callaway*
353rd Infantry, 89th Division

Nothing more unmilitary in appearance can be imagined than the long columns of civilian-clad men, each with paper-wrapped or rope-tied bundle, or valise, or suitcase, which wound from train to barracks. The members of most draft boards flaunted banners and signs proclaiming their identity and often expressing the familiar legend: "To Hell with the Kaiser." Some looked very dejected; a few were boisterously drunk; the great majority accepted the situation with that practical American stoicism which is equally far removed from enthusiasm or despair. These men had not chosen war, but since the job was inevitable, they were going to see it through.[17]

—*Captain L. Wardlaw Miles*
308th Infantry, 77th Division

It was a Wednesday afternoon at 3 P.M. and raining like mad when our train pulled into a place called Camp Upton. They had a band of music at the station playing the *Star Spangled Banner* to get us to feel like fighting. It did—the way they played it. A few roughnecks from the regulars received us. The sergeant gave us a command: "Column of twos. Forward, MARCH!" But we bums stood like a bunch of dopes, for we didn't know what a column of twos meant. All the way to the barracks, the one-month veterans were saying: "Wait till you get the needle."[18]

—*Anonymous Recruit*
305th Infantry, 77th Division

Then came the calling of the roll and further discrepancies. Certain men would answer with alacrity to each of three names called, or stand silent while their own name was called as many times. As a typical instance, a man in M Company had answered "here" at every formation for nearly a week before he was discovered to have been left at home on account of illness and never to have reported at camp. Another ghost was laid by the following dialogue:
   "Morra, T."
   "Here."
   "Morra, R."
   [From the same individual] "Here."
   "Does your first name begin with a T or an R?"
   "Yes, sir."
   "Is your first name Rocco?"
   "Yes, sir."
   "What is your first name?"
   "Tony."
   And all in perfectly good faith.[19]

—*Captain W. Kerr Rainsford*
307th Infantry, 77th Division

We were marched off over rough uncompleted roads thick with dust, around heaps of building material, over spur-tracks of the railroad, past half-constructed barracks, all to the tune of carpenters' hammers which clattered with machine-gun-like precision. Reaching a nearly completed barrack, we were halted, and entering were assigned our bunks. To each man was issued his first army equipment, consisted of two olive-drab blankets, a bed-sack to be filled with straw, and a mess-kit. We were then introduced to army "chow" in a manner which became painfully familiar to us. Passing along an over tedious mess line to a counter, and armed with our newly acquired eating utensils, which we juggled with a difficulty born of inexperience, we made the acquaintance of army beans and that fluid which some demented people have called coffee. The [metal] coffee-cup gave us more trouble, perhaps, than anything else, for it seemed to absorb all the heat of its contents. It became so hot that it would have blistered our lips had we attempted to drink from it. When it cooled off a bit we confidently grasped the handle, hoping to wash down a few beans, only to find, too late, that the handle catch was loose, and that the entire content was being swiftly dumped into the beans. Falling into another line, we poured what had now become bean soup into a garbage can and completed our first mess by washing our mess-kits in soapy hot water and rinsing them in clear cold water. Thus endeth the first lesson.[20]

—Sergeant Francis Field
306th Field Artillery, 77th Division

The barracks (there were five of them, strung out in two parallel rows) were long, unpainted, shed-like affairs built on wooden piles which lifted them two or three feet from the ground. In the center of each side was a door, reached by a flight of steps, and within, directly between the doors, a large pot-bellied coal stove stood in a shallow box of ashes. There were electric lights and by day the interior was well-lighted by a row of windows which occupied nearly half the wall space from the height of one's waist to the eaves. Our cots were lined up, all the way around the walls, side by side with narrow spaces between. The mess hall was exactly the same kind of building, with one end fenced off by a counter, behind which were stoves. The company office occupied a separate room in the end of one of the barracks. Our company street—the lane between the two rows of barracks—was an expanse of clay.

We had for breakfast a cereal: oatmeal, cornflakes, or grape nuts, with sausages, fried potatoes, or (occasionally) pancakes with syrup. Milk was always the evaporated variety, watered; I do not remember seeing fresh milk served at any time that I was in the army. For dinner we had beef stew, or fried beefsteak, or beans baked in a shallow pan with bacon and tomato sauce; for dessert, bread pudding, rice pudding, stewed prunes, or dried fruit cobbler (pie made in a large baker with only a top crust). Supper was much like dinner, with

macaroni and cheese a frequent dish. Coffee was served with all
three meals, and we had all the sugar we wished at a time when the
civilian population was being pretty severely stinted.[21]

—*Corporal Frederick A. Pottle*
Evacuation Hospital #8

*T*he new arrivals received still another physical exam. All were also
inoculated with smallpox, typhoid, and paratyphoid vaccines—the
infamous "needle." For many, it was the first inoculation of their lives.

•

We reached a series of low shed-like buildings, and were told to sit
down near our places in the line and wait until they were ready for
us inside.

"What are they going to do to us?" asked one of the crowd of a
passing recruit.

"Do to you, man? This is where you get the 'shot.' It almost kills
you, that's all."

And, with that cheering information, which was passed religiously from one end of the column to the other, we tarried at the
threshold of what we later learned to designate "the mill."

After half an hour of waiting, an officer stepped to the doorway
and called to our group to get on our feet and file in. As we passed
through the door, we were directed to the right and left and ordered
to disrobe. As fast as a man got his clothes off, he was hustled into
another line of nude humanity, and the parade around the "mill"
was on.[22]

—*Corporal Earl B. Searcy*
311th Infantry, 78th Division

As each man entered the medical barracks a number was stamped on
his bare arm—much like the branding of cattle we thought—and
passing into the first room, where a line of doctors awaited to receive
him, he was thoroughly examined. Eyes, ears, heart, lungs, feet,
throat, teeth and other portions of the anatomy all received the careful consideration of the physicians. Recording the location of scars
and other physical marks followed, and then we were placed in the
hands—none too tender—of the vaccinating surgeon, who passed us
on to his partner in crime, the inoculating surgeon. The inoculation
was a hypodermic injection of typhoid anti-toxin, administered three
times, with ten-day intervals. Few of us will forget the effects of the
"needle" or the violent dislike we developed for it.[23]

—*Sergeant Francis Field*
306th Field Artillery, 77th Division

The manner of giving the smallpox vaccine was not attended with any technique. The vaccine came prepared in a glass tube and, as the soldiers passed in line, the tubes were broken and each man was cut across the arm with the jagged glass, inflicting a ragged wound. If the soldier flinched or cried out then he was slashed again for good measure.

Each week after our first appearance we were returned to the infirmary until three shots had been given. I never had any of the diseases which we were supposed not to have, but if the diseases were worse than the preventatives, I am certain I escaped death in its most violent forms.[24]

—Corporal Chris Emmett
359th Infantry, 90th Division

The inspectors concluded the examination by taking our fingerprints (apparently we were to be treated like criminals) and, provided no physical defects were found, we were finally accepted as fit subjects to withstand the privations of military service.

Mustering-in, which took place immediately after the medical examination, consisted of a general survey of the family tree and the opening of an individual service record. We were happy to oblige the army with biographical notes, but completely lost courage when some tired clerk irritably and unfeelingly asked us, "Whom do you want notified in case you're killed?"[25]

—Sergeant Francis Field
306th Field Artillery, 77th Division

There were 12 cages along the wall, screened with chicken wire and with an opening and counter in the front. One man was inside each stall, and as we passed each cage, a bundle of articles was shoved at us; underclothes from one cage and so on, down the line. We were told that we would be allowed 30 minutes to get into uniform and form a company front on "C" Street. It was a mess, as nothing was issued according to size as needed. We were told to trade around for our sizes. The waist of the breeches I received was about 40 inches and I needed 22 inches. The shirt was twice as large as I needed, as were the underclothes. I went to the sergeant in charge, who laughed and said, "See your company tailor." I tried to find someone to trade with to get a couple of items I could use, but even these were too large. I could easily stick my hands inside the fastened canvas leggins. The shoes were of white elk skin and about size eight. I wore size five and a half. The felt hat was so big that I had to fold my ears out to keep it from covering my eyes.

About that time, the whistle sounded, "Fall in." I dashed over to the cage again and demanded another uniform. My request was met with laughter, so I rushed out to get in line. They had already lined and were counting off when I appeared. Sergeant Smith saw me and barked, "You! Front and center!" The entire company was roaring with laughter. I told him that I tried to find a proper sized uniform and that they had just laughed at me. He turned the company over to the other sergeant and took me back to the basement. If one ever heard hell raised, this was it. He sure told them off. An officer in charge came over and he was told about it, too. They tried hard to get me fixed up, but with little success.[26]

—Private Ralph L. Williams
2nd Engineers, 2nd Division

Sept. 20. Some more men came in during the night so that now the building is half full. This morning someone woke me up before daylight blowing on a horn. Everyone had to get up, dress, and get out of doors to answer roll call. After breakfast, we signed some more papers and the doctors gave us another exam. They must have found something wrong with all of us because they "shot" something into our arms. As for me, I felt better before getting the shot than I do now. Spent most of the day picking up cigarette butts around the barracks. Every time I stopped, a man in uniform named Lewis, who seems to have lots of authority, told me to "get busy."

Sept. 21: More men came in today, so that there are nearly a hundred in this one building now. This morning, some of us scrubbed tables in the mess hall until they are nearly worn out, while the rest worked outside the building. After dinner Lt. Foster took us for a long march all around the camp. After that we learned to salute all men in uniform who wear caps and look well dressed. Also to say "Sir" to all of them. I won't be able to do much saluting unless my arm gets better soon.

Oct. 1: Lt. Smith stopped me this afternoon, and asked what I thought the buttons on my coat were for. I asked him what the joke was. Guess there was no joke about it or if there was he couldn't see it, because he got pretty mad and said, "You'll have to get wise to yourself. Keep those buttons buttoned and take some of that junk out of your pockets. You'll get a barrack bag pretty soon that will hold most of it. Stand up straight. Put your hat on the front of your head. Get onto yourself and try to look like a soldier. That's all." When I got away from him I decided that if having one button unbuttoned caused all that trouble, I had better be more careful.[27]

—Anonymous Recruit
303rd Field Artillery, 76th Division

We were at the gates of the camp. The front line was told to go around the building to the left; the back line to the right. It seemed like a good deal of formality, but we adhered to instructions. I was getting along in good shape, as I supposed, when someone tapped me on the shoulder and said: "You're missing all the cigarette butts and cigar stubs. Get them all."

I beheld a corporal whom I hadn't seen before. "What's the big idea, picking up such trash as that?" I queried. "The ground will be covered again before we get around the building."

"Do as you're told!"

There weren't any signs or symptoms of friendliness in the fellow's voice or eyes, so I backed up, and from then on made a better job of it. Before I had made the round, I had enough butts and stubs to supply my grandfather with clippings for a month. I was also beginning to feel a desire to spread someone's nose all over his face.[28]

—*Corporal Earl B. Searcy*
311th Infantry, 78th Division

Most of the officers were very nice to us, but some of the old non-coms gave us hell and told us how dumb we were. Again we began to hear the familiar cry we heard in the Depot Brigade, "Snap into it, and suck up your guts."

Noncom: "Attention. Bring your heels together with a click. Suck up your guts and throw your chest out; that's not your chest." The rookie is trying all he knows how to throw his chest out, but it comes out in the wrong place.

The noncom then explains the position of a soldier at attention, which is: Heels on the same line and as near to each other as the conformation of the man permits. Feet turned out equally and forming an angle of about 45 degrees. Knees straight, without stiffness. Hips level and drawn back slightly; body erect and resting equally on hips; chest lifted and arched; shoulders square and falling equally. Arms and hands hanging naturally, thumb along the seam of the trousers. Head erect and squarely to the front, chin drawn in so that the axis of the head and neck is vertical; eyes straight to the front. Weight of body resting equally on the heels and balls of the feet.

There were only a few uniforms ready, and the men had to drill and work in their civilian clothes and shoes. Some were dressed in overalls, and some in white shirts and collars. In the latter part of November, when the Secretary of War, the Hon. Newton D. Baker, came to camp to review the division, he still found many of the men wearing their summer underclothing, blue overalls, and civilian shoes, and no overcoat as they passed the reviewing stand.[29]

—*Private Rush Young*
318th Infantry, 80th Division

*A*ccording *to the Medical Department of the Army, the average new*
recruit was between 21 and 23 years of age and unmarried. He stood
5′ 7¹/₂″ tall and weighed 141¹/₂ pounds. Seven out of ten of the rookies
arriving at the training camps were draftees. About 31 percent were illiter-
ate. Approximately 18 percent were foreign born, according to later esti-
mates.

Statistics indicate that states from the central section of the country—
Texas, Oklahoma, Kansas, Nebraska, Iowa, Minnesota, and the Dakotas—
provided the healthiest men. Seventy to 80 percent of the draftees from
those states survived both the Selective Service and U.S. Army physical
exams and were accepted for service. Lowest in physical condition were
draftees from the Northeast and the Far West—notably New York, the New
England States and California—where 50 to 59 percent of the candidates
were accepted. Country boys fared better on physical exams than men from
the cities; whites fared better than blacks; and native-born Americans fared
better than immigrants.

•

The officers of the 15th Field Artillery were a very congenial lot.
Most of the detail work was done by the second lieutenants, who
had just come from civilian life. We were all very young—twenty-
three or twenty-four—and in such good physical health that we
could stand nights of no sleep and long hikes. A couple of hours
sleep at any time would put us back into first-rate shape. Most were
recent graduates of Ivy League colleges. Oby Cunningham was Yale
'14, Jim Husted the same; Jim Bruce was Princeton '16; Eddie
LaMarche was Princeton '15; Jack Clark was Amherst '17; Rod
McIntosh was Yale '14; Marsh, our telephone officer, was a recent
graduate of the University of Minnesota; Mike Walsh was Brown '14;
Roger Griswold was Harvard '14; Dick Peabody was Harvard '15, as
was I. Our battalion commander, Major Benjamin M. Bailey, was a
regular army officer as were the three battery captains.[30]

—*Lieutenant Robert W. Kean*
15th Field Artillery, 2nd Division

My own platoon was made up of a gang of the toughest and most
hard-boiled doughboys I ever heard tell of. There were bartenders,
saloon bouncers, ice men, coal miners, dirt farmers, actors, mill
hands and city boys who had growed up in the back alleys and
learned to scrap ever since they were knee high to a duck. They were
mixed up from 'most every country. They could out-swear, out-
drink and out-cuss any crowd of men I have ever knowed. They
sorter looked upon leave-breaking as a divine right. They were

always spoiling to have it out with somebody. They were fighters and that's all about it. If you looked at them sorter sideways for even a second you were in danger of being on the wrong end of a punch. If you didn't drink they kinder regarded you as being ignorant; and if you didn't cuss a blue streak every time you opened your mouth you were considered to be most awful illiterate. A heap of them couldn't talk our own language at all, and any number of them couldn't sign their own names. The only way the captain could get them to larn to write was by telling them they couldn't get their pay unless they could put their signatures to the pay sheets.

I recollect, too we had a couple of farm boys from the South with us. When we were in New York, before sailing, they got their safety razors. They didn't understand them nohow. One of them fixed up his razor and tried to shave with it, but it weren't no good. He looked at it and said: "Anything the government gives you for nothing ain't never no good," and with a sort of disgusted look on his face he threw it away. The other one tried several times without even cutting a hair. Then he threw his away too, and said he "never had no use for the Democrats, now they were in power they had to go and buy razors that wouldn't shave." They were trying to shave with the wax paper on the blades![31]

—Sergeant Alvin York
328th Infantry, 82nd Division

My personal orderly was a French Canadian who had been a cornet player in the orchestra at Keith's in Boston. My horse orderly was a cow puncher from somewhere near Cody, Wyoming. My cook, George the Greek, came from a short order restaurant of which he was the proprietor, in Denver. My sergeant major had been a court stenographer in Rochester, New York. My chauffeur was a mechanic from the Packard factory in Detroit. Another orderly was a farm boy from Iowa. He was only five feet tall, had tried to volunteer, had been turned down on account of his short stature—and then had been drafted! He was the maddest man I ever saw whenever the draft was mentioned.[32]

—Colonel Frederick M. Wise
59th Infantry, 4th Division

I mailed a report to Washington of the religious census of the camp. Seventy-four creeds were protest by the 31,079 officers and men. The Roman Catholics led the list with 10,786 and are followed by 5,624 Methodists, then in order—Baptists, Lutherans and Presbyterians.

The list shows 81 atheists and infidels, 832 Jews, 15 Quakers.

One soldier stated that socialism was his religion. I had never heard of some of the creeds—Golden Rule, Cavantic, and Nazarene.[33]

—*Army Field Clerk Will Judy*
33rd Division

One valuable thing was accomplished during that winter [1917–18] and that was the teaching of English to men of foreign birth. There were thousands of foreigners in Camp Upton, many of whom could speak little or no English when they arrived. The 304th and, indeed, all the artillery regiments, had perhaps fewer than some of the other organizations, but there were enough to make it worthwhile to establish schools. For those men whose commanding officers decided that their ignorance of the language interfered with the proper performance of their military duties, the classes were made compulsory. There were experienced school teachers in the regiment. These men and others, of perhaps less experience but of equal desire to help, took hold of the classes and accomplished remarkable results in overcoming the difficulties, and especially the diffidence, of shy but eager Italians, Greeks and Russian Jews.[34]

—*Chaplain James M. Howard*
304th Field Artillery, 77th Division

We even had a school in "Early English" and 75 men learned to read and write. One G Company man persistently cut classes. A noncom was sent to bring him in, but failed to do so. I sought him out, and on his own confession that he couldn't write and could barely read, gave him a 15-minute talk on the value of an education. It was a fine talk. I waited for a reply. "Hell, Chaplain," he said, "I am going over there to shoot Germans, not to write letters to 'em!"[35]

—*Chaplain Evan A. Edwards*
140th Infantry, 35th Division

We had some very queer characters at Camp Doniphan. One that I especially recall was Haney, known as the "Gold Brick." Haney was from somewhere along the Ozark trail. He was one of those fellows who "didn't know nothing and didn't want to know nothing; didn't never go nowhere and didn't want to go nowhere." If the war could have been won by lying in bed all the time except when busy stowing away a good portion of army grub, Haney would have been a great factor in winning the war. Whenever there was marching to be done he had sore feet or a game leg. Whenever there was digging to be done he had sore arms or a lame back. But I never saw the time when mess call blew that he was not somewhere near the head end of the line with all of his eating apparatus in good repair. We finally got together and conspired to get Haney a discharge on a physical disability certificate, although there was not one thing wrong with him, unless it was hookworm. He was happy to go as we were to get rid of him and he doubtless sits in front of his shack in the Ozarks to this day telling the natives of the wonderful part he took in canning the Kaiser.[36]

—*Captain W.B. MacLean*
130th Field Artillery, 35th Division

The fellow who sat across from me at my squad table used to be called the Chow Hound. He never used a knife or fork to eat. He ate using two tablespoons, just scooping it down with both hands, dribbling down the front of his shirt. I asked him why he didn't use a knife or fork and he said, "Pappy always said, 'If you can't eat it with a spoon, 'tain't fit'n to eat.'" He turned out to be the most decorated man in the company, very religious, and absolutely without fear.[37]

—*Private Ralph L. Williams*
2nd Engineers, 2nd Division

I must not forget to mention a soldier everyone called "General" on account of his being a general nuisance. He was a Russian boy, well-built, a good-looking good-natured kid, but always in hot water, always doing something wrong and the target for many a good-natured jibe.

We were lining up for inspection one day, and while waiting for the inspector were given "At ease!" We were allowed to talk, smoke and move one foot out of position to rest us from standing at attention. General had come into possession of a flashy cigarette case and was proud of it. He took it from his pocket, pressed a button, and enjoyed watching it open with a snap. After a careful survey he selected a cigarette that met his approval. One of the boys said, "Say, General, give me a cigarette!"

"Buy your own cigarettes," snapped General and put the case back in his pocket. He reached for a match, first in one pocket, then in another, then back to the first again. The boys saw what was up, and the General's smile began to fade. They began to pass cigarettes around, and blow smoke in General's face. Finally he asked someone to give him a match.

"Buy your own matches," they chorused. He begged for a light and finally for even a drag, but he got nothing.

General's real name was Marion Stankowick. He was killed in France by a man in his own company named Cox. Cox heard a noise while the men were in the trenches and went wild. He began throwing hand grenades out of the trench and killed poor old General.[38]

—Corporal Carl Noble
60th Infantry, 5th Division

I f the Allies had expected an immediate flood of U.S. troops into the European war, they were sorely disappointed. A trickle of Regulars and National Guardsmen would arrive before the end of 1917, but the vast majority of the hundreds of thousands of draftees and recruits were destined to spend the fall and winter months training in the camps around the U.S. The unvarnished truth was, the United States was woefully unprepared to take an active part in the war. The War College Division on February 27, 1917, had asked the five supply departments of the army how long it would take to obtain supplies for 1,000,000 men. The replies should have been a warning: 9–12 months to procure clothing; 12 months for small arms and equipment, but 30 months to manufacture sufficient field artillery and 18 months to procure the necessary machine guns; estimated delays for other equipment ranged from 6–12 months.

The flood of troops strained the supply of available equipment. A shortage of rifles saw some recruits drilling with wooden sticks. Hand grenades, machine guns, artillery pieces were all in short supply. Indeed, artillery was so scarce that the French would finally supply virtually all of the guns used by the American Expeditionary Force in France.

•

All of us old rookies had visions of being rushed to the firing line with orders to break through, push on to Berlin and capture the Kaiser. We figured they'd shoot us across on the next boat. But we guessed wrong. Instead of sending us to war they sent us to school, to learn how to be soldiers, I guess.[39]

—Lieutenant Sam Woodfill
60th Infantry, 5th Division

Now we had to get up at the sound of reveille. At first it was hard for me to get up at 5:30. It usually took about three minutes to get dressed and fall out on the company street for checking up. It sure was funny when the Top Sergeant would go around and lift up the overcoats of some soldiers and find some of the fellows in their underwear, or as the saying was—"being caught with their pants down." These fellows who were caught would draw some sort of punishment of extra guard duty or detail work of policing the company's camp. On being dismissed we would fall out to our tents, clean up and make our beds. Some of the boys would go right back to sleep for another half or three-quarters of an hour.[40]

—*Private Joseph N. Rizzi*
110th Engineers, 35th Division

Every morning after breakfast Fatigue Call sounded and we had to police our quarters and the company street. The next formation would be for calisthenics, our morning exercise. This always turned out to be a humorous affair. When we were ordered to "hop," "straddle" and "jump," many of the fellows would be going up while others were coming down. They looked like butterflies taking off which was upsetting to the instructors who would keep the entire outfit overtime trying to get everyone coordinated. It finally ended up that some men were called aside and made to go through the exercise until they moved all together. This was called the awkward squad.

Rifles were issued to us along with ammunition belts filled with 30.06 cartridges. Also issued were a first aid packet, canteen, mess kit, bacon can and a condiment can with sugar, coffee, salt and pepper. New wool blankets were issued along with a shelter "half" which was one-half of a pup tent as they were called. A canvas backpack and a rain poncho were included, and each squad was assembled and instructed how to roll blankets into the pack. This turned out to be quite a problem as the blankets had to be folded just the right way or they hung down in the pack. The expression given to this lack of perfection was "Sad Sack." Unless the blankets were wrapped perfectly, they had to be pulled apart and packed over. Some of the men never did get the hang of wrapping a neat pack and it would fall apart when worn. That called for extra duty, working in the kitchen or cleaning the latrines.[41]

—*Private Ralph L. Williams*
2nd Engineers, 2nd Division

In 1918 many infantry divisions, particularly those formed from the drafted contingents, were armed with the model 1917 [bolt action] rifle; a compromise weapon which enabled our manufacturers to use machinery already set up to turn out rifles for the British forces. The 1917 rifle was the English Enfield changed to permit the use of United States Government ammunition. It was a reliable arm, but heavier, clumsier and less accurate than our own Springfield. Naturally the soldiers themselves were quick to appreciate the difference, and [later in France] it was no uncommon sight, when men of a new division passed a battlefield salvage dump, to see them run to a stack of scarred and rusty Springfields and leave a new but despised Enfield in exchange for a rifle of an older but better pattern.[42]

—John T. Cushing
Historian

Due to the total lack of horses, wooden substitutes were used. These were built by the men, and consisted of long, hollow, wooden cylinders mounted on four sticks. Small pegs fastened on the top of the cylinders served to designate the pommel and cantle of the saddle. Under the tutelage of Lieutenant Burke, we executed the commands "Stand to horse," "Prepare to mount," and "Mount." The last command was particularly difficult to execute, for some of the horses were built higher than others and since none of them had stirrups or saddles, considerable discomfort was experienced by the uninitiated, who jumped high and fell heavily in the hard, wooden seats. Other movements of the cavalry drill were practiced as "Low reach," "About face," etc. With so much other simulated work going on for lack of proper facilities, it is a matter for self-congratulation that we were not compelled to groom imaginary manes and polish imaginary hoofs by the numbers.[43]

—Sergeant Francis Field
306th Field Artillery, 77th Division

On the night of August 13th a telegram from the Office of the Commanding General, Eastern Department, to Capt. Robert J. Gill, Commanding Officer, 3rd Co. C.A.C., was received, ordering him to report to Governor's Island, N.Y.

Major Booth, Adjutant, greeted Captain Gill and said: "Captain, I want you to form a Trench Mortar Battery. This battery, designated the 117th Trench Mortar Battery, is to become a part of the 42nd U.S. Infantry Division, which is being mobilized for immediate service in France."

"Very well, sir," said Captain Gill.

"Are there any questions?" asked Major Booth.

"May I ask, sir, what a trench mortar is?" was the Captain's question.

"Damned if I know, but you will soon find out," replied the Major.[44]

—Private Henry D. Stansbury
117th Trench Mortar Battery, 42nd Division

So the days went on—the men learned to throw grenades and to use the bayonet, to shoot the army rifle and to dig trenches. Especially the latter. They dug trenches and dug more trenches. They braided barbed wire by the rod. And then saw the artillery cheerfully blow up both wire and trenches in ten minutes.[45]

—Chaplain Evan A. Edwards
140th Infantry, 35th Division

I got an opportunity to get home once, and it was nice to see my folks, my brothers and sisters, and my girl. Many of us had no money to get home, but the conductor on the train would take our names and what outfit we belonged to, plus our serial numbers, and said we could settle with the railroad when we got paid. Seems as though the railroad got patriotic, because none of us heard any more from it!

When I left home that time, I told my folks that I might be home once more, but I did not know. There were many tears shed, but once I got out and onto the train again and met other soldiers returning to camp, we helped each other to overcome this feeling by singing and exchanging experiences. Once back to camp we had no time to think about home or to get lonesome.

On Tuesday, September 25, 1917, the inevitable happened. The bugler blew "To Arms," and the sergeants were running up and down the company street hollering, "Everybody up! Start rolling packs!" Well, the time was up. We took our bed sacks and emptied them and started rolling packs. Everybody was excited. Barracks bags were packed and placed in the center of the street, and the trucks came along and took them away. We marched to a waiting train, where all shades were drawn, guards placed at the doors, and no talking allowed, and in a few minutes we were on our way—the quickest move yet.[46]

—Corporal Connell Albertine
104th Infantry, 26th Division

Late one afternoon our captain, Berry M. Whitaker, formed the company and, with great solemnity, announced: "This company is going to France. We are going right away. Is there a man here who does not want to go?" No one replied. He commanded: "Dismissed." I have often wondered if that company did not have a pack of silent liars.

Before leaving Texarkana, one of the men put his rifle to an unintended use. He went into one of the toilets of the depot and shot himself through the head. This trouble might have been saved this despondent youngster had he only known with what willingness any German would have done the same for him. Peculiar as it may seem, a suicide in the company created little comment. The men took it as a matter of course and the boy and the incident were soon forgotten.[47]

—*Corporal Chris Emmett*
359th Infantry, 90th Division

My husband [Captain Arthur Hamm] was an ideal American soldier . . . He was physical perfection, tall, slender and of kingly bearing. His carriage was erect and easy, every muscle fit and supple . . . His hair was chestnut brown with glints of gold, his eyebrows were black . . . and his deep-set eyes were a peculiar shade of dark, warm gray. The strong lines in his cheeks deepened into dimples when he laughed, as he did a great deal.

The night before my husband sailed for France he said, "Remember, that if I should die in action, it is after all, a pretty good way to square accounts with the world."[48]

—*Mrs. Elizabeth Hamm*
Long Island, New York

Notes

1. Laurence Stallings, *The Doughboys.* (New York: Harper & Row, Publishers, 1963), p. 4.

2. Pierce G. Fredericks, *The Great Adventure.* (New York: E.P. Dutton, 1960), p. 35.

3. Robert W. Kean, *Dear Marraine.* (n.p., 1969), pp. xi–xii.

4. The sinking of the passenger liner *Lusitania* on May 7, 1915, by the U-20 with the loss of 1,195 lives, including 124 U.S. citizens, persuaded many Americans that the Germans were indeed barbarians.

5. Connell Albertine, *The Yankee Doughboy.* (Boston: Branden Press, 1968), pp. 9–10.

6. Lowell Thomas, *This Side of Hell.* (Garden City, N.Y.: Doubleday, Doran & Co., Inc., 1932), p. 73.

7. J.E. Rendinell and George Pattullo, *One Man's War.* (New York: J.H. Sears & Company, 1928), pp. 3–5.

8. Lt. Gen. Merwin H. Silverthorn, USMC (ret.), interview 1969 (Oral History Collection, Marine Corps Historical Center, Washington, D.C.).

9. Martin J. Hogan, *The Shamrock Battalion of the Rainbow.* (New York: D. Appleton and Company, 1919).

10. *One Hundred Thirteenth Engineers in France.* (Nancy, Fr.: Berger-Levrault, 1919), p. 78.

11. William L. Langer, *Gas And Flame in World War I.* (New York: Alfred A. Knopf, 1965), pp. xviii–xix.

12. Albertine, *The Yankee Doughboy*, pp. 10–11.

13. Horatio Rogers, *The Diary of an Artillery Scout.* (North Andover, Mass.: pvtly printed, 1975), pp. 3–4.

14. Daniel J. Sweeney (ed.), *History of Buffalo and Erie County 1914–1919.* (Buffalo, N.Y.: Committee of One Hundred, 1919), p. 76.

15. *The Battery Book: A History of Battery "A" 306 F.A.* (New York: The DeVinne Press, 1921), p. 6.

16. A.B. Callaway, *With Packs and Rifles*. (Boston: Meador Publishing Co., 1939), pp. 11–12.

17. L. Wardlaw Miles, *History of the 308th Infantry 1917–1919*. (New York: G.P. Putnam's Sons, 1927), p. 71.

18. Frank B. Tiebout, *A History of the 305th Infantry*. (New York: The 305th Infantry Auxiliary, 1919), p. 12

19. W. Kerr Rainsford, *From Upton to the Meuse with the Three Hundred and Seventh*. (New York: D. Appleton and Company, 1920), pp. 3–4.

20. *The Battery Book*, pp. 6–7.

21. Frederick A. Pottle, *Stretchers: The Story of a Hospital Unit on the Western Front*. (New Haven: Yale University Press, 1929), p. 47.

22. Earl B. Searcy, *Looking Back*. (Springfield, Ill.: The Journal Press, 1921), p. 15.

23. *The Battery Book*, p. 7.

24. Christopher Emmett, *Give Way to the Right*. (San Antonio, Tex.: The Naylor Company, 1934), p. 11.

25. *The Battery Book*, p. 7

26. Ralph L. Williams, *The Luck of a Buck*. (Madison, Wis.: Fitchburg Press, Inc., 1985), pp. 11–13.

27. Ward E. Duffy (ed.), *The G.F. Book Regimental History of the Three Hundred and Third Field Artillery*. (n.p., n.d.), pp. 119–121.

28. Searcy, *Looking Back*, p. 17.

29. Rush Young, *Over the Top with the 80th*. (Pvtly printed, 1933), unpaged.

30. Kean, *Dear Marraine*, p. 85.

31. Tom Skeyhill, *Sergeant York*. (Garden City, N.Y.: Doubleday, Doran and Company, 1928), pp. 184–185.

32. Fredrick M. Wise, *A Marine Tells It to You*. (New York: J.H. Sears & Co., Inc., 1929), p. 282.

33. Will Judy, *A Soldier's Diary*. (Chicago: Judy Publishing Co., 1930), p. 51.

34. James M. Howard, *The Autobiography of a Regiment*. (New York: n.p., 1920), pp. 25–26.

35. Evan A. Edwards, *From Doniphan to Verdun: The Story of the 140th Infantry*. (Lawrence, Kans.: The World Company, 1920), p. 19.

36. W.P. MacLean, *My Story of the 130th Field Artillery*. (Topeka, Kans.: The Boy's Chronicle, n.d.), pp. 8–9.

37. Williams, *The Luck of a Buck*, p. 26.

38. Carl Noble, *Jugheads Behind the Lines*. (Caldwell, Idaho: The Caxton Printers, Ltd., 1938), pp. 29–33.

39. Lowell Thomas, *Woodfill of the Regulars*. (Garden City, N.Y.: Doubleday, Doran & Co., 1929), p. 291.

40. Joseph N. Rizzi, *Joe's War*. (Huntington, W.Va.: Der Angriff Publications, 1983), p. 8.

41. Williams, *Luck of a Buck*, pp. 27–29.

42. John T. Cushing and Arthur F. Stone, *Vermont in the World War 1917–1919*. (Burlington, Vt.: Free Press Printing Company, 1928), pp. 10–11.

43. *The Battery Book*, p. 24.

44. Henry D. Stansbury, *Maryland's 117th Trench Mortar Battery in the World War 1917–1919*. Baltimore, Md.: John D. Lucas Printing Co., 1942), pp. 4–5.

45. Edwards, *From Doniphan to Verdun*, p. 45.

46. Albertine, The *Yankee Doughboy*, p. 22.

47. Emmett, *Give Way to the Right*, pp. 26, 32.

48. Elizabeth C. Hamm, *In White Armor.* (New York: The Knickerbocker Press, 1919), pp. v–vii. Captain Arthur Ellis Hamm was killed in action by shellfire on the Lorraine front on September 14, 1918, a few weeks before his twenty-sixth birthday.

CHAPTER 2

Over the Pond

T he great flood of troops that would cross the Atlantic began with a trickle. A detachment from Base Hospital #4 sailed on May 8, 1917. On June 14, 1917, elements of the U.S. 1st Division, "The Big Red One," sailed for France. The 26th "Yankee" Division, comprised of New England National Guard troops, sailed in September, followed by the 42nd "Rainbow" Division.

Shipping was a problem from the beginning. The U.S. merchant marine was comparatively small and there were almost no troopships capable of making the voyage to France and back. Interned German ships were seized—among them the Vaterland, the largest passenger ship in the world at that time. Renamed Leviathan, she carried almost 100,000 Americans to France during the war. Other shipping was chartered from neutrals or loaned by the Allies, but not until the spring of 1918, when the British released large numbers of ships to the effort, did the trickle of American troops become a torrent. From April 1 to October 31 more than 1,600,000 troops made the trip. In July alone, 306,350 doughboys sailed for Europe.

Four out of every five doughboys sailed from New York Harbor, leaving from the piers at Hoboken; most of the rest sailed from Newport News, Virginia. The average trip took 14 days.

•

From Chattanooga to Camp Meritt our trip was a triumphal procession. Red Cross women met us at the stations, showering us with gifts, whistles blew, and everyone shouted and waved flags. The intensity of enthusiasm steadily increased as we went north, until in Pennsylvania it passed all bounds. Every whistle and bell within miles was playing tunes, people crowded the windows of houses and factories, everybody's hat was off, everybody was yelling himself hoarse; Red Cross ladies at every station with apples and ciga-

rettes, pretty girls shaking hands with us through the car windows—I was quite drunk with the excitement of it. The most touching sight was the intense patriotism old people displayed. Time and
again, we would see an old bent, gray-haired woman waving a great
flag at us, or an old man swinging his hat and cheering like a boy.[1]

—*Corporal Frederick A. Pottle*
Evacuation Hospital #8

We left the train at Long Island and took the ferry for New York. It
seemed rather foolish to me to see the way they were trying to camouflage our movements, as it was broad daylight, and anyone with
any sense would know that we were going to a transport. We
arrived at Pier 59 about 12:30. Great precautions had been taken by
the government to prevent people from seeing any of the transports.
The docks were all boarded up, and we even found the gangplank to
the vessel was boarded up. Once on board we were immediately
ordered below deck and were assigned to different sections.[2]

—*Private Henry G. Reifsnyder*
103rd Engineers, 28th Division

It is likely that much the greater part of our boys had never before
been on a ship. Probably a majority had never even seen an ocean-
going vessel. How crude were the ideas of some of these country
lads may be surmised from the fact that occasionally considerable
numbers of them on a ferry en route from Jersey City to a Brooklyn
pier would suppose that already they were off for France and would
make anxious enquiries as to the probable date of arrival.[3]

—*Major General David C. Shanks*
Port of Embarkation, Hoboken

On certain days the chaplain was asked to remain at the pier office
[at Hoboken], which proved at last to be quite a romantic spot. Here
he officiated at many last-minute weddings. Some were the result of
a tearful girl's inability to wait out the war; others born of a natural
dread that the soldier might never return; still others, the hasty
romances of a week, or even a day. In some instances refusal to offi-
ciate was a necessity. Not a few girls of the street attempted to prey
on soldiers by marrying two, or even three, at different places, in the
hope of being mailed the soldiers' pay from their alleged husbands
during the war.[4]

—*Chaplain Richard H. McLaughlin*
Hoboken

On leaving New York each man was furnished with postcards with
the printed statement, "The ship on which I sailed has arrived safely

overseas," which he might sign and address to whom he pleased. These were taken up and held in New York till the safe arrival of the boat was cabled back, and then were released for mailing.[5]

—*Lieutenant Jay M. Lee*
129th Field Artillery, 35th Division

The line going up the gangplank was moving slowly. The men seemed to have lost their voices. The checker was having difficulties in understanding the names and numbers, even though the rolls had been arranged in the order of the march of the men. Finally I stood abreast the checker and yelled at the very top pitch of my voice: EMMETT . . . CHRISTOPHER . . . A.S.N. . . . TWO MILLION EIGHT HUNDRED SEVEN TWO SEVENTY FOUR." And Bill Goodson, following immediately upon my heels and catching the humor of the thing, pitched his piercing stentorian voice above the hubbub and far above my effort and notified the surrounding world that he, too, was going aboard! The checker tilted back his chair and looking up at us shouted: "THANK GOD! AMERICA IS SAVED. TWO LIVE SOLDIERS GOING TO FRANCE."[6]

—*Corporal Chris Emmett*
359th Infantry, 90th Division

Each man was given a cloth tag which was to serve as his meal ticket besides showing the number of his hatch, letter of his deck, number of his bunk and raft or boat number. This tag was to be worn at all times and to be punched at each meal.

Our bunks were made entirely of steel and were in tiers of three which made each man so close to the next that the air seemed very close. One had the same sensation that a man does going into a mine for the first time.

We were all compelled to stay below until dinner time but allowed on the decks all afternoon. Our mess line seemed about a mile long and led through various passages and down stairways to the very bowels of the ship. And our food being cooked with steam and not seasoned was about as palatable as a wet sponge.[7]

—*Corporal Al Burns*
113th Engineers

[On the afternoon of May 17, 1918] we boarded our ship, the S.S. *Calamares*. She was one of the White Fleet of the United Fruit Co., a "banana boat" that carried the fruit of Central America to the United States. She had accommodations for passengers because that was also a part of the business. She still sported the company white diamond painted on her buff colored smoke stack. Otherwise she had splotches of green and gray paint on her hull, forming grotesque shapes that were called camouflage. All ships were either painted a dull gray or with camouflage stripings which blended into the seascape very well.

The *Calamares* was a small ship. Into her hold on the various decks were long aisles of bunks made of 2x4 wood frames and chicken wire to support straw-filled mattresses. These framed up bunks were three tiers high. Chicken wire stretches. The poor fellows in the bottom bunks were dragging their anchors after a few days. We could endure the bunks, but the odor of bananas permeated the whole ship. Access to the hold of the ship where our bunks were located was through the large cargo hatches in the fore and after well decks. It was up and down the ladders we would go morning, noon and night or as restlessness demanded. Below decks there were continuously running crap games, Red Dog, poker and others I had never heard of. Some of those fellows never saw daylight during the whole trip.[8]

—*Private William F. Clarke*
104th Machine Gun Battalion, 27th Division

I do not remember the exact train of my thoughts; I only know that I was held spellbound by the wonder of the fact that here I was actually going to war, I who but a few years before had hardly turned aside a moment from the leisures of my summer vacation to read in the papers of the beginning of a war in Europe. What was before me now?[9]

—*Corporal Louis F. Ranlett*
308th Infantry, 77th Division

Large ships were curiously painted with huge stripes and curves of black and white and vivid colors, until even at a short distance their own builders would not have known them. There, lying against the island were two small vessels, one behind the other, looking so insignificant that no one would ever waste a torpedo on them, and yet closer inspection reveals the optical illusion; it is really a fair sized troopship cleverly disguised. Seen at close quarters, however, the camouflage looked as if it would attract attention rather than reduce visibility, and the most complimentary remark from the doughboys on board the closely packed ships was that "the camouflage man had had a nightmare."[10]

—*Colonel Christian Bach*
4th Division

The enlisted men eat in gangs, a thousand at a sitting, rather a standing, for there are no seats; five shifts of a thousand each stagger through the mess hall at each meal, never standing still but eating as they move. One must step fast or be pushed aside. Each man carries a tag which states his sleeping shifts, his eating shift, his bunk section and his abandon-ship station.[11]

—Army Field Clerk Will Judy
33rd Division

There was also a canteen on board but the prices were so exorbitant that it was far beyond our means to purchase anything. We were compelled to pay fifteen cents for an ordinary five-cent bar of chocolate and twenty cents for a ham sandwich in which it was some job to find the ham. Oranges sold for twenty-five and fifty cents each. A great part of the goods that were being sold by the crew was supposed to be issued to us. The boat was not operated by naval officers and crew, but by a private concern.[12]

—Lieutenant Edward Sirois
102nd Field Artillery, 26th Division

All garbage was deposited in containers on the deck and dumped overboard on favorable nights. It can readily be seen that if several thousand men were allowed to throw refuse overboard at will, the submarines would easily pick up your trail by following the garbage—and then it would be too bad for all concerned. We were allowed outside on deck at certain hours, and the refreshing air was a life-saver. However, you are herded about by guards (soldiers and gobs) with the expression that becomes a famous bugaboo: "You can't stand there, soldier"; "You can't sit there, soldier"; "Get the hell out of there, soldier."[13]

—Corporal Leslie Langille
149th Field Artillery, 42nd Division

Very few of the boys became seasick until the second or third day but when they did there was a rapid diminishing of the mess line. One boy who was "feeding the fishes" was asked by one of the comrades if he didn't have a weak stomach, and he replied, "Oh I don't know. I guess I'm heaving it about as far as the rest of them."[14]

—Corporal Al Burns
113th Engineers

Whenever I think of seasickness the picture rises to my mind of Jock McSweeney during the stormy weather. Full of fresh air and salt spray I blew into the cabin. McSweeney was lying in his lower bunk with his eyes shut, passively sick for the moment.

"Well Jock, cheer up; it's great on deck. What are you doing down here all day?"

His eyes stayed shut but his lips moved. His prayer was to the effect that the blank blank boat might sink to the bottom of the ocean and do it damn soon. Even this effort made him turn green about the gills.

"Come on, snap out of it, Jock. Get a good meal aboard and you will feel fine."

One corner of his mouth twitched as if in a sardonic smile. He gulped. His eyes opened but they didn't see. With a great effort he said in a whisper, "Get out of here, you bastard. If I'm ever on land again, by Christ, I'll come home by way of Siberia if I have to crawl on my hands and knees!" This effort was too much for his tenderly balanced equilibrium and I got out just in time. How wise I had been in taking an upper berth![15]

—*Corporal Horatio Rogers*
101st Field Artillery, 26th Division

On about the fourth day, we neared the danger zone and were introduced to a new outdoor pastime commonly known as "Abandon Ship Drill." At the blast of the bugle, the soldiers would don their life-belts and proceed to an assigned section on deck. In addition to wearing life-preservers, the extra equipment worn for the drill was one blanket, rolled up over the shoulder, and woolen gloves. After arriving at our station, we would receive instructions as how to go overboard in case of necessity. A seasoned naval officer growled out orders to the effect that, if we had to leave the ship, we would first throw the rafts overboard and then jump into the water. As soon as we were in the ocean, which he claimed was not cold, we were to kick the raft away from the sides of the ship, so as to prevent other rafts from coming down on our heads. We were told not to sit on the rafts, but to hang on the sides. At once, we figured that the blankets and woolen gloves were to keep us warm while in the ocean. Undoubtedly, the uppermost thought in everyone's mind was the reliability of the life-belts. With not enough life-boats to accommodate all the troops aboard, some were to use rafts. We drew the latter. Rumors had it that some life-preservers would hold out 18 hours while others would sink with the wearer upon striking the water. Fortunately, the question remained unsettled.[16]

—*Sergeant Howard L. Fisher*
306th Field Artillery, 77th Division

Several different types of life rafts were in use, but in the end the navy found the "doughnut" shaped raft to be the most satisfactory and the easiest to handle.

These are merely hollow cylinders, doughnut shaped, provided with rope "hang-ons" around the perimeter, and having a lattice floor in the interior.

Life rafts of this kind required no launching and could be dropped overboard without risk of danger to the raft.

The larger rafts had a flotation power sufficient to support forty men.

In addition there was a large supply of life preservers, always in excess of the carrying capacity of the ship.

In the early stage of the war our life preservers were of cork; later it was found that the "kapok" life preserver was more service-able.[17]

—*Major General David C. Shanks*
Port of Embarkation [Hoboken]

The most minute precautions were taken to avoid trouble. First of all, every flashlight, every box of matches, and every cigarette lighter was required to be turned in. Anyone who wanted to smoke could borrow a light from one of the sailors. Immediately after sundown the decks were cleared and the doors and portholes closed, so that no light could escape. At an early hour in the evening the lights in the staterooms and cabins, as well as in the men's quarters below decks, were extinguished and the only illumination was the ghastly and feeble light emitted by a few small incandescent globes of blue glass.

Nothing must be thrown into the sea lest it serve as a clue to our presence. The white caps of the sailors must not be worn after sundown. Portholes are closed after dark.

Of entertainment [on board] there was little. The ship boasted a moving picture machine, which was used every night in the mess hall; but there were so many thousand troops on board, and the difficulties of getting from one place to another were so great, especially after the water-tight doors were closed between compartments at night, that our men never had but one chance to go to a show, and few of them succeeded in getting there even then. But the band used to play on deck, and sometimes the men would gather round and sing . . . "Hail, hail the gang's all here," "In the Artillery," and "Over hill, over dale."

What little exercise they got was in the form of calisthenics. Every morning each organization marched up to the long promenade decks and there the men, peeling off their blouses, were put through a short, snappy physical drill. Once or twice there were some boxing bouts.[18]

—*Chaplain James M. Howard*
304th Field Artillery

There was much discussion of the submarines among the men. Bets
were laid on our chances for coming through alive, the odd nega-
tives to these bets little stopping to consider what they would do
with the money they won in case their expectations came to pass.
The submarine discussions always reached their high points following life belt and life boat drills.[19]

—*Corporal Martin J. Hogan*
165th Infantry, 42nd Division

There was supposed to be an order requiring each man to sleep in
his hammock, but we were below the water-line, and we knew the
hopelessness of the trap should a torpedo pierce the boat's hull.
Consequently, many of us who drew positions far back from the
hatchway, folded our hammocks on the hard deck, made pillows of
our life-jackets, and, with our overcoats as cover, passed each night
in the belief that, in the event of emergency, we would have at least a
fighting chance to make the hatchway and get above.[20]

—*Corporal Earl B. Searcy*
311th Infantry, 78th Division

*C onsidering the public furor over German submarines, the crossings
went relatively unscathed. Successful attacks were limited by the convoy system, speed and the difficulty of finding the ships on widely dis-
persed shipping lanes. U-boats succeeded in torpedoing five large troopships. Three of the five—*Antilles, President Lincoln *and* Covington
—sunk and were lost. The other two—the Finland *and* Mt. Vernon—
*made it back to port. All five were on return voyages to the U.S. when
attacked and carried few military passengers. Among the transports sunk
on the way to France were the* Tuscania *on February 5, 1918;* Moldavia
on May 23, 1918; and the animal transport Ticonderoga *on September 30,
1918. A total of 215 soldiers and sailors went down on the* Ticonderoga;
56 men from the U.S. 4th Division were lost on the Moldavia; *and 230
were lost on the* Tuscania.

•

On the afternoon of February 5th we rounded the north of Ireland
[on the *Tuscania*] and were proceeding southward. On either side we
could dimly discern the cliffs of Scotland and those of the rocky Irish
coast.

The earliest knowledge we had of the proximity of a German
submarine was a decided shock which rocked the big ship from end
to end. Simultaneously all lights went out and a deafening crash
echoed and re-echoed through the ship. There was no question we

had been hit, and so, life belts on, we rushed for our stations. Our boat drills had been perfunctory ones at the best . . . Before the crash had died away every man was on his way to his post. The corridors, passageways and stairways were a seething mass of olive drab streaming for the decks. The rush was devoid of all hysterical excitement. Each man was excitedly cautioning his neighbor to "take it easy," "don't rush," "don't crowd; she isn't sinking"; yet was using his elbows, feet and hands in regular mess-line tactics to further a speedy arrival at his lifeboat.

The torpedo had struck us squarely amidships on the starboard side. A great hole was torn in the hull and all the superstructure directly above was a mass of wreckage. Several sets of davits with their lifeboats were utterly demolished, thus diminishing the chances of getting away safely. From the minute of the explosion the ship began listing to starboard. It became exceedingly difficult to walk on deck, and more than one of the boys on losing his grip on the port rail would find himself sprawled against some of the deck machinery, a keg of rope or even the rail on the lower side.

These ten or fifteen minutes elapsing from the moment we were struck were filled with action. With all indications of a speedy sinking staring us in the face, we worked feverishly to lower the lifeboats and cut away the rafts. Pitch darkness made our work more difficult. Here and there a pocket flashlight came into play. Later the auxiliary lights were turned on and we could better see what there was to do.

The work of lowering the lifeboats proved discouraging. Not only had we lost several, due to the terrific effects of the explosion, which had thrown a sheet of flame and debris a hundred feet into the air, but we discovered the boat tackle in many cases to be fouled or rotted and unfit for use. Some of the first boats we attempted to lower were capsized in midair, spilling their occupants into the icy water. The high seas running and the darkness made the rescue of these men almost impossible. Occasionally we got a boat away in good shape with nothing more serious than sprung planks or missing rain plugs. These difficulties were overcome by bailing with service hats which served the purpose very well. On the port side the launchings were accompanied with another handicap. The *Tuscania* had acquired such a list that we found it necessary to slide the lifeboats down the rivet-studded sloping side of the ship with the aid of oars as levers. In all some thirty lifeboats were launched, and perhaps twelve of these were successful.

After acquiring a heavy list, the *Tuscania* seemed to sink no lower in the water. Of those on board, though, the haste to go somewhere else abated not a bit. With the lifeboats gone together with the rafts, the situation looked none too encouraging. The boys showed few signs of nervousness. Standing there, lining the rail, waiting for the next development, some six hundred of them smoked or talked quietly, discussing their plight. The remarkable part of it all was that they took everything in a matter-of-fact way with a sort of "well, what's next?" attitude. Occasionally a few would sing some little song, indicative of their feelings, such as "Where Do We Go From Here, Boys?" or "To Hell With the Kaiser." The absence of any panic or effort and time in prayer was notable.

Suddenly on the starboard, out of the darkness, a tiny destroyer came sidling up to the troopship. With a display of seamanship nothing short of marvelous she approached near enough for the men to be transferred to her deck. Sometimes almost hidden by the roll of the big ship, the destroyer clung to us. Ropes were let over the side and several hundred of the boys went over. When the destroyer was loaded to the limit she steamed away, leaving a few boys dangling from the sixty-foot ropes. It was here that one of our cooks, a 200-pound specimen, surprised us all and no less himself, by climbing all the way up to the deck again. When asked to demonstrate his feat a few days later in our Irish camp, he was unable to climb the height of the rafters in our barracks.

Shortly after the departure of the destroyer-load of troops, another one sidled up to us and completed the work of rescue. She, too, was crowded to the limit, but she stayed till every known person on board had been transferred. No sooner had she pulled away when some of the longitudinal bulkheads gave way, admitting the water to the port holds. Slowly the *Tuscania* resumed an even keel. Very low in the water and considerably so in the bow, she floated for another hour. At about 10 o'clock, four hours after being struck, she took her final plunge. With a muffled explosion as the water reached her boilers, she gently slid, bow first, under the surface.

During all this time the lifeboats and rafts were drifting help-lessly about. It was impossible to make any headway with the oars, as most of the boats were full of water, and there was such a heavy sea that any such effort was useless. In and out among these boats the destroyers raced, looking for traces of the submarine and drop-ping depth bombs where there were any suspicious indications. Each time one of the "ash cans" exploded the boats would shiver and shake with the concussion. Those men who were in the water were knocked breathless with each explosion, and in a few cases were rendered unconscious.

While the work of abandoning ship was in progress, our res-cuers were added to by a number of trawlers and smaller fishing boats which helped in gathering in the survivors. These vessels together with the destroyers combed the vicinity picking up men in lifeboats and rafts. Each bit of wreckage was closely scanned on the possibility of there being someone clinging to it. In this way the majority of the living were rescued. A few swimming alone and helpless were left. Darkness and the wide area over which the rafts and boats were scattered made it impossible to find them all. Three lifeboats, each more than filled with its complement of men, were overlooked. Among the first away from the big ship, they had drifted quite a distance before the rescue work had fairly commenced. With no guidance and at the mercy of the wind and waves, they drifted aimlessly for several hours and then were dashed upon the cliffs of the Isle of Islay, Scotland. Out of more than sixty men in one of these boats, there were but eight saved.[21]

—*Private Henry J. Askew*
20th Engineers

*O*f the doughboys headed overseas, about half disembarked in England *and the others landed in France. Most of those who landed in England went directly to Liverpool, transferred to trains and were then ferried across the English Channel. Most doughboys who went directly to France came through Brest, though others landed at St. Nazaire, Bordeaux and other ports.*

•

Toward the late afternoon the destroyers left us and we saw, far away, a gray tower. We drew nearer; the chimneys of a city and then its general outlines evolved themselves out of the fog and smoke. We entered the river Mersey and progressed toward the Liverpool docks. Crowded ferries dashed by and we cheered them just as we had cheered the New York ferries two weeks before; we cheered the other ships of our convoy as we passed them; the band played furiously; we cheered every tug and row boat, every floating log or orange peel. We sang 'Over There,' which we were not yet 'fed up' with. We made the waterfront echo for an hour. Then, since we were not to land that night, we subsided and began to look round at the crowded shipping, the docks, the buildings on shore, the two-storied electric tramcars, and all the sights of interest. Dominating our vision, commanding the waterfront from the center of a park, was a thing which of all others we saw and remembered: a sign, black, 20-foot letters on a white ground, reading, not 'Welcome,' not even 'Cable crossing, do not anchor here,' but—who would have guessed it—'Spratt's Dog Biscuit.'[22]

—*Corporal Louis F. Ranlett*
308th Infantry, 77th Division

As we marched down the street at Southampton to the Channel transport, again, "Good-bye, Broadway! Hello, France!" was taken up all along the line. Little children, tots two, three and four years old, lined the sidewalks for blocks and patted our hands, as we went swinging along, and cries of "Good luck, soldier boys!" came from all sides. We felt we were really beginning a wonderful thing.[23]

—*Captain Carroll J. Swan*
101st Engineers, 26th Division

We were hiking through the dark streets of Southampton between rows of unlighted houses. A fine rain was falling, but there seemed to be many people on the sidewalks. They would hold out their hands to touch us in the dark. I shook several hands but saw no faces. A woman's voice said, "Keep your pecker up, laddie."

The first halt found us still inside the city. Nevertheless, most of us took the opportunity of relieving ourselves in the gutter. The spectators, if the darkness makes this term permissible, took no notice. Many troops had passed through those streets since the beginning of the war.[24]

—*Corporal Horatio Rogers*
101st Field Artillery, 26th Division

The entrance to the harbor of Brest is most picturesque, very quaint surroundings and very old-world looking. No giant buildings against the sky line, no giant ocean liners against the gigantic piers; here and there an American liner which had landed her troops was anchored. Dotted along the shore were queer looking little wooden boats or a string of barges such as we have seen being towed up the Hudson. The buildings were little low things such as we have seen in our geography and had laughed at their simplicity.[25]

—*Sergeant H.J. Cochrane Jr.*
105th Infantry, 27th Division

I remember one remark which seemed to be appreciated by most of the men on deck who heard it. A Frenchman raised his cap and waved to the soldiers leaning over the rail and cried, "Vive l'Amerique! Vive les Americaines!" A doughboy on the deck called back through his hands, "Vive yourself, you damned frog!"[26]

—*Lieutenant Colonel Charles M. DuPuy*
311th Machine Gun Battalion, 79th Division

Before anyone got off, we were subjected to a lecture by First Lieutenant George Gould in the art of protecting our manly virtues. According to the lieutenant, we were in much danger of being raped the minute we put foot on French soil. Most of the fellows would have been very willing victims of such treatment.[27]

—Corporal Leslie Langille
149th Field Artillery, 42nd Division

Leaving the quay behind we wind up a hill, while on either side of the road, kiddies besiege us with "Donnez moi un cigarette pour le pere dans la trench." Shabby looking little beggars, bare legs and huge wooden shoes that make a sound like a runaway horse as they clank-clank alongside of us. Big sister was much in evidence too as she begged her share of ciggies.

It was in Brest that we saw our first French soldier, better known to us as "Froggie." So this was the chap we had come over to help out. A dirty field blue uniform, spirals of the same color; but behind this uniform of blue he had an élan we had no acquired as yet. We were carefree, we had not suffered the hardships he had endured; we were full of boyish enthusiasm; he had been that way back in 1914.[28]

—Sergeant H.J. Cochrane Jr.
105th Infantry, 27th Division

The smaller boys lined the street asking for pennies and singing songs, the favorite of which was "Hell! Hell! The Gang's All Here!"[29]

—Lieutenant Carrington Williams
Base Hospital #45

Near the docks and in the railway yards we saw many small groups of German prisoners of war, with their little round skull caps and grayish green uniforms, just as they had been captured and brought from the battlefields. Each group was guarded by a French sentry armed with a rifle with bayonet fixed. The sentry carried his rifle slung by the strap on his back, and any prisoner so minded could have been two blocks away before the Frenchman could have been ready to fire his piece.

Just what sort of work the prisoners were performing could not be determined by us. Apparently they ceased operations when our column hove in sight and, as we passed them, they gazed at us with lackluster eyes and a look of apathy. The sentries were just as woe-be-gone in appearance as the Germans and had a sad and lonesome mien. No one urged the prisoners to perform their tasks as we passed. They reminded us for all the world like flocks of sheep attended by their lazy shepherds.[30]

—Lieutenant Colonel George M. Duncan
3rd Division

We had scarcely debarked and had drawn up in company formation on dock before a long train of hospital cars pulled in and stopped alongside us.

We looked, and beheld, for the first time, the horrors of war, fresh from the line of battle. Every coach was full of men suffering from wounds. Heads were bandaged, arms and legs were missing, and body members were wrapped in tape. It was a train-load of English boys who had done their bit, whose bodies had been torn in the doing, and who were bound for "Blighty," as they called England, to recuperate.

The sight struck us dumb. Stout chaps among us looked and shuddered. "In the name of God, is that what we're headed for?" asked a husky lad at my side.

"Looks bad, doesn't it?" I queried in reply.

Presently, some of the wounded men in the coaches began to call to us. "Aye, Yanks! Aye, Sammies!"

We responded. Then, American-like, we started a volley of questions. How lately had they been wounded? How long were they in France before they went up to the lines? How many did they leave behind? Did they think that we Americans would be put in action at once? All these and more. Nor were these cheerful, though crippled, English soldiers particularly consoling.

"They need you where we came from, lads. You better 'ave your wits about you, men. It's an 'ell of a game, it is."

We gained neither information nor solace from those broken lads. They were on their way to "Blighty" and nothing else mattered to them. It chilled us, everyone. If the scene had been staged with the view of hardening us, it could not have gone off better—except that, instead of feeling callous, we sensed fear and vague apprehensions.[31]

—*Corporal Earl B. Searcy*
311th Infantry, 78th Division

Captain Malcolmson of the 6th Manchesters, our British instructor, said, "I want to look your company over at close range as it marches by." As the company passed he inspected them closely and tears filled his eyes. He said, "My God! This is Kichener's army over again. We have nothing like this now; we have nothing left but boys."[32]

—*Captain Henry Maslin*
105th Infantry, 27th Division

Notes

1. Pottle, *Stretchers*, p. 65
2. Henry G. Reifsnyder, *A Second Class Private in the Great World War.* (Philadelphia: Pvtly printed, 1923), pp. 9–10.

3. David C. Shanks, *As They Passed Through the Port*. (Washington, D.C.: The Cary Publishing Company, 1927), p. 10.

4. Nelson Robinson, *St. Lawrence University in the World War 1917–1918*. (Canton, N.Y.: St. Lawrence University, 1931), p. 188.

5. Jay M. Lee, *The Artilleryman*. (Kansas City, Mo.: Press of Spencer Printing Co., 1920), p. 41.

6. Emmett, *Give Way to the Right*, p. 46.

7. *One Hundred Thirteenth Engineers in France*, pp. 29–30.

8. William F. Clarke, *Over There with O'Ryan's Roughnecks*. (Seattle: Superior Publishing Company, 1966), pp. 28–29.

9. Louis F. Ranlett, *Let's Go!* (Boston: Houghton Mifflin Company, 1927), p. 12.

10. Christian A. Bach and Henry Noble Hall, *The Fourth Division*. (n.p.: The Fourth Division, 1920), pp. 40–41.

11. Judy, *A Soldier's Diary*, p. 82.

12. Edward Sirois, *Smashing Through the World War with Fighting Battery C 102nd F.A. Yankee Division*. (Salem, Mass.: The Meek Press, 1919), p. 21.

13. Leslie Langille, *Men of the Rainbow*. (Chicago: The O'Sullivan Publishing House, 1933) p. 37.

14. *One Hundred Thirteenth Engineers in France*, p. 30.

15. Rogers, *Diary of an Artillery Scout*, pp. 19–20.

16. Roswell De La Mater, *The Story of Battery B 306th F.A.—77th Division*. (New York: Premier Printing Company, 1919), p. 20.

17. Shanks, *As They Passed Through the Port*, p. 143.

18. Howard, *The Autobiography of a Regiment*, pp. 43–44.

19. Hogan, *The Shamrock Battalion of the Rainbow*, pp. 19–20.

20. Searcy, *Looking Back*, p. 24.

21. *Twentieth Engineers France 1917–1918–1919*. (Portland, Oreg.: Twentieth Engineers Publishing Association, c. 1919), unpaged.

22. Ranlett, *Let's Go!*, p. 19.

23. Carroll J. Swan, *My Company*. (Boston: Houghton Mifflin Company, 1918), pp. 17–18.

24. Rogers, *Diary of An Artillery Scout*, p. 24.

25. Robert S. Sutcliffe (compiler), *Seventy-First New York in the World War*. (New York: 71st Infantry, New York National Guard, 1922), pp. 108–109.

26. Charles M. DuPuy, *A Machine Gunner's Notes, France 1918*. (Pittsburgh: Reed & Witting Company, 1920), p. 50.

27. Langille, *Men of the Rainbow*, p. 41.

28. Sutcliffe, *Seventy-First New York in the Great War*, pp. 108–109.

29. Stuart McGuire, *History of U.S. Army Base Hospital No. 45 in the Great War*. (Richmond: The William Byrd Press, Inc., 1924), p. 121.

30. George M. Duncan, "I Go to War," unpublished manuscript, pp. 31–32.

31. Searcy, *Looking Back*, pp. 33–34.

32. Sutcliffe, *Seventy-First New York in the Great War*, p. 67.

CHAPTER 3

"Hey Froggie"

*G*eneral John J. "Black Jack" Pershing and the nucleus of officers that would comprise the headquarters of the American Expeditionary Force—the A.E.F.—arrived in France in June. Also among the initial arrivals were elements of the 1st Division—made up of some of the oldest units in the Regular Army. Regiments such as the 18th Infantry, for instance, dated back to the War of 1812. One battalion of the 16th Infantry showed the flag in Paris during a Fourth of July parade. With two-thirds of the outfit made up of recruits, they made a somewhat awkward appearance, but Paris loved it. "Vivent les Americans, Vivent Pershing, Vivent les Etats Unis," shouted the crowd as the U.S. flag passed by. Decked with wreaths and flowers, the doughboys marched to Lafayette's tomb where Pershing said a few not particularly memorable words. Honors went to a staff officer who summed up the spirit of the hour when he rose and announced, "Lafayette, we are here!"*

Things were a bit less dramatic for most of the doughboys as they boarded trains and headed inland to various training areas.

•

Our train was quite a long one and to our unaccustomed eyes the cars looked rather fragile and toy-like. They were freight cars of course and on the side of each car was painted in white letters "40 hommes—8 chevaux," 40 men or 8 horses. Forty men could get into one of these cars if they all stood up and eight horses might be able to make it, also standing up. I do not know if the French *poilu* traveled so crowded, but we never did. The war would have ended as far as the American doughboy was concerned if he was compelled to.

There were at least 20 to 30 men in each car. The cars had been swept out and were fairly clean. There was fresh straw for us to lie on, the only time this happened. There were a few times later on

when we shoveled the manure and smelly straw from the cars
before we could or would ride in them.[1]

—*Private William F. Clarke*
104th Machine Gun Battalion, 27th Division

On the side of each box car was marked "40 Hommes—8 Chevals,"
which means that either 40 men or 8 horses can be crowded in. One
lad said, "We came across the water like a bunch of bananas and
now we are to be shipped like a lot of horses."[2]

—*Captain James T. Duane*
101st Infantry, 26th Division

The towns occupied by the regiment were typical French country
villages. A winding street, lined with stone and plaster houses, each
one like its neighbor, and all like those in every town of its size in
the district—red-tiled roofs and cobblestone streets—no gutters, and
before every house the inevitable pile of manure—such is the pre-
vailing pattern on which French villages are cut.

The dwellings combined the house and barn under one roof
which, while economical in some ways, had its drawbacks. The family lived on one side of the ground floor and the other side was
devoted to barn purposes. The farmer had only to step out of his
kitchen door to take care of his stock, but vice-versa it was just as
easy for the chickens and pigs to enter the kitchen. Over home and
stable there was always a large open hay mow and it was in these
lofts that the majority of the men were billeted, sleeping in the straw.
"Hitting the hay" and "Going to bed with the chickens" ceased to be
merely figures of speech.[3]

—*Captain Raymond M. Cheseldine*
166th Infantry, 42nd Division

I censored a letter in which one of our lads said: "There are three
classes of inhabitants in the houses—first, residents; second, cattle;
third, soldiers."[4]

—*Father Francis Duffy*
165th Infantry, 42nd Division

At Colmiers la Haut we were confronted with the first necessity
always to be found in every French town—that of cleaning up the
town. It was a small village of some 200 population, but there was
more filth and dirt to the person than in any place ever seen by me.
The cows and horses trailed through the streets of the place, early in
the morning and late in the evening, distributing their dung as they
walked, and before we could drill upon the streets of the town we

became scavengers en masse. Back of each residence was a dung pile carefully thrown high by the frugal hands of the Frenchmen, a reeking, stinking, stench-pot, crying out to High Heaven! What a smell! And the French objected when we removed it. Their wealth was measured by the height of their pile![5]

—Corporal Chris Emmett
359th Infantry, 90th Division

Most of our time was spent in small rural villages like Grand. These truly constituted the backbone of the French Republic. Small farms were located on the outskirts of these villages and the people could easily walk to work on them.

By the time we got to France, the only males we would see in these villages were old men, young boys, and disabled French soldiers. The whole rural area was run by women. Women ran the farms, operated the stores and cafes, and for the most part they were a wonderful, strong-willed group of people. They received us with open arms, because we were among the first American troops to arrive. They had so little themselves, yet they generously offered us a portion of their bounty.

The difference in language didn't mean a thing. Those of us from New York City were more sympathetic, I believe, then troops from other parts of the United States except perhaps from those other large cities where there were large numbers of foreign-born. Practically every New York kid knew a few words of German, Italian, or Yiddish and it didn't take him very long to learn a little French. Of course, Italian-Americans caught on very easily.

On the ship across, we had been issued a little pocket dictionary of French phrases. Well, it wasn't much of a dictionary, but it did help, and we were able to pick up enough of the language to get by. We had such fun trying to talk to the French people, because they so enjoyed the mistakes that we made. It just tickled them to death, and we joined in their amusement.[6]

—Private Albert "Red" Ettinger
165th Infantry, 42nd Division

The French soldier, or *poilu*, as he was called, wore a long overcoat which also served as a blanket at night, wrapped leggins, and he carried a gas mask, a haversack which contained "du pain" (black bread), and a canteen which contained "Van Rouge," as our men called it. All of them needed a shave and a bath. The streets were of cobblestone with no drainage, with plenty of dogs and cats in them. Here we were introduced to the French cafe, with its "garcons," red wine, and cognac. We always went for the last when we could get it.

We could not get any American cigarettes at all, and had to smoke a vile French cigarette, which they called *La Grenade*. It was a most appropriate name for it. Here we also met the French lighter, with its long cord and ignition on the end, which never worked.[7]

—*Lieutenant Joseph D Patch*
18th Infantry, 1st Division

The French soldiers were intensely interested in the equipment of our land forces and in the uniforms of both our soldiers and sailors. They sought by questions to get an understanding of the various insignia by which the Americans designated their rank.

One thing that they noticed was a small, round white pasteboard tag suspended on a yellow cord from the upper left hand breast pocket of either the blue jackets of our sailors or the khaki shirts of our soldiers. So prevalent was this tag, which in reality marked the wearer as the owner of a package of popular tobacco, that the French almost accepted it as uniform equipment.[8]

—*Floyd Gibbons*
Chicago Tribune

Not too far from where our platoon formations were held, there was a watering trough to which the natives would bring their animals to water, and alongside the trough was a hand pump where the people could draw water for house consumption. The trough was made of stone, probably hundreds of years old, and it had continuous running water coming from the nearby mountains and running through the farms and fields before flowing to this trough. Due to the fact that the French use all kinds of manure, including human, it was deadly to drink and we were ordered not to drink it. Even the French wouldn't drink this water, and even the poorest families drank wine. Lister bags were hung conveniently at different places in the village and this water was chlorinated by the medical corps and was the only safe drinking water. It didn't taste very good, but it quenched one's thirst and was safe. Several times during extreme cold weather the water in these bags froze, but it would melt during the daytime when the sun was out, enabling us to fill our canteens.[9]

—*Private Connell Albertine*
104th Infantry, 26th Division

Beaumont was fortunate in having water from the mountain streams, clear and cold, piped right into the public square; but the troops in all the towns had to boil or chlorinate their drinking fluid.

"Where are our latrines?" one of our officers asked Beaumont's mayor.

"But, Monsieur le Commandant, we haven't any."

"Well, what are the men to use?"

"Why," exclaimed the French mayor, while a look of surprise came over his face that such a question should be asked, "why, you can use the streets." In fact, the inhabitants did use the streets, the whole family in most every case; and the few toilets in town were under lock and key.[10]

—1st Lieutenant Frederick M. Cutler
55th Coast Artillery

Company G, 168th Infantry
St. Ciergues, France, January 19, 1918

Memorandum:

1. The men of this company are under no condition to enter houses, barns or other private buildings, other than those assigned to them as billets.

2. The hours during which they may enter drinking places are designated and they will take care not to be in such places at other times.

3. Latrines have been constructed, and the men will see to it that there is no pollution of the streets by themselves or visiting troops.

4. Men may wash in the compartments of the horse troughs farthest from the point where water enters. The troughs are usually in three compartments. Use the compartment from which the water overflows into the drain.

5. There will be no smoking or lighting of candles in billets in which straw is stored.

6. Blouses and overcoats must be worn buttoned at all times. Overcoat collars will not be turned up at any time.[11]

—Lieutenant Quincy Sharp Mills
168th Infantry, 42nd Division

We were issued two round aluminum identification tags—dog tags, we called them—and the tags had our names, ranks and serial numbers. At this time we were reminded that if we were captured by the enemy the only information to give was what was on our dog tags and nothing else. With these tags was issued a yard of white cotton tape about half an inch wide. One tag was tied in a loop, lower than the other loop by three inches, and it could be cut off without loosening the security of the other loop around the neck. The tags were to be worn in this position at all times—the reason being that if any one was killed, the chaplain or whoever was in charge of the burial detail would cut the lower tag off and turn it over to the Graves Registration Department. The other tag would remain on the body, and a rough description of just where the body was buried went with the tag taken off the body.

The number on my dog tag was 70490, since we were among the first hundred thousand American soldiers to land in France as the American Expeditionary Forces.[12]

—Private Connell Albertine
104th Infantry, 26th Division

*A*merican combat forces were organized into divisions consisting of some 28,000 officers and men—larger than the Civil War army corps many of their grandfathers had served in. The American divisions were the largest divisions on the Western Front during World War I: British divisions numbered about 15,000 men, while French and German divisions numbered about 12,000 men each. The U.S. formation was the so-called square organization with two infantry brigades, each made up of two regiments. There were three machine gun battalions and one field artillery brigade with three artillery regiments. One trench mortar battery was assigned to each division. The infantry regiments had three battalions of four rifle companies, and one machine gun company each; and each company had four platoons. Each platoon had two sections of four squads each.

•

An infantry regiment consisted of 114 officers and 3,720 enlisted men.

Three battalions, each consisting of 27 officers and 1,000 enlisted men.

Headquarters: 6 officers
Headquarters Company: 7 officers, 336 enlisted men
Supply Company: 6 officers, 156 enlisted men
Machine Gun Company: 6 officers, 172 enlisted men
Medical Detachment: 8 officers, 48 enlisted men.
An infantry regiment has a total equipment of:
Horses (67), Mules (325), Combat Carts (27), Medical Carts (3), Ration Carts (16), Water Carts (15), Rolling Kitchens (16), Combat Wagons (19), Ration Wagons (22), Bicycles (42), Motor Cars (1), Motorcycles with Sidecars (2), Grenade Dischargers (390), One Pounder Guns (3), Heavy Machine Guns (16), Trench Knives (480), 3-inch Stokes Mortars (6), Pistols (1,202), Rifles (3,200), Automatic Rifles (192).[13]

—Chaplain F.C. Reynolds
115th Infantry, 29th Division

Much to the amazement of our French neighbors, we trained in all sorts of weather. When it rained, they went home to their comfortable billets. On one rainy occasion, they marched by some trenches which our men were digging. The bottoms of the trenches were filled with water, and every shovelful was about half water and half mud. This amused them no end and a *poilu*, who had picked up some American cuss words, yelled—"hell, damn, you like, you no like, etc." to which one of the soldiers yelled back, "Oui-la-law you Frawg s.o.b." This kind of exchange was frequently heard between our men and theirs.[14]

—Lieutenant Joseph D. Patch
18th Infantry, 1st Division

All our training that summer was along the lines of trench warfare. Early one morning, right after breakfast, we marched out to the training area, met the French officers, and the day's work started. We dug a series of trenches. We took up the new method of bayonet fighting. Long lines of straw-stuffed figures hanging from a cross-beam between two upright posts were set up. The men fixed bayonets and charged them. British instructors, who had arrived shortly after us, stood over them and urged them on.

The men had to scramble in and out a series of trenches before they got to the swinging dummies. That was to improve their wind. When the dummies were reached, according to the British instructors, you must put on a fighting face, grunt and curse as you lunged, and literally try to tear the dummy to pieces with the thrust. There was special instruction to bayonet them in the belly wherever possible. If you bayoneted a man you were chasing, you must get him through the kidneys and not in the rump. If your bayonet stuck, shoot it out. The British at that time were crazy about the bayonet. They knew it was going to win the war.

The French were equally obsessed with the grenade. They knew *it* was going to win the war. So we also got a full dose of training in hand grenade throwing.[15]

—Colonel Frederick M. Wise
6th Marines, 2nd Division

Four qualities the soldier must possess to attack effectively with the bayonet—nerve, good direction, strength and quickness. The charge with the bayonet should be made amid excitement, amid shouting and noise, for men kill best when little time is had for reflection.

Five feet is the greatest killing range—five feet from eye to eye. Don't stop to measure. Watch your opponent's eyes, not his feet. Rush at the enemy, holding the bayonet level with his throat, and as you come within plunging range, do not lose the one-fifth of a second which determines whether you or he will be killed. The surgeon dresses few bayonet wounds.

Vulnerable parts of the body are the face, chest, lower abdomen, and if the back is turned, the kidneys. A cut in the arm pit is as fatal as a plunge into the throat. Six inches is deep enough for a thrust else the bayonet can not be withdrawn; if it sticks, fire a round to loosen it. Many men have been killed by others of the enemy while trying to pull the bayonet out of the killed man beneath them.

When the knife comes out, if the air is sucked in, the wounded man begins to bleed inside, feels pain, and quickly gives up the spirit.

If the enemy parries the thrust and the fray is at close quarters kick him on the knee cap or in the crotch . . . Don't chase a fleeing enemy to stab him in the back—shoot him.[16]

—Army Field Clerk Will Judy
33rd Division

We were given automatic rifles which the French call "Shoo Shoo" [chauchat] guns. They were heavy unwieldy affairs, hard to carry and none too accurate. But at close range they were wicked and tremendously effective.

We learned to take the Shoo Shoo apart and put it back together blindfolded, naming each of the many parts as we did so. The magazine carried from 15 to 18 shells and the fire could be made very rapid if necessary. We usually fired it in bursts of two or three.[17]

—Corporal Asa B. Callaway
353rd Infantry, 89th Division

The French automatic rifle was never made to hit anything; in fact, the claim was that it was purposely constructed to produce a scattering fire effect and this it surely did, something on the principle of a shotgun, except that it fired one cartridge at a time; it was a cheap-made affair and likened to gas pipe by our men, who did not like it and had no confidence in it whatsoever. If noise counted for anything, it can be said that it performed very credibly in that respect.[18]

—Captain Emil B. Gnasser
126th Infantry, 32nd Division

Each squad had two automatic rifles and four ammunition bags of 2500 rounds to carry. We took turns carrying the ammunition bags. When they checked up after a hike my squad had only 1800 rounds left all told. What a bawling out they give us. Each of the boys throwed away a couple of handfuls every time it come his turn to carry. I throwed away plenty myself.[19]

—Corporal Joseph E. Rendinell
6th Marines, 2nd Division

Until this time we had all worn the broad-brimmed felt campaign hats. Designed primarily for wear in the tropics to protect the soldier from the sun and rain, they were impractical in France and, upon issue of the small and much more useful cloth overseas caps, were all discarded. It is said they were reclaimed into slippers to be used by the wounded in hospitals.[20]

—Lieutenant Robert W. Kean
15th Field Artillery, 2nd Division

On November 2, 1917, we received our trench helmets. At first they felt quite heavy on our heads, but it didn't take long before we got used to them and wore them every day, except when we had a little free time, as on Sundays, when we wore only our overseas caps. These we called our Dinky Caps, and I have an idea that the song, "Hinky-Dinky Parlez-vous," originated from this cap. Considerable time was spent every day with gas mask drills, and after a while we got so that we could put on our masks in a couple of seconds. We had to carry these masks at all times, no matter where we went.[21]

—Private Connell Albertine
104th Infantry, 26th Division

Five kinds of gas were at that time in common use by the enemy. I shall enumerate them briefly:

"Tear Gas"—Named for its reaction on the tear-glands of the eyes. Non-poisonous, but painful and highly annoying.

"Sneezing Gas"—So termed because of its irritating reaction on the membranes of the nose and head. A few whiffs would throw the victim into violent fits of sneezing. The Germans had the habit of throwing over the "tear" and "sneezing" gas for a time, hoping to render the Allied troops unable to keep their masks on, then would follow up with the poisonous varieties. Later we learned a great deal of this practice from experience.

"Chlorine Gas"—A suffocating gas, highly poisonous.

"Phosgene Gas"—Having the odor of musty hay. Very poisonous.

"Mustard Gas"—So named from its smell, which strongly resembled that of ordinary mustard. The fumes from the "mustard" were not dangerously poisonous, unless inhaled at close range; but the liquid was one of the most cruel weapons of the war. The gas was fired in special shells, which burst with little noise, in the hope that the liquid, which was yellowish in color, might splash over the victim, burning him with such violence that no cure at that time was known for it. Some of the most pitiful cases we saw later were men whose faces and bodies had been burned with this merciless liquid called "mustard gas."

We were told, further, that gas was sent over enemy lines in two ways: by the "cloud" method, which meant that it was simply liberated from huge tanks when the wind was right, and by "shell," meaning that the gas was mixed with other ingredients and fired by artillery.[22]

—*Corporal Earl B. Searcy*
311th Infantry, 78th Division

To add to the job, we were presented with gas masks for the horses. The mask was a flannel-hood arrangement saturated with hexamine, and had a pad inside which fitted into the animal's mouth like a bit. The hood covered the horse's nostrils and almost reached to his eyes.

Along came instruction in adjusting respirators on horses. We were told of the value of horses, how scarce they were, and informed that a horse was worth four men. Our government could get a soldier by sending out a post card, but the procurance of a horse was not such an easy task. So, in case of a gas attack, the mask was first to be put on the helpless animal—the men being a secondary consideration. At first it was a "cinch" putting the masks on the *chevaux*, for they thought they were feed-bags, but they could not be fooled a second time. After experimenting a few times with mules, balky horses and the meek little stallions, most of the men resolved that in the case of a real gas attack, they were going to use their own judgment.[23]

—*Sergeant Howard L. Fisher*
306th Field Artillery, 77th Division

T he winter of 1917 was among the worst in memory, both in the United States and in France. For the doughboys, living in draughty barns and chicken coops, short on supplies of all kinds, the weather was especially cruel.

•

Day after day the soldiers awoke to a cold drizzle of rain interspersed with sleet storms and later by snow. Mud, snow and slush were ankle deep. Wood was scarce and almost impossible to be had. Hobnail shoes treated with grease and oil became pounds heavier with the clay mire of the practice trenches and drill fields. Soldiers roused in their billets of hayloft and barn to find the snow sifted onto their blankets. The frugal French could not understand how much the Americans were accustomed to heat during the winter months for to them this condition seemed perfectly normal. It became difficult even to get wood for the kitchen fires of the cooks, the wood details being forced to tramp four miles to the forests for a meager supply of green sticks—and these always cut under the supervision of an experienced French forester. Even after these details returned, the wood was so green it was difficult to make it burn, and the problem was solved only when these major domos of the kitchen saved the grease from the cooking pots and poured it over the wet logs.

Shoes taken off at night would be frozen stiff by morning. To prevent this, many of the boys slept day after day with their shoes on.[24]

—*James H. Fifield*
Historian, 104th Infantry, 26th Division

At night, the boys would take off their shoes and leave them near their bunks, the shoes would freeze, and on several mornings when they could not get them on they were compelled to put a piece of paper in the shoes and set it on fire to melt the ice. They could then pour out the water and put them on.[25]

—*Captain James T. Duane*
101st Infantry, 26th Division

The Quartermaster Department was not yet functioning properly and about the only thing received in the way of clothing in large enough quantities were stockings, and the boys unable to get gloves wore stockings on their hands while at drill.[26]

—*Sergeant George H. Thomson*
104th Infantry, 26th Division

With the cold winter there were cases of pneumonia, and deaths among some of the boys belonging to the division. I remember going to the funeral of one of the men from C Battery, to which I was attached. We marched solemnly, led by the band, with the body on a caisson, the coffin covered by an American flag, to a small cemetery outside the post. The band played Chopin's "Funeral March," usually used by the Army. It was impressive, with the volley over the grave and the playing of taps. But the moment the funeral was over and the band started marching back to the camp, they struck up "Pop Goes the Weasel." It seemed incongruous, but I was told it was on orders. The funeral was over, and from now on they wanted the men to think of more cheerful things. When every few days they heard the funeral march, the men not in the immediate number of mourners used to sing a parody. Congress had voted that to the relatives of every soldier who died in services overseas would be paid $10,000. The men sang to the tune of the "Funeral March":

Ten thousand dollars going back to the folks
Ten thousand dollars going back to the folks
They will buy an auto
They will buy an auto
Ten thousand dollars going back to the folks.

Automobiles in those days were considered a luxury, not a necessity as now.[27]

> —*Lieutenant Robert W. Kean*
> *15th Field Artillery, 2nd Division*

G radually, in a score of different ways, the Americans began to obtain some inkling of the seriousness of what lay ahead. Allied soldiers were clearly tired; the civilian population seemed to consist mostly of women dressed in black, doddering old men, cripples or young boys. Beneath their joy at the arrival of the Americans, there was a sense of desperation.

•

Our company was quartered for the night in the village school, the only building large enough to accommodate the horde. The brick floors in that schoolhouse were cold and hard, and the exhausted soldiers twisted about in their blankets and groaned, and wished for the softer earth outside. There was a little pathetic card in one of the classrooms, with a list of the Jeans and Gabriels and Pierres, and all the rest of the young village boys who had gone away to serve under the Tricolor and had never come back. "Mort pour la patrie."[28]

> —*Private L.V. Jacks*
> *119th Field Artillery, 32nd Division*

I lived in my pup tent with Lou Vinton. Lou was a typical extrovert, full of fun, would shoot craps or play poker until his last cent was gone. He could swear like a pirate and did most of the time. He had not a care in the world, lived each day as it came along and never worried about the future. The first time I noticed a change in Lou was during the train trip from St. Nazaire. I had not thought the war had impressed itself on Lou, but one day we were slowly passing through a city and a hospital train on the other track. Through the large windows of each car could be plainly seen the berths occupied by wounded French soldiers, swathed in bandages, may of which were bloodstained. These soldiers were silent, motionless, staring out the windows and right through us. It was like we were not there or we were wax figures. I was standing in the open door of our little freight car with Lou alongside me. All he could say as he saw these victims was "Oh my. Oh my." We were face to face with the bloody facts of war. It was a sobering experience.[29]

—*Private William F. Clarke*
104th Machine Gun Battalion, 27th Division

As I came to learn more about the way war was being fought, I began to doubt my ever returning to the States. We talked daily with soldiers from the front, and their stories, while they did not disturb us or create in us any fear, did cause a lot of the fellows to look at the whole thing from a sort of fatalistic attitude.[30]

—*Corporal Asa B. Callaway*
353rd Infantry, 89th Division

I remarked to a British officer that extra rations had been received and that I hated to send them back. He said in a surprised way, "Why should you think of sending them back?" And I answered that if I didn't I would have to pay for them. He said convincingly, "Oh, keep them; you will be bloody well killed before a month." I kept the rations and the Britisher was nearly right; 30 days later I was lying helpless in a shell hole and sixty percent of the battalion was either killed or wounded.[31]

—*Captain Henry Maslin*
105th Infantry, 27th Division

Notes

1. Clarke, *Over There with O'Ryan's Roughnecks*, p. 32.
2. Duane, James T. *Dear Old "K".* (Boston: Pvtly printed, n.d.), p. 10.
3. R.M. Cheseldine, *Ohio in the Rainbow.* (Columbus, Ohio: F.J.Heer Printing Co., 1924), pp. 76–77.
4. Francis P. Duffy, *Father Duffy's Story.* (Garden City, N.Y.: Garden City Publishing Co., 1919), p. 40.
5. Emmett, *Give Way to the Right*, p. 100.
6. Albert M. Ettinger, *A Doughboy with the Fighting 69th.* (Shippensburg, Pa.: White Mane Publishing Co., 1992), p. 32.
7. Maj. Gen. Joseph D. Patch, *A Soldier's War.* (Corpus Christi, Tex.: Mission Press, 1966), p. 27.
8. Floyd Gibbons, *And They Thought We Wouldn't Fight.* (New York: George H. Doran Company, 1918), p. 74.
9. Albertine, *The Yankee Doughboy*, p. 51.
10. Frederick M. Cutler, *The 55th Artillery (CAC) in the American Expeditionary Forces, France, 1918.* (Worcester, Mass.: Commonwealth Press, 1920), p. 62.
11. James Luby, *One Who Gave His Life: War Letters of Quincy Sharpe Mills.* (New York: G.P. Putnam's Sons, 1923), p. 304.
12. Albertine, *The Yankee Doughboy*, p. 81.

13. F.C. Reynolds (ed.), *115th Infantry U.S.A. in the World War*. (Baltimore, Md.: The Read Taylor Co., 1920), p. 32.

14. Patch, *A Soldier's War*, p. 50.

15. Wise, *A Marine Tells It to You*, pp. 164–165.

16. Judy, *A Soldier's Diary*, pp. 70–71.

17. Callaway, *With Packs and Rifles*, p. 65.

18. Emil B. Gnasser, *History of the 126th Infantry in the War with Germany*. (Grand Rapids, Mich.: 126th Infantry Association, 1920), p. 110.

19. Rendinell, *One Man's War*, p. 44.

20. Kean, *Dear Marraine*, p. 45.

21. Albertine, *The Yankee Doughboy*, p. 58.

22. Searcy, *Looking Back*, pp. 36–37.

23. De La Mater, *The Story of Battery B 306th F.A.*, p. 29.

24. James H. Fifield, *The Regiment: A History of the 104th U.S. Infantry, A.E.F. 1917–1919*. (n.p.:1946), p. 44.

25. Duane, *Dear Old "K"*, p. 23–24.

26. Herbert L. Adams, *Worcester Light Infantry 1803–1922: A History*. (Worcester, Mass.: Worcester Light Infantry History Association, 1924), p. 412.

27. Kean, *Dear Marraine*, p. 56.

28. L.V. Jacks, *Service Record by an Artilleryman*. (New York: Charles Scribner's Sons, 1928), p. 162.

29. Clarke, *Over There with O'Ryan's Roughnecks*, pp. 37–38.

30. Callaway, *With Packs and Rifles*, pp. 75–76.

31. Sutcliffe, *Seventy-First New York in the World War*, pp. 67, 77.

CHAPTER 4

Murder in the Mud

The first American division to enter the trenches was, fittingly, the 1st Division, which went into the line east of Nancy in October 1917. The 26th Division took its turn in February at Chemin des Dames; the 42nd Division in February near Luneville; and the 2nd Division in March near St. Mihiel. The experiences of later divisions varied, but most spent some time in the trenches to "blood" them before they were committed to the bitter campaigns of 1918.

•

We got orders to go up to the front. All of us boys went out visiting these French people in town. We told them we were going to Verdun because a lot of them have brothers and kinfolks there. Some cried, so we cried too. We sure put on a good act because they kept fetching out the wine and cognac. I guess I must of cried at every house in the village.[1]

—*Corporal Joseph E. Rendinell*
6th Marines, 2nd Division

Just after dark on April 2nd, my company started for the front line trenches. Of course there was mud; there always is. We marched along, singing and laughing. Three miles from the front lines the mud became deeper and we passed several ruined towns. When we were half a mile from the reserve trenches, shrapnel came over and barely cleared the column, bursting and throwing their deadly steel balls into the woods by the side of the road.

We passed through what seemed to be miles and miles of trenches, up and down hill, through mud and water about two feet deep. Arriving at the front line, we were cautioned to be very quiet, and the French guide led us to the auto-rifle post. He led us into our dugouts and showed us our bunks. There would be eight hours in the trench and then eight hours off for each relief, which was half American and French. He also explained the French system of challenging. The U.S. Army system was for the countersign to be passed around every 24 hours, a word, usually the name of some state or city in America. If I am a sentinel and some one approaches, I bring my pistol or rifle to position and call out, "Halt, who's there?" The party approaching halts and answers, "Friend." I would then say, "Advance, friend, and give the countersign." The party then advances and whispers the countersign to me. In the French Army, instead of a word, they use a number. Take seven for example. A French soldier on halting you would call out, "Three," and the person halted would answer, "Four," as four and three are seven. We had to do some quick thinking when we were halted as they called their numbers in French and we had to answer in the same language.[2]

—*Corporal Frank W. Anderson*
23rd Infantry, 2nd Division

Before the division entered the trenches it had been warned (Bulletin No. 37, H.Q.A.E.F., July 25) that military matters were not to be discussed in public places or at any time or place with civilians for the reason that the enemy gained "much information through injudicious remarks dropped by officers and enlisted men and frequently dresses his agents in the uniform of the United States or allied officers to accomplish his ends."

Facts or information which if overheard might be of value to the enemy were not to be discussed in the front line trenches, because the elaborate "listening in" system made it almost sure that the Germans would hear most conversation indulged in close to their lines. Maps or sketches were not to be marked to show our own position. No document, map or letter could be carried into the front line which if captured might be of value to the enemy; one of the most valuable sources of information was the address of a letter received by a soldier. No documents or insignia that might disclose any information if captured or found could be carried on patrol or by raiding parties or attacking units.[3]

—*Colonel Ralph D Cole*
37th Division

The trenches, being prepared for long service, were supplied with duck boards for the floors and sand bags for the parapets . . . Doors to dugouts opened into the trenches and were well reinforced as were the trenches themselves with timber. The dugouts were constructed to accommodate from 10 to 50 men, depending on the importance of the particular part of the trench. Bunks were built with one section above another in the dugouts . . . The depth of the dugout was from 10 to 40 feet.[4]

—Captain Roy C. Hilton
9th Infantry, 2nd Division

When you finally got down to where the troops lived [in the dugouts] you were in utter darkness. You may or may not have a candle. You slept on some type of frame that had a chicken wire for a spring and there were no mattresses, and you had your blanket. Now, that was the abode of rats also, and the greatest concern was crawling in with rats, because when you got down there, even if you did have a candle, it cast a very dim glow. You would take your blanket and ruffle it up, you see, and you didn't know if some rat had crawled in there or not. I mean these were great big field rats, you know. They were animals. They weren't house mice. And the air down there didn't have ventilating systems on account of the gas danger. I have never experienced such foul air as when I slept in dugouts when I was with the French. Of course the bodies of the men hadn't been bathed. They didn't disrobe. They just lay down in their regular clothes. It was the foulest smelling air. Well, those were the dugouts.[5]

—Sergeant Merwin H. Silverthorn
5th Marines, 2nd Division

In front of our trenches was the inevitable tangle of barbed wire wrapped around or tied to posts and stumps and trees, or to wooden or steel frames like overgrown saw-bucks. These would be thrown into the mass to strengthen places suspected of weakness. These masses of wire were usually as high as a man's waist and sometimes higher than his head. Never less than 10 feet wide, they usually were 40 to 50 feet, and at places where changes or other necessities had arisen, one would find a band of wire 100 or 200 yards deep. Behind this might be a trench or passage, probably invisible from the enemy's position, and back of the trench another tangle of wire.[6]

—Clair Kenamore
Historian, 35th Division

At one point in our lines we were very nearly thrown full length by an obstruction sticking out from the trench wall. It was too dark to see what it was and it was ordered removed at daybreak. Daybreak came but the obstruction was not removed. Instead we got some pieces of duck-board, built a box about it and carefully covered it over with earth. Everybody reverently stepped over it thereafter. It

was the foot and ankle of a French soldier who had been buried
there by a shell a long while before. No French troops had been there
for over a year.[7]

—Corporal Harry Adams
105th Infantry, 27th Division

The 1st Division fired the first official American shot of the war at 6:05
A.M. on October 23, 1917, near the village of Bathelmont just north of
Nancy. The gun was a French 75. There was no particular target. The man
on the lanyard, Sergeant Alex L. Arch, sent the shell hurtling in the general direction of the Germans and their Kaiser. The first doughboy wounded
was a second lieutenant, one D.H. Harden of the 26th Infantry. The first
prisoner taken was a German mail orderly from the 3rd Machine Gun
Company, 7th Regiment, 1st Landwehr Division. Badly wounded, he died
the next day.

•

My headquarters were in the middle of the trench sector we were
holding. It was a hole dug out of the back of the trench about ten feet
square. In one corner was a little box on which were a few pieces of
writing paper and a candle. Two blankets hung over the doorway a
few feet apart so when going in and out one blanket would be raised
at one time so as not to let any light shine out. I kept two runners at
my post with me all the time. There were little holes dug in the side
of the trench where the men would cuddle up and sleep in the day
time, and where a few would sleep at night who did guard duty
during the day. Strange as it may seem to you, some of our men preferred to be in the very front line trenches in this quiet sector rather
than in support and reserve positions because there were no working details taken from the trenches and there was nothing much to
do except lie around, write letters home, sleep, eat and talk in the
day time and "stand to" in the early hours of the morning.

Sometimes only a few men would be awake in the front line
trenches out of each platoon, but these men who stayed awake kept
an ever watchful eye over the parapets into No Man's Land. When
their time was out they would wake up other men to keep watch.
But just before daylight every man was awake and at his post. This
is called "stand to." It was just at dawn that most of the trench raids
were made by the enemy.[8]

—Lieutenant Frank A. Holden
328th Infantry, 82nd Division

Food was carried from the company kitchens in Badonviller to the
line in large containers constructed on the principle of fireless cook-

ers, called by the French *marmites*. With a stout pole passed through the handles, it took two men to negotiate one of them. Once in a while they managed to keep the meal lukewarm until it reached the consumer. Bread was brought up, uncut, in burlap sacks; butter in pails; and the other articles in whatever receptacle was handiest. The menu was simple and invariable, the quality first-rate and the quantity sufficient. It consisted of slum, that haphazard melange of meat, vegetables, and whatnot; coffee with sugar and condensed milk; white bread, good butter, boiled rice, molasses or jam.[9]

—Lieutenant John H. Taber
168th Infantry, 42nd Division

Though food was abundant, water, which had to be carried just like food, was comparatively scarce. One was fortunate if he got a canteen-full a day for all purposes: drinking, washing and cleaning his mess kit. The kits were more often scoured with mud and wiped with paper than washed, and each man's small dish towel became even more grease-encrusted than usual. There was hardly any water for toilet purposes; I shaved once during the week, using as a shaving mug my canteen cup from which I ordinarily drank my coffee or ate my rice pudding, and washing my face and hands from the same cupful. Many of the men used coffee for shaving, both because it was hot and because it was more abundant than plain water. The order which made clear that a cake of issue soap was all that was necessary to keep one's uniform free from spots "under all conditions" could not have contemplated such a scarcity.[10]

—Corporal Louis F. Ranlett
308th Infantry, 77th Division

I never saw such rats. Some of them were a foot long, not counting the tail. They were fat and arrogant and full of fight.

One of my men was bitten through the lips by a rat that started to make a meal off his face as the man slept. Those rats swarmed like cockroaches around our galleys. They didn't mind the men at all.

I was walking down the trench one day when a rat on one side saw me come along. He waited until I got opposite him, leaped to my shoulder, and before I could knock him off, leaped to the other side of the trench. He had used me deliberately as a stepping-stone to save him the trouble of climbing down to the bottom of that trench and climbing out the other side.[11]

—Colonel Frederick M. Wise
6th Marines, 2nd Division

Nearly all the dugouts were infested with lice, better known to Americans as "cooties." The soldiers' opinion of these little creatures expressed mathematically was, "They added to the soldier's troubles, subtracted from his pleasures, divided his attention and multiplied like hell."[12]

> —*Captain Roy C. Hilton*
> *9th Infantry, 2nd Division*

There is nothing so personal as a cootie, but hundreds of them infesting your clothes and bodies were sometimes almost unendurable. The name "cootie" was the British soldiers' name for that human body louse, a blood-sucking insect. In appearance it is similar to a potato bug, but much smaller. It laid its eggs in the seams of our underwear and uniforms. Our body heat produced generation after generation of them. The scabies were the result of the cooties' blood-sucking activities and caused an itching of the skin that was almost unbearable. Little sores and scabs would form all over the body.

When we found the time we would remove our clothes and kill the devils by squeezing them between our thumbnails. There was a satisfying snapping sound when they met their deaths. To rid our clothing of the eggs we would go over the inside seams with a lighted candle, cigarette lighter, or matches. This process never killed all the eggs and it did not help to prolong the life of the uniform. The cootie remained with us until the war was over and our clothes went through a delouser. If I remember correctly, our bodies were steam cleaned at the same time.[13]

> —*Private William F. Clarke*
> *104th Machine Gun Battalion, 27th Division*

*A*nticipating bloody battle, the doughboys were surprised to find that life in the trenches was more tedious than exciting; consisting of work detail, dirt and waiting for something to happen.

•

Generally a squad is assigned to dig a section of a trench. The men pair off in couples, one man taking a shovel and the other taking a pick. The man with the pick first loosens the dirt and the other man shovels it out; by the end of the night this gets very monotonous, to say the least.[14]

> —*Private Henry G. Reifsnyder*
> *103rd Engineers, 28th Division*

Long will the members of one working party remember a new section of trench dug for about three hundred yards across this front, where, when the stench became almost unbearable, the officers discovered that they had dug right into a graveyard of Germans made by the French just a few months before. But since the *Corps Du Genie* of the French forces had struck the line following the contours of the ground, the layout must be religiously adhered to. So the next night, fortified with plug tobacco, the platoon hacked out the trench, six feet deep, faithfully carving through the midriffs of a score of dead men with pick-mattock and shovel, one Irishman remarking that it was hardly fair to spoil "Jerry's" appearance by chopping his coat to pieces and leaving his boots and helmet untouched.

In one section of a communications bay leading from the support to the fire bay, the trench made a sudden angle to the right for the obvious reason that a cowhide boot was projecting. The men used to hang their helmets on it for want of a better hat-rack. Crawling on hands and knees up and through the ruins of trenches and mason work, one would discover on return at daybreak that the unusual "slush" of the night before had not been mud or dirty snow but the partly decomposed remains of a dun clad German.[15]

—Captain Daniel W. Strickland
102nd Infantry, 26th Division

We usually went out about 60 yards in front of our first line and if we worked fast and it wasn't too muddy, we could string 75 yards of entanglements in a night. The French and German strung their wire criss-cross, about the height of the knee, to tangle up advancing soldiers, but the Yanks used a different system. We drove a middle stake, leaving about four feet above the ground. The tall men of the platoon had to drive these. We used a wooden mallet covered with a gunny-sack to drown the sound of the blows. Then, on each side of the row of tall stakes, we drove a row of shorter ones and then we strung the wire. Sometimes we had gloves—usually we didn't—and we had to be careful or we either got tangled in our own wire or got our hands badly torn.

A wire was first strung along the tall stakes. No staples were used, the wire was just wound around them. Then wires were strung criss-cross from these stakes to the short ones. on either side and lastly, along the two rows of short ones. Twisting it around the stakes was usually where we tore our hands and swore at the Germans. We blamed everything on them, you know, from the mud, up to delayed letters from our sweethearts.[16]

—Sergeant William Brown
9th Infantry, 2nd Division

I nevitably, there were casualties. The first combat deaths were suffered by the 1st Division in the trenches northwest of Toul less than two weeks after firing America's opening shot of the war. Curious about the activity in

the opposite lines, the Germans brought up a special 100-man assault com-
pany to investigate. At about 3 A.M. November 3, 1917, German artillery
threw a box barrage around a platoon of F Company, 16th Infantry.

•

I saw a wall of fire rear itself in the fog and darkness. Extending to
right and left a couple of hundred yards, it moved upon us with a
roar, above which I could not hear my own voice.

The earth shuddered. The mist rolled and danced. Sections of
the trench began to give way. Then the explosives were falling all
around me. The air was filled with mud, water, pieces of duckboard
and shell splinters.

As I dodged to shelter, the concussion from one blast knocked
me forward on my face. Before I could get up, I was half burned by
another explosion. I had been carrying my rifle in my left hand and
pistol in my right. When I crawled from the debris, I could find neither weapon.

The barrage lifted as suddenly as it had started and I stumbled
on, hoping to get the men out before it enveloped our communication trenches. Almost at once, however, the efficient enemy artillery
threw a curtain of fire over our flanks and rear. We were boxed in. At
the same instant the German infantrymen, who had crept up within
40 yards of our parapet, covered by the artillery, began pouring into
the trench in three columns, each bigger than my entire platoon.
Hundreds of little lights blinked as the Boches switched on the electric lamps fastened to their breasts.

Ahead I saw a chau-chat open up. As its muzzle crimsoned,
some of the lights outside the trench went out. I started toward the
gunner. Then a flare went up and I could see that the space between
us swarmed with men in coal-scuttle helmets. Other Heinies were
running along the duckboards behind me. Halting, I looked around
for something with which to defend myself. An ax was sticking in a
log at the entrance of an unfinished dugout. As I stooped to grab it, a
violent blow in the back of the neck knocked me out.

When I recovered enough to know what was happening I found
myself on the parapet. Two Boches were holding my arms, while a
third searched the pockets of my blouse, much in the manner of a
highwayman. Nearby stood a German officer, smoking a cigar and
viewing the operations of the raiders with satisfaction. I had lost my
helmet and overcoat. The back of my head felt sticky and something
warm was trickling down my spine. Only enemy soldiers were visible in the trench from which I had been lifted. They were running
back and forth, brandishing pistols, knives and hand grenades.

Apparently, they had found no use for the rifles slung over their backs.

My men were no longer offering any resistance. I concluded that they had all been wounded or killed. I could hear some of them screaming in agony.[17]

—Sergeant Ed Halyburton
16th Infantry, 1st Division

In addition to Halyburton, the enemy raiders seized ten doughboy prisoners, some of them wounded. Three other doughboys lay dead in the trench, the first U.S. casualties of the war. Killed were Corporal James B. Gresham, 23, a former teamster from Evansville, Indiana; Private Thomas F. Enright, 31, an Army Regular from Pittsburgh, Pennsylvania; and Private Merle D. Haye, a 20-year-old farmboy from Glidden, Iowa. Haye was found lying in the mud of the trench, his .45 still clutched in one hand. The hard lessons had begun.

•

I was sitting in my dugout, with my hands lying listless on the table in front of me, when exactly at 3 A.M. there was a terrific explosion, which shook the old dugout. My non-coms immediately gave the gas alarm. It seemed to me that for about ten minutes the Boche sent over gas shells, when they changed to H.E. (high explosive) and shrapnel.

Of course all the men except the sentries took to the dugouts. I decided, however, that it was more dangerous in them than out of them, so I ordered all out to their positions and made them lie flat in the bottom of the trenches with the sentries standing watch.

The barrage lasted about 20 minutes longer, when the shells suddenly stopped dropping on us and we could hear them going over our heads. It was at this point that the Hun appeared and the men started to greet him. One man, especially, Corporal Patrick Hendricks, who was given the D.S.C. and afterwards killed in action, did wonderful work with his automatic rifle and accounted for a good many of the Germans.

I think we would have been all right if they had attacked us only on the front, but evidently the Frenchmen on my right were pretty well tore up. The Germans must have gotten in on them first and then continued against my right flank. Of course, I realized that we were done for, as I could see that they greatly outnumbered us. But we were there to hold the position to the last man. We did.

Finally, they managed to get into the trenches with us, and then the thing had become a hand-to-hand fight—kicking, biting, stabbing, scratching, anything to get the other fellow first. I found myself in a turn in a trench with my sergeant, Frank Wagner, and my runner, Private Dietrich, behind me. Six of the Boches started down the trench towards us, waving their 'potato mashers.'

I shot the first two, but the third one, in the meantime, threw his grenade. As he did, I jumped around the turn and yelled to the others, "Look out!" The grenade hit the wall of the trench behind me and dropped between my feet. I looked down, saw it and jumped, drawing both legs up under me. At that moment it exploded and tore off the right foot about six inches below the knee, the leather of my shoe holding the foot on. On both legs it cut me up pretty well.

Fragments of the same grenade hit Wagner in the neck and knee, and Dietrich in the arm and foot. The remaining four Germans rushed on us then, and as we lay stretched out, went through our clothes, taking everything we had. While they were at it a little Italian, Racco Rocco, came up the other end of the trench and started after the four of them with his bayonet. One of them threw a grenade which exploded under him. He died a few days later.

The fighting kept up a little while longer when the Huns evidently thought help was coming up to us, because they suddenly became greatly excited and started back with their booty and prisoners.

As nearly as I can make out, we had 14 killed, 16 wounded, 4 of whom died, and 12 taken prisoners, one of whom died, and nearly all severely wounded.[18]

—*Lieutenant John V. Flood*
308th Infantry, 77th Division

One man was reported missing during a German raid on the doughboys in the Seicheprey sector; his name was Glenn Hill and he had come with some other drafted men to the 104th Infantry, right in the middle of the Apremont fight. He had come straight from a camp in the United States; the machinery of war had seized him upon his arrival in France and had ground him through to his outfit with hardly a stop on the way.

He arrived on the 13th. The battalion was too busy and too tired to notice him; the guide who brought him in turned him over and he simply joined the nearest squad. The company where he found himself was just starting forward.

Later a lieutenant asked him about his experiences. "Did you get a Boche?" he asked.

"Yes, sir."

"Shoot him?"

"No, sir, I stuck him. I ran my bayonet into him twice."

"Didn't he see you coming?"

"Oh, yes, sir," said Hill. "He saw me coming, all right, and he hollered 'mercy, Kamerad,' or something like that. But I told him I didn't come all the way over here to play with him, and I stuck my bayonet into him. Then I stuck him again. But," he added reflectively, "I didn't do it either time the way they taught me in camp, at home."[19]

—*Frank R. Sibley*
Boston Globe *Correspondent, 26th Division*

Early one morning our French artillery, which had moved up during the night, put over a forty-minute barrage; we put over a machine gun barrage—and the infantry went over the top in their first big raid. It was the first concentration of artillery fire we had ever heard. The infantry penetrated the enemy's third line, but the Germans had fled and only two prisoners were taken. One was mortally wounded and died before he was brought within our lines. They laid him in the first aid station at Pexonne, and all day the place was besieged by American soldiers curious to see their first dead German. He was a huge, broad-shouldered, deep-chested Prussian Guard, and though we shed no crocodile tears over him, most of us will admit that we at least felt sorry for his wife and children he had probably left behind him.[20]

—*Private Ray N. Johnson*
145th Infantry, 37th Division

There were twelve of us who crawled up over the parapet. I divided them up in two sections of six men each. I led one and Vick led the other. We headed for a place in the enemy trenches where I had spotted a couple of dugouts close together.

When we were close to the trench I signaled the bunch to rush it. I sailed over the parapet and landed almost on top of a little runt who had a flare pistol in his hand. He was all ready to let one go. Before I could do a damn thing he let me have it in the leg.

There were nine balls in that flare cartridge. Nine red-hot chunks of hell and blazes were sizzling in my leg, and I went cuckoo. I swiped that baby-face and knocked him down and then jumped on him with my hobnails. My automatic was in my hand, but it never came into my mind to use it. Nothing came into my mind, with that hell's firecracker in my hide.

I jumped up and down on him, stamping him into the ground. He yelled bloody murder. He was nothing but a big baby with tears running down his cheeks, but that didn't help him any. Vick came up quickly and said: "Hey, that's not the way. Let me at him." Vick had his bolo in his hand, and he used it in the most effective way.

Vick was a grand fellow. They don't come any better than Vick.[21]

—Sergeant Dan Edwards
3rd Machine Gun Battalion, 1st Division

I remember one German corporal who tried to carry out a raid on our trenches all by himself while we were in the Baccarat sector. He was killed after getting fairly far in. Prisoners from the same company told me a few days later that he had received the Iron Cross and was so set up about it that he undertook this single handed show.

Sometimes, however, such men were taken after being severely wounded. I remember one corporal, I think a Bavarian, who was captured by a patrol which raided an enemy Cossack post in the Baccarat sector. This man was a peasant about 50 years old. He was shot in the belly with a .45 automatic, shot again in the thigh and had one testicle blown off. Then he was slugged on the side of the head with the handle of a trench dagger and obliged to run about half a mile across No Man's Land while our patrol retreated under fire. I saw him at the hospital in Baccarat a few hours later, shortly after he had left the operating table where eight or nine holes in his intestines were sewed up. He sat up in bed as fresh as paint, would tell me nothing, and practically told me to go to blazes. As there were other prisoners who could give us the information we wanted, and as questioning this man was simply "art for art's sake," I respected his courage and let him alone.[22]

—Lieutenant F.R. Wulsin
Intelligence Officer, 42nd Division

Major Hawkins asked if I would like to go along with a patrol. Would I? I was introduced to the patrol commander, Lieutenant George W. Hazelwood. I had never seen him before. As soon as night was on in earnest, we moved out. Major Hawkins and Lieutenants Wood and Hill of our battalion were also along. Several enlisted men too.

Moving about No Man's Land I was badly frightened. The fear of the unknown had me in its grip. Could the Germans see us? Could they hear us? Would they suddenly attack us from the flank?

We moved down between the lines to a point in front of the French position. An old road passed through the German wire here. We were crawling along slowly. I was shaking badly, but swearing to myself I would not run. The road felt track-beaten to me and I was commenting on this mentally when one shot, then a hundred broke loose, flanking us from both sides. Hand grenades were bursting all around and over us and flares had turned the night to day.

I heard Lieutenant Hazelwood shout, "Tell Major Hawkins that Hazelwood is wounded."

There was a terrific explosion right beside me. I turned and a private lay there groaning. "Are you hurt?" I asked. "I think my hip's blown off," he said. I felt his hip and put my hand into a ghastly hole the potato-masher had made.

The patrol broke. I wanted to shoot, but could see no Germans to shoot at. In the flare lights I could see our men escaping, running back out of the wire. Strangely enough, I did not think of running away. I was not even shaking now. Not that I was thinking of those things at the time. I don't know that I was thinking at all. It was a case of being in a hot, tight corner, and somehow or other there was no time to think.

Soon everyone who was not wounded was gone. The terrible firing continued. A short distance from me was a shell hole. I rolled the wounded man beside me into it. I saw several wounded and got them into the one hole. I found Hazelwood with several bullet wounds in his body and one foot blown off by a grenade. None of the wounded were able to do more than carry themselves.

Sergeant Gardner appeared out of the dark. He said Lieutenant Wood was dying in the wire to our left. I could not help him. I had several wounded of my own, but told him I would cover the opening with a rifle until he could get away. He saluted, and got Wood and saved him.

Firing had not slackened. I got the six enlisted men to the edge of No Man's Land and showed them how to get over to our lines, and watched them hobble away, assisting each other. I went back into the wire for Hazelwood. No flare was up. Darkness was complete except for flashes of grenades and rifles. I crawled too far and found myself almost to the enemy trench as a flare went up and showed me German riflemen shooting into the wire about twelve feet away. I lay still. As the flare went out I made my way to Hazelwood and got him on my back.

I started out through the wire. We were doing well, the noise of firing covering our efforts until it ceased suddenly. Every noise we made now could be heard. It seemed to me that the grass crackling under my hand could be heard in Berlin. But we had to get out. As I struggled with Hazelwood, he bled profusely. He soon had my back soaked in blood and it became slippery. He weighed 180 pounds and as I tip the scales at 135 it was hard to keep him balanced. I would have to throw him over the wire entanglements sometimes and crawl after him. This would cause the Boche to shoot up their flares and rake the wire again. We would have to remain mighty still.

Hazelwood was becoming very weak. He begged me to leave him. He constantly wanted to rest. I was afraid he would become unconscious or bleed to death before I could tend to his wounds. The enemy decided we were wounded in the wire and came out to get us. I could hear them talking.

They came into the wire in small groups. I told Hazelwood to remain away from me as I was going to fight them if they discovered us. I would not be taken prisoner. He asked that I stay right by him. If I was killed, he wanted to go too. I took out four grenades, his and the two I carried, and took out my .45 and waited. One party of three Boche came within five feet of us. I kept them covered, for the slightest sign they had seen us was to be my cue to kill them. It was much wiser not to fire otherwise. There were too many others nearby and they would annihilate us sooner or later if we were discovered.

The Germans, by some miracle, missed us. When they returned to the trench I gradually made my way out, with Hazelwood slipping and sliding off and on my back. Out of the wire, although still only 35 yards from the Germans, my relief was so great I actually felt safe. I stood up and undertook to lift my comrade up on my shoulder. As I lifted, I would get him about waist high and he would groan with pain. I cautioned him to be quiet, but each lift brought the same result until I discovered that all of his foot had been blown away except a long piece of skin, to which was attached his big toe. I was standing on this toe, endeavoring to lift him on my shoulder. No wonder he would groan!

This corrected, I carried him down into No Man's Land. I dressed his wounds and put a tourniquet above his knee to check the loss of blood. He had become unconscious. There came the faint sound of breaking sticks. Somebody was walking cautiously about the woods. The password last night was "Nevada." I heard Major Hawkins say, "Kick the brush and say 'Nevada' so if there are any wounded they will answer you." I ran to the edge of the woods and called, "Nevada."

I have never seen Lieutenant Hazelwood since. I learned, however, that his leg was amputated at the knee and he lived.[23]

—*Captain William A. Sirmon*
325th Infantry, 82nd Division

Notes

1. Rendinell, *One Man's War*, p. 59.
2. Oliver L. Spaulding and John W. Wright, *The Second Division*

American Expeditionary Force in France 1917–1919. (New York: The Hillman Press, 1937), p. 246.

3. Ralph D. Cole, *The Thirty-Seventh Division in the World War 1917–1918,* vol. 2. (Columbus, Ohio: The Thirty-seventh Division Veterans Association, 1929), p. 133.

4. Spaulding, *The Second Division,* p. 241.

5. Silverthorn, Interview.

6. Clair Kenamore, *From Vauquois Hill to Exermont.* (St. Louis, Mo.: Guard Publishing Co., 1919), pp. 46–47.

7. Sutcliffe, *The Seventy-First New York in the World War,* pp. 262–263.

8. Frank A. Holden, *War Memories.* (Athens, Ga.: Athens Book Company, 1922), pp. 74–75, 77.

9. John H. Taber, *The Story of the 168th Infantry.* (Iowa City: The State Historical Society of Iowa, 1925), pp. 77–78.

10. Ranlett, *Let's Go!,* p. 102.

11. Wise, *A Marine Tells It to You,* pp. 183–184.

12. Spaulding, *The Second Division,* p. 241.

13. Clarke, *Over There with O'Ryan's Roughnecks,* pp. 73–74.

14. Reifsnyder, *A Second Class Private in the Great War,* p. 54.

15. Daniel W. Strickland, *Connecticut Fights: The Story of the 102nd Regiment.* (New Haven: Quinnipiack Press, 1930), pp. 86–87.

16. William Brown, *The Adventures of an American Doughboy.* (Tacoma, Wash.: Smith-Kinney Co., 1919), pp. 3–4.

17. Ed Halyburton, *Shoot and be Damned.* (New York: Covici-Friede, 1932), pp. 33–35.

18. Arthur McKeogh, *The Victorious 77th Division (New York's Own) in the Argonne Fight.* (New York: John H. Eggers Co., 1919), pp. 12–13.

19. Frank P. Sibley, *With the Yankee Division in France.* (Boston: Little, Brown, and Company, 1919), pp. 127–128.

20. Ray N. Johnson, *Heaven, Hell or Hoboken.* (Cleveland, Ohio: The O.S.Hubbell Printing Co., 1919), pp. 78–79.

21. Thomas, *This Side of Hell,* pp. 186–188.

22. Henry J. Reilly, *Americans: All The Rainbow at War.* (Columbus, Ohio: F.J. Heer Printing Co., 1936), p. 221.

23. W.A. Sirmon, *That's War.* (Atlanta: The Linmon Co., 1929), pp. 164–171.

CHAPTER 5

First to Fight

*I*n the spring of 1918, bolstered by divisions pulled from the Eastern Front following Russia's withdrawal from the war, the German High Command sought to break the stalemate on the Western Front before the arrival of American reinforcements could tip the balance.

The blow fell on March 21 along a 50-mile front between La Fere and Arras. The goal was to separate French and British forces and then destroy them. The British Fifth Army was swept away. The Germans broke into the open, pushing westward, 40 miles in four days to Montdidier.

At that moment there were only six American divisions in France. The 1st was in a quiet sector near Toul; the 26th had just come out of the trenches at Chemins des Dames; the 42nd from the trenches near Luneville; and the 2nd was with the French southeast of Verdun. Also in France was the 41st, which had been redesignated as a depot division to supply replacements to line outfits, and the 32nd Division, composed of Michigan and Wisconsin National Guard units.

The French Supreme Commander Ferdinand Foch needed help and Pershing gave it to him. During the last week in April, the U.S. 1st Division—the soon to be famous "Big Red One"—headed for the Montdidier sector 55 miles northeast of Paris to bolster the French First Army, which had barely managed to stem the German advance near a little village called Cantigny.

The doughboys came in on foot. "Our socks were worn out," recalled Sergeant Dan Edwards. "Most of us were barefoot in our boots . . . We carried full packs, our clothes were crawling with cooties; we were so dirty you could smell us a mile."[1]

•

Just before starting on our march to the front, General Pershing called all of the officers of the division together and gave them a speech that resembled, in many respects, a farewell address. We gathered that we were going into a place where the majority of us would get killed or wounded and it was our duty to put up a splendid showing until this happened. We were to be a glorious example for the many who were to follow in our footsteps and should set them a very high standard.[2]

—Major Thomas F. Farrell
1st Engineers, 1st Division

With all due respect to the commander-in-chief, it was the most gloomy address I ever heard. He not only stressed the importance of our duty at the front, regardless of consequences, but also that this was to be the "swan song" for some of us. After the lecture, Barney Legge said he was going to his billet to prepare his will and advised me to do the same.[3]

—Lieutenant Joseph D. Patch
18th Infantry, 1st Division

The Cantigny sector was wholly disorganized. Front line trenches found their places on the map if "over two feet in depth." There were no dugouts in the front trenches and no communication trenches. My platoon occupied about 200 yards of front in which there were three small trenches. The largest was possibly 75 yards and contained seven or eight bays. The ground of that trench was very chalky and each man experimented in finding cover by digging a hole of some variety in the side of the trench under the parapet. It was better than being rained on. Sometimes a direct hit on the parapet from a 77 would bury the occupant undamaged under a couple of feet of earth. Anything larger than a 77 meant no further worry.[4]

—Lieutenant Jeremiah M. Evarts
18th Infantry, 1st Division

The worst part was the bunch of green replacements. It was the first time they'd been anywhere near heavy shellfire, and some of them just about went cuckoo. They were galloping around in all directions instead of getting under cover and taking it as it came. Some of those poor fool recruits started running away, and the old timers had to get out in the shrapnel and chase 'em back. It was a shame to send raw, untrained men up where they had to take that kind of shellfire for their first taste of it.

I won a bet that day. We used to size up the replacements and bet on how long they'd last in the lines. One man I'd bet wouldn't last more than two days was killed right there, first crack out of the box.[5]

—Sergeant Dan Edwards
3rd Machine Gun Battalion, 1st Division

I took it upon myself to look after a Private Jackson who could not bear the sound of artillery fire. Earlier, he had been hit on the cheek by a stone thrown up by a shell that killed two men; now he could not control himself when under shellfire. The men had threatened to shoot him if he didn't stop weeping and praying, so I took him. He was about 19 and stood 5 feet 7 or 8. His face was freckled, sallow and pale. He was quite thin and had washed out blue eyes. He looked scared and his hands shook.

The German artillery commenced according to schedule. It generally lasted from three quarters of an hour to two hours at that time of day. Jackson commenced to shake badly and he showed his terror in his face more than anybody I had ever seen. Finally he lay flat on his stomach in the mud and water on the bottom of the trench and wept and wept. He shook all over. It was perfectly terrible and I was at a complete loss as to what I should do.

I waited and watched him. I don't know how long, but finally I couldn't stand it any longer and I reached down, grabbed him by the shoulder and dragged him up beside me. He was covered with mud and the tears rolled down his face. I held his shoulder and said, "Now, Jackson, what the hell is the use in doing that? It only makes things much worse for you and it makes me feel like lying down there in the mud and crying myself and that would be a hell of a thing, wouldn't it?"

He went on weeping and I hung on to his shoulder. I told him I was just as scared as he was, if not more so (I think I probably was). Finally I suppose it penetrated his mind that I had hold of his shoulder and was talking to him. I doubt if he had realized it in his agony. He went on shaking, but he stopped crying. Finally he answered me, "Oh Lieutenant, I can't help it, I can't help it!" It was pitiful beyond words. I repeated what I had said before, but he merely moaned pathetically.[6]

—*Lieutenant Jeremiah M. Evarts*
18th Infantry, 1st Division

F or two weeks the doughboys sweated out enemy artillery fire along the two and a half miles of front facing Cantigny. The village and its environs lay less than 1,000 yards away on gently rising ground overlooking the American positions. German artillery fire was incessant: one officer compared his tour in the sector to "living in a room where someone was eternally beating the carpet." Casualties mounted—more than 2,000 men were killed or wounded between April 28 and May 27.

Finally, in mid-May, the French decided to see what the Americans could do on the offensive. The doughboys were ordered to seize Cantigny— or what was left of it—on May 28 in their first offensive action of the war.

The task was assigned to the 28th Infantry Regiment, which would face elements of the German 82nd and 25th Reserve Divisions.

The artillery started in at 5:45 A.M. At 6:45 A.M. the guns switched to a rolling barrage and the doughboys climbed out of their trenches.

•

Cantigny just began to boil up. And it kept on boiling. In a short time we couldn't see it at all, we couldn't see the ground anywheres. The air was full of trees, stones, timber, equipment, bodies, everything you can imagine, all smashed up and whirling around with the dirt. The shells kept right on going overhead in one steady screeching yowl, without a let-up.[7]

—*Sergeant Dan Edwards*
3rd Machine Gun Battalion, 1st Division

It was 6:45 A.M. The tanks were coming out of the woods, escorted by the infantrymen. Nothing could have been less romantic seeming. The tanks looked like haycarts (horseless); the infantry looked like haymakers that carried rifles instead of pitchforks. Nobody was running, or, I should say no American soldier was running, for some Germans had come running out of Cantigny toward the tanks with their arms raised in surrender. But the advance was wonderfully steady, and no one was falling dead, insofar as I could see. If a soldier did fall, it seemed as if he had merely stumbled.

And now our bombardment let up. And our soldiers were entering Cantigny and the smoke was drifting away from Cantigny and revealing that its buildings were no more.

And now our men were walking through what had once been Cantigny and now they were beyond it. They had taken Cantigny. And it wasn't yet 7 A.M. How easy it had been![8]

—*Lieutenant Daniel Sargent*
5th Field Artillery, 1st Division

Information had been passed out that Cantigny was surrounded with deep dugouts that would have to be cleaned out by flame throwers, but we had nothing to do with flame throwers. It was a new stunt to us. We didn't have experience with that kind of work and we didn't have the equipment for it. So the French had loaned us some of their liquid fire men.

One of them was traveling right along behind me, and every once in a while, when there wasn't anything else doing, I'd drop on the ground and watch him. I never had seen anything like it, and it interested me.

This French bimbo was about 50 years old, with a bushy black beard. The weather was hotter than billy-be-damned, but he had on the regulation French Army overcoat with its bottom buttoned back to the knees on each side. On his back he had two long tanks, each with a nozzle, and he had a big sack full of grenades swung on each side of him. He was loaded down.

Well, you'd have thought he was hoeing a garden, the way he worked. Just before we started out, he lighted up his pipe, and he was still puffing away at it the last I saw of him. He was just as calm and cool as if he was working on a farm. Placid and methodical, he walked along, smoking his pipe and looking around for dugouts. When he spotted one, over he'd go. Just as he got to the entrance, he'd unlimber the nozzle of his canned flame and yell: "Raus mit ihm!" in a tone of voice that meant, "Get the hell out of there!" As he yelled, he trained the nozzle down into the dugout and let her rip. Then he'd take out a grenade, tap it on his tin hat and toss it in. Then he'd fall flat and take a long comfortable draw on his pipe, tamping down the tobacco with his forefinger.

After the bang down in the dugout, he'd look it over carefully to be sure it was on fire. He didn't give them a chance to "Raus mit ihm." Then he'd go on to the next one and do it all over again. As mopper-up, that frog was right at the head of the class—a hundred percent plus.[9]

—*Sergeant Dan Edwards*
3rd Machine Gun Battalion, 1st Division

Then at about 7:10 A.M. everything changed. Our artillery fire had pretty much ceased, but a German artillery fire took its place. Huge German shells began to fall on Cantigny and they raised a cloud of yellow smoke, similar to that which we had raised by a bombardment a few minutes ago.

Lieutenant L.C. and I were lying on the ground side by side, squirming now and then to the right or left as if thereby to evade a shell that we heard screaming towards us. While engaged in this futility, Lieutenant L.C. began what seemed to me an inappropriate social conversation. "Lieutenant Sargent," he began. "Do you remember the date of your commission as first lieutenant?" I answered, "September 1917." "But," he said, "my commission was dated August 1917, which makes me your senior, in which case I suppose this foxhole falls to me." At this he ensconced himself in a three-foot foxhole, protruding from it like a jack-in-the-box with a broken spring.

A French captain heard our conversation and he had turned and seen Lieutenant L.C. insert himself into the foxhole and was staring at him not with contempt nor commiseration—but in sheer amazement. In all his war experience, he had never seen the likes of it.

I know now from books that there were during my stay at observation post "Pennsylvania" this day, four separate German counterattacks, two of which took place early in the morning and two in the late afternoon. All of which were repelled, but I could not see them. In fact, it seemed to me that all those hours were taken up by one long German attack, which I knew of only by seeing the bombardment of Cantigny that surely must be accompanying it.[10]

—Lieutenant Daniel Sargent
5th Field Artillery, 1st Division

The first I knew anything was wrong, a big German gets through to me from the right. He loomed up above me suddenly and began forking at me with a haggle-tooth bayonet. I'll never forget that guy. Every move he made is just as clear as it was then. I can see his face yet, all lit up and shining with joy. He looked like a boy scout that's doing his good deed for the day and doing it up brown. His map was just one big joyful glow.

I was astraddle the gun tripod, my legs sticking out, and my shoulders about level with his feet. He stood on the edge of my placement pit and forked down at me from an angle. His first prod knocked my right arm off the gun. Then he began jabbing me in the mid-section. I yelled "Kamerad!" to beat hell. You have no idea what it feels like, cold steel stabbing into you. The angle he was jabbing from kind of handicapped him. I was loaded down with junk which stopped the saw-tooth from going clean through me. But I want to tell you, a haggle-tooth bayonet is a terrific weapon.

He forked me four times and was starting a good vicious jab with a lot of weight on it when I rolled off to the left and away from him. I didn't lose my head entirely and I remember thinking that it was a damn good soldier who was killing me. He had guts to get through to me the way he did. And he took pride in what he was doing; you could see that.

He was all of six foot tall and his smile showed a mouthful of white teeth. I don't know why I remember those teeth, but I do. There was an Iron Cross on his tunic. It surprised me that I wasn't more excited. I could see it was doing me no good to yell "Kamerad!" at that hardboiled bozo, so I shut up. There wasn't anything I could do; there wasn't time. He had me, all right. He didn't intend to capture me.

As I was falling away from that last jab, my hand touched the grip of my automatic accidentally. It was in its holster, but the flap was open. In a jiff the old gun was out and had plugged him three times right about where he'd been giving it to me. He kneeled down slowly on the edge of the pit and a mighty change came over his face. All the pleasure left it. He looked surprised and then disappointed—and then, just as he keeled over, he looked completely hopeless.[11]

> *—Sergeant Dan Edwards*
> *3rd Machine Gun Battalion, 1st Division*

*T*he doughboys beat off the German counterattacks and held on to the village—or what was left of it. In the initial attack, the 28th Infantry lost 522 men dead or wounded out of a total strength of about 3,150. Between April 19 when the 1st Division arrived and July 13 when it finally left, the Big Red One lost 1,033 officers and men killed and 4,197 wounded.

By the standards of the day, Cantigny was practically a skirmish. At home, however, the fight inspired banner headlines. One commander described the fight as "a brilliant local action." But even as the doughboys stormed Cantigny, events were already moving to relegate it to the backwaters of the war.

Early on the morning of May 27, the Germans launched a major offensive on the Ainse front. Coming as a complete surprise to the Allies, the attack carried the formidable Chemin des Dames in the first rush and crossed the Ainse River at about noon on bridges the French failed to destroy. By evening the Germans were south of the Vesle River. By May 29, Soissons had fallen and the French government was preparing to flee Paris. Reserves from every quarter were rushed to the front to meet the threat. Among them was the U.S. 2nd Division—consisting of a brigade of Army and a brigade of U.S. Marines—which went into position northwest of Chateau Thierry near a patch of forest none of them had ever heard of . . . Belleau Wood.

•

Orders had been received that on May 31st the regiment was to move at 4 A.M. It was our understanding that we were to relieve the 1st Division which had been fighting at Cantigny in front of Montdidier. Billeting officers had already been sent ahead to that area. But about midnight word came that we were not to move in this direction, but that we were to start east in the direction where the Germans had just broken through at the Chemin des Dames, east of Soissons. From reports which we had seen in the *Paris Herald*, they had advanced very fast and were now approaching the Marne, with the road seemingly wide open to Paris.

We left Delincourt at 6 A.M. It was a beautiful spring morning.

We rode about two miles to a crossroad. Here we came upon a long line of motor trucks. In them were our division infantry—the 23rd and 9th Regiments and the two regiments of Marines—packed like sardines in camions with little yellow Annamite drivers from French Indochina. They passed in a seemingly endless line of motor trucks raising clouds of dust, towards the east in the direction of the German breakthrough.[12]

—*Lieutenant Robert W. Kean*
15th Field Artillery, 2nd Division

The long caravan of camions took a route that brought us close to Paris. The people in these small villages ran out and yelled, "The Americans are coming." Most of these people had never seen American Marines and soldiers in great numbers as there were now, miles and miles of camions all loaded with American soldiers. We were kidding and joking with them as if we were on a picnic. Children were yelling, "Vive l'Amerique."[13]

—*Corporal Joseph E. Rendinell*
6th Marines, 2nd Division

It was a long ride and a hard one. We passed to the north of Paris, and little did I think then that in a few weeks I would be coming back over the same road, wounded and out of it all.

The road ran by a cemetery.

"Here's a quiet sector," someone shouted with a laugh, "let's take over here."[14]

—*Private Wayne W. French*
5th Marines, 2nd Division

The minute we got outside Meaux, I knew that hell had broken loose. It was the first time I had seen civilian refugees in France. They streamed down the road; old and young; in oxcarts, in horse-drawn wagons, on foot. Some of them trudged along pushing baby carriages in which their household belongings were piled and tied with cord. Old men and old women tottered along. Children walked in groups, too terrified even to talk much. Hundreds carried things in their arms or in bundles on their backs. All looked terror stricken. Then I noticed a couple of steam rollers marked "Soissons," so I knew the Germans had broken through there.[15]

—*Colonel Frederick M. Wise*
6th Marines, 2nd Division

We passed French soldiers going to the rear, on the roads and in the fields, the backwash of an army in retreat. Some turned their heads away, others saluted us disparagingly, while a few even shouted,

"Fini la guerre," and waved for us to go back. They had small faith in our ability to stop the Germans. Well, we had plenty of doubts about theirs, too.[16]

—*Lieutenant Elliott D. Cooke*
5th Marines, 2nd Division

It was rolling country, with small woods scattered all about and farm land in between. From many of the little hills a good view could be obtained of a considerable expanse of beautiful, pastoral landscape.

Of these woods Belleau was the largest, being about two kilometers from north to south and something over a kilometer from east to west. A kilometer is about three fifths of a mile. It was, therefore, not a large forest, but it loomed up before us like a heavy, menacing frown in the landscape. It was a typical piece of well-kept French woodland, which the foresters had thinned and cared for so that the timber was of fairly uniform size and the underbrush fairly well cleared out inside. At the edges there was some undergrowth and smaller trees and sapling. The timber was not large but grew very thickly. The trees were rather tall. I should say they would not average more than five or six inches in diameter, but they were set so closely that when our men got in they found they could see not more than fifteen or twenty feet through the wood, except where ax or shell fire had made small clearings. Belleau Wood stood on high, rocky ground and hid innumerable gullies and boulder heaps.[17]

—*Colonel Albertus W. Catlin*
6th Marines, 2nd Division

The enemy shelled us at short intervals the whole time of our stay in this position. We would shoot craps beside the guns under the camouflage and, when we would hear the whistle of a shell, we would take cover in a small trench we had dug a few feet in rear of our gun. At one time I saw $200 lie on a blanket while everybody had taken cover. At this time everybody had plenty of money as there was no way of spending it.[18]

—*Sergeant Anthony D. Cone*
15th Field Artillery, 2nd Division

When we were up there fighting, they told us to dig in. I did not have a shovel and had to use my hands and bayonet. Some of the boys wanted to pay 100 francs or $20 for a shovel. Gee, it was great seeing those guys looking for shovels. I found a German shovel and dug with that.[19]

—*Corporal Joseph E. Rendinell*
6th Marines, 2nd Division

*O*n June 2 the German advance struck the doughboy line as French resistance melted away. The Marines, trained in the school of the rifle, peered over the sights of their Springfields and waited patiently.

•

The German attack was coming. A long way off over those grain fields I could see thin lines of infantry advancing.

It wasn't the mass formation I had expected to see after what I had heard of German attacks. Those lines were well extended. At least six or seven paces of open space were between the men. There seemed to be four or five lines, about 25 yards apart. They wore the "coal scuttle" helmet. Their rifles, bayonets fixed, were at the ready. They advanced slowly and steadily. I couldn't distinguish any leaders.

They came within close range. Not a shot had come from our lines. Not a man had tried any wild shooting at long range. Those ten months of drastic discipline and terrific training had done their work. From where I stood I could see maybe 500 yards down the line in each direction. In their fox holes the Marines lay motionless, watching over their rifle sights.

Suddenly, when the German front line was about 100 yards from us, we opened up. Up and down the line I could see my men working their rifle bolts. I looked for the front line of Germans. There wasn't any . . . Their second line moved steadily forward. Their rifles were at their shoulders. They were shooting as they came. Suddenly, they, too, crumpled and vanished. That deadly rifle fire seemed to take the heart out of the Germans who were still on their feet. Suddenly, they broke ranks and ran. Back through the grain fields they retreated raggedly, and vanished in the distance.[20]

—*Colonel Frederick M. Wise*
5th Marines, 2nd Division

*G*erman pressure against the Marine line lifted by the night of June 3, but the enemy artillery continued to rip into the doughboy positions. Casualties mounted and the Marine Brigade alone suffered 200 killed and wounded on June 4 when no movement of any kind was attempted.

•

We were caught in an enemy artillery barrage that lasted about two hours. Our first casualty occurred then, a Corporal Johnson was hit by a piece of shell through the back and died a few minutes afterwards.

We sought protection everywhere, falling flat on our faces as we heard shells come screeching down. That was our only protection. We just had to lie flat wondering if the next was going to get us. One shell landed about 15 feet from me and exploded. I heard a scream at the same time and looked up. It had landed in a hole where two chaps from another company were lying. Several of us rushed over to the spot and pulled them out. They were horribly cut up, but not dead. A horse tied to a tree about five feet away was killed instantly. I think it was the poor animal that screamed. An ambulance rolled by at that moment and we stopped it, had the boys' wounds dressed and they were rolled away. I can't begin to describe my state of mind—you will just have to imagine it.[21]

—Private E.A. Wahl
6th Marines, 2nd Division

This is what we seen out there. Some of the boys was using dead Marines for breastworks. At another place there was a pile of them, arms and legs lying around. The Major ordered them buried. The boy he gave the order to says, "Major, they were buried once, sir, but the German's artillery blowed them out again."[22]

—Corporal Joseph E. Rendinell
6th Marines, 2nd Division

Along the road came Lieutenant Herman Zischke, dragging a black Gladstone bag. He had just returned from some officers' school back in the rear areas. And having ridden all night in a boxcar previously used for transporting coal, he was hot, dirty and bedraggled. We cheered right up at the sight of anyone more miserable than ourselves. When Zischke pulled out an American newspaper printed in Paris, we forgot all about Fritz and his artillery.

The name of our outfit was spread across the front page in six-inch headlines. The paper stated that we had saved Paris. It was hard to figure out because we hadn't done enough fighting to save anything. But Zischke explained. "The Frenchmen you relieved did a Paul Revere right into Paris. They warned everybody on a 40-mile front that there was nothing between Paris and the Germans but a few Americans and the whole country migrated south. So when the Germans didn't show up in the Rue de la Paix, the French decided you-all had saved their capital."

That made us laugh, but our chests stuck out a few more inches just the same. If Paris could be saved that easily, we ought to be able to take Berlin without half trying.[23]

—Lieutenant Elliot D. Cooke
5th Marines, 2nd Division

The German line had settled down with the skill of long experience. Their left was tied in on an eminence known as Hill 204, their right on another called Hill 165. Their center lay in Belleau Wood itself. On June 5, General Joseph Degoutte, the Frenchman who commanded the sector, ordered the Marines to attack the line in and west of Belleau Wood. The first attack was to jump off at 5 A.M.; the second, against the wood itself, 12 hours later.

•

Five minutes before five o'clock, the order for the advance reached our pit. It was brought there by a second lieutenant, a platoon commander.

We hurriedly finished the contents of the can of cold corned willy which one of the machine gunners and I were eating. The machine guns were taken down and the barrels, cradles and tripods were handed over to the members of the crew whose duties it was to carry them.

And then we went over. There are really no heroics about it. There is no bugle call, no sword waving, no theatricalism—it's just plain get up and go over. And it is done just the same as one would walk across a peaceful wheat field out in Iowa.

But with the appearance of our first line, as it stepped from the shelter of the woods into the open exposure of the flat field, the woods opposite began to crackle and rattle with the enemy machine gun fire. Our men advanced in open order, ten and twelve feet between men. Sometimes a squad would run forward fifty feet and drop. And as its members flattened on the ground for safety another squad would rise from the ground and make another rush.[24]

—*Floyd Gibbons*
Correspondent, Chicago Tribune

The platoons came out of the woods as dawn was getting gray. The light was strong when they advanced into the open wheat, now all starred with dewy poppies, red as blood . . . One old noncom—was it Jerry Finnegan of the 49th?—had out a can of salmon, hoarded somehow against hard times. He haggled it open with his bayonet and went forward so, eating chunks of goldfish from the point of that wicked knife. "Finnegan"—his platoon commander, a young gentleman inclined to peevishness before he'd had his morning coffee, was annoyed—"when you are quite through with your refreshments, you can damn well fix that bayonet and get on with the war!" "Aye, aye, sir!" Finnegan was an old Haitian soldier, and had a breezy manner with very young lieutenants—"Th' lootenant want some?" Two hours later Sergeant Jerry Finnegan lay dead across a Maxim gun with his bayonet in the body of the gunner.[25]

—Lieutenant John W. Thomason, Jr.
5th Marines, 2nd Division

I was in the first platoon and our platoon was on the right flank of the company, so we advanced a little too fast for the rest of the company and Don (Captain Donald Duncan) came over and made us halt till the rest of the company got on line with us. At that time we were within 600 yards of our objective. While he was over talking to Mr. Lockert, our platoon leader, the bullets were singing all around us and I asked him, as a joke, if he thought we would see much action. He said, "Oh! Yes, we will give and take. But be sure you take more than you give." I guess he meant lives.

Anyway, he started down the hill and it was not a minute till down he went. The top soldier was with him all the time and I was there in a jiffy. We got a naval doctor, a hospital apprentice, the top and myself and carried him to a small clump of trees. All the time he was gasping, hit through the stomach. We no more than laid him on the ground when a big eight-inch shell came in and killed all but myself. I was knocked down, but my helmet saved me.

So I left them and rejoined my platoon, just in time to enter the town and get a bullet through my cartridge belt, and exploded three shells, but still untouched. At last Fritz took me down, with gas.[26]

—Gunnery Sergeant Aloysius P. Sheridan
6th Marines, 2nd Division

We started off in trench warfare formation, the only formation we knew, which consisted of four waves with the first wave and all waves holding their rifles at what is called "high port," not even aiming or firing or hip firing or anything like that. And the first wave, consisting of riflemen and hand grenadiers that were supposed to throw hand grenades to protect the riflemen; the second wave consisting of rifle grenadiers, people who had rifle grenades and riflemen; and then the third wave duplicating the first wave, and the fourth wave duplicating the second wave—with 75 meters between the first wave and the second wave—and then actually the third and fourth waves are replacements for first and second wave . . .

Now we got out of these woods and we moved towards Belleau Woods, which we could see at this high point, nobody firing a shot. Bayonets fixed, moving at a low steady cadence that we had been taught to move, because theoretically a barrage is shooting in front of you and you don't want to go too fast or you'll walk into your own barrage . . . On our left, approximately 200 yards, and I've checked this in peacetime, was the redoubt of Belleau Woods. It's an eminence, a little raised place; the little hunting lodge was up there. It's a rocky place. It was teeming with machine guns; I mean it seemed that way. And nobody, literally nobody was firing a shot at these Germans. They had us enfiladed. They were to our left front; and as we got out far enough, we were perfectly enfiladed from them. So it was absolutely like a shooting gallery and not a single Marine of ours firing a shot. We weren't trained that way. We went on.

Well of course, as soon as we came out of this first band of woods in my platoon (there were approximately 52 men) there were only six people got across the first 75 yards. All the rest were killed, wounded and pinned down. I mean we were down into a ravine which was perfectly enfiladed and just bloop, a few machine guns— and that was it. So the lieutenant and I stopped halfway across this ravine behind some cord wood to get our bearings and then moved on and then got up beyond this, which is still under a hundred yards. The lieutenant looked around and said, "Where the hell is my platoon?" Well, his platoon was mostly killed and wounded; there were six of us. He said, "I'm going on back." Well, he told me to stick with him, and I thought, "Here's where you and I part company, because we just got across this place, and that's the last thing I'm going to do—go back." Nobody ever got in trouble for going toward the enemy.[27]

> —Sergeant Merwin H. Silverthorn
> 5th Marines, 2nd Division

There was yelling and swearing in the wheat, and the lines, much thinned, got into the woods. Some grenades went off; there was screaming and a tumult, and the "taka-taka-taka-taka" of the Maxim guns died down . . .

Then the men who mounted the slope found themselves in a cleared area, full of orderly French wood-piles, and apparently there was a machine gun to every wood-pile. Jerry Finnegan died here, sprawled across one of them. Lieutenant Somers died here. One lieutenant[28] found himself behind a wood-pile with a big auto-rifleman. Just across from them, very near, a machine gun behind another wood-pile was searching for them. The lieutenant, all his world narrowed to that little place, peered vainly for a loophole; the sticks were jumping and shaking as the Maxim flailed them; bullets rang under his helmet. "Here, Morgan," he said, "I'll poke my tin hat around this side, and you watch and see if you can get the chau-chat on them—" He stuck the helmet on his bayonet and thrust it out.

Something struck it violently from the point, and the rifle made his
fingers tingle. The chau-chat went off, once. In the same breath there
was an odd noise above him . . . the machine gun . . . he looked up.
Morgan's body was slumping down to its knees; it leaned forward
against the wood, the chau-chat, still grasped in a clenched hand,
coming to the ground butt first. The man's head was gone from the
eyes up; his helmet slid stickily back over his combat pack and lay
on the ground . . . "My mother," reflected the lieutenant, "will never
find my grave in this place!" He picked up the chau-chat, and examined it professionally, noting a spatter of little thick red drops on the
breech, and the fact that the clip showed one round expended. The
charging handle was back. He got to his feet with deliberation, laid
the gun across the wood-pile and sighted . . . three Boche with very
red faces; their eyes looked pale under their deep helmets . . . He
gave them the whole clip, and they appeared to wilt. Then he came
away from there. Later he was in the little run at the foot of the hill
with three men, all wounded. He never knew how he got there. It
just happened.[29]

—Lieutenant John W. Thomason, Jr.
5th Marines, 2nd Division

Wounded began trickling back. They told conflicting stories. Some
were cheerful and said our gang was licking hell out of the Boche.
But a few seemed depressed, telling stories of whole platoons being
wiped out by machine guns. We gave them cigarettes and went back
and sat in our holes.[30]

—Lieutenant Elliot D. Cooke
5th Marines, 2nd Division

[I took cover.] In order to keep as close to the ground as possible, I
had swung my chin to the right so that I was pushing forward with
my left cheek flat against the ground and in order to accommodate
this position of the head, I had moved my steel helmet over so that it
covered part of my face on the right.

Then there came a crash. It sounded to me like someone had
dropped a glass bottle into a porcelain bathtub. A barrel of whitewash tipped over and it seemed that everything in the world turned
white. That was the sensation. I did not recognize it because I have
often been led to believe and often heard it said that when one
receives a blow on the head everything turns black.

I did not know then, as I know now, that a bullet striking the
ground immediately under my left cheek bone, had ricocheted
upward, going completely through the left eye and then crashing
out through my forehead, leaving the eyeball and upper eyelid com-

pletely halved, the lower eyelid torn away, and a compound fracture of the skull.

I began to take stock of my condition. During my year or more along the fronts I had been through many hospitals and from my observations in those institutions I had cultivated a keen distaste for one thing—gas gangrene. I had learned from doctors its fatal and horrible results and I also had learned from them that it was caused by germs which exist in large quantities in any ground that has been under artificial cultivation for a long period.

Such was the character of the very field I was lying in and I came to the realization that the wound in the left side of my face and head was resting flatly on the soil. With my right hand I drew up my British box respirator or gas mask and placed this under my head. Thus I rested with more confidence, although the machine gun lead continued to pass in sheets through the tops of the oats not two or three inches above my head. Those guns were not a hundred yards away and they seemed to have an inexhaustible supply of ammunition.

Twenty feet away on my left a wounded Marine was lying. Occasionally I would open my right eye for a painful look in his direction. He was wounded and apparently unconscious. His pack, "the khaki doll," was still strapped between his shoulders. Unconsciously he was doing that which all wounded men do—that is, to assume the position that is most comfortable. He was trying to roll over on his back.

But the pack was on his back and every time he would roll over on this it would elevate his body into full view of the German gunners. Then a withering hail of lead would sweep the field. It so happened that I was lying immediately in line between those German guns and this unconscious moving target. As the Marine would roll over on top of the pack his chest would be exposed to the fire. I could see the buttons fly from his tunic and one of the shoulder straps of the back pack part as the sprays of lead struck him. He would limply roll off the pack over on his side. I found myself wishing that he would lie still, as every movement of his brought those streams of bullets closer and closer to my head.

Sometimes there were lulls in the firing. During those periods of comparative quiet, I could hear the occasional moan of other wounded in that field. Very few of them cried out and it seemed to me that those who did were unconscious when they did it. One man in particular had a long, low groan. I could not see him, yet I felt he was lying somewhere close to me. In the quiet intervals, his unconscious expression of pain reminded me of the sound I had once heard made by a calf which had been tied by a short rope to a tree.

The animal had strayed round and round the tree until its entanglements in the rope had left it a helpless prisoner. The groan of that
unseen, unconscious wounded American who laid near me on the
field that evening sounded exactly like the pitiful bawl of that
calf.[31]

> —*Floyd Gibbons*
> *Correspondent,* Chicago Tribune

I felt that I'd hit my knee on a rock; and I looked down and found
there wasn't any rocks. I found that a machine gun bullet had
creased my knee. By this time we were reduced to an automatic rifle-
man and myself. There were two of us. I couldn't run; it felt as if
somebody had hit me with a baseball bat right across the knee cap—
a terrific blow, but no pain.

While I was out there, a friend of mine (his name was Pilcher)
had been hit and was crying and moaning. I asked him where he
was hit and he said in the stomach. I said, "Well, now, you just stay
right there and I will come back after dark and pick you up."

So I got into Belleau Woods, and there it was just as quiet as it is
out here in my garden right now. There wasn't any shooting going
on; there wasn't anybody there or anything else. There was just
nobody there and there wasn't a shot being fired. Well, I became
frightened for the first time—all by myself, and I knew I was pretty
close to Germans . . . so I headed back to Lucy to a dressing station
to get my wound dressed. By that time it was paining a bit and it
wasn't easy to walk. So I went in there and they tagged me to go to a
hospital. But I said, "No, I'm going back to pick up Sergeant
Pilcher." So I got ahold of a stretcher—there were no stretcher bearers—and one man and we went on back. Well, now it's dark and I
found my way by sort of instinct back to this wheat field. It's quite
dark now, so I started calling to Pilcher. And then all the machine
guns that had been shooting at me at six o'clock started shooting at
me again at 11 o'clock. And I said to myself, "Of all the screwy situations. Here you got out of this thing once. You're right back where
you started from." So I stopped calling, and I felt around and I
found Pilcher. I came across him, but he was dead. That was quite a
shock. I shook his body. I said, "Pilcher, here we are. I've got a
stretcher. We're going to take care of you now." But he was dead.[32]

> —*Sergeant Merwin H. Silverthorn*
> *5th Marines, 2nd Division*

*S*ergeant Pilcher was only one among many American corpses lying out
among the poppies. The Marines took Hill 142 just west of Belleau

Wood, the town of Bouresches and a small section of the wood itself, but it cost them 1,087 casualties. June 6, 1918, was to remain the costliest single day in Marine Corps history until the landing at Tarawa 25 years later. And still it wasn't over. For the next 20 days the 2nd Division's Marine Brigade battled for the wood. Still the men clambered out of their shallow foxholes, not so facetiously called "graves," and formed up for attack after attack. They were opposed by members of the German 10th Division, the 461st Regiment of the 237th Division, the 28th Division and finally by the 87th Division, which came in to relieve the survivors of the 237th and 28th.

•

Breasting the ripened wheat north of the Bois de Champillon we passed dead men—plenty of them. A German here and there, and whole squads of Americans. The Yankees had apparently been on a course at right angles to the one we were following, so must have been killed in the attack of the day before. Behind a handful of saplings lay an officer and three men. The officer had been hit high up on the thigh, had pulled down his pants to dress the wound, but had died before being able to stop the blood.[33]

—*Lieutenant Elliot D. Cooke*
5th Marines, 2nd Division

We went into hot fighting on June 11th at 2 A.M. A few hours before I had been on a detail that was bringing up hot coffee from the rear. Hand grenades were distributed and then Captain L.W. Williams lined us up in combat formation. Soon we were going single file through the woods and charging across the open area to where the Germans were secluded in their holes.

My duties were to load a Chauchat, or French automatic rifle. You could run about nine steps and then another clip would have to be inserted. Bullets slit my canteen, hit my scabbard and two or three went through my trousers without touching me. We had advanced in triangle formation about half a mile. I was in the front of the 'V' when three machine gun bullets got me. One went into the neck, another in my left shoulder and the third in my arm.

I tried to keep on in assisting the operation of the automatic, but the blood came up in my throat. I forced my way back and hid in a shell hole in the woods until a little Marine found me. This fellow dragged me 500 yards on his shoulder to a first aid dugout. There a shelter half was used as a stretcher and I was taken back to a larger dressing station.[34]

—*Private F.E. Steck*
6th Marines, 2nd Division

Our men were yelling as if they were in a football game. We crossed an open space of nearly a mile when we discovered we had hit the Germans' second line trench. Still we kept going. Of the 25 who were with me, only four remained. Suddenly we spotted a machine gun. Without a thought, the four of us started to charge it. Two of the men were killed instantly. I was shot in the right leg. The last man escaped.

I lay wounded for nearly an hour. For a while I hardly dared to breath. I was right in line with the machine gun's fire. The bullets sped past my ears so closely that I couldn't hear them whiz or buzz. There was nothing but a loud crackety-crack-crack as they went by. It was just like having your head near the muzzle of the gun. Soon the camouflage, consisting of high weeds, around me was shot away. Fortunately, the machine gun tried for another target about that time and ceased firing in my direction. I tried to crawl off, but couldn't make it very far.[35]

—Private John C. Geiger
6th Marines, 2nd Division

I heard a noise, a sort of moaning and crying. We listened to hear where it came from. There, out in a shell hole, was one of our buglers acting as a runner, with a leg shot off. I put a tourniquet on his leg to stop the flow of blood, gave him my canteen of water, and left him.

. . . Two runners were sent out, a boy by the name of Reynolds and myself. We both started out with a message apiece to the same commander, two different routes. I delivered my message and on my way back I came across Reynolds. He had no head. We did not have anything to eat. I rolled him over and looked in his pack for bacon and found only a set of barber tools.[36]

—Corporal Joseph E. Rendinell
6th Marines, 2nd Division

We came across a German officer seated comfortably with his knees crossed. Before him was spread a little field table on which was cake, jam, cookies and a fine array of food. A knife and fork was in either hand. Beside the officer was seated a large, bulky sergeant who had been knitting socks. The darning needles were still between his fingers. Both their heads had been blown off by a large shell.[37]

—Private F.E. Steck
6th Marines, 2nd Division

Captain Charley Dunbeck told me how Lieutenant Heiser had died. Leading an attack on a German machine gun nest, Heiser had been literally decapitated. His head had been cut clean from his body by a stream of machine gun bullets that caught him in the throat.[38]

—Colonel Frederick M. Wise
5th Marines, 2nd Division

Going through a barrage with a message, I kept throwing myself flat when one busted close to me. Once I fell right on top of a dead German. He was fat and ripe and his face came away under my hand.[39]

—Corporal Joseph E. Rendinell
6th Marines, 2nd Division

We got a lot of prisoners and they were mighty glad to be captured; at least, they said they were. I was talking to one in the ambulance who said that the war is over for them. He also said that he was going to get his family from Berlin and come to the States after the war. I told him to get that idea entirely out of his head, as we were going to lynch them as fast as they came. Just two hours before he had been mowing our men down with a machine gun, and now he is figuring on going to America to live in peace. Can you beat that for nerve?[40]

—Corporal H.A. Leonard
6th Marines, 2nd Division

I met a sergeant who had two prisoners. "Here, Corporal, take them, I'm in an awful hurry."

"So am I, Sarge," I says.

I saw him a few minutes later. I asked him who took those prisoners back. He said, "Oh, they had the dropsy disease. They both died of heart failure."[41]

—Corporal Joseph E. Rendinell
6th Marines, 2nd Division

Once, when we were going to attack on 23 June, and I had gone forward to reconnoiter, I passed an American soldier whose body had been completely cut in two, quite likely by a piece of high explosive shell. Actually, the parts of his body were on either side of the trail. Upon bringing my platoon up to its line of departure, I made a detour so that the platoon would not have to march between the portions of this unfortunate's body.[42]

—Sergeant Merwin H. Silverthorn
5th Marines, 2nd Division

It seemed that so many of the first to be killed were the really nice ones; we wondered why that should be. I even asked the chaplain about this and he said, "It's in the book. When your time comes, you'll be called." I used to read my pocket testament often, and asked him many questions. I found some comfort in his presence.[43]

—Private Ralph L. Williams
2nd Engineers, 2nd Division

O n June 26 Belleau Wood finally fell after a 14-hour bombardment fol- lowed by an assault by the 3rd Battalion, 5th Marines. The battalion commander reported, "Wood now U.S. Marine Corps entirely." The cost over the previous three weeks was some 5,200 U.S. casualties—about 750 of them killed—more than 50 percent of the Marine Brigade's strength. The French changed the name of the wood to Bois de la Brigade de la Marines and the resulting publicity on behalf of the Marine Corps continued to ran- kle U.S. Army officers and men long after the guns of this War to End All Wars fell silent. But for the survivors, all that mattered now was that it was over. The 26th Division was coming in to take over the sector.

•

We found only a handful of Marines holding these woods; the rest had been killed or wounded. They told us they had had no time to string barbed wire and that the Boches were approximately 500 yards away. What sights we saw! This part of the woods was literal- ly covered with dead Boches and Marines. The stench from these bodies was sickening, and again many of us vomited. There was no protection here at all. The Marines had used the drainage gullies alongside the cow paths for fox hole protection. They had gathered pieces of trees torn apart by shellfire and laid them over these gul- lies—safe from shrapnel, but no good for direct hits. There was no time to bury the dead because the Boches shelled the woods contin- ually, as we discovered when making the relief . . . The expressions on the faces of some of these dead was frightening. German and American equipment was strewn all over the woods. The Marines, who were getting ready to go to the rear, also told us that a lot of their buddies had been wounded or killed by tree splinters, so we must stay under the roofs of these quickly made fox holes as much as possible.[44]

—Private Connell Albertine
104th Infantry, 26th Division

The dead out in the wheat fields near Belleau Wood laid where they had fallen. We had no chance to bury them. There were Frenchmen, Marines and Germans laying together. One place a Marine corporal and three Germans lying together in a heap. At another place, a Marine in a prone position with his rifle to his shoulder and finger on the trigger, just as he died. Another with his bayonet still in a German and both dead . . .

Alarm Clock Bill from Chicago. I forget his name, but a shell exploded under him and we found only his shoe. Young Venn from Detroit and Beatty from the same state, coming out of Bouresches, a shell lit under both of them. Venn was only 17 years old. He got in as a bugler and changed for a rifle. The only thing left alive in Lucy was a chicken. We took it and kept it for the 3rd Battalion pet.

Some of the boys heard I had barber tools. Their hair was getting all matted up under their helmet and they asked me to cut it. Okay. We were standing in some fox holes when they asked me. I sat on the parapet and they stood up and I gave 15 or 16 of them a haircut apiece. One bozo says, "Ho, the last guy who cut my hair got bumped off." He didn't get no haircut from me.[45]

—*Corporal Joseph E. Rendinell*
6th Marines, 2nd Division

[Taken from an intelligence report of the German Army Headquarters, June 17, 1918.]

Examination of Prisoners of the Second American Infantry Division, from the 5th, 6th, 9th and 23rd Regiments, captured from June 5th to 14th in the Bouresches Sector.

The Second American Division may be classed as a very good division, perhaps even as assault troops. The various attacks of both regiments on Belleau Wood were carried out with dash and recklessness. The moral effect of our firearms did not materially check the advances of the enemy. The nerves of the Americans are still unshaken.

VALUE OF THE INDIVIDUAL—the individual soldiers are very good. They are healthy, vigorous and physically well-developed men, ages ranging from eighteen to twenty-eight, who at present lack only necessary training to make them redoubtable opponents. The troops are fresh and full of straightforward confidence. A remark of one of the prisoners is indicative of their spirit: "We kill or get killed."

MORALE—the prisoners in general make an alert and pleasing impression. Regarding military matters, however, they do not show the slightest interest. Their superiors keep them purposely without knowledge of the military subjects. For example, most of them have never seen a map. They are no longer able to describe the villages and roads through which they marched. Their idea of the organization of their unit is entirely confused. For example, one of them told us that his brigade had six regiments and his division twenty-four. They still regard the war from the point of view of the "big brother" who comes to help his hard-pressed brethren and is therefore welcomed everywhere. A certain moral background is not lacking. The majority of the prisoners simply took as a matter of course that they have come to Europe to defend their country.

Only a few of the troops are of pure American origin; the majority is of German, Dutch and Italian parentage, but these semi-Americans, almost all of whom were born in America and never have been in Europe before, fully feel themselves to be true born sons of their country.[46]

—Von Berg
Lieutenant and Intelligence Officer

Dearest Folks:

Still out thank Heaven, hope we get a good long rest. The hardships and dangers we endured, and they were not light, seem as nothing to the thought that we were among those few thousand devoted Americans who saved Paris and perhaps the whole outcome of the war. We do not talk much about it, but way deep down in our hearts we believe it . . .

I started this letter hours ago, but have had so many brother officers dropping in for visits that I could not finish. We are so happy to see each other again and so childishly glad to be alive.[47]

—Lieutenant Lambert A. Wood
9th Infantry, 2nd Division

Notes

1. Thomas, *This Side of Hell*, pp. 179–180.

2. *A History of the 1st U.S. Engineers 1st U.S. Division.* (Coblenz, Ger.: n.p., 1919), p. 19.

3. Patch, *A Soldier's War*, p. 83.

4. Jeremiah Evarts, *Cantigny: A Corner of the War.* (N.p.: Pvtly printed, 1938), pp. 1–2.

5. Thomas, *This Side of Hell*, p. 198.

6. Evarts, *Cantigny: A Corner of the War*, pp. 11–15.

7. Thomas, *This Side of Hell*, pp. 202.

8. Daniel Sargent, "Cantigny" (unpublished memoir), pp. 13–14.

9. Thomas, *This Side of Hell*, pp. 204–205.

10. Sargent, "Cantigny," pp. 14–18.

11. Thomas, *This Side of Hell*, pp. 210–212.

12. Kean, *Dear Marraine*, pp. 90–91.

13. Rendinell, *One Man's War*, pp. 91–92.

14. Craig Hamilton and Louise Corbin, *Echoes from Over There.* (New York: The Soldiers' Publishing Company, 1919), p. 58.

15. Wise, *A Marine Tells It to You*, p. 193.

16. Elliott D. Cooke, *We Can Take It and We Attack.* (Pike, N.H.: The Brass Hat, n.d.), p. 4.

17. A.W. Catlin, *With the Help of God and a Few Marines.* (Garden City, N.Y.: Doubleday, Page & Company, 1919), p. 104.

18. Anthony D. Cone, *E Battery Goes to War.* (Washington, D.C.: Pvtly printed, 1929), p. 19.

19. Rendinell, *One Man's War,* p. 137.

20. Wise, *A Marine Tells It to You,* pp. 202–204.

21. Kemper F. Cowing and Courtney R. Cooper, *Dear Folks at Home.* (Boston: Houghton Mifflin Company, 1919), p. 142.

22. Rendinell, *One Man's War,* p. 96.

23. Cooke, *We Can Take It,* p. 8.

24. Gibbons, *And They Thought We Wouldn't Fight,* pp. 308–309.

25. John W. Thomason, Jr., *Fix Bayonets!* (New York: Charles Scribner's Sons, 1927), pp. 9–10.

26. Cowing and Cooper, *Dear Folks at Home,* p. 271.

27. Silverthorn, Interview.

28. Thomason himself, apparently.

29. Thomason, *Fix Bayonets,* p. 13.

30. Cooke, *We Can Take It,* p. 7.

31. Gibbons, *And They Thought We Wouldn't Fight,* pp. 313–320.

32. Silverthorn, Interview.

33. Cooke, *We Can Take It,* p. 10.

34. Catlin, *With the Help of God,* pp. 150–151.

35. *Ibid.,* pp. 151–152.

36. Rendinell, *One Man's War,* p. 120.

37. Catlin, *With the Help of God,* p. 150.

38. Wise, *A Marine Tells It to You,* p. 221.

39. Rendinell, *One Man's War,* p. 123.

40. Cowing and Cooper, *Dear Folks,* p. 138.

41. Rendinell, *One Man's War,* p. 121.

42. Silverthorn, Interview.

43. Williams, *The Luck of a Buck,* p. 120.

44. Albertine, *The Yankee Doughboy,* pp. 152–153.

45. Rendinell, *One Man's War,* pp. 106–108, 123.

46. Gibbons, *And They Thought We Wouldn't Fight,* pp. 301–303.

47. Mrs. Frank Wilmot, *Oregon Boys in the War.* (Portland, Oreg.: Glass & Prudhomme Co., 1918), p. 6.

CHAPTER 6

Ebb and Flow

On June 16—even as the U.S. 2nd Division was locked in the battle for Belleau Wood—the New York Times *headlined the news that one million American troops would have arrived in France by July. So far, only a handful of the doughboys had participated in actual combat, but their moment was fast approaching.*

The mighty German assaults on the Allies, beginning in March and continuing into June, had failed to force a decision. But the German High Command remained tuned to the offensive. During June and early July the Germans gathered themselves for one final effort to end the war with the Friedensturme, *or "Peace Offensives." Initially, three armies would improve the German position in the Marne salient by pushing the French from the area around Rheims. Following this success, General Erich von Ludendorff intended to launch a decisive attack against the British in Flanders.*

This time, however, Ludendorff would not enjoy the advantage of surprise. The Allies anticipated another attack. Prisoners soon revealed the details, the date (July 15), and even the exact hour. The French prepared a defense in depth. East of Rheims, the U.S. 42nd Division was brought in to stiffen the French front line. But the main U.S. participation would be by the U.S. 3rd Division and elements of the 28th Division along the Marne River line just east of Chateau Thierry. The 3rd Division had been in place since mid-June, conducting patrols and digging in. The 28th had come in during the first week of July.

•

When the United States 3rd Division took up its positions on the Marne the French were positively pitiful in their state of nervous tension. We were given orders to speak to French officers and men only in the most optimistic terms. They said, "We are war-worn and

101

war-weary." When asked, "Are you beaten?" almost invariably their God-given spirit responded, "Oh no, but we are very tired."[1]

—Captain Jesse W. Woolridge
38th Infantry, 3rd Division

A cting on their intelligence coup, the French opened up on enemy lines with an artillery barrage at 11:45 P.M.—less than a half an hour before the German assault was to begin. Shortly after midnight, the Germans replied and at 1:10 A.M. two German divisions—the 10th and the 36th—launched pontoon boats and started across the Marne River toward the Americans. The French defenders ran. The doughboys stayed put, dug in along the river and a railway embankment parallel to the Marne.

•

The German artillery had our trench cold; the place was full of dead and wounded. Three direct hits had accounted for 15.

I was so frightened myself, I could scarcely get the men together. One sergeant, cool as a cucumber, came up and gave me an immense sense of help. There were three or four maniacs from shell shock whom we had to overpower. We dug some of the poor devils out and started them up the hill. The faint sounds and stirrings in the caved-in banks were terrible. Some we could not reach in time and one of these was smothered. We had one party of wounded all together and started up the hill at once, when a big shell fell right in their midst. I saw men blown into the air. Awful confusion again . . . The state of a wounded man, wounded again, and still under fire, is beyond description.[2]

—Lieutenant Hervey Allen
111th Infantry, 28th Division

Private Joseph D. Engle, two other men and myself were on outpost when the German drive started. Engle mistook some Germans for Frenchmen and went out to talk to them. Before that, I wanted to shoot, but he said, "Don't shoot, they are French."

Engle said something to them which I could not hear, discovered his mistake and shot down one of the Germans. They fired and he groaned and fell. He didn't struggle. We fired and the Germans ran. I crawled out to Engle and felt his pulse and listened to his heart and found no signs of life. We fell back and the Germans took the ground.[3]

—Private Louis Bell
110th Infantry, 28th Division

The fog and the smoke were clearing. Directly in front of us and down by the railroad I could see German infantrymen, wearing overcoats, coming straight toward us in approach formation, similar to that used by our army.

As they approached up the hill, they dropped out of sight until they drew close to us. The German infantry and machine gunners came on at a slow walk, as steadily as though on a drill ground. An officer at the head of them was swinging a walking stick. They were not hindered by artillery or machine gun fire.

Because of B Company stragglers coming across our front and because I judged it would be more effective to hold our fire, we waited until the Germans came as close as the British did at Bunker Hill, perhaps 30 yards, being more or less on different parts of the line. Near the center, two Germans were down on their knees. My impression at the time was that they were cutting our wire, but that could have hardly been the case, as they could have easily stepped over it. Presumably, they were getting a light machine gun ready for business.

I gave the order to fire, battle sights. One of our men near the center called out, "Don't shoot, they are Company B men!" I answered back, "They are Germans, commence firing!"

They did a good job of it all along the line. The man next to me, and I do not know who he was, quietly said, "Lieutenant, I am hit. May I go to the rear?" The breast of his coat was torn by a bullet. The automatic rifle squads were making their chauchats rattle like machine guns. The two Germans in the front were conspicuous and drew an undue amount of the first burst of fire. They were riddled instantly and time and again afterwards did I overhear different men of the platoon say that they knew they had killed at least two, as they described what happened to the kneeling men. Every man who fired at them seemed to be convinced that he killed them and to be unconscious of the firing done by others.[4]

—Lieutenant William Ryan
30th Infantry, 3rd Division

Lieutenant Mercer M. Phillips, in command of my first platoon to meet the shock from the forward edge of the railway bank, had been superficially wounded in the head. Corporal Delsoldarto was trying to dress it when a charge came over the top. Phillips seized Delsoldarto's rifle and bayoneted a Prussian officer five times through the body, and then this officer, with a supreme effort, steadied his hand by pressing his elbow on the ground and in his dying gasp shot Phillips, who stood six feet four and a half, through the brain.

One of my men, the littlest chap in the U.S. Army (it will always be a mystery how he got in), was a peculiar combination of insect, fowl and fish. He wore a disorganized expression of material calamity—the loose perplexity of unemployment. He was a fixture in the awkward squad and I tried every known system to get him out—discharged. He was with us, but never of us. He didn't belong, but here he was, even in France, drawing his breath, rations and seventy-five per.

Sometime during the morning of July 15th, while the fighting was at its fever heat, I heard a vigorous "Ughh" at my side. I looked down when I had time and saw this lionhearted little recruit coolly removing a beautiful Luger automatic and its holster from the body of a Prussian officer he had just bayoneted.

Later a staff colonel asked me for a pistol of that kind. I remembered the above incident and asked this quiet little hero if he would like to give his Luger to the colonel. He said, "Yes," and handed it over. I said, "No, you give it to him yourself." I wanted him to have the honor, although I well knew the tongue-tied embarrassment of a modest private in the presence of royalty.

He delivered the pistol without a word, and the colonel, to express his appreciation and make a pleasant remark, said, "Did you kill him?"

Replied the 'tongue-tied' private, "Did I kill him?! Why, @!*$%^ him, you could hang your pack on my bayonet sticking through his back!"[5]

—Captain Jesse W. Woolridge
38th Infantry, 3rd Division

*B*y nightfall, it was clear that the German assault had failed. Lieutenant Kurt Hesse, a member of the 5th Grenadiers, which had been shot to pieces by the 3rd Division doughboys, recalled, "I have never seen so many dead; never have I seen such a frightful war sight. On the other bank, the Americans, in close combat, had completely annihilated two of our companies. Lying down in the wheat they had allowed our troops to approach and then annihilated them by fire at a range of 30 to 50 paces. This enemy was coldhearted; this was already recognized; but this day he gave proof of a bestial brutality. 'The Americans kill everyone' was the cry of fear on July 15, and which for a long time, caused our men to tremble."[6] That night the German survivors began withdrawing back across the river.

•

[The next morning] Lieutenant Frank Glendenning and I took some men and went back to the fourth platoon trench. We took shelter halves and blankets and went through the ditch and picked up arms and hands and everything else. Some things we just turned under, and the most we buried in a great shell hole. Then we pulled out the men that were smothered in the dirt; some were cut in pieces by the shell fragments and came apart when we pulled them out of the bank. Lieutenant John Quinn, a Pittsburgh boy, who had just got his commission a week before, was so mixed up with the two men who had lain nearest to him that I do not know yet whether we got things just right. But we made three graves, and buried them in a very well-marked position, one man on each side of the lieutenant, just as they had died . . . A Catholic priest, one of our chaplains, came and said a few words, some of the boys knelt and it was all over. I got Quinn's watch, which was still going, and gave it to his brother a few weeks later on. We did not feel this so much at the time. Trying to get the identification tags is the worst, but you get numbed after a while.[7]

—*Lieutenant Hervey Allen*
111th Infantry, 28th Division

The failure of the assault across the Marne River concluded four months of offensive action by the German Army. The end result was an enemy salient some 37 miles in length along the base—from six miles west of Soissons to just west of Rheims—and about 20 miles deep, bulging out to the U.S. 3d Division's sector at Chateau Thierry on the Marne.

With the Germans now on the defensive, General Foch prepared a counterstroke. The target was the western face of the enemy bulge near Soissons. A penetration here would force the Germans to evacuate the salient at the very least, and possibly even trap sizable forces at the tip of the bulge. To lead the attack, the French chose the U.S. 1st and 2nd Divisions, both in reserve below the Marne River and brought up to full strength since the fighting in May and June. The two brawny divisions, each twice the strength of a French or German division, would launch a surprise attack at Soissons, going in on either side of the French 1st Moroccan Division, and what was left of the French Foreign Legion, the best troops the French had left.

On the night of July 17–18, the doughboys were hustled forward along forest trails toward the jump-off line amid a flurry of last minute confusion.

•

We hastily loaded into trucks, and after a hectic all-night ride, the 2nd Battalion, 5th Marines was dumped off in the edge of a large forest and told to take cover. There for the first time we had intimation that an attack was coming up. Lieutenant James Legendre, our battalion adjutant, arrived with notes and parts of a French directive. Legendre spoke French like a native—sort of with his tonsils.

"One does not note the precise day of the attack," he translated—as easily as though reading English. He rattled on to that part dealing with pyrotechnics. "A yellow smoke from an airplane signifies that a counterattack is coming. A green caterpillar from the ground will direct the airplane to have the artillery lengthen the barrage."

Captain Lester Wass jerked his head up from the helmet he had been using as a pillow.

"We don't have caterpillars, green or any other color," he protested. "As a matter of fact, we don't even have Very lights."

Legendre scratched his head for a perplexed moment and then brightened into a grin.

"Well," he shrugged, "we probably won't have any airplanes either, so what's the difference?"

The orders were brief and businesslike. Major Ralph Keyser knelt in the gathering dusk before the only map available in our whole battalion. The rest of us crowded in close, hoping to get some idea of where we were and where the fight was going to take place.

Being the junior officer present, I didn't rate much of a view. From my position I couldn't see the hachures on the map well enough to tell a hill from a valley. As it was, by standing on tip-toe and stretching my neck, I could barely distinguish a large blotch of woods under Major Keyser's finger.

Major Keyser paused while we scribbled notes. Then, without looking up, he continued: "One officer and twenty men from each company will be left behind."

In the silence following that statement I asked a question. It was more for the relief of saying something than to get information.

"I only have 160 men now, Major. Why leave any behind?"

Major Keyser's eyes remained on the map as he answered my query. "They will be needed as a nucleus to build new companies after the attack."

Well, I got what I had asked for and wished I had kept my mouth shut. So did everybody else.[8]

—*Lieutenant Elliot D. Cooke*
5th Marines, 2nd Division

I ran into the CO of the Foreign Legion battalion which was to jump off on our right. He was a big, fierce-looking French officer with a big black mustache and wore a Croix de Guerre with a long ribbon stretching almost from his shoulder to his waist, on which there were so many palm leaves that it was hard to count them. He was going over his area also. He gave me a drink of their 'eau de vie,' which was 'white lightning' and about 120 proof. We had a nice visit and he said he hoped it would be sunny on the morrow, as it was much better weather for killing Germans, and that he was looking forward to it. He looked as if he meant it, too. I confess I was not too keen about it, and had some misgivings as to what the next day held. This proved to be the commandant's last hunt, however, for he was killed the next morning just about the same time I was wounded.[9]

—Lieutenant Joseph D. Patch
18th Infantry, 1st Division

We sat there and waited. Waiting around is the worst part. When you know you're going over next day it sure does make you think back. You wonder about everybody you ever done a wrong to and you don't hardly say a word to anybody. You don't seem to recognize anybody. I hardly seen them and that's a fact. You're sort of walking in your sleep. Then every so often you begin to figure "Well, what'll we find over there in the enemy's lines?" And also, "What'll they do to me if they catch me?"

That waiting around before you go over always gets my goat. Gee it makes me nervous. After I get started it is different, but that waiting around sure gets on a guy's nerves. It makes your mouth dry. Everybody kept asking, "What time is it?" They would ask it a thousand times.[10]

—Corporal Joseph E. Rendinell
6th Marines, 2nd Division

Graham came to me very much upset. He had lost his Croix de Guerre ribbon, which he had worn all during the war. He had been with the French prior to our entry and considered this loss an omen of ill luck. I had never seen him so disturbed before. He said he had a hunch that the Germans had his number this time and now he was sure of it. He wasn't cold, but his lips were blue and his teeth were chattering. I was very much worried because I had charged him with maintenance of our direction during the attack and couldn't talk him out of his state of mind.

He did have the right hunch. I was not near him when he met his fate, but was told afterwards that the top of his head was cut off by machine gun bullets, and his death was of course instantaneous.

Graham and I had become great friends. He was a man of about my age and had done quite a bit of civil engineering in South America. He loved music and his favorite tune was "Poor Butterfly."

Every time I hear that tune now, it recalls sadness instead of pleasure and it takes me back again to Graham and the wheatfields
south of Soissons on that hot summer day of July 18, 1918.[11]

—*Lieutenant Joseph D. Patch*
18th Infantry, 1st Division

We hadn't reached the trenches yet, and morning wasn't far off. We
were right ahead of the artillery positions, and that meant we must
be six or seven kilometers behind the front lines. Artillery was
always that far off. I took out a cigarette and struck a match, and
before I could even light it, the nearest officer lammed it out of my
hand. "Cut that out," he ordered. "We're going over the top in two
minutes." Well, I thought he must be kidding and so did the others
that heard him . . .[12]

—*Sergeant Dan Edwards*
3rd Machine Gun Battalion, 1st Division

There was mists hanging low down close to the ground but it was a
right pretty day. Too nice a day to die. The country was rough and a
hard one to fight over. Plenty of woods and wheatfields and there
was stone quarries, too, all full of Germans. The wheat stood as high
as your waist in the fields.[13]

—*Corporal Joseph E. Rendinell*
6th Marines, 2nd Division

Waiting for zero hour within a stone's throw of the German lines
was a nerve-wracking experience. There was desultory artillery and
machine gun fire during the night by both sides . . . As dawn
approached and the enemy front line could be dimly seen, a figure
appeared on the skyline in the familiar outline of the squat helmet of
the German soldier. At first he appeared to be engaging in some
weird calisthenics, bending and twisting about with his arms working like flails. As visibility increased, we saw that he was mending
the barbed wire in front of his trench, working rapidly to complete
his task before daylight.

At 4:30 our artillery preparation cut loose with a roar, and the
German wire-mender disappeared in a shower of dirt, broken tim-
bers, stakes and wire as the shells shattered the Boche emplacements. The artillery barrage continued for five minutes and then
shifted back to the enemy support positions; our whistles shrilled
the 'Follow me' signal of the infantry and the Ainse-Marne offensive
was underway.

The new men of my company conducted themselves splendidly.
Lacking the caution of the old timers, they crossed fire-swept areas

without hesitation. I don't believe they recognized the buzz of rifle and machine gun bullets for what it really was.[14]

—Captain John A. Ballard
9th Infantry, 2nd Division

We moved forward at a slow pace, keeping perfect lines. Men were being mowed down like wheat. A whiz bang (high explosive shell) hit on my right and an automatic team which was there a moment ago disappeared, while men on the right and left were armless, legless or tearing at their faces.

We continued to advance until about 50 yards from the woods when something hit me and I spun around and hit flat. I didn't know where I was hit, so I jumped up to go forward again, but fell. I crawled to a shell hole near by. I don't see how I ever got there, as the ground was being plowed by machine guns. I heard later that my company had one officer and 29 men left when we reached the objective. We had gone to this sector with eight officers and 250 men.[15]

—1st Lieutenant Samuel C. Cumming
5th Marines, 2nd Division

Our boys were going forward in waves across the wheatfields, one line about ten or twenty paces behind the other. They were walking slow and held their rifles at the firing-from-the-hip position. They had pretty good distance, too, about five paces apart. Sometimes there would be a gap before you seen how, then another man from the rank behind stepped up to fill the place. In five minutes I seen one man move up from the fourth line to the first.[16]

—Corporal Joseph E. Rendinell
6th Marines, 2nd Division

I was in the fourth wave. The first two waves are much better than the others. After going over for about 600 yards and about 100 yards from a small town which was one of our objectives, I received my wound when two big shrapnel shells exploded beside the squad I was in, receiving it in my leg. The next fellow got his left hand blown off, the next was shellshocked and lost his voice, and so on. I could use all the paper in the 'Y' telling how each of us got wounded or killed. It sure is horrible. It is something that is impossible to express, but there is something humorous about it. As when we just started over, a high explosive shell lit right behind one fellow on my right and as you know, most of the power of a shell goes before it, so in this case, it didn't hurt the fellow, but just raised him off the ground about three feet. Then turning around, he said, "That one sure had whiskers!" The same fellow had his bayonet taken away by a large shell.[17]

—*Private Kenet Weikal*
6th Marines, 2nd Division

I particularly remember one wounded German. He was hitching along the ground, trying to get under cover, and he was in bad shape. One of our men drew a bead on him, but another of our chaps knocked his gun sideways and yelled, "Save your ammunition! He's done for, anyhow." But the thing that sticks in my memory is that I couldn't hear a word of it, although I was right up close when he yelled. I must have read his lips. That's the kind of noise it was.[18]

—*Sergeant Dan Edwards*
3rd Machine Gun Battalion, 1st Division

I encountered a major of the 23rd Infantry. I attached myself to him for a short time, but he was very rattled. He only had one or two runners, had completely lost control over his battalion and did not, in fact, know where his own troops were. Isolated platoons were attacking the ravine on the right, but there seemed no control nor liaison by regimental or battalion commanders. It was a case of the enlisted men and platoon leaders continuing forward with utmost bravery, with the higher officers incapable of controlling them. These platoon leaders were inexperienced, had no maps, did not know exactly what was expected of them, and isolated groups of enlisted men were wandering around asking only to be led, completely at a loss as to what they should do next.[19]

—*Lieutenant Robert W. Kean*
15th Field Artillery, 2nd Division

We received orders to advance to join the front line, and took off on the run. We heard what we thought were sparrows chirping, and something that sounded like a .22 rifle cracking. The 'chirps' were bullets whizzing past and the closest ones sounded like .22 shots. Those low bullets cut the wheat, folded it down, and made 'lanes' through the field that looked as though someone had drawn lines across it.

We had about one hour of rest, if it could be called that. The Germans kept up a sweeping fire through the wheat. A friend named Dick had dug in about three feet to my right and kept telling me to dig deeper, or my butt would catch a bullet! I said, "Yeah, buddy, better keep your head down!" He was looking at me when the funniest expression came across his face, which seemed to elongate about three inches. Then blood was trickling down his face. A bullet had hit his helmet and gone through his head.[20]

—*Private Ralph L. Williams*
2nd Engineers, 2nd Division

Ahead of me our boys kept on going. A lot of men went down but the lines never stopped. I would see a man walking across the fields with his rifle at his hip and suddenly he would take another step and there wouldn't be no step there and he would go down. Some fell flat. Some grabbed at their wounds and sort of crumpled down. And some would sit down slow like they were sitting down in a chair. I don't remember ever seeing a man throw up his arms and fall back. Maybe that's because they are moving forward and they've got the weight of the rifle and bayonet in front. I passed a lot of dead and wounded. It was terrible to hear the wounded moaning and crying. "First aid! First aid! First aid men here!"[21]

—*Corporal Joseph E. Rendinell*
6th Marines, 2nd Division

We soon were out of the wheat field. The infantry advanced by short rushes. As I moved forward, a half dozen infantrymen would get behind me in Indian file so that my body would protect them from German machine gun bullets. If I swung to the left, they would swing behind me to the left; if I went to the right, they would swing behind me to the right.[22]

—*Lieutenant Robert W. Kean*
15th Field Artillery, 2nd Division

All of a sudden the ground opened up unexpectedly in front of me. There was a trench there. Nobody was in it; it was deserted. I had to jump down into it. But first I wanted to drop my machine gun ammunition which seemed like it was cutting right down to the bone on my left shoulder. It didn't take but a second to ease the strap off my shoulder, but it was just one second too long. A one-pound shell came along with my number on it.

It hit the machine gun I had on my right shoulder and exploded. It knocked me for a double loop. It lifted me clean up off the ground and I didn't know what was happening until I came down again. And I didn't quite know what it was all about even then.

I landed in a funny sort of way with my feet off the ground. My right arm had somehow gotten wedged in between the wall of the trench and the lattice work, and there I hung. Shot and hung all at once. Not so good.

I tried to jerk my arm loose. I was kind of rattled, but I still had enough of my wits to know that I was in a beastly mess and that I had better get out of it damn quick.

The wall of the trench had caved in with me, and a rock had caught my arm and pinned it. I tried every way to get it loose. There wasn't any way in God's world I could budge that rock.

Then I began to notice that arm, in behind the lattice. It had felt sort of numb. Now I woke up to the fact that pieces of shell had cut it up. The fingers were cut clean off the hand, and dangling down, hanging to the thumb by a little strip of skin. A gash run down through the wrist and split the thumb in two, and just above the wrist the arm bones were cut through; not much but a little skin held the arm together there. Another cut split the forearm in two parts, up as far as I could see.

But it didn't hurt any. There just wasn't any feeling in it. But it made me feel sort of queer to look at it. I mean when I thought of it and remembered it was my own arm.

The way blood was pouring out of it, I had to do something quickly or I'd be a goner in jig time. Well, I got a footing in the dirt, against the side of the trench and pulled with every ounce of strength I had. But even with that leverage I couldn't get loose.

I tugged three or four times, hard as I could. Then I stopped to think what to do next. Suddenly I heard voices. I looked over the corner of the trench and saw eight Germans coming my way on a dog trot.

The trench I was in was a communication trench. The main trench joined it at an angle, about five yards from where I was hanging. I could see the tops of eight helmets, coming bobbing along the main trench.

In one way, I was in an ideal position. Jogging along as they were they couldn't very well see me before they rounded the corner of the trench into my part of it. I took out my gun with my left hand and waited for them.

It seemed like it took them an awful long time to get there. The pressure of the rock on my arm seemed to help stop the blood, but it was trickling and dripping down the lattice the whole time. Finally they drew into sight, still on the run, and I let 'em have it. Catching them at a disadvantage that way, I piled up four before they even knew where the fire was coming from.

The other four who were left reached for the sky and began to yell, "Kamerad!" They were armed with rifles, and they didn't have any grenades. So I yelled to 'em to throw down their guns and then motioned to them to come near. They did. One was a big tall hombre, six foot two at least, with an Iron Cross on his tunic. Another was a youngster, maybe 20; and the other two were 30 or older. And one wore glasses, sort of like an owl. All their uniforms were spick and span and they looked combed and brushed and sort of out of place.

They stared at me goggle-eyed. I had to straddle one leg across to the other side of the trench, to ease off the strain a little. And I could see them thinking what fools they were to give in to any guy who was hung. I motioned them with the gun to come up and help me get my arm out. The rock wouldn't budge. They strained and heaved, but it was no use. They couldn't move it with their bare hands, and I wouldn't let them get hold of any of the timber laying around for fear they'd crown me.

I was losing blood—too much. I couldn't go on. There was only one thing to do, and I did it. I made the four prisoners back off a little ways and stand where I could see them. I laid the automatic in a handy place. Then I pulled my bolo knife and got a good grip on it with my left hand, settled my right elbow solid on the parapet, and swung the bolo down on it with a quick, clean blow. The stump of my arm came free, then. I landed down on my feet with the automatic. A sort of haze came over me, but just for a second. I had them bozos covered, all right, and they were staring as though they had seen a ghost. With my left hand I whipped off my belt, made a loop out of it and got it over the stump of my arm. Then with a piece of stick put in through the buckle I twisted it until the blood didn't do more than trickle.

The boys had seen something of what had happened. They'd seen me make the run with my machine gun and saw the shell plunk me. After that they didn't see any more of me and they gave me up. They figured I was a goner. Then suddenly I come popping up, with four Heinie prisoners.

They yelled their heads off.[23]

—Sergeant Dan Edwards
3rd Machine Gun Battalion, 1st Division

We were receiving enemy fire on both flanks. The most severe fire, however, was coming from guns south of the Cravancon Farm. These guns were in the lane of the Foreign Legion. While I was trying to find out where this fire was coming from, something hit me on the shoulder and knocked me down on my back. I felt as if I had been hit by a baseball bat. I got to my feet, but my left shoulder was numb. I thought I had been hit by a shell splinter as shells were falling also, but could see no blood, and then I began spitting blood and fell down again. This time I could hardly breath and was carried into a shell hole by a sergeant and a private whose names I do not know to this day. Before I passed out, I remember that the hole was a great big one, and sitting across from me was a dead German. He had no helmet, but wore that funny little round cap on his head. He was a brunette and his sightless black eyes were looking right at me.[24]

—*Lieutenant Joseph D. Patch*
18th Infantry, 1st Division

We were running across a field and that is the last I remember. When I came to, the sun was a way up in the sky. I tried to get up, but could not. My combat pack was full of holes, my rifle was broken. I crawled over in a shell hole. My nose and ears was bleeding, blood ran out of my mouth. I thought I was going to die.

Shells were bursting everywhere. That screeching sound, it is fierce. There were hundreds of wounded going back. I yelled for help. Then I crawled out of the shell hole and started back to head-quarters on my hands and knees.

Albaugh and Trindad came back looking for me. They found me crawling along. "Gee, kid, I thought you were a goner. We left you for dead. The shell lit about three feet alongside of you. It knocked me down. We got up and seen you still laying there."

At the field hospital I seen Joe Humbler. He was suffering terrible. He died in my arms. Seen Bill Sweeney, he was hit in the leg. When he was going up to the front line I wished him good luck and God bless you and he said the same to me. "Well," says Bill, "we'll get a nice rest now, anyhow."

The field hospital was in a big cave and was full of wounded and the moaning was pathetic. Private Vance came in with half a jaw shot off . . . Keeler, from *Cleveland Plain Dealer,* was shot in the arm. "I'll get a fine rest now," he says. Later, Sweeney, Keeler and myself left the cave to go back and find an ambulance. Keeler run after a truck and got on. A shell hit right in the center of the truck and killed seven and took Keeler's arm clean off. Two other wounded boys come by and I asked for help. One of them got me a branch of a tree for a crutch and we got going to the rear.[25]

—*Corporal Joseph E. Rendinell*
6th Marines, 2nd Division

Beaurepaire Farm was in much confusion. The courtyard, the tables, the outside of the farm, were full of wounded. There had been no efficient provision made for taking care of our wounded. There were no ambulances. Only one doctor—a battalion surgeon from the 9th Infantry—was there, and he was totally incapable of taking care of one-tenth of the number of wounded at the farm. The rest of the medical officers had established their headquarters, unintelligently, so far to the rear that the wounded could not be gotten there. The one 9th Infantry doctor there soon got in such a state from overwork that he was practically useless. Many men were dying from lack of attention.

I remember particularly one wounded German officer. He was lying propped up against the wall of the courtyard. He was evidently in some pain, for he would wince from time to time, gritting his teeth. He was very good looking, smartly dressed even in the midst of battle. He seemed aristocratic to his fingertips. Though owing to the many American wounded little attention could be paid to him, he did not complain. I hope he survived.[26]

—Lieutenant Robert W. Kean
15th Field Artillery, 2nd Division

Some of the men appeared interested in their wounds, some paid no attention to them, while others were horrified and wanted to die. I remember one fellow who attempted to shoot himself, but the piece of shell that had crippled him had broken his revolver, too. Boys with shattered legs begged their comrades to shoot them. I shall always remember how they pleaded. We passed one such in an advance one morning and returned that night by a different route. When we went up the same place the next morning, we found this same soldier dead with a bullet in his head; but we never knew whether he did it himself or whether some German patrol shot him in the night.[27]

—Sergeant William Brown
9th Infantry, 2nd Division

During that afternoon, to my surprise, there appeared over the hill to our right a detachment of French cavalry. They were a beautiful sight—the horses shining and well groomed. (The cavalrymen had nothing much else to do for four years but groom their horses.) They were splendid animals with long arching tails, and not at all like the scrubby half-starved beasts which we had to pull our guns. Each man was carrying a long lance, which seemed a most extraordinary weapon for modern warfare and brought back the memory of the pitched charges of Napoleon's day.

The cavalry disappeared on the trot over the hillside in a gentle cloud of dust, and I did not see them again. However, I heard the next day that as they trotted towards the German lines machine guns opened up and that soon that weapon of modern warfare completely disorganized man and beast and they hastily retreated to the rear, to again, I suppose, groom their horses and shine up their lances for the rest of the war.[28]

—Lieutenant Robert W. Kean
15th Field Artillery, 2nd Division

L ater, both the French and Germans would comment on the élan displayed by the doughboys as they advanced stubbornly against the enemy machine guns. But the doughboys had paid a terrible price for this praise. One battalion of the 16th Infantry lost all its officers and half its men fighting around the village of Chaudun—ending up under the command of a wounded sergeant. As night fell, the wounded and dead of both sides remained littered about in the wheat.

•

The battlefield was very quiet. There was no firing going on in the vicinity. All the guns were silent, evidently in the process of being moved into new positions to take up the battle again in the morning. It was very dark, though the stars were shining bright. It was a pitiful walk through the wheat field. The ground was full of fallen figures. And on hearing my footsteps, the air became full of the calls of the wounded—in French, in English and in German.

An old Frenchman (he looked at least 50) in a tattered blue uniform was walking slowly down the road carrying on his back, towards the dressing station, a wounded American doughboy. Every time I have felt annoyed since then at France, this picture comes to mind and my anger softens.

I will never forget that walk back through those wheat fields. All along I heard groans—cries for help in English, in French, in German—pleas for water and babblings of delirious men, all the way back. The fields were full of dead and dying and nothing could be done for them. When we left this sector a week later the fields were still full of American dead—officers and men—several good friends of mine among them. Our regimental chaplain did wonders in getting a good many of them buried, but there were too many to handle.[29]

—Lieutenant Robert W. Kean
15th Field Artillery, 2nd Division

T he fighting resumed the next day as the exhausted doughboys somehow found the determination to continue. By July 19 the 2nd Division had established itself just short of the Soissons–Chateau Thierry highway. The *division was relieved that night by a French division. The doughboys and Marines had driven the enemy back six miles, captured 3,000 prisoners and 75 guns. They suffered 4,000 casualties in the process, including 750 dead.*

The 1st Division remained in action until the night of July 22 after bitter fighting for the town of Berzy le Sec. That town had originally been the objective of a French division that failed to capture it after several attempts. Relieved the night of July 22, the Big Red One had advanced seven miles, captured 3,500 prisoners and 68 guns from seven different German divisions. Its own losses were horrendous—about 6,900 officers and men, including nearly 2,000 dead.

•

What was left of E Company marched in single file from the railroad crossing to the Bois de Ritz. It was dark, we were not shelled, and I was more tired than I have ever been. The men were subdued, perhaps more exhausted than I because they carried more equipment. I announced there would be no reveille and gave that order to the bugler. I told the company to lie down where they were and go to sleep. That met with instant approval.

The next thing I knew was that someone was kicking me in the ribs. I said, "What the hell are you kicking me for?" It was the bugler and he sounded off reveille. "I told you there would be no reveille," and he kicked me again, motioning to his left. I looked. There was the 1st Division commander General [Charles P.] Summerall! He had come alone to express to us his appreciation for the accomplishments of the 18th Infantry in the battle of Soissons. Standing in a semicircle, we listened to the general. Then we went back to sleep. I am sure that General Summerall made a good speech, but I am also sure that none of us remembered a word of it.[30]

—*Lieutenant Jeremiah M. Evarts*
18th Infantry, 1st Division

Passing through Vierzy, there was a spot in the road where a large German shell had evidently fallen three days before, and there were half a dozen Marine dead, still lying scattered about there, all wearing their gas masks—probably to go through the acrid smoke caused by very heavy shell fire.

Above the ravine—where our artillery battery was—between it and Vauxcastille, I found the bodies of two 23rd Infantry officers, evidently killed leading their troops towards the ravine where the Germans held up our advance for a couple of hours in the middle of the day of July 18. One of the lieutenants, Ken Fuller, I recognized, for I had known him in Harvard where he was in the class below me.

It was a peculiar thing, but the German dead nearly always were in grotesque positions, with arms and legs spread out, while the American and French dead seemed to have just crouched down on the ground and stayed there. Perhaps this was owing to the fact that the Allied soldiers were advancing and leaning forward when they were killed—while the Germans were probably standing still or backing up.

Not a cent was found on the bodies of any American dead. Their pockets had always been rifled and their belongings scattered on the ground near their bodies. The Moroccan division, including the Foreign Legion who had been on our left, were tough and brave fighters, but they evidently felt that money was of no use to a dead man and had wandered into the adjoining sector and taken all there was to take from the bodies.[31]

—Lieutenant Robert W. Kean
15th Field Artillery, 2nd Division

Our troops are doing fine work. They gave the Hun the hard knock of the last few days. The success in this particular has a very good effect materially and psychologically. The spirit of every one is away up. This is what we wanted. The French and all the Allies now take off their hats to the American fighting man. We can well be proud of him . . . This may be the "turning of the tide."[32]

—Lieutenant Colonel Hugh Drum
General Headquarters, American Expeditionary Force

Base Hospital No. 20, A.E.F.

Dear Brownie—I'm a very lucky hombre. Went over the top at 8:20 A.M. [July 18]. High explosive shell hit the road alongside of me and never touched me. The gas blinded and choked me and I fell into a shallow dugout alongside the road. Just then the dugout was blown up and the last of my sensations was of floating up, up, up, minus my left leg. Some time later, when I got back to earth, a hospital apprentice assured me I was all there. Considering all this, I'm feeling pretty good.

I've been to the land from which only cooks and chaplains return. And I've got all my arms and legs! Why? I don't know unless God and Our Country has further use for me before the Kaiser puts my address on a shell. An English Tommy told me before I went up to the battlefront that if I were lucky my trials and troubles would end the first day and were I extremely out of luck, I'd duck along for a year or two. I smiled incredulously then. But he was right. I believe that if it is ever necessary for me again to endure what the last seventeen days have battered in and out of me, I should be a raving maniac.[33]

—Sergeant Arthur Ganoe
6th Marines, 2nd Division

Notes

1. J.W. Woolridge, *The Giants of the Marne.* (n.p., 1923), p. 12.

2. Hervey Allen, *Toward the Flame.* (New York: Farrar & Rinehart, 1926), pp. 47–49.

3. *History of the 110th Infantry.* (Pittsburgh: The Association of the 110th Infantry, 1920), p. 209.

4. Edmund L. Butts, *The Keypoint of the Marne.* (Menasha, Wis.: George Banta Publishing Company, 1930), pp. 118–119.

5. Woolridge, *Giants of the Marne*, pp. 48–9, 53–58, 62.

6. *The German Offensive of July 15, 1918.* (Fort Leavenworth, Kans.: The General Services Schools Press, 1923), p. 672.

7. Allen, *Toward the Flame*, pp. 47–49.

8. Cooke, *We Can Take It*, p. 21–22.

9. Patch, *A Soldier's War*, pp. 125–127.

10. Rendinell, *One Man's War*, pp. 147–148.

11. Patch, *A Soldier's War*, pp. 130–132.

12. Thomas, *This Side of Hell*, p. 261.

13. Rendinell, *One Man's War*, p. 149.

14. Robinson, *St. Lawrence University in the World War*, pp. 95–96.

15. Cowing and Cooper, *Dear Folks*, p. 90.

16. Rendinell, *One Man's War*, pp. 149–150, 152–153.

17. Catlin, *With the Help of God*, pp. 193–194.

18. Thomas, *This Side of Hell*, pp. 264–265.

19. Kean, *Dear Marraine*, pp. 148–149.

20. Williams, *Luck of a Buck*, pp. 141–142.

21. Rendinell, *One Man's War*, pp. 152–153.

22. Kean, *Dear Marraine*, p. 155.

23. Thomas, *This Side of Hell*, pp. 276–283.

24. Patch, *A Soldier's War*, p. 132.

25. Rendinell, *One Man's War*, pp. 162–165.

26. Kean, *Dear Marraine*, pp. 150–151.

27. Brown, *The Adventures of an American Doughboy*, pp. 69–70.

28. Kean, *Dear Marraine*, pp. 151–152.

29. *Ibid.*, pp. 157–159.

30. Jeremiah Evarts, *Recollections of a Vermonter 1896–1918.* (New York: pvtly printed, n.d.), pp. 47–48.

31. Kean, *Dear Marraine*, pp. 165–166.

32. Edward M. Coffman, *The War to End All Wars.* (New York: Oxford University Press, 1968), p. 267.

33. Catlin, *With the Help of God*, pp. 211–212.

CHAPTER 7

The Turn of the Tide

*W*hile the U.S. 1st and 2nd Divisions were locked in battle at Soissons, the Germans were also being pressed on other fronts. General Foch's constant refrain was "Attaquez! Attaquez!" With the arrival of the Americans, he was able to fulfill this aggressiveness.

Two U.S. divisions, 4th and 26th, were already attacking the side of the Marne salient to the south—the 26th at Belleau Wood, the 4th west of the main highway from Soissons to Chateau Thierry, its battalions mixed in with French units. Both had jumped off July 18 after a short artillery barrage. Three days later the U.S. 3rd Division attacked across the Marne River over floating footbridges and began moving against the hills to the north.

The divisions were a mixed bag. The 4th was a Regular Army division that was "regular" in name only. Filled out with draftees and rookies, the men of one of its regiments arrived near the front having yet to fire their rifles. The men of the division's field signal battalion arrived in France with holsters, but no pistols—they stuffed their empty holsters with scrap paper to give the illusion of weaponry. That lack had been largely remedied by July 18, but the Ivies—as they were called after their ivy leaf divisional insignia—had never seen combat, not even a quiet tour of the trenches, since arriving in France in May. They were an unknown quantity.

The 26th Division had more experience, but even the New England Guardsmen making up the division had never faced machine guns in open maneuver. Similarly, the 3rd Division, fresh from its magnificent stand on the Marne on July 15, had no other combat experience to speak of. All three divisions would learn many hard lessons in the days ahead; their teachers would be the boys in the feld grau uniforms and coal-scuttle helmets.

•

This was our boys' first fighting against machine guns and at the beginning they had many losses because they would insist on charging the guns frontally. The French never did this; if they were held up, they telephoned back for artillery and sat down until the big guns had reduced the nests. One of our boys in the 103rd, a Greek, undertook to charge a machine gun all alone, out in the open. Of course, the gun was turned on him and the stream of bullets practically cut him in two at the waist.

The German machine gunners would fire on our men, as they came, till the last moment. Then they would throw up their hand and cry "Kamerad!" It was astonishing that boys who had gone through the spray of death could restrain themselves even when they were ordered. They had seen their comrades drop all the way up, one by one. Heaven only knows how they could keep from killing the Germans, even when they surrendered. As a matter of fact, there were fewer prisoners than might have been expected.[1]

—*Frank R. Sibley*
Boston Globe *Correspondent,*
26th Division

The Germans had placed a long line of machine guns at the bottom of the very gradual slope. These were completely hidden by the tall wheat. Not an enemy could be seen. The Americans were permitted to come halfway down the slope, then all then machine guns opened at a preconcerted signal. They fired low, shooting through the wheat. The slaughter was terrible. Hardly a soldier was hit in the head; nearly all the dead had chest or abdominal wounds.[2]

—*Colonel Christian A. Bach*
4th Division

The Yankees pushed the attack on July 22. No sooner had the men started to move forward, bayonets fixed, than the deadly chatter of a dozen enemy machine guns began anew and the ripe heads of wheat spouted like fountains in the air.

The new men became demoralized by the withering fire and constantly sought cover without orders. This checked the rush of the advance and it became necessary for squad leaders to drive their men forward in some cases by force. Greenhorns in the rear tried to fire through the ranks ahead and increased the casualties. It developed that morning that the last batch of replacements sent up could not even load a rifle, much less fire it. These men had been sent to the two companies, "B" and "D," in the woods just before the great advance and had only landed in France on July 4th![3]

—*Captain Daniel W. Strickland*
102nd Infantry, 26th Division

When our company finally cleared the wheat field it was only to be pinned down at the edge of a strip of woods. A road ran along just there, and the Germans had it covered with machine gun fire. A group of our men led by a lieutenant, the last of our company officers, tried to cross the road. The lieutenant dropped. The rest of the men dived back beside the road. A sniper's bullet had got the lieutenant and the machine guns then opened up. Mike and I were trying to drag the lieutenant back to cover in the ditch; several men ran out to help us. The machine gun bullets began to spray around us; we gave it up and made for the ditch again.

We found one of our sergeants commanding what was left of the company. The sergeant completely lost his head. He sent a detail out to bring the lieutenant in. They were all hit before they got to him. And the fire they drew resulted in the lieutenant's being shot again, in the leg.

The sergeant ordered me to form another detail, go out in close formation and come back with the lieutenant. I asked the sergeant to wait a little, then let me take Mike and go out alone. "We'll get him in our own way, " I said. "There's no use killing any more soldiers by sending them out there now."

The sergeant calmed down at that and let us have our way about it. When we figured that the Germans had had time enough to shift their attention from the road, Mike and I wormed our way out and got back into the ditch with the lieutenant. There wasn't much shelter there any more, but we had nowhere else to leave him while we went on.

The bullet had hit the left side of his head and come out in the middle of his forehead. His brain was lying out there on his forehead—but he was alive and he could talk. He was still alive when they found him there that night and took him back to the dressing station. I never knew what became of him afterward.[4]

—*Private John L. Barkley*
4th Infantry, 3rd Division

Sergeant Craig, a big husky fighting man, came through with an odd experience. A Boche dropped a potato masher grenade and ran for it. He ducked into a dugout and Craig picked up the grenade and pulled the string. "Come out, Boche," he yelled at the man in the pit and flung his missile at the same moment. The German popped his head out just in time to catch the grenade squarely on the forehead. It burst at the instant it struck, blowing the German's head to pieces. And the sight, so unexpected, sickened Craig so that he was unfit for duty for nearly half that day.[5]

—*Frank R. Sibley*
Boston Globe *Correspondent, 26th Division*

O *rders for a gradual withdrawal from the Marne salient had been issued by the German High Command the night of July 18. The retirement began the night of July 19–20. Withdrawal was conducted in successive stages as the Germans attempted to save what they could of the huge quantities of supplies and ammunition in the salient. Behind them they left a screen of machine guns and delaying parties.*

The professionalism of those efforts could be measured in the casualties of the U.S. divisions. By July 23, the 26th Division had suffered serious casualties—approximately 4,000 men—and all four of its infantry regiments were so thoroughly intermingled they had nearly lost their identity.[6]

•

I saw rows of wounded boys on stretchers just brought in. Those rows were four deep and extended several hundred yards. In all of these places I probably saw a thousand or more of our American soldiers with every conceivable kind of wound—some with legs or arms blown away, some with eyes shot out, many with chins gone, others with every muscle in their bodies shaking as with palsy, shell-shocked, some with bodies burned by gas so badly that they were black.[7]

Captain Carroll J. Swan
101st Engineers, 26th Division

We buried our dead in little groups of three to fifteen, with just a blanket or a shelter half wrapped around them. The prisoners we had knew where some of our boys lay dead, and they were marched back under guard to these spots and made to bring back our dead on litters for burial. Some of the bodies were beginning to discolor, and the stench was almost unbearable. The body of Lieutenant Hugh Blanchard was brought in. For some reason his chest had expanded, and when I stuck my two fingers through the upper part of his blouse to retrieve one of his dog tags, my fingers broke a big blister and made a noise like when one punctures a balloon. That really scared me and I started running—running nowhere. Chaplain de Valles, who was officiated at these burials, called me back and assured me that the man was not coming back to life.

Rudely constructed crosses were made and set up on the graves, and their names written on them. In some cases a rifle was stuck at the head of the grave with the Yank's helmet on it, and his name on the chin strap. Each soldier was buried with one dog tag around his neck for future identification. Some were buried unknown. These graves were carefully recorded by the chaplain. All personal effects were removed from the dead and wrapped separately, and each package had a dog tag tied securely to it and sent to the Graves Registration Department, who in turn forwarded the effects to the next of kin.[8]

—*Private Connell Albertine*
104th Infantry, 26th Division

Sometimes we found something pleasant to remember. One German prisoner came into Division Headquarters wearing a tag in his buttonhole. The tag read, "This man when captured was giving water to a wounded American soldier." And three other German Red Cross men were actually bandaging up wounded Yankees on the field when they were taken.[9]

—*Frank R. Sibley*
Boston Globe *Correspondent, 26th Division*

A s the Germans fell back, American troops poured into the vacuum: the 28th, the 32nd, and the 42nd Divisions, along with artillery and support units.

●

There were many fine houses in Essomes, and I went into several near our courtyard. The German soldiers had evidently urinated against the wallpaper in a good many places, and I saw feces in most of the rooms. Brocaded curtains, lace, and silk dresses were the favorite substitutes for toilet paper.

In the business section [of Chateau Thierry] all the shop windows were broken and the shops looted. Here the Germans had found more scope for their originality. I noticed a derby hat full of feces and, in a shoe store, a pair of ladies' dancing slippers full of urine. Many of the places had been burned, but not all.[10]

—*Corporal Horatio Rogers*
101st Field Artillery, 26th Division

Essomes had been badly looted by the Boche and one of the curious impressions made by the place upon a visitor was the clouds of feathers drifting about streets and dwellings. Either in a spirit of destruction or more probably in the search for money which he thought might be concealed in them, the German appeared to have slit open every feather bed, pillow or feather quilt in the town and their contents eddied about in every breeze.[11]

—*Anonymous Artilleryman*
102nd Field Artillery, 26th Division

As we went along, we came to many dead Germans. Some had been pulled off the road. At one place we saw many of them lined up for burial. They smelled quite dead, but the French driver of the truck insisted on stopping to look them over. "Boche, mort, bon," he said over and over. I would translate this as "Dead Boche, or German, is a good German."

French soldiers standing alongside the road held their noses and laughed and said, "Tomorrow." They weren't in a hurry to put their enemies under ground. Sanitary crews and engineers were cleaning up as fast as they could, but a bit farther on we started to pass dead soldiers—Germans—still lying upon the road. I saw German soldiers sitting beside the road quite dead. Their arms and heads were bandaged. They had had a bit of attention, but had died anyway.

My French driver had a hatred for the Germans and a strong stomach, too, for he ran over every dead German he could reach with his truck. He zig-zagged along from dead German to dead German, driving his huge truck over them and smashing them as completely as the rabbits and skunks we see killed along our own roads so often. Then he would stop and look at them and laugh.[12]

—Lieutenant Bob Hoffman
111th Infantry, 28th Division

About 100 yards downstream [of the Marne] one of our men and a *poilu* were "fishing" by throwing hand grenades into the Marne. The wisdom of eating fish at this time was doubtful; the river must have been full of dead Germans, and the conclusion, at least for me, was obvious.

We were issued beef in immense quantities, sometimes having to bury a whole quarter of it. It became tainted very easily, where of course there was no possible means of refrigeration. This meat ration came wrapped in burlap, generally reasonably fresh; but once open, it had to be carried around in the ration carts, and unless quickly cooked, it spoiled very rapidly, especially in those hot summer days along the Marne when the sun was hot.

Another thing which hastened the destruction of perishable food was the immense amount of decay all along the front. All those rotten woods were filled with dead horses, dead men, the refuse, excrement and the garbage of armies. The ground must have been literally alive with pus and decay germs. Scratch your hand, cut yourself in shaving, or get a little abrasion on your foot, and almost anything could happen.[13]

—Lieutenant Hervey Allen
111th Infantry, 28th Division

Horses are huge when they become bloated, swell to twice their normal size. Their legs are thrust out like steel posts and it requires a hole about ten feet square and six feet deep to put a horse under. If the legs were off, a hole hardly more than half that size is required. At times we succeeded in using an ax and saw to cut off the horses' legs. It was a hard task and unpleasant, but it had to be done.[14]

—Lieutenant Bob Hoffman
111th Infantry, 28th Division

Here we again ran across some of the 26th U.S. Division. At that time they had seen so much more fighting than we, that they seemed veterans by comparison. Their clothes were in very bad shape, the set expression of their faces, and their small platoons advertised what they had been through. They sat along the roads and told us stories of the fights and recounted details of their losses. I thought it disheartening for our men, but the "Yanks" did not seem to feel that way about it. They held an absolutely fatalistic viewpoint, telling us we would never get through the game. "Wait," they said, "wait." Later on I understood. There was a great pride about these fellows.[15]

—Lieutenant Hervey Allen
111th Infantry, 28th Division

I thought I would take a little walk with some of the fellows to see whether we could gather in some souvenirs. We walked from the back of our dugout across a little field and into a piece of woods. There must have been very heavy fighting along here, as I noticed shell holes all through the field. We had gone a short distance into the woods when we noticed a place where the Germans had had a battery of artillery. Judging by the destruction, one of our six-inch shells must have hit in the midst of it; I counted 12 Germans scattered in through there who had evidently been killed two or three days before. Some of them were whole and some were pretty well cut up. While we were standing looking at this awful sight, a fellow from the 26th Division came up and seeing a ring on the hand of one of the Germans, he took out his knife and cut off the finger, keeping the ring for a souvenir. It made shivers run up and down my back. I don't think I will ever be cold-blooded enough to do a thing like that.[16]

—Private Henry G. Reifsnyder
103rd Engineers, 28th Division

The boys were forever dressing up in things they found in deserted villages. In practically every French home there was a silk hat, and these were the doughboys' delight. They were always of ancient vintage and quaint shape. Practically every company had at least one joker with a battered old tile on his head, and many a mule was conducted down the endless columns of traffic by solemn, silk-hatted, khaki-shirted, muddy-shod drivers.

One man, "Happy" Carabash of Webster, belonging in Company M of the 104th Infantry, went over the top into Belleau carrying an umbrella he had found, and his rifle. He hadn't any more pack than a jack rabbit, but he had found the umbrella in a farm, and it was raining, so he carried it. The wonder is that the umbrella didn't make him so conspicuous a target as to get him killed.[17]

—*Frank R. Sibley*
Boston Globe *Correspondent, 26th Division*

A medical unit had established a dressing station in a barn. The wounded lay along the road in rows, some sitting, and many blood-soaked and unattended. Some were in a frightfully nervous state, shrieking when a battery of 75s fired, which it did every few minutes. The guns were set right out in the fields and along the road, with their trail pieces newly dug in. The noise was terrific, making us stagger as we passed. It was like being close to a blast when it unexpectedly goes off. They were shelling a wood directly opposite us, so the pieces were laid almost level. Even in daylight there was a blinding glare like taking a flashlight photograph, then a blow of sound and air followed as if one were being shoved by a drunken man.

Backed into the ditch near one battery was a Ford ambulance which had been struck by shrapnel. The driver had been killed. He was sitting with his head resting on the wheel, his hands hanging down, dripping blood. A wounded man on the upper row of stretchers was also dead. We could look in as we passed. The stiff angle of the feet was characteristic, and the dark purple stains of the blood on his khaki showed he had been dead some time. Old blood stains look as though someone had wiped his hands on brown clothes after picking elderberries—dark and purple.[18]

—*Lieutenant Hervey Allen*
111th Infantry, 28th Division

While I was loafing about the entrance of our dugout I noticed that there was quite a lot of excitement along the road and I looked down and saw about 200 Boche prisoners. This is the first time I have seen such a number and they surely are a pretty sad looking bunch of soldiers. I suppose our men would look just as badly if they were taken prisoners. These fellows wore dirty and torn uniforms, but their physical condition seemed very good; they were not half starved as the usual wild rumors had reported. Some of our fellows ran down and tore the buttons and shoulder straps from their uniforms, and even went so far as to take their hats as souvenirs. We are certainly a great gang for collecting souvenirs. The Boche prisoners certainly looked dumb and offered no resistance; in fact, some of them tore their buttons off and handed them to our boys. I guess they were afraid they were going to be killed.[19]

—*Private Henry G. Reifsnyder*
103rd Engineers, 28th Division

*B*y July 25 the German withdrawal was 16 kilometers from Chateau Thierry—the old high-water mark—but the retreat was no rout. The enemy was merely retreating to yet another defense line, this one along the heights of the Ourcq River—more of a creek by American standards—where they stopped to confront the U.S. 42nd (Rainbow) Division. The Rainbows came in for the 26th and 28th Divisions the night of July 25. The 32nd Division came in for the U.S. 3rd Division on July 29.

On Sunday morning, July 28, the 42nd Division doughboys rose from their bivouacs south of the Ourcq and started forward to drive the Germans from the heights to the north of the stream. Moments later the Maxim machine guns began their chug-chugging and Rainbow blood began to flow.

•

Whoever first thought of using barbed wire as a battlefield impediment could have given lessons in pragmatism. It certainly works. It is a dreadful handicap and makes quick progress impossible. The German engineers made a practice of stringing a tight wire under the grass in front of the fence, wherever the grass was thick enough to hide it. Men tripped over the wire and plunged headlong into the entanglement behind it. Most of the wiring I saw was but knee-high, but members of the Rainbow Division told me that they had met much higher wiring in some of their fights. A favorite form consisted of three fences, with intervals of seven or eight feet, two or three wires to each fence, some slack, some tight, and cross wires running irregularly hither and thither, backward and forward over the post tops, and a few loose wires on the ground. Generally, wires were alternately drawn tight and left slack and men floundering through this mess, while it clutched and hampered them, made easy targets for German snipers to shoot at leisure.[20]

—*Private L.V. Jacks*
119th Field Artillery, 32nd Division

Men plunged to earth to the right and left of me. Almost at every stride some comrade fell, stumbling forward lifeless, or falling to [catch his] wind and rock for a while through the first disordering sting of a fatal wound. Others just slipped down and lay low and still, too badly wounded and spent to go on with the advance. I saw these incidents, little nightmare incidents, flashed upon the screen of my vision in jumbled, jerky fashion, and I ran on feeling that the whole thing was just a dream, stopping to aim and fire as some chance gray uniform showed, and then blindly running on.

I was winded, so were we all, but on such a field and at such a time one never seems to notice things like that. The mind is detached from the work of the field and the actions of the body are automatic, going on and on. It is a good thing, when the fight goes warm, that one can't think too much.[21]

—*Corporal Martin J. Hogan*
165th Infantry, 42nd Division

The damaging fire was coming from our left and right, the source completely invisible but yet a sheaf of bullets through the young wheat. A man crouches to run forward. He is shot through the legs, drops to hands and knees, is hit in the legs and arm, down flat and is again hit in the head. A bullet cuts my coat on the back of my shoulder but barely scratches. The men of my headquarters group are all hit but one, a terrible feeling of helplessness because there seems no one to fight against and it is the officers' responsibility to pick the targets and reduce the enemy fire by your own. 180 degrees of emptiness. We fired on every possible bit of cover but it seemed pretty futile there were so many.[22]

—*Captain Van S. Merle-Smith*
165th Infantry, 42nd Division

As our company advanced over the Ourcq we were held up on the crest of Hill 212. I was ordered by my captain, Everett Jackson, to go out with my squad on the left flank of Company F to protect a machine gun detachment of two guns. We met a very stubborn fire from the enemy. The machine gunners were all killed. George Schwend and myself were the only two left. A very heavy patrol of the enemy was trying to get around our left to cut off Company E and also to get us caught in an enfilade fire.

Neither Schwend nor myself knew anything about a machine gun, but we happened to pull the right trigger. I am happy to say we drove back the heavy patrol of the enemy and saved Company F from being wiped out. About this time a young chap of Company F lay badly wounded about ten yards from me. As I looked at him he was pleading for a drink of water. I could not stand the pitiful look in his eyes. I did not have a canteen of water with me, but I noted that just beyond me lay a dead American soldier with a canteen on his side. I told Schwend that I was going to get that canteen for the dying boy. He told me I was crazy, that a sniper would surely get me, but I did not stop. I got the canteen from the dead soldier and luckily it was filled with water.

I came back to this chap and as I held up his head and gave him a drink, he clasped my hand and said, "Corporal, you're a regular guy." He died a few minutes later, but with a dying buddy looking up and saying, "You're a regular guy," I felt at that time that it was worth getting shot for.

Just a few minutes later I was shot through the right leg. The bones were shattered, so I was helpless to move. George Schwend, seeing this, carried me about a half mile in his arms under heavy fire. We had at least three or four narrow escapes from shells and machine guns, but my buddy George Schwend would not leave me, though I begged him to go on and that I might be able to crawl to our line. He carried me to safety with no thought to his personal safety and I am happy to say we both returned to our home state of Alabama after the war.[23]

—*Corporal Harry Drysdale*
167th Infantry, 42nd Division

We remained in position [past Croix Rouge Farm] for over three hours, expecting the rest of the army to arrive. I finally ordered the machine gun dismounted. Paul, the gunner, took the gun from the tripod. Harry Martensen, the loader, reached to take the traversing head from the tripod when he was hit by an explosive bullet. Paul slit his blouse and belt right through to the wound in the center of the back. Paul used his own first aid kit. He put the dressing right into the wound, just as it was. Martensen remained for an hour and like others was crying out in pain. The only place of concealment was where we jumped off, about 500 yards from the Ourcq.

I picked up Martensen and started to carry him back. He was apologizing for all the trouble that he was causing. We had only walked about 50 feet when I saw that he did not have his helmet on. I was carrying him on his side, trying to ease his pain. We reached a point about 100 yards from the Ourcq when Harry was hit again in the back, by a sniper. His stomach pushed against mine, he gasped and passed away.[24]

—*Sergeant Thomas J. Devine*
165th Infantry, 42nd Division

F ighting for the heights to the north of the Ourcq continued over the next four days. Villages such as Sergy, Cierges, places like Croix Rouge Farm and the Ourcq itself became names survivors would one day utter with a pride touched with horror.

•

Sergy before the war was an unpretentious village in the valley of the Ourcq. The river itself is only a few feet wide and in places can be easily taken at a leap. Many American officers when they first crossed it, reported that they had passed a creek, but were unable to find the river.[25]

—*Colonel Christian A. Bach*
4th Division

We joked with [the French liaison officer] Rerat about the size of the French rivers. I told him that one of our soldiers [Jack Finnegan] lay badly wounded near the [Ourcq] river and I offered him a pull at my canteen. Raising himself on one elbow and throwing out his arm in a Sir Philip Sydney fashion, he exclaimed, "Give it to the Ourcq, it needs it more than I do."[26]

—*Father Francis Duffy*
165th Infantry, 42nd Division

Although a great story, it has a sad ending. Like many of our grand boys, Jack died of his wound.[27]

—*Private Albert "Red" Ettinger*
165th Infantry, 42nd Division

The roads were strewn with our doughboys, gray faces in the mud, blue hands frozen to their guns. Near the Ourcq, a 16-inch shell had blown a German from his grave for the third time. His face bore such real resentment that some doughboy wrote a sign and hung it on his chest: "For the love of God, leave me alone. I got appendicitis." In the poppy fields the living lay with the dead; it was hard to tell which was which.[28]

—*Private Charles A. MacArthur*
149th Field Artillery, 42nd Division

The moral courage which accompanied the physical courage of the Americans in Europe was grimly demonstrated during the worst of the congestion in one of the Chateau Thierry hospitals by a wizened Alabama doughboy. The tattered remnant of the body of Bishop M. Lee, bearing several severe trunk wounds and minus one leg, was delivered to the hospital by an ambulance. His case was hopeless and he knew it. He confided his dying words to the ward-master and asked for paper and pencil to write to his mother. The letter was started but never finished. When the paper was taken from his death grip, it read: "Dear Mother: I have been slightly wounded and am in the hospital. It was just a scratch, so don't worry. I—."[29]

—Captain Josiah C. Chatfield
117th Sanitary Train, 42nd Division

Shot down by a spray of bullets just as he reached his platoon commander with a message, Private Martin A. Treptow of Company M left behind him another message that was as effective against the enemy as a score of machine guns. In a little blood-stained book found in his breast pocket, he had painstakingly copied:

America shall win the war.
Therefore I will work,
I will save,
I will sacrifice,
I will endure,
I will fight cheerfully and do my utmost,
as if the whole issue of the struggle
depended on me alone.[30]

—Lieutenant John H. Taber
168th Infantry, 42nd Division

An officer from the Supply Company was on the road to the Regimental P.C. one day when he met a bloody soldier slowly making his way toward a dressing station. He was gripping his abdomen with both hands. "What's the hurt, buddy, can I help?" he called out.

"I'm shot through here, sir," the man replied. "If I take my hands away, everything will fall out. I haven't far to go now, I'll make it."[31]

—Captain Raymond M. Cheseldine
166th Infantry, 42nd Division

The P.C. was crowded with men who had come from the field. Into it stumbled a man from Company A, so cruelly wounded that it took courage to face him. He had been shot in the face. Unable to talk, for a bullet had clipped off part of his tongue, with an ear hanging by a shred, cheek laid open, blood dripping over his shirt and dyeing his hands crimson, he yet listened intently as he was given directions to the dressing station. Accompanied by another who had only lost a finger, he started back, one of the many walking cases. There were no stretcher-bearers up this far. They had their hands full with the men who had already struggled back part of the way to the aid station. There was an almost continuous line of maimed men walking, crawling, staggering along the road back of Hill 212. The aid stations were, of course, choked, and, like every other spot in the vicinity, were being heavily shelled.[32]

—Lieutenant John H. Taber
168th Infantry, 42nd Division

Lieutenant Farrell D. Minor, of Beaumont, Texas, an officer of Company K but attached to Company I in the Croix Rouge Farm fight, was shot through the head. It was thought to be a hopeless case, but the officer lived two months after receiving the wound. When he was being carried back in an ambulance it appeared that he wanted to say something. He would raise his head now and then and count, "1, 2, 3, 4."[33]

—William H. Amerine
Historian, 167th Infantry, 42nd Division

We went through the town of Beuvardes . . . and it was a sight, nothing but death and destruction. Some of the cannoneers even had to come and clean the road for the pieces to get through. Most of the buildings were still burning, buildings were caving in and explosions could be heard throughout the town, all of the dead Americans had been taken away, but German dead were still lying about the street, some of them hanging out of windows, some of them with their feet upon the sidewalks and their heads in the gutters, others welled up so that their clothes were simply cutting them through, and black and blue, all over from the effects of the gas. Helmets were still on their heads, in fact they dropped there with everything they owned and the stench was so sickening that some of the boys got sick.[34]

—Sergeant Elmer Straub
150th Field Artillery, 42nd Division

We went back into the woods which we ourselves took over a week ago, awaiting someone else to relieve us from this support position. As we came in the night of our last relief, a wagon train made for the grounds of the [nearby] chateau. It was dark, wet and disagreeable. A major general named Cameron . . . who had just arrived and taken possession, ordered the train away. An Irishman named Gilhooley, who did not know that this man was a general who was talking, and perhaps would not have cared if he did know, said, "This is a hell of a note, we go and capture this place and you guys come and live in it."

The general rated him roundly and said there were too damn many flies around there now without bringing a lot of animals in the yard, and Gilhooley answered, "Flies, is it? If it is flies you want, go up on the hillside and you will see thousands of them feasting on the blood of our men."

The general said nothing more. The train stayed in the chateau yard that night.[35]

—Major William T. Donovan
165th Infantry, 42nd Division

O n July 31 the Wisconsin and Michigan Guardsmen of the 32nd Division came in on the 42nd Division's right with orders to attack toward Cierges.

•

On approaching Beuvardes, the first American dead soldier was passed. He was on a litter and died while being carried to the field hospital. A little farther on, the dead body of a doughboy was lying in the gutter, his head having been blown off by a shell.

The 42nd Division had fought through these woods and the American and German dead had not yet been buried. Some ghastly sights met our eyes. One American doughboy was killed while firing his rifle from a kneeling position. His head was split in two, one half remaining erect and the other falling on his raised arm, while the body remained in its former kneeling position.[36]

—Captain Emil B. Gnasser
126th Infantry, 32nd Division

Glancing about the plain as one walked across it, small knobs would be apparent here and there. A closer inspection would identify each as the rounded top of an American helmet, and on carefully study-ing the object one could discern under the rim the thin features and staring eyes of the occupant of the burrow. Most men when digging would go straight down for a distance of about three feet, excavating a pit just large enough for the owner to kneel or crouch entirely below the surface. From time to time a roaring blast of shrapnel or glancing machine gun fire would sweep by like a hurricane. Then the knobs would disappear, sinking softly down under the level of the earth. After a minute, here and there they would begin cautious-ly to rise again, and in another moment the dusty surface of the plain would once more be dotted by helmets and peering faces.

The 121st put their kitchen in a hole in which they thought the enemy could not hit it, but none the less they calculated wrongly, for the Germans dropped a shell squarely into the hollow. Quite a num-ber of men were near. One started to run. The explosion lifted him from the earth, hurling him forward like a sack of meal for twelve or fifteen feet. He fell on his face in the mud and, raising himself up on his hands, tried to crawl along. He actually did move two or three feet, with his face turned up toward the sky and his legs trailing helplessly, for he was mangled almost beyond recognition. He threw back his head and screamed, as he struggled along leaving a red trail in the mud. His agony seemed to last hours, though it was not more than two or three seconds till he sank down on his face and died. A second man standing in front of me fell over dead with a piece of the shell in his heart. He was lucky and died quickly. A third nearby was terrible torn, his chest shattered so that one could see his heart beating, and he, too, died in a few moments. The others were less seriously hurt and survived. That first shell was a shock, to say the least.[37]

—Private L.V. Jacks
119th Field Artillery, 32nd Division

We were in Bellvue Farm when Captain Harry Williams, the regimental personnel adjutant, hurried into the room in some excitement and explained, "That soldier lying on the trench out there where all those Boches are floating around in the water is Otto Haugen. His brother, "Mother" Haugen, is on the way here now with the Headquarters Company. We ought to take care of the body before he arrives.

This was a tough situation, and yet what could we do? Everyone in the group knew "Mother" Haugen, the first sergeant of Headquarters Company. Some of us had known him for years, for he was one of the old timers in the Wisconsin National Guard. Many of us knew that the Haugen family of Nellsville had contributed four sons to the service. Otto out there in the rain was the next to the youngest and had been a private first class. Now he lay upon the fresh earth at the edge of the German trenches while below a half dozen sodden figures floated in the dirty yellow water that half filled it.

It was not long before the Headquarters Company did arrive and some comrade told Haugen the sorrowful news. When the chaplain came up, he found Haugen dejected and alone and after the long silent handclasp that says so much at times, finally said, "Well, Haugen, we can't leave the boy this way; let's do what we can for him now."

To take his mind off of the gruesome work of the burial squads, they sent Haugen to find a blanket in which to wrap the body. After a long search, he returned, unable to find one. As he talked with the chaplain, Captain Thomas Watson of Fond du Lac, who was standing nearby, overheard the conversation and without a word, took off his own slicker and handed it over, saying, "Here, sergeant, this will be better than nothing and I can salvage another someplace," and turned to his company in the rain.

After the burial, Captain Arnold and our adjutant suggested to Haugen that he take a few days leave to recover his bearings, but Haugen was a soldier and all his friends and buddies were up there on a rainswept hill awaiting the word to resume the war. He now had a personal interest in that war and looking off to the north where pillars of smoke marked the German retreat, declared he would stay with his outfit.

The Legion post at Nellsville is named after Otto A. Haugen.[38]

—Lieutenant Colonel G.W. Garlock
128th Infantry, 32nd Division

Corporal Otto Chudobba was wounded in the arm by a bursting shell when we attacked the Germans at Cierges. It was a painful wound and caused Otto much agony. Buck Krause, who stood near and helped to dress the wound, said to him, "What in hell are you crying for? You ought to be glad, for now you can go to the hospital and lay between white sheets." Then, pointing to the spot where Frank Novak with his head blown off was lying, he said, "How would you like to be like him?"[39]

—Captain Paul W. Schmidt
127th Infantry, 32nd Division

While in this position we saw some of the worst cases of shell-shock. One individual behaved in most violent fashion and could hardly be dragged along by two companions who were trying to get him to a field hospital. His face had been partly crushed in and blackened by the blast of a close shell explosion and his expression was horrible in the extreme. His insane shrieks were only surpassed by frantic and senseless bursts of laughter.

The nights were continually disturbed by such incidents, and by the cries of shell-shocked men. Most of those outbursts began with a howling peal of laughter, a laugh to make one's skin creep and his hair rise, and ended in a shuddering wail, frequently followed by tears. The shell-shocked men seemed to laugh and to cry almost interchangeably, and some whose faces were drawn up as if in great merriment had tears running down their cheeks, at the height of the convulsion. These men had become totally insane, and some of them caused no little trouble to their comrades trying to care for them.[40]

—Private L.V. Jacks
119th Field Artillery, 32nd Division

I heard talk of an examination of German prisoners recently captured. While my colonel was conferring with staff officers, I went outside in a court to see these first prisoners of war. There were three or four men in the field gray of the German Army. Their faces were marked by lines of fatigue. Major Paul B. Clemens, G-2, and Lieutenant Niederpruem were making the examination. Lieutenant Niederpruem, who came from Detroit, spoke German perfectly and questioned the prisoners and interpreted their answers.

An effort was made to learn whether the Germans were fighting a delaying action on the hills north of us or intended to stabilize their lines there. "What orders do you have?" asked Niederpruem.

"Just to stay there," answered the German soldier.

"How long were you told to stay there?"

The answer was, "We were not told how long, just to stay there."

"But suppose three times or five times as many troops attacked you, would you stay then?" asked the lieutenant.

"Yes, we must stay."

"But if many of your force were killed or wounded, would you still stay?"

The soldier spoke slowly and carefully as he replied, "Well, if but ten remained out of every hundred, then it might be excused if they retired."

I left the scene with considerable respect for these men who understood a soldier's duty in such stern terms.[41]

—*Lieutenant Colonel G.W. Garlock*
128th Infantry, 32nd Division

T he reduction of the Ainse-Marne salient was completed when Allied troops reached the Vesle River in early August. Because the counterattack had achieved its purpose and the Germans clearly intended to hold the Vesle line in force, the general attack on that front was stopped on August 6. However, the fighting was not over. The 4th, 32nd, 28th, and 77th Divisions each took a turn in bitter fighting along the Vesle River in the vicinity of Fismes through the rest of the month and into September.

•

For several days we had been crawling around Fismes, firing from windows, cellars, attics and from behind the stone wall in the back of the house yards. This got tiresome and finally the fellow next to me—a candidate by the name of Vaugn (a man who had qualified for an officer's commission through a special course of study and was waiting only for a vacancy to receive it)—raised up, laid his gun upon the top of the wall and started to shoot over the wall. This was more comfortable and it was easier to see what was being shot at. I should have known better with my previous battle experience, but I thought, "If Vaugn can shoot over the wall, I can, too."

Soon we were banging away merrily. But after several shots each, I suddenly saw Vaugn's helmet go sailing down over the slight hill. I looked at him and the entire top of his head was off—apparently a dum-dum type of bullet had flattened against his helmet or tin hat and had taken his head off to a level with his eyes and ears. He had been kneeling; his buttocks went back a bit, his head forward and his brains ran out there in front of me like soup from a pot. I did not fire over another wall.

The sniper had his choice to pick one or the other of us. For some unknown reason, he chose Vaugn. I'm here and he's gone.[42]

—*Lieutenant Bob Hoffman*
111th Infantry, 28th Division

The company had reached the market place at Fismes and were in comparative safety when a well-directed shell seemed to fall almost in their midst. A wall at the side of the square fell over, instantly killing Sergeant George I. Strawbridge and Private Salesky. Corporal William Lutz was horribly mangled. His grieving comrades crowded around him, but his only thoughts seemed to be of the folks at home. "It will be all right," he said. "Don't any of you write home about it," and again, "Only don't tell my mother." He died that same night in the field hospital.[43]

—*J. Bennett Nolan*
Historian, 108th Machine Gun Battalion, 28th Division

Everybody is sick this morning. Not from gas but dysentery. It is not the fatal kind apparently—just a miserable condition. It has affected every man in the area and comes from a mixture of causes among which flies, decaying bodies, bad water and the heat are primary— though we must not leave out canned food, which is always bad.

Flies—millions and millions of them. In spots, the air is black with the cloud of them. At mess you get a dish full of stuff, carry it away to a shady spot and sit down to eat. When you get there it is covered with flies so thick, that an observer would think we had "currant pudding," for every meal throughout the day. You wave one hand over it—grab a spoonful of the mess with your other—and then, blowing on it to chase away the last hundred or two from the spoon, gulp it quickly. If you are lucky, you don't swallow one or more insects. If you are not—then the fly is unlucky too.[44]

—*Anonymous Artilleryman*
120th Field Artillery, 32nd Division

Dear Mother,

We came across two dead American soldiers from the 59th Machine Gun Company. They were regulars. A shell must have hit them direct, they were so badly mangled. These two infantry fellows started going through their pockets, and I asked them what they were up to. I thought at first they were ransacking all the dead soldiers. But they told me that they were from H Company of the 308th Infantry, and that they had been sent out to bury all American soldiers. So they started to dig into the embankment, and after a half hour, had a big enough hole to shovel the remains of the two bodies into it. There wasn't anything left of those poor devils but large pieces of their torsos and a couple of legs. There were no heads around at all. Thousands of flies were all over them and the stench was something terrible.

The two infantry men doing the burying were peculiar looking fellows and didn't seem to mind the job at all. We found out later that they were a little dopey and had been selected for the job on that account. They made a cross out of two branches and put two battered helmets on top of the grave with the papers and wallets which they found in the pockets under the helmets to identify them later on. They couldn't find any of the identification tags which we have around our necks. I am wondering if those poor devils will ever be shoveled out of that hole someday and how they will be able to separate them. They must have been buddies and were snuffed out together.[45]

—*Private Charles F. Minder*
306th Machine Gun Battalion, 77th Division

O ne low point in the campaign occurred in the final days of August. Two weeks earlier, elements of the 28th Division had captured the village of Fismette on the German side of the Vesle River. Dominated by enemy-held high ground, it wasn't much of a prize. American officers pleaded for permission to withdraw, but French higher command refused. On August 27 the Germans counterattacked and overran the village. Of the approximately 230 doughboys in the village, only about 30 survivors escaped back across the river. One of them was Lieutenant Bob Hoffman.

•

I saw the Germans coming down the street. Clumpety-clump they were going with their high boots and huge coal bucket helmets. I can see them coming yet—bent over, rifle in one hand, potato masher grenade in the other; husky, red-faced fellows, their eyes almost popping out of their heads as they dashed down the street, necks red and perspiring. Far down the street was the barrier usually occupied by Americans. They were centering their attack on that part of town and never dreamed that we were in the houses so far up the street.

I was standing back in the small hall of this house on the corner when in popped a powerful young German. He did not see me. It was not quite light and his eyes could not penetrate the semi-darkness of the interior of the house. He leaned well out of the doorway, planning to run to another doorway. This was their usual system in making an attack. What was I to do? What would you have done—shoot him at close quarters, yell at him to turn around and fight a bayonet duel with him; or just stick the bayonet in him? I chose the latter system as being the safest and easiest. He was so surprised, and died on the end of my bayonet.

The attack had passed. There were only 50 or so of them, but none came back. We had them between the defenders of the barricade and ourselves, and picked them off as they continued down the street and tried to return.[46]

—Lieutenant Bob Hoffman
111th Infantry, 28th Division

The Germans used a captured Company H man as a shield. He came down the street and when he got to our P.C. he stuck his head in the door. "You'd better surrender, the town is full of Germans," he said.

I was just pulling him into the building when a dozen Germans came rushing in right after him. Our boxes of grenades were gone, our chauchat ammunition was long since exhausted. All we had left was our pistols, and I don't believe even then, realizing we were surrounded, that we would have given up had it not been for the fact that the Germans took us by surprise.

Even after we were captured and the Germans were marching us up the hill, one American continued to pick our guard off. I saw a blue spot in one Hun's temple and he crumpled up; then another man on the other side of me dropped. Then I saw a piece of head go by and another German fell, and still another soldier gave a shriek and fell, a crumpling mass on the street. I'd like to meet that game American sniper some day, believe me.

What surprised me most were the details that the Germans knew regarding our organization. The [German] adjutant seemed to know more about the disposition of our own troops than I did. He told me that Colonel Rickards was in command of the 112th and that Colonel Shannon was in charge of the 111th.

A German boy who could speak English also told me that he had eaten in my mess line the night before, and to prove it, he told me just what we had for supper and all about it.

He had come over in an American uniform and, mingling with the replacements which we had recently received, had secured a good piece of white bread, all the information he could take with him and got safely back.[47]

—Captain Edward Schmelzer
112th Infantry, 28th Division

The 28th Division seemed to be having a bad time around Fismes. All day long officers were coming in on stretchers from the operating room. A Texas major, a great whale of a man, was put in the cot beside me, gloriously drunk with ether. I heard muttering to himself: "The best looking bunch of Huns I ever seen—them were regular fellows." Then he lifted a red, unshaven face from the pillow to blink at me. "Say," he whispered confidentially, "them pertater-smashers is great. I seen three men trying to get out of one window to get rid of one of them fellows." A pause while he vomited over the side of the bed, then with a chuckle, "and they done it, too—I was one of 'em."[48]

—Anonymous Officer
77th Division

Six American divisions participated in the fighting from the Marne to the Vesle between July and September 1918. Together they had advanced over 20 miles, removing any enemy threat to Paris, freeing important rail nets and proving to all that the American soldier was to be the decisive factor in the war. But the price of that proof came high. The 3rd Division lost 6,570 men; the 26th Division lost 4,644; the 28th Division lost 4,548; the 32nd lost nearly 4,000; the 42nd lost 5,476; and the 77th, in fighting along the Vesle from August 12 to September 16, lost about 4,600. The casualties left many of the officers and men reflective.

•

We arrived in France at a time when all the French soldiers and civilians could talk about and think was defensive action. It was quite natural for them to stress training for defensive action. I am convinced the American soldiers and officers gave just as good an account of themselves and accomplished the desired results in such defensive action just as well as did the French who were our instructors. It was in offensive action that our defects in leadership and training showed up so prominently. However, we blundered through the early months of the 1918 fighting—losing more men than we should have and won our part of the war in spite of our delinquencies.

There also existed through the chain of command an ever present tendency to rush troops forward and keep pushing them against enemy machine guns without adequate support from machine guns, howitzers and artillery. General officers and field officers were the guilty ones in this respect. They generally had never commanded troops in large bodies and against a first-class well-armed enemy. Many of them employed the same driving tactics they used in smaller commands in the Philippine Islands and in other similar campaigns.

They would not take the word of the officer in the front lines as to the opposing forces and weapons but kept driving troops forward inadequately supported by artillery. Along the Ourcq there were outstanding examples of this sort of thing. Men were constantly driven against machine guns well placed with ample ammunition and with orders to hold the Yankees back. Finally it dawned upon the General Officers they were sacrificing their infantry. When they massed enough artillery to blow the machine guns loose and the way was cleared.

Had artillery been turned loose on those positions the first day our infantry would have just walked over Hill 212 and the Germans would never have been able to organize along their next line.[49]

—Major Lloyd D. Ross
42nd Division

*D*espite it all, they had won. There was no doubt about that.

•

Two things I remember about the march to Gommeville [as we left the Ainse-Marne campaign]. One was the people in the towns through which we passed near sunset. They thronged the roadside at the first sound of our wheels and swarmed about as the head of the column rolled into the village street, laughing, crying, holding babies up to touch our hands and giving us flowers from the fields. We put the flowers in our helmet straps. The people in this region had gotten the idea that we were their preservers who had stopped the German advance from reaching their homes.

The other thing I remember was Jack Hart, the saddler, drunk as a lord, and myself herding him along a moonlit road about a mile behind the column. He would run zigzag until he got well ahead of me and fell into a ditch from which I would pull him and start him on another run. I finally got him to Gommeville, where he spent the rest of the night digging a latrine.[50]

—Corporal Horatio Rogers
101st Field Artillery, 26th Division

Notes

1. Sibley, *With the Yankee Division in France*, p. 211.

2. Bach, *The Fourth Division*, p. 85.

3. Strickland, *Connecticut Fights*, p. 89.

4. John L. Barkley, *No Hard Feelings!* (New York: Cosmopolitan Book Corporation, 1930), pp. 125–127.

5. Sibley, *With the Yankee Division in France*, p. 232.

6. Among the dead on the field was former President Theodore Roosevelt's youngest son, Quentin. A fighter pilot, he was shot down and killed on July 14.

7. Swan, *My Company*, p. 204.

8. Albertine, *The Yankee Doughboy*, pp. 160–161.

9. Sibley, *With the Yankee Division in France*, pp. 223–224.

10. Rogers, *The Diary of an Artillery Scout*, p. 193–194.

11. *History of the One Hundred Second Field Artillery.* (Boston: Pvtly printed, 1927), p. 92.

12. Robert Hoffman, *I Remember the Last War.* (York, Pa.: Strength & Health Publishing Co., 1940), pp. 156–157.

13. Allen, *Toward the Flame*, pp. 85–86, 112.

14. Hoffman, *I Remember the Last War*, p. 161.

15. Allen, *Toward the Flame*, p. 120.

16. Reifsnyder, *A Second Class Private in the Great World War*, p. 64.

17. Sibley, *With the Yankee Division in France*, p. 226.

18. Allen, *Toward the Flame*, pp. 102–103.

19. Reifsnyder, *A Second Class Private in the Great World War*, pp. 61–62.

20. Jacks, *Service Record by an Artilleryman*, pp. 112–113.

21. Hogan, *The Shamrock Battalion of the Rainbow*, pp. 157–158.

22. Reilly, *Americans All*, p. 387.

23. *Ibid.*, pp. 377–378.

24. *Ibid.*, pp. 404–405.

25. Bach, *The Fourth Division*, p. 97.

26. Duffy, *Father Duffy's Story*, p. 222.

27. Ettinger, *A Doughboy with the Fighting 69th*, p. 149.

28. Charles MacArthur, *War Bugs.* (Garden City, N.Y.: Doubleday, Doran & Co., 1929), pp. 107–108.

29. *Iodine and Gasoline.* (Kingsport, Tenn.: Kingsport Press, 1919), p. 95.

30. John H. Taber, *The Story of the 168th Infantry.* (Iowa City: The State Historical Society of Iowa, 1925), p. 361.

31. Cheseldine, *Ohio in the Rainbow*, p. 215.

32. Taber, *The Story of the 168th Infantry (vol.2)* pp. 12–13.

33. William H. Amerine, *Alabama's Own in France.* (New York: Eaton & Gettinger, 1919), p. 314.

34. Straub, Elmer F. *A Sergeant's Diary in the World War.* (Indianapolis: Indiana Historical Commission, 1923), pp. 136–137.

35. Reilly, *Americans All*, pp. 395–396.

36. Gnasser, *History of the 126th Infantry*, pp. 93–95.

37. Jacks, *Service Record by an Artilleryman*, pp. 121–122, 137–138.

38. G.W. Garlock, *Tales of the Thirty-Second.* (West Salem, Wis.: Badger Publishing Co., 1927), pp. 124–125.

39. Paul W. Schmidt, *Co. C, 127th Infantry in the World War.* (Sheboygan, Wis.: Press Publishing Co., 1919), p. 159.

40. Jacks, *Service Record by an Artilleryman*, pp. 74–75.

41. Garlock, *Tales of the Thirty-Second*, p. 85.

42. Hoffman, *I Remember the Last War*, pp. 167–168.

43. J. Bennett Nolan, *The Reading Militia in the Great War.* (Reading, Pa.: The Historical Society of Berks County, n.d.), pp. 141–142.

44. *The 120th Field Artillery Diary.* (Milwaukee: Historical Committee, 120th Field Artillery Association, 1928), p. 224.

45. Charles Minder, *This Man's War.* (New York: Pevensey Press, 1931), pp. 243–244.

46. Hoffman, *I Remember the Last War*, p. 285.

47. James A. Murrin, *With the 112th in France.* (Philadelphia: J.B. Lippincott Company, 1919), pp. 207, 209–211.

48. Rainsford, *From Upton to the Meuse with the Three Hundred and Seventh*, p. 138.

49. Reilly, *Americans All*, pp. 516–517.

50. Rogers, *Diary of an Artillery Scout*, p. 198.

Members of the 32nd Division snack on French onions on their way to the front. PHOTO: U.S. ARMY/SIGNAL CORPS

A doughboy herds German prisoners to the rear. PHOTO: U.S. ARMY/SIGNAL CORPS

Doughboys from the 1st Division wear gas masks as they man frontline trenches in January 1918. PHOTO: U.S. ARMY/SIGNAL CORPS

Doughboys from the 28th Infantry, 1st Division, charge toward Cantigny in one of the earliest U.S. actions of the war. PHOTO: U.S. ARMY/SIGNAL CORPS

A phosphorous shell rains fire during action along the Vesle River in August 1918. PHOTO: U.S. ARMY/SIGNAL CORPS

A doughboy examines the field of fire of a captured German heavy machine gun near Grandpre. PHOTO: U.S. ARMY/SIGNAL CORPS

Doughboys of the 33rd Division keep a watchful eye on the German lines near Forges in October 1918. PHOTO: U.S. ARMY/SIGNAL CORPS

A German prisoner helps two wounded doughboys to an aid station.
PHOTO: U.S. ARMY/SIGNAL CORPS

A burial detail inters the dead of the 79th Division on the edge of Bois de Consenvoye in November 1918. PHOTO: U.S. ARMY/SIGNAL CORPS

Dead of the 79th Division are gathered for burial during the battle for the Meuse-Argonne. PHOTO: U.S. ARMY/SIGNAL CORPS

CHAPTER 8

Wounded

In 200 days of battle the American Expeditionary Force lost 35,560 men killed in action. Another 14,720 died of wounds. For every man killed in battle, six others were wounded, taken prisoner, or reported missing. Statistics compiled after the war indicated that 205,690 American servicemen were wounded. Of these, 90,830 were wounded severely; 80,480 were wounded slightly; and the rest were wounded "degree undetermined."

When possible, initial first aid was rendered in the front line. The casualty then walked or was carried on a litter to the battalion aid station. Here any further emergency care was given and diagnosis tags were filled out. Anti-tetanus serum was administered and the proper notation made by a "T" marked on the forehead with indelible pencil. The casualty was treated for shock if necessary.

The patient was then brought to an ambulance dressing station— established at the farthest point forward that ambulances could reach with reasonable safety—and the patient was evacuated to a field hospital.

After the war, statisticians crunched the available numbers and found that the bulk of wounds suffered by American soldiers were caused by artillery fire. Gas also inflicted numerous casualties, followed by bullets. Bayonet wounds were rare.

Among the thousands of casualties was Corporal William McGinnis, a young artilleryman from Lawrence, Massachussetts, who was wounded by shellfire on July 23 during the Ainse-Marne campaign.

•

Suddenly without the least warning I heard a terrific explosion. I was dazed for a moment and did not know what to do but as my vision became clearer I observed the branches of the trees overhead trembling and the leaves falling to the ground. The odor of burned powder seemed to choke me; I seemed to be floating in space; everything was turning red, I was losing control of myself. I made an effort to stand up, but my legs refused to support me and I fell flat on the ground. I did not know that I was hit. I was conscious of something having happened, but what it was I could not tell. I wanted to talk, but somehow my tongue was cleaved to the roof of my mouth. Peculiar sounds were running in my head. Soon, I felt a burning sensation in my chest, near my throat and in my left shoulder. My left arm was lying stiff across my chest and my head refused to move from right to left. I realized that something was wrong. I pulled myself together again but found I could not stand erect. However, I started off. I had no idea where I was going, but I felt this was no place for me. I wanted to speak to somebody, to learn what was the matter. I was afraid that I had gone insane from the concussion of the exploding shell. Someone in the battery ran out and grabbed me. Sgt. Clarence Davis and Corporal William Hart were lying on the ground having their wounds dressed. When I saw the bandage being placed on them, the thought came to me in a flash that I was hit. Captain William Howe held me while Norman Barteaux, our first aid man, cut my shirt off so that he could place a bandage on.

As the shirt lay on the ground there was no doubt in my mind that I had been bumped because the color of the shirt decided that question. A good drink of cool water was worth more than anything that I possessed in the world at that time, but water could not be found here. Someone gave me a cigarette . . . In the meanwhile, the doctor arrived and made out my field service tag, which was tied onto me, describing the nature of the wound. It was marked G.S.W. (gun shot wound) left chest and left shoulder. I also received an injection of anti-tetanus to prevent lockjaw. I was placed on a stretcher and carried about three hundred meters to the rear, to a dressing station. The station was situated on the edge of a wood and there was a continual stream [of wounded] coming out of these woods to this point, awaiting ambulances. We were placed in the ambulances and started off, four in each car. One of the boys in the lower tier who was from the infantry and who had a fragment enter his stomach died in the ambulance before we reached the clearing station. This place was in an old church in a small village about eight kilometers from the front. Several operating tables were set up and the surgeons with aprons covered with blood were attending to the worst cases, mostly amputations. Here I was tagged for evacuation to a hospital. There were several hundred stretcher cases laid out on the floor. The yard surrounding the church was also full of men, with bandaged heads, arms and legs. The groans of the severely wounded were terrible to listen to and over the cries of agony could be heard the everlasting cry for water and cigarettes. I was getting weaker, owing to the fact that I was bleeding quite freely. I distinctly remember a peculiar buzzing sound in my ears; everything seemed to change color; I took one hasty glance at the corner [where the dead were being placed] and made one supreme effort to pull myself together, but failed and lapsed into unconsciousness.[1]

—Corporal William McGinnis
102nd Field Artillery, 26th Division

C orporal McGinnis was fortunate. He regained consciousness in a hospital, was operated on and recovered from his wounds in time to rejoin his unit eight months later. Lieutenant Colonel George M. Duncan's war ended when he was wounded in the Argonne fighting later that fall.

•

Major Woolworth and I entered a small building. Glancing around for something to sit on, we noticed an officer's bedding roll in the corner just inside the opening. Suddenly without the slightest warning there was a terrific explosion directly in front of us. The lightninglike blast blotted out everything, and it seemed surely the end of the world. The normal functions of my brain apparently were stunned for a moment or two, with a feeling one would experience after a violent fall to the ground. There was a severe pain in the left side of my face and I could not see. There was also a sharp pain in my left hand and wrist. Raising my right hand to my face to find out the reason for my lack of vision, my fingers came in contact with a mass of warm sticky matter, which I knew at once was blood and lacerated flesh.

I knew at once I was badly wounded, but I could not determine just where except my face. I believed death was ready to claim me, for I was sure my face and eyes had been blown away. I remember a feeling of disgust and loathing, as the thought of dying in that Godforsaken hole raced through my mind.

When my eyes finally pierced the gloom of dust and smoke, the first thing I saw was a severed foot, it had been cut off just above the ankle as though with a giant cleaver. The foot was standing upright in its army shoe, and the bloody stump was a sickening sight. At first I thought, "My God, that is one of my feet!" but as I gazed closer, I saw the bloody remnant of a woolen wrap legging clinging to the top of the shoe. I was sure then it was not one of my feet as I never had worn woolen leggings, and a feeling of relief ran through my mind.

There were portions of human bodies scattered about on the

floor as though torn to pieces and fought over by monster wild animals. As I looked with horror upon the shambles before me, someone entered the doorway and flashed the beams of a pocket light about, evidently my legs were unnoticed as the man stepped directly on one of them. The pain was agonizing and I screamed.

The first aid operation in the field is very simple, just expose the wound, open one of the individual containers of iodine, saturate the injury, place a compress bandage, and the patient is ready for removal toward the rear areas. The dressing of my wounds being completed, one of the surgeons produced a large syringe, the size of which led me to believe the doctor belonged to the Veterinary Corps. He told me he would then administer the anti-tetanus serum. Opening my coat he exposed my abdomen, and without a word jabbed that darning needle into my middle, just missing the navel. I let out a yell, at the same time asking the Doc if he did not think I had enough holes in me as it was.

By the time I was ready to be moved I had grown very weak. The GMC ambulance already had two wounded men in the upper litters, and I was shoved in on the bottom. The man above me was crying out with pain. I called to him and asked where he was hurt, what his name was and what outfit he belonged to. Between moans he told me he was Lieutenant Frederick Edwards of the 18th Field Artillery, of our division. He said, "I am badly wounded in the stomach by a large piece of high explosive and my guts are hanging out."

When we reached the hospital at Very we were all taken out to ascertain our condition, whether anyone needed immediate attention or not. When we were reloaded I was placed on the top tier and Lieutenant Edwards on the bottom. I believe the doctors thought the lieutenant would ride more comfortably nearer the ambulance chassis, as the top swayed terribly passing over the rough roads.

We were rolling along at a pretty good clip, and were beyond the reach of enemy shells except the long range ones. The road was rough and my wounds were beginning to pain terrible, when without the slightest warning the left wooden rail of my litter broke in two at the center, and I fell through the opening, landing on top of Lieutenant Edwards. The lieutenant screamed shrilly when the weight of my body crushed into his terrible wound, but the ambulance rolled on, swaying dizzily from side to side. I shouted for the driver to stop at the top of my voice, but nothing happened. The noise of the passing traffic and the roar of our own vehicle drowned out the sound of my voice. I tried vainly to reach the curtain at the front of the ambulance, separating us from the men sitting in front, but my awkward position and the pain of my many wounds prevented me from turning far enough to touch the curtain.

I was becoming desperate and frantic, as the speed of our death house on wheels rolled on, it seemed there must be a dead man at the wheel. The man next to me in the top of the car and the one in the litter next to Edwards had not made a sound up to then. Both of them had body wounds I believe and must have been in a semi-conscious state. My weight was resting partly against the man next to Edwards and he began to grown horribly, making sounds like the death rattle from a human throat, only much louder, then the man above started to whine and moan like a dying animal. Edwards by that time I think was unconscious and beyond the feeling of human suffering.

I then started screaming like a wild man. When we finally reached a point on the road where there were no other vehicles for the time being, the men in front heard my shouting and stopped. My three companions in misery were quiet. I knew they were all unconscious, and perhaps some of them were dead.

As we jolted along my chest seemed to be wet, raising my right hand and placing it on my breast I knew the sticky fluid was blood seeping down from Edward's body, now placed above me.

About 9:30 P.M. our ambulance stopped and we were unloaded at once. Through the darkness I could discern many long, one-story squatty buildings as my litter was borne through the entrance of one of them. I found myself in a long receiving ward filled to capacity with suffering men, awaiting their turn on the operating tables. Nailed to the wall along one side of the room, about 18 inches from the floor, there was a two by four and about five feet from the wall, running the length of the room, was another two by four supported by short lengths of the same material, about 12 inches high. My litter was deposited atop the supporting two by four rails, and I realized the elevation was for the benefit of the nurses administering aid to the stricken soldiers. I learned I was in American Red Cross Hospital #114 at Fleury.[2]

—Lieutenant Colonel George M. Duncan
3rd Division

The nerve that the boys display when they come in wounded is certainly remarkable. They don't even whimper, and some of them even walk in when they are so shot up that they can hardly "tottle" along. I held one American doughboy's hand as he died. He tried to say something to me but he was too far gone so I covered him with a blanket and left him to the chaplain. Then Perry Lesh and I unloaded a whole ambulance which will hold six men, five of them we got out all right but the sixth one we could not get out so easily and Perry climbed into the ambulance to help get the head end

loose. It seemed as if his arm was sticking some place and I asked
him whether or not he could move his arm a little but he did not
answer. Finally we got him out and when I looked at him I knew the
reason for his silence; he was dying and gasping and could not talk,
he had already lost consciousness; so we covered him with a blanket
and stood him aside with the dead. It was sure a mess of blood at
the first aid station and it finally "got to" Perry and I so we stopped
and went to tend to our horses.[3]

—*Sergeant Elmer F. Straub*
151st Field Artillery, 42nd Division

Upon arrival at the field hospital, the cases were sorted and classi-
fied according to their transportability. Most attention was given to
the proper disposition of shock cases. These cases were immediately
taken to the shock room for special treatment. The litter bearing the
patient was placed on two [saw] horses and the surgeon made a hurried examination to determine any open or concealed hemorrhage. If
none was found, the patient was covered with warm blankets and
heat applied beneath the litter. The heat was supplied by burning
generally four cans of solidified alcohol well protected by metal
boxes open at one end only. The blankets were then dropped over
the sides of the litter to the ground. Further, the patient was fortified
by warm drinks in small quantities, provided of course he did not
have an abdominal wound or that he was not slated for an early
operation. The heart was stimulated by subcutaneous injections of
caffeine citrate or camphorated oil. Morphine was freely used for its
relief of pain and for its general beneficial effect. (It was an important adjunct to the suppression of internal hemorrhage.)

During the early days of the division's active campaigning,
when the weather was warm and the soldiers were still in good condition both mentally and physically, the number of shock cases was
relatively small. It was also observed during this period that even
those cases in severe shock responded gratifyingly to treatment.
(Youthful enthusiasm rose to the surface. The men laughingly
recounted tales and experiences along the battle line. Furthermore,
though recently snatched from the jaws of death, they eagerly
inquired how long it would be before they could return to the line.)

In striking contrast was the clinical picture presented by the
wounded during the closing weeks of the war. Not only were the
shock cases greater in number, running from 17–20% of the severely
wounded, but they were far graver in character and reacted very
slowly to the most energetic treatment. Worn out by long fighting,
with little chance for rest, exposed to the cold with insufficient protection or warmth, constantly wet and insufficiently fed by cold food

because of the risk of building fires along the line, the men were at the low water mark of fitness both mentally and physically. Their reserve was gone so that the type of shock then exhibited was more profound than that theretofore encountered. Soldiers with only moderate wounds began to arrive at the hospitals in deep shock, from which they often failed to rally under any form of treatment.[4]

—Colonel D.S. Fairchild
Medical Officer, 42nd Division

I was carried to another building which proved to be the operating room. It was unnecessary for anyone to tell me what the place was used for, because, when I was carried into the brightly lighted room, there were 12 to 15 men, bloody and groaning, lying upon as many operating tables, surrounded by surgical crews. My litter was carried past probably ten of those tables and I certainly had a bird's eye view of a human slaughter house.

Everything seemed to work perfectly. I was hardly on the table until the ether cone was in front of my face. The anesthetic cone was placed over my mouth and nose with instructions about inhaling and exhaling, and I quickly had a sensation of falling off the table and into oblivion.

The next thing I remember was a terrible nightmare. I dreamed I was floundering about in a horrible, slimy, slippery sea of mud. Surrounding me on all sides were fierce Hun soldiers, slowly advancing upon me with bayonets at the position for thrusting. In the dream I was terrified and must have cried out, for I awakened and when my eyes became accustomed to the dim light, I could discern an electric bulb overhead and then realized I was in the hospital.

Sitting by my cot and holding my hand was a young hospital orderly. He spoke to me softly and soothed me as one would a child. I asked what kind of a ward I was in. The young man told me I was in the ether ward, and as soon as possible I would be removed to a surgical ward.

My chart showed I had been on the operating table well over an hour, therefore a large amount of ether had been necessary and oh how sick it made me. The young man stayed with me, held and bathed my head and face, but I thought sure I was going to die. The retching sapped every ounce of strength left in my body, and it felt as though every inner organ in my being must be coming out through my mouth.

Except for the young orderly, my surroundings were ghastly. There seemed to be about 50 men in the long, narrow building, every one of whom had recently been carried in from the operating room. Many of the patients were groaning and moaning, others retching and ether sick like myself. A number of orderlies were moving about silently attending the suffering men. I was carried to another ward just as day was breaking.[5]

—*Lieutenant Colonel George M. Duncan*
3rd Division

When I came to from the operation, I was in a ward for the severe cases. I was vomiting something that smelled like ether. There were ten of us, three Germans, seven Americans. A German, quite close to me, had had most of his face shot out. He would sip a little milk. But the blood would trickle down into his stomach and he would puke blood and milk. From him I first learned of old age pensions and social insurance. He said they had been started under Bismarck. It was very difficult for him to talk, but he spoke English. "If I do not die," he said, "I will take a long vacation and get well. The surgeons are now great. They make new faces." But within an hour, with horrible paroxysms, he died.[6]

—*Lieutenant Maury Maverick*
28th Infantry, 1st Division

A large proportion, probably 85 percent, of the wounds are made by shell fragments. It is not shrapnel as is so commonly believed but high explosive. The shells burst into thousands of jagged pieces of all shapes and sizes and they are most effective. One would scarcely credit the damage that one of these tiny bits of metal can accomplish. A modest little hole may cover a shattered thigh and a pulpified mass of destroyed muscles, torn vessels and severed nerves.

The operation most frequently called for in battle wounds was new to us. It is called by the French debridement. It consists of opening a wound and removing all foreign material, such as dirt, clothes, bits of bone and metal, and of paring away all the destroyed tissue, that if left will slough and cause trouble. Often one can clip out the dead muscle and skin and leave a wound that can be stitched at once. As a rule, however, the wound is kept open and treated with antiseptic solutions (usually Dakin's solution) until a bacteriological examination shows it to be free of germs when it is closed like a new wound.[7]

—*Dr. William L. Peple*
Base Hospital #45

If I hadn't already seen war in its worst stages, some of the sights in that hospital would have been too much. Hopeless cripples, men whose memories would never be the same again—the German had left his indelible mark. Around some of the beds a scaffolding had been built to adjust pulleys and ropes for arms and legs and temporarily paralyzed bodies. Some of the men had both arms in slings of ropes. Others had one or both legs. Armless fellows, protected by asbestos bibs, forgot their troubles in nerve-healing smokes, and by means of lighting contrivances suspended above their heads by other ropes were able to light their own cigarettes.

The regular army and other ward surgeons were not unsympathetic, but their very profession inured them to the sight of suffering; they were dealers in pain and as such could feel no great emotion toward it. With a brisk, businesslike air they made their appointed rounds, viewing unusual cases with scientific interest, almost pleasure. They bestowed resolutely cheerful smiles upon all patients and inquired of those who had lost arms or legs, "Well, how's your stump coming along today?"

It didn't take much to make the fellows happy. A deck of cards, a cigarette, an illustrated magazine no matter how many years old— proved diversion enough for hours. Letters from home—which generally had to be forwarded several times and scarcely ever reached the hospital while the soldiers for whom they were intended were there—sent the recipients into ecstasies.

Sometimes there were treats when philanthropic organizations distributed chocolate bars or stationary. Once the word was spread that a delicacy almost unheard of in rural France was being passed around—ice cream. We were all excited; it was almost like home again. As we lay in our smooth white beds and counted the minutes till our turn might come, an apologetic orderly entered and informed us that the store of boxes of ice cream had been exhausted in the next ward—and there wouldn't be any for us.[8]

—*Private Lawrence O. Stewart*
Sanitary Detachment, 42nd Division

There were dozens of correspondents around the Chateau-Thierry bridgehead, but who among them ever described such a tent as I recall somewhere around Coulommiers, where some of us there suffered from gangrene? Valor they wrote of, yes—but never the cost of it. A lieutenant I loved would alternately emerge from his delirium to apologize for the noise he knew he must have been making; what prayerful thanks we gave when the green of his groin mercifully reached the valves of his heart and the gravedigger came for him. Seeing the backwash of the Korean War a generation later, I marveled at the fine condition of men flown into the Naval Hospital at Oakland six days after receiving wounds which, at Coulommiers, would have meant months of agony. There were no miracle drugs, no sulpha, or antibiotics to quiet the canvas air at Coulommiers. There was only morphine sulphate; yet such was the fellowship of those who survived that tent, I know of none who failed to rid himself of morphine's toxic baggage when he reached the solid wards. You could tell who was quitting the drug by watching the cigarettes glowing among the night lights, where some lad stretched his arm aloft and bared a biceps nostalgic for the poison he had willed from his veins forever, as he began his withdrawal from narcotics and his acceptance of pain. "Tough, eh?" "Yeah, I think I'll ask the nurse for a goddamn aspirin." The Doughboy was a humorist throughout his ordeals—a trait by which soldiers everywhere make war bearable.[9]

—Lieutenant Laurence Stallings
5th Marines, 2nd Division

Usually the first question the surgeon asked a man preparatory to operation was what outfit he came from. This was because we were so busy with our shift in the operating room and with seeing our patients in the wards afterwards that we could hardly follow the progress of a battle in any other way. The Wildcat Division from South Carolina was in front of us at one time, and when one of the wounded men was asked about his outfit, he replied, "I was a wildcat, but I ain't so wild now."[10]

—Corporal Frederick A. Pottle
Evacuation Hospital #8

I got the works—an exploding shell sent fragments into my left hip and stomach. I'll never forget the sensation—there didn't seem to be any sharp pain—it was more like a heavy blow by a mallet which almost right away produced a paralyzing effect.

I recuperated fast in the surgical hospital so that in a few days they took me on a litter to an ambulance and drove me to a hospital tent ward right beside the railroad track. In this place they had the double decker beds. On the whole I was feeling pretty good, but just above me the patient was suffering some pain—he'd lost a leg. We talked and I tried to take his mind off of his trouble to the best of my ability but I was not too successful. Pretty soon he needed the urinal and called to the sergeant attendant sitting at the desk near the door of the tent. This fellow paid no attention to the call so my friend above kept wailing for it. Pretty soon the attendant bawled out—I'm going out for lunch in a few minutes; when my relief comes in he'll bring you the urinal. I was dumbfounded, I'd never heard of anyone behaving in such a brutal manner, so I entered the fray. At the very top of my lungs I ordered the sergeant to bring the urinal to my friend above or I'd get up and get it myself—and if I did that he'd find himself in the hottest court martial he'd ever heard of. Well, he brought the urinal, but boy oh boy the dirty look he gave me—he didn't know just who I was but he believed he'd better not take any chances.

We were laid off on the platform and finally German prisoners came along and carried us up into the wards in the hospital. I wound up in a room with about seven other patients. One of our patients was indeed a pitiful person to contemplate. He was a handsome young man about 22 years of age. He had been badly wounded and had lost both legs right up to his hips. I don't believe I ever in my life saw or experienced such magnificent morale. He was always joking about himself and inviting the nurses to go to the dance with him next Saturday night.

In the ward next to us another patient had evidently lost a leg—as was customary, the doctors and nurses changed our dressings and gave us saline solution on the wound if necessary each day. The boy next door apparently suffered a lot of pain when his dressing was changed and every day we would hear him moan, "Oh my poor leg, my poor leg." Our friend in the ward finally said, "I'm getting tired of that boy moaning over his leg—tomorrow if he sounds off again I'm going to fix him." Sure enough we heard the same moanful expression of self-pity—so when the doctors came to dress our young man he cried at the top of his voice, "Oh my poor two legs—my poor two legs." It worked and we never heard from our friend next door again.[11]

—*Major William G. Weaver*
8th Machine Gun Battalion, 3rd Division

*N*umerous casualties were also caused by gas, the two most common being burns from mustard gas and respiratory failure from phosgene. After admission to a hospital, gas casualties stripped and showered. Those too serious to do so on their own were bathed while still on their stretchers. Medics sprayed eyes, nose, and throat with bicarbonate of soda. Special treatments might include alkaline, oxygen, and sometimes venesection (bleeding) to counter the effects of the gas. Soldiers who had ingested gas contaminated food or water were given olive or castor oil to coat the irritated stomach linings. Fortunately, while a significant producer of casualties, gas was not a great killer. About 27.3 percent of all AEF casualties were caused by gas, but most were not fatal. Of 70,552 men hospitalized as gas casualties, 1,221 died in the wards. As for immediate deaths on the battlefield, it has been estimated that only 200 were caused by gas. Nevertheless, being gassed was no trivial matter.

•

One of the saddest sights of the war was to see the men who were badly gassed being taken to the dressing stations, groaning and squirming in agony, with their bodies burned raw by mustard gas, their eyes burning, clutching their throats as they were gasping for breath. It was indeed a sad picture when one thought of the contrast of these same boys only a few days before as they marched up in the direction of the lines, singing, whistling and with a gay spirit as they swung along the highways. They now looked so different as hundreds of them came back to the field dressing stations, some walking, dragging their tortured bodies along on exhausted legs, others being carried on stretchers, and a few of the blind being guided by less seriously wounded buddies. The scenes of gas cases in the hospitals were also pitiful ones. Ward after ward was filled with these gassed forms, some with oxygen tubes in their mouths, in order to maintain what little life there was left, others with arms strapped and bleeding from incisions made just above the elbows in order to free all the poisonous black blood in the system.[12]

—*Captain James T. Duane*
101st Infantry, 26th Division

Those dreadful mustard gas cases were probably the most painful we had to witness in all our service. As a matter of fact, the majority were in much less serious plight than the wounded men. Mustard gas (it has nothing to do with mustard) is a heavy liquid, which though fairly volatile will remain for some time clinging to grass and undergrowth, and will burn any flesh with which it comes in contact. It is especially adapted for use by a retreating army. By soaking down with mustard gas the area through which the pursuing American troops had to advance, the Germans made sure that a large number of the advancing force would be incapacitated. The soldier's clothing soon becomes impregnated with the stuff as he brushes through the undergrowth, and the burns develop through the help of moisture. Those parts of the body subject to excessive perspiration are especially affected. The burns are extremely painful, but in general not fatal unless the gas has been inhaled, or (as with other surface burns) a third or more of the total skin area has been effected.

A bad feature of mustard gas, however, is that it almost invariably produced temporary, but complete, blindness. Nothing demoralizes a man so much as the fear of losing his sight, and telling him he will see again in a day or two generally fails to reassure him.

The gas patients began to arrive at Juilly as early as June 12. Since most of them were immediately evacuable, we made temporary wards for them in the great cloisters which ran around two sides of the court in front of Wards F and G. By the 16th there were nearly 700 gassed men there, just out of the glare of the sunny court, lying fully dressed on blanket-covered cots, some of them badly gassed in the lungs and fighting horribly for breath, which could be a little prolonged by giving them oxygen; nearly all blinded, many delirious, all crying, moaning, tossing about.

For most of the patients there was nothing to do but renew frequently the wet dressings which relieved somewhat the smart of the burns, and try to restore their lost morale. For those who had been gassed worst, nothing effectual could be done. They were spared much by being in general delirious, but it required the constant attention of several orderlies to keep some of them in bed. Later on, the hospital service was so organized that the gas cases were handled by special gas hospitals. After we left Juilly we almost never received gas victims unless they were also wounded.[13]

—*Corporal Frederick A. Pottle*
Evacuation Hospital #8

Phosgene was quickly recognized by its pungent odor, somewhat similar to the odor of old, moldy hay. The effect of this gas differed in many respects from that of chlorine, and on the whole, it was far more efficient and deadly. If breathed in high concentrations, it killed immediately. In small concentrations, its effect was almost limited to the little terminal air cells in the lungs. Its action so hindered the lining of these little air cells and of the small blood vessels in the cell walls that the fluid part of the blood leaked out of the blood vessels into the air cells. In addition to the blood vessels there was another system of vessels known as the lymphatics, which, from our point of view, may be looked upon as sewers to remove secretion. The symptoms of phosgene poisoning might be delayed for a considerable time, because the sewers at first were able to carry off the greater part of the secretion; a time came, however, when it was impossible for those sewers to remove the secretion as fast as it was excreted from the blood vessels. Consequently, the air cells began to fill up with fluid, which was at first thin and which later became thicker, almost like pus. The result was that death from phosgene poisoning was a slow and prolonged drowning in the subject's own body fluid, a drowning infinitely worse than in water, because instead of eight to ten minutes, it required eight to ten days. The symptoms were those of drowning; the subject was blue, and struggled for breath. The fluid ran out of his mouth and nose. A pool of fluid was often on the floor beside his bed, where he had hung over his head to let it be drained or coughed out. As the case progressed, the patient became bluer, colder, unconscious, and finally, after eight or nine days of suffering, died from inability to get sufficient air to maintain life.[14]

—*Sergeant Fred A. McKenna*
103rd Field Artillery, 26th Division

The patients we retained were generally desperately wounded: fracture cases, amputations, abdominal, chest and head wounds. They required constant and tender attention. Many of them were quite helpless and had to be fed and bathed like infants.

Soon after breakfast the surgeon appeared and the dreadful ordeal of dressing the wounds began. The nurse accompanied him from cot to cot, an orderly pushing along a white-enameled cart bearing fresh sterile dressing, Dakin solution, and tubes, bandages and necessary instruments. The orderly would cut the bandages and lay bare the great wound. The surgeon, equipped with sterilized gown and gloves, would pull out all the old packing and tubes, often having to probe deep with the points of his instrument. Then he would swab it out with a gauze sponge soaked in Dakin solution, push new tubes and gauze back into it, and the orderly would replace the bandage. All this caused the patient excruciating agony.

The wards in the morning, when wounds were being dressed, were dreadful places. It was in the first dressing that the wounded realized the extent of their injuries. Sometimes a poor lad found out then for the first time that he had lost a leg, the absence of which he had been unable to feel. They tried to be brave, but who could quietly endure that pain after such long sapping of strength. After one or two experiences of carrying amputated legs down to the incinerator, it was impossible to get a thrill of horror out of such commonplace events. Indeed, we developed a most unbecoming levity with regard to them. But in the wards one was in constant contact with dreadful agony, which expressed itself in irrepressible moans and shrieks. One had to deal with cringing fear, with unreason, with selfishness in a spirit of charity that always saw these men as not masters of themselves but drained of their strength and courage. One had to be ready to give endlessly those unpleasant attentions which bedridden men demand.[15]

—Corporal Frederick A. Pottle
Evacuation Hospital #8

When a man was dying, they would move him out. It was bad enough for him to die without his comrades, who did not know when their own turn might come, having to watch him die. Some of the men went out screaming when they were moved. The nurses would try to ease their going by telling them that they were only going to the operating room for minor treatment or to the dressing room to have their bandages changed.

The fellows soon learned to observe whether the little bag which held their personal belongings—sometimes a helmet or a coat—came with them. If it remained behind, they could expect to come back; but if it too was moved, then they were sure that worse was in store for them. Some begged to be left here to die with their friends around them, not to be placed with a lot of near corpses who were complete strangers.

The more pitifully wounded did not wish to live. They constantly begged doctors and nurses, sometimes at the top of their voices, to put an end to them. Some made attempts to end their lives with a knife or fork. It became necessary to feed these wounded and never leave a knife or fork with them. One of the orderlies told me that a blinded man who was suffering greatly and did not wish to live had killed himself at one time with a fork. It was hard to drive it deep enough through his chest to end his life, and he kept hitting it with his clenched fist to drive it deeper.

There was a limit to how many pain tablets could be given to any man—how many his heart would stand. But most of them begged for another tablet the minute they recovered sufficiently from the former tablets and once again felt severe pain. Seldom was it quiet at night. Men whose nerves broke would be screaming all night.

There were many cases of shell shock. Horrible cases of mustard gas were everywhere. Some of these men were blinded and had to lie for endless days with their heads covered with bandages. Some of the men later were able to walk straddle-legged down the aisles. I was told that their testicles in some cases shriveled up like dry peas in a pod.[16]

—Lieutenant Bob Hoffman
111th Infantry, 28th Division

[I recall] an American operated [on in October]. As he lay on the table, you would never have guessed how horribly he was wounded. His face was unscarred. I think he was one of the most handsome men I ever saw, with blue eyes and long waving tawny yellow hair. He was shot nearly in two in the region of the abdomen, and died on the table. They gave him an anesthetic, of course, and the surgeon attempted a hasty operation. I remember how he took up two large gauze drains sheathed with rubber tissue, and held them a moment in his hand pondering whether he should waste them on this patient or not. The nurse discontinued the anesthetic, wiped his face and smoothed out his hair, and we all stood there a few moments watching him as he died, quite peacefully, with only a little sob or gasp at the end like a child dropping off to sleep after a fit of crying. I wonder what you will think when I say that the only feeling I experienced was an eager curiosity to know what he was experiencing. I felt no sorrow, and no horror.[17]

—Corporal Frederick A. Pottle
Evacuation Hospital #8

Our hospital room was so crowded it was difficult for the doctors and nurses to attend us. The roster of officers then included Captain Killion, 313th Infantry, from Malden, Massachusetts; Lieutenants Shisler, 313th Infantry, West Virginia; Shultz, 11th Infantry, Chicago, Illinois; Markus, 35th Division, Joplin, Missouri; Humphrey, 11th Machine Gun Battalion, Herrington, Kansas; and myself.

I cannot remember the nature of wounds carried by each officer. Lieutenant Markus, though, seemed to suffer more than anyone else in the room, a machine gun bullet had shattered his left elbow and he had to lie in one position continually. His arm was lashed to a board so arranged to minimize the pain if he moved, and there was a rubber tube in the wound for draining. Markus seldom spoke to anyone, his pain seemed too great to make the effort. The surgeons were making a valiant fight to save his arm, but from what I could gather the arm was badly infected and nothing seemed to overcome the poison. I never knew the outcome of the lieutenant's injury.

Lieutenant Shisler was my bunkie, that is he was in the bed next to mine. He seemed very young and suffered a great deal. His wounds were inflicted by machine gun bullets, in the left leg, one in the thigh which was not so bad, and one in the lower leg. The latter was a serious wound, the bullet having traversed from just below the knee to a point just above the ankle. Evidently there was infection, as there was a rubber tube almost ten inches long in the leg. Shisler suffered the tortures of the damned when the surgeon on his morning rounds had to remove the tube, and after flushing the wound, insert a new tube. Shisler and I were so close together we could hold hands while our dressings were being removed, and holding one another's hands tightly assisted us wonderfully in enduring the pain. Shisler later recovered and returned home, but his left leg was several inches shorter than his right. I suppose he felt lucky to have any of the leg left.[18]

—*Lt. Colonel George M. Duncan*
3rd Division

All of the one-eyed cases and some of the no-eyed cases received attention in one certain ward, and it was to this ward after my release from the hospital that I used to go every day for fresh dressing for my wounds. The greatest excitement in the ward prevailed one day when one of the doctor's assistants entered carrying several flat, hardwood cases, each of them about a yard square. The cases opened like a book and were laid flat on the table. Their interiors were lined with green velvet and there on the shallow receptacles in the green velvet were just dozens of eyes, gleaming unblinkingly up at us.

A shout went up and down the ward and the Cyclopians gathered around the table. There was a grand grab right and left. Everyone tried to get a handful. There was some difficulty reassorting the grabs. Of course, it happened, that fellows that really needed blue or grey ones, managed to get hold of black ones or brown ones, and some confusion existed while they traded back and forth to match up proper colors, shades and sizes.[19]

—*Floyd Gibbons*
Correspondent, Chicago Tribune

We had to question each man as to whether he had a good reason for being wounded; or why he shot himself in the right hand instead of the left, or some less important member of his body, further classifying him as to whether he was accidentally wounded, a battle casualty or the victim of self-inflicted wounds, for every self-inflicted wound a poster bearing S.I.W. must be placed above the bed on the wall conspicuously.[20]

—*Dr. Alvah L. Herrring*
Base Hospital #45

The nearest I ever heard to a complaint or reproach against fate came from a soldier named William Skidmore. He was caught close to a high explosive shell. His right thigh and leg were badly torn in ten or more places. The shaft of the thigh was shattered just above the knee. Gas gangrene had developed and was slowly filtering through the muscles. A big piece of metal had torn through the left ankle joint and lay buried in the tissues of the leg. A large piece had lodged in his temple and taken away the sight of his left eye. Somewhere in his journey his watch, money and valuables, together with a picture of his wife and children, had all been lost. He hung for days between life and death, but finally began to mend. In making my round one day I asked him how he felt. I shall never forget his face as he turned his head slowly and said, "Major, I am a young man. I have a wife and two little children at home, and here I am just a wreck, broken all to pieces. This war business," he said. "This war business. There is just nothing to it." Then he closed his eyes and lay still.[21]

—*Dr. William L. Peple*
Base Hospital #45

In addition to physical wounds, there were psychological breakdowns to deal with. Whole hospitals were set aside to deal with what the doughboys themselves referred to as "shell shock," but which the psychiatrists preferred to describe as "anxiety neurosis."

•

A high percentage of men evacuated from the front line as "gassed" were really cases of fatigue, exhaustion, and emotional disturbance . . . In the last group there were the neuroses with tremors, speech and hearing disorders, ataxias and stupors. The severe cases were evacuated as promptly as possible to the army neurological hospitals, while the milder cases were retained, treated and returned to duty. The proportion retained was usually determined by the exigencies of the campaign.

Aside from the milder cases of exhaustion, sorted out from among the gassed and medical groups, the largest number of psychiatric cases was the exhausted with nervous symptoms. Men who were worn out, upon seeing their comrades killed or injured, and possibly being knocked over themselves by an exploding shell, lost their nerve, cried, shook all over and felt afraid, crouched and put up their arms as if to protect themselves each time they heard a shell coming or exploding. These responded promptly to medical treatment at the front.

The sick and wounded were tagged either by a medical officer, or, as generally was the case, by enlisted men of the regimental sanitary detachments, indicating in a general way that the man was wounded, gassed, sick or nervous. The sanitary personnel had all been instructed to use only the term "N.Y.D. (nervous)" for the latter group of cases. This was an important matter as it was surprising to see with what tenacity men clung to a diagnosis of "shell shock" or "neurosis" even though the tag had been made out by one of the enlisted sanitary personnel. Sometimes soldiers would wander into dressing stations and cheerfully announce that they were "shell shocked." By using the term "N.Y.D. (nervous)" they had nothing definite to cling to and no suggestion had been given to assist them in formulating in their own minds their disorder into something which was generally recognized as incapacitating and as warranting treatment in a hospital, thus honorably releasing them from combat duty. The patients were therefore open to the explanations of the medical officers and to the suggestion that they were only tired and a little nervous, and that with a short rest they would be fit for duty again.[22]

—Lieutenant Colonel Frank W. Weed
U.S. Army Medical Corps

A.P., pvt. Co. 95, 6th U.S.M.C. Age 19; race, white; service 1 year; date of admission [to hospital] July 11, 1918. Enlisted June, 1917; France September, 1917. While in training camp did not like the instructors, but was not unhappy and not sorry he enlisted. After coming to France he liked it. Went into front lines during March and

April. Shelling did not bother him. Shelling was constant, "but it didn't amount to much because we had dugouts." During May was in rear. Became rather disgusted with excessive drilling; thought his outfit should have been given rest. Went into front lines at Chateau Thierry in June and welcomed the opportunity to get some open warfare. For first four days he rather enjoyed it and although under shell fire and seeing a goodly number of casualties, he was not conscious of any fear, merely wondered whether one of the shells would "get him." June 5 his company advanced under fire to relieve the French. He saw many French dead, with heads shot off and others staring at him. He was detailed to assist in burial. This disgusted and horrified him because he never could bear to touch a corpse. He then began to realize for the first time what shell fire was. For several nights he could not sleep because the dead Frenchmen would be constantly before him. At the same time shells began to terrify him. He began to tremble under fire but tried to conceal his fear and to carry on. His condition was exaggerated by the fact that his own artillery was not working very efficiently. June 14, while under heavy shelling in open, and after position of company had been changed several times, he began to tremble, became weak and had to go to dressing station. He quieted down as soon as he was in quiet hospital. For first few weeks had terrifying dreams. Dreams have been absent for weeks. Says he feels fine now. Knows that he will not continue to feel so well if kept in hospital. Other patients make him nervous. They shake and jump at every little noise. He says he was always unable to look at people who were shaking, or to listen to people who were stammering. Does not think that he is unusually susceptible just at present. Wants to go back to company.[23]

—*Base Hospital #117 Report*
La Fauche, France

A. P., the 19-year-old Marine, apparently recovered. Others were not so fortunate. Post-war hospitals would spend years dealing with men whose shattered minds and emotions were beyond repair.

•

G.C., private. It was impossible to obtain the family or previous histories, or any information relative to the origin of his present condition. He was evacuated to the army neurological hospital from the Argonne front. He appeared to be constantly in a confused state, and refused to make any replies to questions put to him. He occasionally would mumble some words in Polish which were evidently of a religious character, assuming at the same time an attitude of prayer. He was rather emotional and would weep without provocation. He lay quietly on his bed showing no interest in his surroundings. Frequently his lips were observed to move as though praying. He was dull, stolid and stupid in his manner, frequently put his head on the table and wept, occasionally nodded his head in reply to a question, but would not talk. When asked why, he pointed to his larynx. He was evacuated to the rear in two days showing no change in his mental state. His condition was one of confusion associated with some negativism and depression.[24]

—*Base Hospital #117 Report*
La Fauche, France

Notes

1. Sirois, *Smashing Through the World War with Fighting Battery C*, pp. 126–129.

2. Duncan, "I Go to War," pp. 334–346; Lt. Edwards died that night in the hospital operating room.

3. Elmer F. Straub, *A Sergeant's Diary in the World War.* (Indianapolis: Indiana Historical Commission, 1923), pp. 210–211.

4. Reilly, *Americans All*, pp. 767–768.

5. Duncan, "I Go to War," pp. 349–352.

6. Maury Maverick, *A Maverick American.* (New York: Covici Friede Publishers, 1937), pp. 135–136.

7. McGuire, *History of U.S. Army Base Hospital No. 45*, pp. 238–241.

8. Lawrence O. Stewart, *Rainbow Bright.* (Philadelphia: Dorrance, 1923), pp. 98–99.

9. Stallings, *The Doughboys*, pp. 2–3.

10. Pottle, *Stretchers*, pp. 256–257.

11. W.G. Weaver, *History of the 8th Machine Gun Battalion.* (Ann Arbor, Mich.: Edwards Brothers, Inc., 1965), pp. 142–146.

12. Duane, *Dear Old K*, p. 88.

13. Pottle, *Stretchers*, pp. 117–118.

14. Fred. A. McKenna (ed.), *Battery A 103rd Field Artillery in France.* (Providence, R.I.: Pvtly printed, 1921), p. 145.

15. Pottle, *Stretchers*, pp. 154–155.

16. Hoffman, *I Remember the Last War*, pp. 144–145.

17. Pottle, *Stretchers*, pp. 236–237.

18. Duncan, "I Go to War," pp. 361–362.

19. Gibbons, *And They Thought We Wouldn't Fight*, pp. 350–351.

20. McGuire, *History of U.S. Army Base Hospital No. 45*, p. 174.

21. *Ibid.*, p. 244.

22. Frank W. Weed (ed.), *The Medical Department of the United States Army in the World War*, vol. 10, *Neuropsychiatry.* (Washington, D.C.: GPO, 1929), pp. 310–311.

23. *Ibid.*, pp. 389–390.

24. *Ibid.*, p. 348.

CHAPTER 9

Experience of War

*H*undreds of thousands of American men saw combat during World War I. Most of them found combat was not what they had expected. The mud, the blood, and the dismembered bodies of their buddies were eons away from the flag waving and glorious charges depicted in the popular press. Most men did their jobs; here and there a hero appeared; some few others failed to measure up.

•

During the entire war I performed the work that was necessary (someone had to do it), but I was as careful as could be during all the months of the war. I never got careless; I always had my gas mask. I always carried a shovel and a pick with me throughout the war. Some men became tired and threw their entrenching tools away, but not I. I was the champion digger of the American army. Every time we stopped I dug a hole.[1]

—Lieutenant Bob Hoffman
111th Infantry, 28th Division

In the regiment we had a lieutenant who was rather a loud-mouthed talker and always boasting what he would do when he got to the front. But when he did get there he became very nervous and was useless as an officer, transmitting his nervousness to the enlisted men. There were several men like this who could not hide their fear. We were all naturally scared and afraid at the front, but most of us had calm enough nerves so that we could control them and not let others see how we really felt.

I always tried to appear as calm as possible, though I did not feel calm. Thus when I went over the top with the infantry at Soissons, I took out and lit a cigar which I had in my map case. Of course I

171

could not keep the cigar lighted, but hoped that it would at least keep up an appearance of nonchalance.

Those of us who were to be witnesses at the officer's court martial were kept in an adjoining room in the little farm house and were not allowed into the room where the trial was going on. I was finally called in before the board of high and important appearing officers. It was a difficult position for me, as the lieutenant had at one time been a member of my mess and naturally I had a friendly feeling towards him. However, I was forced to testify. I refused to accuse him of cowardice, which was the charge, but stated that I thought he was temperamentally unfit to serve at the front. He was, of course, sitting there and it was very unpleasant to testify.

I afterwards heard he had been ordered to the rear and given a position in the Service of Supplies. However, he never recovered from the disgrace and when the flu epidemic came along I heard that he had come down with pneumonia and died.[2]

—*Lieutenant Robert W. Kean*
15th Field Artillery, 2nd Division

An older temporary lieutenant, Stephen S. Nease, became my adjutant, supply officer and general factotum. A native of Kansas and graduate of Kansas University, he spoke French fairly fluently, but with a Kansas accent that the French found difficult to understand. Indicative of his character, Stephen was possessed with the fear that his age, 33, might prevent him from getting into combat. He felt that if he returned home without a wound to prove his valor, he would be disgraced for life. Upon rejoining the 6th Infantry in August, he acquainted his battalion commander with his fear and begged to remain with a rifle company. His wish was granted and in the battle of St. Mihiel in September he gained the wound which was to be a permanent reminder of his valor—loss of his right leg.[3]

—*Captain Vernon G. Olsmith*
6th Infantry, 5th Division

They were pitiful sometimes, these men who took clean sportsmanship and decency to France. It's such a poor way of preparation.[4]

—*Private Elton E. Mackin*
5th Marines, 2nd Division

From a position far out to our left came, late each evening, the staccato "chat . . . chat . . . chat" of a machine gun. The bullets zipped and whined about our position. So persistent was the firing that our men began to dread the hour of this activity. An officer came into the shallow trenches (trenches were always shallow when American boys had to dig them!) and commanded a sergeant to get a squad of men and "go get that machine gun." The sergeant departed to remain away only a short time. When he returned, the officer was waiting. "Did you get that gun, sergeant?" "No, sir. They were *using* it!"[5]

—*Corporal Chris Emmett*
359th Infantry, 90th Division

In addition to training in front line duty, the men of the 38th were learning something about another form of soldiering. That is "salvaging." If a discarded helmet or gas mask were picked up, it was obviously salvaged. But during those days along the Marne a hundred and one articles not to be found in any army manual came in the same category. If Private Jones caught sight of a thick, downy feather comforter and added it to his two blankets for bedding, his explanation to his platoon leader was, "It was salvaged." If Private Brown found that some civilian had fled southward leaving a ripe, inviting truck garden behind, he lost no time in supplying his squad with radishes, lettuce and asparagus. And if Private Smith of the same squad found a shed full of charcoal and built a fire in the billet, knowing it was safe because charcoal fires do not smoke, and cooked all the vegetables for dinner, the whole thing was "salvaged." It was nothing more or less.[6]

—*Lieutenant C.E. Lovejoy*
38th Infantry, 3rd Division

When the line became stabilized, an order was issued to the effect that soldiers were not to interfere in any way with civilian property. It was soon after this order was made public that Private Kennedy found an exceptionally fine single bed with a feather mattress which he decided to move to his billet. He was proceeding up the street of the village with the bed balanced on his head when he met an artillery officer who sternly asked Kennedy where he was going.

"Sir," said Kennedy, "I found this bed yesterday, but my sergeant won't allow me to keep it, so I am returning it now."

The officer accepted the explanation and Kennedy continued on the way to his billet with the prize.

Corporal Hartley was a member of a surveying detail. One day, while the party was at work two kilometers from the front line, Fritz started shelling the road near them. All beat a hasty retreat toward a linesman's dugout and came tumbling down the steps together. After getting his breath, one of the party said, "I never ran so fast in my life."

"I wasn't running much," said Hartley, "but I passed several that were."[7]

—*Sergeant Jesse R. Hinman*
29th Engineers

For two weeks [in the Argonne] we slept with all our clothes on, usually in shell holes or holes dug in the ground a few feet deep so that one's body would not be blown to atoms if a shell landed nearby. These high explosive shells were terrifying and our first impulse was to run to get away from the whistling and screeching sound they made as they came sailing through the air toward us, but we soon learned that the only thing to do was to jump into a hole if there was one nearby, if not to throw ourselves flat on the ground and trust to luck that the shell would not drop on the exact spot we occupied. One had to adopt the doctrine of a fatalist, with respect to the probability of being hit by artillery fire, in order to relieve the constant tension under which he lived. One could never tell if a step too few or a step too many, a step too quick or a step too slow, a step too long or a step too short, would not put him on the danger spot when the shell landed.[8]

—*Lieutenant P.E. Deckard*
371st Infantry, 93rd Division

I had never heard a shell explode so close and I thought the whole world was coming to an end. It is the weirdest sound to hear those shells traveling through the air, and I cannot describe it very well—a sort of whirring sound; the larger the shell the deeper the whir, and the closer the shell, the shorter the sound.[9]

—*Private Henry G. Reifsnyder*
103rd Engineers, 28th Division

To be shelled is the worst thing in the world. It is impossible to imagine it adequately. In absolute darkness we simply lay and trembled from sheer nerve tension.

There is a faraway moan that grows to a scream, then a roar like a train, followed by a ground-shaking smash and a diabolical red light. Let me remark that if you are one of those who think everybody is brave under shell fire like that, you are wrong. "Everybody simply shakes and crawls . . . falling trees, screams, the flop-flop of gas shells; white-faced men digging like mad or standing up under it according to their temperament—some cool, some shaking, some weeping; a few grim jokes, but mostly just dull endurance; a hunching of the shoulders when another comes, and the thought—How long, how long?" There is nothing to do. Whether you get through or not is just sheer chance and nothing more. You may and you may not. *C'est la guerre.*[10]

—*Lieutenant Hervey Allen*
111th Infantry, 28th Division

One of my friends was a little Greek acrobat, a professional, by the name of Pagamemos. He was quite the smallest man in our company . . . Pagamemos said, "Bob, I feel sorry for you."

"Why?"

"Because you are so big. You'll be the first to get hit. I'm so small they can hardly see me—certainly not shoot me."

Poor Pagamemos! I'm here with perfect health and all my arms and legs, while he was actually the first man hit, losing both legs and one arm as a result of it.[11]

—*Lieutenant Bob Hoffman*
111th Infantry, 28th Division

The Austrian 88 is commonly called the "Whiz-Bang," because of the speed with which it sends its shells in your direction. You actually hear the explosion before you hear the report of the gun, the shell traveling faster than the sound. It is a wicked baby and does not give you a chance to duck—it simply says "Whiz-Bang!" and if the "Bang!" happens to be too close, well, you don't have to listen to it any more, and your folks back home get a telegram from the War Department stating that their hero has gone to meet his Maker.[12]

—*Corporal Leslie Langille*
149th Field Artillery, 42nd Division

At 2:10 A.M. we heard the boom of the German signal gun. Almost immediately we were in the midst of an intense barrage of everything in the book. As we had been instructed to do, we picked up our machine gun and crawled into our saps or fox holes. Shrapnel, mortar shells, machine gun bullets, whiz-bangs were landing and exploding all around us. Their fragments, stones and showers of dirt rained on our metal roof. It seemed nothing could save us. It was not possible that we could be saved from a direct hit. I sat with my back against the end of the fox hole, my legs pulled up under my chin, my arms and hands clamped like a vise around my shins. My whole body went into a muscle spasm. I shook. I trembled; my teeth and my mouth chattered. I was enveloped in tremendous fear. I was beyond any ability to exert muscular control. The noise was deafening as the Niagara of shells, bullets and stones descended upon us. With my head bent forward, I pushed my steel helmet back to protect my neck. Our metal roof was rocking like a boat on the rough sea. Dirt and stones were gradually burying us as they poured down the sides of the foxhole. I tried to speak but I could not form any words, nor would a sound emerge from my mouth. I tried to speak without stuttering and trembling, but that was not possible.

Ed Stanton was sitting in front of me in the same position I was in. We were fearful we would touch each other. We must not let the other feel our trembling. I finally spoke, but the four words I uttered sounded like they were coming from an idiot. They were: "Pretty tough, isn't it?" I did not know if Ed heard me. I thought he had not and I was glad because my gibberish would expose my fear. The answer did come in a like stuttering sound, "It sure is." Profound observations of the situation, were they not?[13]

—Private William F. Clarke
104th Machine Gun Battalion, 27th Division

Many of the guns were christened, often with girls' names, and sometimes the crews of each would talk of each great lumbering weapon as if it were alive and an actual sentient member of the outfit. Occasionally, individual gunners would hug the dull monsters they served, and boast feelingly of the destruction each gun had accomplished, of what it could do, and of how carefully they used it.[14]

—Private L.V. Jacks
119th Field Artillery, 32nd Division

"Funk holes" were the usual methods of obtaining protection from the hostile fire of shells. Holes, six feet in length and about 18 inches deep, were dug with the ordinary spade of which there was a plentiful supply. The small shovel or pick, which is standard equipment in the American Army, serves quite effectively for "digging in," particularly under fire. The small shovel could be worked with one hand under the body until, ultimately, you were in the earth.[15]

—Sergeant Leonard Kurtz
312th Infantry, 78th Division

The entrenching shovel, we found, was a very important weapon and our shovel is a small affair, the handle and blade being 18 inches long, and it is made so it can be carried on the pack. Its size didn't meet the approval of the doughboys, who found out that when he had to dig for cover, the faster he did so, the better it was for him.

Now the Germans were equipped with a real shovel. It was a regular size shovel, except the handle was cut down to about three feet in length. These shovels could be picked up almost anywhere on the battlefield and almost every soldier discarded his own and equipped himself with a German shovel. It made no difference how long or awkward it was to carry so long as it gave the service. Even the officers had them. Company commanders could be seen going into action carrying one of these shovels over their shoulders, looking for all the world like a member of a ditching crew. It was hinted that officers were readily recognized because of having the longest-handled shovels.[16]

—Captain Emil Gnasser
126th Infantry, 32nd Division

We also commenced to develop a strong friendship with the steel helmets, popularly known as "tin hats" or "Tin Lizzies" (since they had been produced by the Ford factories). Up to our first introduction to shell-fire, we felt some animosity toward these helmets; they were heavy and, notably during the hikes and maneuvers in August, during our training, attracted and retained the sun's heat like small, fireless cookers. When we got into action, the weight promptly disappeared. The tin hat became a life-saver for many, and serious wounds were avoided when shell splinters struck and were deflected by these helmets. They were also used as pillows, wash basins and shovels.[17]

—Lieutenant Bryant Wilson
364th Infantry, 91st Division

Some of the troops, more often infantrymen, threw away their identification tags because of sheer superstition; they coupled the number on the disk with the colloquial expression to "get their number," and resolved to do all in their power to camouflage their numerical identity. The methodical German was accustomed to stamp a numeral on each unit of artillery ammunition. When, one day, an American infantryman experienced a narrow escape from an exploding shell and presently, examining a fragment of the projectile which chanced to fall beside him, discovered upon it the very group of figures which he wore on his identification tag, he raised a loud outcry. "The Hun has done his worst to get my number, and has failed; he can never hurt me now." And this man immediately lost all nervousness. The absence of tags, however, was a great handicap to burial parties, who were often unable to identify the remains which they interred.[18]

—Lieutenant Frederick M. Cutler
55th Coast Artillery Corps

My squad found shelter in an old German trench, in the bottom of which had been buried half a dozen Americans the day before we reached the woods. In making our way back and forth, it was necessary to walk over the shallow graves, though we regretted having to do it. We were careful not to knock down the little improvised crosses with their identification tags. In the afternoon, a shell, exploding a short distance from one of our platoon headquarters, tore up a freshly made grave, exhumed most of a soldier's body and entirely severed the head. We re-buried the poor lad. Nowhere could we find his identification tag. All we knew was that he was an American. I have often wondered how many American bodies in France got mixed up in their removal to the large cemeteries, or lacked identification entirely.[19]

—*Corporal Earl B. Searcy*
311th Infantry, 78th Division

I remember once when a soldier had been killed and almost buried by a high explosive shell. Only his arm still stuck up out of the earth.

A signal man came by with his wire and not finding anything else, wound it around the upright hand and from there to the stump of a tree that had been blown to pieces by artillery fire.

Another signal man came by with a touch of sentiment in him and took time to scribble something on a piece of wood and stick it up beside the upright arm. It was, "Still doing his bit." It showed the spirit of our boys—game to the end.[20]

—*Sergeant William Brown*
9th Infantry, 2nd Division

I had become as vicious as the rest. Our nerves were mighty strained. We were crabbing about everything in general—hunger, cold and fatigue. Still, the last puff of a cigarette would be split up; the last bit of chewing tobacco was passed around; the last can of corned willie shared. You see, we were all buddies. The canteen of water was passed around. The one who had the water would be the last to drink and he sure would cuss at the fellows if they would insist on his drinking first. It was the same with the smokes or eats or what have you. God never could create human beings so unselfish, so devoted and so tender as my buddies. The beautiful memories of loyalty and comradeship still linger, memories deeply implanted in our souls.[21]

—*Private Joe Joe Rizzi*
110th Engineers, 35th Division

Meier confessed to me [one] night, while I was with him for a few minutes, that he had not lived a model life and had been prone to get drunk quite often. He said he could now see the error of his ways and if God would let him live he would lead a model life and never take another drink. God let him live, but Meier forgot his promise soon after we were relieved and he was out of danger.[22]

—Lieutenant Joseph D. Lawrence
113th Infantry, 29th Division

*O*f all the weapons utilized during World War I, probably none prompt- ed more public revulsion than gas. The first effective use of gas on the Western Front occurred on April 22, 1915, near Ypres when the Germans released 168 tons of chlorine from 1,600 large and 4,130 small cylinders, relying on favorable winds to carry the gas cloud over the enemy. Two French divisions collapsed, leaving a four-mile gap in the Allied line—a success the Germans had not been prepared for and failed to exploit.

As time went on, the antagonists developed various gases and more effective means of delivery, including artillery shells, mortars, and projec- tors. Chemists on both sides investigated over 3,000 chemical agents. About 30 agents were used in combat and about a dozen were found to be successful. In 1917 the Germans introduced mustard against the Allies. Although called "mustard gas," it was actually a volatile liquid that caused severe burns and blisters.

The A.E.F. suffered 34,249 "immediate" deaths on the battlefield. An estimated 200 of these were caused by gas. Another 224,089 men were evacuated with wounds to medical facilities; 70,552 of these were reported as suffering from gas wounds. Of these, 1,221 died. In total, 27.3 percent of all A.E.F. casualties were caused by gas.

•

There were many forms of poisonous gases, and many schemes used in delivering the gas. There was the projector shell (each shell con- taining about thirty pounds of gas), the regular artillery shell, hand grenades and cloud gas. The cloud gas was contained in cylinders, usually placed in grooves in the front line trenches, and with tubes attached leading over the top of the trench. At a given signal the cylinders are opened and with a loud hiss the gas is sent on its way into the enemy lines. This gas rolls along at a height of about six feet and in the form of a cloud. The depth of effect depends entirely on the wind velocity.

The regular gas shell can be identified from the other explosive shells very easily by the burst. The gas shell lands and bursts with a sort of splashing thud instead of the usual sharp report, as with the others.

The enemy used many tricks in sending over their gas. On many occasions they sent over the gas known commonly as "tear gas."

This would affect the eyes and make it difficult to see for a long period. They would follow that with the commonly called "sneezing gas," which would keep one sneezing for a spell, and after putting on the mask it was a difficult feat to keep it on. After the above slightly harmful gases, and while the men had their masks off for relief, they would follow with their mustard, chlorine or phosgene gas, and either of those would cause the desired effect if all were not alert.

It was difficult to detect gas at times if one was not familiar with it. One gas had an odor similar to new-mown hay. Another was like sweet chocolate.

On the arrival of gas shells in the sector, an alarm was given by the sounding of klaxon horns. This alarm would be taken up by the groups on the right and left and rear.[23]

—Captain James T. Duane
101st Infantry, 26th Division

The mask covered most all of the face. It was made of a rubberized cloth with elastic around its edges so the mask would fit securely around the face. Two elastic straps fitted over the top of the head to hold the mask in place. The bottom of the mask fitted snugly against the chin. There were two large eyepieces to look through. They were double clear lenses, with air space between them, but that did not prevent the eyepieces from clouding up. We carried with us a tube of salvelike material to rub on the glass to prevent fogging.

One never saw soldiers with beards in this war. The face must be clean shaven every day so that the gas mask would fit tightly around the face. A stubble of whiskers would allow the poison gas to penetrate the mask. Our razors were a very necessary part of our equipment. A daily shave was a military order. When in combat this is not an easy thing to obey, but we managed somehow. There were many times when I shaved in a half cup of coffee, after drinking the first half. At other times I shaved with just enough water from my canteen to moisten my face. It was pure torture, but worth the price when one's life might be at stake.[24]

—Private William Clarke
104th Machine Gun Battalion, 27th Division

The horses wore gas masks also . . . Neat little bundles perched atop the nose and soaked every time the animal took a drink. A horse without a gas mask can live about five minutes. With a gas mask he can live about five minutes. It takes only about eleven minutes to convince the horse that he ought to wear the gas mask. And there you are.

There are many things one can do while wearing the mask—the principal thing is sleep. The periods of sleep aren't particularly long. The flutter valve has a habit of catching against the trachea tube when one exhales. This can be remedied by sleeping only when inhaling.

Inscriptions on the mask carriers became more numerous every day. Some were embroidered with khaki thread, some just marked with pen or pencil—"I Need Thee Every Hour," "Always in the Way," "People's Gas Light & Coke Co.," "Tango Lizard," "Old Man of the Sea," "War Bride." And the last one was probably the most descriptive.[25]

—Lieutenant Robert Casey
124th Field Artillery

The men had been taught to put the gas mask on and to give the alarm at the slightest indication or sniff. This, of course, was nonsense, as around the front one came into contact with and breathed more or less gas of one kind or another half the time, especially in the woods. Given a condition such as existed, however, with the men trained to believe that a light sniff might mean death, with nerves highly strung by being shelled more or less for a month or so, and the presence of not a few who really had been gassed—it is no wonder that a gas alarm went beyond all bounds. It was remarked as a joke that when someone yelled, "Gas!" everybody in France put on the mask. At any rate, the alarm often spread for miles.[26]

—Lieutenant Hervey Allen
111th Infantry, 28th Division

When you decide there really is gas about and settle down in your mask to stick it out—then gas mask pains and miseries begin to drive you wild. The straps over your ears make them burn and sweat and itch—the tension on your forehead and temples is a perfect ache producer—the eye pieces cloud up and keep you wiping—the gas comes thru and stings a bit—so that your eyes smart and water, while your nose runs and you want to sneeze. But sneeze you dare not, for the reaction is invariably a gasp, and you're likely to get a lungful if you risk it.

All the while the rubber tube in your mouth, tightly clenched between your teeth, makes you drool like a baby, and slobber all over your chin, while your jaws ache like thunder.

After half an hour, the temptation to pull the blamed thing off, and take a chance on the gas being gone, is almost too great to resist. But if you're wise, you wait awhile, even tho it be in cussing and grumbling, and you stick a finger under the mask, opening a crack

from time to time thru which you sniff ever so faintly for the unmistakable odor. Perhaps it's still there, and you have to sleep in the
mask, which is almost an impossibility. And if you succeed, you
need a man on guard to keep you from removing it unconsciously. If
you have to run in the thing, you are exhausted in a hundred yards,
and your valve refuses you enough air to revive you. All this may
last all night or half an hour. Happen once in a week or a dozen
times a day.[27]

> —Anonymous Artilleryman
> 120th Field Artillery

*M*en were not the only ones who suffered in this lethal environment.
The armies of World War I relied heavily on animals—particularly
for transport, pulling guns and wagons—and they too died miserably on
the battlefield, knowing even less about the reasons why than their
masters.

•

It was a rule in the field artillery that the horses must be taken care
of before the men. We heard of two reasons for this, one being that a
man could take care of himself while a horse couldn't, and the other
that if a man was lost, another could take his place, but horses were
scarce![28]

> —Private George Mozley
> 102nd Field Artillery, 26th Division

The mule plays an important part in the army and is subject to many
dangerous tasks. He carries a gas mask while near the front and has
an operation performed on the nose that takes away his bray. Mules
are used generally in teams of four, or to carry packs. A mule team is
supposed to haul 3,000 lbs. on any road. They are rationed by the
army like men, that is to say, their substance consists of a fixed number of pounds of oats per day and is drawn from the Q.M.C. once a
week. However, it is often necessary to forage around the country so
that they may be properly fed.

   The private has a certain amount of sympathy for him, a feeling
of kinship as it were. On the battlefield, especially in the Argonne,
many of them were lying dead side by side with the soldiers.[29]

> —Private Max Foster
> 21st Engineers

Men could get under cover during shell fire or at least lie flat, or in a
shallow trench. But the horses had to stand, to be the target for any
shells or shrapnel which came their way. Many of them died from

gas, but still more of them lingered on for weeks or months with their lungs half eaten away, continuing to do their duty as long as they were able.

One of my most painful memories at the front was seeing a shell drop near two artillery horses. The horses broke away from the tree to which they were secured and galloped through the field. One of the horses was hit in the abdomen; its intestines dropped out, dragged on the ground, and soon its feet were entangled in its own intestines to the point where it fell down and could not run any farther. It lay there with its head up for what seemed to be an endless period. It seemed to be more surprised, concerning how it had become entangled in its own parts, than to be in pain.[30]

—Lieutenant Bob Hoffman
111th Infantry, 28th Division

M ost of the rolling kitchens, facetiously nicknamed "soup guns" by the doughboys, were horse or mule drawn. When the kitchens were in operation, the doughboys received hot food. A staple was stew or "slum." Rice, canned tomatoes, potatoes, and bacon were also common. In the line, canned corned beef or salmon, along with hard crackers, were the general fare, eaten on a catch-as-catch-can basis. When supply lines broke down completely, which was not infrequent in combat situations, the soldiers had to forage for themselves.

•

Food in general during the drives was quite limited, and a feeling of gnawing hunger prevailed almost from the period at which campaigning began to the point where it ended. Usually a meal a day was the most you could expect on the march and, at the front, almost complete dependence was placed upon canned goods. One soldier summarized the situation perfectly when he heard we were entering the lines, by the suggestion: "Throw away your mess kit, for you won't need it anymore." Canned goods contained several types of meat. Corned beef was the "old standby." Roast beef was also put into cans and was quite palatable, the soldiers calling it "monkey meat." Salmon, designated as "Gold fish," was used in large quantities, as was also corned beef hash.[31]

—Sergeant Leonard Kurtz
312th Infantry, 78th Division

We never had any regular food supply. We had to find our own food mostly. Much of our food [at Belleau Wood] was found from the dead soldiers, the 7th Infantry who had come in with full packs. More than once I've gone into a dead soldier's pack and gotten some sugar and bacon and hard tack. You might have a can of Australian beef, which for some reason not known to me was called "monkey meat." It was red. I've never eaten monkey meat, but anyway, it wasn't very palatable and it was called "monkey meat." It was a small tin, something on the order of a tin of tuna fish nowadays— only a couple of inches thick and about three or four inches in diameter. We had Sterno. Once in a while a lieutenant would get a can of Sterno, which was solidified alcohol, and he could bring one bucket of water to a boil on this one can and make coffee for his platoon.[32]

—Sergeant Merwin H. Silverthorn
5th Marines, 2nd Division

Our bread rations during most of the war consisted of the big round French loaves which were quite palatable. The bread was brought up to the front, piled high in open trucks. It was handled, time and time again, by men who almost never had the opportunity to wash. It was piled along the road, fell off the trucks to roll through the excrement of animals, then back on the trucks. But we ate it with relish when we received it. Dirt seldom kills.[33]

—Lieutenant Bob Hoffman
111th Infantry, 28th Division

Food at Battalion Headquarters was satisfactory, though I remember being present when a barrel of dried prunes was opened and seeing them all full of little white worms. I have not been able to eat dried prunes since. Another objection, to me, was that the coffee given us was already sweetened. Not liking coffee with sugar, it was no pleasure to drink. One great treat was a form of corn syrup called Karo. We used to put this on bread for dessert. It was such a treat that when I went home I suggested to my mother that she buy Karo instead of maple syrup, but then I found it was nothing but a sweet sickly syrup with no taste![34]

—Lieutenant Richard Kean
15th Field Artillery, 2nd Division

L iving in dirt and filth, the doughboys became infested with body lice— the infamous "cooties." Behind the lines, clothes could be cleaned in the big steam delousing machines that traveled among units. In the line, there was no such luxury.

•

Dear Mother,
      The cooties have been bothering us something awful. They are

lucky, for they always have something warm to eat. We take off our shirts and kill them by the thousands, and an hour later we are full of them again. I don't know where they come from so quickly. A mother cootie must lay a million eggs at a time. The fellows kid about them in spite of being tortured. If one sees another holding his shirt up, looking for cooties ["reading his shirt"], he asks him, "What's the latest news, buddy?" Of course there is nothing to do but laugh. We all have them.[35]

—Private Charles F. Minder
306th Machine Gun Battalion, 77th Division

I discovered a can of kerosene. My cooties had been getting pretty bad, so I thought this was a good chance to kill them off. I undressed, went all over the seams of my clothes with kerosene, and for good measure rubbed myself down with it. By the time I had my clothes on again I was in agony. The stuff burned like fire, and for the rest of the day I roamed around like a dog with a can tied to its tail. It didn't kill the cooties, either.[36]

—Corporal Horatio Rogers
101st Field Artillery, 26th Division

October 6th, a delousing machine was secured after great effort. This was our first real bath in almost three months. After the bath, we were supplied with second-hand underwear. It was the first under-wear issued to K Company since June 3rd. The socks worn by the boys were worn every day and night for more than a month and the soles became as hard as boards and often cracked in two while being removed from the feet.[37]

—Captain James T. Duane
101st Infantry, 26th Division

O verexposed to virulent Allied propaganda, many doughboys came to France firmly convinced that their German enemy was an immoral barbarian. The term "Boches," coined by the French and adopted by the doughboys to refer to the Germans, translates to "Beasts." While it is diffi-cult to develop much affection for someone who is trying to kill you, most doughboys gradually came to realize the Germans were just men—albeit, often dangerous ones.

•

There was intense fighting at a place called Sergy—and the usual atrocity stories. We heard many of them. They went something like this: "At Malines, a two-year-old child got in the way of the marching column of German troops. A soldier bayoneted it and carried it away on his bayonet." "In Tamines, children were slaughtered for no apparent motive. The soldiers tied up civilian prisoners, prodded them with bayonets, put lighted cigarettes in their noses and ears and shot them. Eyes were burned out with red hot pokers. Civilian snipers were tortured in every possible way. In Vomille they had been spread-eagled in the public square; a rat would be placed under an iron kettle upon the man or woman's bare abdomen, then a fire built upon the top of the kettle. The victim was tortured first by the frantic running around of the rat on his or her bare abdomen when it became nearly smothered and terror-stricken and pain-filled from the smoke and heat; then it would eat down through the human living flesh to escape." "We found the dead body of a girl. Her arms were nailed to the door in extended fashion; her left breast was cut half away. A young boy of five or six years of age lay on a doorstep with his two hands nearly severed from the arms, but still hanging to them. At another place were the dead bodies of a man and a woman, a girl and a boy; each of them had both hands cut off at the wrists and both feet above the ankle. Child of seven beheaded. A whole family killed, including a young girl, because the girl would not give herself to the Germans. Burned to death in their houses. All the women violated. The entire German regiment drunk," etc.

The above are exact quotations from the Bryce Report which specialized in outrages against women and children. They are samples of the sort of stories we were always hearing.[38]

—Lieutenant Bob Hoffman
111th Infantry, 28th Division

Rumors were likewise prevalent that the Germans had committed unheard-of atrocities on captured wounded or killed, such as cutting a body in two by a cross-cut saw or returning a prisoner with his tongue out. Efforts were made to suppress these rumors; but to believe that one's "buddy" might be mistreated in defiance of the rules of civilized warfare aroused in us the resolution to die fighting to the very end rather than be taken alive—and, if we were victors, to show little mercy to the enemy. Without question, the number of prisoners captured by our division throughout the war was materially less than what it should have been. Two thoughts the men bore in mind: "The only good German is a dead German" and "Every German killed brings the end of the war nearer."[39]

—Sergeant Arthur C. Havlin
102nd Machine Gun Battalion, 26th Division

When the Germans remained in a place for any length of time they made their quarters quite livable. They even built bungalows with bomb proofs extending back into the hills for their protection during shell and artillery fire. They planted gardens, raised rabbits, and lived the best life they could. Of course this was not possible on an active sector such as this. But they had constructed little rustic bowers and seats, cleverly woven in a style similar to that used in rustic porch furniture. The paths were lined with seats and white stones and across from Potsdamer Place was a little beer garden, with bar, tables and chairs all made of roots and saplings.

At times I felt that the Germans weren't quite human, but this little homelike touch to the places they had left showed them to be men like ourselves who could enjoy the simple pleasures of life.[40]

—Lieutenant Bob Hoffman
111th Infantry, 28th Division

During the many stormy days of autumn we found much varied literature abandoned by the enemy. Their reading matter included everything from Lutheran hymn books to Von der Goltz and Clausewitz on the art of war. Post cards flourished like fungi, in all their positions; more or less official journals, private diaries and stray personal records of different sorts, with endless newspapers, littered the ground.

The French soldiers were not as much given as were the Germans to carrying libraries into the lines. I saw sets of Lessing and Goethe scattered about on the muddy fields among Feldgesang-bucker, torn diaries, and lurid cheap romances.

I stumbled on a magnificent four-volume Schiller. It lay in a little muddy plot near a dugout formerly used by German officers. It was all in calf, beautifully gold-tooled, gilt all around, Japan paper, and was illustrated and enscrolled with hundreds of marginal decorations in true Munich style. Any bibliophile would have shed a fountain of tears to see that book in the mud. I carried it along for a while and reviewed the "Wallenstein" trilogy and "William Tell," but I had no way to protect it from the weather, and some days later a German gas shell ended the problem.[41]

—Private L.V. Jacks
119th Field Artillery, 32nd Division

There were two ways in which the Germans seemed to enjoy having their photos taken. One way was looking as fierce as they possibly could, with their bayoneted rifles, knives and bombs strung in their belt so that they would look like dangerous customers. Another way was looking as happy as possible, sitting at little rustic tables made of branches of birch trees, at their card games, with bottles of beer or seltzer, smiling and happy—showing it was a pretty nice war after all . . .

We had heard so many reports of regiments of women, of Amazons, who had vowed to fight to the death. This was always of interest to the soldiers. Many of them thought that it would be nice to capture and try to tame an Amazon. Usually we had been away from women for so long that even a woman behind a machine gun would add interest to our existence. There was a lot of talk about women who were fighting with the men.

A French lieutenant said that these were just stories; occasionally women were at the front, or rather behind the lines in the big dugouts, but they were entertainers of some sort—singers and dancers, not unlike American actresses who entertained the American soldiers in advanced points at the front with singing, dancing and comedy; or the WAAC's Queen Mary's Women's Auxiliary Corps of the British army, who entertained the soldiers and tried to make their lives more livable. Sometimes too the female costumes which were found in reserve dugouts had been worn by female impersonators. There were shows held by our own division after the war in which all the chorus girls were men, and many of them made good imitations, too.[42]

—Lieutenant Bob Hoffman
111th Infantry, 28th Division

Among our German prisoners taken after we crossed the Marne was a small chubby-faced German private who was about five foot two inches in height, very fat, and who said he was 15 years of age. We always grouped our prisoners near the rolling kitchens if possible, so we would not have to march them back and forth to meals. One noon while watching the feeding of prisoners, I noticed this young German back of the kitchen scrubbing some pots and pans. He was certainly a comical sight, his uniform being several sizes too large and he evidently had given no thought to the possibility of being captured, for he was still wearing his large coal scuttle helmet which was also too large and was resting on his ears. (In nearly every case when a German realized he was about to be captured or the moment after he surrendered, he cast away his steel helmet and donned his little round skull cap which he carried conveniently around his person.)

When I inquired of the supply officer about this youngster working in the kitchen, he told me the German had begged one of the German-speaking American sergeants to allow him to help the cooks. Permission was given and no harm came of it. When the time arrived for this group of prisoners to start for the rear, the schoolboy begged to remain with us. He promised to work hard and not give us any trouble. Through the interpreter he appealed tearfully to me, but I had no authority to allow such a procedure, and the young man went sadly to the rear, weeping as he departed.[43]

—*Lieutenant Colonel George M. Duncan*
3rd Division

Only a few wounded came into the hospital [after the St. Mihiel operation], and those mainly German prisoners. I remember one splendid young Austrian officer, wounded by a machine-gun bullet through both thighs, who quite overawed us with his excellent English and imperious manner. We expected gratitude, and even a little cringing, but he simply took us for granted as a quite-to-be-expected servile agency, especially provided for his comfort. Only once did we see him lose his self-composure. As we transferred him from the litter to the operating table, the pain forced from him a shriek of agony for which he made no apology. But when he spoke again, it was with the same old arrogance.[44]

—*Corporal Frederick A. Pottle*
Evacuation Hospital #8

F or some Americans, the experience of war and their acquaintance with the enemy came in German prisoner of war camps. In 19 months of war, the American Expeditionary Force lost 4,480 men as prisoners. Swept up in counterattacks, failed assaults or in trench raids, these men found themselves at the mercy of the enemy.

•

In case of capture, the division was warned as a necessity of knowing how to act in order to keep from disclosing valuable military information.

"Remember that there are two sorts of men in every army. A percentage of men are brave soldiers who would no more give information away to betray their country than they would fly. These are not the men we fear. The men we fear are those of a weak character. If you are captured it is only necessary for you to give your name and rank. Outside of this answer nothing. If you must talk, then the following answers by a German prisoner are good examples of what to say:

"'It was dark and we did not know the roads; we slept in a village but did not know the name; the wires were all right but we paid no attention to them; we knew there were dugouts but did not know how many steps, etc.'

"The other method is best. Refuse to talk. If you do talk, and give the enemy information, you are traitors to your country and worse than all, traitors to your own pals," division instructions declared.[45]

—Colonel Ralph D. Cole
37th Division 37th Division

On 3rd September, Company A, 145th Infantry was in reserve and stationed about 25 kilometers from Strausburg. Just about 50 yards in front of No. 8 post on the front line was a small stone blockhouse. I had been on No. 8 post for about six days and nights just before going back in reserve. I never saw any activity at this blockhouse. So, on the above date, about 1:30 P.M., accompanied by Harvey Metz from Pittsburgh and a sergeant and one other private, we went "over the top" to see what was in the block house. After Metz and myself had investigated this house we went a little father. I saw a German rifle lying on the ground and I reached down to pick it up, when it went off and I saw a German on the other end of it.

The fire from the rifle burned my face and at the same time there was firing from the rear of us and on both sides. We made a rush to the rear but were cut off by Germans so we lay close to the ground and let them fire at us. After about 20 minutes the Germans advanced from all around us, firing at the same time. They came up to us and thinking we were dead picked us up. As we had no chance (there being only Metz and myself) we were forced to give ourselves up as none of our men fired a shot from the rear. The first officer that spoke to me in the German trench spoke English. They took us about five miles to the rear and turned us over to other guards who put us on a small train and hauled us several miles back into Germany.

About dark, they put us in a wagon and we rode until after midnight. When we arrived at German Headquarters, a German officer was waiting for us. He began to question us as to our movements. He asked our age. I said I was only 18 years; he said, "So you enlisted to fight Germany?" Metz was 28 years old and did not hesitate to tell him that he was a drafted man.

After questioning we were taken to Strausburg and locked up in what we called a dungeon. The building was of stone with concrete floors and very damp. We had to sleep on the floor without blankets of any kind. There was a German sergeant major over us and he used to come in and give us a kick in the ribs just for fun and "run us out" into the yard. When we would get out in the yard and begin to enjoy the fresh air and sunshine, he would walk around the prison wall and laugh at us. After ten minutes he would come down and give us another kick and "run us" inside. He said he had lived nine years in Boston before the war. (I would like to meet him in this country now.)

After about 28 days we were taken to Rastatt prison camp and registered; my number was 81,229. This number was chosen merely for propaganda as the first American captured was given the number of 80,000 as nearly as I could understand, so I was really only the 1,229th American captured. Two other prisoners and myself were sent away to some little German town and the Germans would see our number which we had sewed on our coats. Naturally they thought 81,000 Americans had been captured.[46]

—*Private Charles E. Sargent*
145th Infantry, 37th Division

The entire POW camp was surrounded by barbed wire fences, twelve feet high with double strands at the top, making escape somewhat difficult.

Every seventy feet was a sentry box at which was stationed a member of the "Landstrum," or reserve soldier in the German army.

Within the camp, which was subdivided into sections with a certain number of barracks to a section, barbed wire separated the French from the Americans. A dirt path ran between the French quarters and the American quarters, which was six feet wide and terminated at one end in the barracks and guard-house, where our captors lived, and at the other at the main entrance to the camp.

The French would sometimes throw their black bread rations across the barrier to the Americans and there followed a wild scramble for the possession of the precious "staff of life." Right here I may say that the German bread contained about as much nourishment as a piece of wet sawdust, and tasted very similar.

At Darmstadt the soup consisted mostly of meal gruel, cow turnips, black mushrooms, beans and sometimes a potato.

Upon our arrival at Darmstadt, we were asked our occupations and we thought the work would be based on our answers, but later learned through bitter experience that a doughboy who said he was a traveling salesman was usually assigned to a coal mine and that one who signed as a farmer or day-laborer stayed in camp on Red Cross Committees or received work which required a minimum amount of muscle. The worst detail was shoveling coal and the best was package detail.

We were quartered in barracks which were clean and airy; we received two blankets, a bed sack filled with bits of paper, rags and thread and also a bowl for soup. Outside each barracks were wash-stands and faucets providing running water which was also "Trinken wasser," and as such was fit to drink without chlorination or boiling. Every morning we received our bowl of "acorn water" and our thin ration of black bread, which had to do us all day.[47]

—Private Clifford M. Markle
102nd Infantry, 26th Division

Seventy-five of us were sent to Waghosuel to work in a sugar facto-ry. We worked 12 hours a day and had a small bowl of soup for breakfast and a very small piece of blood-wurst for dinner. We were badly treated and almost starved until after the Armistice. We were then taken back to Rastatt and stayed there, almost starving until 6th December, 1918, about 10 P.M. when word came that we were going back to France. We made a rush to the depot where we boarded a train with Swiss soldiers as guards on it and crossed the Rhine into Switzerland, through Berne and Geneva into Vickery, France, where we were quarantined for 30 days; then we were shipped back to our companies and I returned to America in July 1919 and was dis-charged.[48]

—Private Charles E. Sargent
145th Infantry, 37th Division

Notes

1. Hoffman, *I Remember the Last War*, pp. 53–54.
2. Kean, *Dear Marraine*, p. 176.
3. Vernon G. Olsmith, *Recollections of an Old Soldier.* (San Antonio, Tex.: Pvtly printed, 1963), pp. 26–27.
4. Elton E. Mackin, *Suddenly We Didn't Want to Die.* (Novato, Calif.: Presido, 1993), p. 55.
5. Emmett, *Give Way to the Right*, p. 226.
6. C.E. Lovejoy, *The Story of the Thirty-Eighth.* (Coblenz, Ger.: n.p., 1919), p. 63.
7. Jesse Hinman, *Ranging in France with Flash and Sound.* (Portland, Oreg.: Press of Dunham Printing Company, 1919), pp. 108, 50.
8. Chester D. Heywood, *Negro Combat Troops in the World War.* (Worcester, Mass.: Commonwealth Press, 1928), p. 191.
9. Reifsnyder, *A Second Class Private*, p. 43.
10. Allen, *Toward the Flame*, pp. 43–45, 48.
11. Hoffman, *I Remember the Last War*, pp. 84–85.
12. Langille, *Men of the Rainbow*, pp. 145–146.
13. Clarke, *Over There with O'Ryan's Roughnecks*, pp. 55–56.
14. Jacks, *Service Record by an Artilleryman*, pp. 285–286.
15. Leonard P. Kurtz, *Beyond No Man's Land.* (Buffalo, N.Y.: Foster & Stewart, 1937), p. 30.

16. Gnasser, *History of the 126th Infantry*, pp. 130–131.

17. Bryant Wilson and Lamar Tooze, *With the 364th Infantry in America, France, and Belgium.* (New York: The Knickerbocker Press, 1919), pp. 72–73.

18. Cutler, *The 55th Artillery (CAC)*, p. 158.

19. Searcy, *Looking Back*, pp. 64–65.

20. Brown, *The Adventures of an American Doughboy*, p. 37.

21. Rizzi, *Joe's War*, p. 93.

22. Joseph D. Lawrence, *Fighting Soldier.* (Boulder: Colorado Associated University Press, 1985), p. 109.

23. Duane, *Dear Old K*, pp. 82–88.

24. Clarke, *Over There with O'Ryan's Roughnecks*, pp. 67–68.

25. Robert Casey, *The Cannoneers Have Hairy Ears.* (New York: J.H. Sears & Company, Inc., 1927), pp. 49–50.

26. Allen, *Toward the Flame*, pp. 91–92.

27. *The 120th Field Artillery Diary*, p. 222.

28. George Mozley, *Our Miracle Battery.* (n.p., 1920), p. 48.

29. *An Historical and Technical Biography of the Twenty-First Engineers Light Railway United States Army.* (New York: Twenty-First Engineers [Light Railway], 1919), p. 146.

30. Hoffman, *I Remember the Last War*, pp. 176–177.

31. Kurtz, *Beyond No Man's Land*, p. 36.

32. Silverthorn, Interview.

33. Hoffman, *I Remember the Last War*, p. 183.

34. Kean, *Dear Marraine*, p. 83.

35. Minder, *This Man's War*, p. 342.

36. Rogers, *Diary of an Artillery Scout*, p. 217.

37. Duane, *Dear Old K*, pp. 122–123.

38. Hoffman, *I Remember the Last War*, pp. 185–186.

39. Arthur C. Havlin, *The History of Company A 102nd Machine Gun Battalion Twenty-Sixth Division, A.E.F.* (n.p.: Pvtly printed, 1928), p. 66.

40. Hoffman, *I Remember the Last War*, p. 124.

41. Jacks, *Service Record by an Artilleryman*, pp. 227–230.

42. Hoffman, *I Remember the Last War*, p. 104–105.

43. Duncan, "I Go to War," pp. 154–155.

44. Pottle, *Stretchers*, p. 212.

45. Ralph D. Cole, *The Thirty-Seventh Division in the World War 1917–1918*, vol. 2 (Columbus, Ohio: The Thirty-seventh Division Veterans Association, 1929), pp. 134.

46. *Ibid.*, pp. 353–355.

47. Clifford M. Markle, *A Yankee Prisoner in Hunland.* (New Haven: Yale University Press, 1920), pp. 13–15.

48. Cole, *The Thirty-Seventh Division in the World War*, pp. 355–356.

CHAPTER 10

The Doughboys

In a small town cemetery in central Connecticut stands a boulder erected as a monument by World War I veterans after the war in honor of their comrades. It reads simply, "Buddies Forever."

Over two million Americans served in France during World War I. In many respects they were like soldiers of all ages—homesick, bored, hungry for women, hungry for chow, sometimes terrified, the last to know and the first to go. Looking back through the years, there was also a certain poignancy about these men. Like their country, they were brash and eager and disingenuous. Most had never been far from home and hearth—now they were in the army and on the other side of an ocean. It was an experience that would bind them together for all time.

•

In the [French] streets, round the pumps and stone horse troughs, the men were continually washing in the running water, though the air was still nipping and frosty—brushing their teeth, soaping their hair, their arms, their necks; shaving before their little steel mirrors or bits of broken glass; washing the cakes of sticky mud from their rubber boots—in short, striving against all obstacles to keep clean.

Dressed in their khaki uniforms they looked strangely alike, emanating a powerful impression of ruddy, clean-shaven youth, of lithe, athletic bodies with strong, clean limbs—the only really youthful army in the field in 1918.[1]

—Captain Ernest Peixetto
Combat Artist

Almost nine-tenths of the soldier's conversation concerns stories about women, the location of wine shops, the likelihood of being able to purchase cigarettes, the next trip to a bath house, what the censor did to the last batch of letters, what is the popular song back in the United States, what's the idea of fighting for France when they charge us high prices, and above all other subjects—"when do we eat?"[2]

—Army Field Clerk Will Judy
33rd Division

A French officer, having served awhile with an American division, reported back to his own French division commander. The French general said, "I don't want any long histories, but tell me a few incidents which you saw which will illustrate for me the characteristics of the Americans."

The young officer replied, "My General, they are the most restless troops I have ever seen. At the end of a long march when they are apparently exhausted they take off their packs, put aside their rifles, get out their mess kits, fall in line at their kitchen to get their supper. Almost immediately and before they have eaten they start jiggling around banging on their mess kits and impatiently asking 'Well, where do we go from here?' They have no sooner eaten when they are all over the place and even miles away apparently instantaneously."[3]

—Brigadier General Henry J. Reilly
42nd Division

Marching, marching, down splendid French roads—dusty roads—so dusty that one could not tell the color or nationality of troops which passed us in motor lorries, so heavily were they coated with dust. Lombardy poplars lined all the roads of France—two rows of trees and a white ribbon of road as far as one could see. We were always climbing hills and going down in little valleys; invariably seeing the steeple of the village church from a considerable distance as we approached the town . . . marching for twenty minutes—the pound, pound of feet . . . The packs got heavier and heavier in spite of the fact that they shrank at nearly every halting. United States equipment was spread from the sea to the front. My huge pack, which had bumped my heels at Calais, shrank to a shelter half, a single blanket, to one of the seventeen Red Cross sweaters friends and relatives at home had so patiently knitted, and still the pack was heavy. Strong as I was, far far stronger and more enduring than average, my back would ache excruciatingly after a few minutes of hiking. At every pause for a moment I would place my rifle under the pack to ease my back, and at the end of twenty minutes of hiking the bugle would blow and we would fall out for ten minutes. Normally an

army marched fifty minutes and rested ten. But we had to modify
that system by marching twenty and resting ten.[4]

—Lieutenant Bob Hoffman
111th Infantry, 28th Division

During the hikes we sang the customary songs of the period until
we stopped for want of breath. "Where do we go from here, boys?"
"All we do is sign the payroll," Home, boys, it's home we ought to
be," Madelon," and "There's a long, long trail a-winding" were a
few of the many songs that seemed to shorten the monotonous
miles in the cold and rain. During the regular ten minutes' rest
every hour, we eagerly sought a few "drags" off a butt, stamped our
feet, and blew on our hands to keep warm; then off again, stiffer
than ever.[5]

—Sergeant Arthur C. Havlin
102nd Machine Gun Battalion, 26th Division

Our regiment loved to sing on the march. To say our songs were
risqué would be putting it mildly. They were as bawdy as the collec-
tive imaginations of 3,000 horny men could conceive.

On the last day of our journey to Exermont, the sun came out,
and we were able to march into our staging positions during the late
afternoon. To bolster our morale, I suppose, the officers let us sing. It
was quite a sight to see the whole regiment under march singing
away at the top of their lungs. As a dispatch rider, I used to be able
to watch them, but this time I was in the ranks with the mortar platoon. I happened to look up, and there was Father Duffy standing on
a bluff at the side of the road, giving his benediction to the troops as
we were "banging away on Lulu" under full field pack and full
throat. He didn't care what we were singing, as long as we were
alive and singing.

Some weeks later in the hospital at Allerey, I picked up an issue
of the *Literary Gazette,* and there was a beautiful photograph of
Father Duffy with arms outstretched in benediction as the regiment
filed below. The caption read: "Father Francis P. Duffy, regimental
chaplain of the 165th New York Infantry, blesses his troops as they
march into battle singing 'Onward Christian Soldiers.'"

Oh God, I laughed—a Protestant hymn, no less![6]

—Private Alfred "Red" Ettinger
165th Infantry, 42nd Division

As I remember the soldiers' favorite ballads, four classics had high
ranking:

Ka-Ka-Katie! You're the only Gi-Gi-Girl I adore!
When the M-Moon comes over the woodshed
I will meet you at the Ki-Ki-Kitchen door!

There's a long, long trail a-winding
Unto the land of my dreams
Where the nightingale is singing
And the pale moon beams.

Pack up your troubles in your old kit bag
And smile, boys, smile!
While you've got a lucifer to light your fag
Smile, boys, that's the style.

Where do we go from here, boys,
Where do we go from here?
Anywhere from Harlem to the Jersey pier.
And Pat would grab me by the arm and whisper in my ear
Oh! Boy! Oh! Joy! Where do we go from here?

●

As for the famous *Mademoiselle from Armentieres*, I do not recall ever
having heard it in Toul.[7]

—*Captain Carter Harrison*
American Red Cross

Oh! the War is long, the War is hard,
Parlez vous?
The War is long, the War is hard,
But thank the Lord for French 'pinard,'
Hinky-dinky, parlez vous?[8]

—*Anonymous Engineer*
101st Engineers, 26th Division

I miss much of our songs in France; we hear them seldom. Our
favorite, "There's a long, long trail a-winding," is not heard from
civilian throats. "Beautiful K-K-K-Katy" must have met her lover by
the cowshed. Even the soldier who was going to kill the bugler has
forgotten "Oh, how I hate to get up in the morning."

Sometimes we sing for our own ears "Good morning, Mr. Zip!
Zip! Zip! With your hair cut just as short as, just as short as mine," or
the English favorite, "Pack up your troubles in your kitbag and
smile, smile, smile."

"Keep the home fires burning" was a favorite not of ours but of the people back home. "It's a long way to Tipperary" was old and not American. "The Star Spangled Banner" was sung very seldom, never of our own accord. The air "Over There" always has been popular; it is original and likely worthy of preservation. "There are smiles" never lost its appeal. "When Yankee Doodle learns to parlez-vous" maintained a steady existence. But the old reliable, in rest camp, in battle line, sailing for France and coming back, was and is "Hail, hail, the gang's all here."[9]

—*Army Field Clerk Will Judy*
33rd Division

I n idle moments there was always "Joe Latrinesky"—the rumor mill—for entertainment; home to think about; letters to write and letters to await.

•

One of the chief topics for conversation was getting back home, and "Joe's" most famous and most believed remark was, "There's a big sign on the Statue of Liberty which says *Welcome Home, 26th Division.*" This "Joe" spread all through our division. It was surprising the number of men who actually believed it and that our division was going home for work in America and then return later. They had the officers' baggage at one of the base ports; they had our ship all picked out, and even the date of the parade up Broadway. Many thought we were going home to help in the third Liberty Loan drive, and they had some good arguments, too. We had received a beautiful Christy poster, the caption being "Fight or Buy Bonds." The boys added a line at the bottom which read, "We Do Both."[10]

—*Captain Carroll J. Swan*
101st Engineers, 26th Division

[From a letter, August 15, 1918]
    I make it a point to censor the letters of a number of men from each company, in order to get a line on how they are feeling. You have no idea how pathetic they are, those letters. When I am dealing with them as a company, I can think of them as soldiers; but when I come to read their letters, they become individuals with a vengeance, the poor devils! They are so pathetic, and so cheerful. It is mighty hard on them, this war, for they do not know where they are, or have any idea of what is going to happen to them. They write very cheerful letters, but they are so inarticulate, and express so little, or rather so inadequately, the love which the men feel; but I hope

that the wives and mothers can read between the lines, as I can who know the circumstances. There are certain things that run through all of them, that are very interesting. Almost without exception they have told their families that the war will be over before Christmas—a statement that I have not heard for years and one that I am entirely unable to account for.[11]

—Captain Branton H. Kellogg
163rd Infantry, 41st Division

All letters were subject to the strictest censorship, but that fact did not deter voluminous epistles from pouring into the hands of these officers for censorship, who in turn would pour them into the postal channels for transport to the folks back home. Each had to be read, signed and sealed. After the censor had finished clipping out all unauthorized information, the letters looked as though a child armed with a pair of scissors had been amusing itself by cutting paper dolls out of them. A sentence which started out interestingly with "the chow is rotten" would end up with "the chow is—" followed by a mysterious blank, which the folks at home would naturally assume stood for "excellent" and conclude that their John had acquired that charming French modesty.[12]

—Lieutenant Bryant Wilson
364th Infantry, 91st Division

The mail came in just before chow call. I had a letter from my mother, and several from others in the family. And I had one from my girl. I put the rest in my pocket and tore that one open.

Dear Jack," she began, "I'm going to make this very brief and to the point."

And she did. She thought a lot of me, but I'd never get out alive anyway, so it wouldn't make any difference to me. She was going to marry the boy she'd been going places with, to try to keep him from having to go into the army.

I went down to supper. I tried to drink some coffee, but I couldn't down even that. I threw my "slum" into the garbage can and went back to camp. Norosoff was sleeping in the tent with me and when he came in he knew something was wrong. "What's the matter?" he asked.

"Nothing. I just want to go to bed."

"I'll go too, then," he said.

But I couldn't lie still.

Finally Norosoff sat up. "Listen," he said. "You can't kid me. Something's eatin' you. What is it? Bad news from home?"

"Yes. But keep your mouth shut about it."

"Sure," he said.

He lay down again, on his back. I was lying on my side. I felt a little better when I had told him. All he said was, "Gee, that's tough . . ." And then, after a while, "Maybe you ain't got this thing straight, Barkley. Maybe it ain't so bad when you know about it."

"I got it straight all right," I said.[13]

—Private John L. Barkley
4th Infantry, 3rd Division

Except for the name of the man and woman concerned, the story I am about to tell is true. An officer of the Headquarters Company came before me and said, "I have a man in my outfit who desires to execute a proxy marriage by affidavit." I wondered to myself that there is still romance in this Godforsaken land.

First there is a letter from a Red Cross chapter in Boston. It reveals no romance, just a sordid war camp story. "Annie Cox is a mother but not a wife . . . Wells B. Dawes, A.E.F. soldier, is the father of the child and acknowledges its paternity . . . If he marries the mother she and their child can receive aid as the wife and child of a soldier . . . A legal marriage may be effected by the soldier's affidavit that he takes her as his wife and her affidavit that she takes him as her husband . . ."

Presently the officer who left the papers returns with another officer and two soldiers. One of the soldiers is Dawes. "You desire to go through with this and you understand all that it implies and that when it is completed you will be legally married to this woman?" I asked Dawes.

The answer was, "Yes, sir."

I directed him to raise his right hand and then read, "I, Wells B. Dawes, a private in Hdq. Co. 128th Inf. A.E.F. do solemnly swear that I take Annie Cox as my lawful wedded wife." The soldier said, "I do," dropped his hand and signed; the paper was witnessed by the other three, I affixed my signature and the A.E.F. end of this marriage is complete. I never saw Wells B. Dawes again. Two months later Dawes stopped something in the Argonne and died of wounds in late October.

To complete this marriage Annie Cox must also go before a military officer to execute an affidavit and swear that she takes Welles B. Dawes as her lawful wedded husband. In February 1919 she took such action before the Judge Advocate of the Northeastern Department of the Army at Boston. Why she waited so long or whence the delay I do not know. At any rate when she solemnly swore she took Dawes as her husband, the soldier had been in his grave for over three months.[14]

—Lieutenant Colonel G.W. Garlock
128th Infantry, 32nd Division

B *ehind the lines, the doughboys lived in barns and haylofts. Officers were billeted in the houses. Most of the able-bodied Frenchmen were gone—killed or in the army. The fieldwork was done by women, old men, and children. It seemed, recalled a doughboy, that all the civilians were dressed in black.*

•

To Americans used to every convenience, the French billet had little to offer as regards comfort. In these little villages the houses were of stone, cement and mud, generally built in blocks along the main highway with a few very short side streets. Separated from the house by only the wall was the barn with one or two doors leading into the living rooms. In most cases the room used as the kitchen occupied most of the lower part of the house. In the lofts of the barns were quartered the soldiers. Floors in most cases were of rough boards, many of them loose, and the roofs were leaky. Access to the loft was by ladder. Owing to the danger of fire, lights were strictly prohibited so that at night the soldiers' billet was a gloomy place. Below the soldiers' sleeping quarters were the owners' cattle, horses, hens, pigs and rabbits—all of which did not add to the purity of the air. Then there were rats which scampered around. After some time tiny barrack wood stoves were procured which were not of much value except for drying wet clothes. With green wood, these stoves produced a great deal of smoke, which added to the discomfort of the soldiers.[15]

—Captain Edward J. Connelly
104th Infantry, 26th Division

The French people gathered the impression, at times, that the Americans were having difficulties with their language, but no American soldier was ever heard to admit that he was anything but a fluent conversationalist in the French tongue. The average vocabulary contained such words as *oeufs*, variously pronounced as erfs or just plain oofs, *monjay, cooshay, frites, omeletes, vin rouge, toot sweet, combien*—all pronounced with a magnificent disregard for phonetics and as no Frenchman had ever before heard them pronounced. *Oui* and *Oo la la!* were the only expressions in which they really approximated the proper accent, and these were somewhat overworked.

If the natives did not understand, the difficulty was usually laid to their stupidity. Some thought by waving the hands and interspersing here and there a "ze" and a "oui" that they could make themselves intelligible. Someone happened to be listening in on a conversation between a French woman and an H Company man which ran something like this:

Madame—ah—Mademoiselle—ah—Madam—vooly voo washa ze clothes for ze lieutenant? Wash, Madame? Yes, wash clothes. Compree—*compree*? What, you fathead, don't you understand your own language?"

A sergeant in K Company once volunteered to get some straw for the men in his section, no one else being able to think of the word. He marched up to the rosy-cheeked madame, and after a proper salutation inquired:

"Madame, avvy voo straw—Straw? Compree straw?"

"Comprends pas."

"Too bad boys, the old bird says she ain't got none."[16]

—*Lieutenant John H. Taber*
168th Infantry, 42nd Division

Occasionally we would encounter French girls along the way and whenever this occurred there was a red hot exchange of greetings. Some of those girls had evidently encountered American soldiers before for we were occasionally regaled by some pretty red-cheeked mademoiselle with a peculiarly attractive twist of her nose, blurting out some hard-boiled expression in English which we knew came originally from the reckless lips of some fun-loving Yank. These uncouth expressions coming from the red lips of a pretty village girl shocked us at first, but we soon learned that the poor girls had not the slightest idea what the words meant. Not that it would have made any difference with some of them if they had known, however. Probably some of them did know exactly what they were putting out.

On the way over we had been issued little phrase books to study but our pronunciation of the French was undoubtedly off color for when we attempted to talk to them, the girls would wrinkle up their noses and shrug their shoulders and say, "No compree." This was a decided jolt to some of our fellows who had trained faithfully at their French, expecting to be able to cut a wide swath at once with the French maidens about whom they had heard so much.[17]

—*Corporal Asa B. Callaway*
353rd Infantry, 89th Division

The women had big feet and looked like sausage balloons, but rigors of the front had materially affected any fixed ideals of our dreams. Most of the boys had a very low boiling point, anyhow.[18]

—*Private Charles MacArthur*
149th Field Artillery, 42nd Division

Four of my buddies picked up a peachy French blonde apiece one night and of course the skirts steered them into a swell restaurant.

My, how those girls did order food. They must have been starved waiting for the Americans to get to France. Then they topped it off with four bottles of cognac. The bill those birds got must of been the number of U.S. troops in France. Between the four of them Marines they had exactly 27 francs, so they told the girls to wait a minute, they would be right back. I am wondering how long they waited.[19]

—*Corporal Joseph E. Rendinell*
6th Marines, 2nd Division

Prostitution was a big business in France at that time. It was a source of revenue to the government. It was legal, and licensed by the civil authorities. The houses where it was practiced were subject to medical inspection, as were their occupants. In St. Omer I remember seeing long lines of soldiers outside these houses.

Our army did not definitely prohibit its men from patronizing these houses, but it did try by moral suasion and by threat of court martial if one contracted one of the social diseases consequent to the action. Every soldier who had such contact was required to report to his medical officer for a prophylactic treatment. To me this would have been a humiliating experience. I think it was on the Sunday before the day I left home for army service that my Dad and I attended Mass together at our parish church. One of the things very much on his mind must have been this type of temptation I would be subject to as a soldier. I do not remember, as we were walking home, the exact phrasing my father used, but, in substance, he hoped I would treat every woman I met as a gentleman should, and show each one the same respect I would want everyone to show my sister and mother. I told him I was sure I knew what he was talking about, and assured him he would have no cause to worry about my behavior.[20]

—*Private William F. Clarke*
104th Machine Gun Battalion, 27th Division

[The bordello] was a fine-looking house between Baccarat and Denevre. At first, I was kind of embarrassed because I'd never before seen women dressed, or rather undressed, that way, draped all over the room. But soon I became keen on a girl no older than I. She was absolutely lovely, and after a most pleasant sojourn, I took my leave. Before proceeding to Deneuvre, however, I checked in at the aid station in Baccarat for a prophylaxis.

After returning to HQ, the first person I ran into was Hennessy. "Hey, Red, what's it like?" he inquired. I told him the story, embellishing here and there and after I finished he was positively drooling. Nothing to do, he took off that very same night for Deneuvre and joined the same girl I had been with. But he didn't bother with a prophylaxis, and several days later, he came down with a dose. He never forgave me—and he accused me of having infected that beautiful, sweet young girl!

Not long after the regiment arrived and settled in around the various suburbs of Baccarat, our MPs put that bordello off limits—which was a damn dirty trick, because the officers were having a ball with these ladies . . . but the poor enlisted men had no place to go.[21]

—*Private Albert M. Ettinger*
165th Infantry, 42nd Division

Prophylaxis stations were in all the camps. At Beaune there were several, one in nearly every one of the eight areas. At these stations medical men were in attendance throughout the night. A "Y" man who had sleeping quarters nearby told me the traffic for treatment was such, so constant, he had to get a room elsewhere in order to get sleep.

When the young man has exposed himself to the disease he must apply for treatment at some station within three hours. If he neglects to do this and the disease develops later, he is court martialed, not for exposing himself but for failure to apply for treatment. The treatment, he is assured, is nearly 100 percent effective . . . However, in practice, in some of the stations, the treatment was left to the young men themselves. The medical officer, tired of the late hours and disagreeable work, sometimes signed up lots of blanks in advance and gave them out, saying, "Oh, go treat yourself." This last I got from a man in the service who was in a position to know. Some ninety cases were treated at one station during one night.

Notwithstanding all this work and in the face of an order that any soldier suffering from venereal disease would not be allowed to return home till cured, in one camp of detention in France there were, about July 1, 1919, 12,000 soldiers suffering from venereal diseases.[22]

—*George Thayer*
YMCA Secretary

*W*hile the average doughboy probably didn't give it much thought, the Americans were guests in a foreign country. Being Americans, the soldiers were endowed with supreme confidence in the superiority both of themselves and of their country—after all, had they not crossed an ocean to come to the rescue of "the frogs"? And, if the truth be told, the French were not always lovable. Inevitably there were problems and misconceptions as support troops and combat soldiers back from the line mingled with the civilian population.

•

There exists a strong strain of avarice in the French peasantry. Mere Blanc, who ran a combination wine shop and epicerie on the corner of Arches, was one with her eyes always on the francs.

A soldier would enter her shop. "Eggs today, Madame?"

"Oui, Monsieur," Mere Blanc would reply. "Five francs, Monsieur."

"Why is it you are charging me five francs for a dozen of these when you sell them to the French for two francs?" he would ask.

"Pas compris, Monsieur."

The soldier would pay the five francs and leave. The reason the French paid no more than two francs for eggs was because Mere Blanc knew they would pay no more. The Americans paid five francs because Mere Blanc knew that if he wanted them bad enough he would pay ten.[23]

—Musician Carl E. Haterius
137th Infantry, 35th Division

We had great fun buying things, though. One of the boys wanted eggs, so he spotted one of these little dairy stores, went in and crowed. He got the eggs.[24]

—Sergeant William Brown
9th Infantry, 2nd Division

After Government Insurance and Compulsory and Voluntary Allotments, the average private had some six dollars and thirty cents coming to him per month; the noncoms drew a little more. Six dollars and thirty cents was about thirty-two francs and in francs to the Yank seemed quite an amount. In America, we had of course figured with the dollar as the unit; and in France, with the franc as the basic coin in our calculations, we seemed to have five times as much spending money. The Yank therefore bore the reputation of being a millionaire. There is no question about it, whenever an American soldier struck a village or a town in France—whether on pass or on leave—the French shop-keeper became almost wealthy (for a Frenchman) overnight. The American eagerly bought some embroidered silk handkerchiefs or some similar article for five francs, which, up to then, had been unsalable at thirty centimes. Stock which had littered up the store shelves for years and which could not be sold at any price, was snatched at by the American soldier. He just wanted to buy—no matter what it was.[25]

—Major Stanton Whitney
105th Machine Gun Battalion, 27th Division

We could never realize the value of the paper francs. Fifty or even a hundred meant nothing to us. If we had francs we paid any price

asked; the French people quickly learned this and the price of everything went sky high when American troops were around.[26]

—Lieutenant Bob Hoffman
111th Infantry, 28th Division

Of course our men had included in their equipment their dice
("bones," "galloping dominoes"). In most places where we were billeted, until after the Armistice, there was not much to buy, and pay
day, consequently, saw some of the best "rollin'" you ever laid your
eyes on. The first time the French saw our men sit down, roll the
bones and pick up anywhere from 20 to 500 francs at one cast of the
dice, they nearly died. A day or so after pay-off, most of the money
in each company would be found in the possession of a few artists
whose "bones" responded to special pleadings or on whom Lady
Luck had smiled.[27]

—Captain Chester Heywood
371st Infantry, 93rd Division

*The doughboy perception of French avarice was enhanced by civilian
claims against the soldiers for transgressions that often seemed petty to
the Americans, who expected more gratitude from those they had come to
save from the clutches of the Hun.*

•

Our company pitched their pup tents in a field and dug in. The
farmer who owned the field did not want us there and his wife felt
the same way and took pains to let us know it. Of course nobody
would care to have his best pasture dug out but this was war and as I
had received orders to dig in, the farmer was S.O.L. [Shit Out of
Luck]. These people knew they would be reimbursed for any damage
done and their only reason for howling was to forestall any arguments regarding the large and somewhat unreasonable claim for
damages they would eventually present and Uncle Sam would pay.
One farmer, on being told soldiers would camp on his land the next
day, hitched up his plow, ran a few furrows and presented a claim for
a crop of vegetables. That's patriotism for you with a vengeance.[28]

—Major Raymond Hodgdon
105th Infantry, 27th Division

On the trip up to the training area some of our young men lifted a
few cans of jam and corn syrup from an open gondola car in the big
railroad yards at Nevers. Another group emptied a wine keg in a little French stand near the railroad at Is-sur-Tille. The news of such
diversions in France always traveled fast. Claims aggregating $600

were ready for us as soon as the troops were settled in the billets. The two claims, accompanied by scandalized remarks by Division came to me for investigation. I dug up some evidence and later collected 3650 francs and turned them in. This was the beginning of many investigations of claims. If a soldier burned up an old board, chopped down a bush or broke off a branch from a wayside fruit tree there was sure to be a claim placed against our army. I have sometimes thought that half our war debt must have been incurred through the payment of French claims against the A.E.F.[29]

—*Lieutenant Colonel G.W. Garlock*
128th Infantry, 32nd Division

It is no surprise that the soldiers of the 61st Brigade should have become disgusted with France and her people. But even these low grade Frenchmen had many virtues for which they should be commended; their relations with each other and with the Americans were always smoothed by an innate politeness, even their slightest request being accompanied by an "if you please," and ownership of property was sacred to them that any kind of little articles, such as clothing and fruit, were entirely safe from their molestation. Americans think nothing of stepping into the orchard of a stranger and helping themselves to a peach or a pear, but these French people consider such an act as outrageous and entirely unlawful, under no circumstances to be permitted. They live in such close contact with each other and are so congested that they have long since learned to oil their relations with politeness, and their appreciation of property rights has been forced upon them because of their slender individual means.[30]

—*Private Rex Harlow*
61st Field Artillery Brigade

Since my youth, I had had a watch which was treasured because of the associations. It was a good timepiece but the scars on the hunting case had been put here by falls from horses or other accidents, which marked events in my life.

The watch stopped. I gave it to my sergeant and requested him to have a jeweler fix it. We got hurry-up orders to move. Neither he nor I thought of the watch till miles away. He did not know what jeweler had it. I gave the watch up for lost, and thought no more of it. Perhaps a month later it came to me addressed in my name with the supplemental address of "320th Infantry, A.E.F." Wrapped with the watch was a bill for 16 francs. Now, I ask you, what American jeweler would have done such a thing?[31]

—*Captain John S. Stringfellow*
320th Infantry, 80th Division

A lso familiar to any doughboy who served overseas was the ubiquitous French café with its vin rouge, vin blanc, cognac and even more potent concoctions such as mirabelle—liquid fire brewed from plums.

•

It had really been extremely difficult and expensive for a man in uniform to procure liquor in the United States. I cannot remember that I ever saw a drunken soldier at Camp Oglethorpe. In France, the natives were supposed not to sell liquor to anyone except between certain hours, and not to sell distilled liquor to Americans at any time. As a matter of fact, it was easy enough, provided you had the money, to obtain anything you wanted whenever you wanted it.[32]

—*Corporal Frederick A. Pottle*
Evacuation Hospital #8

The men spent what money they had freely, especially for wine and cognac.

There was always an order against drinking anything except light wines and beer. The censorship decided that no mention might be made in stories sent home of any drinking whatever. "So far as the censorship is concerned," said a censor to me, "the lips of the American Expeditionary Force never touch liquor."[33]

—*Frank R. Sibley*
Boston Globe *Correspondent, 26th Division*

There was an abundant supply of *vin rouge* and *vin "blink"* at varying prices: three, five, and ten francs a copy, to be exact. The first grade was diluted vinegar, the second fair Pinard, and the third plain bottled hell. On getting fried, the custom was to visit the Y.M.C.A. canteen, a secondhand stable operated by a human scantling with a bad temper. This bozo passed out paper and envelopes, but never had both at the same time; what's more, he didn't want any remarks about the shortage.[34]

—*Private Charles MacArthur*
149th Field Artillery, 42nd Division

The French are great on brandies made from all sorts of fruits. Cassis, made from cherries, is very palatable, but most of them I do not care for at all. The most virulent of all of them is mirabelle, made from plums. It is a fiery white liquor corresponding to American "third rail" or "white lightning," and three drinks of it will make you climb a steel high-tension pole and bite the insulators right off the crossarms. I know, for I've tried it—once. Never again![35]

—*Lieutenant Quincy Sharpe Mills*
168th Infantry, 42nd Division

Some of our men were becoming restless and hard to handle and a certain number of "bad actors" were going AWOL every chance they found. They were going back to a town called Coulommiers, the town nearest us where wine, women and song could be found. That was not their only offense; they were stealing the trucks and motor-cycles with sidecars belonging to our organization and on several occasions taking transportation belonging to other outfits with which to make their trips. They could travel more comfortably back and forth in their own vehicles than they could begging rides from truck drivers. Many of the motor vehicles were damaged while in possession of these runaways and caused us endless trouble recover-ing and returning them from the roadside or other locations where they had been abandoned by those rascally misfits.

When I asked them why they continued to go AWOL they were surly, almost insulting. Their only excuse was, "They wanted to have a good time." Good men in my outfits were beginning to grumble because they felt those offenders were taking it easy and escaping all the long hours on traffic post and other duties. Something had to be done.

The next morning, several of those reckless men were brought before me for trial on the same old charges of AWOL and drunk and disorderly conduct. I immediately decided to take drastic measures. I secured a log chain about 30 feet in length and selected 14 of the most desperate characters from the guardhouse, handcuffed them by one wrist to the chain, this in turn being securely fastened to heavy fence posts supporting the wire around a cow pasture. We left them there under the watchful eyes of the sentry in front of the guardhouse nearby with orders to give them nothing but bread and water. The colonel approved of the step taken and said, "Let them remain there for fourteen days."[36]

—*Lieutenant Colonel George M. Duncan*
3rd Division

From La Ferte to Meaux was ten kilometers, and from Meaux to Paris, twenty. It looked easy, but the entire distance was lousy with Marine M.P.s. They patrolled the railroads, hid in the bushes, lined the streets and came out of the floor in every café and coeducational centre. Always they wanted to know who we were, where we were going, what we were doing, and were we looking for trouble? It was pretty hot, and we had shed a few clothes, so they yapped:

"Where the hell's your blouse?"

The answer to this one was easy and immediate:

"I left it up at the front where they ain't no Marines."

The M.P.'s usual reaction to this remark was to shove a .45 automatic in the wisecracker's face with the right hand and slug him with the left. Mr. Colt certainly brought a lot of injustice into the world with his inventions.[37]

—*Private Charles MacArthur*
149th Field Artillery, 42nd Division

Between Soissons and the Saint-Mihiel show, things were fairly dull. When I noticed a couple of soldiers unloading a truck, I asked them where they were headed. "Back to Paris," they answered. I talked real fast and persuaded them to let me hide in the truck and hitch a ride to Paris.

On my second day in Paris, I ran into Sergeant Henry Topping, the father of Dan Topping, who later owned the New York Yankees. Henry was a chauffeur for some Army general stationed in Paris. At the moment, Henry's general was out of town and Henry was celebrating his absence with a few drinks. The least I could do was help him, with the result that, come midnight, we were both pretty wobbly. As we reeled down the Champs Elysees, we passed a large, unprotected plate-glass store window. Looking at the window, Henry said, "I wonder how much noise it would make if we kicked in that window." "Why don't we find out?" I came back and WHAM! We kicked at the same time. The answer to Henry's implied question was—a hell of a lot. Pieces of glass shattered down, some on the sidewalk. That accomplished, we staggered on as far as the corner, where two MPs grabbed us. We were taken to Sainte-Anne prison, located in the Military Police headquarters on Rue Sainte-Anne where they wanted to see our dog tags. My AWOL status had caused me to carefully hide mine in a sock. Henry mentioned the name of his general and talked them into letting him call one of the general's aides. Henry and I then went to sleep. The aide contacted must have been beholden to Henry, for by early dawn he had effected our release, after guaranteeing that we would pay for replacing the window. By train and truck I wangled my way back to my outfit and was glad to find that, in the topsy-turvy condition between fronts, I'd hardly been missed.[38]

—*Private Ben Finney*
5th Marines, 2nd Division

Forty-eight hour leaves were granted, some regimental commanders accepting the most ingenious excuses imaginable from their subalterns. It was even possible in those few halcyon days to get to Paris, though standing orders were that no leaves should be granted for Paris.

That was for officers. As to the doughboys and cannon feeders, the mule wranglers and camion drivers, they simply leaked in. The American soldier discovered that he could travel on a French train without money or ticket; if "no compree" didn't get him by, any old stamped piece of paper would go as a pass. He was equally ingenious about getting into Paris past the military police at the station.

I met one of the boys in the street in Paris. He explained how he had gone absent without leave; how he had jumped a train at La Ferte by the simple expedient of going down the track a piece and jumping the train on the far side.

"But how did you get into Paris?" I asked.

"I didn't come into Paris," said he. "I got off at a place called 'Interdite' and climbed up to the street."

Now 'Interdite' is a sign that is placed by a stairway from the cut outside the station. It means simply 'Forbidden.' But as its existence—and the fact that the trains all stopped there before being switched to their station track—became known, 'Interdite' got to be the American A.W.O.L. station.[39]

—*Frank R. Sibley*
Boston Globe *Correspondent, 26th Division*

When the French conductor would approach and ask for fares, they would hand out a long line of real foolish talk and appear as though they were there proceeding on a very important mission. Often they would shrug their shoulders and say, "*Pas comprenons,*" and if this didn't work they produced any kind of a paper which had an official looking stamp on it; and as the conductor could not *comprenait Anglais,* the boys got away with it. Once in a while even a United Cigar Store coupon was presented, and with success. The conductor on the train carried a small mouth horn which was blown as the signal to start the train. It did not take the boys from home very long to get onto this scheme and in a short time more than a dozen of these small horns were blowing on each train. These horns in the hands of our boys were the bane of the conductor's life.[40]

—*Captain James T. Duane*
101st Infantry, 26th Division

The doughboy in France whenever possible avoided salutes. He could spot an officer a block away, no matter how crowded the walk; at the psychological moment he would turn to a show window and gaze at whatever was exposed, be it a line of Parisian millinery creations, a display of female *lingerie* or the daintiest of *layettes.* When the officer had passed he would take up the stroll. Infraction of orders became so pronounced shavetails [2nd lieutenants] were sent

from the Provost Marshal's office and followed by a pair of M.P.s
whose task was the trapping of offending privates![41]

—Captain Carter Harrison
American Red Cross

My buddy and I arrived in Paris through one of the railroad stations.
As we were walking down the Rue des Italiens we spotted two
Marine M.P.s coming toward us. We hailed a taxicab and told the
driver, "Alley toot sweet." We sat down on the floor of the rear of
the cab so that we could not be seen, and after a very fast ride the
taxi driver stopped the cab and said we were now safe. This ride
cost us three francs, including tip, about sixty cents in our money.
We didn't know where we were, but proceeded down this beautiful
boulevard, when as we reached the corner to cross over, two Marine
M.P.s grabbed us and ushered us down a side street to a building
called St. Agnant. We had heard of this place, which was said to be
under the command of a Lieutenant Hard-Boiled Smith, and he was
having his men beat up with billies all enlisted men picked up.
There were several other soldiers ahead of us in the line leading to
the desk. We got thinking very fast, and seeing no M.P.s around
except the one at the desk, we made for the door, falling and sliding
down the whole flight of seven marble steps on our backsides. Upon
reaching the bottom, we ran out double time to the street. A passing
cab was hailed on the run, and it was again, "Alley toot sweet." The
cab took us around three or four blocks and then let us out right in
front of the Cafe de la Paix. After paying the cab driver we ran into
the restaurant and asked if we could buy a meal. The waiter said
that all that was needed was French francs. We looked over the
menu and ordered cheese omelet, French fries and a bottle of wine.
This came to eighteen francs, including the tip.

We then proceeded to the Folies Bergeres. After some confusing
directions, and keeping our eye out for the M.P.s, we found the
place. We bought two tickets costing twenty-eight francs ($5.60 in
American money). The usher took our tickets and seated us in the
third row orchestra. We were no sooner seated when the curtain
went up and several very beautiful girls came out and sang in
French and danced. The speaking was all in French; some we got
some we didn't. My buddy and I started to laugh at what we
thought was a funny scene, but no one else was laughing with us.
Finally an usher came down and told us that it was nothing to laugh
about and if we couldn't be quiet we would have to leave the theater. There was a short intermission, and looking around we saw the
theater was packed and the interior decoration was gorgeous. One

would hardly know there was a war going on. We were the only Americans in the theater.[42]

—Private Connell Albertine
104th Infantry, 26th Division

While most of the A.W.O.L.s entertained notions no more serious than seeing "Paree" or embarking on a vin rouge bender, some were intent on avoiding combat or resuming criminal careers that had been interrupted by the draft board. With over a million Americans in France by July of 1918, it was inevitable that a certain percentage of criminal types would surface.

•

In the spring of 1918 the A.W.O.L. man, better known as a deserter, began to make his appearance in many of the smaller towns and cities. With so many American welfare organizations giving away food and furnishing lodgings he could easily subsist and was able to work the railroads to travel over large portions of the country. Not content with freedom from military duty he soon gave bent to his criminal instincts, if so inclined . . . The military police, originally confined to camp duties and localities nearby, soon had to be enlarged to include all France. Highway robberies, burglaries and even murders had become more or less frequent, according to locality. In Le Mans, a city of 65,000 people, from August 1918 to January 1919, 25 murders were committed, not to mention the other crimes on the list. Women were used by the American soldiers to lure victims to robbery. As a result a veritable reign of terror existed in some sections of France in 1918 and the early part of 1919.

A co-worker of mine, while in the motor transport service not far from Verdun, was not allowed by the M.P. to stop in the town because of trouble there one day, a double murder. Two American soldiers, deserters, had become infatuated over the same French girl with the result that one deserter killed the girl and her deserting comrade.

The Department of Criminal Investigation, plainclothes men, was later organized to supplement the work of the M.P. One day shortly before I left, a D.C.I. man, in attempting to arrest a deserter just outside Paris, was shot through the head and instantly killed. Trouble arising from desertions and other crimes continued on the increase till in the late summer and early fall of 1918, the average of arrests each week in one city, Paris, was 500. This rate continued during the months of August, September and October, 1918, at a time when every soldier was needed in the final drive in the

Argonne. Up to June 30, 1919, 10 American soldiers were executed in France. In the entire army up to June 30, 1919, death penalties were adjudged in 165 cases. During the year ending June 30, 1919, more than 16,000 men were before a general court martial of which number 85 percent were convicted, in the cases of enlisted men one-half having been convicted of desertion, absent without leave, disobedience and sleeping on post.[43]

—George B. Thayer
YMCA Secretary

S ocial welfare organizations such as the YMCA, Red Cross, Salvation Army, Knights of Columbus, among others, attempted to tend to doughboy morale—and morals. The organizations sold or gave away cigarettes, candy, and other items. In more established areas, they provided "huts" or tents where the doughboys could find stationary and a place to write home or sit and read, listen to music or play cards. Ironically, many of the doughboys came to regard the do-gooders—the YMCA in particular—as price gougers.

•

The Y.M.C.A. man attached to our regiment came and held his sale right in front of the major's quarters on a little rutted road. He would have a few cartons (called "cartoons" by the men) of cigarettes, or baskets full of small jellies put up in pasteboard cups, and little cakes wrapped in wax paper. There was always a dense ring formed around him right away, and things were bought up like mad, the officers snatching off the cigars, and everyone wanting to get more than his share. There was also much discontent at prices, and haggling over change, which was very difficult to make, the men's pay generally being in franc notes of large denominations. The harassed "Y" men were for the most part very patient, but the nature of their business, selling gum drops and cakes when civilization hung in the balance, was so petty that they were bound to be despised by the very men for whom they labored.[44]

—Lieutenant Hervey Allen
111th Infantry, 28th Division

The American public maintained the Red Cross with huge subscriptions for the single purpose of advancing the physical, mental and moral welfare of its soldiers. Small account was taken of how the moneys would be spent; that was left to the judgment of the organization. Its desire was to make the boys comfortable, to add a mite to the happiness of the hale and strong, to ease the sufferings of the sick and wounded. While the army would look out for absolute necessities, there were things it would fail to supply, not classing them as necessities, which in the eyes of American parents were essential to the boys' well being; for these things Red Cross funds were intended.

The supplies most in demand were cigarettes, candies, chocolates, cookies, chewing gum, jam, smoking tobacco and the like luxuries. Cigarettes ranked easily first, practically every hospital patient in France not only wanted his fag, but got it. The sole exceptions were pneumonia and gas patients. Often I have seen a boy on a stretcher in a hallway on the way to his bed after a bad operation, with a cigarette hanging from the corner of his mouth. Camels, Lucky Strikes, Fatimas, so ran the preference.

To the above list must be added as necessities or luxuries toothbrushes, toothpaste, safety razors, razor-blades, shaving soap, toilet soap, towels, combs, brushes, handkerchiefs, underwear, socks, sweaters, comfort kits, Dorothy bags . . . most of the boys, when wounded or taken sick, usually reached the hospital with the clothes on his back and nothing more.[45]

—*Captain Carter Harrison*
American Red Cross

[From a letter]

We are at present attached to the 77th Division which is, as you know, the New York drafted bunch. It is, I believe, a unique division and to me a most interesting one. It looks as though they had taken a cross section of New York City and divided it into battalions, regiments, companies and all the different units and branches of the service which go to make up a division. The officers are almost entirely from the "four hundred" so called, and the enlisted men from the lower East Side, Italians, Polish Jews, Greeks, Serbs, in fact, representatives from most every country in the world. Many of them can't even speak English intelligibly and I have been thankful for my scraps of Italian, French and even German to make them understand me. They are a ferocious looking lot for the most part and always sure that I am trying to skin them. It's rather pathetic and I try to be patient and make them understand that the "Y" may have made mistakes unintentionally but that we are not in France to profiteer. It's a bit discouraging at the end of a long hot day to have some boy throw the change you have given him down on the counter and announce in a loud voice that the "Y girl" is trying to cheat him. They haven't learned the value of French money, not having been over here long and are tremendously suspicious of what they call "that tin Chinese money" (the French have punctured their smaller coins in the center in order to save metal) and are always sure that you are trying to put something over on them.[46]

—*Marian Baldwin*
YMCA Worker

How much of the criticism of the "Y" was deserved? The air was too surcharged with it, the doughboys' wrath too outspoken to leave doubt its secretaries had committed grave blunders. My experience was so mixed, I could take either side of the argument. Boys had come to me again and again with cigarettes just bought in Toul's "Y" canteen that were plainly marked: "Gift of the American People through the American Red Cross." The "Y" insisted the cases had been bought at the Is-sur-Tyl army commissary. Even if true, they should have been exchanged; selling gift cigarettes that were plainly marked as such, was unpardonable.

I heard often of "Y" canteen personnel, with fixed hours for keeping open, refusing to sell to tardy boys. There surely were cases where a remote unit and road conditions had caused the delay. It fell with poor grace on a doughboy coming fresh from the hell of the trenches to get cigarettes or candy for "the gang," to hear the cold voice of a noncombatant, physically well and little older than himself: "Closed, can't open again; you must be on time!" The boy did not argue; he just turned away, embittered forever and a day against the "Y" and all its works. Wherever doughboys congregated, the "Y" was "roasted from hell to breakfast."[47]

—*Captain Carter Harrison*
American Red Cross

Commissary prices were fixed by the Army law at factory cost plus nothing. Y prices must be computed on the actual cost delivered. And the Y, because the Army had been unable to keep its pledge as to shipping tonnage, had been forced on the one hand to buy commercial tonnage and on the other to purchase in European markets at prices madly inflated by the war.

But the doughboys, buying an article at the Y for one price, and later seeing the same thing at a neighboring commissary for a lesser sum, understood none of these things. "Grafters!" said he. "Profiteers!" said he, and spread the scandal broadcast.

Yet in spite of this, our American Army actually enjoyed at least four times more welfare service than did any other army in the war. This was rendered by the various welfare societies associated with the A.E.F. and ninety percent of the whole was, according to official Army reckoning, performed by the Y alone. With forty percent of the

required personnel, with forty percent of the required ocean tonnage, with thirty percent of the land transportation required for a
covering job, the Y performed ninety percent of all the welfare work
done overseas for the best-served army in the war.

And yet that Army damned the Y.[48]

—*Katherine Mayo*
YMCA Worker

N o discussion of the American Expeditionary Force would be complete
without reference to the black Americans who served. Approximately
*200,000 blacks were sent overseas with the A.E.F. As the U.S. Army was
still segregated in 1918, most served in all-black labor or stevedore units.
Two African American divisions—the 92nd and the 93rd—were also
formed. Units of the 92nd served with the French; the 93rd saw some combat in the closing months of the war. The two divisions suffered a combined
total of about 5,000 casualties.*

*As the A.E.F. was overwhelmingly white, with its members reflecting
the racial attitudes of American society at large, it goes almost without saying that the black soldiers were subjected to the same disparagement from
their white "brothers in arms" that they endured at home.*

•

At Base 210, two large rooms were assigned for the Red Cross hut;
one room was restricted to whites, the other to colored men, a Jim
Crow arrangement which I doubt existed elsewhere in the AEF.
Strange to say, the officer who ordered the segregation was not from
the South. The arrangement made the Red Cross hut worker's labors
more than difficult, for, as she put it, with the men jumbled together
in one room, it was easy to ignore the color line, while work in a
room with no occupants save blacks caused mutual embarrassment.

As was to be expected, disputes were frequent, many verging on
the serious. Negroes of the 92nd Division, whose notions of the
rights of man had grown in association with French women and
men, who are notoriously free of racial prejudice and rarely draw
the color line, resented segregation as a wanton affront. One day a
few hardier spirits violated orders by entering the quarters set aside
"For Whites Only" and refused to withdraw. Attempts at expulsion
led to resistance. How far the trouble went I did not learn, beyond
the fact that M.P.s had been summoned, weapons drawn and a number of whites and blacks retired to the wards, while others were confined in the guard house. With a change of command, the Red Cross
worker tried in vain to get the order withdrawn. Finally her
entreaties prevailed and she threw open the doors of the two huts to

doughboys, irrespective of color. Strange to say, few colored men would now use what hitherto had been forbidden quarters; rather they herded up in the old room to croon soft melodies, and, I am forced to confess, to indulge in shooting craps.[49]

—*Captain Carter Harrison*
American Red Cross

As we entered Nixeville, I recognized an officer in a side car. It was Major ———. He had been with us at Camp Lee, but was transferred to a negro division [the 92nd]. I dismounted and went over to him. "Why, Major, what are you doing around here? I thought you were with the negro division?"

"I was, Stringfellow, I was until one night we were in the trenches. We were waiting for zero hour. Finally, about dawn it came. They were ordered over the top and wouldn't budge. At last the colonel came up in the trenches and going along the lines kept saying, "Men, you are making history for your race!" Tell you, Stringfellow, the thing I was most afraid of was that some of those Germans across No Man's Land would hop up with white sheets on and start for us. I'd have been trampled to death.

After I had a good laugh, he continued, "Following that, the division was taken out, broken up and turned into labor battalions."

Now that story is as it was given me by a Southern man, who knew his onions. I never made any effort to check its truth. It is given here simply as one more negro story. The army was full of them.

The negro race will always be hampered by the many restrictions put upon it by the whites and should never be required to make the supreme sacrifice in the white man's wars. None are braver than some negroes. My position is—do not ask them to fight your battles unless you are prepared to give them true equality, which you are not.[50]

—*Captain John Stringfellow*
321st Infantry, 80th Division

We were not located near any large cities, but there were no restrictions when the black soldiers went into small towns. Some of the men went on leave to Paris and came back with no complaints. There was a good relationship between the white officers and the black enlisted men. I never saw any black soldier treated any differently than a white soldier would have been treated under similar circumstances. The only "color" remark I heard was in Company K. We had an orderly in Company Headquarters to run errands, etc. One day something happened—I don't remember what it was—but a lieutenant said, "I'll get that little nigger," in a joking voice. The top sergeant happened to hear the remark, and turning to the lieutenant, said, "Lieutenant, I thought that in the Army there were no more 'niggers.'" The lieutenant apologized and that was the end of that incident. That is the only time color of a soldier's skin came up—to my knowledge. We were never stationed too close to white troops, but on one occasion I heard that some white troops objected to the French selling wine to black troops. The French, as a rule, treated the black troops quite well, as many were from the New Orleans area and could speak French fluently.[51]

—Lieutenant Ernest E. Wade
806th Pioneer Infantry (Colored)

When the 311th troops alighted from the troop special early on the morning of their arrival, the station and avenues of approach to the town were guarded by American negro M.P.s, members of the 164th Artillery Brigade, who had arrived in the town several weeks previous and had made themselves at home with the natives.

An element of negro troops had started the story on its rounds among the guileless French peasants that the white troops, who had just arrived, comprised the "Scum of America," and that they (the negroes) were the real Americans; the whites being the so-called "American Indians." Admonition was added that the white arrivals were dangerous and corrupt and the French should refrain from associating with the new arrivals.

Thus there was created an intense and bitter racial feeling that loomed gigantic and threatened open racial hostilities as the white and colored American troops traveled the same streets of a foreign village; were admitted to the same cafes and vied with each other for the friendship of the French people. Street fights were not infrequent, while scenes in cafes were enacted wherein whites refused to sit in the same room with colored troops or vice versa.[52]

—Private William E. Bachman
311th Field Artillery, 79th Division

While observing a 10-minute rest period, and seated alongside the road, an amusing incident took place. We were watching a company of colored engineers filling in the holes and crevices of the highway. They were working during the nighttime as a precaution against enemy observers. They were large, awkward-appearing Texas negroes, and as they came nearer, one of our lads, desiring to know what state they hailed from, addressed one burly-looking fellow with, "Hey, Rastus, where are you men from?" The colored gent, glancing up and resting momentarily on his implement, replied in all proudness and sincerity, "D'on you all know? I'se from de *United States.*" And brother, he was proud of the fact.[53]

—*Musician Carl E. Haterius*
137th Infantry, 35th Division

Notes

1. Ernest Peixotto, *The American Front.* (New York: Charles Scribner's Sons, 1919), p. 35.
2. Judy, *A Soldier's Diary*, p. 125.
3. Reilly, *Americans All*, p. 861.
4. Hoffman, *I Remember the Last War*, pp. 62–63.
5. Havlin, *The History of Company A*, p. 60.
6. Ettinger, *A Doughboy with the Fighting 69th*, p. 150.
7. Carter Harrison, *With the American Red Cross in France 1918–1919.* (n.p.: Ralph Fletcher Seymour, 1947), p. 86.
8. *History of the 101st United States Engineers.* (Cambridge, Mass.: University Press, 1926), p. 220; one of the tamer of the some 3,000 verses of the *Mademoiselle from Armentieres.*
9. Judy, *A Soldier's Diary*, p. 215.
10. Swan, *My Company*, pp. 131–132.
11. M.A. DeWolfe Howe, *Memoirs of the Harvard Dead in the War Against Germany*, vol. 4 (Cambridge: Harvard University Press, 1921–24), p. 426.
12. Wilson, *With the 354th Infantry*, pp. 32–33.
13. John L. Barkley, *No Hard Feelings!* (New York: Cosmopolitan Book Corporation, 1930), pp. 161–163.
14. Garlock, *Tales of the Thirty-Second*, pp. 193–195.
15. *History of the Richardson Light Guard.* (Wakefield, Mass.: Item Press, 1926), p. 144.
16. Taber, *The Story of the 168th Infantry*, pp. 202–203.
17. Callaway, *With Packs and Rifles*, pp. 52–53.
18. MacArthur, *War Bugs*, p. 124.
19. Rendinell, *One Man's War*, pp. 36–37.
20. Clarke, *Over There with O'Ryan's Roughnecks*, pp. 18–19.
21. Ettinger, *A Doughboy with the Fighting 69th*, p. 91.
22. George B. Thayer, "Army Influence over the Y.M.C.A. in France," pp. 51–52.
23. Carl E. Haterius, *Reminiscences of the 137th U.S. Infantry.* (Topeka, Kans.: Crane & Company, 1919), pp. 33–34.
24. Brown, *Adventures of an American Doughboy*, p. 11.
25. Stanton Whitney, *Squadron A in the Great War 1917–1918.* (New York: Squadron A Association, 1923), pp. 20–21.
26. Hoffman, *I Remember the Last War*, p. 65.
27. Heywood, *Negro Combat Troops in the World War*, p. 35.
28. Sutcliffe, *Seventy-First New York*, pp. 158–159.
29. Garlock, *Tales of the Thirty-Second*, p. 15.
30. Rex F. Harlow, *Trail of the 61st.* (Oklahoma City: Harlow Publishing Company, 1919), pp. 124–125.
31. John S. Stringfellow, *Hell! No!* (Boston: The Meador Press, 1936), pp. 165–166.

32. Pottle, *Stretchers*, p. 94.

33. Sibley, *With the Yankee Division*, pp. 35–36.

34. MacArthur, *War Bugs*, pp. 60–61.

35. Luby, *One Who Gave His Life*, p. 434.

36. Duncan, "I Go to War," pp. 99–101.

37. MacArthur, *War Bugs*, p. 119.

38. Ben Finney, *Once A Marine—Always A Marine*. (New York: Crown Publishers, 1977), p. 28.

39. Sibley, *With the Yankee Division*, pp. 244–245.

40. Duane, *Dear Old K*, p. 110.

41. Harrison, *With the American Red Cross in France*, p. 284.

42. Albertine, *The Yankee Doughboy*, pp. 164–165.

43. Thayer, "Army Influence over the Y.M.C.A.," pp. 8–9.

44. Allen, *Toward the Flame*, p. 181.

45. Harrison, *With the American Red Cross in France*, pp. 55–56, 65, 96.

46. Marian Baldwin, *Canteening Overseas 1917–1919*. (New York: The MacMillan Company, 1920), pp. 105–106.

47. Harrison, *With the American Red Cross in France*, pp. 259–261.

48. Katherine Mayo, *That Damn Y*. (Boston: Houghton Mifflin Company, 1920), p. 381.

49. Harrison, *With the American Red Cross in France*, p. 88.

50. Stringfellow, *Hell No!*, pp. 244–247.

51. Moses N. Thisted, *Pershing's Pioneer Infantry of World War I*. (Hemet, Calif.: Alphabet Printers, 1982), p. 154.

52. William E. Bachman, *The Delta of the Triple Elevens*. (Hazleton, Pa.: Standard-Sentinel Print, 1920), pp. 68–69.

53. Haterius, *Reminiscences of the 137th U.S. Infantry*, pp. 123–124.

CHAPTER 11

The St. Mihiel Picnic

*U*p until the late summer of 1918, units of the American Expeditionary *Force had fought largely under French direction and army command. It was a regiment that took Cantigny in May; a division that drove the Germans out of Belleau Wood in June; and a corps that fought at Chateau Thierry and Soissons in July and early August. Through it all, General John J. Pershing had not lost sight of his desire for an independent army organization in France. The Allies, largely for political reasons, had poised many obstacles to this goal, but finally, in August of 1918, the independent American First Army was formed.*

The First Army's first operation was to be against a position familiar to the doughboys since late 1917—the St. Mihiel Salient, 150 miles east of Paris. Jutting 16 miles into Allied lines southeast of Verdun, the salient had been created in 1914 during the early months of the war, the by-product of a failed German attempt to strangle Verdun. Retained as a potential springboard for future attacks, it had resisted attacks by French troops earlier in the war, but now was held by eight, largely second-rate German divisions. Pershing's plan was to eradicate the salient, free the Paris-Nancy and Toul-Verdun railroads, and threaten Metz and the German lateral railroad net. The assault by nine U.S. divisions organized into three corps, with attached French organizations, was set for September 12. The divisions began gathering around the salient in late August. A total of 550,000 Americans and 110,000 French were involved—the greatest aggregation of U.S. troops for a battle up to that time—more than the combined Union and Confederate forces at Gettysburg. The air forces concentrated 1,481 planes, the largest number ever brought together for a single operation up until that time. Like the thousands of pieces of artillery being gathered, most of the aircraft were of French or British manufacture, though crewed by Americans.

•

A well-known French observer, attached to 89th Division Head-quarters for a time, was asked what he thought of the prospects of success for the American plan of driving the Germans out of the St. Mihiel Salient in ten days. He is reported to have used that expressive, inimitable, typically French gesture, or combination of gestures, that involves simultaneous movement of ears, nose, eyes, shoulders and hands and said, "In six months—perhaps." And there was much stress on the "perhaps." They all felt that way about it. Nobody was confident, except the men and officers of the American First Army. It never entered their minds that failure was even remotely possible.[1]

—*Captain Arthur L. Fletcher*
113th Field Artillery

The orders were no lighting of matches, no cigarettes, no smoking and no talking. We hiked all night with an occasional rest until daybreak, when we pulled into dense woods. Cold corned beef and hardtack were served and then we pitched pup tents and tried to get some sleep. Even though it was daylight, the density of the woods made it almost pitch dark. Some fell asleep, while others just sat in their tents singing or having a bull session. At dusk we were again served a cold meal and then took our tents down, rolled our packs, and soon we were on what was supposed to be a road but turned out to be a cow path. It was very dark, we couldn't see a hand in front of us, and to make it worse it started to rain. Luckily we all had raincoats. Some who had lost theirs in the Chateau Thierry Drive got them back in La Ferte. We marched all night with short rests now and then. A slight wind came up, blowing the chill rain in our faces. The cow path, having just dirt for a foundation, became very muddy. Our trench hobnail shoes, having been impregnated so many times with dubbin, were as waterproof as any shoes could be. No other kind of shoes would have lasted so long under such adverse conditions. Each of us had two pairs of woolen socks on and as far as our feet were concerned, there was no complaint. But the mud stuck like glue and the farther we marched the deeper it got and it just kept on raining.[2]

—*Private Connell Albertine*
104th Infantry, 26th Division

If you've never seen French mud, you've never seen real mud. Get a layer started on your feet, and it just keeps "taking unto itself more mud" until one has a width and thickness of five or six inches of it. It takes strength to lift shoes coated like that, on a long hike, with the rain pouring down.[3]

—*Sergeant William Brown*
9th Infantry, 2nd Division

During one of these night marches, one of the boys forgot himself and started to light a cigarette. Major [Thomas J.] Hamond spotted the light and, turning his horse quickly, headed for this soldier and lashed him across the head and face with his riding crop. No one really blamed Major Hammond, for he was doing his duty and might have saved many boys from being killed. As small a light as a match would magnify greatly in this kind of darkness and if the Boches spotted it, they could easily pinpoint the spot and start artillery firing.[4]

—Private Connell Albertine
104th Infantry, 26th Division

The last lap of this terrible hike was up a stiff steep grade, with the driving rain coming down harder than ever. Most of us were having trouble with our feet; rain, mud and sharp gravel had finally worn our hobnails to a frazzle. We reached Regnieville, the mud squashing between our toes, our shoes having given up the battle. We were in a frame of mind, if given the chance, to drive Jerry clear back to Berlin.[5]

—Private Ernest L. Wrentmore
60th Infantry, 5th Division

Five days we waited for the impending attack—five days during which we watered and scrubbed and manicured the nags, tried to send German helmets home, and renamed the guns.

The first piece was christened: "There's a Reason." To supplement the idea, Jack Walsh painted a large German soldier on the shield. The German was quite terrified, his hair standing every which way, and his arms high in the air. A balloon issuing from his mouth contained the words: "I Give Up."

We were a little nervous about this design. Not all the Germans were that way, and we were likely to run into a few of them personally one of these days.

The second piece was named "Hell's Belle" and revealed a lady in a red Venetian mask. This was considered the cat's whiskers—quite equal to the moniker Indiana had painted on one of their guns—"Old Dutch Cleanser."

"Americanische Bluff" were the fighting words applied to the third piece; and "The Reaper" designated the fourth, which carried a portrait of Death making marmalade out of eight Germans with a big scythe. All things considered, naming the guns registered the last burning moment of passionate patriotism that we experienced in the entire war.[6]

—Private Charles MacArthur
149th Field Artillery, 42nd Division

For the most part, the [veteran] doughboys with whom we came in contact in a walk of a kilometer or so were merely kids who didn't look to be a day over sixteen. Probably the average age was a year or so higher than the average apparent age—but not much, if any, more than a year. They were clean-looking kids—might have been the pick of the freshman class in any big American university—lean, straight, well set-up even in army issue uniforms.

But there was something depressing about them—probably the psychic message that they themselves are depressed. If there's any joke about this war, they seem to have missed it. They didn't sit around as our men did, cracking jokes and thinking up bright remarks to embroider on gas masks. These lads had the serious faces of old and disillusioned men.[7]

—*Lieutenant Bob Casey*
124th Field Artillery

*B*y the night of September 11–12, the doughboys were in position in the wet woods around the salient. On the southern face of the salient was I Corps with the 82nd, 90th, 5th, and 2nd Divisions in the line and the 78th in reserve, and IV Corps with the 89th, 42nd, and 1st Divisions in the line and the 3rd in reserve. Attacking on the western face as part of a pincer movement to nip off the salient was IV Corps with the U.S. 26th Division, French 15th Colonial Division, and part of the U.S. 4th Division in the line. The Americans had about 400 French tanks—including 144 manned by Americans. About 3,000 pieces of artillery stood ready, stockpiled with some 3,300,000 rounds of artillery ammunition. The barrage was scheduled to begin at 5 A.M.

•

Nowhere else in our experience did we see so much wire as there was in this sector. Elsewhere there had been belts, anywhere up to 30 yards across; here belt followed belt, and there were literally miles of wire entanglements.

At the No Man's Land area, the woods were, of course, blown to bits. Gaunt skeleton tree trunks stood here and there, but the position had remained as it was for so long that thick underbrush had grown up round the trees, and travel was almost impossible, even for unburdened, free-going foot passengers, in peace. It was awful country.[8]

—*Frank R. Sibley*
Boston Globe *Correspondent, 26th Division*

We artillerymen were amazed at the infantry's perfect sang-froid and indifference on the eve of what everyone expected to be the fastest American offensive of the war. They filed past the ammunition sergeant, who issued to each man his share of light and heavy hand grenades, incendiary bombs, rifle grenades, flares, Very lights, etc., which were carelessly stuffed into overcoat pockets and distributed about the person like so many green apples.[9]

—Anonymous Gunner
101st Field Artillery, 26th Division

"This time tomorrow where will we be?" shouted someone.

"Back in rest camp," another answered.

"Like fun," exclaimed a lieutenant. "You'll be sprouting daisies maybe then."[10]

—Corporal Martin J. Hogan
165th Infantry, 42nd Division

At 1 o'clock we halted and word was passed that we were about to enter a thick wood, probably to spend the night. "If we're near the lines, it's the quietest damned sector I ever heard of," commented Corporal Rafferty, whom I had buddied with a great deal.

A moment later, it seemed as if the whole top of the world had blown off. The horizon in front of us, and to either side, leaped forward in a mad blaze of jumping flashes. Crashes for an instant were distinguishable, but they settled quickly into a roar, much after the fashion of an airplane motor which, at slackened speed, misses, then, as the propeller gains momentum, emits a steady din. We gazed, every man of us, stunned. For five minutes, no attempt was made to pass orders. Officers and men watched the spectacle in awe.[11]

—Corporal Earl B. Searcy
311th Infantry, 78th Division

All the thunderstorms that ever happened on this old globe put together wouldn't begin to measure up to that the great American artillery made that morning. That front billed as a quiet sector, too. We couldn't hear ourselves think on our side and no living thing could last long on the other. The bombardment lasted about four hours and it is claimed that more shells were fired in this battle than in any previous one the Allied Powers were in. It sounded to me like the end of the world. One of the boys cupped his hands and yelled full strength into my ear: "Say, boy, some Fourth of July we're having!" His voice sounded like a whisper to me. What he said was the truth, believe me.[12]

—Sergeant William Brown
9th Infantry, 2nd Division

The crack of each gun seemed to drive down upon us an increasing downpour. The quiver of the elements following the explosion shook the water from the skies like drops from the leaves of trees. Water began to accumulate in our trench. We arose to our feet, leaning against the muddy banks. Our hands were slimy with the oozy clay. Our feet now felt the chill of the penetrating cold. I sat down in the slush again, no longer being able to hold the weight of my body on my feet. The mud was cold and the water seeped through my dirt-encrusted uniform. Shivers ran over my body . . . and I wanted to do something . . . go somewhere . . . just anything . . . anywhere![13]

—Corporal Chris Emmett
359th Infantry, 90th Division

I felt that if the Germans were ready for us and had organized the position, as they were able to, that we would have a terrible time. With 65 percent new men and 75 percent new officers, it would be a terrific task to keep things going. I knew my job was cut out for me and frankly I never expected to come through.

But as I lay on the ground that night and saw our tremendous artillery—1700 guns—with not an answering German shot, I said to the men beside me, "The Germans are pulling out."[14]

—Major William Donovan
165th Infantry, 42nd Division

It was raining slightly, there was a mist and dawn was not yet breaking when the machine gun barrage which took the men over began to fire. The men began to whisper among themselves, "That's our stuff; no it's not, yes it is." Then everybody jumped up and started forward.[15]

—Father Francis Duffy
165th Infantry, 42nd Division

Men were rising from the mud all along the trenches. I looked to the left. A soldier was moving from his concealment into the open. He stood erect, limned against a faint skyline, his rifle grasped in his left hand, and without taking a step, the rifle fell. Slowly he bent over, just perceptibly. Down on his face with a thud! He was dead . . . dead from a machine gun bullet. Momentarily, I could not understand what had taken place so suddenly before my eyes.

I stood with my head above the parapet. Old "Lord" George was crawling up the bank. I caught his foot and boosted him and he lay flat on his belly. Reaching back for my extended hand, he yanked at me. *Zip . . . zip . . . zip . . . pst . . . pst . . .* a peculiar noise, like a fast flying insect, almost touched my face. I struck at the "insect." "What the hell, Lord, is that biting at us?"

"You damn numskull. Get down or you'll never find out. Machine gun bullets."[16]

—Corporal Chris Emmett
359th Infantry, 90th Division

The doughboys were scrambling out of the trenches, clicking bayonets into place and yelling obscure things to each other. Their officers ran after, yelling: "Dress on the right, you gosh damn lousy doughboys!" The lines filled up and trailed abreast of the tanks, which dipped and bobbed like cautious old ladies. They stopped at shell holes and seemed to hesitate. You felt they had left their rubbers home. Then a flash from the turret. A one-pounder into a patch just ahead, and two German machine gunners with their hands in the air.

The doughboys strung along like crowds following a golf match, slowly and deliberately—dressing on the right whenever they were told. Here and there a man stumbled and fell. The line moved on under a cataract of shrapnel and high explosive.[17]

—Private Charles MacArthur
149th Field Artillery, 42nd Division

It was like a moving picture battle. Tanks were crawling up along the muddy rods and khaki-colored figures could be seen moving about in ones and tows and fours along the edges of the woods and across the grassy plains. Toward the rear were passing ever larger groups of prisoners in their blue-gray uniforms, carrying their personal belongings, and in many cases their own wounded as well as ours on improvised litters. Overhead the shells were still screaming from our heavy artillery with a good deal of answering fire from the German batteries, which caused most of our losses.[18]

—Father Francis Duffy
165th Infantry, 42nd Division

Fritz had worked for four years laying his acres of barbed wire entanglements, but our artillery tore them all to pieces. The mass of wire bothered us a little though, for it tore through our leggins and cut our legs. After we had gone a short ways, at least a third of the boys had no leggins left.[19]

—Sergeant William Brown
9th Infantry, 2nd Division

Going into a draw, I had begun my ascent of the other slope when to my astonishment two German soldiers with rifles in their hands walked out of a dugout on the side of the hill facing me. I stepped behind a small evergreen and was on the point of pulling off a bit of sniping when a big shell lit squarely in front of them. I saw the man in front raise his arms and seemingly rise in the air as the shell exploded. The form of the man disappeared as if by magic and when the smoke from the shell had slightly cleared I saw but one form; that of the one who had been in the rear of the foremost. He was sliding down into the shell hole and was mangled horribly. His companion had been blown to pieces. I rushed up and reaching over grasped his arm and pulled him upon the ground beside the shell hole. He died immediately. His legs were mangled and a big piece of the shell had passed through his breast. I could have run my hand through the hole. Thinking I that I heard noises below, I stepped to the door of the dugout and yelled, "Rouse mit you." Hearing no further sounds but to make sure I was leaving no chance to be shot in the back, I took out a hand grenade, pulled the cotter pin and threw it down into the dugout. I stepped to one side of the door and waited. A few seconds later it exploded and I turned and went on my way to find the other fellows.[20]

—Corporal Asa B. Callaway
353rd Infantry, 89th Division

Our division was advancing very rapidly. On the advance we passed thousands of prisoners, many of them wounded and gassed. One of the Germans was crawling toward us with his heel shot off when a doughboy rushed at him with a fixed bayonet. He was about to run it through him when I yelled at the top of my voice, "You damn fool, give him a chance, he's wounded." The young fellow then felt ashamed of himself and walked away. I stopped and gave the Hun a drink of water and a few hard tacks. He certainly had appreciated what I had done for him, for he said a lot, but his German was all Greek to me.[21]

—Private J. Herbert Ambler
150th Machine Gun Battalion, 42nd Division

We took a cut across the field to avoid the crossroads and went on in to Pannes. There we ran into a German canteen and in it was anything a fellow could want, officer's quarters, maps, books, field glasses, pistols, automatics, food, horses and any kind of equipment one could wish for. Right in front of the canteen stood a wagon all loaded with things from some German officer's quarters. We went through it and found ivory toilet sets, the best of Turkish towels and a thousand other things worth real money. We went into the canteen and there we got cigarettes, cigars, candies, soap, towels, matches, cakes and much other food and then we went down into the cellar of the canteen and there to our surprise sat two American doughboys, dirty, just full of mud, packs on their backs and rifles at their sides, but Oh, Boy! they were sure drunk because the cellar was filled with champagne and beer and they certainly had gotten their share of it.[22]

—Sergeant Elmer F. Straub
151st Field Artillery, 42nd Division

It was most interesting over the battlefield. Like the books but much less dramatic. The dead were about, mostly hit in the head. There were a lot of our men stripping off buttons and other things but they always covered the face of the dead in a nice way.

I saw one amusing thing which I would have liked to have photographed. Right in the middle of a large field where there had never been a trench was a shell hole from a 9.7 gun. The hole was at least 8 feet deep and 15 across. On the edge of it was a dead rat, not a large healthy rat but a small field rat not over twice the size of a mouse. No wonder the war costs so much.[23]

—Colonel George S. Patton
U.S. Tank Corps

*A*s it turned out, the U.S. attack caught the Germans at the beginning of a planned withdrawal from the salient. On the southern face, the German 77th Reserve Division, opposite the U.S. 89th and 2nd Divisions, crumbled like rotten wood. The doughboys on the right of I Corps encountered stiffer resistance as German troops fought to protect the base of the salient and prevent a major breakthrough. Fighting was especially severe in the 90th Division's sector where the advance led through a shattered woods defended by units of the German 255th Division in trenches and concrete pillboxes.

•

I scampered from hole to hole, sometimes running, sometimes crawling, taking advantage of cover wherever possible. In one of my leaps into a hole for safety I fell upon Corporal Ross. Upon my arrival, he raised up, then fell backwards, whimpering, "I am shot." His pallid face convinced me he was mortally hit. I stripped his pack for him, searching for the tell-tale blood but found none. "Where are you hit?"

"Here," and he indicated his left shoulder with his right hand. I ripped off his jacket and saw nothing. Then I stripped down his shirt and a small trickle of blood oozed from just below the clavicle. Bending him over so I could see the point of exit of the bullet, I found a clean wound bleeding very little. Feeling over the bones, I found no fractures, and as he bled little, I concluded he was not severely wounded. He contended he was going to die. Consoling him the best I could while I took his emergency kit to staunch the trickle of blood, I left him lying flat, scared and pale.[24]

—Corporal Chris Emmett
359th Infantry, 90th Division

Private Alexander Swain and I were on the extreme left and while advancing through the knee high weeds, caught sight of two Boches on ahead of us some 200 yards. They glanced back and seeing us turned and fired. Crouching low, we kept advancing, but before we could overtake them, a machine gun came to their rescue and we were compelled to lie down. Finally, we got up on hands and knees and after crawling for about 50 yards we passed through the machine gun fire and began our stalking tactics again. We caught sight of the two Germans and in a minute were almost upon them. Then they passed through an opening in a hedge fence that ran almost at right angles with our course. Believing that they had stopped and hidden themselves on the sides of the opening, we dropped to our knees and fired several shots apiece into the hedge on both sides of the opening.

When we got to the hedge we could see them running through the weeds a short distance beyond. Seeing us emerge through the opening, they turned and began firing again but their aim was bad and the bullets passed harmlessly over our heads.

"Take the one on the right and I'll get the bird on the left," shouted Swain. "And be sure of your aim," he added.

Dropping to our knees, we both took careful aim. Swain's rifle cracked and out of the corner of my eye I saw his man throw up his arms, stagger, grasp at his helmet and fall forward upon his face. Aiming at the base of the other fellow's skull, I pulled the trigger just as he plunged headlong into the hedge.

I circled to the right until I reached the hedge and then approached the place where the German had disappeared. Then I saw him. There he lay, flat on his back, his body in the hedge and his legs extending outward. Swain came up and we stood over the German as he died.

"This is bad business," I said as I saw his body quiver. The fellow's face was turning purple. His eyes had a glassy no-seeing look.

"Sure," said Swain grimly. "It's mean work, but they started it."

Turning the body over, I saw the tiny hole just where I had

aimed. The bullet had gone through the neck and came out through the mouth. As I stood looking down at this fallen foe, my very soul revolted at such a deed.[25]

—Corporal Asa B. Callaway
353rd Infantry, 89th Division

A large shell had made a direct hit upon four boys. All were dead. Limbs were mangled, bodies were torn. It was a sight revolting beyond description. Of one of my comrades I could find only small fragments of his poor body. None were larger than my hand . . . with the exception . . . there lay his head, jerked completely from his body. The skin from his neck was stripped back to the crown of his skull. Bare white bones of his head, smeared over with a pinkish thin blood not yet congealed glistened in the light. The powder-blackened face of a young Jewish boy stared immobile into eternity. Nearby was his hand which had been popped off at the arm just back of the wrist. On the bleeding stub was a wristwatch. And I looked at the others . . . Their spent distorted bodies, with muscles still twitching . . .

A sergeant came along. He was rather old for a soldier in the ranks. He was florid of face and his neatly trimmed red mustache showed in contrast to his fast graying hair. I called to him to assist me with a wounded lieutenant. Indiscreetly, he stood up. With a grunt, he sat down, gurgling, "I am shot. Through the chest." A gas shell popped above us and we stuck our heads into our masks. Looking at the freshly wounded sergeant, who was now sitting with his head in his hands, I realized he was unable to put on his mask and would surely die without it. I grabbed it. To my horror, I found the pipe leading to the inhalation tank punctured by the bullet which had entered his chest. Frantically I repaired the pipe and fitted it to his face. When last I saw him he was leaning over, breathing laboriously. A frothy, pinkish spume blubbered from his nose and mouth.[26]

—Corporal Chris Emmett
359th Infantry, 90th Division

T hree hours after I and IV Corps jumped off against the Germans on the southern face of the salient, the 26th Division attacked on the west against mixed resistance.

•

To see a regiment of soldiers on the drill field, one would think that there was a large number of men, but to see that same regiment go "over the top" in combat formation, there is a vast difference. They are so scattered that they look to be but a handful. We thought we were to go over behind tanks, but in this conjecture we were wrong. As soon as we started over the top and were on No Man's Land, I said to myself, "Here's where this outfit gets annihilated." And I really thought we would.[27]

—*Private F.C. Wilder*
101st Infantry, 26th Division

I kept glancing at my wristwatch. Precisely at 8:00 I scrambled up the top of the trench, crying out to my platoon, "Over the top and give them hell!" What induced me to use these melodramatic words, I don't know, but in any event, the platoon understood my meaning and followed me out through paths in the barbed wire into No Man's Land.

Meeting no resistance, we advanced about 100 yards to the rear portion of their first line of defense . . . I suddenly saw a German soldier coming out of a dugout with an automatic rifle at the ready. Seeing that he was covered, he showed no disposition to fight and he went back into the dugout to leave his rifle. He then came up the steps with his hands up. Not wishing to use one of my men to guide only one prisoner, I took the chance of leading him back a little way through the trenches and then forcibly making signs to him to go in the direction of our lines. Judging from subsequent events, I think that many of the enemy were quite willing to give up and they did not need to be heavily guarded.[28]

—*Lieutenant Eliot Carter*
103rd Infantry, 26th Division

There were very few dead around. As the column stopped at intervals in the woods, men would rummage around, going into dugouts, visiting gun emplacements and seeing all they possibly could, and especially on the lookout for souvenirs. Spiked helmets were much sought. One of our men after going through a barrack, came out with a dozen helmets, some of felt and a few patent leather ones, the latter which were the most popular because of their brass eagles surmounted with the inscriptions, "Got Mitt Uns."

As we were going along, a group of Austrian litter bearers was seen coming our way. They were carrying an American doughboy. The latter had been picked up by them while they were out on duty. They had bandaged the man well and headed for our lines. The man was however, too badly wounded to be saved and he died on the wayside where our column was passing by. A few feet from the spot, the body of a boy attracted us. "Poor kid," the men murmured as they looked at it. The boy had the traits of the Slav and was undoubtedly one of the many young conscripts of the Austrian Army.[29]

—Corporal Ernest E. LaBranche
102nd Field Artillery, 26th Division

We met a lot of doughboys in the woods. They were trudging alone in single file, their rifles slung on their backs, and they were hung all over with souvenirs. They were loaded with the little bags of sweet hardtack. Some carried German helmets in a bunch, like carrots, and some had several pairs of German field glasses hung around their shoulders. They were willing to sell or swap anything they had, but preferred to wait until they got behind the lines where they could get good prices from the Y.M.C.A. secretaries, MPs and others. However, I saw a Luger pistol that I liked the looks of, and as they were popular and hard to find, I bought it for a few francs.[30]

—Corporal Horatio Rogers
101st Field Artillery, 26th Division

B y afternoon, Pershing knew he had won an overwhelming victory. Unit after unit was reaching their objectives well before schedule. Thousands of German prisoners were streaming toward the rear.

•

The tactics of one enemy gun crew were described thus:
"M.G. fire until close approach of our infantry.
Threw grenades when our troops advanced to 30 yards.
Called 'Kamerad' at 20 yards.
Attached to A.E.F. for rations at 0 yards."[31]

—Historian
5th Division

Near sundown, troops still moving rapidly, my wagons got blocked once more. It was again necessary to make a detour and I rode off to find a way. Riding at good speed through some trees, I came to a dead right turn, face-to-face with a band of German soldiers!

I was scared to death and nearly fell off my horse. My knees banged up against the horse. I think even the horse was scared. I expected to be shot full of holes. To my amazement, they all dropped their guns and held up their hands. There were 26 of them. They did not run up and say "Kamerad! Kamerad!" as the story books say. What they did was to move up closer, but at a fairly respectable distance, and beg me, in the worst English I ever heard in Europe, to save their lives. By this time I was getting very brave and patronizing.

They said they wanted to surrender. I said that was all right with me, and they could go ahead and surrender. I pointed to the Allied lines and said, "Beat it!"

But they wanted to be personally escorted. They said that if I turned them loose, they would get shot before they could reach the prison camp. They pleaded with me pitifully. Two of the younger lads were crying. My emotions were changing fast. First I had been scared; then I was proud of myself for having 26 men begging for their lives; and the latest emotion was brotherly love.

I agreed to take them back. We headed for the main road, where they could join the main line of prisoners going back to prison camp. I rode my horse and my 26 captives trudged along beside me like a pack of hunting dogs with a huntsman. When we parted, one of them offered me a piece of sausage, and they wanted to stop and express their thanks, but I waved them on with a gesture and said, "Allez! Allez!" I didn't know any German. Their leader saluted me very stiffly and clumsily in a fond farewell.

I have read stories of heroes, and have met them, but there are many illusions about the hero business.[32]

—Lieutenant Maury Maverick
28th Infantry, 1st Division

Just before noon the 90th Division escorts marched several hundred German prisoners to the rear. As they passed our positions, the men of the regiment helped themselves to Fritz helmets, bayonets, belts and other souvenirs of war. Later in the day one of the prisoners' escorts stopped at one of our kitchens for supper. He was a little Italian chap, perhaps an inch taller than Bud Fisher's Jeff. Suspended over his shoulders was a pair of eighth-power German field glasses.

"Where'd you get the glasses, private?" asked one of our majors.

"Off'n a German captain, sir," he brokenly replied.

"Did he give them to you?" was the battalion commander's next question.

The little fellow's eyes stuck out far enough to allow most anyone to hang a derby on them. "Did he gimme 'em, sir? Did he gimme. Damn it all, Major, he gotta gimme 'em," he exploded.[33]

—Sergeant Major William E. McCarthy
309th Field Artillery, 78th Division

Approaching the railroad station in Toul I saw a long line of German prisoners marching toward the railway yards where they were loaded in box cars and transported southward. The prisoners came from our corps cage. They had been organized into companies of 250 men each and a number of their own officers assigned to handle them.

There were about 3,000 in that one column, but just a few American troops had been detailed to guard them. They all seemed well satisfied with their fate and appeared perfectly happy except they were in a hurry to get aboard the box cars and escape the jibes and jeers of the French populace. The civilians were out in force just as though it were a circus parade, they lined the route of march five and six deep and pressed forward until the guards became intermingled with the prisoners at one point. Many of the French women spat on the Huns and their caustic reproaches were full of venom and sarcasm.

The women taunting the Germans were much worse than the men. Several of the women were shouting something into the ears of the prisoners I did not understand. Upon inquiry, I learned they were asking the question, "Are you on your way to Paris?" That having been the cry of the German nation from the start of the war.[34]

—*Lieutenant Colonel George M. Duncan*
3rd Division

*F*or all intents and purposes, the battle of St. Mihiel was over within 48 hours. U.S. forces eradicated the salient, captured about 16,000 prisoners and 450 artillery pieces in the initial push. The U.S. 2nd Division, which had punched through the heart of the German 77th Reserve Division, led the tally with more than 3,000 prisoners, 118 guns, and a complete hospital train. U.S. casualties had been far lower than anticipated—about 7,000, including the slightly wounded. It had been a stunning success for the American First Army's initial offensive. But the doughboys' most severe test was yet to come.

Notes

1. A.L. Fletcher, *History of the 113th Field Artillery 30th Division.* (Raleigh, N.C.: The History Committee of the 113th F.A., 1920), p. 81.

2. Albertine, *The Yankee Doughboy,* p. 178.

3. Brown, *The Adventures of an American Doughboy,* p. 61.

4. Albertine, *The Yankee Doughboy,* pp. 178–179.

5. Ernest L. Wrentmore, *In Spite of Hell.* (New York: Greenwich Publishers, 1958), p. 90.

6. MacArthur, *War Bugs,* pp. 133–134.

7. Casey, *The Cannoneers Have Hairy Ears,* pp. 55–56.

8. Sibley, *With the Yankee Division in France,* pp. 261–262.

9. *Battery A of the 101st Field Artillery.* (Cambridge, Mass., Brattle, 1919), p. 157.

10. Hogan, *The Shamrock Battalion of the Rainbow,* p. 206.

11. Searcy, *Looking Back,* p. 52.

12. Brown, *The Adventures of an American Doughboy,* p. 61.

13. Emmett, *Give Way to the Right,* p. 170.

14. Reilly, *Americans All,* pp. 562–563.

15. Duffy, *Fighting Father Duffy,* p. 236.

16. Emmett, *Give Way to the Right,* p. 172.

17. MacArthur, *War Bugs,* pp. 142–143.

18. Duffy, *Fighting Father Duffy,* p. 239.

19. Brown, *The Adventures of an American Doughboy,* p. 64.

20. Callaway, *With Packs and Rifles,* pp. 140–141.

21. Reilly, *Americans All,* p. 571.

22. Straub, *A Sergeant's Diary,* p. 174.

23. Martin Blumenson, *The Patton Papers 1885–1940.* (Boston: Houghton Mifflin Company, 1972), p. 640.

24. Emmett, *Give Way to the Right,* p. 176.

25. Callaway, *With Packs and Rifles,* pp. 142–144.

26. Emmett, *Give Way to the Right,* pp. 184–185.

27. F.C. Wilder, *War Experiences.* (Belchertown, Mass.: Lewis H. Blackmer, 1926), pp. 95–96.

28. Eliot A. Carter, *Lanes of Memory.* (Boston: Thomas Todd Co., 1963), p. 126.

29. Ernest E. LaBranche, *An American Battery in France.* (Worcester, Mass.: Belisle Printing & Publishing Co., 1923), p. 187.

30. Rogers, *Diary of an Artillery Scout,* p. 212.

31. *The Official History of the Fifth Division U.S.A.,* (Washington, D.C.: The Society of the Fifth Division, 1919), p. 117.

32. Maverick, *A Maverick American,* pp. 123–124.

33. William E. McCarthy, *Memories of the 309th Field Artillery.* (n.p., 1920), pp. 82–83.

34. Duncan, "I Go to War," p. 247.

Machine gun set up in railroad shop. Company A, 9th Machine Gun Battalion, Chateau Thierry, France. PHOTO: U.S. ARMY/SIGNAL CORPS

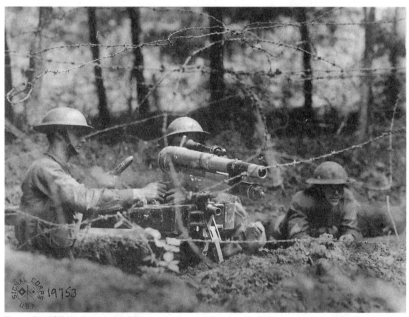

French "37" in firing position on parapet in second-line trench in Dieffmatten, Germany. This gun had a maximum range of 1.5 miles, was more accurate than a rifle, and could fire twenty-eight rounds a minute. PHOTO: U.S. ARMY/SIGNAL CORPS

A soldier of Company K, 110th Infantry Regiment (formerly 3rd and 10th Infantry, Pennsylvania National Guard), receives first-aid treatment from a comrade in Varennes-en-Argonne, France. PHOTO: U.S. ARMY/SIGNAL CORPS

Antiaircraft machine gun of the 101st Field Artillery (formerly 1st Massachusetts Field Artillery, New England Coast Artillery), firing on a German observation plane at Plateau Chemin des Dames, France. PHOTO: U.S. ARMY/SIGNAL CORPS

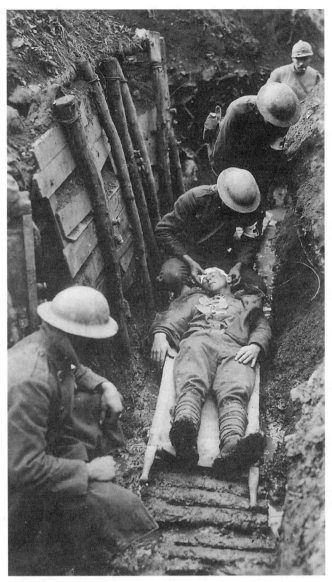

Marine receiving first aid before being sent to hospital in rear
of trenches in Toulon sector, France. PHOTO: U.S. ARMY/SIGNAL
CORPS

Soldiers tried out their gas masks in every possible way. Here a
soldier of the 40th Division puts his to good use while peeling
onions. PHOTO: U.S. ARMY/SIGNAL CORPS

American soldiers on the Piave front hurl hand grenades into Austrian trenches near Varage, Italy. PHOTO: U.S. ARMY/SIGNAL CORPS

Men of the 35th Coast Artillery load a mobile 14-inch railroad gun on the Argonne front near Baleycourt, France. PHOTO: U.S. ARMY/SIGNAL CORPS

On a field near Petite Sythe, France, the 148th American Aero Squadron makes
preparations for a daylight raid on German trenches and cities.   PHOTO: U.S.
ARMY/SIGNAL CORPS

1st Lt. Eddie Rickenbacker of the 94th Aero Squadron stands up in his Spad
plane near Rembercourt, France.   PHOTO: U.S. ARMY/SIGNAL CORPS

The skipper and gunner of a "whippet" tank with the hatches open, northwest of Verdun, 1918. PHOTO: U.S. ARMY/SIGNAL CORPS

American troops going forward to the battle line in the Argonne, September 26, 1918. PHOTO: U.S. ARMY/SIGNAL CORPS

Battery C of the 6th Field Artillery fired the first American shot on the Lorraine front. PHOTO: U.S. ARMY/SIGNAL CORPS

Gun crew from Regimental Headquarters Company, 23rd Infantry, firing 37-millimeter gun during an advance against German entrenched positions.
PHOTO: U.S. ARMY/SIGNAL CORPS

Cutting hair at the 166th Field Hospital, Baccarat, France. PHOTO: U.S. ARMY/SIGNAL CORPS

American snipers of the 166th Infantry (formerly the 4th Infantry, Ohio National Guard) picking off Germans on the outer edge of town in Villers sur Fre, France. PHOTO: U.S. ARMY/SIGNAL CORPS

The results of an Ordnance Department test of body armor at Fort de la Peigney, Langres, France. PHOTO: U.S. ARMY/SIGNAL CORPS

Gen. John J. Pershing at Chaumont, France.

CHAPTER 12

Into the Argonne

A s the fighting at St. Mihiel wound down, U.S. troops were already on the move toward what was to be the biggest and costliest operation of the war for the A.E.F.—the Meuse Argonne.

Under plans agreed upon with the Allied commander-in-chief in early September, the American Army was to advance northward between the Meuse River and the Argonne Forest. The French Fourth Army would attack on the west, while French and British operations continued on other parts of the Western Front.

The American advance was directed toward the critical German lateral railways in the vicinity of Sedan, within 35 miles of the battle line. An Allied success in these areas would divide the German armies and force a collapse of the German position on the Western Front.

This danger was appreciated by the Germans, who had used the ideal defensive terrain with its east-west ridges to construct a practically continuous zone of trenches, barbed wire, and other fixed fortifications to a depth of about 10 miles.

Three main barriers—each appropriately named after a Wagnerian witch—had been constructed behind an outlying complex of defenses. The Giselher Stellung lay anchored on the hill of Montfaucon at the center of the American line. Five miles behind were the Romagne Heights, site of the Kriemhilde Stellung. Five miles behind that was the last ditch defense line, the Freya Stellung. The enemy would prove to be well armed and determined. "Every goddamn German there who didn't have a machine gun had a cannon," recalled a doughboy.[1]

Pershing's plan called for three U.S. Corps to attack on a 20-mile front from the Argonne Forest on the left to the Meuse River on the right. I Corps on the left consisted of the 77th, 28th, and 35th Divisions. V Corps in the center consisted of the 91st, 37th, and 79th Divisions. III Corps on the right consisted of the 4th, 80th, and 33rd Divisions.

The movement of men and materiel was made under cover of darkness *starting in mid-September. French soldiers remained in the front lines to conceal the influx. During this narrow time-frame, about 220,000 Allied soldiers were moved out of the area and 600,000 American soldiers moved in.*

•

Evidences that we were nearing the front began to make themselves felt. Military traffic began to appear on the roads. As we turned into a great highway, there loomed in the darkness long trains of camions. Some hurried past us toward the rear, empty, but most of them were rumbling along in our direction, loaded with French and American infantry. Something unusual was afoot. A bewildered M.P. on a crossroad, questioned by one of our officers, said that troops had been pouring through for hours, and we could well believe him, for from every road that we passed new columns of men and guns and wagons streamed in to swell the volume of the mighty river of war traffic that moved on toward the front.[2]

—Captain James H. Howard
304th Field Artillery, 77th Division

Other troops were there, men from high-number divisions who had previously been holding the sector. They stared inquisitively at us, our horses lean and gaunt, our guns battered and scarred, equipment shattered, clothes in rags, and our men thin-faced and sunken-eyed. Evidently they doubted that this was the 32nd Division. It more nearly resembled "When We Dead Awaken."[3]

—Private L.V. Jacks
119th Field Artillery, 32nd Division

Our ranks had been depleted by deaths, wounds and illness. While officers and platoon sergeants were assembled at headquarters for their thrilling instructions, a welcome issue of replacements was received from the 40th Division. Most of these new men had been in civilian clothes on the Pacific Coast in July. They had had almost no practice with the gas mask. Very few of them, if any, had ever thrown a live grenade. Some had fired not more than 15 rounds with the service rifle. A Camp Upton veteran actually collected a five-franc note for teaching one of his new comrades how to insert a clip, and thought he had pulled a good one! What he expected to do in the woods with a five-franc note, no one knew; yet it was just as safe in one pocket as in another.[4]

—Captain Frank B. Tiebout
305th Infantry, 77th Division

The detailed plans and orders for the attack began to arrive. Among them came the order (Par. 17, Order No. 12, 91st Div. 23 Sep. 18) which later was strictly observed and keenly felt: "The troops will go into action carrying only their ammunition, reserve rations and water. They should not expect to receive any supplies, except ammunition, other than those carried on the person, for possibly 48 hours after the commencement of the action." No blankets, no overcoats, no raincoats, no extra weight to hold back the attack and consequently little to keep out the cold and rain.[5]

—*Captain Harold H. Burton*
361st Infantry, 91st Division

Some of the arrangements and plans in the 35th Division were pitiful. Very pistols were issued to be used for signaling. Then ammunition was issued. It was for pistols of another bore. Just a few hours before the battle an appendix to battle orders was issued, giving the code readings of rockets and flares. It was a long and valuable thing. Six white balls of lights in a rocket was a call for a barrage, one white and one green meant one thing and two reds and a blue met another, and so on down the list. Then the materials were obtained and they were all "yellow smoke." There was no code on the list for yellow smoke. The signalers could only fire that one sign and it did not mean anything.[6]

—*Clair Kenamore*
35th Division Historian

It was with inexpressible relief that we came presently to our "positions." Never before had I seen such a place selected for artillery fire. We were on top of a ridge that ran directly across the forest, parallel, in a general way, to the front line trenches somewhere to the north. On each side was a deep ravine. Everywhere there were magnificent great trees that completely shut off the view. Our guns were to be placed almost wheel to wheel just off the road, and in the midst of this vast forest. I thought my adjutant had gone crazy to select such a place, for it would have been impossible to fire in any direction without hitting a tree.

He saw my look of amazement, and, with a wave of his hand toward all the other guns, big and little, which lined the road, he said, "It was the only available position."

"But what about the trees?"

"They are all to be sawed through and ready for felling just before the attack."

It was then that the magnitude of the operation in which we were about to engage first dawned upon me, for what Frenchman

would have permitted the beautiful Bois de la Chalade to be thus
laid waste unless great things were to come of the sacrifice?[7]

—*Major Alvin Devereux*
304th Field Artillery, 77th Division

The days and nights of waiting in the forest had been under almost
constant shell fire and there had not been a great deal of sleeping.
After dark the infantry moved forward through the woods in
approximately the formation they were to employ the following day.
The men lay down among the big guns and tried to sleep. Each one,
according to orders, first loaded and locked his rifle.

Each infantryman carried his rifle, bayonet, steel helmet and gas
mask. He had 250 rounds of rifle ammunition, carried in his belt,
and two bandoleers, each one swung over one shoulder and under
the other arm. On his back was his combat pack, in his packcarrier.
This contained his raincoat, if he was not wearing it, his mess-kit
and two days' "iron rations," which usually was two cans of corned
beef and six boxes of hard bread. This is the improved form of the
famed hardtack of the Civil War, and as issued now is a thick crack-
er, palatable and full of nutrition, but hard. A few men had a loaf or
half a loaf of the excellent white army bread fresh from the baker.
This usually was carried on the rifle with the fixed bayonet run
through it. All carried a full canteen of water, about a quart.
Occasional details carried Stokes mortar ammunition, four shells to
a man, each shell weighing 10 pounds, 11 ounces. Infantry also carried ordinary explosive grenades, gas grenades, rifle grenades and
incendiary grenades, but most of these were thrown away.[8]

—*Clair Kenamore*
35th Division Historian

At 11:30 the regiment was assembled and we went out of the woods
onto the muddy road and seemed to be traveling in an easterly
direction. Going up this first road, we met some French troops who
had just been relieved by some of our own men. As we passed them
we would yell, "Fini la guerre," and they would respond with the
same expression and seemed tickled to death about it.[9]

—*Sergeant Major George W. Cooper*
111th Infantry, 28th Division

The air of expectancy grew as the hour of 2:30 A.M. approached. We
were about to witness our first real barrage. Precisely on the hour,
there came the crack of a 75 to our immediate rear. This appeared to
be the signal for the vicinity, for it was followed immediately by a
half dozen more, at various distances to the right and left, and then

more and more in ever increasing numbers until the whole blended into a continuous crackling roar, interspersed with the full-throated navy guns several kilometers back. The close-up horizon to the rear was a thin line of lightning flashes, reaching as far to left and right as the eye could see. From then until 5 A.M. conversation was only possible by shouting close to the ear of the man one wished to talk to.[10]

—*Captain Dale Brown*
145th Infantry, 37th Division

Mess Sergeant Byram, who was a veteran of the war with Spain, was sitting on the tongue of the rolling kitchen. He listened attentively to the roar of the guns for over ten minutes. Suddenly he looked around and remarked dryly, "I've heard more shooting in the last ten minutes than I heard during the whole damn Spanish-American War!"[11]

—*Private Ray N. Johnson*
146th Machine Gun Battalion, 37th Division

T he attack jumped off at 5:30 A.M. as the infantry of nine U.S. divisions got up out of the mud and headed into the fog.

•

The day was just breaking and the sky was obscured by a heavy fog which hung over the valley of the Meuse. The white and black bursts of shrapnel could be seen for miles along the edge of the fog bank, which was intensified by smoke shells. Thermite shells threw their awful flares of flame in all directions. Here and there the ground heaved upward in geysers of earth as the "heavies" exploded.[12]

—*Captain George N. Malstrom*
131st Infantry, 33rd Division

Special details had been previously sent out to cut dozens of paths through our barbed wire entanglements. Pouring out through these lanes like a black flood we formed our combat groups and began an orderly movement toward the German lines. We had no sooner begun our advance than the enemy sent up great flares. Myriads of star-shells burned overhead with bluish-white light; rockets burst in showers of little stars; broad fan-like flares mounted the heavens like the flames from a hundred smelters; green, red and white signal rockets, like the fiery balls of Roman candles, hung in the sky, flickered and went out; long squirming "caterpillars" sailed upward to float high in the air, their little chains of lights burning steadily and then, one by one, disappearing. It was the most magnificent display of fireworks any of us had ever witnessed; the whole horizon seemed enveloped in a great conflagration, so stupendous in its proportions that we were momentarily awed and shaken.

Our advance continued steadily. Only the shrill whistles could now be depended upon to convey orders above the titanic, churning shriek and roar of shells. When the flares were brightest we crouched in the thousands of shell holes or froze rigidly in our tracks. We could see the bellying smoke and flying earth in the garish light where our barrage was falling. When the light died down we trudged on toward the goal.[13]

—*Private Ray N. Johnson*
146th Machine Gun Battalion, 37th Division

As we crossed No Man's Land we passed a battalion of the 77th Division who were just going in on our left. As we proceeded further, we saw the skull of a man and about twenty feet further there was a shoe with the bone of a leg up to the knee sticking in it. Apparently they were the remains of some soldier who had been killed out there on a patrol at night and his body had never been recovered.[14]

Sergeant Major George W. Cooper
111th Infantry, 28th Division

The heavy fog had kept the powder smoke down, and as morning began to lighten I found myself, with my striker and two runners, adrift in a blind world of whiteness and noise, groping over something like the surface of the moon. One literally could not see two yards, and everywhere the ground rose into bare pinnacles and ridges, or descended into bottomless chasms, half filled with rusted tangles of wire. Deep, half-ruined trenches appeared without system or sequence, usually impossible of crossing, bare splintered trees, occasional derelict skeletons of men, thickets of gorse, and everywhere the piles of rusted wire. It looked as though it had taken root there among the iron chevaux-de-frise and had grown; and it was so heavy that only the longest handled cutters would bite through it.

There seemed to be very little rifle fire going on and the shelling was still almost all in front and growing more distant. I remember trying to light a pipe, but the tobacco was so saturated with powder smoke and gas that it was impossible. At the end of an hour's time I had collected two squads of infantry with a few engineers and together we steered on by compass over the seemingly limitless desolation.[15]

—*Captain W. Kerr Rainsford*
307th Infantry, 77th Division

Only a few dugouts had escaped destruction; the balance were nothing but a sagging mass of splintered wood or concrete. Trees had been uprooted bodily and added to the already well-nigh insurmountable tangle of barbed wire and underbrush. A light railway track running through the woods had been struck by shells and the rails bent into fantastic curves from the explosions. Near the edge of the wood and alongside the road were the bodies of several Germans. One body was that of a comparatively elderly man. He lay with his head cushioned upon his arm, with wide open eyes staring glassily toward the road. As some of the men passed, they imagined that the eyelids of the German slowly closed and opened, but a closer examination proved him to be quite dead.

In a ditch near a former machine gun emplacement, three bodies in field gray lay in a tangled heap, evidently the result of a shell. One of the dead presented a horrible sight, with his head swollen to abnormal proportions from a dreadful wound in his jaw. Another, a sergeant, evidently hit squarely by the shell, had a charred mass of burned uniform and flesh where his legs should have been. The third lay in a pool of blood with the top of his head completely blown off. Nearby, a horse, minus a head and neck, completed the gruesome picture.[16]

—*Major F.W. Marcolin*
145th Infantry, 37th Division

At 9:30 we came to a town called Cheppy. I went past the infantry as we were supposed to have taken the place. But all at once we got shot at from all sides. Pretty soon some of our infantry came running back. So, as none of my men had any rifles, I went back with the infantry, but stopped before they did. Also I stopped in a better place just back of a crest.

When we got here it [the weather] began to clear up and we were shot at to beat hell with shells and machine guns. Twice the infantry started to run but we hollered at them and called them all sorts of names so they stayed. But they were scared some and acted badly, some put on gas masks, some covered their face with their hands but none did a damned thing to kill Boches. There were no officers there but me. So I decided to do business. Some of my reserve tanks were stuck by some trenches. So I went back and made some Americans hiding in the trenches dig a passage. I think I killed one man here. He would not work so I hit him over the head with a shovel. It was exciting for they shot at us all the time but I got mad and walked on the parapet.

At last we got five tanks across and I started them forward and yelled and cussed and waved my stick and said come on. About 150 doughboys started but when we got to the crest of the hill the fire got fierce right along the ground. We all lay down. I saw that we must go forward or back and I could not go back so I yelled, "Who comes with me?" A lot of doughboys yelled, but only six of us started. My striker, me and four doughs. I hoped the rest would follow but they would not. Soon there were only three but we could see the machine guns right ahead so we yelled to keep up our courage and went on. Then the third man went down and I felt a blow in the leg but at first I could walk so I went about 40 feet when my leg gave way. My striker, the only man left, yelled, "Oh God, the Colonel's hit and there ain't no one left." He helped me over to a shell hole and we lay down and the Boches shot over the top as fast as he could. He was very close. The tanks began getting him and in about an hour it was fairly clear [of bullets].

Some of my men carried me out under fire which was not at all pleasant. Finally I got to a hospital at 3:30. I was hit at 11:15.

The bullet went into the front of my left leg and came out just at the crack of my bottom about two inches to the left of my rectum. It was fired at about 50 meters so made a hole about the size of a silver dollar where it came out.[17]

—*Colonel George S. Patton*
Tank Corps

As we started on the downslope, we picked up the major, part of the battalion and our 4th Platoon. Here we moved across the place where a company of the 138th had been moving in on the village of Cheppy, just ahead, when the fog lifted. Most of 'em were still there. They'd tried to do a "Charge of the Light Brigade," only they didn't have horses to get away on. The stretcher men were gathering 'em in and lining 'em up in a clump of trees.

Halfway through town my auto squads scattered for action. About 200 yards ahead were five Jerries carrying something out of a building on the left side of the street and setting it down on the sidewalk. Looked like a machine gun. But I'd been fooled a couple of times that morning, so I told 'em to hold it, and took a squad of rifles up the right side, hugging the walls. When we got closer we found it was a stretcher and they were [U.S.] medical men. I asked the fellow in charge if he was a doctor and he said, "Yes, where is the hospital?" I hadn't the least idea. "Well, it's too late for this one. He was hit thirteen times." He was right. Some second lieutenant out of the 138th, and there were half a dozen bullet holes in sight. So they rolled him off and went to the rear, looking for more business . . .

About this time a fellow named Garrett pulled off a wild stunt. He'd always wanted one of those German watches with the waterproof cover, and had rolled several Jerries without finding one. So he got away on his own, crawled up to the right along that bushy low ground and rushed himself a Jerry machine gun crew.

They saw him when he got close, and got him plenty from the knees to the waist, but he bombed it out with 'em!

The right flank squad found him later when we went in again, and saw he wasn't worth wasting bandages on, but he'd gotten his watches—two of 'em, plus five belt buckles and an Iron Cross.[18]

—*Sergeant William F. Triplett*
140th Infantry, 35th Division

We came upon a Boche machine gun crew of four men who had been killed. I remember one man had four bullets through his face and another was shot in the stomach, the former, having evidently died instantly, was lying on his right side and the other, who had evidently lingered some time, had crawled up and put his arms around him. Who knows but what they might have been buddies. Further on a shell had struck a wagon, killing the two horses and the driver, and just before I reached my troops I came upon a great German truck: I sent one of my men to run it, but it would not work. I remember we passed two wounded Boche lying in a shell hole, one a middle-aged man and the other a boy about 19, the latter had had part of his foot torn away by a shell. I do not know how the other had been injured. The boy was eating a piece of schwarzbrot.[19]

—*Captain Ashby Williams*
320th Infantry, 80th Division

The elements of the 79th advanced steadily against the withering fire of the machine guns, but with frightful losses in killed and wounded. The floor of the valley for several hundred yards was thickly dotted with their dead. The German gunners, though, paid dearly for their stubborn resistance. We saw a number of German machine guns along the ridge badly wrecked and broken. Surrounding their guns were the bodies of the gun crews, shot and bayoneted, lying cold in death.

All of those enemy gunners were naked to the waist and for a moment we were puzzled. It was entirely too cold and wet for human beings to exist half naked, even machine gunners. But the truth soon dawned on us. It was undoubtedly the work of the loath-some ghouls, who had hesitated on their forward movement long enough to rip or cut the clothes from the dead and search the gar-ments as they walked along, in their eternal quest for valuables or souvenirs.[20]

—*Lieutenant Colonel George M. Duncan*
3rd Division

We advanced six kilometers over shell-torn roads. In some places we had to wait until engineers repaired the road. Dead Germans were scattered along the roads and fields. Some were cut up badly, with their legs and arms off, and quite a few had their heads completely severed.

While waiting for a small stretch of road to be repaired, our bat-tery was halted in front of a first-aid station that had just been estab-lished in a shell-torn house. Immediately afterwards hundreds of wounded American boys were there. Many had their arms and legs hanging on by threads, others were shot in the chest, head and other parts of the body. It was such a piteous and sorrowful sight.[21]

—*Corporal David S. Garber*
107th Field Artillery, 28th Division

For the first couple of hours the advance was very slow because of the poor visibility and liaison difficulties. Wounded men began to come back. Many of these casualties came from following our own barrage too closely. We passed many dugouts around the opening of which were scattered promiscuously the personal effects of the retir-ing enemy. Apparently the attack was at least partially a surprise because it appeared that those vacating had thrown all their effects into blankets and, after carrying them a short distance, had opened the blankets and selected the things they could carry further, and then left the rest.

Our left battalion came upon a kitchen with hot coffee still on the stove. Thousands of reserve rations of sanitary white bags of small square crackers were captured by our troops, who had already begun to learn the lesson of acquiring all the rations possible for approaching emergencies.

By eight or nine o'clock, prisoners began to come back. The smoke screen had long since been left in the rear and on all sides over the terribly mutilated terrain could be seen single files of Germans, going toward our rear. Some of them were marching with their hands above their heads, if they happened to be accompanied by an especially vindictive doughboy.[22]

—*Captain Dale Brown*
145th Infantry, 37th Division

P *rogress the first day was considered very satisfactory, except in the vicinity of Montfaucon, a dominating hill in the 79th Division's zone. The hill had been heavily fortified and the defenders inflicted heavy casualties on the attacking doughboys. The 35th Division on the right of I Corps also ran into heavy fighting, but seized the heights at Vauquois and Very. In the Argonne Forest itself, the 77th Division advanced about a mile.*

It was an indication of the campaign to come that eight Medals of Honor were won that first day of the Meuse-Argonne attack, two of them posthumously. Among the surviving heroes was a 33rd Division infantry captain, George H. Mallon. The 41-year-old Minnesotan led nine soldiers forward and captured nine hostile machine guns without the loss of a man, then led an attack on a battery of four 155-mm howitzers that were still in action, rushing the position and capturing the battery and its crew—personally assaulting one of the enemy gunners with his fists. Another medal-winner, Private Nels Wold of the 35th Division, was less fortunate. Having already silenced a number of machine gun nests, captured 11 prisoners, and rescued a comrade who was about to be shot by a German officer—killing the officer during the exploit—he was killed while attempting to rush a fifth machine gun nest.

Montfaucon fell on the second day of the assault, but the delay allowed the enemy to rush reinforcements into positions north of the hill. The American advance on the first day had also outrun most of its artillery support, so the amount of ground seized on day 2 was not so great. By September 28, U.S. forces seized the ground directly in front of the German third position—the Kriemhilde Stellung along the Romagne Heights—and there they were stopped. Efforts to advance on September 29 were hit by strong enemy artillery concentrations and counterattacks by fresh enemy troops. Gains were made in some isolated spots, but most had to be relinquished. The 35th and 79th Divisions suffered especially heavy casualties.

•

A very large proportion of the dead of the 35th Kansas-Missouri Division around our headquarters were shot through the ankles and shins and through the top of the head in the case of those within a short distance of former German machine gun nests. I also noticed that these machine gun nests were not placed on the "military crest," but were pushed well forward in front of it. This enabled the Germans to deliver a surprise fire at close quarters from machine gun nests, which because of their unusual location had not been discovered and destroyed by artillery fire. This low fire had mowed down the men of the 35th Division by shooting them through the legs and ankles and then as they fell forward through the top of their heads.[23]

—*Colonel William N. Hughes, Jr.*
42nd Division

There were so many corpses of the 79th Division on the hillsides that some had to be dragged away to make a path through which ammunition could be brought to the guns without driving over the bodies. The aversion that the soldiery showed to stepping on a dead man was only equaled by the horror of the horses, in the same situation. A perfect windrow of the 79th lay behind our battery, 39 bodies being piled in one heap.[24]

—Private L.V. Jacks
119th Field Artillery, 32nd Division

It is a cruel necessity of war which requires . . . that ambulances taking wounded to the rear must be held up to let the guns and ammunition go forward. Hour after hour the long trains of ambulances lay in the congested roads, some of the wounded singing in defiance, some moaning in pain, some would become silent for a while and some became silent forever. One of the few advantages of a regular battle is that there is no restriction on noise. You may talk, sing or shout, curse or pray and nobody cares. Occasionally a man of the Salvation Army, the Y.M.C.A., the K. of C. or some other service would work his way through, giving cigarettes to the wounded, but usually it was the ambulance drivers who supplied their passengers with smokes.[25]

—Clair Kenamore
35th Division Historian

Reaching the vicinity of Malancourt I came upon the most pitiful and heart-rending sight I witnessed during the war. Hundreds of trucks and ambulances were standing on the road unable to move rearward. The blockade stretched away for several miles, and I was told the vehicles had only moved a few feet at a time for hours. Every truck and ambulance was loaded to capacity with men, wounded so badly they could not stand. Many of them were unconscious. Others were moaning and crying, suffering from the pain of their hurts. The cry of "water, water" came from nearly every conveyance. There was one good Samaritan on the job though. He was a short, chubby lieutenant of the Medical Corps. How long he had been traveling up and down that line of vehicles administering to those stricken men, I never knew, but his eyes were sunken, and through the dirt and whiskers which covered his face, his skin was as white as snow. He was practically dead from lack of sleep and rest, but he never stopped his work. I understood later the duty he was performing was entirely voluntary, he was just passing by with his organization and saw the plight of those men. At one of the evacuation hospitals a few days later, I learned many of those wounded men were in the trucks and ambulances for 56 hours.[26]

—*Lieutenant Colonel George M. Duncan*
3rd Division

When we were attacking over that ground, I hadn't thought about how many men we were losing because you can't see everything, and when you make a report that you've lost six or a dozen men, it doesn't mean anything. It's just figures, and you're thinking mostly about the number of rifles and autos you have left for the next shove.

But when you go back with time to look around and see 'em laid out in rows, or dotted all over, with fellows you know saying, "Try to get a stretcher up for me," it makes you feel pretty low . . . especially when you remember that the stretcher men are two or three days behind their schedule right now.[27]

—*Sergeant William F. Triplett*
140th Infantry, 35th Division

Our men were falling in such numbers that it was no longer possible to send those who had made the great sacrifice back to the burial grounds in the rear; they must be buried on the battlefield. I was given a burial detail to assist me in this work. Bodies were borne on stretchers and accumulated in convenient, easily designated spots where burial grounds were created, each burial ground being carefully marked on field maps so it could be located later. All valuables were take from the body and marked to be sent home. One identification tag was left on the body, the other fastened to the marker, which was often made either from canned goods boxes or split sticks and placed at the head of each grave. Where possible, religious services were held at each interment but often we worked under such heavy shell fire that there was opportunity to utter only a word of prayer as we lowered the bodies into their temporary resting places.[28]

—*Chaplain Hal T. Kearns*
79th Division

The invisibility of the Germans was one of their strong points. Their camouflage was good and they took advantage of every possibility for concealment. Some of our men never saw a German except those who had surrendered.

A typical experience was that of Sergeant C.G. McCorkle of E Company of the 138th Infantry, who fought from the jumping off day to the 29th when he was wounded, but in all that time he never saw a German with a rifle in his hands. All he saw either had their hands high in the air, surrendering, or were using them to work a machine gun.

Another man, he was a south Missourian and we spoke the same language of the Ozarks, said to me in the Charpentry dressing station, "I've fought for three days and I hain't seen a German yet while he was fighting. Now I got shot through the knee and I won't get me airy one."[29]

—*Clair Kenamore*
35th Division Historian

We were in a skirmish line . . . Sergeant Albert H. Cole was about four yards in the rear of the front line and I was on his left. Sergeant Sherl Gibboney was on Sergeant Cole's right. A shell hit directly in rear of Sergeant Gibboney, and we dropped. Cole didn't get down all the way. He was sort of leaning back on his hand. Shell struck him directly in the right eye and right above the left eye. One piece went through his gas mask—he had it at the alert. He fell face downward—he had his face covered with his hands. Sergeant Gibboney and I reached him at the same time. Sergeant Gibboney rolled him over on his back and inquired if he was hit. Sergeant Cole replied, "Yes." Those were the only words he said. I hollered for the first aid man; together with them and Private James C. McCauley, we started to carry him to a hedge about two hundred yards in the rear of the line—we stopped once and gave him aromatic spirits of ammonia.

We finally reached the place where a litter was waiting. Osborne, one of the medics, said there was no use carrying him further; he had passed away on the way down. And after making sure of that, we sort of put him [back] about 25 or 30 yards so he wouldn't be in sight, so there wouldn't be any chance of him being seen and fired on again by the Germans. We then rejoined the company. I should judge it was about 10 o'clock, September 27, 1918. He was buried about 200 feet from that hedge in the valley just north of Ivoiry. I saw his grave. I saw it twice.

He was an excellent soldier. He was a good companion—I lived with him seven months, part of the time in Camp Sherman and while we were in France.[30]

—*Sergeant Leo S. Brumberg*
148th Infantry, 37th Division

At daybreak September 28th, we looked around us and Germans were everywhere. They seemed to be getting ready for an attack. One German approached the shell hole where we Americans were.

He seemed to be looking for a place to plant a machine gun. We ordered him to surrender and get into the shell hole with us. He turned to run, but we fired and he fell dead near the shell hole.

The Germans then made a rush upon us, but we resisted and drove them back, wounding some and killing others. But with the aid of a machine gun and hand grenades, the Germans closed in again. Lieutenant [Charles R.] Gesner said, "Men, it's no use to resist any longer." And we (there were six of us, Lieutenant Gesner, two corporals and three privates) tied a towel to a bayonet and stuck it up out of the hole. The Germans ceased firing and rushed up excitedly. A dozen or more of the Germans kicked at us and attempted to strike us with their fists or guns, but others seemed to be trying to keep their comrades from treating the Americans with cruelty . . . On our way back as prisoners, we carried two Americans and a German to a dressing station. There were many dead Germans behind their lines. Our artillery was playing havoc with their men. We expected to be shot after the questioning, for on the way back an officer told one of the guards to kill us, but the guard would not. I made up my mind to fight like hell if it looked like they meant business.[31]

—Corporal James Baranek
137th Infantry, 37th Division

About 2:30 I was standing talking to Corporal Robinson, watching the Jerries still walking across on our right front, when we got the artillery support we'd been looking for the last two days. The first shell hit a tree just behind us and a slug as big as my hand buzzed between our heads. It took the bayonet square off Robinson's rifle about three inches from the muzzle. Another one exploded in a tree top and unraveled about six inches of a grenadier's backbone.

I started a runner to the captain to have the artillery fire lifted about half a mile, and damned if a tiny piece of steel didn't hit him low on the side of the neck. He started to breathe pink fuzz right away, so I had to send another man.

Somebody in the right front rifle squad yelled for a stretcher, and turned out to have a chunk through the palm of his hand. Can you beat it? We hadn't seen a stretcher since the first day and most of us would have snapped at his chance to walk out. He and the runner started out down the road together. We found the runner that evening about 300 yards down the back trail.[32]

—Sergeant William F. Triplett
140th Infantry, 35th Division

The wounded and dying were groaning and calling for help. "I'm hit, for God sakes help me," was the cry. It was almost unbearable.

Some were shell-shocked and were screaming maniacs. From the way they were screaming you would think they were shot to pieces.[33]

—*Private Rush Young*
318th Infantry, 80th Division

Our position was in a valley on a slight slope of a hill. On the opposite side of the valley were many dead Americans, who were unburied. Some were in their original firing position, with their guns to their shoulders. In a clump of trees nearby there were four machine gun emplacements sunk in the ground. They were made of armor-plate with small openings to fire through. Directly in front of these nests were twenty dead Americans, killed while charging these machine gun emplacements.[34]

—*Corporal David S. Garber*
107th Field Artillery, 28th Division

We ran across an old trail, sunk down a foot or so, and we piled into it. I counted up and had only thirteen or fourteen men left. Over twenty down! They'd sure been hard on us that time.

I crawled over to Wilson and told him that I thought we'd better stay where we were until it got dark because I didn't think we'd ever make it; but he said the battalion was coming up and we were supposed to stay on their left flank. Said we could take it on the run to the hedge to our front. I thought we might as well go finish it now as later, so I climbed out.

They came right after me, too, and surprised me. If they had felt about it like I did they'd have stayed there and to hell with it. But they came out like they never thought of doing anything else.

Just then I got smacked on the shoulder and knocked back down in the rut again. I was certain my arm was gone at the shoulder and was glad of it. Anything was better than staying out in that storm.

Wilson was howling, "On the run!" and they broke into a trot. My arm was there all right, only I couldn't use it. There were just two small holes in the raincoat so I felt fine.

The platoon was almost to there when I noticed Wilson sitting down about 50 yards out, filling his pipe. Having been hit once I felt lucky and bullet-proof and went out to see how he was getting along.

He was hit through the shinbone just below the knee and had started to unroll his leggin. I was kneeling alongside watching when another one cracked me on the head.

The next thing I knew somebody was saying, "By God! The

Sergeant got it right, didn't he?" and Wilson said, "Yep, right through the head, but it's funny, I can't find where the bullet came out." The news didn't seem to bother me a bit. A corpse can't worry.

But then for a week or so Wilson kept making me take a drink out of a canteen and telling me I wasn't hurt. Then he'd put on my mask, take it off, give me a drink, and say I wasn't hurt. All I wanted to do was die, so I could get away from the headache, which beat anything I'd ever had and was getting worse.

After a while I was able to ask him how things were going. He said we were both okay. His leg was busted but not bad. My shoulder was in the same shape. The bullet that socked me on the head had bounced off again. Said he didn't know whether we ought to call 'em wide hits or close misses, but I couldn't laugh for fear my brains would fall out.

Then he began telling me the latest about the battle. Johnson was not far off with a leg gone at the waistline. Hayes was hit in the side and had passed by on his way back. According to Hayes, Porto had got shot on his belt full of hand grenades and had disappeared with a loud bang down at the hedge.

For about another hour we laid there, getting the latest news, all bad, from the cripples going past, and hearing the fellow in the next hole saying, "Take me back with you, buddy, take me back, won't you?" Finally he didn't say anything more.

Wilson said he thought he could use his rifle for a crutch and my cane to lean on, so we climbed out and started back. My helmet looked like it had been hit with an axe where the slug had bounced through and I wouldn't trust an American hat again anyway, so I picked up a Jerry helmet. It was heavy and made the headache worse, but it felt very snug.[35]

—Sergeant William F. Triplett
140th Infantry, 35th Division

As I rode toward Montfaucon, my attention was attracted to a large number of soldiers coming down the valley, some of them carrying litters containing dead men, and others were carrying dead men on their shoulder, then I noticed a long shallow trench, freshly dug, and not over 15 feet from the road.

The gatherers of the dead laid their burdens in a row on the far side of the trench, then, identification being made and the dog tag secured from the neck of the victim, the body was lifted into the trench and laid close to his brother in death. There must have been more than 200 of those bodies at that one spot and they were not a pleasant sight. The weather was cool and decomposition had not set in, but rigor mortis was complete and arms and legs were set in every conceivable manner. It was a horrible sight.

Many of the men going forward along the edge of the road had never been under fire before, probably many of them had never seen the dead body of a human being before in their lives. As I watched them coming forward, most of them seemed carefree enough, although their faces had a stern expression as though they fully realized what was before them in the coming attack, but when they reached a point on the road where all the horrible aftermath of battle was unfolded like a panorama before their eyes, their expressions changed instantly, instead of quiet mobile faces going toward the front, there was fear, terror and horror in their eyes. Many of those young men stopped in their tracks at the sight of all those bloody dead men, only to move forward once more as the men in rear of them pressed on. Some of the young soldiers crowded into their comrades toward the left in an effort to get as far away from the dead as possible.[36]

—Lieutenant Colonel George M. Duncan
3rd Division

At the road where the litters were taken, we came upon two other stretcher cases just brought down the north slope . . . a couple of German lads. One had taken a piece of HE in the lungs. The other had a machine gun bullet through his guts. The boy with the belly wound was about 13 years old. He was jabbering to anyone who would talk to him. "This other boy is my brother," he said. "His name is Rudolph. We haven't been in this war very long . . . Only about a month . . . And the Red Cross man says we are going where there aren't any shells."

There was something pathetic about this baby and his eager interest in the strange country that lay back of the lines. Somebody translated for the benefit of the Medical Corps lieutenant who had examined our wounded. He shook his head. "I guess there won't be any shells where that kid is going," he admitted. "He probably won't live til they get him to the dressing station."

The boy, who could not understand, seemed to think that the lieutenant was agreeing with him in the matter of safety from shells. He pulled out of his blouse a thick nickel watch. Spare wheels and corners of brass fell out of it through a jagged hole. A bullet had gone clean through it. "Do you think I can get my watch fixed in this country?" he asked me.

I gulped. "I think so," I said. "The French are very good at fixing watches."

"I hope so," he said. "My mother gave it to me just before I came into this war and I shouldn't want her to think I had been careless with it."

I tried damn hard not to bawl at that. I don't believe I succeeded. The kid was still smiling when they loaded him into the ambulance.[37]

—Lieutenant Bob Casey
124th Field Artillery

[First Army Summary of Intelligence Oct. 5, 1918. Translation of a German Document dated Sept. 29, 1918.]

1. The American infantry is very unskilled in the attack. It attacks in thick columns, in numerous waves echeloned in depth, preceded by tanks. This sort of attack offers excellent objectives for the fire of our artillery, infantry and machine guns.

On condition that the infantry does not allow itself to be intimidated by the advancing masses and that it remains calm, it can make excellent use of its arms, and the American attacks fail with the heaviest losses. For example, the 150th Regiment of the 37th Infantry Division yesterday repelled 10 American attacks and today 3, without losing any ground and suffering relatively light losses.

The Americans are very much afraid of the artillery fire and especially gas shells. A few yellow cross shells are sufficient to start the gas alarm and considerable confusion. Therefore, it is recommended to continue the use of the salvos of yellow cross shells, especially at night.

As to the American tanks, the troops after recovering from their first fright have been able to defend themselves excellently . . . Several times it has happened that the tanks have been put out of commission by grenades thrown through the loopholes by the infantry . . .

The general opinion of the troops of the Meuse West Group is that the American troops are not a dangerous adversary when their method of fighting is known beforehand.[38]

Notes

1. Stallings, *The Doughboys*, p. 225.
2. Howard, *The Autobiography of a Regiment*, p. 154.
3. Jacks, *Service Record by an Artilleryman*, pp. 177–178.
4. Tiebout, *A History of the 305th Infantry*, pp. 143–145.
5. Harold Burton (ed.), *600 Days' Service: A History of the 361st Infantry Regiment of the United States Army*. (n.p., c. 1919), p. 45.
6. Clair Kenamore, *From Vauquois Hill to Exermont*. (St. Louis, Mo.: Guard Publishing Co., 1919), pp. 139–140.

7. Howard, *The Autobiography of a Regiment,* pp. 160–161.

8. Kenamore, *From Vauquois Hill to Exermont,* pp. 88–89.

9. George W. Cooper, *Our Second Battalion.* (Pittsburgh, Pa.: Second Battalion Book Company, 1920), p. 145.

10. Cole, *The Thirty-Seventh Division,* p. 212.

11. Johnson, *Heaven, Hell or Hoboken,* pp. 105–106.

12. *Illinois in the World War: An Illustrated History of the Thirty-Third Division,* vol. 1 (Chicago: States Publications Society, 1921), pp. 238–239.

13. Johnson, *Heaven, Hell or Hoboken,* p. 93.

14. Cooper, *Our Second Battalion,* p. 145.

15. Rainsford, *From Upton to the Meuse,* pp. 166–168.

16. Cole, *The Thirty-Seventh Division,* p. 206.

17. Blumenson, *The Patton Papers,* pp. 665, 668–670.

18. William F. Triplett, *Sergeant Terry Bull: His Ideas on War and Fighting in General.* (Washington, D.C.: The Infantry Journal, 1943), pp. 119–120, 143–144.

19. Ashby Williams, *Experiences of the Great War.* (Roanoke, Va.: The Stone Printing and Manufacturing Company, 1919), p. 86.

20. Duncan, "I Go to War," pp. 286–287.

21. David S. Garber, *Service With Battery C.* (Philadelphia: Innes & Sons, 1919), pp. 71–72.

22. Cole, *The Thirty-Seventh Division,* p. 212.

23. Reilly, *Americans All,* pp. 658–659.

24. Jacks, *Service Record by an Artilleryman,* p. 204.

25. Kenamore, *From Vauquois Hill to Exermont,* pp. 142–143.

26. Duncan, "I Go to War," pp. 289–291.

27. Triplett, *Sergeant Terry Bull,* pp. 171–172.

28. Robinson, *St. Lawrence University in the World War,* p. 336.

29. Kenamore, *From Vauquois Hill to Exermont,* p. 111.

30. William Cadwallader, *Major Conelly's Front Line Fighters in France and Belgium.* (Cleveland, Ohio: Pvtly printed, 1919), p. 73.

31. Haterius, *Reminiscences of the 137th U.S. Infantry,* p. 163.

32. Triplett, *Sergeant Terry Bull,* pp. 153–154.

33. Young, *Over the Top with the 80th,* unpaged.

34. David S. Garber, *Service with Battery C.* (Philadelphia: Innes & Sons, 1919), p. 78.

35. Triplett, *Sergeant Terry Bull,* pp. 165–170.

36. Duncan, "I Go to War," pp. 301–302.

37. Casey, *The Cannoneers Have Hairy Ears,* pp. 200–201.

38. *The 120th Field Artillery Diary,* p. 339.

CHAPTER 13

Death in the Forest

During the first days of October, one of the most celebrated episodes of the war unfolded in the Argonne Forest on the First Army's left. While struggling through the dense forest, elements of a battalion of the 77th Division's 308th Infantry—mostly New York City area draftees—had been pinched off and surrounded by German forces.

Led by a thin, bespectacled former New York lawyer, Major Charles W. Whittlesey, the doughboys held out from October 3 to the night of October 7 when they were finally relieved. Whittlesey was awarded the Medal of Honor and became a national hero. His unit became known as the "Lost Battalion," a misnomer since they were never lost, either literally or figuratively. Later, asked about his ordeal, Whittlesey, who seems to have had a flair for understatement, recalled quietly, "The men swore a great deal."[1]

•

The so-called Lost Battalion, consisting of 679 men, with other forces of the American and Allied armies, lined up in front of the forest with orders to go over the top and clear the wood of Germans. Our battalion succeeded in clearing that portion of the forest directly in front of it to a greater depth than the adjoining troops, and pushed down one hill, across an open valley perhaps 100 yards wide, and took up a position on the south slope of a hill nearly one mile northeast of Binarville.

That was on the 2nd day of October, 1918. We had gone so fast that we pushed through the German lines and they closed in on us from the rear, entirely cutting us off from our rations and allies. Night came on and we sent our patrols in all directions. Not a man came back. On the following day a company of about 60 men was sent out to make a survey of our position. A small handful of them came back, bleeding. We then realized for the first time that we were not only cut off, but that we were in a pocket completely surrounded by the Huns.

On the second day a piece of shrapnel tore through my left shoulder, coming out of my back under the right shoulder blade; my musette bag was torn and a bullet was stopped by a little pocket-book in the bag. This one would have plowed through my stomach. Another struck me in the right knee. The only souvenir of clothing I brought home was my riddled overcoat.

All our medical attention fell under the withering fire on the first day, and our wounded could only receive crude aid. We were in shell holes all the time, in groups according to the size of the hole—some held two, some four and some larger ones held a dozen men. I was on the extreme left in a small hole that two of us could lie down in. It rained almost constantly and we wallowed in mud, but the mud made our bed softer.

While we were cut off we had no rations and were forced to eat brush, leaves and roots. When our supply of tobacco was exhausted we smoked dry leaves. Our water supply was mostly from shell holes, though at night some of the men would crawl out to a little slough at the foot of the hill and fill their canteens. Dead soldiers were lying all around.

The Germans crept up on us and made five attacks while we were cut off, but we silenced each attack. They were so close to us that we could hear them talking and they would occasionally throw over a hand grenade. Sometimes we could toss them back before they exploded.

We were constantly under fire of machine guns, for the enemy had located us from various directions. Six times a day we were subjected to a heavy trench mortar bombardment. Every day we could watch the Americans attacking on the hills south of us trying to break through. On one afternoon we were shelled by artillery from 2:30 to 4:30. During this bombardment the hill was shaking like an earthquake for the entire two hours. Two shells burst within ten feet of the hole I was in and we were nearly buried alive.[2]

—*Lieutenant Maurice V. Griffin*
308th Infantry, 77th Division

[On October 3] Lieutenant Marshall G. Peabody got the whole burst of a machine gun in one leg just below the knee. Somebody put a tourniquet on the leg . . .

[Still alive on October 6] Peabody sat on the edge of a funk hole twisting his lips to a smile when anyone was looking at him, giving quiet intelligent answers to questions. The pain of his shattered leg was fierce; when no one looked he moaned. They had given him the one overcoat in the outfit for his gallantry, but as he sat draped in it that afternoon under a machine gun barrage, his tired reflexes did not respond quick enough to the danger signal.

Without a sound he came flopping down the hill right on top of signalman Larney, through the hole and out again into another depression, his arms flung grotesquely wide.

Larney looked at Richards and Cepeglia who were in the hole with him, then edged down on his belly like a crawling lizard, and with the remark that the lieutenant must have been alive when he fell and dead when he stopped, began to pull off the overcoat.

"Don't do that! It's bad luck to take a dead man's coat."

"I couldn't have any worse luck than I got right now."

"Butts on the coat then."[3]

—*Thomas M. Johnson*
A.E.F. War Correspondent

On the morning of October 7, 1918 . . . a sergeant came over to where myself and several comrades were lying in our funk holes and told us the major (meaning Major Whittlesey) had asked that eight men volunteer to try to get through to our support lines, to report our condition and get rations. I, among others, having visions of food and rest, volunteered to go. I did not at the time know the sergeant's name nor have I ever been able to find out what company he was with or from whom he received his orders to start us out on this fool's errand. I only know that I had one driving thought and that was the desire for food and anything that would help me secure it was all the incentive needed.

Through a light fog and mist myself and seven comrades started in the general direction of our support lines and crept down the hillside away from the beleaguered battalion . . . [T]here was one man among the eight of us who was a full-blooded Indian from Montana and we delegated him as our leader and guide, as several times while crossing that little valley he had kept us from taking wrong paths or trails. He only permitted us to go short distances and then take rests to preserve what little strength we had left. We moved very carefully, going quite a bit of the way on our hands and knees. It was right after one of these rest periods when we were again moving that the Indian stopped short and motioned for the rest of us to halt by raising his hand high above his head and I knew then the Indian had scented danger. We stopped dead in our tracks and in a silence so dense you could hear your own heart beat, the machine guns suddenly started their deadly "rat-tat-tat" and we all dropped flat to the ground. We did not know where the firing was coming from, we only knew it was close and as the bullets began to cut away the brush and twigs around us, knew they had our range, yet we dared not move.

As the bullets came closer and closer I noticed little spurts of dirt kicking up ahead and around me and wondered to myself "What will happen next." Then wondered how the other boys were faring, and even had a despairing wish that I was back with the rest of the battalion on the hill. Just about that time a peculiar feeling or sort of chill came over me and I thought "this is the last" and fell into a sort of coma or daze. I have no idea how long that deadly "rat-tat-tat" of the machine guns kept up, it may have been for only a few minutes or longer but it seemed like eternity to me. I had no idea how many of the other fellows were alive, but I did know that the boy directly in front of me was dead as I had seen the jagged bullet holes in his head, although I do not remember him stirring or even uttering a sound.

[A]bout that time a German appeared from behind a bush not six feet from me and held a long Luger leveled at my head. The German half smiled, half sneered and I instinctively raised my hands and said the only German word I knew, "Kamerad." Perhaps a second passed between the time I said "Kamerad" until he slowly lowered his gun, but it seemed several lifetimes to me. After the German lowered his gun he smiled a great big smile and what a lovely looking German he was. As he stood there in his gray uniform fully six feet tall, his smile seemed to broaden and broaden, then he started walking toward me. I suppose the reason his smile is still in my mind is because it was so unexpected, as I had been taught to hate and expect fearful things from the Germans should they ever capture me.

The German stepped over to me and started talking in his own language and pointed at my leg. I half turned and looked to where he was pointing and saw blood spouting from my leg near the knee. For the first time I realized I had been hit. Then other Germans appeared and began looking at my comrades and then I knew how they had fared. Of my seven buddies I found four had been killed outright and all the rest wounded. Our Indian guide was one of those who had been killed.

The first thing each new [German] would do was go through my pockets, but none of them took any of my belongings. The one thing that interested all [of them] was my Gillette razor and they all wanted it. Two of them offered to buy it and another to trade his straight razor for it, but when I made known by gestures that I had declined, he put it back in my pocket.[4]

—Private Lowell Hollingshead
308th Infantry, 77th Division

After six days of isolation under constant fire, we were rescued. There were 252 survivors out of the 679 who went into the fire. Every man who laid down his life sold it dearly—every man fought to the last breath. The hour we were relieved there was less than an average of 15 rounds of ammunition to each living man. The Germans were preparing to lay down a liquid fire attack that night and they probably would have succeeded in burning alive the remaining survivors had not succor come just when it did.

In all this experience I never saw a tinge of cowardice on the face nor in the action of a single member of the Lost Battalion. Every man expected to die, but he did not flinch—nor surrender.[5]

—Lieutenant Maurice V. Griffin
308th Infantry, 77th Division

At 7 P.M. October 7, Lieutenant Richard K. Tillman of the relieving force, the 307th Infantry, lifted his nose to the breeze. It stank like a glue factory, and the next minute he was stumbling into a shell hole in the dark, right onto a man who cried at him like a puppy. He just managed to throw himself sidewise from the silvery flash of a bayonet and could make out that the helmet and the arm that held the weapon were American.

"What's the matter with you?" snapped Tillman. "I'm looking for Major Whittlesey."

"I don't give a damn who you are and what you want," said the man with the bayonet. "You just step on my buddy again and I'll kill you."[6]

—Thomas M. Johnson
A.E.F. War Correspondent

Our flanks having come up, the Boche, of course, had to pull out and we were relived. The next day a captain from the left flank came and said something to the Major about having been glad to have been one of them who helped to "rescue" us. "Rescue, hell," said the Major, "if you had come up when we did, you wouldn't have put us in that fix."[7]

—Lieutenant William J. Cullen
308th Infantry, 77th Division

*W*hittlesey's predicament was indicative of the situation along most of the U.S. front. Recovering from their initial surprise, the German defenders took advantage of the difficult terrain and resistance grew stiffer by the day. According to the army history of the campaign, "fighting all along the front from that time on was of the most desperate character. Each *foot of ground was stubbornly contested, the hostile troops taking advantage of every available spot from which to pour enfilading and cross fire into the advancing Americans."*[8]

As the First Army paused to regroup, some exhausted divisions were relieved from the line, replaced by fresh organizations. Among the hardest hit was the 35th Division, composed of Kansas and Missouri National Guardsmen, which had been shattered in five days of fighting, losing over 6,000 men. Soon to be relieved by the veteran 1st Division, it would not see serious action again in the war. The 91st Division, drawn largely from the Pacific Northwest and also seeing its first fighting, suffered over 4,700 casualties between September 26 and October 7. It was finally relieved by the 32nd Division, composed of Michigan and Wisconsin National Guardsmen. The 79th Division, also new to the line, had lost nearly 3,500 officers and men in the fighting around Montfaucon. It was replaced on October 1 by the 3rd Division, veterans of the Marne.

•

Dozens of front line doughboys came to our kitchen to mooch some hot coffee and a handful of willy. None of them seemed to belong to any outfit, nor seemed anxious to do anything but sit and watch the artillery. I questioned one, trying to find out whether GHQ had decided to send in reinforcements one man at a time or what the what.

"We ain't replacements," he said. "I don't know about the rest of this gang. They ain't in my outfit. But me, I came back to get some coffee and a night's sleep. All our officers is gone and we more or less shift for ourselves. I think I'll try a new sector the next time I go in. I was up at Eclis Fontaine and it's too damned hot."

There was something downright startling about this naive confession. We had been hearing from our liaison details that the 91st was just about out of officers and that the men were fighting as individuals rather than tactical units. Here was evidence that parts of the line must be totally shattered.

These men came from the West Coast of the United States and, according to all reports, were excellent shots. Victims of hard luck and spotty leadership, they were fighting a back-to-the-wall fight up there. But they were making no effort to retreat. They had discovered an excellent arrangement whereby they might commute to the war with their bellies full of hot coffee. Presently they would be starting for the front again to take up their jobs where they had left them last night. MPs over near Very were beginning to round them up. But they required no persuasion. It was one thing to fight a war on a piecework basis and quite another to quit a job and leave one's friends holding the sack.[9]

—Lieutenant Bob Casey
124th Field Artillery

Dear Mother,

The rumor is that the Germans are licked, but by the way they are bombarding us with their big shells, you wouldn't think so. For the past week, we have been getting them pretty heavy and it sure is demoralizing. Some of the fellows get down on their knees now and pray. The funny part is that the ones that are praying are the fellows who were always so tough and foul-mouthed back in Camp Upton. Since they have been in dangerous zones, with the ever-present danger of being snuffed out at hand, they have become very meek and pure in their speech. What a change comes over a man when death is all around him! It is remarkable!

There is one fellow in our platoon, his name is Hamilton, who doesn't believe in God at all. When he sees the fellows down on their knees, he ridicules them, and says, "What the hell good is all that praying going to do you? If your name is on one of those shells, you are going to get it no matter how much you pray. Don't you think the men who have been killed already in this war for the past four years prayed? Don't you think their wives and mothers prayed for them? What the hell good did it do them?" Of course, there is no answer. He seems to be right.[10]

—Private Charles F. Minder
306th Machine Gun Battalion, 77th Division

Oct. 1st, Fleury

We have unquestionably been severely handled. The 35th Division on the right of 1st Corps lost three of its four colonels, all of its lieutenant colonels and majors, and probably most of its captains and subalterns. The 79th came out much bedraggled, and General Brewster says it will probably be broken up or have its number changed, as there's not use trying to build up an *esprit* from a unit with a bad name. The National Army has not made such a good showing as expected.[11]

—Dr. Harvey Cushing
U.S. Medical Corps

As we marched on [to relieve the 35th Division on October 1], we heard a rattling of equipment. Men were rushing toward us. It was a black night. I yelled at them to stop. They came on and we threw down two chau-chat rifles, little antique French machine guns, and told them we would kill them if they came further, for we thought it was a German trick. We let one man come up. "Oh sir, they are killing us," the poor fellow cried. "Out there today I saw six men crucified upon trees, even as our Lord Jesus was crucified upon the cross."

A great shrieking nose came, then a dull explosion. Gas! Gas! We put on our gas masks. Soon we marched on, holding hands and marching single file. I stumbled. It was the body of a dead man. I could see nothing. We were getting lost. I took off my mask. The dead man stunk, and he was soft and rotting and slippery.[12]

—Lieutenant Maury Maverick
28th Infantry, 1st Division

The fields were covered with soldiers' packs and equipment that they had discarded when they went over the top. Some French soldiers were looting these packs and taking whatever suited their fancy—shoes or anything they happened to find. An old American sergeant told them to stop stealing the shoes.

The French soldier said, "No compris," and the sergeant gave the Frenchman three or four real kicks in the seat of the pants to help him understand. He "compreed" all right and the rest of the pilfering Frenchmen did also, for they dropped what they were carrying and ran as fast as they could to get out of the way of the Americans.[13]

—Corporal Carl Noble
60th Infantry, 5th Division

R *esumption of the attack along the First Army front was ordered for October 4. At this time the bulk of the U.S. forces east of the Argonne faced the outpost zone of the Hindenburg Line. The army order of battle from the Meuse River to the west was: the 33rd, 4th, and 80th Divisions in III Corps; the 3rd and 32nd Divisions in the line in V Corps (with the 91st withdrawing to reserve); and the 1st, 28th, and 77th in I Corps. The attack was launched with great force at about daybreak October 4. Enemy resistance was characterized as "desperate in the extreme."[14]*

•

The American Division [35th] was still retreating when we went in; they had broken; other soldiers were needed. I was back with the infantry, and Frank Felbel, a little Jew, was commander of my company. He was shy. He spoke of art and the opera. I knew little about such subjects and was not very responsive.

October 4, we attacked. Five thirty-five in the morning was the H hour. It was thick black dark.

Just before the attack, up and down the lines you could hear the American lieutenants yelling "God damn it, don't you know we're going over the top at 5:35." On the German side there was only empty silence, a vacuum. We began to think that they had retreated.

Working through some barbed wire, little ditches and mud-holes, we were in proper line to advance under our own barrage at the minute of 5:35. We started, but the Germans were there. We had reckoned without a German rear guard action. And no doubt they had heard us telling our men to get ready.

They were soldiers who had trained four years at the front. They had left their lines checkerboarded with machine guns, had left their men in the rear to fight to the death, and had slowly moved out the heavy masses of troops. Most of us who were young American officers knew little of actual warfare—we had the daring but not the training of the old officer of the front. The Germans simply waited, and then laid a barrage of steel and fire. And the machine gunners poured it on us.

Our company numbered two hundred men. Within a few minutes about half of them were either dead or wounded. Felbel was killed outright, and I did not even see his body. A runner came to me and told me he had been killed. I took command of the company. There was not a single sergeant.

At this moment of 5:35 everything happened that never happens in the storybooks of war. We literally lost each other. There were no bugles, no flags, no drums, and as far as we knew, no heroes. The great noise was like great stillness, everything seemed blotted out. We hardly knew where the Germans were. We were simply in a big black spot with streaks of screaming red and yellow, with roaring giants in the sky tearing and whirling and roaring.

I have never read in any military history a description of the high explosives that break overhead. There is a great swishing scream, a smash-bang, and it seems to tear everything loose from you. The intensity of it simply enters your heart and brain and tears every nerve to pieces.

Although so many men had been killed, there was nothing to do but keep on going. I remember very distinctly that I held my head down a bit, figuring that a bullet would bounce off the steel helmet—which I thought I was wearing. Then I figured that at that particular angle if one hit me on my chin it would tear my chin off and leave me disfigured for the rest of my life. Then holding my head up, I began thinking that it would hit me and knock all of my teeth out and probably my eyes, and make me blind.

I suddenly realized that I had no steel helmet at all. I had been wearing the helmet on top of my overseas cap and it slipped off without my feeling it. But this was no time to be worrying about hats. We had to advance. And in front were dense growths of trees and barbed wire to keep us from going farther. There was a lane down the middle and no other way to go ahead. Dead men lay along the lane, all Americans. I felt sure that there was a German machine gun on the other side. I did not want to go through that lane. But the men began to waver a little and I figured it would not be right for me to lay down or stop, so I moved ahead. I said to myself, "This is one of the finest dilemmas I have ever been in. I must go through that lane, call for my men if I don't get killed, and get a hat. I need a hat. I need a hat."

So I started on through the lane and reached down and borrowed a hat from a poor fellow who had no further use for it. But it didn't fit. It was much too small. "I'll find a bigger one," I said to myself. I got through the lane and my men came through, too, without being killed. Then I looked on the battlefield for a hat to fit my seven and five-eighths head, and tried several, and found one. So, with a new headpiece, I re-formed my lines. On the other side of the open space I found, as I had suspected, a German machine gun nest. But the Germans were dead; one of them was hanging over his gun.

We started to advance again. A shell burst above my head. It tore out a piece of my shoulder blade and collar bone and knocked me down. It was a terrific blow, but I was not unconscious. I think it was the bursting of the shell, the air concussion, which knocked me down, and not the shell itself. It was not five seconds, it seemed, before a Medical Corps man was dressing my wounds. He cut my coat away from the wound and wrapped up my shoulder in such a way that it would not bleed too much. As he lifted me from the ground, I looked at my four runners, and I saw that the two in the middle had been cut down to a pile of horrid red guts and blood and meat, while the two men on the outside had been cut up somewhat less badly, but no less fatally. It reminded me of nothing I had ever seen before, except a Christmas hog butchering back on the Texas farm.

Leaving the field, I was forced to walk slowly. Suddenly I found I had been walking around in circles. For in clear view ahead was a German machine gun nest. I had circled back into the German lines. I was wearing only my breeches and shoes. My undershirt had been cut off and the torn blouse had been thrown over me like a cape. Because of my wound, my left arm was useless. But I had an automatic in my right hand. I decided to get heroic and kill a couple of Germans. There were six or seven of them.

Their helmets stuck up a little above the smoke on the battlefield. The place where I stood had been thoroughly shelled and was still being shelled. There was no wind, and the smoke lay close to the ground. As I remember it, one of the Germans was standing, but the others were close down and plugging away. So I thought it would be a swell idea to take a crack at them. I cocked my pistol and got ready.

But I realized that my automatic pistol would not even reach them. They were out of my range. But I was in range of their machine gun; if I had shot, they would have heard the pistol, turned and knocked me off. So a spirit of good humor, or good sense, came over me. It was then that I remembered the words of Captain Bill Tobin, Fire Chief of the great city of San Antonio, who came to me as I left for France, and said with a solemn face: "My son, remember this: It is better to be a live son-of-a-bitch than a dead hero." And so I turned around. It was the smartest thing I ever did in the war.[15]

—Lieutenant Maury Maverick
28th Infantry, 1st Division

It was apparently to be close fighting, so I exchanged my rifle for a sawed-off shotgun. I had my pistol too with about 35 rounds of ammunition in clips, my trench knife, and two grenades.

Our battalion moved forward slowly with frequent halts. We were trying to make no noise, and we couldn't have made any speed if we'd wanted to. It had rained so heavily that the ground was a slippery quagmire, and it was still misting. Our orders said two of our companies were to assault the woods, the other two were to constitute the support.

Suddenly a heavy rifle and automatic rifle fire opened directly ahead. I heard somebody yell, "Let's go!" and we ran straight forward. At the same time the Germans on the right end of the line opened up on us with dozens of machine guns.

The company on our right was having a tough time making the woods, but it was putting up a good fight. There was a lot of hand-to-hand fighting going on. I crowded up behind them, and just as I did so a party of the enemy rushed them. They closed in to meet the attack, firing from the hip.

In the mix-up that followed, one of our own crowd swung his rifle back over his head to meet an oncoming German, and the rifle got me across the side of my helmet. It only knocked me out for a moment; almost immediately I was back on my feet. But my shotgun was gone. And there was too much going on around there for me to spend time looking for it.

The fight swayed farther to the right. I saw a chance to get into a better position, and started to run across a little open place toward the woods. Halfway across, I fell headlong into a hole. The wind was knocked completely out of me, and I cracked my hip against a machine gun which was mounted at the side of the hole.

As I turned over and sat up, someone else slid into the hole. He stepped on my left hand. His boots were German boots, and as I moved he made an exclamation in German.

My pistol was still in my right hand, and I fired three shots as fast as I could pull the trigger. He fell toward me and pinned me against the machine gun. He was lying across my chest, and just as I'd succeeded in rolling him over my legs and getting to my feet, another fellow lit beside us.

He had evidently been running. He came in head first just as I had. I pushed my gun into his back. But when he yelled, in perfectly good New York English, "Where in hell's the rear?" I took it away again. He didn't wait for an answer. He scrambled out of the hole and disappeared in the darkness.[16]

—Private John L. Barkley
4th Infantry, 3rd Division

So alert were the Germans, so instantly was any movement we made met with a storm of shelling or machine gun fire, that it was impossible to get our wounded out by day. Four men to a stretcher, we got them out under cover of the dark . . . We found one man still living with eight bullet holes in him; too weak to move or call out. He had lain in the brush under that steady rain for a week before we found him. As he was being sent to the rear, I told one of my men to take a memo about him. If he recovered, it was worth knowing. But the man who took the memo was killed next day and I never learned how that wounded man came out.[17]

—Lieutenant Colonel Frederick Wise
59th Infantry, 4th Division

We kept gaining ground, but always at a stiff price. The new men were suffering most; they tried to hurry things too much. The old-timers had learned how to go slow and make their fire count. There was a lot of bayonet fighting.[18]

—Private John L. Barkley
4th Infantry, 3rd Division

*T*he attack of October 4 had not been entirely successful, but important gains were made against fierce German resistance. Pershing directed that the attacks continue. On October 8 an attack was launched east of the Meuse by the French XVII Corps of the American First Army. The corps, made up of three French divisions reinforced by the U.S. 29th and 33rd Divisions, cleared the enemy from the heights east of the Meuse and eliminated much of the serious flanking fire directed at troops west of the river. This was followed on October 9 by attacks by the 3rd and 80th Divisions, which penetrated the Hindenburg Line in and near Bois de Cunel, while the 37th Division penetrated the line south of Romagne. On October 10, *attacks were general along the Hindenburg Line. Again, fighting was fierce. Survivors of the 131st Infantry, 33rd Division chronicled their losses in this particular push.*

•

On October 10, 1918, we took part in the Bois de Chaume and Bois du Plat Chene Offensive. About 8 A.M. we started up the hill to our final objective. The enemy shot many shells in the valley. One of these landed a few feet behind Private Sam Buchman, taking off one of his legs and mangling the other so it was hanging by a skin. His face was black from the powder of the shell. We placed him on a stretcher and started to carry him to the rear, but he died in a few minutes. Except for crying for help, he did not speak after he was hit, until he died.[19]

—Private Robert M. Digler
131st Infantry, 33rd Division

Private Albin Fingal was hit about 2 o'clock by shrapnel from a shell bursting about ten feet away. One leg was blown off and one large piece of shrapnel lodged in his back, which was the cause of his death. He died on a stretcher about an hour after being hit. When hit, he was in a shallow trench with the company about two miles east of Consenvoye. When last seen, he was on a stretcher on which he died at the edge of the woods bout one mile east of Consenvoye. Fingal was conscious up to the moment he died. The shell that struck him also wounded 18. Fingal was in great pain and he kept on saying, "I'm going to die, kill me."[20]

—Sergeant Harold E. Stavers
131st Infantry, 33rd Division

The company had taken a position on a bald hill about a kilometer north of the Bois de Plat Chene. About 8:30 in the morning Private Albert Gerkin and myself were advancing up the hill when Private Gerkin threw up his arms and fell, saying, "I am hit!" Before continuing on, I endeavored to give him a drink of water, but he shook his head. He did not speak and seemed to be but semi-conscious. When I was able to get back about a half an hour later, I found him dead.[21]

—Corporal John C. Swanson
131st Infantry, 33rd Division

Corporal Holger Haunstrup was wounded while making an advance through Bois de Chaume. He was hit by a machine gun bullet, the bullet passing through his bladder. He was wounded about

9:30 A.M. His last words to me were, "I'm done for, give me my hat, my head is cold." He then became unconscious and died at the hospital.[22]

> —*Private George J. Prentice*
> *131st Infantry, 33rd Division*

While directing fire of the platoon after reaching the final objective on the hill north of Bois Plat Chene at about 10:30 A.M., Lieutenant Harding Horton was struck in the forehead by a machine gun bullet fired from a position near Villeneuve Farm. He died about 4 P.M. in the afternoon without regaining consciousness. I was about 20 feet to the right of the lieutenant when he was hit and remained in this position until the second night when the line was moved back.[23]

> —*Private Joseph Branigan*
> *131st Infantry, 33rd Division*

In the battle at Bois de Chaume we had reached our final objective and about an hour after we had dug in, around 2 o'clock in the afternoon, the Germans counterattacked. I was about four feet from Private Maurice Norman when a high explosive shell hit the front of the trench he was in and I saw him blown up in the air. To the best of my knowledge, he was killed instantly.[24]

> —*Corporal William C. Doran*
> *131st Infantry, 33rd Division*

After reaching our final objective, we dug in and were preparing to defend our position. Private Louis Platt left his place in the newly dug trench to obtain ammunition from the bodies of some dead American soldiers about 100 feet distant. Securing the ammunition, he came back to his place in the trench and he had barely deposited the ammunition at his side when he was hit by two machine gun bullets, one hitting him in the forehead and another entering his heart. Groaning, he fell and died instantly, uttering no word.[25]

> —*Sergeant William Jones*
> *131st Infantry, 33rd Division*

On the afternoon after the attack on the east bank of the Meuse, Private George Walz was wounded slightly in the head by a machine gun bullet. I was helping him back to the first aid station and had to pass through Bois de Chaume which was being heavily shelled by the enemy. A shell exploded about 10 feet in front of us and a piece of shrapnel struck Private Walz in the throat, killing him instantly.[26]

> —*Private Sidney Kohn*
> *131st Infantry, 33rd Division*

T he bloodbath ebbed on October 12 as the First Army again paused to regroup. By now the doughboys faced the main strength of the Hindenburg Line along most of their zone and had managed to penetrate the line along a front of about three miles. But progress on the maps brought little comfort to the front lines where the soldiers endured appalling conditions. There were frequent rains and the days and nights were turning colder. Living in holes scraped in the ground, shot at, gassed, and shelled, with supplies often nonexistent due to the difficulty of getting transport forward to the front lines, the doughboys suffered great hardships.

•

The morale of the American soldier during this most trying period was superb. Physically strong and virile, naturally courageous and aggressive, inspired by unselfish and idealistic motives, he guaranteed the victory and drove a veteran enemy from his last ditch. Too much credit cannot be given him; his patriotism, courage and fortitude were beyond praise.

Upon the young commanders of platoons, companies and battalions fell the heaviest burden. They not only suffered all the dangers and rigors of the fight but carried the responsibility of caring for and directing their men, often newly arrived and not fully trained.[27]

—General John J. Pershing
American Expeditionary Force

The feelings of misery and overwhelming fatigue which all members of the division experienced at this time can best be illustrated by the desperate answer which Lieutenant Devine of the 308th Field Artillery gave an angry major general en route.

Devine was struggling along with part of his battery through the mud and rain one night when the battery cooker, showing less resistance than a human being, collapsed in a hopeless fashion, blocking the whole road. While he was looking at the wreck and wondering where the hot rations and coffee for his men were going to come from without a cooker, a limousine rolled up and was stopped by the wreck. An angry head popped out of the window and demanded to know who was in command of this battery. Devine presented himself and saw he was talking to a major general. The latter hotly asked what he meant by blocking the road, and without waiting for an answer shouted: "Young man, instead of being in command of a battery, you ought to be in jail!" A vision of a warm, dry building with a bunk, dry clothes, no mud, hot meals, and no responsibility for weary, hungry men passed through Devine's mind. Then he drew himself up and said: "Sir, I wish to God I *was* in jail!" And the general went on.[28]

—Lieutenant Colonel Thomas F. Meehan
78th Division

We started for the rear and rest, south of Cuisy. The Germans must have gotten on to our plans and they began to drop shells mixed with gas back on us. The gas corporal, Kemp Rush, with his prickly nose, began to shout, "Gas! Gas!" The sirens were also sounding.

The captain ordered us to put on our masks and hold fast to the man next to us and not to let loose until we were out of the woods. It was almost impossible to hold on to the man next to you. We were falling in shell holes, over limbs, tearing our masks off, losing our helmets, and getting whiffs of chlorine gas before we could get our masks back on. Some were gassed badly. The lenses were getting sweaty and we could not see, the clips kept coming off our noses and the masks were puffing in and out like bellows. We were hot and the slobbers were streaming from the flutter valves like horses that had been eating grass. Finally the order was passed along, "All clear, All clear," and off came the masks. We marched rearward through the early morning hours and finally the light of dawn began to come under the light fog.

We were getting sick from the gas and the impure water we drank while on the lines. Our bowels were getting loose. The farther we hiked the sicker we got. Boys were breaking the ranks all along, their packs going one way and their overcoat the other but sometimes it was too late. They would pick up their coat and pack with a disgusted look and start hobbling along.[29]

—Private Rush Young
318th Infantry, 80th Division

Dear Mother,
It started to rain and we became soaking wet. We put our raincoats on over our overcoats and the rain soaked through. Whoever sold these raincoats to the government ought to be shot. If we throw them away, we'll have to pay for them. Some of the fellows sold theirs to the French people back in the villages for food and wine.[30]

—Private Charles F. Minder
306th Machine Gun Battalion, 77th Division

Most of us were scared stiff, to the point that some of the boys had diarrhea. I had diarrhea, too, and because of the constant shelling could not stop and go, and so it just came out, trickled down, and lodged at my knees. Because of the wrap leggins that were wrapped from our ankles to our knees, the stool just stayed put. Soon we could all smell this stool odor from each other. There was nothing in this experience to be ashamed of, because it happened to all of us, and it didn't make any difference whether you were an officer or an enlisted man, but we were all reluctant to talk about it. While resting in a small gully, some of us took the spoons from our mess kits and, lowering our breeches, tried to scoop up this stool from around our knees, for besides the odor it was very uncomfortable.[31]

—Private Connell Albertine
104th Infantry, 26th Division

Dear Mother:

We saw some pretty bad damage all along the hike today. I saw at least 200 dead bodies lying all over the place, in every possible position. I saw one fellow, with his head bandaged, down on his knees. He passed on while kneeling. One fellow was completely blown to pieces, and half of his body was hanging on a branch of a tree, one arm on the ground and his two legs about ten yards away. It was the most ghastly sight I've ever seen. The smell of the dead is terrible in the woods. I guess the burial detail is on the job by now, it's some job to bury them. What I wonder about is how they are ever going to find the bodies, for the underbrush is so thick that it will grow over the graves and completely hide them. The whole ground is like honeycomb all through this sector from the shellholes.[32]

—Private Charles F. Minder
306th Machine Gun Battalion, 77th Division

Moving forward to our new position, we found time to investigate some of the trenches that Heinie had evacuated during this drive. While passing an opening to a dugout, we were hit with a horrible odor. Entering the dugout, we found several dead Boche. Some doughboy had tossed a grenade into the dugout, making a clean sweep of all the occupants. What a mess!

On all sides were the bloated carcasses of dead mules and horses, the demolished remains of soup carts and many other types of equipment. There were bodies of many doughboys who had given their all, lying by the roadside, most of them covered by blankets or overcoats. Ammunition, rifles, bayonets, packs and supplies of every description covered the fields. God! It was nothing but complete desolation. To me, it seemed like the beginning of the end of the world.[33]

—Private Ernest L. Wrentmore
60th Infantry, 5th Division

Gas was very thick, as it rolled down the hill in the rear of us and just laid in the valley we were in, it was not strong enough to make one wear a gas mask but nevertheless everybody was sneezing and crying most of the time.[34]

—Sergeant Elmer T. Straub
150th Field Artillery, 42nd Division

One afternoon I was out alone repairing telephone wire in the waste of shell holes behind and to the left of our position when I heard faint groaning. I found two doughboys in a shell hole. They had been sleeping there when a shell exploded just inside the shell hole, blowing off their legs. They had done the best they could with first aid packets and tourniquets but they were moribund when I found them. There was nothing I could do. The same night I found a dead stranger in the trench leading to our kitchen hole. The back of his head was crushed in, I suppose by a large shell fragment. All this was beginning to get on my nerves.[35]

—Corporal Horatio Rogers
101st Field Artillery, 26th Division

A shell landed fifty feet away from us. A clod of earth as big as a house flew up and came down on two men who were in the next shell hole chewing the rag over a tin of corn willy. The argument stopped pronto. A half dozen of the rest of us crawled over to dig 'em out. We expected to find 'em in pieces, but they weren't even hurt, just stunned considerable. Their rifles had been hurled out of their hands and the barrels twisted up like corkscrews.

We started back to our own fox hole. Another shell was coming. We heard its whine and dropped flat. Bang! square in a shell hole over to the right—a direct hit. A column of mud and rags, blood and brains and muscle, shot into the air and sprayed us from head to foot. There was nothin' more left of the two men who had been there than of a tomato when you throw it against a brick wall.[36]

—Lieutenant Sam Woodfill
60th Infantry, 5th Division

Early the next morning, October 13, Lieutenant R.N. Derrickson suddenly appeared at the dugout door, stood there for a moment as if dazed, and blurted out: "Grassey, what are you going to do about it? Something has got to be done."

"What's the matter with you?" said Grassey. "Are you crazy?"

"The men are all crazy and I am going crazy," replied Derrickson. "The minenwerfers are blowing us to pieces."

"I will send Lawrence down to relieve you if you can't stand it," said Lieutenant Grassey.

That did not sound so good to me.

Derrickson then said, with much dignity, "I will never desert my men."

"All right," said Grassey. "Go on back."

Derrickson turned and left the dugout and picked his way back to the battered line.[37]

—*Lieutenant Joseph D. Lawrence*
113th Infantry, 29th Division

On the morning of Sunday, October 13th, we were greeted with the news, telephoned down from corps and division headquarters, that Germany and Austria had agreed to President Wilson's terms for an armistice. That they had asked for terms we knew, and also that the President had replied that no armistice could be granted so long as their troops occupied invaded territory and their submarines were engaged in unlawful practices at sea, nor so long as their governments were responsible to anyone except the people themselves. To this the two Central Powers had now replied that they would withdraw their forces from France and Belgium and recall their submarines, and pointed out that such changes had taken place in the governments that those in control were now answerable to the people. This looked like the beginning of capitulation, and hopes ran high that an armistice might be proclaimed which would, at least, give the army a chance to rest. Some grew so hopeful as to place bets that an order to suspend hostilities would be forthcoming within 24 hours. No such order came, however. Rather we were told to increase our efforts to crush and break the German lines.[38]

—*Captain James H. Howard*
304th Field Artillery, 77th Division

The main attack was to resume the second week of October. U.S. divisions in the line from east to west were the 29th and 33rd (26th in reserve); west of the Meuse was III Corps with the 4th, 3rd, and 5th Divisions in the line; V Corps with the 32nd and 42nd Divisions in the line (89th in reserve); and I Corps with the 82nd and 77th Divisions in the line and the 78th in reserve. The 1st, 80th, 90th, and 91st Divisions were in army reserve. Opposing this force were 17 German divisions in the line and six in reserve, but they were largely understrength and weary. The American attack, launched on October 14, was overwhelming.

•

We were suddenly ordered forward to relieve another division, the 1st. The same old jumble of troops and camions and trains on the road, only now the roads more slippery and more in need of repair. Our way led past freshly killed and yet unburied Germans, through unmistakable smell of dead horses to a farm in a valley where we parked our wagons and disposed of our men. The farmhouse had been used as a dressing station for one of the regiments of the other division. Outside was a huge collection of torn and bloody litters, broken salvaged equipment, reddened underclothing and discarded uniforms, all of our own men—the cast off of the dead and wounded. Within, however, was a nice fat Y.M.C.A. man in a suit of blue overalls and a sombrero. He was in attendance at a big cauldron of cocoa while on a stand beside him was bread, and best of all, beef. There could have been no better meal.

The division preceding us had a terrific fight just three days before and the ground was a stew of dead—Boche and American. One attack had evidently been made in the morning mist and as it cleared an entire company was caught on a little rise. The bodies were laid out in rows. It was easy to determine the formation and the plans of the different leaders. In one hole we found a wounded German who had lain there three days afraid to come out—in another, a wounded German and wounded American who had crawled to the same hole, shared their water and cigarettes, and then, rolling into the German's blanket, had gone to sleep. If we read that in a storybook we would not have believed it.[39]

—*Colonel William Donovan*
165th Infantry, 42nd Division

I remember going out in an open space that morning. What I saw I will never forget. There on the ground lay dead Germans and Americans from the 1st Division. I looked them over. One dead U.S. doughboy sat up against a tree where he had died, his rifle leaning against the tree. Another dead U.S. doughboy lay there with a hole in his head big enough for me to lay my hand in.

I needed tobacco bad, and there lay a sack of Bull Durham. It was wet from the rain, but I used it as I knew he never would again. Then a little farther away lay a dead German in a foxhole, a bullet hole in the center of his forehead and a hand grenade clasped in his hand. He lay there on his back stretched out with his eyes wide open. I can still see him there as he lay. I'll never forget that.

That evening our first platoon, which was in the line, needed help, so our platoon was called up there to help them. Along about 2:30 A.M. two of our boys lost both legs halfway to the knees by shell fire as they were sleeping in their foxhole together. I remember it very well as I was called to help them to the dressing station about a mile back. That was terrible too, as we tried to locate a stretcher, but couldn't, so had to use two shelter halves to carry them, causing such suffering as I hadn't seen before. We'd go about 200 feet and then give them a rest. It took three men to carry each man. Doty kept asking for water. We'd give it to him and to Woods also. We were not allowed to smoke, of course. They did want a cigarette so badly. We couldn't give it to them. Towards morning we got them back okay. I've never seen either since. Doty lived and married a war nurse, but I hear Woods died.[40]

—Private Lloyd F. Kindness
150th Machine Gun Battalion, 42nd Division

Early on the morning of the 14th we received orders that the attack would be made in the morning. There were a multitude of things to do and the orders coming so late they could not be done properly. The hour struck and promptly the leading battalion moved out. The Germans at once put down a heavy barrage and swept the hill we had to climb with indirect machine gun fire. The advance did not go well. There were green company commanders with the companies; liaison was not maintained; the barrage was not followed closely; there was not enough punch. There were times when I had to march at the head of the companies to get them forward. They would follow me. New men need some visible symbol of authority. I could see nothing coming up on our right or left. They were crowding in, the resistance was becoming stronger. The preparation had been hurried, proper instructions had not been sent; officers had been killed or wounded. We fought our way to within 500 meters of the line. You know the Germans were entrenched with three parallels of wire and a position they proposed holding. The attack, as is always the case, finally languished. I sent for another battalion. It was late in arriving and in coming into position. Not until 8 P.M. did I get it across, but it too was beaten back. Orders then came to stabilize for the night. I was in a little shell hole with my telephone operator. For mess I had an onion, which was delicious and raw, and two pieces of hard tack. At 1 A.M. the telephone went out and it was impossible to get in touch with the rear. Patrols were sent out to tie with elements on our right and left. I knew an attack would come in the morning, but I had no orders. I did not know how or where it would be launched, what artillery preparation, nothing. The night passed all too quickly. I sent back for food but the lieutenant with his party never returned. Ammunition came up and then at 6.20 the orders for an attack at 7.30. A heavy mist was hanging. I went around to the men and talked to them. All of this was close to the German line. We had gained two kilometers the first day, the 14th.

Tanks were to be near to help us. Zero hour came but no tanks, so we started anyway. I had walked to the different units and was coming back to the telephone when—smash, I felt as if somebody had hit me on the back of the leg with a spiked club. I fell like a log, but after a few minutes managed to crawl into my little telephone hole. A machine gun lieutenant ripped open my breeches and put on the first aid. The leg hurt, but there were many things to do. There was more defense than we thought and the battalion was held up. Messengers I sent through were killed or wounded and messages remained undelivered. We were shelled heavily. Beside me three men were blown up and I was showered with the remnants of their bodies. No communication with the rear as the telephone was still out. Gas was then thrown at us, thick and nasty. Five hours passed. I was getting very groggy but managed to get a message through, withdrawing the unit on the line and putting another in place. Then they carried me back in a blanket. I told them to put me down but they said they were willing to take a chance. At the battalion first aid station they tied a tag to me—Lt. Col. W.J. Donovan G.S.W. right knee, Corbet, M.O., meaning I had received a gunshot wound in the right knee. From there I was carried on a stretcher about $1^1/_2$ kilometer to the regimental dressing station where my wound was dressed and I was placed in an ambulance. A tough three kilometers ride over shell-torn roads to the field hospital. I was hauled out and placed on the ground. It then being determined that there was no immediate need of an operation I was sent back to the Mobile Unit. This was about four kilometers further back and all these rides were damned uncomfortable.

At this hospital I was taken in during a pounding rain. They took a complete record of my name, regiment, rank, nature and date of wound. Then they stripped me and rubbed me over with a warm sponge. It being the first in many days, it was very welcome. Then the anti-tetanus injection. Then on a stretcher and put in a row in the waiting room off the operating room awaiting my turn. Placed on the operating table they saw no need for an operation and putting my left leg in a splint turned me into a ward. I was put between sheets—Think of it! Beside me was an officer shot through the stomach and dying, across two officers coming out of ether and asking the nurse to hold their hands or smooth their brows. In the next ward, a bedlam of delirium. Early in the morning the man next to me died still calling for his wife and children.[41]

—Colonel William Donovan
165th Infantry, 42nd Division

We arrived at what was commonly known as Dead Man's Hill (Samogneaux) on the morning of October 14. Although there was considerable artillery activity, our men found no difficulty in sleeping on the counterslope of this hill. We were eating one meal a day which was served about 6 P.M.

The attack was to be made just at dawn [October 15]. It was made to look comparatively easy, particularly due to the fact that we were to have five French tanks along with us.

The tanks were advancing in echelon formation and four of our men and myself were ahead of them; the remaining men of our platoon flanking these tanks. From the very moment that we jumped off there was an attack upon us from three sides. A flare was sent up from the German lines to inform their commanding officers the attack had started. We found ourselves surrounded, our support units cut off by a concentrated machine gun barrage at the jumping off point. The tanks which were to be of so much assistance to us all stopped within 400 yards of the starting point of the advance. Surviving occupants of these tanks left them and I could see them running toward our lines. Whether they ever reached there, I never learned.

Up to this point about 400 yards out, I was leading the advance platoon. Seventy-five percent of the men of our platoon had either been killed or wounded, and the possibility of any of them getting out alive looked rather doubtful. I was struck by a German hand grenade (potato masher) which opened a gash 13 inches long across my spine. It was pouring rain at the time and that, together with the fact that I was able to crawl to a big shell hole that was filled more than waist high with ice cold water, kept me conscious. The Germans continued throwing hand grenades from the woods we had just passed, and a knee-high infiltration of machine gun bullets playing on our rear prevented our support from coming up. Fortunately, this cold water kept me in pretty good spirits for when I finally reached the dressing station the doctor told me that I should have been dead long before and even went so far as to say he did not expect I would reach the field hospital.

While in this shell hole I had a most unusual experience. Two Germans crawled into the hole with me and apparently thought I was dead, for by this time only the ugly wound was showing above water and I was lying head down with just my nose exposed for breathing purposes. One was so near that he touched me. Both were using this vantage point from which to fire at our men. I watched my opportunity and got rid of one of them which, of course, attracted the other one, and we had a little fight all our own in the shell hole. I received a pistol bullet in the shoulder and have no recollection of what became of him.

It was practically as difficult to get back to the lines as it had been to go forward but I managed after some six hours of crawling to reach the dressing station. I passed many of my men who lay dying on the field and for whom I was unable to get assistance.[42]

—*Lieutenant Ralph W. Robard*
104th Infantry, 26th Division

After dark I inspected the line and found that the men were holding on determinedly but were in bad shape—hungry, wet, caked from head to foot with mud and filth, suffering from dysentery caused by the gas (the woods reeked with gas, and many of the men were care-less about using their masks and consequently were affected before they realized it). When night came I heard someone slipping through the bushes, quickly investigated and found one of my men attempting to slip to the rear; the poor fellow wanted only a few minutes of relief from the hell on the line. This kept up all night, making it necessary for me to patrol the line, at considerable risk; I would drive one man back to his position and another would try to slip by.[43]

—*Lieutenant Joseph D. Lawrence*
113th Infantry, 29th Division

We were expecting confidently to be relieved. So it was something of a blow to us when Captain William Kelley called the sergeants to his P.C. and told us that we must take the hill opposite that day. He was cool and reassuring, but his anxiety for his men was evident.

"We will attack at 11 o'clock this morning," he told us. "There will be a barrage. I know it's tough that we've got to hit it again, but the brigade has been ordered to take the hill, even if it is wiped out in doing it.

"Now, men, it's serious. We're going to have losses. We've only 85 left. We must keep casualties as low as possible. We'll advance one man from each squad at a time. I think that way we can hold losses to the minimum.

"Go back to your men and get them busy at something. Get them to polishing up their rifles, so they know that they'll shoot. Get them to digging to warm up and to take their minds off things. Get their morale as high as you can; we'll need it."

So we told each other, "It won't be very bad," and we knew it would be terrible.

It was terrible. After I had got back to the hospital the next day I still heard the crack-crack-crack of the machine guns we faced all day, and could not sleep.[44]

—*Sergeant Harold N. Denny*
168th Infantry, 42nd Division

Over to my right a shell broke in the middle of the road, right among some infantry, killed about four or five of them. We then went over that way and got into the path of that shell fire. A shell would come and we'd drop down in the ditch. We went on like this until about midnight. I was the gunner then. I am small anyway. That Hotchkiss [machine gun] sure was heavy. We came to a steep hill with a road at the bottom. As we went down that hill, they started shelling again heavy. I fell head first, gun and all. I got up and went to the bottom very carefully after that. They told us not to talk aloud, only whisper, and be as quiet as we could. Finally I got on the road at the bottom of the hill.

Some of our men stumbled into some wire that the Germans had placed there as a trap. When they did that why the Germans opened up with the machine guns and this was the closest call I'd had for some time. I dropped flat on the ground and could hear the bullets sing and whistle all around me. I laid my gun down against the bank and took my pack off and laid it down and got so I could use it for protection. It wasn't much of a protection, but I felt it was a stone wall next to me. Suddenly I heard a dull thud and the man right next to me let out a yelp and said, "I'm hit." I said, "You are," in a low tone and then told him to be as quiet as he could, but he would not be quiet. He got shot in the leg and went back and I have never seen him since. I would like to, though.

Finally the Germans let up their fire after some of our men went down there and bayoneted them. I could hear some German shout, "Heinie, wasser, wasser." Some German wanted his partner to bring him water, but he never got water, as he died soon.[45]

—Private Lloyd F. Kindness
150th Machine Gun Battalion, 42nd Division

The 17th of October, 1918, at about 11:30 A.M., twelve of us were picked from the Machine Gun Company, 165th Infantry, to take a machine gun nest, situated about 300 yards to the left of our position. We left in squad formation. About 200 yards from the enemy position, we spread out and moved slowly ahead under extremely heavy shell fire, large and small caliber.

Nick O'Neil, the champion cigarette bummer, was crawling along on his belly in a ditch. Private Henderson carried the musette bag with the clips and extra barrel. I carried the tripod and other attachments. These things always weigh a ton under the circumstances. After advancing about 100 yards, we crossed a steep embankment which had a 60 degree angle drop. We figured it was a good spot to set up the gun, as there were three trees a little back of us.

In crossing the embankment, a shell came over; missing the tops of our heads, it dug a hole which seemed to us as big as the Grand Canyon. Afterwards we were told it buried several men alive. Another hit the roots of the tree nearest us, knocking it down. By some miracle, it missed Henderson and myself in falling. The branches of the tree just brushed us while fragments of the shell slightly wounded both of us. A third shell hit the stony part of the embankment, spraying shrapnel over us and adding more misery as it broke my leg in two places. The shells seemed to rain around us at this point. They dropped all around the corner of the embankment, under which we were luckily sheltered by the three trees which had fallen across one another, giving us some protection and undoubtedly saving our lives.

Fearing loss of blood would finally bring unconsciousness, I dragged myself slowly and as best I could by using some shrubbery growing along the embankment. When I finally got to the top, I found that the shelling had increased. However, I cheered up on finding that there were four men in a shell hole not far off. They were unable to reach me because of the shells which forced them to stay put. I crawled back down the embankment. In coming down this steep slope, my leg, which had been broken above the knee, flopped over and the heel of my hobnail shoe hit me on the head in back of the ear. It almost knocked me unconscious. However, I was only dazed for few minutes.

Soon after the shelling ceased and four men from B or D Company came over the embankment to my aid. Using a blanket as a stretcher, they wormed their way out to our dressing station situated in an orchard.

Just as they were approaching the dressing station, the blanket split right down the middle and I found myself in the mud. I hit it like a ton of brick. Just then a gas shell came over, so the boys had to beat it again for a hole and adjust their masks. After about twenty minutes, they came back, picked me up and carried me to a dressing station.[46]

—Private Joseph B. Connolly
165th Infantry, 42nd Division

Diary: Oct. 19: Going to and from the O.P. we also go through a valley that has gained the name of "Death Valley" because the Germans shell it so much and never fail to get at least one each time. All through this valley one can see American dead lying about and it seems as if the first aid men who are supposed to litter these men off do not do their work properly because these dead Americans ought to be taken away immediately after they are killed; it is certainly a gruesome looking place. On our way back I took a shortcut and got into some sneezing gas. I was afraid to run my horse as he is so poor that I thought he would drop dead; I have been sneezing ever since.

Diary: Oct. 22: Last night just after we had all gone to bed (they always wait until after we have gone to bed) Lieut. [Charles D.] Clift blew his whistle for all noncoms and twenty minutes later found all of them assembled in the Captain's dugout. The Captain then read an order and it sure was a 'peach,' since our infantry is so shot up and have failed to take their objective they have asked each artillery outfit for 68 privates, 4 corporals, 3 sergeants and one second lieutenant to act as infantry during the next attack. They asked for volunteers and most of the fellows jumped for the chance. I put my name in with the rest of them, but they would not let me go. All the men were to get rifles, ammunition belts and doughboy packs immediately and be ready at a moment's notice to go . . .

From 2 until 4:30 we watched the effect of our fire on two small woods; while we were there an infantry major came up and told us a lot of the reports given out by General Pershing while inspecting our sector. They say that he relieved several of the officers of their high commands. He also said that we would stay here until we had reached our objective and held it. He also said if there were only two men left that the Brigade Commander should take them over the top. Failure to gain an objective would be no explanation.[47]

—*Sergeant Elmer T. Straub*
150th Field Artillery, 42nd Division

There has been . . . a tendency to exaggerate losses and casualties by the use of some of the following expressions:
"All shot to pieces."
"Held up by machine guns or machine gun fire."
"Suffered enormous losses."
"Men all exhausted."
All officers and soldiers are forbidden to use such expressions in official messages, reports, conversations or discussions. They are generally misleading and always do harm. An exact statement of the facts will convey the necessary information.[48]

—*V Corps Directive*
Major General Charles P. Summerall

General Order No. 35, Hdqrs. III, American Corps, stated: "This soldier absented himself from his organization in time of battle or impending battle, with no apparent cause except fear."

The foregoing was to be sent as a letter to the father, mother or nearest relative of the soldier; copies will be sent to the postmaster and the mayor of his hometown, and to his sweetheart, if she is known. A copy was to be posted on the company street.

I think a coward wrote this order. Only a coward could know so well what another coward dreads. Every soldier at the moment of battle trembles, is afraid and wishes he could escape from it. The noise is dreadful; the men rush forward, never walk; each one is watchful lest a companion may read fear in his face; no one cries out lest he be shot down; thus the whole regiment goes into battle, playing the part of bravery, yet sick of the whole business.[49]

—Army Field Clerk Will Judy
33rd Division

Four of us occupied a place in an unfinished dugout, which was just large enough for us if we lay on our sides. But to turn over was impossible. The cooties bothered me too much and as I was unable to defend myself, I crawled out and went down the stairs still further. I had gone down about 30 steps when I heard someone breathing. I said, "Who's here?"

"Are you after me?" anxiously asked a voice.

"No," I replied. "Why do you ask?"

"Because I am hiding here. I have been here almost two days."

"What are you hiding for?" I asked.

"To be honest with you, I am afraid." Then he continued, "I am from Company———and I know that this war is nearly over. I have been through the whole thing and have never been a coward before. But I'll admit that I am one now. I want to go back to the States and I know that if I go over the top again, I will be killed."

"Don't be afraid of me squealing. The best of luck to you."

The enemy had the range of that dugout and all night long could be heard the plop of machine gun bullets in the mud at the entrance. They came over about every ten minutes.[50]

—Private F.C. Wilder
101st Infantry, 26th Division

None of the Company K officers was on hand; two had been wounded, one lost his mind temporarily from fright and fled to the rear, and the captain remained in a dugout, winning for himself the nickname of "Dugout Pete." The lieutenant, Young, who fled to the rear, mistook me for a German in his ravings and nearly shot me before I could convince him otherwise. All of Company M's officers had been killed or wounded except Fred Sexton, and he was killed the next night.[51]

—Lieutenant Joseph D. Lawrence
113th Infantry, 29th Division

There was a dead infantryman lying beside the road just opposite the kitchen. One day someone covered the face with a slicker to keep the rain off, but the next day the wind had blown the slicker away. He was still there when we left.[52]

—Corporal Horatio Rogers
101st Field Artillery, 26th Division

Combat wagons kept passing us, loaded with dead. Once a long train of them went by us. They were trucks, 12 or 14 feet long, four feet deep and three or four feet wide, each drawn by six mules. They were loaded to the top. It seemed to me that not another leg or another arm could have been crowded into them.

It was still raining. The road was a quagmire. The mules were struggling and straining through the mud. As one of the wagons passed us, a body fell out and we helped put it back. He was a young fellow. His back was so stiff you couldn't bend it.

Along in the afternoon we found a soldier lying in the mud at the side of the road. He was through, he said. He'd made up his mind to lie down there and die. We had a tough time getting him up and making him try to go on with us. Every few minutes he'd stop and start to lie down again. When we wouldn't let him, he'd cry and say all he wanted to do was die.

Finally Floyd jabbed him with his trench knife and said, "Damn you, I'll kill you if you don't shut up and keep goin'!"

He staggered along after that. We didn't hear any more about his wanting to die.[53]

—Private John L. Barkley
4th Infantry, 3rd Division

My people at home, hearing what I was passing through, expected me to come back hard, brutal, callous, careless. But I didn't even want to take a dead mouse out of a trap when I was home.

Yet over there I buried 78 men one morning. I didn't dig the holes for them, of course, but I did take their personal belongings from them to return to their people—their rings, trinkets, letters and identification tags. They were shot up in a great variety of ways and it was not pleasant, but I managed to eat my quota of bread and meat when it came up with no opportunity to wash my hands

One night I was hiking along through the darkness. We fell out for a moment by the side of the road and I sat on what I thought was a partially buried sandbag. After resting there for a time, a comrade told me that I was sitting on a dead man. I didn't even move. I didn't think he would mind.

At times men died in such a position that they were hard to bury. The ground was hard; there was danger of shell fire . . . We'd try hard to make the graves as decent as possible. So often men were buried in the holes other men had dug along the side of the road as they advanced. A rifle or bayonet would be thrust in the ground at the head of the grave and a man's identification tag placed on it.

Soon the remainder of the army would be moving up—the machine gunners, the artillery, the supply trucks. They would have to pass on a narrow road. The truck would run over the grave and knock down the improvised cross; there was no other way to identify the dead man.

When a man died in a sitting or kneeling position it was impossible to straighten him out—difficult to dig a deep enough hole to cover him. More than once I would try to straighten out the body—stand on the legs and the head would come up; finally compromise by burying the upper body, letting the legs stick up for a cross and hanging the helmet and gas mask to the human cross. Other times it was necessary to put a big man in a comparatively small hole. We would step on his middle and bend it sufficiently to make him fit the hole.[54]

—Lieutenant Bob Hoffman
111th Infantry, 28th Division

*A*s the fighting dragged on and casualties mounted, more and more replacements, many with only cursory training, were fed into the lines as the demand for manpower outstripped the time needed to adequately train the troops. Among the newcomers arriving in France that fall was Corporal Richard A. Pierce.

•

We drilled in the so called mud camp [Camp Wadsworth, S.C.] for a few days; we were given a lot of instruction about "saluting," and then were shipped to Hoboken for shipment to France. [In France] we were given 5 *minutes* of rifle instruction. It went like this: "Unstrap your gun, get in prone position, and aim at the enemy between the legs above the knees. In the excitement of battle, you will shoot higher and probably hit his stomach."[55]

—Corporal Richard A. Pierce
57th Pioneer Infantry

At this time enough replacements were received to bring the regiment up to approximate battle strength. The first detachment consisted of 320 splendid men from the National Guard of Texas and Oklahoma, who, having seen months of service in the States, were well-trained, well-disciplined, and fully equipped.

So much could not be said of the 647 men who came to us in two groups soon after. They were for the most part drafted men from the East, far below the mental and physical standard of the original cadre. Many of them were unable to read, write or speak English; and, more than that, most of them had never fired a rifle. They had never heard of a skirmish line, and couldn't have told the difference between a grenade and a platoon. This is the report that was turned in from the Second Battalion: "Investigation discloses the fact that not more than half of them have had over a month's training of any sort, and that few of them have had any instruction whatsoever in gas protection, or in the use of rifle, auto-rifle, and grenades."

The commander of Company H reported that out of one group of 43 assigned him one man had had but one week of training; four had had two weeks; 20, three weeks; six, four weeks; and the rest anywhere between one and three months.[56]

—*Lieutenant John H. Taber*
168th Infantry, 42nd Division

About 10 o'clock in the morning a chow detail of 15 men joined us. There were also several signal corps men and six officers. The chow they had brought was canned salmon and canned apricots. I drew salmon. It made me sick. And I wasn't the only one.

The new officers began making themselves unpopular as soon as they arrived. They were replacements. Not a front line officer in the lot. The men were all too desperate to be bothered with forms and they weren't very respectful.

One of the officers said, "What's the matter with this goddamn hard-boiled outfit? They go round here getting sick like babies!"

About noon a lieutenant from one of the 7th Infantry companies worked his way up to us. He was a front line officer and he got plenty of respect. He had three of his own men with him. The lieutenant told [us] we'd done pretty well and ordered us to stay where we were. He left us one of the new officers and took the rest away with him. They came under fire just as they left the position. One of the new men we hadn't liked was knocked off. He'd been at the front just long enough to get his boots muddy.[57]

—*Private John L. Barkley*
4th Infantry, 3rd Division

Notes

1. Thomas M. Johnson and Fletcher Pratt, *The Lost Battalion.* (New York: The Bobbs-Merrill Company, 1938), p. 307.

2. A. Lincoln Lavine, *Circuits of Victory.* (Garden City, N.Y.: Country Life Press, 1921), pp. 568–569.

3. Johnson and Pratt, *The Lost Battalion*, pp. 205–206.

4. L.C. McCollum, *History And Rhymes of the Lost Battalion.* (n.p., 1929), pp. 65–74.

5. Lavine, *Circuits of Victory*, p. 569.

6. Johnson and Pratt, *The Lost Battalion*, p. 253.

7. Miles, *History of the 308th Infantry*, p. 243.

8. American Battle Monuments Commission, *American Armies and Battlefields in Europe.* (Washington, D.C.: GPO, 1938), p. 175–176.

9. Casey, *The Cannoneers Have Hairy Ears*, pp. 204–204.

10. Minder, *This Man's War*, pp. 331–332.

11. Harvey Cushing, *From a Surgeon's Journal.* (Boston: Little, Brown and Company, 1936), p. 462.

12. Maverick, *A Maverick American*, p. 127.

13. Noble, *Jugheads Behind the Lines*, pp. 129–130.

14. American Battle Monuments Commission, *American Armies and Battlefields in Europe*, p. 178.

15. Maverick, *A Maverick American*, pp. 127–133.

16. Barkley, *No Hard Feelings*, pp. 169–170.

17. Wise, *A Marine Tells It to You*, p. 278.

18. Barkley, *No Hard Feelings*, p. 181.

19. Joseph B. Sanborn, *The 131st Infantry in the World War.* (Chicago: n.p., 1919), p. 317.

20. *Ibid.*, p. 326.

22. *Ibid.*, p. 328.

23. *Ibid.*, p. 332.

24. *Ibid.*, p. 335.

25. *Ibid.*, p. 349.

26. *Ibid.*, p. 351.

26. *Ibid.*, p. 359.

27. American Battle Monuments Commission, *American Armies and Battlefields in Europe*, p. 183.

28. Thomas F. Meehan, *History of the Seventh-Eighth Division in the World War 1917–18–19.* (Wilmington, Del.: Mercantile Printing Company, 1921), p. 84.

29. Young, *Over the Top With the 80th*, unpaged.

30. Minder, *This Man's War*, pp. 323–324.

31. Albertine, *The Yankee Doughboy*, pp. 221–223.

32. Minder, *This Man's War*, pp. 354–355.

33. Wrentmore, *In Spite of Hell*, pp. 138–139.

34. Straub, *A Sergeant's Diary*, p. 204.

35. Rogers, *Diary of an Artillery Scout*, p. 230.

36. Thomas, *Woodfill of the Regulars*, p. 291.

37. Lawrence, *The Fighting Soldier*, p. 117.

38. Howard, *The Autobiography of a Regiment*, p. 186.

39. Sweeney, *History of Buffalo and Erie County*, p. 289.

40. Reilly, *Americans All*, pp. 713–715.

41. Sweeney, *History of Buffalo and Erie County*, p. 289.

42. Fifield, *The Regiment*, pp. 291–295.

43. Lawrence, *The Fighting Soldier*, p. 123.

44. Taber, *The Story of the 168th Infantry*, p. 188.

45. Reilly, *Americans All*, pp. 838–839.

46. *Ibid.*, pp. 702–703.

47. Straub, *A Sergeant's Diary*, p. 199.

48. Charles F. Dienst, *They're from Kansas: History of the 353rd Infantry.* (Wichita, Kans.: Regimental Society, the 353rd Infantry, 1921), p. 111.

49. Judy, *A Soldier's Diary*, pp. 150–151.

50. Wilder, *War Experiences*, p. 113.

51. Lawrence, *Fighting Soldier*, p. 102.

52. Rogers, *Diary of an Artillery Scout*, p. 236.

53. Barkley, *No Hard Feelings*, pp. 257–258.

54. Hoffman, *I Remember the Last War*, pp. 165–167.

55. Moses N. Thisted, *Pershing's Pioneer Infantry of World War I.* (Hemet, Calif.: Alphabet Printers, 1982), p. 29.

56. Taber, *The Story of the 168th Infantry*, pp. 58–59.

57. Barkley, *No Hard Feelings*, pp. 232–234.

CHAPTER 14

To the Bitter End

*E*ven as Americans and Germans slaughtered each other by the thou- *sands in the Meuse-Argonne, another insidious killer made its appear- ance—Spanish Influenza, or "the flu." Among the first to be stricken was an enlisted man of Company D, 42nd Infantry, who reported to the infir- mary at Camp Devens, Massachusetts, in September with a sore throat, fever, and severe pain in his back. The next day, 12 more soldiers from the same unit reported with similar symptoms. By September 18, 600 men were bedridden and there were so many dead the corpses had to be stored in the quartermaster sheds. On September 20 alone there were 1,543 new cases.*

It was the start of the most terrible epidemic the United States had ever known. In the army camps in the United States, one of every four men came down with influenza; one of every 24 developed pneumonia; one of every 67 died. There was no cure. The epidemic reached its peak in September- October-November, then gradually tapered off. But before running its course, the flu took a worldwide toll of 21,642,000 men, women, and chil- dren. A total of 548,452 Americans, soldiers and civilians at home and in France, died. In some places there weren't enough coffins for all the dead.

•

Men in apparently splendid health and perfect physical condition were suddenly desperately ill, and many of them dead in less than 48 hours. One week in October 1918, there was a series of nearly 100 "flu" and pneumonia cases of whom over 80 percent died. Of course some of these were nearly dead when we took them out of the ambulances, and never rallied, dying a few hours after they reached the wards. In fact, it happened more than once when a large convoy of ambulances came in from around St. Mihiel or up towards Verdun that one or more had died on the way.[1]

—Dr. John G. Nelson
Base Hospital #45

We had proceeded but a short distance to the New York docks when it was discovered that the men were falling out of ranks, unable to keep up. The attention of the commanding officer was called to the situation. The column was halted and the camp surgeon was summoned. The examination showed that the dreaded influenza had hit us. Although many men had fallen out we were ordered to resume the march. We went forward up and up over the winding moonlight road leading to Alpine Landing on the Hudson where ferry boats were waiting to take us to Hoboken.

The victims of the epidemic fell on either side of the road unable to carry their heavy packs. Some threw their equipment away and with determination tried to keep up with their comrades. Army trucks and ambulances following, picked up those who had fallen and took them back to the camp hospital. How many men or how much equipment was lost on that march has never been determined.

On board the transport men continued to be stricken and 100 of these were taken off and returned to shore before sailing. On Sunday afternoon Sept. 29th, tugs pulled the great ship into midstream, turned her bow in the direction of the open ocean, the great propellers began to turn and we were off to the Great Adventure. We had on board 9,033 officers and men and about 200 army nurses on their way to hospitals in France. The presence of the nurses was very fortunate as it afterwards turned out. The ship was packed, conditions were such that the influenza bacillus could breed and multiply with extraordinary swiftness. We went much of the way without convoy. The U-boat menace made it necessary to keep every port hole closed at night, and the air below decks where the men slept was hot and heavy. The number of sick increased rapidly. Washington was appraised of the situation, but the call for men for the Allied armies was so great that we must go on at any cost. The sick bay became overcrowded and it became necessary to evacuate the greater portion of Deck E and turn that into sick quarters. Doctors and nurses were stricken. Every available doctor and nurse was utilized to the limit of endurance.

The official government report now on file with the Navy Department has this to say in regard to the conditions on board the *Leviathan:* "The conditions during the night cannot be visualized by anyone who has not actually seen them. Pools of blood from severe nasal hemorrhages of many patients were scattered throughout the compartments, and the attendants were powerless to escape tracking through the mess, because of the narrow passages between the bunks. The decks became wet and slippery, groans and cries of the terrified added to the confusion of the applicants clamoring for treatment, and altogether a true inferno reigned supreme."

We landed at Brest October 7th and all who were able to march were moved to the mud flats beyond the Pontanezan Barracks, where we remained until October 11th. Several hundred of the men never reached camp or their organizations. They were picked up by the Y.M.C.A. and K.C. [Knights of Columbus] men or by army ambulances and taken to hospitals as soon as they were unable to walk. Official records show that within a few days after landing 123 of the men died at Kerhuon Hospital, about 40 at Base Hospital No. 33, several at Naval Base Hospital No. 5 and at the hospital at Landernau.

Nearly 200 of the regiment were buried in the American cemetery at Lambezellec.[2]

—Colonel E.W. Gibson
57th Pioneer Infantry

The young women nurse interns from the Vassar Camp were placed at once on the "firing line" in the more than thirty hospitals where they had chosen to complete their nursing education. Here, as in nearly all hospitals, influenza patients overflowed the wards in the worst epidemic the world has ever known, not to exclude the Black Death. Patients had to be placed in beds made on chairs, on the floor, even on shelves. At Ann Arbor, Michigan, the second floor of an old gymnasium was converted into a flu ward—and the floor collapsed. It was common for ambulances to bring in soldiers, sailors and civilians during an evening. By morning, the undertaker's cars were at the doors to claim them. The disease seemed to have a special affinity for those of fine physique. When they had apparently recovered from the initial attack, they were stricken by pneumonia, became cyanosed, and died when their lungs filled. They actually drowned in their own fluids. Together with pneumonia germs, a deadly red-blood cell dissolver known as streptococcus hemolytic abetted the work of the unknown cause of the influenza attack. Pfeiffer's bacillus was accused, but the doctors felt that the cause must be a virus, although they could not isolate it.

Dr. Martha Wollstein of the Rockefeller Institute believed the organism was a filterable virus, capable of many mutations. This was verified by the electronic microscope by the year 1933. Other types of influenza virus were isolated and reproduced in ferrets in the laboratory but the true virus of Spanish Influenza has never been discovered. It was found that the port of entry was through the nasal mucous membrane. The influenza virus A and B under the electronic microscope resembles a fluffy cotton ball with twenty to thirty million organisms on a spot as large as a pin head.[3]

—Gladys B. Clappison
Nurse

The beds in the medical wards were soon filled, and an order was received from the Surgeon-General's Office that only emergency operations should be performed. Gradually the beds in the surgical wards were filled with patients suffering from influenza. Ambulances were constantly bringing patients and soon barracks were taken over as wards. Officers as well as enlisted men were stricken. One of the first to die was the Commanding Officer of the Hospital, Colonel Doer, a fine type of gentleman, loved and respected by both officers and enlisted men.

The mortality from the epidemic was exceedingly high and there were periods when it was impossible to obtain coffins for several days. Corpses accumulated in the morgue and shipment of bodies to homes was delayed. Extra beds and cots were placed in the wards and the nurses, orderlies and medical officers were obliged to work there with but little rest.

At the peak of the epidemic the scene in the wards was most depressing. Patients were being admitted and corpses removed. Sometimes a patient was obliged to remain on a litter until a body was removed from a bed. Delirious patients were noisy and at times it was difficult to keep them in bed. Often restraint was necessary. There was incessant coughing and moaning. Nurses were stricken and several died. The nursing corps was overworked but continued to spend long hours in the wards.

The medical profession was impotent to control the disease. An attempt was made to prevent communication of the disease by requiring officers, nurses and orderlies to wear masks, made of several layers of gauze, placed over the mouth and nose. These masks were worn for about three weeks, and gave those wearing them a grotesque appearance.

I was constantly reminded of the days of the Black Plague, and the fact that men and women kept their heads indicates that civilization has made progress since the Dark Ages.

Anxious friends were telephoning and telegraphing for reports, and frequently came long distances to be near a sick son, brother, husband, or sweetheart. In several instances the visiting member of the family was taken ill and had to be sent to a hospital in Washington. One mother came from a state in the Middle West in response to a telegram announcing the serious illness of her son. She arrived in the afternoon of a dark day in early November. The boy was dead. The frail middle-aged mother, plainly dressed in black, was overwhelmed by silent grief and requested to be alone. She wandered along a road through the woods, and when looked for by a nurse, late in the evening, was found seated on a log. She declined the urgent request of the nurse to come to the Nurses' Home, and spent the night alone in the woods. In the morning, she appeared at the hospital, composed. She had found herself, and with wonderful poise gave directions for shipping the remains of her son and left for her home in the afternoon.

It seems impossible [now, in 1931] that such grief and human sacrifice can appear so far away.[4]

—*Dr. Grant C. Mandill*
Camp Humphries, Va.

M *eanwhile, back in the Meuse-Argonne, the fighting ground on. By mid-October, the blood toll stood at 75,000 doughboys—with another 11,000 a week being felled by influenza. But there was growing evidence that the Germans were nearing collapse.*

•

On the morning of the 22nd a number of Germans opposite our right position appeared and indicated they wanted to surrender. Our men indicated to them to come one at a time, but the French on the right caught sight of them, and not knowing what was up, opened fire and they ducked for cover, thus spoiling a good-sized surrender. About noon an English-speaking German asked for permission to advance and leave a paper. This was granted and he advanced to within a short distance of the line, leaving a note which said, "In the night not shooting." A little later another German came over and left a German newspaper and a note which said, "If we must shoot, we shoot high. What will you make?"[5]

—*Captain James Brown*
104th Infantry, 26th Division

On the 102nd's front, the Boche trenches were only one hundred yards away from our own. They were held by Saxons of a Landwehr regiment, and on the 20th of October, some of the Boches came out of their trench and began to make gestures to our men to come over.

The Yankees stayed where they were but waved to the Germans to come over to them. This the Huns were afraid to do. Finally Sergeant Major Wax and Mechanic Rechen, both of whom spoke German, jumped out of the trench, went across No Man's Land and up to the Boche trench, to see what was wanted. The man who had waved to them, and thirty-seven other Germans—one of whom was a lieutenant—came and gathered round the Americans.

"What did you want?" asked Wax.

"We want you to stop shooting at us," said the spokesman for the Huns. "We are Saxons here. We know that the war is over. There is no use in going on fighting; we are not barbarians and we don't want to kill unnecessarily."

"You'd better come over and surrender, the whole bunch of you," said the Americans.

"No, we won't do that. We should be sent far away into the interior of France, and the war is so nearly over that the long journey isn't worthwhile."

"You'd get good treatment."

"We can't do it anyway . . . But we don't want to kill Americans. We have had plenty of chances to shoot you in the last few days and haven't done it. When we have been ordered to fire by our officers we have fired high, purposely."

"Why don't your people retreat, then?" asked the Yankees.

"They can't. If they could only go in peace, they would. But if we retreat, your artillery will shoot us in the back. We can't retreat without being killed. Anyway, we won't fire on you unless we are attacked. You can go out without fear to bury your dead; in fact, we have buried some of your dead ourselves. We know the war is over and we know the Hohenzollerns are out of power. We are going to have a republican government in Germany."

"Well," said the Yankees, "the only way you Germans can get peace is to stop fighting, and the easiest way to stop fighting is to come over and surrender. You'd better think it over till tomorrow about this same time, and then tell us what you think."

The Yankees sauntered back to their own trench and the war was on again.[6]

—Frank R. Sibley
Boston Globe *Correspondent, 26th Division*

*T*he American First Army planned to renew the attack in overwhelming force on November 1. Order of battle from the Meuse River to the west was: the III Corps with the 5th and 90th Divisions in the line and the 32nd in reserve; V Corps with the 89th and 2nd Division in the line and the 1st and 42nd in reserve; and I Corps with the 80th, 77th, and 78th Division in the line and the 6th and 82nd in reserve. The 3rd, 29th, and 36th Divisions made up the First Army reserve.

The capture of Barricourt Heights in the V Corps sector was expected to compel a German retirement across the Meuse.

•

We had been under fire almost continuously the last week of October, making no reply. The soldiers' nerves were strained nearly to breaking. It was random firing but that was no consolation to the men who were hit. Every night we were encouraged by the enormous loads of ammunition shipped up to us, and, from the huge and stealthy preparations, we knew that the drive in contemplation would be crushing. Guns were massed more thickly than ever before, in places hub to hub, and extra infantry of the best caliber were brought, we were told, from other sectors.[7]

—Private L.V. Jacks
119th Field Artillery, 32nd Division

We left the trucks at Sainte-Menehould and followed a winding, climbing road up into the tree-clad hills of the lower Argonne. There had been very little rain for some time and an early frost had had a chance to work its magic in the trees. Men said it was the most beautiful autumn they could remember. You watched them grab at vivid-colored leaves that drifted by or kick their way through windblown piles along the roads the way that children do.[8]

—Private Elton E. Mackin
5th Marines, 2nd Division

*T*he American assault jumped off at daybreak, November 1, after a two-hour barrage. The progress of the attack exceeded all expectations.

•

In the morning, at the jump-off, I followed the first wave of Marines up to the edge of the woods. I stayed there a while watching. As like all mornings in that position, there was a mist coming up from the ground. You couldn't see much at first. I never heard any artillery like it.

As the light came up and the mist cleared, it looked as if a volcano was riding right up the hill to the front. The Marine units just marched behind it in a line of skirmishers and the usual attack formation. I suppose, though, that coming through the woods and trenches must have broken it up as it didn't look any too regular at that stage.

After the first couple of battalions had passed, I went down towards the town to see what had happened. Just before I left the edge of the woods, a German came in with his hands up. Spoke broken English. He hadn't been hit. He said that he hadn't seen anything like that barrage in four years. He told one of my men that he had been a bartender in Brooklyn. Then I joined the outfit and went back.[9]

—Major Thomas T. Reilly
165th Infantry, 42nd Division

After our shoot we decided to go over with the first wave of infantry and see if we had actually landed any bombs in the enemy machine gun emplacements. You can imagine our delight when we found that we had actually completely destroyed a graveyard with its trench system and two strongly fortified machine gun emplacements.

While we were looking over the damage we had caused and were collecting souvenirs from the many dead enemy, the Germans changed their barrage and laid it down along the road and in the town. When the shells began to fall we naturally sought cover in the trenches. We all headed for a shallow dugout. In the scramble we landed practically in the laps of a German medical lieutenant and two orderlies. For a few minutes nobody knew who was surrendering to whom as there was so much "Kamerading" going on.

Finally, after the barrage had lifted, we left the dugout to continue our survey and collection of souvenirs after sending the prisoners to the rear. The German lieutenant told us we had caught the machine gun section in the midst of a relief and had practically wiped out both detachments. We found a German major among the dead with his head practically blown off, dressed in a brand new uniform with a gorgeous pair of new Cordovan boots and belt of the same material. He had on all his campaign ribbons. He looked like he might have been dressed to attend a formal military function instead of being in the front line on the eve of a major battle. There was considerable scrambling for his decorations, belt and pistol.[10]

—Captain J. Woodall Greene
117th Trench Mortar Battery, 42nd Division

By 7:30, groups of Boche prisoners began to appear, driven along by Marines. The latter were on the right of the 80th Division and they seemed to be living up to their reputation. All day, in gradually increasing numbers, their captives marched past our positions. Someone counted those that went by along one road: there were 1,563. We went out and spoke with some of them as they halted at a crossroads. A miserable lot they were, for the most part, pale and worn and dirty, and apparently glad to be out of the fight.

"When do you think the war will end?" we asked several.

"In about a week," was the usual reply.

Now and then an officer marched, grim and defiant, with his men. One of these was standing by while the privates were hustled into a truck to be taken to the rear.

"Now then, you get aboard," ordered the driver when the men were all in. The officer started to climb up into the seat. "No, not here. Get in with the rest," said the driver.

"Do you mean to say," said the officer, in perfect English, "that you expect an officer to ride with the privates?"

"Oh, so that's bothering you, is it? We'll soon fix that." Ripping out his knife, he cut the shoulder straps from the officer's uniform. "Now," said he, "you're a private. Get in!"[11]

—*Captain James H. Howard*
304th Field Artillery, 77th Division

*O*n the first day of the attack V Corps crushed all opposition. By early afternoon the doughboys had advanced about six miles and captured the Barrincourt Heights, clinching the success of the operation. On the right, III Corps also made a deep advance. On the left, I Corps, facing the unbroken Hindenburg Line on most of its front, attacked and made an average gain of about a half mile.

Their artillery positions overrun, the German High Command issued orders the night of November 1 for a withdrawal from west of the Meuse—a decision that required a general retirement along the whole battle line as far as Holland if the Germans were to avoid a decisive military defeat.

•

It was almost 3 A.M. November 3 when we reached the town of Marcq, where we halted to await orders. The men found shelter in barns and deserted houses.

The first thing noticed, when going through the houses, was the evidence of the hasty retreat. The former German quarters were in terrible disorder; unfinished meals were on the tables, and one in particular held five portions of sauerkraut all ready to be eaten.

For the souvenir hunter, it was a harvest. Nothing in that line, from a life-sized photograph of the Kaiser to a mustache curling iron, was unavailable. German officers' helmets were plentiful. In one building, a German flag had been cast in a corner of the floor like a rag. Posters, urging money from the public to carry on the war for the Vaterland, were tacked everywhere. Entrance to most of the houses was blocked by the debris inside. Beautiful antique furniture, clocks, bric-a-brac and other works of art were piled up in huge masses of rubbish.

A few hundred yards from the village church, a house had been used for a German hospital. Inside were operating tables, many surgical instruments, bottles of hermetically sealed medicine, bandages, splints and other valuable articles which had been left behind in the haste of the retreat. On the wall was a huge red poster picturing a dragon, its head a caricature of President Wilson. In its claws were clutched bags of gold. Close by, a German soldier was poised ready to slay the dragon with a spear. Underneath was an appeal for money, to help do away with the Americans. It made one smile, for the booming of the guns was becoming fainter and fainter as the Germans, instead of doing away with the Americans, ran away from them as fast as possible.

One of the officers found a letter in his quarters written by a German officer to his wife. One portion of it, translated, read as follows—"The Americans are here. We can kill them but we can't stop them."[12]

—Sergeant Howard L. Fisher
306th Field Artillery, 77th Division

We arrived in position at 10 P.M. on November 5th, hiking eight kilometers. We laid our guns and went to bed in the mud and rain with nothing to cover us but a tarpaulin. We got up in the morning and as we were almost barefooted and our socks were wet, we went out to look for some German boots and socks. We found plenty of boots and socks as the Germans left all kinds of equipment behind them. There were also a number of German dead by their machine guns. We could see that the guns had been used continuously, as there were thousands of empty cartridges on the ground. After we changed socks and put on the German boots we started to look around. We saw a big monument about three hundred meters to the right of the main road. This monument was on a hill and parallel with it were three lines of German machine gun emplacements, which were pretty well camouflaged. Our infantry had run right into these trenches and were surprised by the Germans. They met with heavy losses as we could see them stretched all over the fields where they had been shot down. There were a few dead Germans who had been bayoneted by our men. All of the dead soldiers, and there were about five hundred, had their pockets turned inside out; someone had looked through them during the night for money and valuables.[13]

—Sergeant Anthony D. Cone
15th Field Artillery, 2nd Division

The roads became a morass. Animals died in traces trying to pull loads through. Tractors were being used continuously to pull out stalled trucks. During the day casualties piled up in the advanced positions with no ambulances available for evacuation; they were not able to get forward. To add to the "horrors of war," men were becoming ravaged with dysentery. Slightly wounded men sent to the rear by walking, died on the way from the combination of wounds, exposure and dysentery. The use of our trucks for emergency moves seemed improbable during the day, and they were offered for the evacuation of wounded. Over 600 wounded were thus sent to the rear, the trucks bringing up ammunition and supplies on their return trips.[14]

—Lieutenant Wendell Westover
4th Machine Gun Battalion, 2nd Division

Losses had been heavy. Some were due to battle—wounds and death—but most were caused by sickness, dysentery and flu. Men, weakened, sought a place of fancied shelter in the brush. They sometimes wrapped a sodden blanket around them and slept. And in sleeping, they died. Exposure, hunger, and sickness took a toll in other ways. One fellow used a bullet on himself and found relief.[15]

—Private Elton C. Mackin
5th Marines, 2nd Division

Captain Arthur Y. Wear had recently been discharged from the hospital and was weak and nervous. His command had been through severe fighting . . . Evidently his mind gave way under the strain of events and of his depleted physical condition. . . . [G]oing a little aside from his headquarters in the dismal woods, at about 3 o'clock in the morning, he ended his life by shooting himself through the head.[16]

—Lieutenant Colonel George H. English
89th Division

Up on the Meuse, where Captain Wear died, we had been advancing night and day for five days. The pace was killing and the strain on him with the responsibility of the whole battalion must have been terrible. We were trying to cross the river, but the Germans had blown out all of the bridges and it was impossible. The battalion was in an exposed, dangerous place. Captain Wear gave the order to withdraw the battalion, then shot himself. I am positive in my mind that he believed that he was saving his men at the cost of his own life.

I was nowhere near him at the time. He sent word to me by his orderly to write his brother, Jim, and say simply that he was "weary and tired."[17]

—Lieutenant Joseph J. Hook
356th Infantry, 89th Division

Though the doughboys could not know it, the end was near. On November 3 elements of the 5th Division managed to establish a bridgehead across the Meuse River. By November 6, the doughboys were across the river in strength and the Germans had no chance of stopping them.

The German government had already extended peace feelers to the Allies. The Kaiser abdicated and Germany erupted into revolution. On the night of November 7 a German armistice delegation crossed into the French lines. At 5:10 A.M. on November 11, the Germans signed the armistice agreement. There were no Americans present, though doughboys held 21 percent of the front (83 miles) and had two million men in France.

Peace was to go into effect at 11 A.M. on November 11. The doughboys were ordered to keep the pressure on until the last tick of the clock.

●

It was another very misty, cold morning, and it felt as if it was going to snow. A Medical Corps man arrived and gave the boys who had colds some aspirin tablets. At ten thirty—it was November 11, 1918—a few shells fell at the foot of the hill. We heard someone shout, "Medical Corps men—litter bearers—hurry—hurry!" A soldier from the 104th Machine Gun Company by the name of Gerrior had been mortally wounded. By the time we got him on a litter and were trying to get him back to a more safe cover, he had died. Chaplain de Valles administered the last rites of the church, and without any other ceremonies we began to dig a shallow grave with our bayonets so we could at least bury him. As the Boches were shelling this particular spot quite heavily we just about had him covered when a shell came so close that the dirt and stones and pieces of shrapnel fell all around us. The Chaplain decided we had better move, so we ran back to the brow of the hill, leaving the dead soldier covered except for his toes, which were sticking up about four inches.[18]

—*Private Connell Albertine*
104th Infantry, 26th Division

As the 11th hour drew near, preparations were begun for the attack. Many of the boys were looking to their guns and fixing bayonets. And there were several boys there who did not know very much about a rifle for they had just been sent to join the division the night before and were in the line for the first time.

I found that my only weapon was a pair of field glasses, so I picked out a heavy noncom who had a pistol and decided to follow him and take that pistol if he got hit. We moved forward about 100 feet when the barrage had stopped—and then we received the order to halt. For a long time nothing was heard and everyone was hoping that it was all over. After a while we all began to cheer up, some of the boys lit fires and we all gathered around them. Several of the men who had never been up there before swore that they would say their prayers every night if the thing was over. At last it was made known that the armistice was signed—and a happier bunch of boys could never be seen.

And yet I can say that I never heard one of them complain when the orders for the attack had been given, even though they knew that they were fighting the last moments of the war.[19]

—Lieutenant Archie B. Fairly
26th Division

The artillery kept it up till the last minute. So did the Boche guns. But there seemed to be little hate in that morning's barrage. The guns weren't pointed anywhere in particular; they were just headed in the general direction of Germany and turned loose as fast as they could be fired.

As the hour approached, officers and men of the artillery gathered at the batteries, all eager to fire "the last shot in the war." In one battery each man took a shell and waited in line for his turn to fire the gun. In another battery, five officers took hold of the lanyard and all fired the last shot together. In still another a long rope was made fast to the lanyard of each of the four guns. Some two hundred men got a handle on each rope, and one man, with a watch, went out forward. At the hour, he dropped a handkerchief. A thousand men sagged back on the firing ropes; four guns barked simultaneously, and a thousand Americans let out a yell that must have been heard in Bocheland.

And then they sat down in the mud.[20]

—Frank Sibley
Boston Globe *Correspondent, 26th Division*

All of a sudden our artillery stopped firing and we were all up on our feet wondering just what had happened . . .

At this moment, looking directly to our rear where our artillery was, we saw some French artillerymen throwing their helmets in the air. Then at this moment—and what a moment—one that will live with us as long as we live—an officer from G Company came running down the trench, practically breathless and very excited, shouting, "The war is over . . . the war is over . . . an armistice has been signed."[21]

—Private Connell Albertine
104th Infantry, 26th Division

It was a funny feeling all of us had. Everybody was listening and watching for shells to come over. On my way back to Beaumont I had to stop and listen every once in a while. After months of constant roar of the guns and exploding shells, to have everything stop all at once, the quietness was too much for us; we couldn't believe it was true and we were lost without the noise. I couldn't get my mind to believe the war was ended.[22]

—*Private John A. Hughes*
15th Field Artillery, 2nd Division

We were all fixed up [November 11], ready to load on the trucks. We were sure this time we were headed for Metz. But the final orders to move didn't come through. About 9 o'clock in the evening we heard wild commotion in the little town. The French people, old and young, were running through the streets. Old men and women we'd seen sitting around their houses too feeble to move, were out in the streets yelling, "Vive la France! Vive la France! Vive l'America!"

We couldn't imagine what was the matter. "Hell seems to have broken loose. What's it all about?" Jesse said to me.

"Search me!" I said. "It looks like all the frogs in town are going nuts."

Down the street came a soldier. He was telling everybody the armistice had been signed. I said, "What's an armistice?" It sounded like some kind of a machine to me. The other boys around there didn't know what it meant either.

When the official word came through that it meant peace, we couldn't believe it. Finally Jesse said, "Well kid, I guess it really does mean the war is over."

I said, "I just can't believe it's true."

But it was.[23]

—*Private John L. Barkley*
4th Infantry, 3rd Division

Notes

1. McGuire, *History of U.S. Army Base Hospital No. 45*, p. 252.
2. Cushing, *Vermont in the World War*, pp. 7–9.
3. Gladys B. Clappison, *Vassar's Rainbow Division 1918*. (Lake Mills, Iowa: The Graphic Publishing Company, Inc., 1964).
4. Robinson, *St. Lawrence University in the World War*, pp. 182–184.
5. Fifield, *The Regiment: A History of the 104th U.S. Infantry*, p. 300.
6. Sibley, *With the Yankee Division*, pp. 327–328.
7. Jacks, *Service Record by an Artilleryman*, p. 289.
8. Elton E. Mackin, *Suddenly We Didn't Want to Die*. (Novato, Calif.: Presidio, 1993), p. 220.

9. Reilly, *Americans All*, pp. 755–756.

10. *Ibid.*, p. 758.

11. Howard, *The Autobiography of a Regiment*, pp. 199–200.

12. De La Mater, *The Story of Battery B 306th F.A.*, pp. 69–73.

13. Anthony D. Cone, *E Battery Goes to War*. (Washington, D.C.: Pvtly printed, 1929), pp. 46–47.

14. Wendell. Westover, *Suicide Battalions.* (New York: G.P. Putnam's Sons, 1929), pp. 257–258.

15. Mackin, *Suddenly We Didn't Want to Die*, p. 247.

16. George H. English, Jr., *History of the 89th Division, U.S.A.*, (Denver: The War Society of the 89th Division, 1920), p. 205.

17. George H. Nettleton (ed.), *Yale in the World War.* (New Haven: Yale University Press, 1925), p. 33.

18. Albertine, *The Yankee Doughboy*, pp. 228–229.

19. Henry T. Samson and George C. Hull, *The War Story of C Battery.* (Norwood, Mass.: The Plimpton Press, 1920), p. 196.

20. Sibley, *With the Yankee Division*, pp. 340–341.

21. Albertine, *The Yankee Doughboy*, p. 233.

22. Spaulding, *The Second Division*, p. 187.

23. Barkley, *No Hard Feelings*, pp. 270–272.

CHAPTER 15

Peace and Home

*T*he front-line doughboys were more stunned than ecstatic at the end of the war. In some sectors, it was the Germans—closing the door on over four years of war—who showed the most elation. Fraternization between the two sides was strictly forbidden, but someone forgot to tell the boys from Berlin.

●

We were stupefied to see crowds of Boches running over to us between the mine fields with their hands up and yelling like mad. They were crazy for cigarettes and chocolate. They had some cigars but they were awful. They were big fellows in sloppy uniforms; 328th Infantry. Some of them had been to America and talked English. They said their food had been vile. We had some burned rice that our boys wouldn't eat and they fell on it like wolves. They showed us where the mines were. This getting together lasted for only about an hour when our officers stopped it and chased the Germans back to their lines. All that night we could hear them singing and burning Very Lights and bon fires. There wasn't much doing with our crowd as they were all played out and wanted sleep.[1]

—Private Carl Stuber
42nd Division

Everywhere little camp fires began to smoke and glow, and the rations came swiftly up to the line. Commanding officers came forward to inspect, and the majors, red-eyed with fatigue, dirty and unshaven for many days, and so hoarse with gas that they could not speak aloud, reported their lines.

The early dusk came down, pearly with moisture and with the

promise of a fair night. All the automobiles lighted their lamps and went glowing down the rough roads among the shining of thousands of little bonfires.

"Put out those lights!" the doughboys would yell at the passing motors.

"Put out those fires!" was the appropriate response. And then the delighted soldiers would yell in chorus, "Hoo-oo!"[2]

—*Frank R. Sibley*
Boston Globe *Correspondent, 26th Division*

We found a five-gallon jug of schnapps and proceeded to celebrate. Some of the boys began to feel pretty good and started singing. Towards night it grew cold and we all built fires. It seemed funny to see so many fires now when twenty-four hours before we could not even strike a match. Our cook got busy and scouted around Muzon where he found a large supply of flour and sauerkraut. We brought the flour to our position and the boys had lots of hot cakes and biscuits. They ate sauerkraut until they were filled up.[3]

—*Sergeant Anthony D. Cone*
15th Field Artillery, 2nd Division

"The enemy has capitulated. It is fitting that I address myself in thanks directly to the officers and soldiers of the American Expeditionary Forces who by their heroic efforts have made possible this glorious result. Our Armies, hurriedly raised and hastily trained, met a veteran enemy, and by courage, discipline and skill always defeated him. Without complaint you have endured incessant toil, privation and danger. You have seen many of your comrades make the supreme sacrifice that freedom may live. I thank you for the patience and courage with which you have endured. I congratulate you upon the splendid fruits of victory which your heroism and the blood of our gallant dead are now presenting to our nation. Your deeds will live forever on the most glorious pages of America's history. Those things you have done. There remains now a harder task which will test your soldierly qualities to the utmost. Succeed in this and little note will be taken and few praises will be sung; fail, and the light of your glorious achievements of the past will be sadly dimmed. But you will not fail. Every natural tendency may urge towards relaxation in discipline, in conduct, in appearance, in everything that marks the soldier. Yet you will remember that each officer and each soldier is the representative in Europe of his people and that his brilliant deeds of yesterday permit no action of today to pass unnoticed by friend or foe. You will meet this test as gallantly as you have met the tests of the battlefield. Sustained by your high ideals and inspired by the heroic part you have played, you will carry back to our people the proud consciousness of a new Americanism born of sacrifices. Whether you stand on hostile territory or on the friendly soil of France, you will so bear yourself in discipline, appearance and respect for all civil rights that you will confirm for all time the pride and love which every American feels for your uniform and for you."—Pershing.[4]

—General John J. Pershing
Commander, American Expeditionary Force

Before passing in review, General Pershing with his staff and General O'Ryan with his staff and General Read with his staff, walked slowly down each aisle or file of troops, 25,000 of them, spread in precise order over this vast field. We were all "At Attention." The progress of the generals was so slow it seemed we would be there in our rigid position forever. General Pershing inspected every man with an all-apprising look from the top of his steel helmet to the toes of his shoes. With many who wore wound stripes or a decoration, or both, he would pause for conversation. This thing would never end. Our backs were stiff and straight, our chins in and our chests out.

At last the personal inspection was completed, but no "At Ease" command would be given until the general had returned to the front and center of the division. The group, and it was a large one, moved off to my left. Only a few of us of the entire division could still see the group from the corner of our eyes. Suddenly the group stopped. It formed a circle, all facing outwards. The General of the A.E.F. had to perform an act of nature. The few of us who witnessed the event wondered if the 27th Division was the only division in the A.E.F. to stand at attention while its commander in chief performed an act of nature.[5]

—Private William F. Clarke
104th Machine Gun Battalion, 27th Division

D uring the weeks, then months following the end of the war, work began to break up the huge U.S. forces in France and transport them back to the United States. Other troops were designated for occupation duty in Germany. It would be 1923 before the last of them came home.

•

From the moment the firing ceased, the boys' talk changed. Before this one might hear them say, "If I ever get back to the States," but now everyone was saying, "When I get back." All was over. They were going back. They began to wonder how soon. Some thought we would start at once and be back early in December. Others thought it would be Christmas time or New Year's Day before we saw the States again. I thought we wouldn't make it before February. It was July before we left Europe and I reached home August 2.[6]

—Corporal Carl Noble
60th Infantry, 5th Division

In all the little towns we passed through the French people made a lot of fuss about us. They would crowd into the streets and wave American flags that they'd made themselves. Most of the flags were pretty good, but there were some funny ones, too. Some had red, white and blue stripes with one or two stars. Some had the stripes running the wrong way.

I was glad to be going into Germany, for a wanted to see what the German people were really like. We'd heard so much that it didn't seem possible they could be like the rest of the world. But when we marched through the little German towns, and they crowded out in the streets to watch us go by, they didn't seem much different from the people I'd always known. Not as different as the French.

Aside from the clothes some of them wore, and their language, the only thing that seemed queer about them was the scared look on their faces. We couldn't figure that out at first. But when we called out friendly things to them they'd look at each other in surprise, and their faces would light up. After that they wouldn't act afraid any more. It dawned on us then what was the matter. They'd been told worse things about us than we'd been told about them! They were just finding out that they'd been fooled.

The ex-soldiers still felt pretty bitter. When there was one of them in the crowd he'd look at us as if we were some kind of wild beasts. But when you thought what he'd probably been through to try to win this war, you couldn't exactly blame him.[7]

—Private John L. Barkley
4th Infantry, 3rd Division

"The Commander-in-Chief has called on us to deal fairly with the German people. Our great nation entered this war to give to oppressed people a square deal. With our Allies, we have won the victory which guarantees this square deal. Our Army of Occupation is here to secure this square deal. We demand it, we enforce it and we will also give it.

"Security and protection of troops on the march or at halts must never be neglected.

"Until further orders, enlisted men will not go beyond the outposts established by their command, except on duty. Officers will not travel without arms, and troops will habitually be formed and marched under arms. The unpoliced portion of larger towns must not be frequented by individuals. Single individuals will not, as a rule, be sent on any duty.

"The use of light wines and beer is not prohibited, but intoxication will be punished severely and the use of strong drink of whatever kind prevented. The beverage called 'Schnapps' is prohibited."[8]

—General Order No. 103
89th Division

On December 15th, 1918, we arrived at Bodendorf, Germany, after a hard month's march from France. We were tired and wanted a place to rest. We were told that we had reached the end of our journey. So we looked around.

I and my section were assigned to a small house. As we entered, we were met by a family of Germans: man, wife and children. They showed us a small room where we were to live. It was about 6-foot by 12-foot. Not enough room for two men, much less a section of machine gunners. And it seemed as if all the chairs, stands, etc. were put in this room.

I yelled for the Kraut to come and remove his furniture. He refused. I had the men remove it in no gentle terms. As I went to remove a large canvas painting of the Kaiser from the wall, the whole family let out a howl, telling us in no uncertain terms that he was the Kaiser. I saw that they would obey the Kaiser if no one else. So I drew my Colt .45 automatic and smashed the glass. Then I took the picture down and put it outside with the rest of the furniture. I then took from my pocket a photo of myself taken in France and hung it on the wall in the same place, telling them, "Hoch, dat is der Kaiser."

They looked at the photo and at me. I made them salute the new photo, which they did after a little argument. Within an hour's time all of the village knew of it. The other families came in, looked at the photo, then at me. Some were silent, others smiled and spoke. I told them all that I would be the Kaiser of Bodendorf. And all during our four months stay there I was known as the "Kaiser of Bodendorf." I even had a charge account at Meitzer's General Store under that name.[9]

—Sergeant Earl E. Young
150th Machine Gun Battalion, 42nd Division

On February 20, 1919, the following instructions were received from the army commander:

"The billeting capacity of every available house including pri-

vate dwellings, regardless of the social status or class of the inhabitants, will be carefully checked up and no exceptions will be made in
the case of any house. The use of kitchens will be left to inhabitants
and sufficient sleeping quarters to permit of each female occupant
over the age of twelve years having her own bed. Aside from this, no
bed or separate room need be left for any adult male German
between the ages of twelve and sixty years where such procedure
would result in an American officer or soldier not being provided
with a bed."[10]

—Captain Charles F. Dienst
353rd Infantry, 89th Division

I stayed with a German family from January until we left in July. A
son of this family had been a machine gunner in the German Army. I
slept in a feather bed, and this son slept on the floor. Two other
Americans shared my room. They slept in one bed, together, and I
had a bed to myself.[11]

—Corporal Carl Noble
60th Infantry, 5th Division

Fraternization with the German civilians was strictly prohibited and
the ruling was rigidly enforced. Conversation with the German civilians except on matters of business was classed as fraternization and
soldiers found talking to Germans on the streets or drinking with
them in cafes were subject to arrest. In the homes, however, where
our soldiers were billeted, it was impossible to enforce this rule, and
in many cases German women insisted on making friends with the
American soldiers billeted in their houses.

Food was very scarce, the natives living principally on a diet of
potatoes and cabbage with a beverage made out of burnt wheat. Fats
could not be bought at any price. Probably the most grievous shortage was soap, a bar of which had a wonderful purchasing power as
the American soldier soon found out. A cake of sapolio was worth
its weight in gold. To hand out a piece of chocolate was the same as
giving them a share in a gold mine, and the Dutch kids would run
blocks for a stick of gum.[12]

—Lieutenant William R. Wright
148th Field Artillery

*M eanwhile, hundreds of thousands of doughboys remained in France
with only one thought on their minds—home. Morale suffered and
army routine seemed pure drudgery for men who were, in their own minds,
now merely civilians in uniform.*

But for all too many others, there were no medals, no boredom, no longings for home. They were dead, their remains littering the battlefields of the last 12 months, or hastily interred in shallow graves. Work had already begun to account for the missing and gather the dead for interment in central cemeteries. Many would later be sent home for burial at their families' request. The gruesome task of digging up the dead frequently fell to labor outfits made up of African Americans. To add insult to their uninviting work, their efforts were not always appreciated.

●

Graves Registration Service was making a big central cemetery in Romagne. We found them living in board shacks with a big tent camp of some 2,000 or 4,000 niggers up on the hillside. And all along the slopes to the east of town were great yawning graves six feet wide and about 100 feet long, wherein they are planting the boys who are lying now in scattered graves all over the country thereabout.

The total dead of the U.S. in this war is somewhere around 50,000. Of these about 17,999 were killed and buried here in one small tract of the Argonne. And not so very distant—to be gathered up now and placed in this cemetery. There are all told about 26,000 bodies, they say—or about half our dead.

The officers welcomed us. Visitors are, strangely enough, not infrequent. Nearly every day, they say, some 10 to 20 officers drop in from just such trips as ours, looking over old scenes, hunting graves of friends, etc.

Sitting over back of the roaring stove, one of the medical lieutenants talked to me at length. He had been here but three weeks and the work evidently got on his nerves. He didn't like it. "The worst job in the A.E.F.," he emphatically announced, "digging up the dead."

He said that the niggers seemed about equally divided—some of them seeming to actually glory in the work and never tired of talking about it. But that the other half saw approximately a million ghosts every night after they went to bed, and were hard to handle.

It's ugly work—and so utterly foolish, I think. I know if I were dead over here, I'd much rather be lying on some windswept hilltop, where friendly hands of comrades had buried me, than to have a bunch of niggers taking my bones out of Mother Earth's kind embrace and sticking me in with a hundred others. Why don't they let the dead rest in peace![13]

—Anonymous Artilleryman
120th Field Artillery

All companies check up on their men when relieved, but First Lieutenant Clovis Moomaw could not be accounted for [when the outfit came out of the line]. Meanwhile, the War Department at Washington had notified his people that he was wounded, condition undetermined, another letter they stated killed in action and still another not accounted for.

His brother in Washington tried to get the War Department to send him to France, they refused. He joined the American Red Cross, went to France, got a month's leave of absence and went to the Headquarters of the 80th Division for information. No one seemed to know, then he went to the Captain of each company of the 1st Battalion, still he found out nothing until he got to Captain Douglas of Company B. He stated he knew nothing about Lieutenant Moomaw except: "I saw a man blown to atoms just at the edge of the woods on the evening of October 5, that man was never accounted for and it might have been him. If you care to investigate this I will furnish you with maps as to the location, and furnish a sergeant that is familiar with the territory. At this place you will find one shell hole much larger than the rest and that is it."

Mr. Moomaw and the sergeant started out on their journey. About a week later he returned, having discovered his brother's dismembered body. He identified his brother by the wristwatch still attached to the bones of his hand. At this time he had been killed almost six months. Thus the error was corrected. First Lieutenant Clovis Moomaw, Company D, killed in action.[14]

—Private Rush Young
318th Infantry, 80th Division

A famous war correspondent, Percy Hammond, wrote for the *Chicago Tribune* a description of an Argonne Wood he visited some weeks after the Armistice.

We saw a bruised and barren Hell's Half Acre of trampled, wounded landscape, in the center of which was a German machine gun nest. The guns were still there, some of them in the forks of trees on the outskirts. All about them the ground was thick with a litter of blankets, helmets, caps, bayonets, rifles, shells, cartridge belts, mess-kits, canteens, grenades, trench spades, rolls, tunics, boots, a bugle and letters—scores of letters—and post cards.

We could not imagine the Americans coming across the road we had just left, pushing their way through the small trees and underbrush, knee-deep in mud, in the face of German machine gunners and riflemen. It seemed incredible. Yet we stood in the midst of the tragic evidence of it. We could tell that there had been no flight in this tiny and unrecorded conflict. The soldiers in it had killed or been killed, it was to the death and hand to hand.

The thing we looked at longest was a colossal and erstwhile Prussian. He lay on top of the ground in the corner of the field and was apparently turned to stone. His face, to employ a fantastic comparison, was like that of an old-time clown in the circus, or a waxed figure in a shop window, dead white with cardinal lips and blank eyes.

His mustachios, as though by the elements, were upturned and truculent. His helmet was on his head, the strap still holding under his chin. His boots and uniform were almost as good as new, and his Mauser, with bayonet fixed, was nearby, not much rusted. We could see his wallet in his pocket. His path of glory had not led him even to the grave, but he did not seem to care. There was an ugly brown hole in his throat.

What young American in a troop of heroes undistinguished, we wondered, had vanquished this giant, and how? What had they muttered to each other as they came to the clinches and the German fell? Where is the American now? Was he a drug clerk, or a teamster, or a lawyer, or a junior at Yale, or a reporter on a newspaper or a traveling salesman? Was he from Manictowuwoc or Baltimore. Did he push along the hillside and drop, and is his helmet the one I picked up nearby with a hole in its rim? Or is he now in some lonely German village, standing in a long line with his comrades, mess-kit in hand, after mashed potatoes and corned beef and thinking of home?

For awhile we stood and watched the wet wind blow the dead German's coat to and fro in the quiet twilight. Then we groped our way to our comfortable limousine and set sail for Verdun, 20 miles away, for dinner and lodging.[15]

—Wagoner Ralph J. Robinson
113th Ambulance Company, 29th Division

G *radually, the troops in France were transported home. Within two months of the Armistice, the army had discharged 818,532 men and by the end of June 1919 more than 2,700,000 soldiers had been discharged, out of a total war strength of 3,703,273. As is the army way, the exit had its strictures.*

•

On January 21st we rolled our packs and hiked fifteen kilometers to the delouser at St. Denis. Here we got a sort of bath, and our clothes and blankets were put in a delouser under live steam. The shower baths were a mere single fine stream of warm water and usually were cut off just when we were nicely soaped up! The delouser presumably killed the cooties, but we found out quickly enough that it only got about half of them. Private Clayborn Greenleaf cussed because his clothes came out barely warm and the cooties still ready for business. He swore it was a damned cootie incubator—not a delouser.

Cootie orders from headquarters now began to come in. We were instructed to get rid of them by any means available. We were advised to "press the seams of our clothing with hot irons"—but no one could tell us where to get the irons![16]

—Private Ray N. Johnson
145th Infantry, 37th Division

We were assigned, at the extreme end of the camp, to the once-familiar octagonal army tents, in which were wooden floors, iron cots and mattresses.

We were promptly assembled and warned that we were not to visit other plots, that all marching was to be in column of twos, that no individuals could buy at the "Y" or similar organizations—goods could be bought only by and for an organization—and so on through a long list of instructions. Certainly we were not to ask the M.P.s, "Who won the war?" for the whole outfit would be punished.

The schedule of calls at this time is enlightening as to army efficiency: first call, 6 A.M.; assembly, 6:15; mess, 7:07; drill, 7:50; recall, 11:30; mess, 12:37 P.M.; drill, 1:30; recall, 4:30; retreat, 5; taps, 10. There were no calls on Sundays or holidays.

Perhaps the most impressive ceremony of the schedule was preparations for meals. The kitchens were so efficiently handled that approximately 180 men were served in each kitchen per minute.

We turned in our French money (if we had any) and received American money. It had been so long since we had handled any that at first it seemed very strange.[17]

—Sergeant Arthur C. Havlin
102nd Machine Gun Battalion, 26th Division

After a very cold night, we woke to find two inches of snow on the ground. That day the battery went through a place known as "The Mad House." It reminded me of "The Pit" at Natasket Beach Amusement Park. With our packs, we entered a large wooden building in single file, and were steered into a bath department where we took off all our clothes and threw them away. Then we filed into a sort of steam chamber where a soapy water fell on us from the ceiling. In the room beyond we were painted all over with some white disinfectant by men with large whitewash brushes. Then we progressed to a shower room, after which we were given towels and told to use them. At the door of the next department the towels were taken away from us and we were given a complete set of clothes, with no regard for our different sizes. After getting dressed, we were herded into a large hall where we found our packs waiting for us. We then lined up, took distance, and opened our packs, each man laying out all his worldly possessions according to the prescribed pattern. Strange embarkation officers made a minute inspection and pulled out a few men who were deficient in something, a cake of soap or a can of dubbin or a fork. I never knew what happened to these unfortunates. I was too busy watching my own stuff to see what went on around me. When it was over and our packs made again, we were marched out into a torrent of rain. It rained all that night.[18]

—Corporal Horatio Rogers
101st Field Artillery, 26th Division

On the night of Wednesday, March 12th, we went through the camp delouser. Our clothing was hung on moveable racks, and while we were under the showers, was subjected to a dry heat of exceedingly high temperature. We went through a regular "by the numbers" bath. It was a new one on us! The soldiers in charge of the place seemed to enjoy this chance to "boss us around." Absolute silence was required and half the joy of the bath was taken away because we couldn't shout and yell. We were lined up under the showers and at a signal the water was turned on. "Soak yourselves," we were ordered. We "soaked" for half a minute and then the water was shut off. "Soap yourselves—soap is in the troughs," came the sing-song voice. We lathered our bodies with a peculiar soft soap like wallpaper paste and then, at the order, "Under the showers," we stood shivering on the wet slatted floor. They kept us waiting a sufficient length of time to properly impress it upon our minds that we were at the mercy of the S.O.S. and then turned on the water. We scarcely had time to rinse off the soap when the water was again cut off and we were shunted into another room where we received clean underwear and our deloused clothes.[19]

—Private Ray N. Johnson
145th Infantry, 37th Division

We found out that one outfit was all set aboard a transport when some Yank yelled out, "To hell with France!" and the embarkation officer ordered this outfit back to camp. We made up our minds this was not going to happen to us. After a pep talk, we marched to the embarkation pier. While the troops that were to embark were lined up on the dock, an officer from the Port of Embarkation told us that anyone having any souvenirs such as German Luger pistols, binoculars, spiked helmets, etc. was to get rid of them at once by setting them on the dock, and that anyone found with any of these articles aboard the boat would be court-martialed. Some of the boys got scared, so they took their souvenirs from their packs and threw them on the dock. This was no sooner done, when some officers who had probably fought the war in the Service of Supply came along and helped themselves to the souvenirs.

We were each given a tag to tie on the buttonholes of our coats, to remain for the duration of the trip. These tags, we were told, were for the second sitting. There were going to be six sittings of 1,000 at each sitting, and a half-hour was allocated for each sitting. Each sitting had a different colored tag, and as one group was filing out of the galley, another group was all assembled and filing in. Each table accommodated ten men, and the food was placed in several tin cans nestled on top of each other at the end of each table. There were no benches to sit on, so everybody had to stand. These sittings were supervised by Navy petty officers. The instructions were to file in, and no one was to touch any of the food until the petty officer blew his whistle. It was very hot in this galley, and between the heat, foul air, and the vibration of the ship, it made several of the boys at my table sick and they started to heave. Being packed in so close, elbow to elbow and back to back, there was no place for the boys to heave but right on the table. This made other boys sick, so no one at our table was able to eat, and before we knew it the whistle blew again to file out. The boys that did the heaving had to clean up the mess, and what a mess it was!

The second day out, details were assigned to the ship's kitchen to slice hundreds of pounds of bologna. It was so hot in the kitchen that many of the boys fainted and had to be carried up on deck and revived by throwing cold water in their faces. Some of the boys felt that this was no way to treat the best soldiers in the Expeditionary Forces. Perhaps now that the war was over no one cared about heroes.[20]

—Private Connell Albertine
104th Infantry, 26th Division

The wounded men [aboard ship] were on the whole cheerful and contented. I don't recall hearing a word of complaint from one. Most of the cases were machine gun wounds. One diminutive infantryman, from the Argonne, had four holes neatly bored through him; he couldn't tell which one he got first. "They just all got me at once." He was getting alone nicely and would soon be out, as he said, sound and well as ever.

One poor chap who had been badly gassed came upon the deck daily and sat for hours looking wistfully at the sea. I tried to talk with him, but he couldn't speak above a whisper. He was thin, pale and weak. I don't think he was long for this world. The transport was so crowded that there was no separate space on the deck available for the wounded and most of the wounded preferred to stay below in their own quarters rather than be jostled by the men on the crowded troop decks.

There was a great deal of good-natured chaff and bantering among the wounded men. All arms of the service were represented and nearly all nationalities, including Japanese and negroes. Some one would call out, "Who won the war?" The answer was, "The Marines." Then the argument started and the few Marines among the wounded would be in for a "chafing." There were nearly 5,000 Marines at Chateau Thierry and 100,000 doughboys. The Marines are sure great little advertisers. Devil Dogs, say the rest of us, got hell sure. But nobody ever heard of anybody but the Marines.[21]

—Colonel Robert L. Moorhead
139th Field Artillery

There were about 125 wounded officers on the ship. We were an assorted set of cripples, but all could walk unaided fairly well. We managed to get about and have a little amusement. We had plays and skits in the middle of the ocean and forgot our troubles.

One night, in the dining room, we sat talking about the various armies. The parson, who looked like a baboon, and had less sense, was making a great speech about what awful cowards the Germans were. Another parson who had not been at the front joined in with an oration on war atrocities.

I got pretty well bored with this kind of guff and nonsense. I suggested that if our opponents were mere cowards, then we weren't such brave men for having whipped them. Then the parson, both brave and bold, stood up and pointed his accusing finger at me: "Do you mean to tell me that you admire the German fiends, the despoilers of women, the destroyers of churches, the Huns, the vandals—?" and so on, and so on.

By that time I was sore. With barrack-room language, I repeated that the Germans were just as good soldiers as we were. I said something else about Christian preachers urging men to kill each other.

As for the German soldiers, I said that from a military viewpoint, they were bound to be better trained then we were, for they had been at it longer.

When we arrived at the hospital on Staten Island, there was a colonel from the Inspector General's Department waiting to investigate me and others. By radio we had been charged with making remarks "derogatory to the morale of the American troops," which was a damned lie. Fortunately, the colonel had some brains. In about fifteen minutes he dismissed us all and told us to go to town and enjoy ourselves.[22]

—*Lieutenant Maury Maverick*
28th Infantry, 1st Division

There was much discussion among the boys as to what they were going to do when they were discharged from the army. One Yank said the first thing he was going to do was to drink a gallon of milk. Another said he was going to eat ice cream until it came out of his ears. Many said they were going to get married. A few said they were going to join the Regular Army. Some wondered if their jobs would still be available.[23]

—*Private Connell Albertine*
104th Infantry, 26th Division

While we were waiting for release from quarantine in New York a tug bearing the sign, "Mayor's Welcoming Committee of the City of New York," came out to meet us. She pulled alongside and the band aboard her began to play a popular air. The effect was electrical—the boys swarmed to the starboard side and cheer after cheer rent the air, completely drowning the music. A husky riverman mounted the tug's bridge and hurled bundles of New York newspapers into the seething, yelling, madly cheering crowd of soldiers. We cheered until we were hoarse.[24]

—*Private Ray N. Johnson*
145th Infantry, 37th Division

Soon we were steaming slowly by Coney Island. Scores of boats came out to meet us. Ferry boats, tugboats, launches and lighters escorted us up the bay and past the Statue of Liberty. They were loaded to overflowing with friends and relatives who did nearly everything to demonstrate their welcome but jump overboard. Over the side of one boat hung a large banner inscribed with the name "Geiger." There were wild calls for Geiger to come and see his friends. Other names were similarly displayed, and each man so honored was summoned to a place of vantage in order that he might respond. The office of the Bon Ami Company, in which "Rip" Ring had formerly been employed, spelled his name across the office suite by placing huge posters, each containing one letter of his name, in four of its windows. When "Rip" saw this enormous "R-I-N-G" confronting him, he must have felt as if his trip to France was worthwhile after all. Before long we were opposite our pier in the North River. A few minutes after 11 we were at dock and debarkation began immediately. While we waited for our turn to leave the ship, a Knights of Columbus boat, together with two or three tugs, came alongside and put over a barrage of oranges, newspapers and chocolate. Most of it fell in the river, but that seemed to make no difference whatever, for the bombardment continued at a terrific rate. Salvation Army workers came aboard and distributed telegram blanks on which to write messages to our families.

When we left the *Agamemnon* we were stationed in the great warehouse beside the vessel. A high wire fence separated us from the eager crowd of friends and relatives awaiting a glimpse of their own. Except for the fence and the M.P.s who guarded it, there would probably have been a stampede, and as it was there was considerable confusion. Fathers, mothers, wives, sisters and brothers cried for joy when they caught sight of their "brave hero," and another barrage of food and newspapers was directed at us. Anything was ours for the asking. Whole pies, quart boxes of ice cream and pounds of candy were thrown over the fence by total strangers, who seemed as eager to serve a man they had never seen before as to welcome their own sons. Some of the spectators tried to burst the wire with their bare hands in order to shake hands with us; soldiers were kissed through the openings in the wire; women begged to be allowed inside the enclosure; and one woman, recognizing her son, literally flew at the fence, and ended by falling back into the crowd in a dead faint.[25]

—Sergeant Francis Field
306th Field Artillery, 77th Division

There were 9,000 soldiers on our ship. We made the crossing in five and one-half days. It was raining when we landed, and everyone got wet; but we were very glad to reach home. I felt a thrill as my feet trod American soil. I stopped and picked up a handful of dirt. It had been trampled by millions of feet, but it was part of our country. Someone asked me what I was doing. I said I was just shaking hands with America. Several of the men reached down and felt of the ground.

We were en route for Fort D.A. Russell, Wyoming. This trip was quite different from our trip from Camp Green to Camp Merritt in the spring of 1918. I suppose the people had seen so many soldiers and troop trains during the past two years that it was an old sight; they had become indifferent. There was little shouting, cheering or hand waving. In one town in my native state, Ohio, the train stopped for a few minutes. I got off the train and rushed across the street to buy a watermelon. I bought the melon and started to leave the store, when a gentleman spoke to me: "I beg your pardon, but I would like to know how much the lady charged you for that melon." I said I had paid 75 cents for it.

"I thought so," he said. "I thought that was what she charged you. Those melons have been selling for 25 cents. Come with me and I'll see that you get your 50 cents back." The train whistle was blowing and I told him I must go. The girl who had sold me the melon could hear our conversation, and looked perturbed. As I started for the train the man who had accosted me said, "Soldier, I'm going to do my part to see that this doesn't happen again." I thought of the Y.M.C.A. chap who had made the speech when we went into the Argonne: "Men, when you get back to America and see anything you want, do not ask the price; just pick it up and walk off with it, and you will have carpets strewn with flowers to walk on!"[26]

—*Corporal Carl Noble*
60th Infantry, 5th Division

We arrived at Camp Devens late in the afternoon—the train moved slowly so that people could see us—and we marched to the quarantine area for further delousing and inspection, just in case, before going to nice clean barracks. We had to take all our clothes off, tie them in a bundle, and pass in a single file to the delousing machine. These bundles of clothes were thrown into what looked like a big circular boiler, then the door was securely clamped and steam let into the boiler. This was done to make sure that we had no lice in our clothes. In the meantime, we were ushered into showers with plenty of hot water, soap and clean fluffy towels. When we got through our showers, we picked up our bundles of clothes and proceeded to dress. The terrific pressure of the steam had wrinkled our uniforms very badly. We all looked a mess, and it was all very discouraging. Fine way to send us home on pass with our uniforms all wrinkled up! Not only that, but the synthetic chocolate-colored buttons all shrank so that it was impossible to keep our blouses buttoned. These synthetic buttons had replaced the brass buttons overseas because the chocolate-colored buttons did not shine out at night, and there might have been a brass shortage. These uniforms had been deloused before at Brest, France, but the buttons were not damaged then. Some eager beavers soon obtained other buttons from friends that knew someone in the Quartermaster's Department, so most of us got new buttons and later we sewed them on.[27]

> —*Private Connell Albertine*
> *104th Infantry, 26th Division*

We were broken up on the 12th, the soldiers from different states going to different barracks; and as the remnant of our old outfit marched before us, all the boys felt like crying. Many a tear was shed when we saw our old colors march by. Everyone saluted. I guess we stood at attention for five minutes after the colors passed us, not a word spoken. I felt then, as I have often felt, that silence is the greatest tribute. Little did we realize the attachment that had grown among us until that moment.

Several of us hired a cab and went to a hotel in Trenton and found they were not anxious to accommodate us. Quite a contrast from a year or two before. Human nature was taking its course and the events of the past three years had been forgotten.[28]

> —*Private John A. Hughes*
> *15th Field Artillery, 2nd Division*

Quite a number of French girls came in without appointment [as men returned to the U.S.]. Many of them said they had been engaged to American soldiers and that letters they had sent to the United States had been returned, there being no such address as the one the soldier had given them. Some brought in babies and wanted to know how they could find the soldier-father and how they could get support for the half-American child. Some of the soldiers had even given fictitious names which were not on any Army roster. Unfortunately, there was little we could do for them.[29]

> —*Lieutenant R.W. Kean*
> *15th Field Artillery, 2nd Division*

Notes

1. Nolan, *The Reading Militia in the Great War*, p. 173.
2. Sibley, *With the Yankee Division*, p. 341.
3. Cone, *E Battery Goes to War*, pp. 48–49.
4. Strickland, *Connecticut Fights*, p. 299.
5. Clarke, *Over There with O'Ryan's Roughnecks*, pp. 126–127.
6. Noble, *Jugheads Behind the Lines*, p. 162.
7. Barkley, *No Hard Feelings*, pp. 273–274.
8. Dienst, *They're from Kansas*, p. 159.
9. Reilly, *Americans All*, pp. 873–874.
10. Dienst, *They're from Kansas*, p. 167.
11. Noble, *Jugheads Behind the Lines*, pp. 199–200.

12. *A History of the Sixty-Sixth Field Artillery Brigade.* (Denver: Smith-Brooks Printing Co., n.d.), pp. 78–79.

13. *The 120th Field Artillery Diary,* pp. 505–506.

14. Young, *Over the Top With the 80th,* unpaged.

15. Ralph Robinson, *Ambulance Company 113, 29th Division.* (Baltimore, Md.: n.p., 1919), pp. 147–148.

16. Johnson, *Heaven, Hell or Hoboken,* p. 170.

17. Havlin, *The History of Company A,* p. 197.

18. Rogers, *Diary of an Artillery Scout,* pp. 264–265.

19. Johnson, *Heaven, Hell or Hoboken,* p. 175–176.

20. Albertine, *The Yankee Doughboy,* pp. 268, 270–271.

21. Robert Moorhead, *The Story of the 139th Field Artillery, American Expeditionary Force.* (Indianapolis: The Bobbs-Merrill Company, 1920), p. 153.

22. Maverick, *A Maverick American,* pp. 138–139.

23. Albertine, *The Yankee Doughboy,* p. 273.

24. Johnson, *Heaven, Hell or Hoboken,* pp. 181–182.

25. *The Battery Book,* pp. 158–159.

26. Noble, *Jugheads Behind the Lines,* pp. 204–205.

27. Albertine, *The Yankee Doughboy,* p. 278.

28. Spaulding, *The Second Division,* p. 291.

29. Kean, *Dear Marraine,* p. 240.

Epilogue

The last Americans returned from occupation duty in Germany in early 1923. By then, President Woodrow Wilson was dead, and along with him his dream for American participation in the League of Nations. The harsh terms of the allied-imposed peace had already sown the seeds for another world war.

In the United States, the returning doughboys were greeted by the nation's ill-conceived experiment with prohibition. They were not immune to the social change: they too had changed, not all of them for the better. William A. Pinkerton of the famed Pinkerton Detective Agency noted that, "The increase in daylight robbers [after the war] was due in large measure to unemployment among discharged soldiers. The methods used are those of men accustomed to taking great risks, men who will brook no interference. They constitute a new class of criminals. They are not professionals, but are usually men between 20 and 30 years of age who will kill if resisted."[1]

Other thousands, such as Ralph Grimm, a former blacksmith and coal miner, faced even higher hurdles than simple unemployment. Grimm, who lost both legs at about hip level to a German shell in the Argonne, would spend the rest of his life in a wheelchair. Through occupational courses at Walter Reed Hospital in Washington, he learned to become an expert jewelry craftsman and eventually opened his own shop. Some of his even less fortunate comrades, crippled and broken, would end their days in veterans hospitals.

By far the majority of veterans, of course, returned home and tried to pick up their lives as best they could on the farm or in the factory, as if the war had been a mere interlude. Many, having faced death, came back to civilian life determined to succeed. They founded businesses, went into politics, became stalwart citizens. By 1924 no less than 45 veterans of the war were seated in the 68th Congress, including five U.S. senators.

Veterans also founded the American Legion to preserve a sense of their comradeship and to look after their interests. For years after the war, the

327

American Legion Magazine *carried plaintive appeals from mothers, brothers, sisters, and other relatives, seeking information on loved ones who had been killed or were still listed as missing in the fighting overseas. Other veterans wrote back and gave them information if they could.*

The veterans also found, like combat soldiers before them and those who came after, that outsiders could never fully grasp what they had endured. That experience remained uniquely theirs, a cup both bitter and sweet to be shared most fully only with one another.

•

We felt on our return "let down" and disappointed over something. What that something is, I do not know. I wish I did. We criticize no one for it. I would not go two blocks now to hear Lieutenant Rene Fonck, the French ace, tell how he downed three German planes in 23 seconds, or tell of his experience in downing 75 planes officially credited to him and the 40 others that he claims. I would not go two blocks to hear [Medal of Honor winner] Sergeant Alvin York tell of how he killed 20 Germans and captured 132, and I doubt if there are many others who would.[2]

—*Lieutenant Frank A. Holden*
328th Infantry, 82nd Division

"The boys won't talk about the war." That is not true. But it is true that the boys do not talk about the war. The reason is not because the war is something not to be thought of. The boys would talk if the questioners would listen. But the questioners do not. They at once interrupt with "It's all too dreadful," or, "Doesn't it seem like a terrible dream?" or, "How can you think of it?" or, "I can't imagine such things." That is as bad as telling a humorist you've heard that one before. It shuts the boys up.[3]

—*Lieutenant Louis F. Ranlett*
23rd Infantry, 2nd Division

Early on the morning of October 15, 1918, Sherwood and I were reminiscing about home. I wanted to smoke and had plenty of tobacco and paper for making cigarettes, but, damn it, I didn't have a match, and Sherwood didn't smoke, so he didn't have a match. Consequently, I went over to the next foxhole to get some matches.

In the next foxhole was our color sergeant, Bill Sheahan, and another doughboy I didn't know. I got some dry matches from them and squeezed back into our foxhole. No sooner had I rolled and lit a cigarette than there was a terrible explosion! Both Sherwood and I were stunned and buried in mud. We managed to dig ourselves out of our hole, heard shouts, and discovered that the shell had landed in the adjacent foxhole where those two men had been. There was no sign of Bill Sheahan, and the other fellow had both legs blown off. He was being carried down the slope to the aid station, but you could tell it was useless.

Everyone was mystified as to what had happened to Sheahan. I told Tom Fitzsimmons he had been in that hole, because I had spoken to him only a few minutes before the shell exploded. At dawn, we looked around and soon came across what appeared to be a piece of roast beef strapped by a web belt, and the initials "W S" were burned into the belt. Those were the mortal remains of Bill Sheahan.

Twenty years later, in 1938, we held a service in the 69th Regiment Armory in memory of our comrades who had been killed during the war. A beautiful plaque was unveiled on which were engraved the names of the men who had died in France. A man sitting next to me introduced himself as the brother of William Sheahan; then he introduced me to a woman next to him, who was Bill's sister. They had traveled all the way from Ireland for this occasion. I was nonplused when he told me that, during the war, Bill's body had been returned to his hometown in Ireland for burial. I wondered what in God's name had been returned. Then his brother confided: "You know, Father Duffy told us that he was killed by shell concussion, and there wasn't a mark on his body."

Although shocked, I managed to reply, "Father was right, sir, that's what happened."[4]

—Private Albert M. Ettinger
165th Infantry, 42nd Division

A one-armed soldier came into my office one day after the war to see if he could get help in finding a job. He sat down, we began to talk things over, and then we got on the subject of his experiences in France. He spoke of what a terrible thing the war was, yet said that in some ways he had hated to have it end and to give up his friends and the spirit there was in his company. He missed the comradeship of it and the lift of it.[5]

—Colonel Arthur Woods
American Expeditionary Force

The war brings out the worst in you. It turns you into a mad fightin' animal, but it also brings out something else, something I jes don't know how to describe, a sort of tenderness and love for the fellows fightin' with you. I had kinder got to know and sorter understand the boys around me. I knowed their weakness as well as their strength. I guess they knowed mine. If you live together for several months sharing and sharing alike, you learn a heap about each other. It was as though we could look right through each other and knowed everything without anything being hid. I'm a telling you I loved them-there boys in my squad. They were my buddies.[6]

—Sergeant C. Alvin York
328th Infantry, 82nd Division

We remember them as friends. When Lieutenant [Clinton L.] Whiting was shot through the lungs at the cemetery in the Argonne, and was being sent to the hospital from which he never returned, I told him how splendidly I felt he had done. Up to that time he had been smiling in spite of pain, but there were tears in his eyes and a sob in the words as he choked out his short good-bye: "Oh, Whit, I don't want to leave the men."

When, on one of the last days in the "Pocket" [of the Lost Battalion], after other runners had, one by one, been killed or captured in trying to get through the enemy that surrounded our detachment, Joseph Friel was asked whether he thought he could carry a message to Regimental Headquarters. "I know I can," he said, and he said it with a smile. He was found later, dead, not far beyond the outposts.

Such men we are richer to have known.[7]

—Lieutenant Colonel Charles W. Whittlesey
308th Infantry, 77th Division

The nurses asked me while I was laying in the hospital, "When was you scared most?"

I said, "All the time."
And that's the truth.[8]

—Corporal Joseph Rendinell
6th Marines, 2nd Division

Notes

1. Thayer, "Army Influence over the Y.M.C.A. in France," pp. 12–13.
2. Holden, *War Memories*, pp. 12–13.
3. Ranlett, *Let's Go!*, p. vii.
4. Ettinger, *A Doughboy with the Fighting 69th*, p. 162.
5. Markham W. Stackpole, *World War Memoirs of Milton Academy 1914–1919*. (Cambridge, Mass.: Riverside Press, 1940), p. 323.
6. Skeyhill, *Sergeant York*, pp. 212–213.
7. Joseph P. Demaree, *History of Company A (308th Infantry) of the Lost Battalion*. (New York: George U. Harvey, 1920), pp. 7–8.
8. Rendinell, *One Man's War*, p. 177.

Selected Bibliography

Adams, Herbert L. *Worcester Light Infantry 1803–1922: A History.* Worcester, Mass.: Worcester Light Infantry History Association, 1924.

Albertine, Connell. *The Yankee Doughboy.* Boston: Branden Press, 1968.

Allen, Hervey. *Toward the Flame.* New York: Farrar & Rinehart, 1926.

Amerine, William H. *Alabama's Own in France.* New York: Eaton & Gettinger, 1919.

American Battle Monuments Commission. *American Armies and Battlefields in Europe.* Washington, D.C.: GPO, 1938.

Bach, Christian A., and Henry Noble Hall. *The Fourth Division.* N.p.: The Fourth Division, 1920.

Bachman, William E. *The Delta of the Triple Elevens.* Hazleton, Pa.: Standard-Sentinel Print, 1920.

Baldwin, Marian. *Canteening Overseas 1917–1919.* New York: MacMillan, Company, 1920.

Barkley, John L. *No Hard Feelings!* New York: Cosmopolitan, 1930.

Battery A of the 101st Field Artillery. Cambridge, Mass.: Brattle, 1919.

The Battery Book: A History of Battery "A" 306 F.A. New York: DeVinne, 1921.

Blumenson, Martin. *The Patton Papers 1885–1940.* Boston: Houghton Mifflin, 1972.

Brown, William. *The Adventures of an American Doughboy.* Tacoma, Wash.: Smith-Kinney, 1919.

Burton, Harold (ed.). *600 Days' Service: A History of the 361st Infantry Regiment of the United States Army.* N.p., c. 1919.

Butts, Edmund L. *The Keypoint of the Marne.* Menasha, Wis.: George Banta, 1930.

Cadwallader, William. *Major Conelly's Front Line Fighters in France and Belgium.* Cleveland: n.p., 1919.

Callaway, A.B. *With Packs and Rifles.* Boston: Meador, 1939.

Carter, Eliot A. *Lanes of Memory.* Boston: Thomas Todd, 1963.

Casey, Robert. *The Cannoneers Have Hairy Ears.* New York: J.H. Sears, 1927.

Catlin, A.W. *With the Help of God and a Few Marines.* Garden City, N.Y.: Doubleday, Page, 1919.

Cheseldine, R.M. *Ohio in the Rainbow.* Columbus, Ohio: F.J. Heer, 1924.

Clappison, Gladys B. *Vassar's Rainbow Division 1918.* Lake Mills, Iowa: Graphic, 1964.

Clarke, William F. *Over There with O'Ryan's Roughnecks.* Seattle: Superior, 1966.

Coffman, Edward M. *The War to End All Wars.* New York: Oxford University Press, 1968.

Cole, Ralph D. *The Thirty-Seventh Division in the World War 1917–1918.* Vol. 2. Columbus, Ohio: The Thirty-seventh Division Veterans Association, 1929.

Cone, Anthony D. *E Battery Goes to War.* Washington, D.C.: n.p., 1929.

Cooke, Elliott D. *We Can Take It and We Attack.* Pike, N.H.: The Brass Hat, n.d.

Cooper, George W. *Our Second Battalion.* Pittsburgh: Second Battalion, 1920.

Cowing, Kemper F., and Courtney R. Cooper. *Dear Folks at Home.* Boston: Houghton Mifflin, 1919.

Cushing, Harvey. *From a Surgeon's Journal.* Boston: Little, Brown, 1936.

Cushing, John T., and Arthur F. Stone (eds.). *Vermont in the World War 1917–1919.* Burlington, Vt.: Free Press, 1928.

Cutler, Frederick M. *The 55th Artillery (CAC) in the American Expeditionary Forces, France, 1918.* Worcester, Mass.: Commonwealth, 1920.

De La Mater, Roswell. *The Story of Battery B 306th F.A.—77th Division.* New York: Premier, 1919.

Demaree, Joseph P. *History of Company A (308th Infantry) of the Lost Battalion.* New York: George U. Harvey, 1920.

Dienst, Charles F. *They're from Kansas: History of the 353rd Infantry.* Wichita, Kans.: Regimental Society, the 353rd Infantry, 1921.

Duane, James T. *Dear Old "K".* Boston, Mass.: n.p., n.d.

Duffy, Francis P. *Father Duffy's Story.* Garden City, N.Y.: Garden City, 1919.

Duffy, Ward E. (ed.). *The G.P.F. Book Regimental History of the Three Hundred and Third Field Artillery.* N.p., n.d.

DuPuy, Charles M. *A Machine Gunner's Notes, France 1918.* Pittsburgh: Reed & Witting, 1920.

Edwards, Evan A. *From Doniphan to Verdun: The Story of the 140th Infantry.* Lawrence, Kans.: World, 1920.

Edwards, Frederick T. *Fort Sheridan to Montfaucon.* DeLand, Fla.: n.p., 1954.

Emmett, Christopher. *Give Way to the Right.* San Antonio, Tex.: Naylor, 1934.

English, George H., Jr. *History of the 89th Division, U.S.A.* Denver: The War Society of the 89th Division, 1920.

Ettinger, Albert M. *A Doughboy with the Fighting 69th.* Shippensburg, Pa.: White Mane, 1992.

Evarts, Jeremiah. *Cantigny: A Corner of the War.* N.p., 1938.

Evarts, Jeremiah. *Recollections of a Vermonter 1896–1918.* New York: n.p., n.d.

Fifield, James H. *The Regiment: A History of the 104th U.S. Infantry, A.E.F. 1917–1919.* N.p., 1946.

Finney, Ben. *Once A Marine—Always A Marine.* New York: Crown, 1977.

Fletcher, A.L. *History of the 113th Field Artillery 30th Division.* Raleigh, N.C.: The History Committee of the 113th F.A., 1920.

Fredericks, Pierce G. *The Great Adventure.* New York: Dutton, 1960.

Garber, David S. *Service with Battery C.* Philadelphia: Innes & Sons, 1919.

Garlock, G.W. *Tales of the Thirty-Second.* West Salem, Wis.: Badger, 1927.

The German Offensive of July 15, 1918. Fort Leavenworth, Kans.: General Services School, 1923.

Gibbons, Floyd. *And They Thought We Wouldn't Fight.* New York: George H. Doran, 1918.

Gnasser, Emil B. *History of the 126th Infantry in the War with Germany.* Grand Rapids, Mich.: 126th Infantry Association, 1920.

Halyburton, Ed. *Shoot and Be Damned.* New York: Covici-Friede, 1932.

Hamilton, Craig, and Louise Corbin. *Echoes from Over There.* New York: The Soldiers' Publishing Company, 1919.

Hamm, Elizabeth C. *In White Armor.* New York: Knickerbocker, 1919.

Harlow, Rex F. *Trail of the 61st.* Oklahoma City: Harlow, 1919.

Harrison, Carter. *With the American Red Cross in France 1918–1919.* N.p.: Ralph Fletcher Seymour, 1947.

Haterius, Carl E. *Reminiscences of the 137th U.S. Infantry.* Topeka, Kans.: Crane, 1919.

Havlin, Arthur C. *The History of Company A, 102d Machine Gun Battalion, Twenty-Sixth Division, A.E.F.* N.p., 1928.

Heywood, Chester D. *Negro Combat Troops in the World War.* Worcester, Mass.: Commonwealth, 1928.

Hinman, Jesse. *Ranging in France with Flash and Sound.* Portland, Oreg.: Dunham, 1919.

An Historical and Technical Biography of the Twenty-First Engineers Light Railway United States Army. New York: Twenty-First Engineers (Light Railway), 1919.

A History of the 1st U.S. Engineers 1st U.S. Division. Coblenz, Ger.: n.p., 1919.

History of the 101st United States Engineers. Cambridge, Mass.: Harvard University Press, 1926.

History of the One Hundred Second Field Artillery. Boston: n.p., 1927.

History of the 110th Infantry. Pittsburgh: The Association of the 110th Infantry, 1920.

History of the Richardson Light Guard. Wakefield, Mass.: Item, 1926.

History of the Seventh Field Artillery. N.p., 1929.

History of the Seventy-Seventh Division August 25th, 1917–November 11th, 1918. New York: The 77th Division Association, 1919.

A History of the Sixty-Sixth Field Artillery Brigade. Denver: Smith-Brooks Printing Co., n.d.

A History of the 313th Field Artillery U.S.A. New York: Thomas Y. Crowell, 1920.

Hoffman, Robert. *I Remember the Last War.* York, Pa.: Strength & Health, 1940.

Hogan, Martin J. *The Shamrock Battalion of the Rainbow.* New York: D. Appleton, 1919.

Holden, Frank A. *War Memories.* Athens, Ga.: Athens, 1922.

Howard, James M. *The Autobiography of a Regiment.* New York: n.p., 1920.

Howe, M.A. DeWolfe. *Memoirs of the Harvard Dead in the War Against Germany.* 5 vols. Cambridge: Harvard University Press, 1921–24.

Illinois in the World War: An Illustrated History of the Thirty-Third Division. 2 vols. Chicago: States Publications Society, 1921.

Iodine and Gasoline. Kingsport, Tenn.: Kingsport, 1919.

Jacks, L.V. *Service Record by an Artilleryman.* New York: Scribner's, 1928.

Johnson, Ray N. *Heaven, Hell or Hoboken.* Cleveland, Ohio: The O.S. Hubbell Printing Co., 1919.

Johnson, Thomas M., and Fletcher Pratt. *The Lost Battalion.* New York: Bobbs-Merrill, 1938.

Judy, Will. *A Soldier's Diary.* Chicago: Judy Publishing, 1930.

Kean, Robert W. *Dear Marraine.* N.p., 1969.

Kenamore, Clair. *From Vauquois Hill to Exermont.* St. Louis, Mo.: Guard, 1919.

Kenamore, Clair. *The Story of the 139th Infantry.* St. Louis, Mo.: Guard, 1920.

Kurtz, Leonard P. *Beyond No Man's Land.* Buffalo, N.Y.: Foster & Stewart, 1937.

LaBranche, Ernest E. *An American Battery in France.* Worcester, Mass.: Belisle, 1923.

Langer, William L. *Gas And Flame in World War I.* New York: Knopf, 1965.

Langille, Leslie. *Men of the Rainbow.* Chicago: O'Sullivan, 1933.

Lavine, A. Lincoln. *Circuits of Victory.* Garden City, N.Y.: Country Life, 1921.

Lawrence, Joseph D. *Fighting Soldier.* Boulder, Colo.: Colorado Associated University Press, 1985.

Lee, Jay M. *The Artilleryman.* Kansas City, Mo.: Spencer, 1920.

Lovejoy, C.E. *The Story of the Thirty-Eighth.* Coblenz, Ger.: n.p., 1919.

Luby, James. *One Who Gave His Life: War Letters of Quincy Sharpe Mills.* New York: Putnam, 1923.

Mackin, Elton E. *Suddenly We Didn't Want to Die.* Novato, Calif.: Presidio, 1993.

MacLean, W.P. *My Story of the 130th Field Artilery.* Topeka, Kans.: The Boy's Chronicle, n.d.

Markle, Clifford M. *A Yankee Prisoner in Hunland.* New Haven: Yale University Press, 1920.

Maverick, Maury. *A Maverick American.* New York: Covici Friede, 1937.

Mayo, Katherine. *That Damn Y.* Boston: Houghton Mifflin, 1920.

MacArthur, Charles. *War Bugs.* Garden City, N.Y.: Doubleday, Doran, 1929.

McCarthy, William E. *Memories of the 309th Field Artillery.* N.p., 1920.

McCollum, L.C. *History And Rhymes of the Lost Battalion.* N.p., 1929.

McGuire, Stuart. *History of U.S. Army Base Hospital No. 45 in the Great War.* Richmond: William Byrd, 1924.

McKenna, Fred. A. (ed.). *Battery A 103rd Field Artillery in France.* Providence, R.I.: n.p., 1921.

McKeogh, Arthur. *The Victorious 77th Division (New York's Own) in the Argonne Fight.* New York: John H. Eggers, 1919.

Meehan, Thomas F. *History of the Seventh-Eighth Division in the World War 1917–18–19.* Wilmington, Del.: Mercantile, 1921.

Miles, L. Wardlaw. *History of the 308th Infantry 1917–1919.* New York: Putnam, 1927.

Minder, Charles. *This Man's War.* New York: Pevensey, 1931.

Moorhead, Robert. *The Story of the 139th Field Artillery, American Expeditionary Force.* Indianapolis: Bobbs-Merrill, 1920.

Mozley, George. *Our Miracle Battery.* N.p., 1920.

Murrin, James A. *With the 112th in France.* Philadelphia: J.B. Lippincott, 1919.

Nettleton, George H. (ed.). *Yale in the World War.* New Haven: Yale University Press, 1925.

Noble, Carl. *Jugheads Behind the Lines.* Caldwell, Idaho: Caxton, 1938.

Nolan, J. Bennett. *The Reading Militia in the Great War.* Reading, Pa.: The Historical Society of Berks County, n.d.

The Official History of the Fifth Division U.S.A. Washington, D.C.: The Society of the Fifth Division, 1919.

Olsmith, Vernon G. *Recollections of an Old Soldier.* San Antonio, Tex.: N.p., 1963.

120th Field Artillery Diary. Milwaukee: Historical Committee, 120th Field Artillery Association, 1928.

One Hundred Thirteenth Engineers in France. Nancy, Fr.: Berger-Levrault, 1919.

Patch, Maj. Gen. Joseph D. *A Soldier's War.* Corpus Christi, Tex.: Mission, 1966.

Peixotto, Ernest. *The American Front.* New York: Charles Scribner's, 1919.

Pottle, Frederick A. *Stretchers: The Story of a Hospital Unit on the Western Front.* New Haven: Yale University Press, 1929.

Rainsford, W. Kerr. *From Upton to the Meuse with the Three Hundred and Seventh.* New York: D. Appleton, 1920.

Ranlett, Louis F. *Let's Go!* Boston: Houghton Mifflin, 1927.

Regimental History Three Hundred and Forty-First Field Artillery. Kansas City, Mo.: Union Bank Note Company, 1919.

Reifsnyder, Henry G. *A Second Class Private in the Great World War.* Philadelphia: n.p., 1923.

Reilly, Henry J. *Americans: All The Rainbow at War.* Columbus, Ohio: F.J. Heer, 1936.

Rendinell, J.E., and George Pattullo. *One Man's War.* New York: J.H. Sears, 1928.

Reynolds, F.C. (ed.). *115th Infantry U.S.A. in the World War.* Baltimore, Md.: Read Taylor, 1920.

Rizzi, Joseph N. *Joe's War.* Huntington, W.Va.: Der Angriff, 1983.

Robinson, Nelson. *St. Lawrence University in the World War 1917–1918.* Canton, N.Y.: St. Lawrence University, 1931.

Robinson, Ralph. *Ambulance Company 113, 29th Division.* Baltimore, Md.: n.p., 1919.

Rogers, Horatio. *The Diary of an Artillery Scout.* North Andover, Mass.: n.p., 1975.

Samson, Henry T., and George C. Hull. *The War Story of C Battery.* Norwood, Mass.: Plimpton, 1920.

Sanborn, Joseph B. *The 131st Infantry in the World War.* Chicago: n.p., 1919.

Schauble, Peter L. *The First Battalion: The Story of the 406th Telegraph Battalion Signal Corps, U.S. Army.* Philadelphia: The Bell Telephone Company of Pennsylvania, 1921.

Schiani, Alfred. *A Former Marine Tells It Like It Was, and Is.* New York: Carlton, 1988.

Schmidt, Paul W. *Co. C, 127th Infantry in the World War.* Sheboygan, Wis.: Press Publishing, 1919.

Searcy, Earl B. *Looking Back.* Springfield, Ill.: Journal, 1921.

Shanks, David C. *As They Passed Through the Port.* Washington, D.C.: Cary, 1927.

Sibley, Frank P. *With the Yankee Division in France.* Boston: Little, Brown, 1919.

Sirmon, W.A. *That's War.* Atlanta: Linmon, 1929.

Sirois, Edward. *Smashing Through the World War with Fighting Battery C 102nd F.A. Yankee Division.* Salem, Mass.: Meek, 1919.

Skeyhill, Tom. *Sergeant York.* Garden City, N.Y.: Doubleday, Doran, 1928.

Spaulding, Oliver L., and John W. Wright. *The Second Division American Expeditionary Force in France 1917–1919.* New York: Hillman, 1937.

Stackpole, Markham W. *World War Memoirs of Milton Academy 1914–1919.* Cambridge, Mass.: Riverside Press, 1940.

Stallings, Laurence. *The Doughboys.* New York: Harper & Row, 1963.

Stansbury, Henry D. *Maryland's 117th Trench Mortar Battery in the World War 1917–1919.* Baltimore, Md.: John D. Lucas Printing Co., 1942.

Stewart, Lawrence O. *Rainbow Bright.* Philadelpia: Dorrance, 1923.

Straub, Elmer F. *A Sergeant's Diary in the World War.* Indianapolis: Indiana Historical Commission, 1923.

Strickland, Daniel W. *Connecticut Fights: The Story of the 102nd Regiment.* New Haven: Quinnipiack, 1930.

Stringfellow, John S. *Hell! No!* Boston: Meador, 1936.

Sutcliffe, Robert S. (compiler). *Seventy-First New York in the World War.* New York: 71st Infantry, New York National Guard, 1922.

Swan, Carroll J. *My Company.* Boston: Houghton Mifflin, 1918.

Sweeney, Daniel J. (ed.). *History of Buffalo and Erie County 1914–1919*. Buffalo, N.Y.: Committee of One Hundred, 1919.

Taber, John H. *The Story of the 168th Infantry*. Iowa City: The State Historical Society of Iowa, 1925.

Taft, William H. (ed.). *Service with the Fighting Men*. 2 vols. New York: Association, 1922.

Thisted, Moses N. *Pershing's Pioneer Infantry of World War I*. Hemet, Calif.: Alphabet, 1982.

Thomas, Lowell. *This Side of Hell*. Garden City, N.Y.: Doubleday, Doran, 1932.

Thomas, Lowell. *Woodfill of the Regulars*. Garden City, N.Y.: Doubleday, Doran, 1929.

Thomason, John W., Jr. *Fix Bayonets!* New York: Scribner's, 1927.

Tiebout, Frank B. *A History of the 305th*. New York: The 305th Infantry Auxiliary, 1919.

Triplett, William F. *Sergeant Terry Bull: His Ideas on War and Fighting in General*. Washington, D.C.: The Infantry Journal, 1943.

Twentieth Engineers France 1917–1918–1919. Portland, Oreg.: Twentieth Engineers Publishing Association, c. 1919.

Weaver, W.G. *History of the 8th Machine Gun Battalion*. Ann Arbor, Mich.: Edwards Brothers, 1965.

Weed, Frank W. (ed.). *The Medical Department of the United States Army in the World War*. Vol. 10, *Neuropsychiatry*. Washington, D.C.: GPO, 1929.

Whitney, Stanton. *Squadron A in the Great War 1917–1918*. New York: Squadron A Association, 1923.

Wilder, F.C. *War Experiences*. Belchertown, Mass.: Lewis H. Blackmer, 1926.

Williams, Ashby. *Experiences of the Great War*. Roanoke, Va.: Stone, 1919.

Williams, Ralph L. *The Luck of a Buck*. Madison, Wis.: Fitchburg, 1985.

Wilmot, Mrs. Frank. *Oregon Boys in the War*. Portland, Oreg.: Glass & Prudhomme, 1918.

Wilson, Bryant, and Lamar Tooze. *With the 364th Infantry in America, France, and Belgium*. New York: Knickerbocker, 1919.

Wise, Fredrick M. *A Marine Tells It to You*. New York: J.H. Sears, 1929.

Woolridge, J.W. *The Giants of the Marne*. N.p., 1923.

Wrentmore, Ernest L. *In Spite of Hell*. New York.: Greenwich, 1958.

Young, Rush. *Over the Top with the 80th*. N.p., 1933.

Unpublished

Duncan, George M. "I Go to War." Author's collection.

Sargent, Daniel. "Cantigny." Author's collection.

Silverthorn, Merwin H., USMC (ret.), interview 1969 (Oral History Collection, Marine Corps Historical Center, Washington, D.C.)

Thayer, George B. "Army Influence over the Y.M.C.A. in France." Author's collection.

Index

About the Book

This multilayered history of World War I's doughboys recapitulates the enthusiasm of scores of soldiers as they trained for war, voyaged to France, and, finally, faced the harsh reality of combat on the Western Front.

Drawing on journals, diaries, personal narratives, and unit histories, Hallas relates the story of men in combat—the men behind the rifles. He has crafted a vivid pastiche that portrays the realities of all the major campaigns, from the first experiences in the muddy trenches to the bloody battle for Belleau Wood, from the violent clash on the Marne to the seemingly unending morass of the Argonne. His moving account reveals what the doughboys saw, what they did, how they felt, and the impact the Great War had on them.

James H. Hallas is publisher of the *Glastonbury Citizen*, a newspaper in Glastonbury, Connecticut, and author of *The Devil's Anvil: The Assault on Peleliu; Squandered Victory: The American First Army at St. Mihiel;* and *Killing Ground on Okinawa: The Battle for Sugar Loaf Hill.*

Stackpole Military History Series

Real battles. Real soldiers. Real stories.

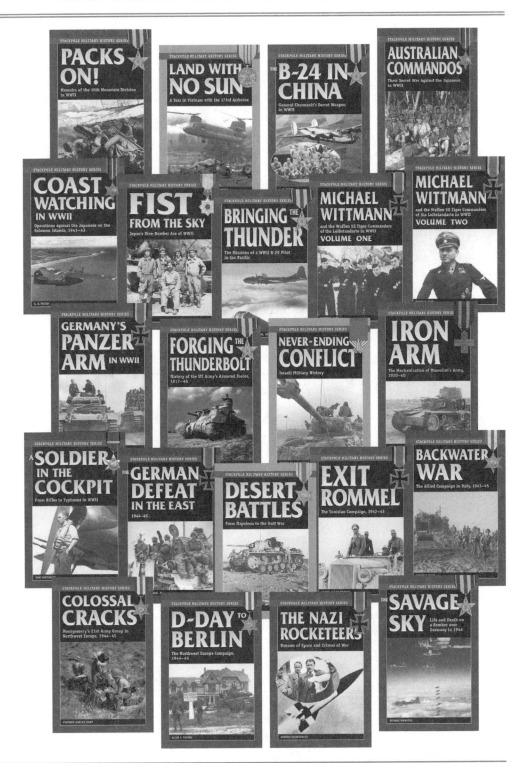

Stackpole Military History Series

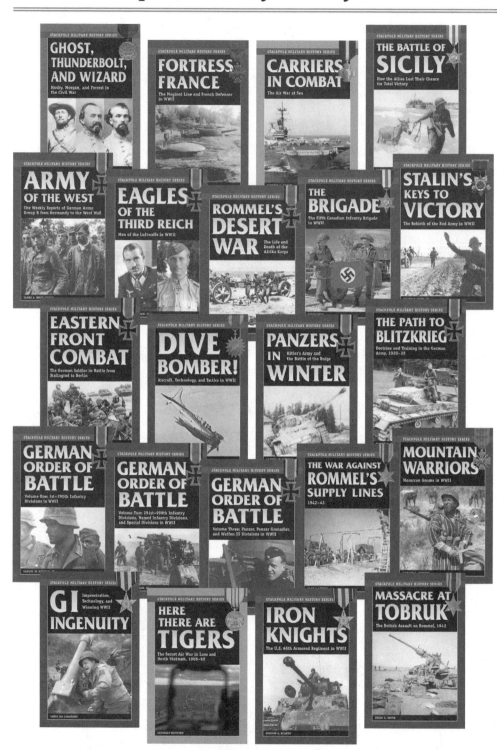

Real battles. Real soldiers. Real stories.

Stackpole Military History Series

STACKPOLE MILITARY HISTORY SERIES

PANZERS IN NORMANDY
General Hans Eberbach and the German Defense of France, 1944

SAMUEL W. MITCHAM, JR.

STACKPOLE MILITARY HISTORY SERIES

TRIUMPHANT FOX
Erwin Rommel and the Rise of the Afrika Korps

STACKPOLE MILITARY HISTORY SERIES

TANK TACTICS
From Normandy to Lorraine

NEW for Spring 2009

STACKPOLE MILITARY HISTORY SERIES

ROMMEL'S LIEUTENANTS
The Men Who Served the Desert Fox, France, 1940

STACKPOLE MILITARY HISTORY SERIES

WOLFPACK WARRIORS
The Story of WWII's Most Successful Fighter Outfit

ROGER A. FR

STACKPOLE MILITARY HISTORY SERIES

ARMOURED GUARDSMEN
A War Diary from Normandy to the Rhine

ROBERT BOSCAWEN

STACKPOLE MILITARY HISTORY SERIES

DOUGHBOY WAR
The American Expeditionary Force in WWI

EDITED BY JAMES H. HALLAS

STACKPOLE MILITARY HISTORY SERIES

PHANTOM REFLECTIONS
An American Fighter Pilot in Vietnam

MIKE McCARTHY

Real battles. Real soldiers. Real stories.

STACKPOLE MILITARY HISTORY SERIES

GOODWOOD
The British Offensive in Normandy, July 1944

IAN DAGLISH

STACKPOLE MILITARY HISTORY SERIES

DESTINATION NORMANDY
Three American Regiments on D-Day

STACKPOLE MILITARY HISTORY SERIES

EXPENDABLE WARRIORS
The Battle of Khe Sanh and the Vietnam War

BRUCE B. G. CLARKE

STACKPOLE MILITARY HISTORY SERIES

D-DAY DECEPTION
Operation Fortitude and the Normandy Invasion

STACKPOLE MILITARY HISTORY SERIES

RED STAR UNDER THE BALTIC
A Soviet Submariner in WWII

NEW for Spring 2009

STACKPOLE MILITARY HISTORY SERIES

HITLER'S NEMESIS
The Red Army, 1930–45

WALTER S. DUNN, JR., WITH A FOREWORD BY DAVID GLANTZ

STACKPOLE MILITARY HISTORY SERIES

PENALTY STRIKE
The Memoirs of a Red Army Penal Company Commander, 1943–45

ALEXANDER V. PYL'CYN

Stackpole Military History Series

D-DAY TO BERLIN
THE NORTHWEST EUROPE CAMPAIGN, 1944–45
Alan J. Levine

The liberation of Western Europe in World War II
required eleven months of hard fighting, from the beaches
of Normandy to Berlin and the Baltic Sea. In this crisp,
comprehensive account, Alan J. Levine describes the Allied
campaign to defeat Nazi Germany in the West: D-Day, the
hedgerow battles in France during the summer of 1944, the
combined airborne-ground assault of Operation Market-
Garden in September, Hitler's winter offensive at the Battle
of the Bulge, and the final drive across the Rhine that
culminated in Germany's surrender in May 1945.

$16.95 • Paperback • 6 x 9 • 240 pages

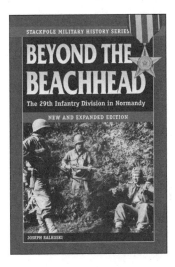

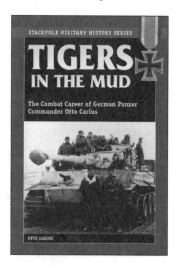

Stackpole Military History Series

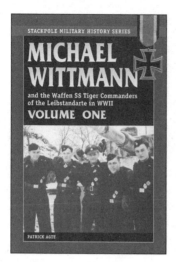

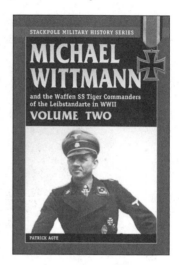

MICHAEL WITTMANN AND THE WAFFEN SS TIGER COMMANDERS OF THE LEIBSTANDARTE IN WORLD WAR II

Patrick Agte

By far the most famous tank commander on any side in World War II, German Tiger ace Michael Wittmann destroyed 138 enemy tanks and 132 anti-tank guns in a career that embodies the panzer legend: meticulous in planning, lethal in execution, and always cool under fire. Volume One covers Wittmann's armored battles against the Soviets in 1943–44 at places like Kharkov, Kursk, and the Cherkassy Pocket. Volume Two picks up with the epic campaign in Normandy, where Wittmann achieved his greatest successes before being killed in action. The Leibstandarte went on to fight at the Battle of the Bulge and in Austria and Hungary before surrendering in May 1945.

Volume One: $19.95 • Paperback • 6 x 9 • 432 pages
383 photos • 19 maps • 10 charts
Volume Two: $19.95 • Paperback • 6 x 9 • 400 pages
287 photos • 15 maps • 7 charts

Stackpole Military History Series

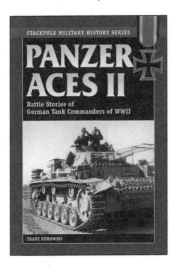

PANZER ACES II

BATTLE STORIES OF
GERMAN TANK COMMANDERS OF WORLD WAR II

Franz Kurowski,
translated by David Johnston

With the same drama and excitement of the first book,
Franz Kurowski relates the combat careers of six more
tank officers. These gripping accounts follow Panzer
crews into some of World War II's bloodiest engage-
ments—with Rommel in North Africa, up and down
the Eastern Front, and in the hedgerows of the West.
Master tacticians and gutsy leaders, these soldiers
changed the face of war forever.

$19.95 • Paperback • 6 x 9 • 496 pages • 71 b/w photos

WWW.STACKPOLEBOOKS.COM
1-800-732-3669

Stackpole Military History Series

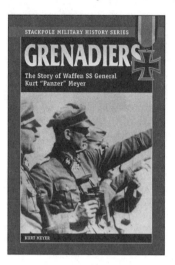

GRENADIERS

THE STORY OF WAFFEN SS GENERAL
KURT "PANZER" MEYER

Kurt Meyer

Known for his bold and aggressive leadership, Kurt Meyer was one of the most highly decorated German soldiers of World War II. As commander of various units, from a motorcycle company to the Hitler Youth Panzer Division, he saw intense combat across Europe, from the invasion of Poland in 1939 to the 1944 campaign for Normandy, where he fell into Allied hands and was charged with war crimes.

$19.95 • Paperback • 6 x 9 • 448 pages • 93 b/w photos

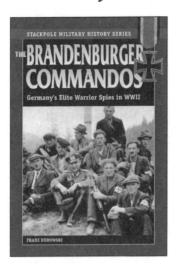

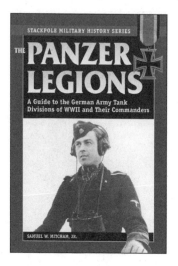

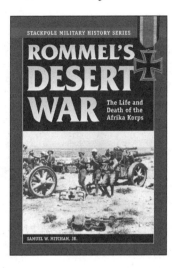

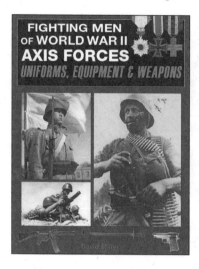 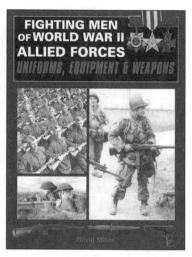